D1487405

Ivan Soll

Art and Philosophy

Second Edition

Second Edition

Art and Philosophy

Readings in Aesthetics

W. E. KENNICK
Amherst College

St. Martin's Press · New York

To A. H. K.

Library of Congress Catalog Card Number: 78–65213
Copyright © 1979 by St. Martin's Press, Inc.
All Rights Reserved.
Manufactured in the United States of America.
32109
fedcba
For information, write St. Martin's Press, Inc.,
175 Fifth Avenue, New York, N.Y. 10010

Cover design: Melissa Tardiff

ISBN: 0–312–053908

Preface to the Second Edition

THIS BOOK IS A SUBSTANTIAL REVISION of the first edition of *Art and Philosophy*. Most of the selections are new—only about one-third remain from the first edition. In addition, two topical sections from the first edition, "The Work of Art and the Aesthetic Object" and "The Arts," have been dropped, the former because the question of the so-called ontological status of the work of art, although interesting, has come to seem less important to me and my students than some alternative topics, and the latter because I have found it a hopeless task to teach "the arts," one after another, *as philosophy*. The topical sections in the new edition are "The Nature of Art," "Artistic Creativity," "Understanding Works of Art," "Aesthetic Experience," "Aesthetic Judgment," and "Critical Judgment."

Changes in the selections have been largely in the direction of updating material on topics broached in the first edition. I have also included selections by Hume and Kant, in whom, happily, there has been a renewed interest of late. The updating was motivated not by a desire to modish, trendy, or "with it," but by a desire to get better—more lively, more imaginative, more "rigorous," less dreary—philosophy into the hands of students. This has meant the inclusion of quite a few younger American philosophers who have been doing really interesting work in aesthetics in the last decade or so.

This book is designed as an introduction to aesthetics but not as an introduction to philosophy. A student should have had at least one course in philosophy (such as logic, ethics, introduction to philosophy) before taking the course for which this book is designed. Although some of the essays included here are not easy to read, I have included nothing that an able or persistent undergraduate cannot cope with. I base this judgment on personal teaching experience with most of the materials here assembled. The book is fairly long. Instructors, however, are obviously free to choose from among its contents or to emphasize some sections at the expense of others.

Two features of the first edition that were especially well received have been retained. First, each section is prefaced with a brief introduction. Lengthy introductions to unfamiliar material are rarely helpful: before the student has become engaged with the problems, the introduction is meaningless; afterwards, it is otiose. Second, a frequently followed practice is therefore reversed and there is appended to each section a brief essay. The aim of these essays, which are largely interrogative, is not to set students straight about aesthetics or to give them "the answers." It is rather to raise provocative questions about the collected materials which,

I hope, will generate in students' minds a friction productive of thought, and to indicate lines along which further discussion and investigation might profitably be pursued.

The title of one of the selections, that by Peter Kivy, has been added by me.

I am indebted to many persons who have helped me with this book: to my students in Philosophy 31 who, over the years, have been my best critics; to those colleagues at other colleges and universities who have offered helpful comments on and criticisms of the first edition and the provisional prospectus of this second edition; to Lela Cryz, who typed all of my words and caught at least some solecisms; and finally to A. H. K., who helped in many ways and to whom this second edition, like the first, is dedicated.

W. E. K.

Contents

IV AESTHETIC EXPERIENCE

V AESTHETIC JUDGMENT

VI CRITICAL JUDGMENT

Abbreviations Used in the Bibliographies

Am. Phil. Quart.: American Philosophical Quarterly
Aust. J. Phil.: The Australasian Journal of Philosophy
B.J.A.: The British Journal of Aesthetics
Can. J. Phil.: The Canadian Journal of Philosophy
Crit. Inq.: Critical Inquiry
J.A.A.C.: The Journal of Aesthetics and Art Criticism
J. Phil.: The Journal of Philosophy
P.A.S.: Proceedings of the Aristotelian Society
P.B.A.: Proceedings of the British Academy
Phil.: Philosophy
Phil. and Phen.: The Journal of Philosophy and Phenomenological
　Research
Phil. Quart.: Philosophical Quarterly
Phil. Rev.: The Philosophical Review
Phil. Studs.: Philosophical Studies
Rev. Met.: The Review of Metaphysics

What Is Aesthetics?:
A Brief Introduction

But—it is in the very nature of philosophy never
to make things easier but only more difficult.

(Heidegger)

THE NATURE OF AESTHETICS IS ITSELF a matter of philosophical dispute,
although there is a fairly widespread consensus about what questions
fall within the domain of aesthetics as a branch of philosophy. In his
A History of Aesthetics of 1892, the British philosopher Bosanquet defined
aesthetics as "the philosophy of the beautiful"[1]; and this definition, or
something like it, has been embalmed and entombed in our dictionaries.[2]
Although it stems from Kant and has his magisterial authority behind it,
few if any philosophers would accept it today. It is simply too restrictive.
What Bosanquet calls "the philosophy of the beautiful" is still a part of
aesthetics (although one not as heavily emphasized as it used to be), but
the subject is nowadays more broadly conceived.

Closer to present-day thinking is Monroe Beardsley's conception of
aesthetics. In his *Aesthetics from Classical Greece to the Present: A Short
History*,[3] Beardsley holds that "we can distinguish at least three levels, so
to speak, on which questions may be asked that have a bearing on works
of art"[4]—which at once makes art, and not beauty, the central topic of
aesthetics. "First, one can ask particular questions about particular works:
'Is this melody in the Phrygian mode?' 'Where is the peripety in *Oedipus
Rex?*'"[5] Such questions Beardsley assigns to the critic, "not the aesthetician." Second, "one can ask such questions as: 'What is a musical
mode?' 'What are the fundamental, or general, characteristics of
tragedy?'"[6] Such questions Beardsley assigns to "the literary or musical
theorist, or systematic critic," although he admits that some of them—
for example, the second as opposed to the first of the two given—are "of
interest to the aesthetician, and are often considered part of his business."[7] "On the third level, one can ask questions about criticism itself,
about the terms it uses, its methods of investigation and argument, its
underlying assumptions. These questions obviously belong to philosophical aesthetics."[8] So aesthetics, according to this conception, is the
philosophy (or, to use expressions popular in certain circles, the "logic,"
or the "grammar") of art criticism, where criticism is broadly conceived,
not as so-called textual criticism, but as an amalgam of activities that can

conveniently be categorized under the headings of interpretation and judgment or evaluation.

To put what I take to be Beardsley's point another way, aesthetics as a branch of philosophy (the word, of course, signifies other enterprises as well) is concerned with a range of conceptual problems, problems having to do with our understanding of certain concepts, especially controversial concepts—such as those of art, of tragedy, of creativity, of beauty, of goodness in art, as opposed to those of the Phrygian mode, of peripety, of a sestina, of an etching, or of a barrel vault—that we use in thinking and speaking about art. "What is a sestina?" is easily answered, and a respectable dictionary will answer it for you; but "What is art?" is not easily answered, and no dictionary is likely to be of much help to anyone troubled by this question. (Why this is, or should be, so is itself an interesting question for philosophical reflection and inquiry.) Conceptual problems, problems having to do with what Wittgenstein called the "grammar" of expressions (including full sentences) can thus sometimes be readily resolved by appeal to a dictionary or some similar source; but sometimes they cannot, and where they cannot philosophy enters the picture. This is the way it has been with philosophy since at least the time of Socrates.

Just to illustrate what a less than obvious conceptual problem is, let us consider a few relatively easy cases. (1) Suppose someone asks, "Can you make a touchdown or score a goal in tennis?" The answer is no, but how would you explain this answer? (2) Again, suppose someone asks, "Can a chair be in pain? Can you hurt it by hitting it with a hammer or by driving a nail into it?" Here again the answer is no—or is it? But how would you explain a negative answer to this question? Is it enough to say that a chair has no central nervous system? Just what is the relation between being susceptible to pain and having a central nervous system, anyway? (3) "Could someone have a feeling of ardent love or hope for the space of one second—*no matter what* preceded or followed this second?"[9] This is a tougher one, but again the answer seems to be no. But why? Finally, (4) consider the following two comic-book figures:

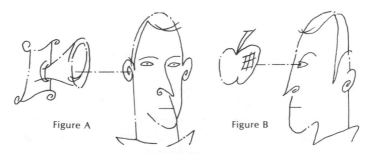

Figure A   Figure B

In what direction do the dotted lines go in each case? Despite the fact that sound travels to the ear and light to the eye, we end to "read" the dotted line in Figure A as going from the speaker to the ear and the dotted line in Figure B as going from the eye to the apple. But why?[10]

These problems or puzzles have to do with the concepts of (1) tennis and making a touchdown or scoring a goal, (2) being in pain, (3) having a feeling of ardent love or hope, and (4) hearing and seeing, ear and eye.

Oddly enough, as even these puzzles show, the concepts with which philosophy, and hence philosophical aesthetics, deals are quite familiar to all or most of us. Confining our attention to some of the concepts with which aesthetics deals, we use such expressions as "work of art," "to create," "to interpret," "to represent or depict," "metaphor," "fiction," "aesthetic," "beautiful," and "good" frequently and without hesitation. But as soon as someone asks us, or the question occurs to us, "What is art?"; "What is it to create a work of art?"; "What is it to interpret or understand a work of art?"; "Are incompatible interpretations of works of art jointly acceptable?"; "How can a piece of music be joyful or melancholy?"; "What is it for a picture to represent an object or event?"; "What is it for fiction to depict persons and their actions?"; "Is there a distinctively aesthetic attitude or way of looking at something or kind of experience?"; "What is beauty?"; "How can we tell whether a painting or a poem is a good one?"; we are in the position of St. Augustine, who, when confronted with the question "What is time?," observed, "I know well enough what it is, provided that nobody asks me; but if I am asked and try to explain I am baffled." And it is precisely by asking such questions and trying to answer them that, as Heidegger puts it, "it is in the very nature of philosophy never to make things easier but only more difficult."[11]

Some people are inclined to say—students often do say it—"But this is just a matter of semantics." And in a way they are right. But the tone in which they say it suggests either that it makes no difference what one says—for example, whether one says that something is or is not a work of art—or that what one says is somehow "arbitrary." But is this really the case? Does it make no difference, is it really arbitrary whether one says that abortion is or is not murder, for example? What we say is intricately and intimately connected with our whole way of life; and if that makes no difference, it is hard to see what could make a difference. Whether art is a necessity of life, as opposed to biological survival, is a question worth pondering, but all people appear to have some form of art and to take it quite seriously. And if art is to be taken seriously, then thinking as clearly as we can about it, and about what we say about it, is surely to be taken seriously as well. I can imagine no more important justification for aesthetics. It is true, as Schopenhauer once put it, that "no one ever became an artist by studying aesthetics," but aesthetics has never pretended to make people artists or, one might add, art critics. It does enough if it can make us more sensitive to the content and implications of what we think and say about art and art criticism.

Notes

1. Bernard Bosanquet, *A History of Aesthetic* (London, 1892), p. 1. The connection between aesthetics as the philosophy of the beautiful and aesthetics as the philosophy of art is made by Bosanquet's assumption that "Fine Art may be accepted, for theoretical purposes, as the chief, if not the sole representative of the world of beauty" (p. 3).

2. Thus according to the Shorter O.E.D. aesthetics is "the philosophy of taste, or of the perception of the beautiful"; and according to Webster's New World Dictionary of the American Language it is "the study or philosophy of beauty; theory of the fine arts and of people's responses to them."

3. New York, 1966.

4. P. 13.

5. *Ibid.*

6. *Ibid.*

7. P. 14. Of these questions Beardsley says, "Such questions call for an inquiry into the nature of music or literature, or some important features of these arts—for theory and explanation, analysis and induction" (pp. 13–14). This is not very helpful, because it leaves open what is meant by "an inquiry into the nature of" something, by "theory and explanation," and by "analysis"—if not by "induction." For at least two things can be meant by these expressions. One can inquire into the nature of aspirin, for example, analyze it, give a theory or explanation of its properties in the way a chemist does. This is an empirical, or theoretico-empirical, investigation. Similarly, one might inquire into the nature of tragedy or comedy, analyze tragedies or comedies and give a psychological, sociological, or historical explanation of their existence. But this presupposes that one already knows, in some way, what a tragedy or comedy is; for without this knowledge one would be unable to carry out the kind(s) of investigation in question. But the question "What is it for something to be a tragedy or a comedy at all?" is another matter. Here inquiry into the nature of tragedy or comedy, analysis of the concept of tragedy or comedy, theory or explanation of the "essence" or "nature" of tragedy or comedy is not analogous to the work of the chemist, but is philosophy pure and simple. (The most famous treatise on the nature of tragedy, Aristotle's *Poetics*, appears to be a mixture of these two modes of investigation.)

8. P. 14.

9. Ludwig Wittgenstein, *Philosophical Investigations*, G. E. M. Anscombe, trans. (Oxford, 1953), #583.

10. Consider the following as at least partial answers. "We do not see the human eye as a receiver, it appears not to let anything in, but to send something out. The ear receives, the eye looks. (It casts glances, it flashes, radiates, gleams.) One can terrify with one's eyes, not with one's ear or nose. When you see the eye you see something going out from it. You see the look in the eye." Ludwig Wittgenstein, *Zettel*, G. E. M. Anscombe and G. H. von Wright, eds., G. E. M. Anscombe, trans. (Oxford, 1967), #222. ". . . it is of the nature of hearing that what is heard comes *from* someplace, whereas what you can see you can look *at*."

Stanley Cavell, *The World Viewed: Reflections on the Ontology of Film* (New York, 1971), p. 18.

11. Martin Heidegger, *An Introduction to Metaphysics*, Ralph Manheim, trans. (New Haven, 1959), p. 9. Cf. Ludwig Wittgenstein, *Zettel*, #456: "Some philosophers (or whatever you like to call them) suffer from what may be called 'loss of problems.' Then everything seems quite simple to them, no deep problems seem to exist any more, the world becomes broad and flat and loses all depth, and what they write becomes immeasurably shallow and trivial." This is surely true not only of "some philosophers (or whatever you like to call them)," but of most of us most of the time.

I

The Nature
of Art

Introduction

O NE QUESTION central to aesthetics is "What is art?" Despite its apparent simplicity, the question itself is unclear; but it is usually taken as a request for a definition of art. Although there are many kinds of definitions,[1] the one that has figured most prominently in philosophy since at least the time of Socrates and has often been thought of as the ideal—if not the only—form of definition is a statement of the features common and peculiar to at least a possible plurality of things, by virtue of which they are things of a certain kind, or by virtue of which we properly apply the same term to them: for example, "A hexapod is an animal having six feet." Thus, Aristotle (*Topics* 101 b 38) says, "A definition is a form of words (*logos*) signifying a thing's essence." (The Greek phrase here rendered as "essence" means literally "the what-it-is-to-be." Therefore, a definition of a so-and-so, for example, a hexapod, tells us what it is to be a so-and-so as opposed to something else.) And Aristotle makes it clear, here and elsewhere, that the form of words signifying a thing's essence, the so-called *definiens,* should give us the genus and differentia of the thing, or kind of thing, to be defined, the so-called *definiendum.* Thus, "A hexapod is an animal having six feet" tells us that the hexapod belongs to the genus of animals and that what differentiates hexapods from other animals is that hexapods alone have six feet.

A modern version of Aristotle's view is that a definition should give the logically necessary and sufficient conditions of something's being a so-and-so. Again, "A hexapod is an animal having six feet" will fill the bill. For it tells us that if something is to be a hexapod it *must* (1) be an animal and *must* (2) have six feet—1 and 2 thus being severally logically *necessary* conditions of being a hexapod—and that if something satisfies both conditions, 1 and 2, then it is a hexapod—1 and 2 being jointly logically *sufficient* conditions of being a hexapod. In short, something is a hexapod if and only if it is an animal having six feet. For convenience, we can refer to this kind of definition as a *formal definition.*[2]

The authors of the selections to be found in this section appear to be looking for the defining feature(s) of art. Tolstoy says that he is looking for "the characteristic sign of a work of art," and he explicitly refers to what he is doing as defining. Bell says that he is searching for "the quality common and peculiar to works of art." Langer, that she is trying to spell out "the principles that obtain wholly and fundamentally in every kind of art." And Dickie, in the face of a frequently voiced skepticism about whether art can be formally defined, indeed in the face of claims that it cannot be so defined, offers what he takes to be an adequate formal definition of art. Although Croce is silent on just what he is doing, his procedure leaves no doubt that he too is trying to define art.

Because "art" refers to a certain human activity, or group of related activities, as well as to the products of that activity, or those activities, "What is art?," as a request for a formal definition, suffers from what is called "process-product ambiguity." It may mean one, or both, of two things: (1) What distinguishes art as an activity from other activities? (2) What distinguishes works of art from other objects? Tolstoy and Croce emphasize the activity; Bell emphasizes the object, as does Dickie too in an unusual way; and Langer seems to straddle the fence. Tolstoy, himself a great artist, argues that art is a means of communication singular in its capacity to transmit the feelings of one person to others; other modes of communication transmit thoughts. According to Croce, the most famous philosopher of modern Italy, the communicative function of art is incidental; essentially, art is the expression of a nonintellectual intuition, a spiritual activity that culminates in a nonconceptual insight that is identical with its expression. Restricting himself almost entirely to the visual arts,[3] Bell, who was a renowned art critic, finds nonrepresentational "significant form" to be the essence of art. Langer, a distinguished American philosopher, sees art, as does Tolstoy, as essentially communicative. But, in contrast to Tolstoy, she holds that the capacity of a work of art to transmit feelings is incidental; what is essential is that it be a symbol expressive of what is logically or conceptually ineffable, namely, what the artist knows about human sentience —which makes her view similar to Croce's. Finally, Dickie, a younger American philosopher, does not look for the essence of art in any of the "exhibited" or perceptually detectable properties of works of art or in any distinctive activity of artists. Rather, a work of art is any artifact that has had a certain status duly conferred upon it by persons in a position to confer that status, just as a knight or a Ph.D. is a person who has had a knighthood or a doctorate in philosophy duly conferred upon him.

The theories of art presented in this section by no means cover the range of answers that have been given by philosophers and others to the question "What is art?" When it comes to theories of the nature of art, aesthetics suffers from an embarrassment of riches. But the theories presented here are typical of the *kind* of answers that aestheticians offer to the question; and some of them have been very influential, not merely on other philosophers, but on critics and other persons seriously concerned with the arts.

The main body of this section is preceded by Kristeller's important and influential essay on the modern—that is, on our—conception of the arts. Until relatively recent times, no one had the notions of the automobile, of air mail, of the light bulb, of space rockets, and of countless other things. The reason for this is simple: such things did not exist, and no one had yet thought of them. But, although we think of art as having been in existence since at least the days when men lived in caves, it was not until the middle of the eighteenth century, as Kristeller demonstrates, that what we think of as art was thought of as *art*. Hence, the question "What is art?," as *we* understand it, is of relatively recent provenance.

In *The Genealogy of Morals*, Nietzsche remarks, "Only that which has no history can be defined." His point appears to be that anything that has a history, as art does, is constantly changing and developing, so that any attempt to define it will quickly be subverted by the changes and developments in what is to be defined. Be that as it may, we are all aware of the fact that the arts, notably the visual arts, have changed radically in this century. We are constantly being confronted by, or told about, objects—if indeed some of them can properly be called "objects" at all— that are presented as works of art but that baffle and confuse us. We do not know what to make of them. They seem so remote from anything we recognize as being clearly *art* that we are tempted to reject them as being art at all, or to suspect that some sardonic joke is being played on us; at best, they call for a great deal of explaining. It is this situation that is addressed by Rosenberg's and Danto's essays appended to this section; but how successfully the reader will have to judge for himself.

Notes

1. For the most thorough discussion of various kinds of definition, see Richard Robinson, *Definition,* Oxford, 1950.

2. Consider the following three sentences: (1) "a hexapod is an animal having six feet"; (2) " 'hexapod' means an animal having six feet"; (3) " 'a hexapod' means the same as 'an animal having six feet.' " Statement 1 gives us the necessary and sufficient conditions of something's being a hexapod. Statement 2 defines the word "hexapod" and gives us the necessary and sufficient conditions of its correct application to something. Statement 3 tells us that two phrases, "a hexapod" and "an animal having six feet," are synonymous and may therefore be substituted for one another in a sentence without altering the sense of the sentence. All three are commonly called "definitions." But 1 is sometimes said to express an *analytic* proposition, according to Kant's use of the term, or to be an analysis of the *concept* of a hexapod; or the proposition it expresses is said to be true *by definition*. For if 2 or 3 expresses a true statement about what the word "hexapod" means, then 1, by substitution, reduces either to "a hexapod is a hexapod" or "an animal having six feet is an animal having six feet"—which is clearly a tautology. Similarly, if 1 expresses an analytic proposition, one that is indeed true by definition, then there must be some such sentence as 2 or 3 that expresses a true proposition about the meaning of the word "hexapod" and relative to which the proposition expressed by 1 is analytic or true by definition. In this way 1, 2, and 3 may be said to be equivalent.

Although "a hexapod is an animal having six feet" tells us what all, and only, hexapods have in common, it does not rule out the possibility that all, and only, hexapods may have *other* features in common; if they do, however, the statement that they do is not a definition of a hexapod.

3. For Bell's views on literature, see his "The 'Difference' of Literature," *New Republic,* 33 (1922), 18-19.

PAUL OSKAR KRISTELLER

The Modern System of the Arts

I

THE FUNDAMENTAL IMPORTANCE of the eighteenth century in the history of aesthetics and of art criticism is generally recognized. To be sure, there has been a great variety of theories and currents within the last two hundred years that cannot be easily brought under one common denominator. Yet all the changes and controversies of the more recent past presuppose certain fundamental notions which go back to that classical century of modern aesthetics. It is known that the very term "Aesthetics" was coined at that time, and, at least in the opinion of some historians, the subject matter itself, the "philosophy of art," was invented in that comparatively recent period and can be applied to earlier phases of Western thought only with reservations. It is also generally agreed that such dominating concepts of modern aesthetics as taste and sentiment, genius, originality and creative imagination did not assume their definite modern meaning before the eighteenth century. Some scholars have rightly noticed that only the eighteenth century produced a type of literature in which the various arts were compared with each other and discussed on the basis of common principles, whereas up to that period treatises on poetics and rhetoric, on painting and architecture, and on music had represented quite distinct branches of writing and were primarily concerned with technical precepts rather than with general ideas. Finally, at least a few scholars have noticed that the term "Art," with a capital A and in its modern sense, and the related term "Fine Arts" (Beaux Arts) originated in all probability in the eighteenth century.

In this paper, I shall take all these facts for granted, and shall concentrate instead on a much simpler and in a sense more fundamental point that is closely related to the problems so far mentioned, but does

From *Journal of the History of Ideas*, 12 (1951), pp. 465-527; 12 (1952), pp. 17-46. Copyright 1951, 1978, *Journal of the History of Ideas, Inc.* Reprinted by permission of the *Journal of the History of Ideas* and the author. The footnotes have been omitted here and may be found in the original articles published in *Journal of the History of Ideas*.

not seem to have received sufficient attention in its own right. Although
the terms "Art," "Fine Arts" or "Beaux Arts" are often identified with
the visual arts alone, they are also quite commonly understood in a
broader sense. In this broader meaning, the term "Art" comprises above
all the five major arts of painting, sculpture, architecture, music and
poetry. These five constitute the irreducible nucleus of the modern system
of the arts, on which all writers and thinkers seem to agree. On the other
hand, certain other arts are sometimes added to the scheme, but with
less regularity, depending on the different views and interests of the
authors concerned: gardening, engraving and the decorative arts, the
dance and the theatre, sometimes the opera, and finally eloquence and
prose literature.

The basic notion that the five "major arts" constitute an area all by
themselves, clearly separated by common characteristics from the crafts,
the sciences and other human activities, has been taken for granted by
most writers on aesthetics from Kant to the present day. It is freely employed even by those critics of art and literature who profess not to
believe in "aesthetics"; and it is accepted as a matter of course by the
general public of amateurs who assign to "Art" with a capital A that
ever narrowing area of modern life which is not occupied by science,
religion, or practical pursuits.

It is my purpose here to show that this system of the five major arts,
which underlies all modern aesthetics and is so familiar to us all, is of
comparatively recent origin and did not assume definite shape before the
eighteenth century, although it has many ingredients which go back to
classical, medieval and Renaissance thought. I shall not try to discuss any
metaphysical theories of beauty or any particular theories concerning
one or more of the arts, let alone their actual history, but only the systematic grouping together of the five major arts. This question does not
directly concern any specific changes or achievements in the various arts,
but primarily their relations to each other and their place in the general
framework of Western culture. Since the subject has been overlooked by
most historians of aesthetics and of literary, musical or artistic theories,
it is hoped that a brief and quite tenative study may throw light on some
of the problems with which modern aesthetics and its historiography
have been concerned.

II

The Greek term for Art (τέχνη) and its Latin equivalent (*ars*) do not
specifically denote the "fine arts" in the modern sense, but were applied
to all kinds of human activities which we would call crafts or sciences.
Moreover, whereas modern aesthetics stresses the fact that Art cannot be
learned, and thus often becomes involved in the curious endeavor to
teach the unteachable, the ancients always understood by Art something

that can be taught and learned. Ancient statements about Art and the arts have often been read and understood as if they were meant in the modern sense of the fine arts. This may in some cases have led to fruitful errors, but it does not do justice to the original intention of the ancient writers. When the Greek authors began to oppose Art to Nature, they thought of human activity in general. When Hippocrates contrasts Art with Life, he is thinking of medicine, and when his comparison is repeated by Goethe or Schiller with reference to poetry, this merely shows the long way of change which the term Art had traversed by 1800 from its original meaning. Plato puts art above mere routine because it proceeds by rational principles and rules, and Aristotle, who lists Art among the so-called intellectual virtues, characterizes it as a kind of activity based on knowledge, in a definition whose influence was felt through many centuries. The Stoics also defined Art as a system of cognitions, and it was in this sense that they considered moral virtue as an art of living.

The other central concept of modern aesthetics also, beauty, does not appear in ancient thought or literature with its specific modern connotations. The Greek term καλόν and its Latin equivalent (*pulchrum*) were never neatly or consistently distinguished from the moral good. When Plato discusses beauty in the *Symposium* and the *Phaedrus*, he is speaking not merely of the physical beauty of human persons, but also of beautiful habits of the soul and of beautiful cognitions, whereas he fails completely to mention works of art in this connection. An incidental remark made in the *Phaedrus* and elaborated by Proclus was certainly not meant to express the modern triad of Truth, Goodness and Beauty. When the Stoics in one of their famous statements connected Beauty and Goodness, the context as well as Cicero's Latin rendering suggest that they meant by "Beauty" nothing but moral goodness, and in turn understood by "good" nothing but the useful. Only in later thinkers does the speculation about "beauty" assume an increasingly "aesthetic" significance, but without ever leading to a separate system of aesthetics in the modern sense. Panaetius identifies moral beauty with decorum, a term he borrows from Aristotle's *Rhetoric,* and consequently likes to compare the various arts with each other and with the moral life. His doctrine is known chiefly through Cicero, but it may also have influenced Horace. Plotinus in his famous treatises on beauty is concerned primarily with metaphysical and ethical problems, but he does include in his treatment of sensuous beauty the visible beauty of works of sculpture and architecture, and the audible beauty of music. Likewise, in the speculations on beauty scattered through the works of Augustine there are references to the various arts, yet the doctrine was not primarily designed for an interpretation of the "fine arts." Whether we can speak of aesthetics in the case of Plato, Plotinus or Augustine will depend on our definition of that term, but we should certainly realize that in the theory of beauty a consideration of the arts is quite absent in Plato and secondary in Plotinus and Augustine.

Let us now turn to the individual arts and to the manner in which they were evaluated and grouped by the ancients. Poetry was always most highly respected, and the notion that the poet is inspired by the Muses goes back to Homer and Hesiod.The Latin term (*vates*) also suggests an old link between poetry and religious prophecy, and Plato is hence drawing upon an early notion when in the *Phaedrus* he considers poetry one of the forms of divine madness. However, we should also remember that the same conception of poetry is expressed with a certain irony in the *Ion* and the *Apology,* and that even in the Phaedrus the divine madness of the poet is compared with that of the lover and of the religious prophet. There is no mention of the "fine arts" in this passage, and it was left to the late sophist Callistratus to transfer Plato's concept of inspiration to the art of sculpture.

Among all the "fine arts" it was certainly poetry about which Plato had most to say, especially in the *Republic,* but the treatment given to it is neither systematic nor friendly, but suspiciously similar to the one he gives to rhetoric in some of his other writings. Aristotle, on the other hand, dedicated a whole treatise to the theory of poetry and deals with it in a thoroughly systematic and constructive fashion. The *Poetics* not only contains a great number of specific ideas which exercised a lasting influence upon later criticism; it also established a permanent place for the theory of poetry in the philosophical encyclopaedia of knowledge. The mutual influence of poetry and eloquence had been a permanent feature of ancient literature ever since the time of the Sophists, and the close relationship between these two branches of literature received a theoretical foundation through the proximity of the *Rhetoric* and the *Poetics* in the corpus of Aristotle's works. Moreover, since the order of the writings in the Aristotelian Corpus was interpreted as early as the commentators of late antiquity as a scheme of classification for the philosophical disciplines, the place of the *Rhetoric* and the *Poetics* after the logical writings of the *Organon* established a link between logic, rhetoric and poetics that was emphasized by some of the Arabic commentators, the effects of which were felt down to the Renaissance.

Music also held a high place in ancient thought; yet it should be remembered that the Greek term μουσική, which is derived from the Muses, originally comprised much more than we understand by music. Musical education, as we can still see in Plato's *Republic,* included not only music, but also poetry and the dance. Plato and Aristotle, who also employ the term music in the more specific sense familiar to us, do not treat music or the dance as separate arts but rather as elements of certain types of poetry, especially of lyric and dramatic poetry. There is reason to believe that they were thus clinging to an older tradition which was actually disappearing in their own time through the emancipation of instrumental music from poetry. On the other hand, the Pythagorean discovery of the numerical proportions underlying the musical intervals led to a theoretical treatment of music on a mathematical basis, and con-

sequently musical theory entered into an alliance with the mathematical
sciences which is already apparent in Plato's *Republic*, and was to last far
down into early modern times.

When we consider the visual arts of painting, sculpture and architecture, it appears that their social and intellectual prestige in antiquity
was much lower than one might expect from their actual achievements
or from occasional enthusiastic remarks which date for the most part
from the later centuries. It is true that painting was compared to poetry
by Simonides and Plato, by Aristotle and Horace, as it was compared to
rhetoric by Cicero, Dionysius of Halicarnassus and other writers. It is
also true that architecture was included among the liberal arts by Varro
and Vitruvius, and painting by Pliny and Galen, that Dio Chrysostom
compared the art of the sculptor with that of the poet, and that Philostratus and Callistratus wrote enthusiastically about painting and
sculpture. Yet the place of painting among the liberal arts was explicitly
denied by Seneca and ignored by most other writers, and the statement of
Lucian that everybody admires the works of the great sculptors but would
not want to be a sculptor oneself, seems to reflect the prevalent view
among writers and thinkers. The term δημιουργός, commonly applied to
painters and sculptors, reflects their low social standing, which was related to the ancient contempt for manual work. When Plato compares
the description of his ideal state to a painting and even calls his world-
shaping god a demiurge, he no more enhances the importance of the
artist than does Aristotle when he uses the statue as the standard example
for a product of human art. When Cicero, probably reflecting Panaetius,
speaks of the ideal notions in the mind of the sculptor, and when the
Middle Platonists and Plotinus compare the ideas in the mind of God
with the concepts of the visual artist they go one step further. Yet no
ancient philosopher, as far as I know, wrote a separate systematic treatise
on the visual arts or assigned to them a prominent place in his scheme
of knowledge.

If we want to find in classical philosophy a link between poetry, music
and the fine arts, it is provided primarily by the concept of imitation
(μίμησις). Passages have been collected from the writings of Plato and
Aristotle from which it appears quite clearly that they considered poetry,
music, the dance, painting and sculpture as different forms of imitation.
This fact is significant so far as it goes, and it has influenced many later
authors, even in the eighteenth century. But aside from the fact that
none of the passages has a systematic character or even enumerates all of
the "fine arts" together, it should be noted that the scheme excludes
architecture, that music and the dance are treated as parts of poetry and
not as separate arts, and that on the other hand the individual branches
or subdivisions of poetry and of music seem to be put on a par with
painting or sculpture. Finally, imitation is anything but a laudatory
category, at least for Plato, and wherever Plato and Aristotle treat the

"imitative arts" as a distinct group within the larger class of "arts," this group seems to include, besides the "fine arts" in which we are interested, other activities that are less "fine," such as sophistry, or the use of the mirror, of magic tricks, or the imitation of animal voices. Moreover, Aristotle's distinction between the arts of necessity and the arts of pleasure is quite incidental and does not identiy the arts of pleasure with the "fine" or even the imitative arts, and when it is emphasized that he includes music and drawing in his scheme of education in the *Politics*, it should be added that they share this place with grammar (writing) and arithmetic.

The final ancient attempts at a classification of the more important human arts and sciences were made after the time of Plato and Aristotle. They were due partly to the endeavors of rival schools of philosophy and rhetoric to organize secondary or preparatory education into a system of elementary disciplines (τὰ ἐγκύκλια). This system of the co-called "liberal arts" was subject to a number of changes and fluctuations, and its development is not known in all of its earlier phases. Cicero often speaks of the liberal arts and of their mutual connection, though he does not give a precise list of these arts, but we may be sure that he did not think of the "fine arts" as was so often believed in modern times. The definitive scheme of the seven liberal arts is found only in Martianus Capella: grammar, rhetoric, dialectic, arithmetic, geometry, astronomy, and music. Other schemes which are similar but not quite identical are found in many Greek and Latin authors before Capella. Very close to Capella's scheme and probably its source was that of Varro, which included medicine and architecture in addition to Capella's seven arts. Quite similar also is the scheme underlying the work of Sextus Empiricus. It contains only six arts, omitting logic, which is treated as one of the three parts of philosophy. The Greek author, Sextus, was conscious of the difference between the preliminary disciplines and the parts of philosophy, whereas the Latin authors who had no native tradition of philosophical instruction were ready to disregard that distinction. If we compare Capella's scheme of the seven liberal arts with the modern system of the "fine arts," the differences are obvious. Of the fine arts only music, understood as musical theory, appears among the liberal arts. Poetry is not listed among them, yet we know from other sources that it was closely linked with grammar and rhetoric. The visual arts have no place in the scheme, except for occasional attempts at inserting them, of which we have spoken above. On the other hand, the liberal arts include grammar and logic, mathematics and astronomy, that is, disciplines we should classify as sciences.

The same picture is gained from the distribution of the arts among the nine Muses. It should be noted that the number of the Muses was not fixed before a comparatively late period, and that the attempt to assign particular arts to individual Muses is still later and not at all uniform. However, the arts listed in these late schemes are the various branches of poetry and of music, with eloquence, history, the dance, grammar, geometry, and astronomy. In other words, just as in the schemes of the liberal arts, so in the schemes for the Muses poetry and music are grouped with some of the sciences, whereas the visual arts are omitted. Antiquity knew no Muse of painting or of sculpture; they had to be invented by the allegorists of the early modern centuries. And the five fine arts which constitute the modern system were not grouped together in antiquity, but kept quite different company: poetry stays usually with grammar and rhetoric; music is as close to mathematics and astronomy as it is to the dance, and poetry; and the visual arts, excluded from the realm of the Muses and of the liberal arts by most authors, must be satisfied with the modest company of the other manual crafts.

Thus classical antiquity left no systems or elaborate concepts of an aesthetic nature, but merely a number of scattered notions and suggestions that exercised a lasting influence down to modern times but had to be carefully selected, taken out of their context, rearranged, reemphasized and reinterpreted or misinterpreted before they could be utilized as building materials for aesthetic systems. We have to admit the conclusion, distasteful to many historians of aesthetics but grudgingly admitted by most of them, that ancient writers and thinkers, though confronted with excellent works of art and quite susceptible to their charm, were neither able nor eager to detach the aesthetic quality of these works of art from their intellectual, moral, religious and practical function or content, or to use such an aesthetic quality as a standard for grouping the fine arts together or for making them the subject of a comprehensive philosophical interpretation.

III

The early Middle Ages inherited from late antiquity the scheme of the seven liberal arts that served not only for a comprehensive classification of human knowledge but also for the curriculum of the monastic and cathedral schools down to the twelfth century. The subdivision of the seven arts into the Trivium (grammar, rhetoric, dialectic) and Quadrivium (arithmetic, geometry, astronomy and music) seems to have been emphasized since Carolingian times. This classification became inadequate after the growth of learning in the twelfth and thirteenth centuries. The classification schemes of the twelfth century reflect different attempts to combine the traditional system of the liberal arts with the threefold division of philosophy (logic, ethics and physics) known through Isidore, and with the divisions of knowledge made by Aristotle or based on the order of his writings, which then began to become known through Latin translations from the Greek and Arabic. The rise of the universities also established philosophy, medicine, jurisprudence and theology as new and distinct subjects outside the liberal arts, and the latter were again reduced from the status of an encyclopaedia of secular knowledge they had held in the earlier Middle Ages to that of preliminary disciplines they had held originally in late antiquity. On the other hand, Hugo of St. Victor was probably the first to formulate a scheme of seven mechanical arts corresponding to the seven liberal arts, and this scheme influenced many important authors of the subsequent period, such as Vincent of Beauvais and Thomas Aquinas. The seven mechanical arts, like the seven liberal arts earlier, also appeared in artistic representations, and they are worth listing: *lanificium, armatura, navigatio, agricultura, venatio, medicina, theatrica* [fabric making, armament, commerce, agriculture, hunting, medicine, theatrics]. Architecture as well as various branches of sculpture and of painting are listed, along with several other crafts, as subdivisions of *armatura*, and thus occupy a quite subordinate place even among the mechanical arts. Music appears in all these schemes in the company of the mathematical disciplines, whereas poetry, when mentioned, is closely linked to grammar, rhetoric and logic. The fine arts are not grouped together or singled out in any of these schemes, but scattered among various sciences, crafts, and other human activities of a quite disparate nature. Different as are these schemes from each other in detail, they show a persistent general pattern and continued to influence later thought.

If we compare these theoretical systems with the reality of the same period, we find poetry and music among the subjects taught in many schools and universities, whereas the visual arts were confined to the artisans' guilds, in which the painters were sometimes associated with the druggists who prepared their paints, the sculptors with the goldsmiths, and the architects with the masons and carpenters. The treatises also that were written, on poetry and rhetoric, on music, and on some of the arts and crafts, the latter not too numerous, have all a strictly technical and professional character and show no tendency to link any of these arts with the others or with philosophy.

The very concept of "art" retained the same comprehensive meaning it had possessed in antiquity, and the same connotation that it was teachable. And the term *artista* coined in the Middle Ages indicated either the craftsman or the student of the liberal arts. Neither for Dante nor for Aquinas has the term Art the meaning we associate with it, and it has been emphasized or admitted that for Aquinas shoemaking, cooking and juggling, grammar and arithmetic are no less and in no other sense *artes* than painting and sculpture, poetry and music, which latter are never grouped together, not even as imitative arts.

On the other hand, the concept of beauty that is occasionally discussed by Aquinas and somewhat more emphatically by a few other medieval philosophers is not linked with the arts, fine or otherwise, but treated primarily as a metaphysical attribute of God and of his creation, starting from Augustine and from Dionysius the Areopagite. Among the transcendentals or most general attributes of being, *pulchrum* does not appear in thirteenth-century philosophy, although it is considered as a general concept and treated in close connection with *bonum*. The question whether Beauty is one of the transcendentals has become a subject of controversy among Neo-Thomists. This is an interesting sign of their varying attitude toward modern aesthetics, which some of them would like to incorporate in a philosophical system based on Thomist principles. For Aquinas himself, or for other medieval philosophers, the question is meaningless, for even if they had posited *pulchrum* as a transcendental concept, which they did not, its meaning would have been different from the modern notion of artistic beauty in which the Neo-Thomists are interested. Thus it is obvious that there was artistic production as well as artistic appreciation in the Middle Ages, and this could not fail to find occasional expression in literature and philosophy. Yet there is no medieval concept or system of the Fine Arts, and if we want to keep speaking of medieval aesthetics, we must admit that its concept and subject matter are, for better or for worse, quite different from the modern philosophical discipline.

IV

The period of the Renaissance brought about many important changes in the social and cultural position of the various arts and thus prepared the ground for the later development of aesthetic theory. But, contrary to a widespread opinion, the Renaissance did not formulate a system of the fine arts or a comprehensive theory of aesthetics.

Early Italian humanism, which in many respects continued the grammatical and rhetorical traditions of the Middle Ages, not merely provided the old Trivium with a new and more ambitious name (*Studia humanitatis*) but also increased its actual scope, content and significance in the curriculum of the schools and universities and in its own extensive literary production. The *Studia humanitatis* excluded logic, but they added to the traditional grammar and rhetoric not only history, Greek, and moral philosophy, but also made poetry, once a sequel of grammar and rhetoric, the most important member of the whole group. It is true that in the fourteenth and fifteenth centuries poetry was understood as the ability to write Latin verse and to interpret the ancient poets, and that the poetry which the humanists defended against some of their theological contemporaries or for which they were crowned by popes and emperors was a quite different thing from what we understand by that name. Yet the name poetry, meaning at first Latin poetry, received much honor and glamor through the early humanists, and by the six-

teenth century vernacular poetry and prose began to share in the prestige
of Latin literature. It was the various branches of Latin and vernacular
poetry and literature which constituted the main pursuit of the numerous
"Academies" founded in Italy during that period and imitated later in
the other European countries. The revival of Platonism also helped to
spread the notion of the divine madness of the poet, a notion that by the
second half of the sixteenth century began to be extended to the visual
arts and became one of the ingredients of the modern concept of
genius. . . .

Still more characteristic of the Renaissance is the steady rise of painting and of the other visual arts that began in Italy with Cimabue and
Giotto and reached its climax in the sixteenth century. An early expression of the increasing prestige of the visual arts is found on the Campanile
of Florence, where painting, sculpture, and architecture appear as a
separate group between the liberal and the mechanical arts. What characterizes the period is not only the quality of the works of art but also the
close links that were established between the visual arts, the sciences and
literature. The appearance of a distinguished artist who also was a
humanist and writer of merit, such as Alberti, was no coincidence in a
period in which literary and classical learning began, in addition to
religion, to provide the subject matter for painters and sculptors. When
a knowledge of perspective, anatomy, and geometrical proportions was
considered necessary for the painter and sculptor, it was no wonder that
several artists should have made important contributions to the various
sciences. On the other hand, ever since Filippo Villani, the humanists,
and their journalist successors in the sixteenth century, looked with favor
upon the work of contemporary artists and would lend their pen to its
praise. From the end of the fourteenth century through the sixteenth the
writings of the artists and of authors sympathetic to the visual arts repeat
the claim that painting should be considered as one of the liberal, not of
the mechanical arts. It has been rightly noted that the classical testimonies
in favor of painting, mainly from Pliny, Galen and Philostratus, were not
as authoritative and strong as the Renaissance authors who quoted them
in support of their claim believed or pretended to believe. Yet the claim
of Renaissance writers on painting to have their art recognized as liberal,
however weakly supported by classical authority, was significant as an
attempt to enhance the social and cultural position of painting and of
the other visual arts, and to obtain for them the same prestige that music,
rhetoric, and poetry had long enjoyed. And since it was still apparent
that the liberal arts were primarily sciences or teachable knowledge, we
may well understand why Leonardo tried to define painting as a science
and to emphasize its close relationship with mathematics.

The rising social and cultural claims of the visual arts led in the
sixteenth century in Italy to an important new development that occurred
in the other European countries somewhat later: the three visual arts,

painting, sculpture and architecture, were for the first time clearly separated from the crafts with which they had been associated in the preceding period. The term *Arti del disegno,* upon which "Beaux Arts" was probably based, was coined by Vasari, who used it as the guiding concept for his famous collection of biographies. And this change in theory found its institutional expression in 1563 when in Florence, again under the personal influence of Vasari, the painters, sculptors and architects cut their previous connections with the craftsmen's guilds and formed an Academy of Art (*Accademia del Disegno*), the first of its kind that served as a model for later similar institutions in Italy and other countries. The Art Academies followed the pattern of the literary Academies that had been in existence for some time, and they replaced the older workshop tradition with a regular kind of instruction that included such scientific subjects as geometry and anatomy.

The ambition of painting to share in the traditional prestige of literature also accounts for the popularity of a notion that appears prominently for the first time in the treatises on painting of the sixteenth century and was to retain its appeal down to the eighteenth: the parallel between painting and poetry. Its basis was the *Ut pictura poesis* of Horace, as well as the saying of Simonides reported by Plutarch, along with some other passages in Plato, Aristotle and Horace. The history of this notion from the sixteenth to the eighteenth century has been carefully studied, and it has been justly pointed out that the use then made of the comparison exceeded anything done or intended by the ancients. Actually, the meaning of the comparison was reversed, since the ancients had compared poetry with painting when they were writing about poetry, whereas the modern authors more often compared painting with poetry while writing about painting. How seriously the comparison was taken we can see from the fact that Horace's *Ars poetica* was taken as a literary model for some treatises on painting and that many poetical theories and concepts were applied to painting by these authors in a more or less artificial manner. The persistent comparison between poetry and painting went a long way, as did the emancipation of the three visual arts from the crafts, to prepare the ground for the later system of the five fine arts, but it obviously does not yet presuppose or constitute such a system. Even the few treatises written in the late sixteenth and early seventeenth century that dealt with both poetry and painting do not seem to have gone beyond more or less external comparisons into an analysis of common principles.

The sixteenth century formulated still other ideas that pointed in the direction of later developments in the field of aesthetics. Just as the period attached great importance to questions of "precedence" at courts and in public ceremonies, so the Academies and educated circles inherited from the medieval schools and universities the fancy for arguing the relative merits and superiority of the various sciences, arts, or other human activities. This type of debate was by no means limited to the arts, as appears from the old rivalry between medicine and jurisprudence, or from the new contest between "arms and letters." Yet this kind of discussion was also applied to the arts and thus helped to strengthen the sense of their affinity. The parallel between painting and poetry, in so far as it often leads to a plea for the superiority of painting over poetry, shows the same general pattern. No less popular was the contest between painting and sculpture, on which Benedetto Varchi in 1546 held a regular inquiry among contemporary artists, whose answers are extant and constitute interesting documents for the artistic theories of the time. The question was still of interest to Galileo. The most important text of this type is Leonardo's *Paragone*, which argues for the superiority of painting over poetry, music, and sculpture. In a sense, this tract contains the most complete system of the fine arts that has come down to us from the Renaissance period. However, the text was not composed by Leonardo in its present form, but put together from his scattered notes by one of his pupils, and again rearranged by most of the modern editors. In any case, architecture is omitted, the separation between poetry and music is not consistently maintained, and the comparison seems to be extended to the mathematical disciplines with which painting, as a science, is closely linked for Leonardo. . . .

Renaissance speculation on beauty was still unrelated to the arts and apparently influenced by ancient models. Nifo's treatise *De pulchro*, still quoted in the eighteenth century, dealt exclusively with personal beauty. Francesco da Diacceto's main philosophical work, which carries the same title, continues the metaphysical speculations of Plotinus and of his teacher Ficino and does not seem to have exercised any lasting influence.

That the Renaissance, in spite of these notable changes, was still far from establishing the modern system of the fine arts appears most clearly from the classifications of the arts and sciences that were proposed during that period. These schemes continued in part the traditions of the Middle Ages, as is clear in the case of such Thomists as S. Antonino or Savonarola. On the whole, however, there is a greater variety of ideas than in the preceding period, and some of the thinkers concerned were neither backward nor unrepresentative. Vives, Ramus, and Gesner largely follow the old scheme of the liberal arts and the university curriculum of their time. Neither Agrippa of Nettesheim nor Scaliger, nor in the seventeenth century Alsted or Vossius, makes any attempt to separate the fine arts from the sciences; they list them scattered among all kinds of sciences and professions, and the same is still true of the eighteenth-century *Cyclopaedia* of E. Chambers. Francis Bacon connects poetry with the faculty of imagination, but does not mention the other arts, and the same is true of Vico, whom Croce considers the founder of modern aesthetics. Bonifacio stresses the link between poetry and painting, but otherwise does not separate the fine arts from the sciences, and the same is true of Tassoni. Even Muratori, who again stresses imagination in poetry and at times compares poetry and painting, when he speaks of the *arti* connected with poetry means eloquence and history, in other words, the *studia humanitatis*. The modern system of the fine arts does not appear in Italy before the second half of the eighteenth century, when such writers as Bettinelli began to follow the lead of contemporary French, English and German authors.

V

During the seventeenth century the cultural leadership of Europe passed from Italy to France, and many characteristic ideas and tendencies of the Italian Renaissance were continued and transformed by French classicism and the French Enlightenment before they became a part of later European thought and culture. Literary criticism and poetic theory, so prominent in the French classical period, seem to have taken little notice of the other fine arts. . . .

Yet the *Siècle de Louis XIV* was not limited in its achievements to poetry and literature. Painting and the other visual arts began to flourish, and with Poussin France produced a painter of European fame. Later in the century Lulli, although of Italian birth, developed a distinctive French style in music, and his great success with the Parisian public went a long way to win for his art the same popularity in France it had long possessed in Italy.

This rise of the various arts was accompanied by an institutional development which followed in many respects the earlier Italian model, but was guided by a conscious governmental policy and hence more centralized and consistent than had been the case in Italy. The Académie Française was organized in 1635 by Richelieu for the cultivation of the French language, poetry, and literature after the model of the Accademia della Crusca. Several years later, in 1648, the Académie Royale de Peinture et de Sculpture was founded under Mazarin after the model of the Accademia di S. Luca in Rome, and tended to detach French artists from the artisans' guilds to which they had previously belonged. Many more Academies were founded by Colbert between 1660 and 1680. They included provincial academies of painting and sculpture, the French Academy in Rome, dedicated to the three visual arts, as well as Academies of Architecture, of Music, and of the Dance. However, the system of the arts that would seem to underly these foundations is more apparent than real. The Academies were founded at different times, and even if we limit ourselves only to the period of Colbert, we should note that there were also the Académie des Sciences and the Académie des Inscriptions et Médailles, which have no relation to the "Fine Arts"; that there was at least a project for an Académie de Spectacles to be devoted to circus performances and other public shows; and that the Académie de Musique and the Académie de Danse, like this projected Académie de Spectacles, were not organizations of distinguished professional artists or scientists, like the other Academies, but merely licensed establishments for the regular preparation of public performances. Moreover, an extant paper from the time of Colbert that proposed to consolidate all Academies in a single institution makes no clear distinction between the arts and the sciences and lends additional though indirect support to the view that Colbert's Academies reflect a comprehensive system of cultural disciplines and professions, but not a clear conception of the Fine Arts in particular.

Along with the founding of the Academies, and partly in close connection with their activities, there developed an important and extensive theoretical and critical literature on the visual arts. The Conférences held at the Académie de Peinture et Sculpture are full of interesting critical views, and separate treatises were composed by Du Fresnoy, De Piles, Fréart de Chambray, and Félibien. Du Fresnoy's Latin poem *De arte graphica*, which was translated into French and English and made the subject of notes and commentaries, was in its form a conscious imitation of Horace's *Ars poetica*, and it begins characteristically by quoting Horace's *Ut pictura poesis* and then reversing the comparison. The parallel between painting and poetry, as well as the contest between the two arts, were important to these authors, as to their predecessors in Renaissance Italy, because they were anxious to acquire for painting a standing equal to that of poetry and literature. This notion, which has been fully studied, remained alive until the early eighteenth century, and it is significant that the honor painting derives from its similarity to poetry is sometimes extended, as occasionally in the Italian Renaissance, to sculpture, architecture and even engraving as related arts. Even the term *Beaux Arts*, which seems to have been intended at first for the visual arts alone, corresponding to *Arti del Disegno*, seems sometimes for these authors to include also music or poetry. The comparison between painting and music is also made a few times, and Poussin himself, who lived in Italy, tried to transfer the theory of the Greek musical modes to poetry and especially to painting.

One of the great changes that occurred during the seventeenth century was the rise and emancipation of the natural sciences. By the second half of the century, after the work of Galileo and Descartes had been completed and the Académie des Sciences and the Royal Society had begun their activities, this development could not fail to impress the literati and the general public. It has been rightly observed that the famous *Querelle des Anciens et Modernes*, which stirred many scholars in France and also in England during the last quarter of the century, was due largely to the recent discoveries in the natural sciences. The Moderns, conscious of these achievements, definitely shook off the authority of classical antiquity that had weighed on the Renaissance no less than on the Middle Ages, and went a long ways toward formulating the concept of human progress. Yet this is only one side of the Querelle.

The Querelle as it went on had two important consequences which have not been sufficiently appreciated. First, the Moderns broadened the literary controversy into a systematic comparison between the achievements of antiquity and of modern times in the various fields of human endeavor, thus developing a classification of knowledge and culture that was in many respects novel, or more specific than previous systems. Secondly, a point by point examination of the claims of the ancients and moderns in the various fields led to the insight that in certain fields, where everything depends on mathematical calculation and the accumulation of knowledge, the progress of the moderns over the ancients can be clearly demonstrated, whereas in certain other fields, which depend on individual talent and on the taste of the critic, the relative merits of the ancients and moderns cannot be so clearly established but may be subject to controversy.

Thus the ground is prepared for the first time for a clear distinction between the arts and the sciences, a distinction absent from ancient, medieval or Renaissance discussions of such subjects even though the same words were used. In other words, the separation between the arts and the sciences in the modern sense presupposes not only the actual progress of the sciences in the seventeenth century but also the reflection upon the reasons why some other human intellectual activities which we now call the Fine Arts did not or could not participate in the same kind of progress. To be sure, the writings of the *Querelle* do not yet attain a complete clarity on these points, and this fact in itself definitely confirms our contention that the separation between the arts and the sciences and the modern system of the fine arts were just in the making at that time. Fontenelle, as some scholars have noticed, indicates in an occasional statement of his *Digression* that he was aware of the distinction between the arts and the sciences.

Much more important and explicit is the work of Charles Perrault. His famous *Parallèle des Anciens et des Modernes* discusses the various fields in separate sections which reflect a system: the second dialogue is dedicated to the three visual arts, the third to eloquence, the fourth to poetry, and the fifth to the sciences. The separation of the fine arts from the sciences is almost complete, though not yet entirely, since music is treated in the last book among the sciences, whereas in his poem, *Le Siècle de Louis le Grand*, which gave rise to the whole controversy, Perrault seems to connect music with the other arts. Moreover, in his prefaces Perrault states explicitly that at least in the case of poetry and eloquence, where everything depends on talent and taste, progress cannot be asserted with the same confidence as in the case of the sciences which depend on measurement. Equally interesting, though unrelated to the *Querelle*, is another writing of Perrault, *Le Cabinet des Beaux Arts* (1690). This is a description and explanation of eight allegorical paintings found in the studio of a French gentleman to whom the work is dedicated. In the preface, Perrault opposes the concept *Beaux Arts* to the traditional *Arts Libéraux*, which he rejects, and then lists and describes the eight "Fine Arts" which the gentleman had represented to suit his taste and interests: Eloquence, Poésie, Musique, Architecture, Peinture, Sculpture, Optique, Méchanique. Thus on the threshold of the eighteenth century we are very close to the modern system of the Fine Arts, but we have not yet quite reached it, as the inclusion of Optics and Mechanics clearly shows. The fluctuations of the scheme show how slowly the notion emerged which to us seems so thoroughly obvious.

VI

During the first half of the eighteenth century the interest of amateurs, writers and philosophers in the visual arts and in music increased. The age produced not only critical writings on these arts composed by and for laymen, but also treatises in which the arts were compared with each other and with poetry, and thus finally arrived at the fixation of the modern system of the fine arts. Since this system seems to emerge gradually and after many fluctuations in the writings of authors who were in part of but secondary importance, though influential, it would appear that the notion and system of the fine arts may have grown and crystallized in the conversations and discussions of cultured circles in Paris and in London, and that the formal writings and treatises merely reflect a climate of opinion resulting from such conversations. A further study of letters, diaries and articles in elegant journals may indeed supplement our brief survey, which we must limit to the better known sources.

The treatise on Beauty by J. P. de Crousaz, which first appeared in 1714 and exercised a good deal of influence, is usually considered as the earliest French treatise on aesthetics. It has indeed something to say on the visual arts and on poetry, and devotes a whole section to music. Moreover, it is an important attempt to give a philosophical analysis of beauty as distinct from goodness, thus restating and developing the notions of ancient and Renaissance Platonists. Yet the author has no system of the arts, and applies his notion of beauty without any marked distinction to the mathematical sciences and to the moral virtues and actions as well as to the arts, and the fluidity of his "aesthetic" thought is shown by the fact that in his second edition he substituted a chapter on the beauty of religion for the one dealing with music.

During the following years, the problem of the arts seems to have dominated the discussions of the Académie des Inscriptions, and several of its lectures which were printed somewhat later and exercised a good deal of influence stress the affinity between poetry, the visual arts and music. These discussions no doubt influenced the important work of the Abbé Dubos that appeared first in 1719 and was reprinted many times in the original and in translations far into the second half of the century. Dubos' merits in the history of aesthetic or artistic thought are generally recognized. It is apparent that he discusses not only the analogies between poetry and painting but also their differences, and that he is not interested in the superiority of one art over the others, as so many previous authors had been. His work is also significant as an early, though not the first, treatment of painting by an amateur writer, and his claim that the educated public rather than the professional artist is the best judge in matters of painting as well as of poetry is quite characteristic. He did not invent the term *beaux-arts*, nor was he the first to apply it to other than the visual arts, but he certainly popularized the notion that poetry was one of the *beaux-arts*. He also has a fairly clear notion of the difference between the arts that depend on "genius" or talent and the sciences based on accumulated knowledge, and it has been rightly observed that in this he continues the work of the "Moderns" in the *Querelle des Anciens et des Modernes*, especially of Perrault. . . .

The decisive step toward a system of the fine arts was taken by the Abbé Batteux in his famous and influential treatise, *Les beaux arts réduits à un même principe* (1746). It is true that many elements of his system were derived from previous authors, but at the same time it should not be overlooked that he was the first to set forth a clearcut system of the fine arts in a treatise devoted exclusively to this subject. This alone may account for his claim to originality as well as for the enormous influence he exercised both in France and abroad, especially in Germany. Batteux codified the modern system of the fine arts almost in its final form, whereas all previous authors had merely prepared it. He started from the poetic theories of Aristotle and Horace, as he states in his preface, and tried to extend their principles from poetry and painting to the other arts. In his first chapter, Batteux gives a clear division of the arts. He separates the fine arts which have pleasure for their end from the mechanical arts, and lists the fine arts as follows: music, poetry, painting, sculpture, and the dance. He adds a third group which combines pleasure and usefulness and puts eloquence and architecture in this category. In the central part of his treatise, Batteux tries to show that the "imitation of beautiful nature" is the principle common to all the arts, and he concludes with a discussion of the theatre as a combination of all the other arts. The German critics of the later eighteenth century, and their recent historians, criticized Batteux for his theory of imitation and often failed to recognize that he formulated the system of the arts which they took for granted and for which they were merely trying to find different principles. They also overlooked the fact that the much maligned principle of imitation was the only one a classicist critic such as Batteux could use when he wanted to group the fine arts together with even an appearance of ancient authority. For the "imitative" arts were the only authentic ancient precedent for the "fine arts," and the principle of imitation could be replaced only after the system of the latter had been so firmly established as no longer to need the ancient principle of imitation to link them together. Diderot's criticism of Batteux has been emphasized too much, for it concerned only the manner in which Batteux defined and applied his principle, but neither the principle itself, nor the system of the arts for which it had been designed.

As a matter of fact, Diderot and the other authors of the *Encyclopédie* not only followed Batteux's system of the fine arts, but also furnished the final touch and thus helped to give it a general currency not only in France but also in the other European countries. Montesquieu in his essay on taste written for the *Encyclopédie* takes the fine arts for granted. Diderot, whose interests included music and the visual arts . . . , criticizes Batteux in his *Lettre sur les Sourds et Muets* (1751), in which he demands a better and more detailed comparison between poetry, painting and music that would take into account the different modes of expression of those arts as they would affect their treatment of even the same subject matter. In the article on the Arts for the *Encyclopédie*, Diderot does not discuss the fine arts, but uses the old distinction between the liberal and mechanical arts and stresses the importance of the latter. Yet in his article on beauty, he does discuss the fine arts. . . .

Still more interesting is D'Alembert's famous *Discours préliminaire*. In his division of knowledge, purportedly based on Francis Bacon, D'Alembert makes a clear distinction between philosophy, which comprises both the natural sciences and such fields as grammar, eloquence, and history, and "those cognitions which consist of imitation," listing among the latter painting, sculpture, architecture, poetry and music. He criticizes the old distinction between the liberal and mechanical arts, and then subdivides the liberal arts into the fine arts which have pleasure for their end, and the more necessary or useful liberal arts such as grammar, logic and morals. He concludes with a main division of knowledge into philosophy, history and the fine arts. This treatment shows still a few signs of fluctuation and of older notions, but it sets forth the modern system of the fine arts in its final form, and at the same time reflects its genesis. The threefold division of knowledge follows Francis Bacon, but significantly d'Alembert speaks of the five fine arts where Bacon had mentioned only poetry. D'Alembert is aware that the new concept of the fine arts is taking the place of the older concept of the liberal arts which he criticizes, and he tries to compromise by treating the fine arts as a subdivision of the liberal arts, thus leaving a last trace of the liberal arts that was soon to disappear. Finally, he reveals his dependence on Batteux in certain phrases and in the principle of imitation, but against Batteux and the classical tradition he now includes architecture among the imitative arts, thus removing the last irregularity which had separated Batteux's system from the modern scheme of the fine arts. Thus we may conclude that the *Encyclopédie*, and especially its famous introduction, codified the system of the fine arts after and beyond Batteux and through its prestige and authority gave it the widest possible currency all over Europe.

After the middle of the century and after the publication of the *Encyclopédie*, speculation on the fine arts in France does not seem to have undergone any basic changes for some time. The notion was popularized and stabilized through such works as Lacombe's portable dictionary of the Fine Arts, which covered architecture, sculpture, painting, engraving, poetry, and music, and through other similar works. The term Beaux Arts, and "Art," in the new sense, found its way into the dictionaries of the French language that had ignored it before. And the Revolution gave the novel term a new institutional expression when it merged several of the older Academies into the Académie des Beaux Arts. Gradually, the further developments of aesthetics in Germany began to affect French philosophy and literature. The second edition of the *Encyclopédie*, published in Switzerland in 1781, has additions by Sulzer, including an article on aesthetics and a section on Fine Arts appended to the article on Art that had not appeared in the first edition. Early in the nineteenth century, the philosopher Victor Cousin, following Kant and the Scottish thinkers of the eighteenth century, as well as what he believed he found in Plato, Proclus and other classical sources, centered his philosophical system on the three concepts of the Good, the True and the Beautiful, understanding by the latter the realm of art and aesthetics. Cousin's wide influence in the later nineteenth century went a long ways toward establishing this triad in modern value theory and toward fortifying the place of aesthetics in the system of philosophical disciplines. It also induced many thinkers and historians to interpret in terms of this scheme a number of ancient and medieval notions that resembled it superficially but had in reality a very different meaning and context....

VII

Having followed the French development through the eighteenth century, we must discuss the history of artistic thought in England. The English writers were strongly influenced by the French down to the end of the seventeenth century and later, but during the eighteenth century they made important contributions of their own and in turn influenced continental thought, especially in France and Germany. . . . Early in the eighteenth century, Jonathan Richardson was praising painting as a liberal art, and John Dennis in some of his critical treatises on poetics stressed the affinity between poetry, painting and music.

Of greater importance were the writings of Anthony, Earl of Shaftesbury, one of the most influential thinkers of the eighteenth century, not only in England but also on the continent. His interest and taste for literature and the arts are well known, and his writings are full of references to the various arts and to the beauty of their works. The ideal of the *virtuoso* which he embodied and advocated no longer included the sciences, as in the seventeenth century, but had its center in the arts and in the moral life. Since Shaftesbury was the first major philosopher in modern Europe in whose writings the discussion of the arts occupied a prominent place, there is some reason for considering him as the founder of modern aesthetics. Yet Shaftesbury was influenced primarily by Plato and Plotinus, as well as by Cicero, and he consequently did not make a clear distinction between artistic and moral beauty. His moral sense still includes both ethical and aesthetic objects. . . .

The philosophical implications of Shaftesbury's doctrine were further developed by a group of Scottish thinkers. Francis Hutcheson, who considered himself Shaftesbury's pupil, modified his doctrine by distinguishing between the moral sense and the sense of beauty. This distinction, which was adopted by Hume and quoted by Diderot, went a long ways to prepare the separation of ethics and aesthetics, although Hutcheson still assigned the taste of poetry to the moral sense. A later philosopher of the Scottish school, Thomas Reid, introduced common sense as a direct criterion of truth, and although he was no doubt influenced by Aristotle's notion of common sense and the Stoic and modern views on "common notions," it has been suggested that his common sense was conceived as a counterpart of Hutcheson's two senses. Thus the psychology of the Scottish school led the way for the doctrine of the three faculties of the soul, which found its final development in Kant and its application in Cousin. . . .

VIII

Discussion of the arts does not seem to have occupied many German writers of the seventeenth century, which was on the whole a period of decline. The poet Opitz showed familiarity with the parallel of poetry and painting, but otherwise the Germans did not take part in the development we are trying to describe before the eighteenth century. During the first part of that century interest in literature and literary criticism began to rise, but did not yet lead to a detailed or comparative treatment of the other arts. . . .

These critical discussions among poets and literati constitute the general background for the important work of the philosopher Alexander Gottlieb Baumgarten and of his pupil Georg Friedrich Meier. Baumgarten is famous for having coined the term aesthetics, but opinions differ as to whether he must be considered the founder of that discipline or what place he occupies in its history and development. The original meaning of the term aesthetics as coined by Baumgarten, which has been well nigh forgotten by now, is the theory of sensuous knowledge, as a counterpart to logic as a theory of intellectual knowledge. The definitions Baumgarten gives of aesthetics show that he is concerned with the arts and with beauty as one of their main attributes, but he still uses the old term liberal arts, and he considers them as forms of knowledge. The question whether Baumgarten really gave a theory of all the fine arts, or merely a poetics and rhetoric with a new name, has been debated but can be answered easily. In his earlier work, in which he first coined the term aesthetic, Baumgarten was exclusively concerned with poetics and rhetoric. In his later, unfinished work, to which he gave the title *Aesthetica*, Baumgarten states in his introduction that he intends to give a theory of all the arts, and actually makes occasional references to the visual arts and to music. This impression is confirmed by the text of Baumgarten's lectures published only recently, and by the writings of his pupil Meier. On the other hand, it is quite obvious, and was noted by contemporary critics, that Baumgarten and Meier develop their actual theories only in terms of poetry and eloquence and take nearly all their examples from literature. Baumgarten is the founder of aesthetics in so far as he first conceived a general theory of the arts as a separate philosophical discipline with a distinctive and well-defined place in the system of philosophy. He failed to develop his doctrine with reference to the arts other than poetry and eloquence, or even to propose a systematic list and division of these other arts. In this latter respect, he was preceded and surpassed by the French writers, especially by Batteux and the Encyclopaedists, whereas the latter failed to develop a theory of the arts as part of a philosophical system. It was the result of German thought and criticism during the second half of the eighteenth century that the more concrete French conception of the fine arts was utilized in a philosophical theory of aesthetics for which Baumgarten had formulated the general scope and program. . . .

The broadening scope of German aesthetics after Baumgarten, which we must now try to trace, was due not only to the influence of Batteux, of the Encyclopaedists, and of other French and English writers but also to the increasing interest taken by writers, philosophers, and the lay public in the visual arts and in music. Winckelmann's studies of classical art are important for the history of our problem for the enthusiasm which he stimulated among his German readers for ancient sculpture and architecture, but not for any opinion he may have expressed on the relation between the visual arts and literature. Lessing's *Laokoon* (1766), too, has a notable importance, not only for its particular theories on matters of poetry and of the visual arts, but also for the very attention given to the latter by one of the most brilliant and most respected German writers of the time. Yet the place of the *Laokoon* in the history of our problem has been misjudged. To say that the *Laokoon* put an end to the age-old tradition of the parallel between painting and poetry that had its ultimate roots in classical antiquity and found its greatest development in the writers of the sixteenth, seventeenth, and early eighteenth century, and thus freed poetry from the emphasis on description, is to give only one side of the picture. It is to forget that the parallel between painting and poetry was one of the most important elements that preceded the formation of the modern system of the fine arts, though it had lost this function as a link between two different arts by the time of Lessing, when the more comprehensive system of the fine arts had been firmly established. In so far as Lessing paid no attention to the broader system of the fine arts, especially to music, his *Laokoon* constituted a detour or a dead end in terms of the development leading to a comprehensive system of the fine arts. It is significant that the *Laokoon* was criticized for this very reason by two prominent contemporary critics, and that Lessing in the post-humous notes for the second part of the work gave some consideration to this criticism, though we have no evidence that he actually planned to extend his analysis to music and to a coherent system of the arts.

The greatest contributions to the history of our problem in the interval between Baumgarten and Kant came from Mendelssohn, Sulzer, and Herder. Mendelssohn, who was well acquainted with French and English writings on the subject, demanded in a famous article that the fine arts (painting, sculpture, music, the dance, and architecture) and belles lettres (poetry and eloquence) should be reduced to some common principle better than imitation, and thus was the first among the Germans to formulate a system of the fine arts. Shortly afterwards, in a book review, he criticized Baumgarten and Meier for not having carried out the program of their new science, aesthetics. They wrote as if they had been thinking exclusively in terms of poetry and literature, whereas aesthetic principles should be formulated in such a way as to apply to the visual arts and to music as well. In his annotations to Lessing's *Laokoon*, pub-lished long after his death, Mendelssohn persistently criticizes Lessing for not giving any consideration to music and to the system of the arts as a whole; we have seen how Lessing, in the fragmentary notes for a continuation of the *Laokoon*, tried to meet this criticism. Mendelssohn also formulated a doctrine of the three faculties of the soul correspond-ing to the three basic realms of goodness, truth and beauty, thus con-tinuing the work of the Scottish philosophers. He did not work out an explicit theory of aesthetics, but under the impact of French and English authors he indicated the direction in which German aesthetics was to develop from Baumgarten to Kant.

What Mendelssohn had merely set forth in a general outline and pro-gram, the Swiss thinker Sulzer, who was well versed in French literature but spent the greater part of his life in Northern Germany, was able to develop in a more systematic and elaborate fashion. Sulzer began his literary activity with a few short philosophical articles in which his interest for aesthetics was already apparent, and in which he also leaned toward the conception of an aesthetic faculty of the soul separate from the intellectual and moral faculties, a conception in whose development Mendelssohn and the philosopher Tetens also took their part. Some years later, Sulzer was prompted by the example of Lacombe 's little dictionary of the fine arts to compile a similar dictionary in German on a much larger scale. This General Theory of the Fine Arts, which appeared in several editions, has been disparaged on account of its pedantic arrangement, but it is clear, comprehensive and learned, and had a considerable importance in its time. The work covers all the fine arts, not only poetry and eloquence, but also music and the visual arts, and thus represents the first attempt to carry out on a large scale the program formulated by Baumgarten and Mendelssohn. Thanks to its wide diffusion, Sulzer's work went a long way to acquaint the German public with the idea that all the fine arts are related and connected with each other. Sulzer's influence extended also to France, for when the great *Encyclopédie* was published in Switzerland in a second edition, many additions were based on his General Theory, including the article on aesthetics and the section on the Fine Arts.

In the decades after 1760, the interest in the new field of aesthetics spread rapidly in Germany. Courses on aesthetics were offered at a number of universities after the example set by Baumgarten and Meier, and new tracts and textbooks, partly based on these courses, appeared almost every year . . .

It is interesting to note the reaction to this aesthetic literature of the leaders of the younger generation, especially of Goethe and of Herder. Goethe in his early years published a review of Sulzer which was quite unfavorable. Noticing the French background of Sulzer's conception, Goethe ridicules the grouping together of all the arts which are so different from each other in their aims and means of expression, a system which reminds him of the old-fashioned system of the seven liberal arts, and adds that this system may be useful to the amateur but certainly not to the artist. This reaction shows that the system of the fine arts was something novel and not yet firmly established, and that Goethe, just like Lessing, did not take an active part in developing the notion that was to become generally accepted. Toward the very end of his life, in the *Wanderjahre*, Goethe shows that he had by then accepted the system of the fine arts, for he assigns a place to each of them in his pedagogical province. Yet his awareness of the older meaning of art is apparent when in a group of aphorisms originally appended to the same work he defines art as knowledge and concludes that poetry, being based on genius, should not be called an art.

Herder, on the other hand, took an active part in the development of

the system of the fine arts and used the weight of his literary authority
to have it generally accepted. In an early but important critical work
(*Kritische Waelder, 1769*), he dedicates the entire first section to a critique
of Lessing's *Laokoon*. Lessing shows merely, he argues, what poetry is
not, by comparing it with painting. In order to see what its essence is, we
should compare it with all its sister arts, such as music, the dance, and
eloquence. . . .

I should like to conclude this survey with Kant, since he was the first
major philosopher who included aesthetics and the philosophical theory
of the arts as an integral part of his system. Kant's interest in aesthetic
problems appears already in his early writing on the beautiful and sublime, which was influenced in its general conception by Burke. He also
had occasion to discuss aesthetic problems in several of his courses. Notes
based on these courses extant in manuscript have not been published,
but have been utilized by a student of Kant's aesthetics. It appears that
Kant cited in these lectures many authors he does not mention in his
published works, and that he was thoroughly familiar with most of the
French, English and German writers on aesthetics. At the time when he
published the *Critique of Pure Reason,* he still used the term aesthetics
in a sense different from the common one, and explains in an interesting
footnote, that he does not follow Baumgarten's terminology since he does
not believe in the possibility of a philosophical theory of the arts. In the
following years, however, he changed his view, and in his *Critique of
Judgment,* which constitutes the third and concluding part of his philosophical system, the larger of its two major divisions is dedicated to
aesthetics, whereas the other section deals with teleology. The system of
the three *Critiques* as presented in this last volume is based on a threefold
division of the faculties of the mind, which adds the faculty of judgment,
aesthetic and teleological, to pure and practical reason. Aesthetics, as the
philosophical theory of beauty and the arts, acquires equal standing
with the theory of truth (metaphysics or epistemology) and the theory of
goodness (ethics).

In the tradition of systematic philosophy this was an important innovation, for neither Descartes nor Spinoza nor Leibniz nor any of their
ancient or medieval predecessors had found a separate or independent
place in their system for the theory of the arts and of beauty, though they
had expressed occasional opinions on these subjects. If Kant took this
decisive step after some hesitation, he was obviously influenced by the
example of Baumgarten and by the rich French, English, and German
literature on the arts his century had produced, with which he was well
acquainted. In his critique of aesthetic judgment, Kant discusses also the
concepts of the sublime and of natural beauty, but his major emphasis is
on beauty in the arts, and he discusses many concepts and principles
common to all the arts. In section 51 he also gives a division of the fine
arts: speaking arts (poetry, eloquence); plastic arts (sculpture, architec-

ture, painting, and gardening); arts of the beautiful play of sentiments (music, and the art of color). This scheme contains a few ephemeral details that were not retained by Kant's successors. However, since Kant aesthetics has occupied a permanent place among the major philosophical disciplines, and the core of the system of the fine arts fixed in the eighteenth century has been generally accepted as a matter of course by most later writers on the subject, except for variations of detail or of explanation.

IX

We shall not attempt to discuss the later history of our problem after Kant, but shall rather draw a few general conclusions from the development so far as we have been able to follow it. The grouping together of the visual arts with poetry and music into the system of the fine arts with which we are familiar did not exist in classical antiquity, in the Middle Ages or in the Renaissance. However, the ancients contributed to the modern system the comparison between poetry and painting and the theory of imitation that established a kind of link between painting and sculpture, poetry and music. The Renaissance brought about the emancipation of the three major visual arts from the crafts, it multiplied the comparisons between the various arts, especially between painting and poetry, and it laid the ground for an amateur interest in the different arts that tended to bring them together from the point of view of the reader, spectator and listener rather than of the artist. The seventeenth century witnessed the emancipation of the natural sciences and thus prepared the way for a clearer separation between the arts and the sciences. Only the early eighteenth century, especially in England and France, produced elaborate treatises written by and for amateurs in which the various fine arts were grouped together, compared with each other and combined in a systematic scheme based on common principles. The second half of the century, especially in Germany, took the additional step of incorporating the comparative and theoretical treatment of the fine arts as a separate discipline into the system of philosophy. The modern system of the fine arts is thus pre-romantic in its origin, although all romantic as well as later aesthetics takes this system as its necessary basis.

It is not easy to indicate the causes for the genesis of the system in the eighteenth century. The rise of painting and of music since the Renaissance, not so much in their actual achievements as in their prestige and appeal, the rise of literary and art criticism, and above all the rise of an amateur public to which art collections and exhibitions, concerts as well as opera and theatre performances were addressed, must be considered as important factors. The fact that the affinity between the various fine arts is more plausible to the amateur, who feels a comparable kind of enjoyment, than to the artist himself, who is concerned with the peculiar aims and techniques of his art, is obvious in itself and is confirmed by Goethe's reaction. The origin of modern aesthetics in amateur criticism would go a long way to explain why works of art have until recently been analyzed by aestheticians from the point of view of the spectator, reader and listener rather than of the producing artist.

The development we have been trying to understand also provides an interesting object lesson for the historian of philosophy and of ideas in general. We are accustomed to the process by which notions first formulated by great and influential thinkers are gradually diffused among secondary writers and finally become the common property of the general public. Such seems to have been the development of aesthetics from Kant to the present. Its history before Kant is of a very different kind. The basic questions and conceptions underlying modern aesthetics seem to have originated quite apart from the traditions of systematic philosophy or from the writings of important original authors. They had their inconspicuous beginnings in secondary authors, now almost forgotten though influential in their own time, and perhaps in the discussions and conversations of educated laymen reflected in their writings. These notions had a tendency to fluctuate and to grow slowly, but only after they had crystallized into a pattern that seemed generally plausible did they find acceptance among the greater authors and the systematic philosophers. Baumgarten's aesthetics was but a program, and Kant's aesthetics the philosophical elaboration of a body of ideas that had had almost a century of informal and non-philosophical growth. If the absence of the scheme of the fine arts before the eighteenth century and its fluctuations in that century have escaped the attention of most historians, this merely proves how thoroughly and irresistibly plausible the scheme has become to modern thinkers and writers.

Another observation seems to impose itself as a result of our study. The various arts are certainly as old as human civilization, but the manner in which we are accustomed to group them and to assign them a place in our scheme of life and of culture is comparatively recent. This fact is not as strange as may appear on the surface. In the course of history, the various arts change not only their content and style, but also their relations to each other, and their place in the general system of culture, as do religion, philosophy or science. Our familiar system of the five fine arts did not merely originate in the eighteenth century, but it also reflects the particular cultural and social conditions of that time. If we consider other times and places, the status of the various arts, their associations and their subdivisions appear very different. There were important periods in cultural history when the novel, instrumental music, or canvas painting did not exist or have any importance. On the other hand, the sonnet and the epic poem, stained glass and mosaic, fresco painting and book illumination, vase painting and tapestry, bas relief and pottery have all been "major" arts at various times and in a way they no longer are now. Gardening has lost its standing as a fine art since the eighteenth century. On the other hand, the moving picture is a good example of how new techniques may lead to modes of artistic expression for which the aestheticians of the eighteenth and nineteenth century had no place in their systems. The branches of the arts all have their rise and decline, and even their birth and death, and the distinction between "major" arts and their subdivisions is arbitrary and subject to change. There is hardly any ground but critical tradition or philosophical preference for deciding whether engraving is a separate art (as most of the eighteenth-century authors believed) or a subdivision of painting, or whether poetry and prose, dramatic and epic poetry, instrumental and vocal music are separate arts or subdivisions of one major art.

As a result of such changes, both in modern artistic production and in the study of other phases of cultural history, the traditional system of the fine arts begins to show signs of disintegration. Since the latter part of the nineteenth century, painting has moved further away from literature than at any previous time, whereas music has at times moved closer to it, and the crafts have taken great strides to recover their earlier standing as decorative arts. A greater awareness of the different techniques of the various arts has produced dissatisfaction among artists and critics with the conventions of an aesthetic system based on a situation no longer existing, an aesthetics that is trying in vain to hide the fact that its underlying system of the fine arts is hardly more than a postulate and that most of its theories are abstracted from particular arts, usually poetry, and more or less inapplicable to the others. The excesses of aestheticism have led to a healthy reaction which is yet far from universal. The tendency among some contemporary philosophers to consider Art and the aesthetic realm as a pervasive aspect of human experience rather than as the specific domain of the conventional fine arts also goes a long way to weaken the latter notion in its traditional form. All these ideas are still fluid and ill defined, and it is difficult to see how far they will go in modifying or undermining the traditional status of the fine arts and of aesthetics. In any case, these contemporary changes may help to open our eyes to an understanding of the historical origins and limitations of the modern system of the fine arts. Conversely, such historical understanding might help to free us from certain conventional preconceptions and to clarify our ideas on the present status and future prospects of the arts and of aesthetics.

LEO TOLSTOY

What Is Art?

"WHAT IS ART?" What a question! Art is architecture, sculpture, painting, music, and poetry in all its forms, usually replies the ordinary man, the art amateur or even the artist himself, imagining the matter about which he is talking to be perfectly clear and uniformly understood by everybody. But in architecture, one inquires further, are there not simple buildings which are not objects of art, and buildings with artistic pretensions which are unsuccessful and ugly and therefore not to be considered works of art? Wherein lies the characteristic sign of a work of art?

It is the same in sculpture, in music, and in poetry. Art in all its forms is bounded on one side by the practically useful, and on the other by unsuccessful attempts at art. How is art to be marked off from each of these? The ordinary educated man of our circle, and even the artist who has not occupied himself specially with aesthetics, will not hesitate at this question either. He thinks the solution was found long ago, and is well known to everyone.

"Art is activity that produces beauty," says such a man.

If art consists in that,—then is a ballet or an operetta art? you inquire.

"Yes," says the ordinary man, though with some hesitation, "a good ballet or a graceful operetta is also art, in so far as it manifests beauty. . . ."

What then is this conception of beauty, so stubbornly held to by people of our circle and day as furnishing a definition of art?

In its subjective aspect, we call beauty that which supplies us with a particular kind of pleasure.

In its objective aspect, we call beauty something absolutely perfect, and we acknowledge it to be so only because we receive from the manifestation of this absolute perfection a certain kind of pleasure: so that this objective definition is nothing but the subjective conception differently

From *What is Art? and Essays on Art* by Leo Tolstoy, translated by Aylmer Maude, World's Classics Series, 1930 and reprinted by permission of Oxford University Press, London.

expressed. In reality both conceptions of beauty amount to one and the same thing, namely, the reception by us of a certain kind of pleasure; that is to say, we call "beauty" that which pleases us without evoking in us desire. . . .

In order to define any human activity, it is necessary to understand its sense and importance; and in order to do this it is primarily necessary to examine that activity in itself, in its dependence on its causes and in connexion with its effects, and not merely in relation to the pleasure we can get from it.

If we say that the aim of any activity is merely our pleasure and define it solely by that pleasure, our definition will evidently be a false one. But this is precisely what has occurred in the efforts to define art. Now if we consider the food question it will not occur to any one to affirm that the importance of food consists in the pleasure we receive when eating it. Everybody understands that the satisfaction of our taste cannot serve as a basis for our definition of the merits of food, and that we have therefore no right to presuppose that dinners with cayenne pepper, Limburg cheese, alcohol, and so on, to which we are accustomed, and which please us, form the very best human food.

In the same way beauty, or that which pleases us, can in no sense serve as a basis for the definition of art; nor can a series of objects which afford us pleasure serve as the model of what art should be.

To see the aim and purpose of art in the pleasure we get from it, is like assuming (as is done by people of the lowest moral development, for instance by savages) that the purpose and aim of food is the pleasure derived when consuming it.

Just as people who conceive the aim and purpose of food to be pleasure cannot recognize the real meaning of eating, so people who consider the aim of art to be pleasure cannot realize its true meaning and purpose, because they attribute to an activity the meaning of which lies in its connexion with the other phenomena of life, the false and exceptional aim of pleasure. People come to understand that the meaning of eating lies in the nourishment of the body, only when they cease to consider that the object of that activity is pleasure. And it is the same with regard to art. People will come to understand the meaning of art only when they cease to consider that the aim of that activity is beauty, that is to say, pleasure. The acknowledgement of beauty (that is, of a certain kind of pleasure received from art) as being the aim of art, not only fails to assist us in finding a definition of what art is, but on the contrary by transferring the question into a region quite foreign to art (into metaphysical, psychological, physiological, and even historical, discussions as to why such a production pleases one person and such another displeases or pleases some one else), it renders such definition impossible. And since discussions as to why one man likes pears and another prefers meat do not help towards finding a definition of what is essential in nourishment, so the solution of questions of taste in art (to which the discussions on art involuntarily come) not only does not help to make clear in what this particular human activity which we call art really consists, but renders such elucidation quite impossible until we rid ourselves of a conception which justifies every kind of art at the cost of confusing the whole matter. . . .

In order to define art correctly it is necessary first of all to cease to consider it as a means to pleasure, and to consider it as one of the conditions of human life. Viewing it in this way we cannot fail to observe that art is one of the means of intercourse between man and man.

Every work of art causes the receiver to enter into a certain kind of relationship both with him who produced or is producing the art, and with all those who, simultaneously, previously, or subsequently, receive the same artistic impression.

Speech transmitting the thoughts and experiences of men serves as a means of union among them, and art serves a similar purpose. The peculiarity of this latter means of intercourse, distinguishing it from intercourse by means of words, consists in this, that whereas by words a man transmits his thoughts to another, by art he transmits his feelings.

The activity of art is based on the fact that a man receiving through his sense of hearing or sight another man's expression of feeling, is capable of experiencing the emotion which moved the man who expressed it. To take the simplest example: one man laughs, and another who hears becomes merry, or a man weeps, and another who hears feels sorrow. A man is excited or irritated, and another man seeing him is brought to a similar state of mind. By his movements or by the sounds of his voice a man expresses courage and determination or sadness and calmness, and this state of mind passes on to others. A man suffers, manifesting his suffering by groans and spasms, and this suffering transmits itself to other people; a man expresses his feelings of admiration, devotion, fear, respect, or love, to certain objects, persons, or phenomena, and others are infected by the same feelings of admiration, devotion, fear, respect, or love, to the same objects, persons, or phenomena.

And it is on this capacity of man to receive another man's expression of feeling and to experience those feelings himself, that the activity of art is based.

If a man infects another or others directly, immediately, by his appearance or by the sounds he gives vent to at the very time he experiences the feeling; if he causes another man to yawn when he himself cannot help yawning, or to laugh or cry when he himself is obliged to laugh or cry, or to suffer when he himself is suffering—that does not amount to art.

Art begins when one person with the object of joining another or others to himself in one and the same feeling, expresses that feeling by certain external indications. To take the simplest example: a boy having experienced, let us say, fear on encountering a wolf, relates that encounter, and in order to evoke in others the feeling he has experienced, describes himself, his condition before the encounter, the surroundings, the wood, his own lightheartedness, and then the wolf's appearance, its movements, the distance between himself and the wolf, and so forth. All this, if only the boy when telling the story again experiences the feelings he had lived through, and infects the hearers and compels them to feel what he has experienced—is art. Even if the boy had not seen the wolf but had frequently been afraid of one, and if wishing to evoke in others the fear he had felt, he invented an encounter with a wolf and recounted it so as to make his hearers share the feelings he experienced when he feared the wolf, that would also be art. And just in the same way it is art if a man, having experienced either the fear of suffering or the attraction of enjoyment (whether in reality or in imagination), expresses these feelings on canvas or in marble so that others are infected by them. And it is also art if a man feels, or imagines to himself, feelings of delight, gladness, sorrow, despair, courage, or despondency, and the transition from one to another of these feelings, and expresses them by sounds so that the hearers are infected by them and experience them as they were experienced by the composer.

The feelings with which the artist infects others may be most various—very strong or very weak, very important or very insignificant, very bad or very good: feelings of love of one's country, self-devotion and submission to fate or to God expressed in a drama, raptures of lovers described in a novel, feelings of voluptuousness expressed in a picture, courage expressed in a triumphal march, merriment evoked by a dance, humour evoked by a funny story, the feeling of quietness transmitted by an evening landscape or by a lullaby, or the feeling of admiration evoked by a beautiful arabesque—it is all art.

If only the spectators or auditors are infected by the feelings which the author has felt, it is art.

To evoke in oneself a feeling one has once experienced and having evoked it in oneself then by means of movements, lines, colours, sounds, or forms expressed in words, so to transmit that feeling that others experience the same feeling—this is the activity of art.

Art is a human activity consisting in this, that one man consciously by means of certain external signs, hands on to others feelings he has lived through, and that others are infected by these feelings and also experience them.

Art is not, as the metaphysicians say, the manifestation of some mysterious Idea of beauty or God; it is not, as the aesthetic physiologists say, a game in which man lets off his excess of stored-up energy; it is not the expression of man's emotions by external signs; it is not the production of pleasing objects; and, above all, it is not pleasure; but it is a means of union among men joining them together in the same feelings, and indispensable for the life and progress towards well-being of individuals and of humanity.

As every man, thanks to man's capacity to express thoughts by words, may know all that has been done for him in the realms of thought by all humanity before his day, and can in the present, thanks to his capacity to understand the thoughts of others, become a sharer in their activity and also himself hand on to his contemporaries and descendants the thoughts he has assimilated from others as well as those that have arisen in himself; so, thanks to man's capacity to be infected with the feelings of others by means of art, all that is being lived through by his contemporaries is accessible to him, as well as the feelings experienced by men thousands of years ago, and he has also the possibility of transmitting his own feelings to others.

If people lacked the capacity to receive the thoughts conceived by men who preceded them and to pass on to others their own thoughts, men would be like wild beasts, or like Kasper Hauser.[1]

And if men lacked this other capacity of being infected by art, people might be almost more savage still, and above all more separated from, and more hostile to, one another.

And therefore the activity of art is a most important one, as important as the activity of speech itself and as generally diffused.

As speech does not act on us only in sermons, orations, or books, but in all those remarks by which we interchange thoughts and experiences with one another, so also art in the wide sense of the word permeates our whole life, but it is only to some of its manifestations that we apply the term in the limited sense of the word.

We are accustomed to understand art to be only what we hear and see in theatres, concerts, and exhibitions; together with buildings, statues, poems, and novels. . . . But all this is but the smallest part of the art by which we communicate with one another in life. All human life is filled with works of art of every kind—from cradle-song, jest, mimicry, the ornamentation of houses, dress, and utensils, to church services, buildings, monuments, and triumphal processions. It is all artistic activity. So that by art, in the limited sense of the word, we do not mean all human activity transmitting feelings but only that part which we for some reason select from it and to which we attach special importance.

This special importance has always been given by men to that part of this activity which transmits feelings flowing from their religious perception, and this small part they have specifically called art, attaching to it the full meaning of the word.

That was how men of old—Socrates, Plato, and Aristotle—looked on art. Thus did the Hebrew prophets and the ancient Christians regard art. Thus it was, and still is, understood by the Mohammedans, and thus it is still understood by religious folk among our own peasantry.

Some teachers of mankind—such as Plato in his *Republic,* and people like the primitive Christians, the strict Mohammedans, and the Buddhists —have gone so far as to repudiate all art.

People viewing art in this way (in contradiction to the prevalent view of to-day which regards any art as good if only it affords pleasure) held and hold that art (as contrasted with speech, which need not be listened to) is so highly dangerous in its power to infect people against their wills, that mankind will lose far less by banishing all art than by tolerating each and every art.

Evidently such people were wrong in repudiating all art, for they denied what cannot be denied—one of the indispensable means of communication without which mankind could not exist. But not less wrong are the people of civilized European society of our class and day in favouring any art if it but serves beauty, that is, gives people pleasure.

Formerly people feared lest among works of art there might chance to be some causing corruption, and they prohibited art altogether. Now they only fear lest they should be deprived of any enjoyment art can afford, and they patronize any art. And I think the last error is much grosser than the first and that its consequences are far more harmful. . . .

There is one indubitable sign distinguishing real art from its counterfeit—namely, the infectiousness of art. If a man without exercising effort and without altering his standpoint, on reading, hearing, or seeing another man's work experiences a mental condition which unites him with that man and with others who are also affected by that work, then the object evoking that condition is a work of art. And however poetic, realistic, striking, or interesting, a work may be, it is not a work of art if it does not evoke that feeling (quite distinct from all other feelings) of joy and of spiritual union with another (the author) and with others (those who are also infected by it).

It is true that this indication is an *internal* one and that there are people who, having forgotten what the action of real art is, expect something else from art (in our society the great majority are in this state), and that therefore such people may mistake for this aesthetic feeling the feeling of diversion and a certain excitement which they receive from counterfeits of art. But though it is impossible to undeceive these people, just as it may be impossible to convince a man suffering from colour-blindness that green is not red, yet for all that, this indication remains perfectly definite to those whose feeling for art is neither perverted nor atrophied, and it clearly distinguishes the feeling produced by art from all other feelings.

The chief peculiarity of this feeling is that the recipient of a truly artistic impression is so united to the artist that he feels as if the work were his own and not some one else's—as if what it expresses were just what he had long been wishing to express. A real work of art destroys in the consciousness of the recipient the separation between himself and the artist, and not that alone, but also between himself and all whose minds receive this work of art. In this freeing of our personality from its separation and isolation, in this uniting of it with others, lies the chief characteristic and the great attractive force of art.

If a man is infected by the author's condition of soul, if he feels this emotion and this union with others, then the object which has effected this is art; but if there be no such infection, if there be not this union with the author and with others who are moved by the same work—then it is not art. And not only is infection a sure sign of art, but the degree of infectiousness is also the sole measure of excellence in art.

The stronger the infection the better is the art, as art, speaking of it now apart from its subject-matter—that is, not considering the value of the feelings it transmits.

And the degree of the infectiousness of art depends on three conditions:-

(1) On the greater or lesser individuality of the feeling transmitted; (2) on the greater or lesser clearness with which the feeling is transmitted; (3) on the sincerity of the artist, that is, on the greater or lesser force with which the artist himself feels the emotion he transmits.

The more individual the feeling transmitted the more strongly does it act on the recipient; the more individual the state of soul into which he is transferred the more pleasure does the recipient obtain and therefore the more readily and strongly does he join in it.

Clearness of expression assists infection because the recipient who mingles in consciousness with the author is the better satisfied the more clearly that feeling is transmitted which, as it seems to him, he has long known and felt and for which he has only now found expression.

But most of all is the degree of infectiousness of art increased by the degree of sincerity in the artist. As soon as the spectator, hearer, or reader, feels that the artist is infected by his own production and writes, sings, or plays, for himself, and not merely to act on others, this mental condition of the artist infects the recipient; and, on the contrary, as soon as the spectator, reader, or hearer, feels that the author is not writing, singing, or playing, for his own satisfaction—does not himself feel what he wishes to express, but is doing it for him, the recipient—resistance immediately springs up, and the most individual and the newest feelings and the cleverest technique not only fail to produce any infection but actually repel.

I have mentioned three conditions of contagion in art, but they may all be summed up into one, the last, sincerity; that is, that the artist should be impelled by an inner need to express his feeling. That condition includes the first; for if the artist is sincere he will express the feeling as he experienced it. And as each man is different from every one else, his feeling will be individual for every one else; and the more individual it is— the more the artist has drawn it from the depths of his nature—the more sympathetic and sincere will it be. And this same sincerity will impel the artist to find clear expression for the feeling which he wishes to transmit.

Therefore this third condition—sincerity—is the most important of the three. It is always complied with in peasant art, and this explains why such art always acts so powerfully; but it is a condition almost entirely absent from our upper-class art, which is continually produced by artists actuated by personal aims of covetousness or vanity.

Such are the three conditions which divide art from its counterfeits, and which also decide the quality of every work of art considered apart from its subject-matter.

The absence of any one of these conditions excludes a work from the category of art and relegates it to that of art's counterfeits. If the work does not transmit the artist's peculiarity of feeling and is therefore not individual, if it is unintelligibly expressed, or if it has not proceeded from the author's inner need for expression—it is not a work of art. If all these conditions are present even in the smallest degree, then the work even if a weak one is yet a work of art.

The presence in various degrees of these three conditions: individuality, clearness, and sincerity, decides the merit of a work of art as art, apart from subject-matter. All works of art take order of merit according to the degree in which they fulfil the first, the second, and the third, of these conditions. In one the individuality of the feeling transmitted may predominate; in another, clearness of expression; in a third, sincerity; while a fourth may have sincerity and individuality and be deficient in clearness; a fifth, individuality and clearness, but less sincerity; and so forth, in all possible degrees and combinations.

Thus is art divided from what is not art, and thus is the quality of art, as art, decided, independently of its subject-matter, that is to say, apart from whether the feelings it transmits are good or bad.

But how are we to define good and bad art with reference to its content or subject-matter? . . .

Art like speech is a means of communication and therefore of progress, that is, of the movement of humanity forward towards perfection. Speech renders accessible to men of the latest generations all the knowledge discovered by the experience and reflection both of preceding generations and of the best and foremost men of their own times; art renders accessible to men of the latest generations all the feelings experienced by their predecessors and also those felt by their best and foremost contemporaries. And as the evolution of knowledge proceeds by truer and more necessary knowledge dislodging and replacing what was mistaken and unnecessary, so the evolution of feeling proceeds by means of art—feelings less kind and less necessary for the well-being of mankind being replaced by others kinder and more needful for that end. That is the purpose of art. And speaking now of the feelings which are its subject-matter, the more art fulfills that purpose the better the art, and the less it fulfills it the worse the art.

The appraisement of feelings (that is, the recognition of one or other set of feelings as more or less good, more or less necessary for the well-being of mankind) is affected by the religious perception of the age.

In every period of history and in every human society there exists an understanding of the meaning of life, which represents the highest level to which men of that society have attained—an understanding indicating the highest good at which that society aims. This understanding is the religious perception of the given time and society. And this religious perception is always clearly expressed by a few advanced men and more or less vividly perceived by members of the society generally. Such a religious perception and its corresponding expression always exists in every society. If it appears to us that there is no religious perception in our society, this is not because there really is none, but only because we do not wish to see it. And we often wish not to see it because it exposes the fact that our life is inconsistent with that religious perception.

Religious perception in a society is like the direction of a flowing river. If the river flows at all it must have a direction. If a society lives, there must be a religious perception indicating the direction in which, more or less consciously, all its members tend.

And so there always has been, and is, a religious perception in every society. And it is by the standard of this religious perception that the feelings transmitted by art have always been appraised. It has always been only on the basis of this religious perception of their age, that men have chosen from amid the endlessly varied spheres of art that art which transmitted feelings making religious perception operative in actual life. And such art has always been highly valued and encouraged, while art transmitting feelings outlived, flowing from the antiquated religious perceptions of a former age, has always been condemned and despised. All the rest of art transmitting those most diverse feelings by means of which people commune with one another was not condemned and was tolerated if only it did not transmit feelings contrary to religious perception. Thus for instance among the Greeks, art transmitting feelings of beauty, strength, and courage (Hesiod, Homer, Phidias) was chosen, approved, and encouraged, while art transmitting feelings of rude sensuality, despondency, and effeminacy, was condemned and despised. Among the Jews, art transmitting feelings of devotion and submission to the God of the Hebrews and to His will (the epic of Genesis, the prophets, the Psalms) was chosen and encouraged, while art transmitting feelings of idolatry (the Golden Calf) was condemned and despised. All the rest of art—stories, songs, dances, ornamentation of houses, of utensils, and of clothes—which was not contrary to religious perception, was neither distinguished nor discussed. Thus as regards its subject-matter has art always and everywhere been appraised and thus it should be appraised, for this attitude towards art proceeds from the fundamental characteristics of human nature, and those characteristics do not change.

I know that according to an opinion current in our times religion is a superstition humanity has outgrown, and it is therefore assumed that no such thing exists as a religious perception common to us all by which art in our time can be appraised. I know that this is the opinion current in the pseudo-cultured circles of today. People who do not acknowledge Christianity in its true meaning because it undermines their social privileges, and who therefore invent all kinds of philosophic and aesthetic theories to hide from themselves the meaninglessness and wrongfulness of their lives, cannot think otherwise. These people intentionally, or sometimes unintentionally, confuse the notion of a religious cult with the notion of religious perception, and think that by denying the cult they get rid of the perception. But even the very attacks on religion and the attempts to establish an idea of life contrary to the religious perception of our times, most clearly demonstrate the existence of a religious perception condemning the lives that are not in harmony with it.

If humanity progresses, that is, moves forward, there must inevitably be a guide to the direction of that movement. And religions have always furnished that guide. All history shows that the progress of humanity is accomplished no otherwise than under the guidance of religion. But if the race cannot progress without the guidance of religion—and progress is always going on, and consequently goes on also in our own times,—then there must be a religion of our times. So that whether it pleases or displeases the so-called cultured people of to-day, they must admit the existence of religion—not of a religious cult, Catholic, Protestant, or another, but of religious perception—which even in our times is the guide always present where there is any progress. And if a religious perception exists amongst us, then the feelings dealt with by our art should be appraised on the basis of that religious perception; and as has been the case always and everywhere, art transmitting feelings flowing from the religious perception of our time should be chosen from amid all the indifferent art, should be acknowledged, highly valued, and encouraged, while art running counter to that perception should be condemned and despised, and all the remaining, indifferent, art should neither be distinguished nor encouraged.

The religious perception of our time in its widest and most practical application is the consciousness that our well-being, both material and spiritual, individual and collective, temporal and eternal, lies in the growth of brotherhood among men—in their loving harmony with one another. This perception is not only expressed by Christ and all the best men of past ages, it is not only repeated in most varied forms and from most diverse sides by the best men of our times, but it already serves as a clue to all the complex labour of humanity, consisting as this labour does on the one hand in the destruction of physical and moral obstacles to the union of men, and on the other hand in establishing the principles common to all men which can and should unite them in one universal brotherhood. And it is on the basis of this perception that we should appraise all the phenomena of our life and among the rest our art also: choosing from all its realms and highly prizing and encouraging whatever transmits feelings flowing from this religious perception, rejecting whatever is contrary to it, and not attributing to the rest an importance that does not properly belong to it. . . .

The essence of the Christian perception consists in the recognition by every man of his sonship to God and of the consequent union of men with God and with one another, as is said in the Gospel (John xvii. 21) .[2] Therefore the subject-matter of Christian art is of a kind that feeling can unite men with God and with one another.

The expression *unite men with God and with one another* may seem obscure to people accustomed to the misuse of these words that is so customary, but the words have a perfectly clear meaning nevertheless. They indicate that the Christian union of man (in contradiction to the partial, exclusive, union of only certain men) is that which unites all without exception.

Art, all art, has this characteristic, that it unites people. Every art causes those to whom the artist's feeling is transmitted to unite in soul with the artist and also with all who receive the same impression. But non-Christian art while uniting some people, makes that very union a cause of separation between these united people and others; so that union of this kind is often a source not merely of division but even of enmity towards others. Such is all patriotic art, with its anthems, poems, and monuments; such is all Church art, that is, the art of certain cults, with their images, statues, processions, and other local ceremonies. Such art is belated and non-Christian, uniting the people of one cult only to separate them yet more sharply from the members of other cults, and even to place them in relations of hostility to one another. Christian art is such only as tends to unite all without exception, either by evoking in them the perception that each man and all men stand in a like relation towards God and towards their neighbour, or by evoking in them identical feelings, which may even be the very simplest, provided that they are not repugnant to Christianity and are natural to every one without exception. . . .

Whatever the work may be and however it may have been extolled, we have first to ask whether this work is one of real art, or a counterfeit. Having acknowledged, on the basis of the indication of its infectiousness even to a small class of people, that a certain production belongs to the realm of art, it is necessary on this basis to decide the next question, Does this work belong to the category of bad exclusive art opposed to religious perception, or of Christian art uniting people? And having acknowledged a work to belong to real Christian art, we must then, according to whether it transmits feelings flowing from love of God and man, or merely the simple feelings uniting all men, assign it a place in the ranks of religious art, or in those of universal art.

Only on the basis of such verification shall we find it possible to select from the whole mass of what in our society claims to be art, those works which form real, important, necessary, spiritual food, and to separate them from all the harmful and useless art and from the counterfeits of art which surround us. Only on the basis of such verification shall we be able to rid ourselves of the pernicious results of harmful art and avail ourselves of that beneficent action which is the purpose of true and good art, and which is indispensable for the spiritual life of man and of humanity.

Notes

1. "The foundling of Nuremberg," found in the market-place of that town on 23rd May, 1828, apparently some sixteen years old. He spoke little and was almost totally ignorant even of common objects. He subsequently explained that he had been brought up in confinement underground and visited by only one man, whom he saw but seldom.

2. "That they may all be one; even as thou, Father, are in me, and I am in Thee, that they also may be in us."

BENEDETTO CROCE

Art as Intuition

Intuition and Expression

KNOWLEDGE HAS TWO FORMS: it is either *intuitive* knowledge or *logical* knowledge; knowledge obtained through the *imagination* or knowledge obtained through the *intellect;* knowledge of the *individual* or knowledge of the *universal;* of *individual things* or of the *relations* between them: it is, in fact, productive either of *images* or of *concepts.*

In ordinary life, constant appeal is made to intuitive knowledge. It is said that we cannot give definitions of certain truths; that they are not demonstrable by syllogisms; that they must be learnt intuitively. The politician finds fault with the abstract reasoner, who possesses no lively intuition of actual conditions; the educational theorist insists upon the necessity of developing the intuitive faculty in the pupil before everything else; the critic in judging a work of art makes it a point of honour to set aside theory and abstractions, and to judge it by direct intuition; the practical man professes to live rather by intuition than by reason.

But this simple acknowledgement granted to intuitive knowledge in ordinary life, does not correspond to an equal and adequate acknowledgement in the field of theory and of philosophy. There exists a very ancient science of intellectual knowledge, admitted by all without discussion, namely, Logic; but a science of intuitive knowledge is timidly and with difficulty asserted by but a few. Logical knowledge has appropriated the lion's share; and if she does not slay and devour her companion outright, yet yields her but grudgingly the humble place of maid-servant or door-keeper—What can intuitive knowledge be without the light of intellectual knowledge? It is a servant without a master; and though a master find a servant useful, the master is a necessity to the servant, since he enables him to gain his livelihood. Intuition is blind; intellect lends her eyes.

Now, the first point to be firmly fixed in the mind is that intuitive knowledge has no need of a master, nor to lean upon any one; she does

From *Aesthetic* by Benedetto Croce, 2nd ed., 1922, translated by Douglas Ainslie, and reprinted by permission of Farrar, Straus & Co. and Macmillan & Company Ltd, London. Published 1953 by the Noonday Press.

not need to borrow the eyes of others, for she has excellent eyes of her own. Doubtless it is possible to find concepts mingled with intuitions. But in many other intuitions there is no trace of such a mixture, which proves that it is not necessary. The impression of a moonlight scene by a painter; the outline of a country drawn by a cartographer; a musical motive, tender or energetic; the words of a sighing lyric, or those with which we ask, command and lament in ordinary life, may well all be intuitive facts without a shadow of intellectual relation. But, think what one may of these instances, and admitting further the contention that the greater part of the intuitions of civilized man are impregnated with concepts, there yet remains to be observed something more important and more conclusive. Those concepts which are found mingled and fused with the intuitions are no longer concepts, in so far as they are really mingled and fused, for they have lost all independence and autonomy. They have been concepts, but have now become simply elements of intuition. The philosophical maxims placed in the mouth of a personage of tragedy or of comedy, perform there the function, not of concepts, but of characteristics of such personage; in the same way as the red in a painted face does not there represent the red colour of the physicists, but is a characteristic element of the portrait. The whole is that which determines the quality of the parts. A work of art may be full of philosophical concepts; it may contain them in greater abundance and they may there be even more profound than in a philosophical dissertation, which in its turn may be rich to overflowing with descriptions and intuitions. But notwithstanding all these concepts the total effect of the work of art is an intuition; and notwithstanding all those intuitions, the total effect of the philosophical dissertation is a concept. The *Promessi Sposi* contains copious ethical observations and distinctions, but does not for that reason lose as a whole its character of simple story or intuition. In like manner the anecdotes and satirical effusions to be found in the works of a philosopher like Schopenhauer do not deprive those works of their character of intellectual treatises. The difference between a scientific work and a work of art, that is, between an intellectual fact and an intuitive fact, lies in the difference of the total effect aimed at by their respective authors. This it is that determines and rules over the several parts of each, not these parts separated and considered abstractly in themselves.

But to admit the independence of intuition as regards concept does not suffice to give a true and precise idea of intuition. Another error arises among those who recognize this, or who at any rate do not explicitly make intuition dependent upon the intellect, to obscure and confuse the real nature of intuition. By intuition is frequently understood *perception*, or the knowledge of actual reality, the apprehension of something as *real*.

Certainly perception is intuition: the perceptions of the room in which I am writing, of the ink-bottle and paper that are before me, of the pen I am using, of the objects that I touch and make use of as instruments of my person, which, if it write, therefore exists;—these are all intuitions. But the image that is now passing through my brain of me writing in another room, in another town, with different paper, pen and ink, is also an intuition. This means that the distinction between reality and non-reality is extraneous, secondary, to the true nature of intuition. If we imagine a human mind having intuitions for the first time, it would seem that it could have intuitions of actual reality only, that is to say, that it could have perceptions of nothing but the real. But since knowledge of reality is based upon the distinction between real images and unreal images, and since this distinction does not at the first moment exist, these intuitions would in truth not be intuitions either of the real or of the unreal, not perceptions, but pure intuitions. Where all is real, nothing is real. The child, with its difficulty of distinguishing true from false, history from fable, which are all one to childhood, can furnish us with a sort of very vague and only remotely approximate idea of this ingenuous state. Intuition is the undifferentiated unity of the perception of the real and of the simple image of the possible. In our intuitions we do not oppose ourselves as empirical beings to external reality, but we simply objectify our impressions, whatever they be.

Those, therefore, who look upon intuition as sensation formed and arranged simply according to the categories of space and time, would seem to approximate more nearly to the truth. Space and time (they say) are the forms of intuition; to have an intuition is to place it in space and in temporal sequence. Intuitive activity would then consist in this double and concurrent function of spatiality and temporality. But for these two categories must be repeated what was said of intellectual distinctions, when found mingled with intuitions. We have intuitions without space and without time: the colour of a sky, the colour of a feeling, a cry of pain and an effort of will, objectified in consciousness: these are intuitions which we possess, and with their making space and time have nothing to do. In some intuitions, spatiality may be found without temporality, in others, *vice versa;* and even when both are found, they are perceived by later reflexion: they can be fused with the intuition in like manner with all its other elements; that is, they are in it *materialiter* and not *formaliter,* as ingredients and not as arrangement. Who, without an act of reflexion which for a moment breaks in upon his contemplation, can think of space while looking at a drawing or a view? Who is conscious of temporal sequence while listening to a story or a piece of music without breaking into it with a similar act of reflexion? What intuition reveals in a work of art is not space and time, but *character, individual physiognomy.* The view here maintained is confirmed in several quarters of modern philosophy. Space and time, far from being simple and primitive functions, are nowadays conceived as intellectual constructions of great complexity. And further, even in some of those who do not altogether deny to space and time the quality of formative principles, categories and functions, one observes an effort to unite them and to regard them in a different manner from that in which these categories are generally conceived. Some limit intuition to the sole category of spatiality, maintaining that even time can only be intuited in terms of space. Others abandon the three dimensions of space as not philosophically necessary, and conceive the function of spatiality as void of all particular spatial determination. But what could such a spatial function be, a simple arrangement that should arrange even time? It represents, surely, all that criticism and refutation have left standing—the bare demand for the affirmation of some intuitive activity in general. And is not this activity truly determined, when one single function is attributed to it, not spatializing it nor temporalizing, but characterizing? Or rather, when it is conceived as itself a category or function which gives us knowledge of things in their concreteness and individuality?

Having thus freed intuitive knowledge from any suggestion of intellectualism and from every later and external addition, we must now explain it and determine its limits from another side and defend it from a different kind of invasion and confusion. On the hither side of the lower limit is sensation, formless matter, which the spirit can never apprehend in itself as simple matter. This it can only possess with form and in form, but postulates the notion of it as a mere limit. Matter, in its abstraction, is mechanism, passivity; it is what the spirit of man suffers, but does not produce. Without it no human knowledge or activity is possible; but mere matter produces animality, whatever is brutal and impulsive in man, not the spiritual dominion, which is humanity. How often we strive to understand clearly what is passing within us! We do catch a glimpse of something, but this does not appear to the mind as objectified and formed. It is in such moments as these that we best perceive the profound difference between matter and form. These are not two acts of ours, opposed to one another; but the one is outside us and assaults and sweeps us off our feet, while the other inside us tends to absorb and identify itself with that which is outside. Matter, clothed and conquered by form, produces concrete form. It is the matter, the content, which differentiates one of our intuitions from another: the form is constant: it is spiritual activity, while matter is changeable. Without matter spiritual activity would not forsake its abstractedness to become concrete and real activity, this or that spiritual content, this or that definite intuition.

It is a curious fact, characteristic of our times, that this very form, this very activity of the spirit, which is essentially ourselves, is so often ignored or denied. Some confound the spiritual activity of man with a metaphorical and mythological activity of what is called nature, which is mechanism and has no resemblance to human activity, save when we imagine, with Aesop, that *"arbores loquuntur non tantum ferae."*[1] Some affirm that they have never observed in themselves this "miraculous" activity, as though there were no difference, or only one of quantity, between sweating and thinking, feeling cold and the energy of the will. Others, certainly with greater reason, would unify activity and mechanism in a more general concept, though they are specifically distinct. Let us, however, refrain for a moment from examining if such a final unification be possible, and in what sense, but admitting that the attempt may be made, it is clear that to unify two concepts in a third implies to begin with the admission of a difference between the two first. Here it is this difference that concerns us and we set it in relief.

Intuition has sometimes been confused with simple sensation. But since this confusion ends by being offensive to common sense, it has more frequently been attenuated or concealed with a phraseology apparently designed at once to confuse and to distinguish them. Thus, it has been asserted that intuition is sensation, but not so much simple sensation as *association* of sensations. Here a double meaning is concealed in the word "association." Association is understood, either as memory, mnemonic association, conscious recollection, and in that case the claim to unite in memory elements which are not intuited, distinguished, possessed in some way by the spirit and produced by consciousness, seems inconceivable: or it is understood as association of unconscious elements, in which case we remain in the world of sensation and of nature. But if with certain associationists we speak of an association which is neither memory nor flux of sensations, but a *productive* association (formative, constructive, distinguishing) ; then our contention is admitted and only its name is denied to it. For productive association is no longer association in the sense of the sensationalists, but *synthesis,* that is to say, spiritual activity. Synthesis may be called association; but with the concept of productivity is already posited the distinction between passivity and activity, between sensation and intuition.

Other psychologists are disposed to distinguish from sensation something which is sensation no longer, but is not yet intellectual concept: the *representation* or *image.* What is the difference between their representation or image and our intuitive knowledge? Everything and nothing: for "representation" is a very equivocal word. If by representation be understood something cut off and standing out from the psychic basis of the sensations, then representation is intuition. If, on the other hand, it be conceived as complex sensation we are back once more in crude sensation, which does not vary in quality according to its richness or poverty, or according to whether the organism in which it appears is rudimentary or highly developed and full of traces of past sensations. Nor is the ambiguity remedied by defining representation as a psychic product of secondary degree in relation to sensation, defined as occupying the first place. What does secondary degree mean here? Does it mean a qualitative, formal difference? If so, representation is an elaboration of sensation and therefore intuition. Or does it mean greater complexity and complication, a quantitative, material difference? In that case intuition is once more confused with simple sensation.

And yet there is a sure method of distinguishing true intuition, true representation, from that which is inferior to it: the spiritual fact from the mechanical, passive, natural fact. Every true intuition or representation is also *expression*. That which does not objectify itself in expression is not intuition or representation, but sensation and mere natural fact. The spirit only intuits in making, forming, expressing. He who separates intuition from expression never succeeds in reuniting them.

Intuitive activity *possesses intuitions to the extent that it expresses them*. Should this proposition sound paradoxical, that is partly because, as a general rule, a too restricted meaning is given to the word "expression." It is generally restricted to what are called verbal expressions alone. But there exist also non-verbal expressions, such as those of line, colour and sound, and to all of these must be extended our affirmation, which embraces therefore every sort of manifestation of the man, as orator, musician, painter, or anything else. But be it pictorial, or verbal, or musical, or in whatever other form it appear, to no intuition can expression in one of its forms be wanting; it is, in fact, an inseparable part of intuition. How can we really possess an intuition of a geometrical figure, unless we possess so accurate an image of it as to be able to trace it immediately upon paper or on the blackboard? How can we really have an intuition of the contour of a region, for example of the island of Sicily, if we are not able to draw it as it is in all its meanderings? Every one can experience the internal illumination which follows upon his success in formulating to himself his impressions and feelings, but only so far as he is able to formulate them. Feelings or impressions, then, pass by means of words from the obscure region of the soul into the clarity of the contemplative spirit. It is impossible to distinguish intuition from expression in this cognitive process. The one appears with the other at the same instant, because they are not two, but one.

The principal reason which makes our view appear paradoxical as we maintain it, is the illusion or prejudice that we possess a more complete intuition of reality than we really do. One often hears people say that they have many great thoughts in their minds, but that they are not able to express them. But if they really had them, they would have coined them into just so many beautiful, sounding words, and thus have expressed them. If these thoughts seem to vanish or to become few and meagre in the act of expressing them, the reason is that they did not exist or really were few and meagre. People think that all of us ordinary men imagine and intuit countries, figures and scenes like painters, and bodies like sculptors; save that painters and sculptors know how to paint and carve such images, while we bear them unexpressed in our souls. They believe that any one could have imagined a Madonna of Raphael; but that Raphael was Raphael owing to his technical ability in putting the Madonna upon canvas. Nothing can be more false than this view. The world which as a rule we intuit is a small thing. It consists of little expressions, which gradually become greater and wider with the increasing spiritual concentration of certain moments. They are the words we say to ourselves, our silent judgments: "Here is a man, here is a horse, this is heavy, this is sharp, this pleases me," etc. It is a medley of light and colour, with no greater pictorial value than could be expressed by a haphazard splash of colours, from among which one could barely make out a few special, distinctive traits. This and nothing else is what we possess in our ordinary life; this is the basis of our ordinary action. It is the index of a book. The labels tied to things (it has been said) take the place of the things themselves. This index and these labels (themselves expressions) suffice for small needs and small actions. From time to time we pass from the index to the book, from the label to the thing, or from the slight to the greater intuitions, and from these to the greatest and most lofty. This passage is sometimes far from easy. It has been observed by those who have best studied the psychology of artists that when, after having given a rapid glance at any one, they attempt to obtain a real intuition of him, in order, for example, to paint his portrait, then this ordinary vision, that seemed so precise, so lively, reveals itself as little better than nothing. What remains is found to be at the most some superficial trait, which would not even suffice for a caricature. The person to be painted stands before the artist like a world to discover. Michael Angelo said, "One paints, not with the hands, but with the brain." Leonardo shocked the prior of the Convent of the Graces by standing for days together gazing at the "Last Supper," without touching it with the brush. He remarked of this attitude: "The minds of men of lofty genius are most active in invention when they are doing the least external work." The painter is a painter, because he sees what others only feel or catch a glimpse of, but do not see. We think we see a smile, but in reality we have only a vague impression of it, we do not perceive all the characteristic traits of which it is the sum, as the painter discovers them after he has worked upon them and is thus able to fix them on the canvas. We do not intuitively possess more even of our intimate friend, who is with us every day and at all hours, than at most certain traits of physiognomy which enable us to distinguish him from others. The illusion is less easy as regards musical expression; because it would seem strange to every one to say that the composer had added or attached notes to a motive which was already in the mind of him who is not the composer; as if Beethoven's Ninth Symphony were not his own intuition and his intuition the Ninth Symphony. Now, just as one who is deluded as to the amount of his material wealth is confuted by arithmetic, which states its exact amount, so he who nourishes delusions as to the wealth of his own thoughts and images is brought back to reality, when he is obliged to cross the *Pons Asinorum* of expression. Let us say to the former, count; to the latter, speak; or, here is a pencil, draw, express yourself.[2]

Each of us, as a matter of fact, has in him a little of the poet, of the sculptor, of the musician, of the painter, of the prose writer: but how little, as compared with those who bear those names, just because they possess the most universal dispositions and energies of human nature in so lofty a degree! How little too does a painter possess of the intuitions of a poet! And how little does one painter possess those of another painter! Nevertheless, that little is all our actual patrimony of intuitions or representations. Beyond these are only impressions, sensations, feelings, impulses, emotions, or whatever else one may term what still falls short of the spirit and is not assimilated by man; something postulated for the convenience of exposition, while actually non-existent, since to exist also is a fact of the spirit.

We may thus add this to the various verbal descriptions of intuition, noted at the beginning: intuitive knowledge is expressive knowledge. Independent and autonomous in respect to intellectual function; indifferent to later empirical discriminations, to reality and to unreality, to formations and apperceptions of space and time, which are also later: intuition or representation is distinguished as *form* from what is felt and suffered, from the flux or wave of sensation, or from psychic matter; and this form, this taking possession, is expression. To intuit is to express; and nothing else (nothing more, but nothing less) than *to express*.

Intuition and Art

Before proceeding further, it may be well to draw certain consequences from what has been established and to add some explanations.

We have frankly identified intuitive or expressive knowledge with the aesthetic or artistic fact, taking works of art as examples of intuitive knowledge and attributing to them the characteristics of intuition, and *vice versa*. But our identification is combated by a view held even by many philosophers, who consider art to be an intuition of an altogether special sort. "Let us admit," (they say) "that art is intuition; but intuition is not always art: artistic intuition is a distinct species differing from intuition in general by something *more*."

But no one has ever been able to indicate of what this something more consists. It has sometimes been thought that art is not a simple intuition, but an intuition of an intuition, in the same way as the concept of science has been defined, not as the ordinary concept, but as the concept of a concept. Thus man would attain to art by objectifying, not his sensations, as happens with ordinary intuition, but intuition itself. But this process of raising to a second power does not exist; and the comparison of it with the ordinary and scientific concept does not prove what is intended, for the good reason that it is not true that the scientific concept is the concept of a concept. If this comparison proves anything, it proves just the opposite. The ordinary concept, if it be really a concept and not a simple representation, is a perfect concept, however poor and limited. Science substitutes concepts for representations; for those concepts that are poor and limited it substitutes others, larger and more comprehensive; it is ever discovering new relations. But its method does not differ from that by which is formed the smallest universal in the brain of the humblest of men. What is generally called *par excellence* art, collects intuitions that are wider and more complex than those which we generally experience, but these intuitions are always of sensations and impressions.

Art is expression of impressions, not expression of expression.

For the same reason, it cannot be asserted that the intuition, which is generally called artistic, differs from ordinary intuition as intensive intuition. This would be the case if it were to operate differently on the same matter. But since the artistic function is extended to wider fields, yet does not differ in method from ordinary intuition, the difference between them is not intensive but extensive. The intuition of the simplest popular love-song, which says the same thing, or very nearly, as any declaration of love that issues at every moment from the lips of thousands of ordinary men, may be intensively perfect in its poor simplicity, although it be extensively so much more limited than the complex intuition of a love-song by Leopardi.

The whole difference, then, is quantitative, and as such is indifferent to philosophy, *scientia qualitatum*. Certain men have a greater aptitude, a more frequent inclination fully to express certain complex states of the soul. These men are known in ordinary language as artists. Some very complicated and difficult expressions are not often achieved, and these are called works of art. The limits of the expression-intuitions that are called art, as opposed to those that are vulgarly called non-art, are empirical and impossible to define. If an epigram be art, why not a simple word? If a story, why not the news-jottings of the journalist? If a landscape, why not a topographical sketch? The teacher of philosophy in Moliere's comedy was right: "whenever we speak, we create prose." But there will always be scholars like Monsieur Jourdain, astonished at having spoken prose for forty years without knowing it, who will have difficulty in persuading themselves that when they call their servant John to bring their slippers, they have spoken nothing less than—prose.

We must hold firmly to our identification, because among the principal reasons which have prevented Aesthetic, the science of art, from revealing the true nature of art, its real roots in human nature, has been its separation from the general spiritual life, the having made of it a sort of special function or aristocratic club. No one is astonished when he learns from physiology that every cell is an organism and every organism a cell or synthesis of cells. No one is astonished at finding in a lofty mountain the same chemical elements that compose a small stone fragment. There is not one physiology of small animals and one of large animals; nor is there a special chemical theory of stones as distinct from mountains. In the same way, there is not a science of lesser intuition as distinct from a science of greater intuition, nor one of ordinary intuition as distinct from artistic intuition. There is but one Aesthetic, the science of intuitive or expressive knowledge, which is the aesthetic or artistic fact. And this Aesthetic is the true analogue of Logic, which includes, as facts of the same nature, the formation of the smallest and most ordinary concept and the most complicated scientific and philosophical system.

Nor can we admit that the word *genius* or artistic genius, as distinct from the non-genius of the ordinary man, possesses more than a quantitative signification. Great artists are said to reveal us to ourselves. But how could this be possible, unless there were identity of nature between their imagination and ours, and unless the difference were only one of quantity? It were better to change *poeta nascitur* into *homo nascitur poeta:* some men are born great poets, some small. The cult of the genius with all its attendant superstitions has arisen from this quantitative difference having been taken as a difference of quality. It has been forgotten that genius is not something that has fallen from heaven, but humanity itself. The man of genius who poses or is represented as remote from humanity finds his punishment in becoming or appearing somewhat ridiculous. Examples of this are the *genius* of the romantic period and the *superman* of our time.

But it is well to note here, that those who claim unconsciousness as the chief quality of an artistic genius, hurl him from an eminence far above humanity to a position far below it. Intuitive or artistic genius, like every form of human activity, is always conscious; otherwise it would be blind mechanism. The only thing that can be wanting to artistic genius is the *reflective* consciousness, the superadded consciousness of the historian or critic, which is not essential to it.

The relation between matter and form, or between *content* and *form*, as is generally said, is one of the most disputed questions in Aesthetic. Does the aesthetic fact consist of content alone, or of form alone, or of both together? This question has taken on various meanings, which we shall mention, each in its place. But when these words are taken as signifying what we have above defined, and matter is understood as emotionality not aesthetically elaborated, or impressions, and form as intellectual activity and expression, then our view cannot be in doubt. We must, that is to say, reject both the thesis that makes the aesthetic fact to consist of the content alone (that is, the simple impressions), and the thesis which makes it to consist of a junction between form and content, that is, of impressions plus expressions. In the aesthetic fact, expressive activity is not added to the fact of the impressions, but these latter are formed and elaborated by it. The impressions reappear as it were in expression, like water put into a filter, which reappears the same and yet different on the other side. The aesthetic fact, therefore, is form, and nothing but form.

From this was inferred not that the content is something superfluous (it is, on the contrary, the necessary point of departure for the expressive fact); but that *there is no passage* from the qualities of the content to those of the form. It has sometimes been thought that the content, in order to be aesthetic, that is to say, transformable into form, should possess some determined or determinable qualities. But were that so, then form and content, expression and impression, would be the same thing. It is true that the content is that which is convertible into form, but it has no determinable qualities until this transformation takes place. We know nothing about it. It does not become aesthetic content before, but only after it has been actually transformed. The aesthetic content has also been defined as the *interesting*. That is not an untrue statement; it is merely void of meaning. Interesting to what? To the expressive activity? Certainly the expressive activity would not have raised the content to the dignity of form, had it not been interested in it. Being interested is precisely the raising of the content to the dignity of form. But the word "interesting" has also been employed in another and an illegitimate sense, which we shall explain further on.

The proposition that art is *imitation of nature* has also several meanings. Sometimes truths have been expressed or at least shadowed forth in these words, sometimes errors have been promulgated. More frequently, no definite thought has been expressed at all. One of the scientifically legitimate meanings occurs when "imitation" is understood as representation or intuition of nature, a form of knowledge. And when the phrase is used with this intention, and in order to emphasize the spiritual character of the process, another proposition becomes legitimate also: namely, that art is the *idealization* or *idealizing* imitation of nature. But if by imitation of nature be understood that art gives mechanical reproductions, more or less perfect duplicates of natural objects, in the presence of which is renewed the same tumult of impressions as that caused by natural objects, then the proposition is evidently false. The coloured waxen effigies that imitate the life, before which we stand astonished in the museums where such things are shown, do not give aesthetic intuitions. Illusion and hallucination have nothing to do with the calm domain of artistic intuition. But on the other hand if an artist paint the interior of a wax-work museum, or if an actor give a burlesque portrait of a man-statue on the stage, we have work of the spirit and artistic intuition. Finally, if photography have in it anything artistic, it will be to the extent that it transmits the intuition of the photographer, his point of view, the pose and grouping which he has striven to attain. And if photography be not quite an art, that is precisely because the element of nature in it remains more or less unconquered and ineradicable. Do we ever, indeed, feel complete satisfaction before even the best of photographs? Would not an artist vary and touch up much or little, remove or add something to all of them?

The statements repeated so often, that art is not knowledge, that it does not tell the truth, that it does not belong to the world of theory, but to the world of feeling, and so forth, arise from the failure to realize exactly the theoretic character of simple intuition. This simple intuition is quite distinct from intellectual knowledge, as it is distinct from perception of the real; and the statements quoted above arise from the belief that only intellectual cognition is knowledge. We have seen that intuition is knowledge, free from concepts and more simple than the so-called perception of the real. Therefore art is knowledge, form; it does not belong to the world of feeling or to psychic matter. The reason why so many aestheticians have so often insisted that art is *appearance (Schein),* is precisely that they have felt the necessity of distinguishing it from the more complex fact of perception, by maintaining its pure intuitiveness. And if for the same reason it has been claimed that art is *feeling* the reason is the same. For if the concept as content of art, and historical reality as such, be excluded from the sphere of art, there remains no other content than reality apprehended in all its ingenuousness and immediacy in the vital impulse, in its *feeling,* that is to say again, pure intuition.

The theory of the *aesthetic senses* has also arisen from the failure to establish, or from having lost to view, the character of expression as distinct from impression, of form as distinct from matter.

This theory can be reduced to the error just indicated of wishing to find a passage from the qualities of the content to those of the form. To ask, in fact, what the aesthetic senses are, implies asking what sensible impressions are able to enter into aesthetic expressions, and which must of necessity do so. To this we must at once reply, that all impressions can enter into aesthetic expressions or formations, but that none are bound to do so of necessity. Dante raised to the dignity of form not only the "sweet colour of the oriental sapphire" (visual impressions), but also tactual or thermic impressions, such as the "dense air" and the "fresh rivulets" which "parch the more" the throat of the thirsty. The belief that a picture yields only visual impressions is a curious illusion. The bloom on a cheek, the warmth of a youthful body, the sweetness and freshness of a fruit, the edge of a sharp knife, are not these, too, impressions obtainable from a picture? Are they visual? What would a picture mean to an imaginary man, lacking all or many of his senses, who should in an instant acquire the organ of sight alone? The picture we are looking at and believe we see only with our eyes would seem to his eyes to be little more than an artist's paint-smeared palette.

Some who hold firmly to the aesthetic character of certain groups of impressions (for example, the visual and auditive), and exclude others, are nevertheless ready to admit that if visual and auditive impressions enter *directly* into the aesthetic fact, those of the other senses also enter into it, but only as *associated.* But this distinction is altogether arbitrary. Aesthetic expression is synthesis, in which it is impossible to distinguish direct and indirect. All impressions are placed by it on a level, in so far as they are aestheticized. A man who absorbs the subject of a picture or poem does not have it before him as a series of impressions, some of which have prerogatives and precedence over others. He knows nothing as to what has happened prior to having absorbed it, just as, on the other hand, distinctions made after reflexion have nothing whatever to do with art as such.

The theory of the aesthetic senses has also been presented in another way; as an attempt to establish what physiological organs are necessary for the aesthetic fact. The physiological organ or apparatus is nothing but a group of cells, constituted and disposed in a particular manner; that is to say, it is merely physical and natural fact or concept. But expression does not know physiological facts. Expression has its point of departure in the impressions, and the physiological path by which these have found their way to the mind is to it altogether indifferent. One way or another comes to the same thing: it suffices that they should be impressions.

It is true that the want of given organs, that is, of certain groups of cells, prevents the formation of certain impressions (when these are not otherwise obtained through a kind of organic compensation). The man born blind cannot intuit and express light. But the impressions are not conditioned solely by the organ, but also by the stimuli which operate upon the organ. One who has never had the impression of the sea will never be able to express it, in the same way as one who has never had the impression of the life of high society or of the political arena will never express either. This, however, does not prove the dependence of the expressive function on the stimulus or on the organ. It merely repeats what we know already: expression presupposes impression, and particular expressions particular impressions. For the rest, every impression excludes other impressions during the moment in which it dominates; and so does every expression.

Another corollary of the conception of expression as activity is the *indivisibility* of the work of art. Every expression is a single expression. Activity is a fusion of the impression in an organic whole. A desire to express this has always prompted the affirmation that the work of art should have *unity,* or, what amounts to the same thing, *unity in variety*. Expression is a synthesis of the various, or multiple, in the one.

The fact that we divide a work of art into parts, a poem into scenes, episodes, similes, sentences, or a picture into single figures and objects, background, foreground, etc., may seem opposed to this affirmation. But such division annihilates the work, as dividing the organism into heart, brain, nerves, muscles, and so on, turns the living being into a corpse. It is true that there exist organisms in which division gives rise to other living beings, but in such a case we must conclude, maintaining the analogy between the organism and the work of art, that in the latter case too there are numerous germs of life each ready to grow, in a moment, into a single complete expression.

It may be said that expression sometimes arises from other expressions. There are simple and there are *compound* expressions. One must surely admit some difference between the *eureka,* with which Archimedes expressed all his joy at his discovery, and the expressive act (indeed all the five acts) of a regular tragedy.—Not in the least: expression always arises directly from impressions. He who conceives a tragedy puts into a crucible a great quantity, so to say, of impressions: expressions themselves, conceived on other occasions, are fused together with the new in a single mass, in the same way as we can cast into a melting furnace formless pieces of bronze and choicest statuettes. Those choicest statuettes must be melted just like the pieces of bronze, before there can be a new statue. The old expressions must descend again to the level of impressions, in order to be synthetized in a new single expression.

By elaborating his impressions, man *frees* himself from them. By objectifying them, he removes them from him and makes himself their superior. The liberating and purifying function of art is another aspect and another formula of its character as activity. Activity is the deliverer, just because it drives away passivity.

This also explains why it is usual to attribute to artists both the maximum of sensibility or *passion,* and the maximum of insensibility or Olympian *serenity.* The two characters are compatible, for they do not refer to the same object. The sensibility or passion relates to the rich material which the artist absorbs into his psychic organism; the insensibility or serenity to the form with which he subdues and dominates the tumult of the sensations and passions.

Notes

1. "Trees speak, not only beasts."

2. *Pons Asinorum*: "asses' bridge," or "bridge of fools." A label affixed, by whom we do not know, to Proposition 5, Book 1 of Euclid's *Elements*. According to the standard explanation, it refers to the difficulties that a poor geometer will have in mastering its proof. Metaphorically, it refers to any sure test of knowledge or ability.

Despite Croce's references to drawing and painting in these paragraphs, the reader should be warned that according to Croce the actual drawing or painting of something is not identical with expression but is in fact incidental to it. As he says in Chapter VI of *Aesthetic*, pp. 50-51, that "The aesthetic fact is altogether completed in the expressive elaboration of impressions. When we have achieved the word within us, conceived definitely and vividly a figure or a statue, or found a musical motive, expression is born and is complete; there is no need of anything else. If after this we should open our mouths . . . to speak, or our throats to sing, that is to say, utter by word of mouth and audible melody what we have completely said or sung to ourselves; or if we should . . . stretch out our hands to touch the notes of the piano, or to take up the brush and chisel, thus making on a large scale, movements which we have already made in little and rapidly, in a material in which we leave more or less durable traces; this is all an addition, a fact which obeys quite different laws from the former, with which we are not concerned for the moment, although we recognize henceforth that this second movement is a production of things, a *practical* fact, or fact of *will*. It is usual to distinguish the internal from the external work of art: the terminology seems to us infelicitous, for the work of art (the aesthetic work) is always *internal*; and what is called *external* is no longer a work of art." Ed.

CLIVE BELL

The Aesthetic Hypothesis

IT IS IMPROBABLE that more nonsense has been written about aesthetics than about anything else: the literature of the subject is not large enough for that. It is certain, however, that about no subject with which I am acquainted has so little been said that is at all to the purpose. The explanation is discoverable. He who would elaborate a plausible theory of aesthetics must possess two qualities—artistic sensibility and a turn for clear thinking. Without sensibility a man can have no aesthetic experience, and, obviously, theories not based on broad and deep aesthetic experience are worthless. Only those for whom art is a constant source of passionate emotion can possess the data from which profitable theories may be deduced; but to deduce profitable theories even from accurate data involves a certain amount of brain-work, and, unfortunately, robust intellects and delicate sensibilities are not inseparable. As often as not, the hardest thinkers have had no aesthetic experience whatever. I have a friend blessed with an intellect as keen as a drill, who, though he takes an interest in aesthetics, has never during a life of almost forty years been guilty of an aesthetic emotion. So, having no faculty for distinguishing a work of art from a handsaw, he is apt to rear up a pyramid of irrefragable argument on the hypothesis that a handsaw is a work of art. This defect robs his perspicuous and subtle reasoning of much of its value; for it has ever been a maxim that faultless logic can win but little credit for conclusions that are based on premises notoriously false. Every cloud, however, has its silver lining, and this insensibility, though unlucky in that it makes my friend incapable of choosing a sound basis for his argument, mercifully blinds him to the absurdity of his conclusions while leaving him in full enjoyment of his masterly dialectic. People who set out from the hypothesis that Sir Edwin Landseer was the finest painter that ever lived will find no uneasiness about an aesthetic which proves that Giotto

First published in 1914 and reprinted from the Capricorn edition of *Art* by Clive Bell by permission of G. P. Putnam's Sons and Chatto and Windus Ltd, London.

was the worst. So, my friend, when he arrives very logically at the conclusion that a work of art should be small or round or smooth, or that to appreciate fully a picture you should pace smartly before it or set it spinning like a top, cannot guess why I ask him whether he has lately been to Cambridge, a place he sometimes visits.

On the other hand, people who respond immediately and surely to works of art, though, in my judgment, more enviable than men of massive intellect but slight sensibility, are often quite as incapable of talking sense about aesthetics. Their heads are not always very clear. They possess the data on which any system must be based, but, generally, they want the power that draws correct inferences from true data. Having received aesthetic emotions from works of art, they are in a position to seek out the quality common to all that have moved them, but, in fact, they do nothing of the sort. I do not blame them. Why should they bother to examine their feelings when for them to feel is enough? Why should they stop to think when they are not very good at thinking? Why should they hunt for a common quality in all objects that move them in a particular way when they can linger over the many delicious and peculiar charms of each as it comes? So, if they write criticism and call it aesthetics, if they imagine they are talking about Art when they are talking about particular works of art or even about the technique of painting, if loving particular works they find tedious the consideration of art in general, perhaps they have chosen the better part. If they are not curious about the nature of their emotion, nor about the quality common to all objects that provoke it, they have my sympathy, and, as what they say is often charming and suggestive, my admiration too. Only let no one suppose that what they write and talk is aesthetics: it is criticism, or just "shop."

The starting-point for all systems of aesthetics must be the personal experience of a peculiar emotion. The objects that provoke this emotion we call works of art. All sensitive people agree that there is a peculiar emotion provoked by works of art. I do not mean, of course, that all works provoke the same emotion. On the contrary, every work produces a different emotion. But all these emotions are recognisably the same in kind; so far, at any rate, the best opinion is on my side. That there is a particular kind of emotion provoked by works of visual art, and that this emotion is provoked by every kind of visual art, by pictures, sculptures, buildings, pots, carvings, textiles, etc., etc., is not disputed, I think, by anyone capable of feeling it. This emotion is called the aesthetic emotion; and if we can discover some quality common and peculiar to all the objects that provoke it, we shall have solved what I take to be the central problem of aesthetics. We shall have discovered the essential quality in a work of art, the quality that distinguishes works of art from all other classes of objects.

For either all works of visual art have some common quality, or when we speak of "works of art" we gibber. Everyone speaks of "art," making a mental classification by which he distinguishes the class "works of art" from all other classes. What is the justification of this classification? What is the quality common and peculiar to all members of this class? Whatever it be, no doubt it is often found in company with other qualities; but they are adventitious—it is essential. There must be some one quality without which a work of art cannot exist; possessing which in the least degree, no work is altogether worthless. What is this quality? What quality is shared by all objects that provoke our aesthetic emotions? What quality is common to St. Sophia and the windows at Chartres, Mexican sculpture, a Persian bowl, Chinese carpets, Giotto's frescoes at Padua, and the masterpieces of Poussin, Piero della Francesca, and Cézanne? Only one answer seems possible—significant form. In each, lines and colours combined in a particular way, certain forms and relations of forms, stir our aesthetic emotions. These relations and combinations of lines and colours, these aesthetically moving forms, I shall call "Significant Form"; and "Significant Form" is the one quality common to all works of visual art.

At this point it may be objected that I am making aesthetics a purely subjective business, since my only data are personal experiences of a particular emotion. It will be said that the objects that provoke this emotion vary with each individual, and that therefore a system of aesthetics can have no objective validity. It must be replied that any system of aesthetics which pretends to be based on some objective truth is so palpably ridiculous as not to be worth discussing. We have no other means of recognising a work of art than our feeling for it. The objects that provoke aesthetic emotion vary with each individual. Aesthetic judgments are, as the saying goes, matters of taste; and about tastes, as everyone is proud to admit, there is no disputing. A good critic may be able to make me see in a picture that had left me cold things that I had overlooked, till at last, receiving the aesthetic emotion, I recognise it as a work of art. To be continually pointing out those parts, the sum, or rather the combination, of which unite to produce significant form, is the function of criticism. But it is useless for a critic to tell me that something is a work of art; he must make me feel it for myself. This he can do only by making me see; he must get at my emotions through my eyes. Unless he can make me see something that moves me, he cannot force my emotions. I have no right to consider anything a work of art to which I cannot react emotionally, and I have no right to look for the essential quality in anything that I have not *felt* to be a work of art. The critic can affect my aesthetic theories only by affecting my aesthetic experience. All systems of aesthetics must be based on personal experience—that is to say, they must be subjective.

Yet, though all aesthetic theories must be based on aesthetic judgments, and ultimately all aesthetic judgments must be matters of personal taste, it would be rash to assert that no theory of aesthetics can have general validity. For, though A, B, C, D are the works that move me, and A, D, E, F the works that move you, it may well be that *x* is the only quality believed by either of us to be common to all the works in his list. We may all agree about aesthetics, and yet differ about particular works of art. We may differ as to the presence or absence of the quality *x*. My immediate object will be to show that significant form is the only quality common and peculiar to all the works of visual art that move me; and I will ask those whose aesthetic experience does not tally with mine to see whether this quality is not also, in their judgment, common to all works that move them, and whether they can discover any other quality of which the same can be said.

Also at this point a query arises, irrelevant indeed, but hardly to be suppressed: "Why are we so profoundly moved by forms related in a particular way?" The question is extremely interesting, but irrelevant to aesthetics. In pure aesthetics we have only to consider our emotion and its object: for the purposes of aesthetics we have no right, neither is there any necessity, to pry behind the object into the state of mind of him who made it. Later, I shall attempt to answer the question; for by so doing I may be able to develop my theory of the relation of art to life. I shall not, however, be under the delusion that I am rounding off my theory of aesthetics. For a discussion of aesthetics, it need be agreed only that forms arranged and combined according to certain unknown and mysterious laws do move us in a particular way, and that it is the business of an artist so to combine and arrange them that they shall move us. These moving combinations and arrangements I have called, for the sake of convenience and for a reason that will appear later, "Significant Form."

A third interruption has to be met.

"Are you forgetting about colour?" someone inquires. Certainly not; my term "significant form" included combinations of lines and of colours. The distinction between form and colour is an unreal one; you cannot conceive a colourless line or a colourless space; neither can you conceive a formless relation of colours. In a black and white drawing the spaces are all white and all are bounded by black lines; in most oil paintings the spaces are multi-coloured and so are the boundaries; you cannot imagine a boundary line without any content, or a content without a boundary line. Therefore, when I speak of significant form, I mean a combination of lines and colours (counting white and black as colours) that moves me aesthetically.

Some people may be surprised at my not having called this "beauty." Of course, to those who define beauty as "combinations of lines and colours that provoke aesthetic emotion," I willingly concede the right of substituting their word for mine. But most of us, however strict we may be, are apt to apply the epithet "beautiful" to objects that do not provoke that peculiar emotion produced by works of art. Everyone, I suspect, has called a butterfly or a flower beautiful. Does anyone feel the same kind of emotion for a butterfly or a flower that he feels for a cathedral or a picture? Surely, it is not what I call an aesthetic emotion that most of us feel, generally, for natural beauty. I shall suggest, later, that some people may, occasionally, see in nature what we see in art, and feel for her an aesthetic emotion; but I am satisfied that, as a rule, most people feel a very different kind of emotion for birds and flowers and the wings of butterflies from that which they feel for pictures, pots, temples and statues. Why these beautiful things do not move us as works of art move is another, and not an aesthetic question. For our immediate purpose we have to discover only what quality is common to objects that do move us as works of art. In the last part of this chapter, when I try to answer the question—"Why are we so profoundly moved by some combinations of lines and colours?" I shall hope to offer an acceptable explanation of why we are less profoundly moved by others.

Since we call a quality that does not raise the characteristic aesthetic emotion "Beauty," it would be misleading to call by the same name the quality that does. To make "beauty" the object of the aesthetic emotion, we must give to the word an over-strict and unfamiliar definition. Everyone sometimes uses "beauty" in an unaesthetic sense; most people habitually do. To everyone, except perhaps here and there an occasional aesthete, the commonest sense of the word is unaesthetic. Of its grosser abuse, patent in our chatter about "beautiful huntin'" and "beautiful shootin'," I need not take account; it would be open to the precious to reply that they never do so abuse it. Besides, here there is no danger of confusion between the aesthetic and the non-aesthetic use; but when we speak of a beautiful woman there is. When an ordinary man speaks of a beautiful woman he certainly does not mean only that she moves him aesthetically; but when an artist calls a withered old hag beautiful he may sometimes mean what he means when he calls a battered torso beautiful. The ordinary man, if he be also a man of taste, will call the battered torso beautiful, but he will not call a withered hag beautiful because, in the matter of women, it is not to the aesthetic quality that the hag may possess, but to some other quality that he assigns the epithet. Indeed, most of us never dream of going for aesthetic emotions to human beings, from whom we ask something very different. This "something," when we find it in a young woman, we are apt to call "beauty." We live in a nice age. With the man-in-the-street "beautiful" is more often than not synonymous with "desirable"; the word does not necessarily connote any aesthetic reaction whatever, and I am tempted to believe that in the minds of many the sexual flavour of the word is stronger than the aesthetic. I have noticed a consistency in those to whom the most beautiful thing in the world is a beautiful woman, and the next most beautiful thing a picture of one. The confusion between aesthetic and sensual beauty is not in their case so great as might be supposed. Perhaps there is none; for perhaps they have never had an aesthetic emotion to confuse with their other emotions. The art that they call "beautiful" is generally closely related to the women. A beautiful picture is a photograph of a pretty girl; beautiful music, the music that provokes emotions similar to those provoked by young ladies in musical farces; and beautiful poetry, the poetry that recalls the same emotions felt, twenty years earlier, for the rector's daughter. Clearly the word "beauty" is used to connote the objects of quite distinguishable emotions, and that is a reason for not employing a term which would land me inevitably in confusions and misunderstandings with my readers.

On the other hand, with those who judge it more exact to call these combinations and arrangements of form that provoke our aesthetic emotions, not "significant form," but "significant relations of form," and then try to make the best of two worlds, the aesthetic and the metaphysical, by calling these relations "rhythm," I have no quarrel whatever. Having made it clear that by "significant form" I mean arrangements and combinations that move us in a particular way, I willingly join hands with those who prefer to give a different name to the same thing.

The hypothesis that significant form is the essential quality in a work of art has at least one merit denied to many more famous and more striking—it does help to explain things. We are all familiar with pictures that interest us and excite our admiration, but do not move us as works of art. To this class belongs what I call "Descriptive Painting"—that is, painting in which forms are used not as objects of emotion, but as means of suggesting emotion or conveying information. Portraits of psychological and historical value, topographical works, pictures that tell stories and suggest situations, illustrations of all sorts, belong to this class. That we all recognize the distinction is clear, for who has not said that such and such a drawing was excellent as illustration, but as a work of art worthless? Of course many descriptive pictures possess, amongst other qualities, formal significance, and are therefore works of art: but many more do not. They interest us; they may move us too in a hundred different ways, but they do not move us aesthetically. According to my hypothesis they are not works of art. They leave untouched our aesthetic emotions because it is not their forms but the ideas or information suggested or conveyed by their forms that affect us.

Few pictures are better known or liked than Frith's "Paddington Station"; certainly I should be the last to grudge it its popularity. Many a weary forty minutes have I whiled away disentangling its fascinating incidents and forging for each an imaginary past and an improbable future. But certain though it is that Frith's masterpiece, or engravings of it, have provided thousands with half-hours of curious and fanciful pleasure, it is not less certain that no one has experienced before it one half-second of aesthetic rapture—and this although the picture contains several pretty passages of colour, and is by no means badly painted. "Paddington Station" is not a work of art; it is an interesting and amusing document. In it line and colour are used to recount anecdotes, suggest ideas, and indicate the manners and customs of an age: they are not used to provoke aesthetic emotion. Forms and the relations of forms were for Frith not objects of emotion, but means of suggesting emotion and conveying ideas.

The ideas and information conveyed by "Paddington Station" are so amusing and so well presented that the picture has considerable value and is well worth preserving. But, with the perfection of photographic processes and of the cinematograph, pictures of this sort are becoming otiose. Who doubts that one of those *Daily Mirror* photographers in collaboration with a *Daily Mail* reporter can tell us far more about "London day by day" than any Royal Academician? For an account of manners and fashions we shall go, in future, to photographs, supported by a little bright journalism, rather than to descriptive painting. Had the imperial academicians of Nero, instead of manufacturing incredibly loathsome imitations of the antique, recorded in fresco and mosaic the manners and fashions of their day, their stuff, though artistic rubbish, would now be an historical gold-mine. If only they had been Friths instead of being Alma Tademas! But photography has made impossible any such transmutation of modern rubbish. Therefore it must be confessed that pictures in the Frith tradition are grown superfluous; they merely waste the hours of able men who might be more profitably employed in works of a wider beneficence. Still, they are not unpleasant, which is more than can be said for that kind of descriptive painting of which "The Doctor" is the most flagrant example. Of course "The Doctor" is not a work of art. In it form is not used as an object of emotion, but as a means of suggesting emotions. This alone suffices to make it nugatory; it is worse than nugatory because the emotion it suggests is false. What it suggests is not pity and admiration but a sense of complacency in our own pitifulness and generosity. It is sentimental. Art is above morals, or, rather, all art is moral because, as I hope to show presently, works of art are immediate means to good. Once we have judged a thing a work of art, we have judged it ethically of the first importance and put it beyond the reach of the moralist. But descriptive pictures which are not works of art, and, therefore, are not necessarily means to good states of mind, are proper subjects of the ethical philosopher's attention. Not being a work of art, "The Doctor" has none of the immense ethical value possessed by all objects that provoke aesthetic ecstasy; and the state of mind to which it is a means, as illustration, appears to me undesirable.

The works of those enterprising young men, the Italian Futurists, are notable examples of descriptive painting. Like the Royal Academicians, they use form, not to provoke aesthetic emotions, but to convey information and ideas. Indeed, the published theories of the Futurists prove that their pictures ought to have nothing whatever to do with art. Their social and political theories are respectable, but I would suggest to young Italian painters that it is possible to become a Futurist in thought and action and yet remain an artist, if one has the luck to be born one. To associate art with politics is always a mistake. Futurist pictures are descriptive because they aim at presenting in line and colour the chaos of the mind at a particular moment; their forms are not intended to promote aesthetic emotion but to convey information. These forms, by the way, whatever may be the nature of the ideas they suggest, are themselves anything but revolutionary. In such Futurist pictures as I have seen—perhaps I should except some by Severini—the drawing, whenever it becomes representative as it frequently does, is found to be in that soft and common convention brought into fashion by Besnard some thirty years ago, and much affected by Beaux-Art students ever since. As works of art, the Futurist pictures are negligible; but they are not to be judged as works of art. A good Futurist picture would succeed as a good piece of psychology succeeds; it would reveal, through line and colour, the complexities of an interesting state of mind. If Futurist pictures seem to fail, we must seek an explanation, not in a lack of artistic qualities that they were never intended to possess, but rather in the minds the states of which they are intended to reveal.

Most people who care much about art find that of the work that moves them most the greater part is what scholars call "Primitive." Of course there are bad primitives. For instance, I remember going, full of enthusiasm, to see one of the earliest Romanesque churches in Poitiers (Notre-Dame-La-Grande), and finding it as ill-proportioned, over-decorated, coarse, fat and heavy as any better class building by one of those highly civilised architects who flourished a thousand years earlier or eight hundred later. But such exceptions are rare. As a rule primitive art is good—and here again my hypothesis is helpful—for, as a rule, it is also free from descriptive qualities. In primitive art you will find no accurate representation; you will find only significant form. Yet no other art moves us so profoundly. Whether we consider Sumerian sculpture or pre-dynastic Egyptian art, or archaic Greek, or the Wei and T'ang masterpieces, or those early Japanese works of which I had the luck to see a few superb examples (especially two wooden Bodhisattvas) at the Shepherd's Bush Exhibition in 1910, or whether, coming nearer home, we consider the primitive Byzantine art of the sixth century and its primitive developments amongst the Western barbarians, or, turning far afield, we consider that mysterious and majestic art that flourished in Central and South America before the coming of the white men, in every case we observe three common characteristics—absence of representation, absence of technical swagger, sublimely impressive form. Nor is it hard to discover the connection between these three. Formal significance loses itself in preoccupation with exact representation and ostentatious cunning.

Naturally, it is said that if there is little representation and less saltimbancery in primitive art, that is because the primitives were unable to catch a likeness or cut intellectual capers. The contention is beside the point. There is truth in it, no doubt, though, were I a critic whose reputation depended on a power of impressing the public with a semblance of knowledge, I should be more cautious about urging it than such people generally are. For to suppose that the Byzantine masters wanted skill, or could not have created an illusion had they wished to do so, seems to imply ignorance of the amazingly dexterous realism of the notoriously bad works of that age. Very often, I fear, the misrepresentation of the primitives must be attributed to what the critics call, "wilful distortion." Be that as it may, the point is that, either from want of skill or want of will, primitives neither create illusions, nor make display of extravagant accomplishment, but concentrate their energies on the one thing needful —the creation of form. Thus they have created the finest works of art that we possess.

Let no one imagine that representation is bad in itself; a realistic form may be as significant, in its place as part of the design, as an abstract. But if a representative form has value, it is as form, not as representation. The representative element in a work of art may or may not be harmful; always it is irrelevant. For, to appreciate a work of art we need bring with us nothing from life, no knowledge of its ideas and affairs, no familiarity with its emotions. Art transports us from the world of man's activity to a world of aesthetic exultation. For a moment we are shut off from human interests; our anticipations and memories are arrested; we are lifted above the stream of life. The pure mathematician rapt in his studies knows a state of mind which I take to be similar, if not identical. He feels an emotion for his speculations which arises from no perceived relation between them and the lives of men, but springs, inhuman or super-human, from the heart of an abstract science. I wonder, sometimes, whether the appreciators of art and of mathematical solutions are not even more closely allied. Before we feel an aesthetic emotion for a combination of forms, do we not perceive intellectually the rightness and necessity of the combination? If we do, it would explain the fact that passing rapidly through a room we recognise a picture to be good, although we cannot say that it has provoked much emotion. We seem to have recognized intellectually the rightness of its forms without staying to fix our attention, and collect, as it were, their emotional significance. If this were so, it would be permissible to inquire whether it was the forms themselves or our perception of their rightness and necessity that caused aesthetic emotion. But I do not think I need linger to discuss the matter here. I have been inquiring why certain combinations of forms move us; I should not have travelled by other roads had I enquired, instead, why certain combinations are perceived to be right and necessary, and why our perception of their rightness and necessity is moving. What I have to say is this: the rapt philosopher, and he who contemplates a work of art, inhabit a world with an intense and peculiar significance of its own; that significance is unrelated to the significance of life. In this world the emotions of life find no place. It is a world with emotions of its own.

To appreciate a work of art we need bring with us nothing but a sense of form and colour and a knowledge of three-dimensional space. That bit of knowledge, I admit, is essential to the appreciation of many great works, since many of the most moving forms ever created are in three dimensions. To see a cube or a rhomboid as a flat pattern is to lower its significance, and a sense of three-dimensional space is essential to the full appreciation of most architectural forms. Pictures which would be insignificant if we saw them as flat patterns are profoundly moving because, in fact, we see them as related planes. If the representation of three-dimensional space is to be called "representation," then I agree that there is one kind of representation which is not irrelevant. Also, I agree that along with our feeling for line and colour we must bring with us our knowledge of space if we are to make the most of every kind of form. Nevertheless, there are significant designs to an appreciation of which this knowledge is not necessary; so, though it is not irrelevant to the appreciation of some works of art it is not essential to the appreciation of all. What we must say is that the representation of three-dimensional space is neither irrelevant nor essential to all art, and that every other sort of representation is irrelevant.

That there is an irrelevant representative or descriptive element in many great works of art is not in the least surprising. Why it is not surprising I shall try to show elsewhere. Representation is not of necessity baneful, and highly realistic forms may be extremely significant. Very often, however, representation is a sign of weakness in an artist. A painter too feeble to create forms that provoke more than a little aesthetic emotion will try to eke that little out by suggesting the emotions of life. To evoke the emotions of life he must use representation. Thus a man will paint an execution, and, fearing to miss with his first barrel of significant form, will try to hit with his second by raising an emotion of fear or pity. But if in the artist an inclination to play upon the emotions of life is often the sign of a flickering inspiration, in the spectator a tendency to seek, behind form, the emotions of life is a sign of defective sensibility always. It means that his aesthetic emotions are weak or, at any rate, imperfect. Before a work of art people who feel little or no emotion for pure form find themselves at a loss. They are deaf men at a concert. They know that they are in the presence of something great, but they lack the power of apprehending it. They know that they ought to feel for it a tremendous emotion, but it happens that the particular kind of emotion it can raise is one that they can feel hardly or not at all. And so they read into the forms of the work those facts and ideas for which they are capable of feeling emotion, and feel for them the emotions that they can feel—the ordinary emotions of life. When confronted by a picture, instinctively they refer back its forms to the world from which they came. They treat created form as though it were imitated form, a picture as though it were a photograph. Instead of going out on the stream of art into a new world of aesthetic experience, they turn a sharp corner and come straight home to the world of human interests. For them the significance of a work of art depends on what they bring to it; no new thing is added to their lives, only the old material is stirred. A good work of visual art carries a person who is capable of appreciating it out of life into ecstasy; to use art as a means to the emotions of life is to use a telescope for reading the news. You will notice that people who cannot feel pure aesthetic emotions remember pictures by their subjects; whereas people who can, as often as not, have no idea what the subject of a picture is. They have never noticed the representative element, and so when they discuss pictures they talk about the shapes of forms and the relations and quantities of colours. Often they can tell by the quality of a single line whether or not a man is a good artist. They are concerned only with lines and colours, their relations and quantities and qualities; but from these they win an emotion more profound and far more sublime than any that can be given by the description of facts and ideas.

This last sentence has a very confident ring—over-confident, some may think. Perhaps I shall be able to justify it, and make my meaning clearer too, if I give an account of my own feelings about music. I am not really musical. I do not understand music well. I find musical form exceedingly difficult to apprehend, and I am sure that the profounder subtleties of harmony and rhythm more often than not escape me. The form of a musical composition must be simple indeed if I am to grasp it honestly. My opinion about music is not worth having. Yet, sometimes, at a concert, though my appreciation of the music is limited and humble, it is pure. Sometimes, though I have a poor understanding, I have a clean palate. Consequently, when I am feeling bright and clear and intent, at the beginning of a concert, for instance, when something that I can grasp is being played, I get from music that pure aesthetic emotion that I get from visual art. It is less intense, and the rapture is evanescent; I understand music too ill for music to transport me far into the world of pure aesthetic ecstasy. But at moments I do appreciate music as pure musical form, as sounds combined according to the laws of a mysterious necessity, as pure art with a tremendous significance of its own and no relation whatever to the significance of life; and in those moments I lose myself in that infinitely sublime state of mind to which pure visual form transports me. How inferior is my normal state of mind at a concert. Tired or perplexed, I let slip my sense of form, my aesthetic emotion collapses, and I begin weaving into the harmonies, that I cannot grasp, the ideas of life. Incapable of feeling the austere emotions of art, I begin to read into the musical forms human emotions of terror and mystery, love and hate, and spend the minutes, pleasantly enough, in a world of turbid and inferior feeling. At such times, were the grossest pieces of onomatopoeic representation—the song of a bird, the galloping of horses, the cries of children, or the laughing of demons—to be introduced into the symphony, I should not be offended. Very likely I should be pleased; they would afford new points of departure for new trains of romantic feeling or heroic thought. I know very well what has happened. I have been using art as a means to the emotions of life and reading into it the ideas of life. I have been cutting blocks with a razor. I have tumbled from the superb peaks of aesthetic exaltation to the snug foothills of warm humanity. It is a jolly country. No one need be ashamed of enjoying himself there. Only no one who has ever been on the heights can help feeling a little crestfallen in the cosy valleys. And let no one imagine, because he had made merry in the warm tilth and quaint nooks of romance, that he can even guess at the austere and thrilling raptures of those who have climbed the cold, white peaks of art.

About music most people are as willing to be humble as I am. If they cannot grasp musical form and win from it a pure aesthetic emotion, they confess that they understand music imperfectly or not at all. They recognise quite clearly that there is a difference between the feeling of the musician for pure music and that of the cheerful concert-goer for what music suggests. The latter enjoys his own emotions, as he has every right to do, and recognises their inferiority. Unfortunately, people are apt to be less modest about their powers of appreciating visual art. Everyone is inclined to believe that out of pictures, at any rate, he can get all that there is to be got; everyone is ready to cry "humbug" and "imposter" at those who say that more can be had. The good faith of people who feel pure aesthetic emotions is called in question by those who have never felt anything of the sort. It is the prevalance of the representative element, I suppose, that makes the man in the street so sure that he knows a good picture when he sees one. For I have noticed that in matters of architecture, pottery, textiles, etc., ignorance and ineptitude are more willing to defer to the opinions of those who have been blest with peculiar sensibility. It is a pity that cultivated and intelligent men and women cannot be induced to believe that a great gift of aesthetic appreciation is at least as rare in visual as in musical art. A comparison of my own experience in both has enabled me to discriminate very clearly between pure and impure appreciation. Is it too much to ask that others should be as honest about their feelings for pictures as I have been about mine for music? For I am certain that most of those who visit galleries do feel very much what I feel at concerts. They have their moments of pure ecstasy; but the moments are short and unsure. Soon they fall back into the world of human interests and feel emotions, good no doubt, but inferior. I do not dream of saying that what they get from art is bad or nugatory; I say that they do not get the best that art can give. I do not say that they cannot understand art; rather I say that they cannot understand the state of mind of those who understand it best. I do not say that art means nothing or little to them; I say they miss its full significance. I do not suggest for one moment that their appreciation of art is a thing to be ashamed of; the majority of the charming and intelligent people with whom I am acquainted appreciate visual art impurely; and, by the way, the appreciation of almost all great writers has been impure. But provided that there be some fraction of pure aesthetic emotion, even a mixed and minor appreciation of art is, I am sure, one of the most valuable things in the world—so valuable, indeed, that in my giddier moments I have been tempted to believe that art might prove the world's salvation.

Yet, though the echoes and shadows of art enrich the life of the plains, her spirit dwells on the mountains. To him who woos, but woos impurely, she returns enriched what is brought. Like the sun, she warms the good seed in good soil and causes it to bring forth good fruit. But only to the perfect lover does she give a new strange gift—a gift beyond all price. Imperfect lovers bring to art and take away the ideas and emotions of their own age and civilisation. In twelfth-century Europe a man might have been greatly moved by a Romanesque church and found nothing in a T'ang picture. To a man of a later age, Greek sculpture meant much and Mexican nothing, for only to the former could he bring a crowd of associated ideas to be the objects of familiar emotions. But the perfect lover, he who can feel the profound significance of form, is raised above the accidents of time and place. To him the problems of archaeology, history, and hagiography are impertinent. If the forms of a work are significant its provenance is irrelevant. Before the grandeur of those Sumerian figures in the Louvre he is carried on the same flood of emotion to the same aesthetic ecstasy as, more than four thousand years ago, the Chaldean lover was carried. It is the mark of great art that its appeal is universal and eternal.[1] Significant form stands charged with the power to provoke aesthetic emotion in anyone capable of feeling it. The ideas of men go buzz and die like gnats; men change their institutions and their customs as they change their coats; only great art remains stable and unobscure. Great art remains stable and unobscure because the feelings that it awakens are independent of time and place, because its kingdom is not of this world. To those who have and hold a sense of the significance of form what does it matter whether the forms that move them were created in Paris the day before yesterday or in Babylon fifty centuries ago? The forms of art are inexhaustible; but all lead by the same road of aesthetic emotion to the same world of aesthetic ecstasy.

Note

1. Mr. Roger Fry permits me to make use of an interesting story that will illustrate my view. When Mr. Okakura, the Government editor of *The Temple Treasures of Japan,* first came to Europe, he found no difficulty in appreciating the pictures of those who from want of will or want of skill did not create illusions but concentrated their energies on the creation of form. He understood immediately the Byzantine masters and the French and Italian Primitives. In the

Renaissance painters, on the other hand, with their descriptive preoccupations, their literary and anecdotic interests, he could see nothing but vulgarity and muddle. The universal and essential quality of art, significant form, was missing, or rather had dwindled to a shallow stream, overlaid and hidden beneath weeds, so the universal response, aesthetic emotion, was not evoked. It was not till he came on to Henri-Matisse that he again found himself in the familiar world of pure art. Similarly, sensitive Europeans who respond immediately to the significant forms of great Oriental art, are left cold by the trivial pieces of anecdote and social criticism so lovingly cherished by Chinese dilettanti. It would be easy to multiply instances did not decency forbid the labouring of so obvious a truth.

SUSANNE K. LANGER

Expressiveness

W HEN WE TALK about "Art" with a capital "A"—that is, about any or all of the arts: painting, sculpture, architecture, the potter's and goldsmith's and other designers' arts, music, dance, poetry, and prose fiction, drama and film—it is a constant temptation to say things about "Art" in this general sense that are true only in one special domain, or to assume that what holds for one art must hold for another. For instance, the fact that music is made for performance, for presentation to the ear, and is simply not the same thing when it is given only to the tonal imagination of a reader silently perusing the score, has made some aestheticians pass straight to the conclusion that literature, too, must be physically heard to be fully experienced, because words are originally spoken, not written; an obvious parallel, but a careless and, I think, invalid one. It is dangerous to set up principles by analogy, and generalize from a single consideration.

But it is natural, and safe enough, to ask analogous questions: "What is the function of sound in music? What is the function of sound in poetry? What is the function of sound in prose composition? What is the function of sound in drama?" The answers may be quite heterogeneous; and that is itself an important fact, a guide to something more than a simple and sweeping theory. Such findings guide us to exact relations and abstract, variously exemplified basic principles.

At present, however, we are dealing with principles that have proven to be the same in all the arts, when each kind of art—plastic, musical, balletic, poetic, and each major mode, such as literary and dramatic writing, or painting, sculpturing, building plastic shapes—has been studied in its own terms. Such candid study is more rewarding than the usual passionate declaration that all the arts are alike, only their materials differ, their principles are all the same, their techniques all analagous, etc. This is not only unsafe, but untrue. It is in pursuing the differences among them that one arrives, finally, at a point where no more differences appear; then one has found, not postulated, their unity. At that deep level there is only one concept exemplified in all the different arts, and that is the concept of Art.

The principles that obtain wholly and fundamentally in every kind of art are few, but decisive; they determine what is art, and what is not. Expressiveness, in one definite and appropriate sense, is the same in all art works of any kind. What is created is not the same in any two distinct arts—this is, in fact, what makes them distinct—but the principle of creation is the same. And "living form" means the same in all of them.

A work of art is an expressive form created for our perception through sense or imagination, and what is expressed is human feeling. The word "feeling" must be taken here in its broadest sense, meaning *everything that can be felt,* from physical sensation, pain and comfort, excitement and repose, to the most complex emotions, intellectual tensions, or the steady feeling-tones of a conscious human life. In stating what a work of art is, I have just used the words "form," "expressive," and "created"; these are key words. One at a time, they will keep us engaged.

Let us first consider what is meant, in this context, by a *form.* The word has many meanings, all equally legitimate for various purposes; even in connection with art it has several. It may, for instance—and often does—denote the familiar, characteristic structures known as the sonnet form, the sestina, or the ballad form in poetry, the sonata form, the madrigal, or the symphony in music, the contredance or the classical ballet in choreography, and so on. This is not what I mean; or rather, it is only a very small part of what I mean. There is another sense in which artists speak of "form" when they say, for instance, "form follows function," or declare that the one quality shared by all good works of art is "significant form," or entitle a book *The Problem of Form in Painting and Sculpture,* or *The Life of Forms in Art,* or *Search for Form.* They are using "form" in a wider sense, which on the one hand is close to the commonest, popular meaning, namely just the *shape* of a thing, and on the other hand to the quite unpopular meaning it has in science and philosophy, where it designates something more abstract; "form" in its most abstract sense means structure, articulation, a whole resulting from the relation of mutually dependent factors, or more precisely, the way that whole is put together.

The abstract sense, which is sometimes called "logical form," is involved in the notion of expression, at least the kind of expression that characterizes art. That is why artists, when they speak of achieving "form," use the word with something of an abstract connotation, even when they are talking about a visible and tangible art object in which that form is embodied.

The more recondite concept of form is derived, of course, from the

naive one, that is, material shape. Perhaps the easiest way to grasp the
idea of "logical form" is to trace its derivation.

Let us consider the most obvious sort of form, the shape of an object,
say a lampshade. In any department store you will find a wide choice of
lampshades, mostly monstrosities, and what is monstrous is usually their
shape. You select the least offensive one, maybe even a good one, but
realize that the color, say violet, will not fit into your room; so you look
about for another shade of the same shape but a different color, perhaps
green. In recognizing this same shape in another object, possibly of another material as well as another color, you have quite naturally and
easily abstracted the concept of this shape from your actual impression of
the first lampshade. Presently it may occur to you that this shade is too
big for your lamp; you ask whether they have *this same shade* (meaning
another one of this shape) in a smaller size. The clerk understands you.

But what is *the same* in the big violet shade and the little green one?
Nothing but the interrelations among their respective various dimensions.
They are not "the same" even in their spatial properties, for none of their
actual measures are alike; but their shapes are congruent. Their respective spatial factors are put together in the same way, so they exemplify
the same form.

It is really astounding what complicated abstractions we make in our
ordinary dealing with forms—that is to say, through what twists and transformations we recognize the same logical form. Consider the similarity of
your two hands. Put one on the table, palm down, superimpose the other,
palm down, as you may have superimposed cut-out geometrical shapes in
school—they are not alike at all. But their shapes are *exact opposites.*
Their respective shapes fit the same description, provided that the description is modified by a principle of application whereby the measures
are read one way for one hand and the other way for the other—like a
timetable in which the list of stations is marked: "Eastbound, read down;
Westbound, read up."

As the two hands exemplify the same form with a principle of reversal
understood, so the list of stations describes two ways of moving, indicated
by the advice to "read down" for one and "read up" for the other. We
can all abstract the common element in these two respective trips, which
is called the *route.* With a return ticket we may return only by the same
route. The same principle relates a mold to the form of the thing that is
cast in it, and establishes their formal correspondence, or common logical
form.

So far we have considered only objects—lampshades, hands, or regions
of the earth—as having forms. These have fixed shapes; their parts remain
in fairly stable relations to each other. But there are also substances that
have no definite shapes, such as gases, mist, and water, which take the
shape of any bounded space that contains them. The interesting thing
about such amorphous fluids is that when they are put into violent mo-

tion they do exhibit visible forms, not bounded by any container. Think of the momentary efflorescence of a bursting rocket, the mushroom cloud of an atomic bomb, the funnel of water or dust screwing upward in a whirlwind. The instant the motion stops, or even slows beyond a certain degree, those shapes collapse and the apparent "thing" disappears. They are not shapes of things at all, but forms of motions, or dynamic forms.

Some dynamic forms, however, have more permanent manifestations, because the stuff that moves and makes them visible is constantly replenished. A waterfall seems to hang from the cliff, waving streamers of foam. Actually, of course, nothing stays there in mid-air; the water is always passing; but there is more and more water taking the same paths, so we have a lasting shape made and maintained by its passage—a permanent dynamic form. A quiet river, too, has dynamic form; if it stopped flowing it would either go dry or become a lake. Some twenty-five hundred years ago, Heracleitos was struck by the fact that you cannot step twice into the same river at the same place—at least, if the river means the water, not its dynamic form, the flow.

When a river ceases to flow because the water is deflected or dried up, there remains the river bed, sometimes cut deeply in solid stone. That bed is shaped by the flow, and records as graven lines the currents that have ceased to exist. Its shape is static, but it *expresses* the dynamic form of the river. Again, we have two congruent forms, like a cast and its mold, but this time the congruence is more remarkable because it holds between a dynamic form and a static one. That relation is important; we shall be dealing with it again when we come to consider the meaning of "living form" in art.

The congruence of two given perceptible forms is not always evident upon simple inspection. The common *logical* form they both exhibit may become apparent only when you know the principle whereby to relate them, as you compare the shapes of your hands not by direct correspondence, but by correspondence of opposite parts. Where the two exemplifications of the single logical form are unlike in most other respects one needs a rule for matching up the relevant factors of one with the relevant factors of the other; that is to say, a *rule of translation,* whereby one instance of the logical form is shown to correspond formally to the other.

The logical form itself is not another thing, but an abstract concept, or better an *abstractable* concept. We usually don't abstract it deliberately, but only use it, as we use our vocal chords in speech without first learning all about their operation and then applying our knowledge. Most people perceive intuitively the similarity of their two hands without thinking of them as conversely related; they can guess at the shape of a hollow inside a wooden shoe from the shape of a human foot, without any abstract study of topology. But the first time they see a map in the Mercator projection—with parallel lines of longitude, not meeting at the poles—they find it hard to believe that this corresponds logically to the circular map they used in school, where the meridians bulged apart toward the equator and met at both poles. The visible shapes of the continents are different on the two maps, and it takes abstract thinking to match up the two representations of the same earth. If, however, they have grown up with both maps, they will probably see the geographical relationships either way with equal ease, because these relationships are not *copied* by either map, but *expressed,* and expressed equally well by both; for the two maps are different *projections* of the same logical form, which the spherical earth exhibits in still another—that is, a spherical—projection.

An expressive form is any perceptible or imaginable whole that exhibits relationships of parts, or points, or even qualities or aspects within the whole, so that it may be taken to represent some other whole whose elements have analogous relations. The reason for using such a form as a symbol is usually that the thing it represents is not perceivable or readily imaginable. We cannot see the earth as an object. We let a map or a little globe express the relationships of places on the earth, and think about the earth by means of it. The understanding of one thing through another seems to be a deeply intuitive process in the human brain; it is so natural that we often have difficulty in distinguishing the symbolic expressive form from what it conveys. The symbol seems to be the thing itself, or contain it, or be contained in it. A child interested in a globe will not say: "This means the earth," but, "Look, this is the earth." A similar identification of symbol and meaning underlies the widespread conception of holy names, of the physical efficacy of rites, and many other primitive but culturally persistent phenomena. It has a bearing on our perception of artistic import; that is why I mention it here.

The most astounding and developed symbolic device humanity has evolved is language. By means of language we can conceive the intangible, incorporeal things we call our *ideas,* and the equally inostensible elements of our perceptual world that we call *facts.* It is by virtue of language that we can think, remember, imagine, and finally conceive a universe of facts. We can describe things and represent their relations, express rules of their interactions, speculate and predict and carry on a long symbolizing process known as reasoning. And above all, we can communicate, by producing a serried array of audible or visible words, in a pattern commonly known, and readily understood to reflect our multifarious concepts and precepts and their interconnections. The use of language is *discourse;* and the pattern of discourse is known as *discursive form.* It is a highly versatile, amazingly powerful pattern. It has impressed itself on our tacit thinking, so that we call all systematic reflection "discursive thought." It has made, far more than most people know, the very frame of our sensory experience—the frame of objective facts in which we carry on the practical business of life.

Yet even the discursive pattern has its limits of usefulness. An expressive form can express any complex of conceptions that, via some rule of projection, appears congruent with it, that is, appears to be of that form.

Whatever there is in experience that will not take the impress—directly or indirectly—of discursive form, is not discursively communicable or, in the strictest sense, logically thinkable. It is unspeakable, ineffable; according to practically all serious philosophical theories today, it is unknowable.

Yet there is a great deal of experience that is knowable, not only as immediate, formless, meaningless impact, but as one aspect of the intricate web of life, yet defies discursive formulation, and therefore verbal expression: that is what we sometimes call the *subjective aspect* of experience, the direct feeling of it—what it is like to be walking and moving, to be drowsy, slowing down, or to be sociable, or to feel self-sufficient but alone; what it feels like to pursue an elusive thought or to have a big idea. All such directly felt experiences usually have no names—they are named, if at all, for the outward conditions that normally accompany their occurrence. Only the most striking ones have names like "anger," "hate," "love," "fear," and are collectively called "emotion." But we feel many things that never develop into any designable emotion. The ways we are moved are as various as the lights in a forest; and they may intersect, sometimes without cancelling each other, take shape and dissolve, conflict, explode into passion, or be transfigured. All these inseparable elements of subjective reality compose what we call the "inward life" of human beings. The usual factoring of that life-stream into mental, emotional, and sensory units is an arbitrary scheme of simplification that makes scientific treatment possible to a considerable extent; but we may already be close to the limit of its usefulness, that is, close to the point where its simplicity becomes an obstacle to further questioning and discovery instead of the revealing, ever-suitable logical projection it was expected to be.[1]

Whatever resists projection into the discursive form of language is, indeed, hard to hold in conception, and perhaps impossible to communicate, in the proper and strict sense of the word "communicate." But fortunately our logical intuition, or form-perception, is really much more powerful than we commonly believe, and our knowledge—genuine knowledge, understanding—is considerably wider than our discourse. Even in the use of language, if we want to name something that is too new to have a name (e.g. a newly invented gadget or a newly discovered creature), or want to express a relationship for which there is no verb or other connective word, we resort to metaphor; we mention it or describe it as something else, something analogous. The principle of metaphor is simply the principle of saying one thing and meaning another, and expecting to be understood to mean the other. A metaphor is not language, it is an idea expressed by language, an idea that in its turn functions as a symbol to express something. It is not discursive and therefore does not really make a statement of the idea it conveys; but it formulates a new conception for our direct imaginative grasp.

Sometimes our comprehension of a total experience is mediated by a metaphorical symbol because the experience is new, and language has words and phrases only for familiar notions. Then an extension of language will gradually follow the wordless insight, and discursive expression will supersede the non-discursive pristine symbol. This is, I think, the normal advance of human thought and language in the whole realm of knowledge where discourse is possible at all.

But the symbolic presentation of subjective reality for contemplation is not only tentatively beyond the reach of language—that is, not merely beyond the words we have, it is impossible in the essential frame of language. That is why those semanticists who recognize only discourse as a symbolic form must regard the whole life of feeling as formless, chaotic, capable only of symptomatic expression, typified in exclamations like "Ah!" "Ouch!" "My sainted aunt!" They usually do believe that art is an expression of feeling, but that "expression" in art is of this sort, indicating that the speaker has an emotion, a pain, or other personal experience, perhaps also giving us a clue to the general kind of experience it is—pleasant or unpleasant, violent or mild—but not setting that piece of inward life objectively before us so we may understand its intricacy, its rhythms and shifts of total appearance. The differences in feeling-tones or other elements of subjective experience are regarded as differences in quality, which must be felt to be appreciated. Furthermore, since we have no intellectual access to pure subjectivity, the only way to study it is to study the symptoms of the person who is having subjective experiences. This leads to physiological psychology—a very important and interesting field. But it tells us nothing about the phenomena of subjective life, and sometimes simplifies the problem by saying they don't exist.

Now, I believe the expression of feeling in a work of art—the function that makes the work an expressive form—is not symptomatic at all. An artist working on a tragedy need not be in personal despair or violent upheaval; nobody, indeed, could work in such a state of mind. His mind would be occupied with the causes of his emotional upset. Self-expression does not require composition and lucidity; a screaming baby gives his feeling far more release than any musician, but we don't go into a concert hall to hear a baby scream; in fact, if that baby is brought in we are likely to go out. We don't want self-expression.

A work of art presents feeling (in the broad sense I mentioned before, as everything that can be felt) for our contemplation, making it visible or audible or in some way perceivable through a symbol, not inferable from a symptom. Artistic form is congruent with the dynamic forms of our direct sensuous, mental, and emotional life; works of art are projections of "felt life," as Henry James called it, into spatial, temporal, and poetic structures. They are images of feeling, that formulate it for our cognition. What is artistically good is whatever articulates and presents feeling to our understanding.

Artistic forms are more complex than any other symbolic forms we know. They are, indeed, not abstractable from the works that exhibit them. We may abstract a shape from an object that has this shape, by disregarding color, weight and texture, even size; but to the total effect that is an artistic form, the color matters, the thickness of line matters, and the appearance of texture and weight. A given triangle is the same in any position, but to an artistic form its location, balance, and surroundings are not indifferent. Form, in the sense in which artists speak of "significant form" or "expressive form," is not an abstracted structure, but an apparition; and the vital processes of sense and emotion that a good work of art expresses seem to the beholder to be directly contained in it, not symbolized but really presented. The congruence is so striking that symbol and meaning appear as one reality. Actually, as one psychologist who is also a musician has written, "Music sounds as feelings feel." And likewise, in good painting, sculpture, or building, balanced shapes and colors, lines and masses look as emotions, vital tensions and their resolutions feel.

An artist, then, expresses feeling, but not in the way a politician blows off steam or a baby laughs and cries. He formulates that elusive aspect of reality that is commonly taken to be amorphous and chaotic; that is, he objectifies the subjective realm. What he expresses, is, therefore, not his own actual feelings, but what he knows about human feeling. Once he is in possession of a rich symbolism, that knowledge may actually exceed his entire personal experience. A work of art expresses a conception of life, emotion, inward reality. But it is neither a confessional nor a frozen tantrum; it is a developed metaphor, a non-discursive symbol that articulates what is verbally ineffable—the logic of consciousness itself.

Notes

1. On p. 91 of *Problems of Art,* Langer writes: "What does art seek to express? (Here again, I can only state my own notions dogmatically): I think every work of art expresses, more or less purely, more or less subtly, not feelings and emotions which the artist *has,* but feelings and emotions which the artist *knows;* his *insight* into the nature of sentience, his picture of vital experience, physical and emotive and fantastic.

Such knowledge is not expressible in ordinary discourse. The reason for this ineffability is not that the ideas to be expressed are too high, too spiritual, or too anything else, but that the forms of feeling and the forms of discursive expression are logically incommensurate, so that any exact concepts of feeling and emotion cannot be projected into the logical form of literal language. Verbal statement, which is our normal and most reliable means of communication, is almost useless for conveying knowledge about the precise character of the affective life. Crude designations like 'joy,' 'sorrow,' 'fear,' tell us as little about vital experience as general words like 'thing,' 'being,' or 'place' tell us about the world of our perceptions. . . ." Ed.

GEORGE DICKIE

What Is Art?:
An Institutional Analysis

THE ATTEMPT TO DEFINE "art" by specifying its necessary and sufficient conditions is an old endeavor. The first definition—the imitation theory—despite what now seem like obvious difficulties, more or less satisfied everyone until some time in the nineteenth century. After the expression theory of art broke the domination of the imitation theory, many definitions purporting to reveal the necessary and sufficient conditions of art appeared. In the mid-1950's, several philosophers, inspired by Wittgenstein's talk about concepts, began arguing that there are no necessary and sufficient conditions for art. Until recently, this argument had persuaded so many philosophers of the futility of trying to define art that the flow of definitions had all but ceased. Although I will ultimately try to show that "art" can be defined, the denial of that possibility has had the very great value of forcing us to look deeper into the concept of "art." The parade of dreary and superficial definitions that had been presented was, for a variety of reasons, eminently rejectable. The traditional attempts to define "art," from the imitation theory on, may be thought of as Phase I and the contention that "art" cannot be defined as Phase II. I want to supply Phase III by defining "art" in such a way as to avoid the difficulties of the traditional definitions and to incorporate the insights of the later analysis. . . .

I

The best-known denial that "art" can be defined occurs in Morris Weitz's article "The Role of Theory in Aesthetics."[1] Weitz's conclusion depends upon two arguments which may be called his "generalization argument" and his "classification argument." In stating the "generalization argument" Weitz distinguishes, quite correctly, between the generic conception of "art" and the various subconcepts of art such as tragedy, the novel, painting, and the like. He then goes on to give an argument purporting to show that the subconcept "novel" is open, that is, that the members of the class of novels do not share any essential or defining characteristics. He then asserts without further argument that what is true of novels is true of all other subconcepts of art. The generalization from one subconcept to all subconcepts may or may not be justified, but I am not questioning it here. I do question, however, Weitz's additional contention, also asserted without argument, that the generic conception of "art" is open. The best that can be said of his conclusion about the generic sense is that it is unsupported. All or some of the subconcepts of art may be open and the generic conception of art still be closed. That is, it is possible that all or some of the subconcepts of art, such as novel, tragedy, sculpture, and painting, may lack necessary and sufficient conditions and at the same time that "work of art," which is the genus of all the subconcepts, can be defined in terms of necessary and sufficient conditions. Tragedies may not have any characteristics in common which would distinguish them from, say, comedies *within the domain of art*, but it may be that there are common characteristics that works of art have which distinguish them from nonart. Nothing prevents a "closed genus/open species" relationship. Weitz himself has recently cited what he takes to be a similar (although reversed) example of genus-species relationship. He argues that "game" (the genus) is open but that "major league baseball" (a species) is closed.[2]

His second argument, "the classification argument," claims to show that not even the characteristic of artifactuality is a necessary feature of art. Weitz's conclusion here is something of a surprise, because it has been widely assumed by philosophers and nonphilosophers alike that a work of art is necessarily an artifact. His argument is simply that we sometimes utter such statements as "This piece of driftwood is a lovely piece of sculpture," and since such utterances are perfectly intelligible, it follows that some nonartifacts such as certain pieces of driftwood are works of art (sculptures). In other words, something need not be an artifact in order to be correctly classified as a work of art. I will try to rebut this argument shortly.

Recently, Maurice Mandelbaum has raised a question about Wittgenstein's famous contention that "game" cannot be defined and Weitz's thesis about "art."[3] His challenge to both is based on the charge that they have been concerned only with what Mandelbaum calls "exhibited" characteristics and that consequently each has failed to take account of the nonexhibited, relational aspects of games and art. By "exhibited" characteristics Mandelbaum means easily perceived properties such as the fact that a ball is used in a certain kind of game, that a painting has a triangular composition, that an area in a painting is red, or that the plot of a tragedy contains a reversal of fortune. Mandelbaum concludes that when we consider the nonexhibited properties of games, we see that they have in common "the potentiality of . . . [an] . . . absorbing non-practical interest to either participants or spectators."[4] Mandelbaum may or may not be right about "game," but what interests me is the application of his suggestion about nonexhibited properties to the discussion of the definition of art. Although he does not attempt a definition of "art," Mandelbaum does suggest that feature(s) common to all works of art may perhaps be discovered that will be a basis for the definition of "art," if the nonexhibited features of art are attended to.

Having noted Mandelbaum's invaluable suggestion about definition, I now return to Weitz's argument concerning artifactuality. In an earlier attempt to show Weitz wrong, I thought it sufficient to point out that there are two senses of "work of art," an evaluative sense and a classificatory one; Weitz himself distinguishes these in his article as the evaluative and the descriptive senses of art. My earlier argument was that if there is more than one sense of "work of art," then the fact that "This piece of driftwood is a lovely piece of sculpture" is intelligible does not prove what Weitz wants it to prove. Weitz would have to show that "sculpture" is being used in the sentence in question in the classificatory sense, and this he makes no attempt to do. My argument assumed that once the distinction is made, it is obvious that "sculpture" is here being used in the evaluative sense. Richard Sclafani has subsequently noted that my argument shows only that Weitz's argument is inconclusive and that Weitz might still be right, even though his argument does not prove his conclusion. Sclafani, however, has constructed a stronger argument against Weitz on this point.[5]

Sclafani shows that there is a third sense of "work of art" and that "driftwood cases" (the nonartifact cases) fall under it. He begins by comparing a paradigm work of art, Brancusi's *Bird in Space*, with a piece of driftwood which looks very much like it. Sclafani says that it seems natural to say of the piece of driftwood that it is a work of art and that we do so because it has so many properties in common with the Brancusi piece. He then asks us to reflect on our characterization of the driftwood and the *direction* it has taken. We say the driftwood is art because of its resemblance to some paradigm work of art or because the driftwood shares properties with several paradigm works of art. The paradigm work or works are of course always artifacts; the direction of our move is from paradigmatic (artifactual) works of art to nonartifactual "art." Sclafani quite correctly takes this to indicate that there is a primary, paradigmatic sense of "work of art" (my classificatory sense) and a derivative or secondary sense into which the "driftwood cases" fall. Weitz is right in a way in saying that the driftwood is art, but wrong in concluding that artifactuality is unnecessary for (the primary sense of) art.

There are then at least three distinct senses of "work of art": the primary or classificatory sense, the secondary or derivative, and the evaluative. Perhaps in most uses of Weitz's driftwood sentence example, both the derivative and the evaluative senses would be involved: the derivative sense if the driftwood shared a number of properties with some paradigm work of art and the evaluative sense if the shared properties were found to be valuable by the speaker. Sclafani gives a case in which only the evaluative sense functions, when someone says, "Sally's cake is a work of art." In most uses of such a sentence "work of art" would simply mean that its referent has valuable qualities. Admittedly, one can imagine contexts in which the derivative sense would apply to cakes. (Given the situation in art today, one can easily imagine cakes to which the primary sense of art could be applied.) If, however, someone were to say, "This Rembrandt is a work of art," both the classificatory and the evaluative senses would be functioning. The expression "this Rembrandt" would convey the information that its referent is a work of art in the classificatory sense, and "is a work of art" could then only reasonably be understood in the evaluative sense. Finally, someone might say of a sea shell or other natural object which resembles a man's face but is otherwise uninteresting, "This shell (or other natural object) is a work of art." In this case, only the derivative sense would be used.

We utter sentences in which the expression "work of art" has the evaluative sense with considerable frequency, applying it to both natural objects and artifacts. We speak of works of art in the derived sense with somewhat less frequency. The classificatory sense of "work of art," which indicates simply that a thing belongs to a certain category of artifacts, occurs, however, very infrequently in our discourse. We rarely utter sentences in which we use the classificatory sense, because it is such a basic notion: we generally know immediately whether an object is a work of art, so that generally no one needs to say, by way of classification, "That is a work of art," although recent developments in art such as junk sculpture and found art may occasionally force such remarks. Even if we do not often talk about art in this classificatory sense, however, it is a basic concept that structures and guides our thinking about our world and its contents.

II

It is now clear that artifactuality is a necessary condition (call it the genus) of the primary sense of art. This fact, however, does not seem very surprising and would not even be very interesting except that Weitz and others have denied it. Artifactuality alone, however, is not the whole story and another necessary condition (the differentia) has to be specified in order to have a satisfactory definition of "art." Like artifactuality, the second condition is a nonexhibited property, which turns out to be as complicated as artifactuality is simple. The attempt to discover and specify the second condition of art will involve an examination of the intricate complexities of the "artworld." W. E. Kennick, defending a view similar to Weitz's, contends that the kind of approach to be employed here, following Mandelbaum's lead, is futile. He concludes that "the attempt to define Art in terms of what we do with certain objects is as doomed as any other."[6] He tries to support this conclusion by referring to such things as the fact that the ancient Egyptians sealed up paintings and sculptures in tombs. There are two difficulties with Kennick's argument. First, that the Egyptians sealed up paintings and sculptures in tombs does not show that they regarded them differently from the way in which we regard them. They might have put them there for the dead to appreciate or simply because they belonged to the dead person. The Egyptian practice does not establish so radical a difference between their conception of art and ours that a definition subsuming both is impossible. Second, one need not assume that we and the ancient Egyptians share a common conception of art. It would be enough to be able to specify the necessary and sufficient conditions for the concept of art which we have (we present-day Americans, we present-day Westerners, we Westerners since the organization of the system of the arts in or about the eighteenth century—I am not sure of the exact limits of the "we"). Kennick notwithstanding, we are most likely to discover the differentia of art by considering "what we do with certain objects." Of course, nothing guarantees that any given thing we might do or an ancient Egyptian might have done with a work of art will throw light on the concept of art. Not every "doing" will reveal what is required.

Although he does not attempt to formulate a definition, Arthur Danto in his provocative article, "The Artworld," has suggested the direction that must be taken by an attempt to define "art."[7] In reflecting on art and its history together with such present-day developments as Warhol's *Brillo Carton* and Rauschenberg's *Bed*, Danto writes, "To see something as art requires something the eye cannot descry—an atmosphere of artistic theory, a knowledge of history of art: an artworld."[8] Admittedly, this stimulating comment is in need of elucidation, but it is clear that in speaking of "something the eye cannot descry" Danto is agreeing with Mandelbaum that nonexhibited properties are of great importance in constituting something as art. In speaking of atmosphere and history, however, Danto's remark carries us a step further than Mandelbaum's analysis. Danto points to the rich structure in which particular works of art are embedded: he indicates *the institutional nature of art.*[9]

I shall use Danto's term "artworld" to refer to the broad social institution in which works of art have their place.[10] But is there such an institution? George Bernard Shaw speaks somewhere of the apostolic line of succession stretching from Aeschylus to himself. Shaw was no doubt speaking for effect and to draw attention to himself, as he often did, but there is an important truth implied by his remark. There is a long tradition or continuing institution of the theater having its origins in ancient Greek religion and other Greek institutions. That tradition has run very thin at times and perhaps even ceased to exist altogether during some periods, only to be reborn out of its memory and the need for art. The institutions associated with the theater have varied from time to time: in the beginning it was Greek religion and the Greek state; in medieval times, the church; more recently, private business and the state (national theater). What has remained constant with its own identity throughout its history is the theater itself as an established way of doing and behaving, what I shall call . . . the primary convention of the theater. This institutionalized behavior occurs on both sides of the "footlights": both the players and the audience are involved and go to make up the institution of the theater. The roles of the actors and the audience are defined by the traditions of the theater. What the author, management, and players present is art, and it is art because it is presented within the theater-world framework. Plays are written to have a place in the theater system and they exist as plays, that is, as art, within that system. Of course, I do not wish to deny that plays also exist as literary works, that is, as art within the literary system: the theater system and the literary system overlap. Let me make clear what I mean by speaking of the artworld as an institution. Among the meanings of "institution" in *Webster's New Collegiate Dictionary* are the following: "3. That which is instituted as: a. An established practice, law, custom, etc. b. An established society or corporation." When I call the artworld an institution I am saying that it is an established practice. Some persons have thought that an institution must be an established society or corporation and, consequently, have misunderstood my claim about the artworld.

Theater is only one of the systems within the artworld. Each of the systems has had its own origins and historical development. We have some information about the later stages of these developments, but we have to guess about the origins of the basic art systems. I suppose that we have complete knowledge of certain recently developed subsystems or genres such as Dada and happenings. Even if our knowledge is not as complete as we wish it were, however, we do have substantial information about the systems of the artworld as they currently exist and as they have existed for some time. One central feature all of the systems have in common is that each is a framework for the *presenting* of particular works of art. Given the great variety of the systems of the artworld it is not surprising that works of art have no exhibited properties in common. If, however, we step back and view the works in their institutional setting, we will be able to see the essential properties they share.

Theater is a rich and instructive illustration of the institutional nature of art. But it is a development within the domain of painting and sculpture—Dadaism—that most easily reveals the institutional essence of art. Duchamp and friends conferred the status of art on "ready-mades" (urinals, hatracks, snow shovels, and the like), and when we reflect on their deeds we can take note of a kind of human action which has until now gone unnoticed and unappreciated—the action of conferring the status of art. Painters and sculptors, of course, have been engaging all along in the action of conferring this status on the objects they create. As long, however, as the created objects were conventional, given the paradigms of the times, the objects themselves and their fascinating ex-hibited properties were the focus of the attention of not only spectators and critics but of philosophers of art as well. When an artist of an earlier era painted a picture, he did some or all of a number of things: depicted a human being, portrayed a certain man, fulfilled a commission, worked at his livelihood, and so on. In addition he also acted as an agent of the artworld and conferred the status of art on his creation. Philosophers of art attended to only some of the properties the created object acquired from these various actions, for example, to the representational or to the expressive features of the objects. They entirely ignored the nonexhibited property of status. When, however, the objects are bizarre, as those of the Dadaists are, our attention is forced away from the objects' obvious prop-erties to a consideration of the objects in their social context. As works of art Duchamp's "ready-mades" may not be worth much, but as ex-amples of art they are very valuable for art theory. I am not claiming that Duchamp and friends invented the conferring of the status of art; they simply used an existing institutional device in an unusual way. Duchamp did not invent the artworld, because it was there all along.

The artworld consists of a bundle of systems: theater, painting, sculp-ture, literature, music, and so on, each of which furnishes an institutional background for the conferring of the status on objects within its domain. No limit can be placed on the number of systems that can be brought under the generic conception of art, and each of the major systems con-tains further subsystems. These features of the artworld provide the elasticity whereby creativity of even the most radical sort can be accom-modated. A whole new system comparable to the theater, for example, could be added in one fell swoop. What is more likely is that a new sub-system would be added within a system. For example, junk sculpture added within sculpture, happenings added within theater. Such additions might in time develop into full-blown systems. Thus, the radical crea-tivity, adventuresomeness, and exuberance of art of which Weitz speaks is possible within the concept of art, even though it is is closed by the necessary and sufficient conditions of artifactuality and conferred status.

Having now briefly described the artworld, I am in a position to specify a definition of "work of art." The definition will be given in terms of artifactuality and the conferred status of art or, more strictly speaking, the conferred status of candidate for appreciation. Once the definition has been stated, a great deal will still remain to be said by way of clarification: A work of art in the classificatory sense is (1) an artifact (2) a set of the aspects of which has had conferred upon it the status of candidate for appreciation by some person or persons acting on behalf of a certain social institution (the artworld).

The second condition of the definition makes use of four variously interconnected notions: (1) acting on behalf of an institution, (2) conferring of status, (3) being a candidate, and (4) appreciation. The first two of these are so closely related that they must be discussed together. I shall first describe paradigm cases of conferring status outside the artworld and then show how similar actions take place within the artworld. The most clear-cut examples of the conferring of status are certain legal actions of the state. A king's conferring of knighthood, a grand jury's indicting someone, the chairman of the election board certifying that someone is qualified to run for office, or a minister's pronouncing a couple man and wife are examples in which a person or persons acting on behalf of a social institution (the state) confer(s) *legal* status on persons. The congress or a legally constituted commission may confer the status of national park or monument on an area or thing. The examples given suggest that pomp and ceremony are required to establish legal status, but this is not so, although of course a legal system is presupposed. For example, in some jurisdictions common-law marriage is possible—a legal status acquired without ceremony. The conferring of a Ph.D. degree on someone by a university, the election of someone as president of the Rotary, and the declaring of an object as a relic of the church are examples in which a person or persons confer(s) nonlegal status on persons or things. In such cases some social system or other must exist as the framework within which the conferring takes place, but, as before, ceremony is not required to establish status: for example, a person can acquire the status of wise man or village idiot within a community without ceremony.

Some may feel that the notion of conferring status within the artworld is excessively vague. Certainly this notion is not as clear-cut as the conferring of status within the legal system, where procedures and lines of authority are explicitly defined and incorporated into law. The counterparts in the artworld to specified procedures and lines of authority are nowhere codified, and the artworld carries on its business at the level of customary practice. Still there *is* a practice and this defines a social institution. A social institution need not have a formally established constitution, officers, and bylaws in order to exist and have the capacity to confer status—some social institutions are formal and some are informal. The artworld could become formalized, and perhaps has been to some extent in certain political contexts, but most people who are interested in art would probably consider this a bad thing. Such formality would threaten the freshness and exuberance of art. The core personnel of the artworld is a loosely organized, but nevertheless related, set of persons including artists (understood to refer to painters, writers, composers), producers, museum directors, museum-goers, theater-goers, reporters for newspapers, critics for publications of all sorts, art historians, art theorists, philosophers of art, and others. These are the people who keep the machinery of the artworld working and thereby provide for its continuing existence. In addition, every person who sees himself as a member of the artworld is thereby a member. Although I have called the persons just listed the core personnel of the artworld, there is a minimum core within that core without which the artworld would not exist. This essential core consists of artists who create the works, "presenters" to present the works, and "goers" who appreciate the works. This minimum core might be called "the presentation group," for it consists of artists whose activity is necessary if anything is to be presented, the presenters (actors, stage managers, and so on), and the goers whose presence and cooperation is necessary in order for anything to be presented. A given person might play more than one of these essential roles in the case of the presentation of a particular work. Critics, historians, and philosophers of art become members of the artworld at some time after the minimum core personnel of a particular art system get that system into operation. All of these roles are institutionalized and must be learned in one way or another by the participants. For example, a theater-goer is not just someone who happens to enter a theater; he is a person who enters with certain expectations and knowledge about what he will experience and an understanding of how he should behave in the face of what he will experience.

Assuming that the existence of the artworld has been established or at least made plausible, the problem is now to see how status is conferred by this institution. My thesis is that, in a way analogous to the way in which a person is certified as qualified for office, or two persons acquire the status of common-law marriage within a legal system, or a person is elected president of the Rotary, or a person acquires the status of wise man within a community, so an artifact can acquire the status of candidate for appreciation within the social system called "the artworld." How can one tell when the status has been conferred? An artifact's hanging in an art museum as part of a show and a performance at a theater are sure signs. There is, of course, no guarantee that one can always know whether something is a candidate for appreciation, just as one cannot always tell whether a given person is a knight or is married. When an object's status depends upon nonexhibited characteristics, a simple look at the object will not necessarily reveal that status. The nonexhibited relation *may* be symbolized by some badge, for example, by a wedding ring, in which case a simple look will reveal the status.

The more important question is that of how the status of candidate for appreciation is conferred. The examples just mentioned, display in a museum and a performance in a theater, seem to suggest that a number of persons are required for the actual conferring of the status. In one sense a number of persons are required but in another sense only one person is required: a number of persons are required to make up the social institution of the artworld, but only one person is required to act on behalf of the artworld and to confer the status of candidate for appreciation. In fact, many works of art are seen only by one person—the one who creates them—but they are still art. The status in question may be acquired by a single person's acting on behalf of the artworld and *treating an artifact as a candidate for appreciation.* Of course, nothing prevents a group of persons from conferring the status, but it is usually conferred by a single person, the artist who creates the artifact. It may be helpful to compare and contrast the notion of conferring the status of candidate for appreciation with a case in which something is simply presented for appreciation: hopefully this will throw light on the notion of status of candidate. Consider the case of a salesman of plumbing supplies who spreads his wares before us. "Placing before" and "conferring the status of candidate for appreciation" are very different notions, and this difference can be brought out by comparing the salesman's action with the superficially similar act of Duchamp in entering a urinal which he christened *Fountain* in that now-famous art show. The difference is that Duchamp's action took place within the institutional setting of the artworld and the plumbing salesman's action took place outside of it. The salesman could do what Duchamp did, that is, convert a urinal into a work of art, but such a thing probably would not occur to him. Please remember that *Fountain's* being a work of art does not mean that it is a good one, nor does this qualification insinuate that it is a bad one either. The antics of a particular present-day artist serve to reinforce the point of the Duchamp case and also to emphasize a significance of the practice of naming works of art. Walter de Maria has in the case of one of his works even gone through the motions, no doubt as a burlesque, of using a procedure used by many legal and some nonlegal institutions— the procedure of licensing. His *High Energy Bar* (a stainless-steel bar) is accompanied by a certificate bearing the name of the work and stating that the bar is a work of art only when the certificate is present. In addition to highlighting the status of art by "certifying" it on a document, this example serves to suggest a significance of the act of naming works of art. An object may acquire the status of art without ever being named but giving it a title makes clear to whomever is interested that an object is a work of art. Specific titles function in a variety of ways—as aids to understanding a work or as a convenient way of identifying it, for example—but any title at all (even *Untitled*) is a badge of status.[11]

The third notion involved in the second condition of the definition is candidacy: a member of the artworld confers the status of candidate for appreciation. The definition does not require that a work of art actually be appreciated, even by one person. The fact is that many, perhaps most,

works of art go unappreciated. It is important not to build into the
definition of the classificatory sense of "work of art" value properties such
as actual appreciation: to do so would make it impossible to speak of
unappreciated works of art. Building in value properties might even
make it awkward to speak of bad works of art. A theory of art must preserve certain central features of the way in which we talk about art, and
we do find it necessary sometimes to speak of unappreciated art and of
bad art. Also, not every aspect of a work is included in the candidacy for
appreciation; for example, the color of the back of a painting is not
ordinarily considered to be something which someone might think it
appropriate to appreciate. . . . The definition of "work of art" should not,
therefore, be understood as asserting that every aspect of a work is included within the candidacy for appreciation.

The fourth notion involved in the second condition of the definition
is appreciation itself. Some may assume that the definition is referring to
a special kind of *aesthetic* appreciation. . . . I do not think there is any
reason to think that there is a special kind of aesthetic appreciation. All
that is meant by "appreciation" in the definition is something like "in
experiencing the qualities of a thing one finds them worthy or valuable,"
and this meaning applies quite generally both inside and outside the
domain of art. Several persons have felt that my account of the institutional theory of art is incomplete because of what they see as my insufficient analysis of apprehension. They have, I believe, thought that
there are different kinds of appreciation and that the appreciation in the
appreciation of art is somehow typically different from the appreciation
in the appreciation of nonart. But the only sense in which there is a
difference between the appreciation of art and the appreciation of nonart
is that the appreciations have different *objects*. The institutional structure in which the art object is embedded, not different kinds of appreciation, makes the difference between the appreciation of art and the
appreciation of nonart. . . .

The definition I have given contains a reference to the artworld.
Consequently, some may have the uncomfortable feeling that my definition is viciously circular. Admittedly, in a sense the definition is circular,
but it is not viciously so. If I had said something like "A work of art is
an artifact on which a status has been conferred by the artworld" and
then said of the artworld only that it confers the status of candidacy for
appreciation, then the definition would be viciously circular because the
circle would be so small and *uninformative*. I have, however, devoted a
considerable amount of space in this chapter to describing and analyzing
the historical, organizational, and functional intricacies of the artworld,
and if this account is accurate the reader has received a considerable
amount of *information* about the artworld. The circle I have run is not
small and it is not uninformative. If, in the end, the artworld cannot be
described independently of art, that is, if the description contains references to art historians, art reporters, plays, theaters, and so on, then

the definition strictly speaking is circular. It is not, however, viciously so, because the whole account in which the definition is embedded contains a great deal of information about the artworld. One must not focus narrowly on the definition alone: for what is important to see is that art is an institutional concept and this requires seeing the definition in the context of the whole account. I suspect that the "problem" of circularity will arise frequently, perhaps always, when institutional concepts are dealt with.

The institutional theory of art may sound like saying, "A work of art is an object of which someone has said, 'I christen this object a work of art.'" And it is rather like that, although this does not mean that the conferring of the status of art is a simple matter. Just as the christening of a child has as its background the history and structure of the church, conferring the status of art has as its background the Byzantine complexity of the artworld. Some may find it strange that in the nonart cases discussed, there are ways in which the conferring can go wrong, while that does not appear to be true in art. For example, an indictment might be improperly drawn up and the person charged would not actually be indicted, but nothing parallel seems possible in the case of art. This fact just reflects the differences between the artworld and legal institutions: the legal system deals with matters of grave personal consequences and its procedures must reflect this; the artworld deals with important matters also but they are of a different sort entirely. The artworld does not require rigid procedures; it admits and even encourages frivolity and caprice without losing its serious purpose. Please note that not all legal procedures are as rigid as court procedures and that mistakes made in conferring certain kinds of legal status are not fatal to that status. A minister may make mistakes in reading the marriage ceremony, but the couple that stands before him will still acquire the status of being married. If, however, a mistake cannot be made *in* conferring the status of art, a mistake can be made *by* conferring it. In conferring the status of art on an object one assumes a certain kind of responsibility for the object in its new status—presenting a candidate for appreciation always allows the possibility that no one will appreciate it and that the person who did the conferring will thereby lose face. One *can* make a work of art out of a sow's ear, but that does not necessarily make it a silk purse. . . .

Notes

1. *Journal of Aesthetics and Art Criticism,* September 1956, pp. 27-35. See also Paul Ziff's "The Task of Defining a Work of Art," *Philosophical Review,* January 1953, pp. 58-78; and W. E. Kennick's "Does Traditional Aesthetics Rest on a Mistake?" *Mind,* July 1958, pp. 317-334.

2. "Wittgenstein's Aesthetics," in *Language and Aesthetics,* Benjamin R. Tilghman, ed. (Lawrence, Kans., 1973), p. 14. This paper was read at a symposium

at Kansas State University in April 1970. Monroe Beardsley has pointed out to me that the relationship between "game" and "major league baseball" is one of class and member rather than of genus and species.

3. "Family Resemblances and Generalizations Concerning the Arts," *American Philosophical Quarterly*, July 1965, pp. 219-228; reprinted in *Problems in Aesthetics*, Morris Weitz, ed., 2d ed. (London, 1970), pp. 181-197.

4. *Ibid.*, p. 185 in the Weitz anthology.

5. "'Art' and Artifactuality," *Southwestern Journal of Philosophy*, Fall 1970, pp. 105-108.

6. "Does Traditional Aesthetics Rest on a Mistake?" p. 330.

7. *Journal of Philosophy*, October 15, 1964, pp. 571-584.

8. *Ibid.*, p. 580.

9. Danto does not develop an institutional account of art in his article nor in a subsequent related article entitled "Art Works and Real Things," *Theoria*, Parts 1-3, 1973, pp. 1-17. In both articles Danto's primary concern is to discuss what he calls the Imitation Theory and the Real Theory of Art. Many of the things he says in these two articles are consistent with and can be incorporated into an institutional account, and his brief remarks in the later article about the ascriptivity of art are similar to the institutional theory. The institutional theory is one possible version of the ascriptivity theory.

10. This remark is not intended as a definition of the term "artworld," I am merely indicating what the expression is used to *refer* to. "Artworld" is nowhere defined in this book, although the referent of the expression is described in some detail.

11. Recently in an article entitled "The Republic of Art" in *British Journal of Aesthetics*, April 1969, pp. 145-56, T. J. Diffey has talked about the status of art being conferred. He, however, is attempting to give an account of something like an evaluative sense of "work of art" rather than the classificatory sense, and consequently the scope of his theory is much narrower than mine.

HAROLD ROSENBERG

On the De-definition of Art

A N EXCITED VIEW, recently become prevalent in advanced artistic and academic circles, holds that all kinds of problems are waiting to be solved by the magical touch of art. So intense is this enthusiasm for what the artist might accomplish that mere painting and sculpture are presented as undeserving of the attention of the serious artist.

"There are already enough objects," writes an artist, "and there is no need to add to those that already exist."

"I choose not to make objects," writes another. "Instead, I have set out to create a quality of experience that locates itself in the world."

And here is a clincher by the sculptor Robert Morris, who concludes in a recent article that "The static, portable indoor art object [a rather nice materialistic way to describe a painting or sculpture] can do no more than carry a decorative load that becomes increasingly uninteresting."

In contrast to the meagerness of art, the artist is blown up to gigantic proportions. He is described as a person of trained sensibility, a developed imagination, a capacity for expression and deep insight into the realities of contemporary life.

The artist has become, as it were, too big for art. His proper medium is working on the world: Ecology—Transforming the Landscape—Changing the Conditions of Life. Among the followers of Buckminster Fuller this super- or beyond-art activity is called, significantly, the World Game.

This aggrandizement, and self-aggrandizement, of the artist seems on the surface to represent an expanded confidence in the creative powers of artists today. Everything can be done through art, and whatever an artist does is a work of art. "Why is *The Chelsea Girls* art?" Andy Warhol reflected in an interview, and answered, "Well, first of all, it was made by an artist, and, second, that would come out as art." You have the choice of answering, Amen!—or, Oh, yeah?

From *The De-definition of Art: Action Art to Pop to Earthworks* by Harold Rosenberg, pp. 11–14, 28–38 (illustrations excluded), Copyright 1972. Reprinted by permission of the publisher, Horizon Press, New York.

Actually, the artist who has left art behind or—what amounts to the same thing—who regards anything he makes or does as art, is an expression of the profound crisis that has overtaken the arts in our epoch. Painting, sculpture, drama, music, have been undergoing a process of de-definition. The nature of art has become uncertain. At least, it is ambiguous. No one can say with assurance what a work of art is—or, more important, what is not a work of art. Where an art object is still present, as in painting, it is what I have called an anxious object: it does not know whether it is a masterpiece or junk. It may, as in the case of a collage by Schwitters, be literally both.

The uncertain nature of art is not without its advantages. It leads to experiment and to constant questioning. Much of the best art of this century belongs to a visual debate about what art is. Given the changing nature of twentieth century reality and the unbroken series of upheavals into which the world has been plunged since World War I, it was inevitable that the processes of creation should have become detached from fixed forms and be compelled to improvise new ones from whatever lies ready at hand. In countries where high art is maintained according to the old definitions—as in the Soviet Union—art is either dead or engaged in underground revolt. So art must undergo—and has been undergoing—a persistent self-searching.

However, it is one thing to think about art in new ways—and another not to think about it at all, but to pass beyond art and become an artist in a pure state. The post-art artist carries the de-definition of art to the point where nothing is left of art but the fiction of the artist. He disdains to deal in anything but essences. Instead of painting, he deals in space; instead of dance, poetry, film, he deals in movement; instead of music, he deals in sound. He has no need for art since by definition the artist is a man of genius and what he does "would," in Warhol's phrase, naturally "come out as art." He need no longer confine himself to a single genre or form of language, such as painting or poetry—or even to a mixture of genres, such as theater or opera—he can go from one medium to the other, and innovate in each through refusing to find out what it is about. Or he can be an inter-media creator who blends the visual, the aural, the physical, into a super-art presumably able to encompass all experience into something he calls a "quality that locates itself in the world."

The post-art artist can go further—he can fashion an "environment" (most potent word in present-day art jargon) in which all kinds of mechanically induced stimuli and forces play upon the spectator and make him no longer a spectator but, willy-nilly, a participant and thus a "creator" himself.

The vision of transcending the arts in a festival of forms and sensations rests upon one crucial question: "What makes one an artist?" This issue is never raised in the post-art world, where it is assumed that the artist is a primal force, a kind of first cause—and that he therefore exists by self-declaration.

In reality, however, an artist is a product of art—I mean a particular art. *The* artist does not exist except as a personification, a figure of speech that represents the sum total of art itself. It is painting that is the genius of the painter, poetry of the poet—and a person is a creative artist to the extent that he participates in that genius. The artist without art, the beyond-art artist, is not an artist at all, no matter how talented he may be as an impresario of popular spectaculars. The de-definition of art necessarily results in the dissolution of the figure of the artist, except as a fiction of popular nostalgia. In the end everyone becomes an artist. Set out for Clayton! (See Chapter 22).[1]

Despite the Great Expectations held for the new open-form fabrications, the individual arts, in whatever condition they have assumed under pressure of cultural change and the actions of individual artists, have never been more indispensable to both the individual and to society than they are today. With its accumulated insights, its disciplines, its inner conflicts, painting (or poetry, or music) provides a means for the active self-development of individuals—perhaps the only means. Given the patterns in which mass behavior, including mass education, is presently organized, art is the one vocation that keeps a space open for the individual to realize himself in knowing himself. A society that lacks the presence of self-developing individuals—but in which passive people are acted upon by their environment—hardly deserves to be called a *human* society. It is the greatness of art that it does not permit us to forget this.

Note

1. Chapter 22 is entitled "Set Out for Clayton!" The reference is to Franz Kafka's fantasy *Amerika*. In the last chapter, the hero, Karl Rossmann, a young man "packed off to America by his parents," sees a placard with the following announcement: "The Oklahoma Theatre will engage members for its company today at Clayton racecourse from six o'clock in the morning until midnight. The Great Theatre of Oklahoma calls you! . . . If you want to be an artist, join our company! Our Theatre can find employment for everyone, a place for everyone! If you decide on an engagement we congratulate you here and now! But hurry, so that you get in before midnight! . . . Down with all those who do not believe in us! Up, and to Clayton!" Franz Kafka, *Amerika*, Edwin Muir trans., New York, 1946, p. 252. Ed.

ARTHUR C. DANTO

Artworks and Real Things

> The children imitating the cormorants,
> Are more wonderful
> Than the real cormorants.
>
> *Issa*

> Painting relates to both art and life . . .
> (I try to work in that gap between the two).
>
> *Rauschenberg*

FROM PHILOSOPHERS bred to expect a certain stylistic austerity, I beg indulgence for what may strike them as an intolerable wildness in the following paper. It is a philosophical reflection on New York painting from circa 1961 to circa 1969, and a certain wildness in the subject may explain the wildness I apologize for in its treatment. Explain but not excuse, I will be told: the properties of the subject treated of need never penetrate the treatment itself; Freud's papers on sexuality are exemplarily unarousing, papers in logic are not logical *merely* in consequence of their subject. But in a way the paper is part of its own subject, since it becomes an artwork at the end. Perhaps the final creation in the period it treats of. Perhaps the final artwork in the history of art!

I

Rauschenberg's self-consciously characterized activity exemplifies an ancient task imposed generically upon artists in consequence of an alienating criticism by Plato of art as such. Art allegedly stands at a certain invidious remove from reality, so that in fabricating those entities whose production defines their essence, artists are contaminated at the outset with a kind of ontological inferiority. They bear, as well,

From *Theoria*, 39 (1973), pp. 1-17. Reprinted by permission of *Theoria*.

the stigma of a moral reprobation, for with their productions they charm the souls of artlovers with shadows of shadows. Finally, speaking as a precocious therapist as well as a true philistine, Plato insinuates that art is a sort of perversion, a substitute, deflected, compensatory activity engaged in by those who are impotent to *be* what as a *pis-aller* they *imitate*. Stunned by this triple indictment into a quest for redemption, artists have sought a way towards ontological promotion, which means of course collapsing the space between reality and art. That there should, by Rauschenberg's testimony, still remain an insulating vacuity between the two which even *he* has failed to drain of emptiness, stimulates a question regarding the philosophical suitability of the task.

To treat as a defect exactly what makes a certain thing or activity possible and valuable is almost a formula for generating platonic philosophy, and in the case of art an argument may be mounted to show that its possibility and value is logically tied up with putting reality at a distance. It was, for example, an astonishing discovery that representations of barbaric rites need *themselves* no more be barbaric than representations of any *x* whatever need have the properties of *x*-hood. By *imitating* practices it was *horrifying* to engage in (Nietzsche), the Greeks spontaneously put such practices at a distance and invented civilization in the process; for civilization consists in the awareness of media as media and hence of reality as reality. So just those who gave birth to tragedy defeated an insupportable reality by putting between themselves and it a spiritualizing distance it is typical of Plato to find demeaning. It may be granted that this achievement creates the major problem of representational art, which is sufficiently to resemble the realities it denotes that identification of it as a representation of the latter is possible, while remaining sufficiently different that confusion of the two is difficult. Aristotle, who explains the pleasure men take in art through the pleasure they take in imitations, is clearly aware that the pleasure in question (which is intellectual) logically presupposes the knowledge that it *is* an imitation and not the real thing it resembles and denotes. We may take (a minor) pleasure in a man imitating a crow-call of a sort we do not commonly take in crow-calls themselves, but this pleasure is rooted in cognition: we must know enough of crow-calls to know that these are what the man is imitating (and not, say, giraffe-calls), and must know that he and not crows is the provenance of the caws. One further condition for pleasure is this, that the man *is* imitating and not just an unfortunate crow-boy, afflicted from birth with a crowish pharynx. These crucial asymmetries need not be purchased at the price of decreased verisimilitude, and it is not unreasonable to insist upon a perfect acoustical indiscernibility between true and sham crow-calls, so that the uninformed in matters of art might—like an overhearing crow, in fact—be deluded and adopt attitudes appropriate to the reality of crows. The knowledge upon which artistic pleasure (in contrast with *aesthetic* pleasure) depends is thus external to and at right angles to the sounds themselves, since they concern the causes and conditions of the sounds and their relation to the real world. So the option is always available to the mimetic artist to rub away all differences between artworks and real things providing he is assured that the audience has a clear grasp of the distances.

It was in the exercise of this option, for example, that Euripides undertook the abolition of the chorus, inasmuch as *real* confrontation, *real* frenzies of jealousy commonly transpire without benefit of the ubiquitous, nosy, and largely disapproving chorus inexplicably (to *him*) deemed necessary for the action to get on by his predecessors. And in a similar spirit of realism, the stony edifying heroes of the past are replaced by plain folks, and their cosmic suffering with the commonplace heartpains of such (for example) as us. So there *was* some basis for the wonder of his contemporary, Socrates (who may, considering his Egyptolatry in the *Laws,* have been disapproving not so much of art as of *realistic* art in the *Republic*), as to what the *point* of drama any longer could be: if we *have* the real thing, of what service is an idle iteration of it? And so he created a dilemma by looking inversely at the cognitive relations Aristotle subsequently rectified: either there is going to be a discrepancy, and mimesis fails, or art succeeds in erasing the discrepancy, in which case it just *is* reality, a roundabout way of getting what we already *have*. And, as one of his successors has elegantly phrased it: "one of the damned things is enough." Art fails if it is indiscernible from reality, and it equally if oppositely fails if it is not.

We are all familiar enough with one attempt to escape this dilemma, which consists in locating art in whatever makes for the discrepancies between reality and imitations of it. Euripidies, it is argued, went in just the wrong direction. Let us instead make objects which are *insistently* art by virtue of the fact that no one can mistake them for reality. So the disfiguring conventions abolished in the name of reality became reintroduced in the name of art, and one settles for perhaps a self-conscious woodenness, a deliberate archaism, an operatic falseness so marked and underscored that it must be apparent to any audience that illusion could never have been our intent. *Non*-imitativeness becomes the criterion of art, the more artificial and the less imitative in consequence, the purer the art in question. But a fresh dilemma awaits at the other end of the inevitable route, namely that non-imitativeness is *also* the criterion of reality, so the more purely art things become, the closer they verge on reality, and *pure* art collapses into pure *reality*. Well, this may after all be the route to ontological promotion, but the other side of the dilemma asks what makes us want to call *art* what by common consent is reality? So in order to preserve a distinction, we reverse directions, hardly with a light heart since the same dilemma, we recall, awaits us at the other end. And there seems, on the face of it, only one available way to escape the unedifying shuttle from dilemma to dilemma, which is to make non-imitations which are radically distinct from all heretofore existing real things. Like Rauschenberg's stuffed goat garlanded with a tire! It is with such unentrenched objects, like combines and emerubies, that the abysses between life and art are to be filled!

There remains then only the nagging question of whether all un-entrenched objects are to be reckoned artworks, e.g., consider the first can-opener. *I* know of an object indiscernible from what happen to be our routine can-openers, which *is* an artwork:

> The single starkness of its short, ugly, ominous blade-like extremity, em-bodying aggressiveness and masculinity, contrast formally as well as symbolically with the frivolous diminishing helix, which swings freely (but upon a fixed enslaving axis!) and is pure, helpless femininity. The two motifs are symbiotically sustained in a single, powerful composition, no less universal and hopeful for its miniature scale and commonplace material.
> [*Gazette des beaux arts,* vol. 14, no. 6, pp. 430-431. My translation]

As an artwork, of course, it has the elusive defining properties of art-works, significant form *compris.* In virtue of its indiscernibility from the domestic utensil, then, one might think it uncouth if not unintelligible to withhold predication of significant form to the latter, merely on grounds of conspicuous *Zuhandenheit* (one *could* open cans with the work the critic of the *Gazette* was so stirred by) or large numbers. For it would be startling that two things should have the same shape and yet one have and the other lack significant form. Or it would be were we to forget for an inadvertent moment the existence of a Polynesian language in which the sentence "Beans are high in protein," indiscernible acoustically from the English sentence "Beans are high in protein" actually means, in its own language, what "Motherhood is sacred" means in English. And it induces profound filial sentiments when audited by native speakers though hardly that with us. So perhaps significant form is supervenient upon a semantical reading, itself a weak function of language affiliation which mere inscriptional congruity happens to under-determine? The question is suitably rhetorical at this point, for my concern is that the logical intersection of the non-imitative and the non-entrenched may as easily be peopled with artworks as by real things, and *may* in fact have pairs of indiscernible objects, one an artwork and one not. In view of this possibility, we must avert our eyes from the objects themselves in a counter-phenomenological turn—*Von den Sachen selbst!*—and see whatever it is, which clearly does *not* meet the eye, which keeps art and reality from leaking hopelessly into one another's territory. Only so can we escape the dilemma of Socrates, which has gen-erated so much art-history through the misunderstandings it epitomizes and encourages.

II

Borges merits credit for, amongst other things, having discovered the Pierre Menard Phenomenon: two art-objects, in this instance two fragments of the *Quixote,* which though verbally indiscriminable have radically non-overlapping and incompatible *artistic* properties. The art-works in question stand to their common physical embodiment in something like the relationship in which a set of isomers may stand to a common molecular formula, which then underdetermines and hence fails to explain the differences in their chemical reactions. The difference, of course, is given by the way the elements recorded in the formula are put together. Of the two *Quixotes,* for example, one is "more subtle" and the other "more clumsy" than its counterpart. That of Cervantes is the more coarse: it "opposes to the fiction of chivalry the tawdry provincial reality of his country." Menard's ("On the other hand . . ."!) selects for *its* reality "the land of Carmen during the century of Lepanto and Lope de Vega." Menard's work is an oblique condemnation of *Salammbô,* which Cervantes' could hardly have been. Though visibly identical, one is almost incomparably richer than the other and, Borges writes, "The contrast in style is also vivid. The archaic style of Menard—quite foreign, after all—suffers from a certain affectation. Not so that of his forerunner, who handles with ease the current Spanish of his time." Menard, were he to have *completed* his *Quixote,* would have had the task of creating at least one character in excess of Cervantes': the author of the (so-called in Menard's but *not* so-called in Cervantes') "Autobiographical Fragment." And so on. Menard's work was *his,* not a copy nor an accidentally congruent achievement of the sort involved in the discovery that the painters of Jupiter are making (there being no question here of cultural diffusion) flat works using the primary colors and staggeringly like Mondrians, but rather a fresh, in its own way remarkable creation. A mere copy would have no *literary* value at all, but would be merely an exercise in facsimilitation, and a *forgery* of so well known a work would be a fiasco. It is a precondition for the Menard phenomenon that author and audience alike know (not the original but) the *other* Quixote. But Menard's is not a quotation either, as it were, for quotations in this sense *merely* resemble the expressions they denote without having *any* of the artistically relevant properties of the latter: *quotations* cannot be scintilating, original, profound, searching, or whatever what is quoted may be. There are, indeed, theories of quotation according to which they lack *any* semantical structure, which their originals seldom lack. So a *quotation* of the Quixote (*either* Quixote) would be artistically null though quite superimposable upon its original. Quotations, in fact, are striking examples of objects indiscernible from originals which are not artworks though the latter are. Copies (in general) lack the properties of the originals they denote and resemble. A copy of a cow is not a cow, a copy of an artwork is not an artwork.

Quotations are entities difficult to locate ontologically, like reflections and shadows, being neither artworks nor real things, inasmuch as they are parasitic upon reality, and have in particular that degree of derivedness assigned by Plato to artworks as class. So though a copy—or quotation—of an artwork is logically excluded from the class of artworks, it raises too many special questions to be taken as our specific example of an entity indiscernible from an artwork though not one. But it is not difficult to generate less intricate examples. Consider, for the moment, *neckties,* which have begun to work their way into the artworld, e.g., Jim Dine's *Universal Tie,* John Duff's *Tie Piece,* etc. Suppose Picasso exhibits now a tie, painted uniform blue in order to reject any touch of *le peinture* as decisively as the Strozzi altarpiece rejects, as an act of artistic will, giottesque perspective. One says: my child could do *that.* Well, true enough, there is nothing beyond infantile capability here: so let a child, with his stilted deliberateness, color one of his father's ties an all over blue, no brush-strokes "to make it nice." I would hesitate to predict a magnificent future in art for this child on the basis of his having caused the existence of something indistinguishable from something created by the greatest master of modern times. I would go further, and say that he has not produced an artwork. For something prevents *his* object from entering the artworld, as it prevents from entering that world those confections by a would-be van Meegeren of Montmartre who sees at once the Picasso tie as a chance for clever forgery. Three such objects would give rise to one of those marvelous Shakespearean plots, of confused twins and mistaken identities, a possibility not a joking one for Kahnwieler (or was it Kootz?) who takes all the necessary precautions. *In spite of which,* let us suppose, the ties get mixed up, and the child's tie hangs to this very day in the Museum of the Municipality of Talloir. Picasso, of course, disputes its authenticity, and refuses to sign it (in fact he signs the forgery). The original was confiscated by the Ministry of Counterfacts. I look forward to the time when a doctoral candidate under Professor Theodore Reff straightens out the attributions by counting threads, though the status of a forgery with an authentic signature remains for philosophers of art to settle. Professor Goodman has an intriguing argument that sooner or later differences are bound to turn up, that what looks identically similar today will look artistically so diverse tomorrow that men will wonder how the case I have described would ever have arisen. Well, sufficient unto the day may be the similarities thereof: tomorrow's differentiations would appear *whichever* of the three ties were to hang in the museum, and I am inclined to feel that any seen differences will ultimately be used to reenforce the attribution, right or wrong, which is the accepted one. But that leaves still unsettled the ontological questions, besides generating a kind of absurdity of connoisseurship by bringing into the aesthetics of this order of object the refined peering appropriate, say, to Poussin or Morandi or Cézanne. None of whom, though clearly not for reasons of artistic ineptitude, would have been able to make an artwork out of a painted tie. So it isn't just that Picasso happens to be an *artist* that makes the difference in the cases at hand. But the further reasons are interesting.

For one thing, there would have been no room in the artworld of Cézanne's time for a painted necktie. Not everything can be an artwork at every time: the artworld must be ready for it. Much as not every line which is *witty* in a given context can be witty in all. Pliny tells of a contest between rival painters, the first drawing a straight line; the second drawing, in a different color, a line *within* that line; the first drawing an ultimately fine line within this. One does not ordinarily think of lines as having sides, but with each inscribed line, a space exists between its edges and the edges of the containing line, so that the result would be like five very thin strips of color. Nested lines, each making space where none was believed possible, shows remarkable steadiness of hand and eye, and bears witness to the singular prowess of Parahesios and his rival here. And the object was a wonder in its time. But not an artwork! No more than the famous free-hand circle of Giotto. But I could see exactly such an object turning up on Madison Avenue today, a synthesis, perhaps, of Barnett Newman and Frank Stella. Such an object in the time of Parahesios would have *merely* been a set-piece of draughtsmanly control. So it is not even as though, on the Berkeleyan assumption that only art-works can anticipate artworks, Parahesios were a predecessor of the contemporary painter of fine stripes. Parahesios could not have modified his perception of art, nor that of his times, to accommodate his *tour de main* as an artistic achievement. But Picasso's artworld was ready to receive, at Picasso's hand, a necktie: for he had made a chimpanzee out of a toy, a bull out of a bicycle seat, a goat out of a basket, a venus out of a gas-jet: so why not a *tie out of a tie*? It had room not only in the artworld, but in the corpus of the artist, in a way in which the identical object, from the hands of Cézanne, would have had room for neither. Cézanne could only have made a mountain out of paint, in the received and traditional manner of such transformations. He did not have the option even of making paint out of paint, in the later manner of the Abstract Expressionists.

But while these considerations serve to show that the identical object could, in one art-historical context be an artwork and in another one not, the problem remains of moving from *posse ad esse*. What, apart from the possibility, makes it actually a work of art in the context of late Picasso? And what makes then the differences between what Picasso did and his contemporaries, the child and the forger, did? Only when the world was ready for "Necktie" could the comedy of mistaken identities have transpired, and while it is easy to see how, given the sharp and exact resemblances, an artwork which was a necktie should have been confused with a necktie which was not an artwork, the task of explicating the differences remains.

One way to see the matter is this: Picasso *used* the necktie to *make a statement*, the forger employed the necktie to copy what Picasso made a statement with, but made *no* statement by means of his. And this would be true even were he inspired by van Meegeren to invent, say, a rose-colored necktie to fill a gap in Picasso's development. The child and Cézanne are simply making noise. Their objects have no location in the history of art. Part at least of what Picasso's statement is about is art, and art had not developed appropriately by the time of Cézanne for such a statement to have been intelligible, nor can the child in question have sufficiently internalized the history and theory of art to make a statement, much less *this* statement, by means of the painted necktie. At least the right relations hold between the four objects to enable a distinction structurally of a piece with that between statement, echo, and noise to be made. And though a real enough object—a hand-painted tie! —Picasso's work stands at just the right remove from reality for it to *be* a statement, indeed a statement in part about reality and art sufficiently penetrating to enable its own enfranchisement into the world of art. It enters at a phase of art-history when the consciousness of the difference between reality and art is part of what makes the difference between art and reality.

III

Testamorbida is a playwright who deals in Found Drama. Disgusted with theatricality, he has run through the tiresome post-Pirandello devices for washing the boundaries away between life and art, and has sickened of the contrived atmospheres of happenings. Nothing is going to be real enough save reality. So he declares his latest play to have been everything that happened in the life of a family in Astoria between last Saturday and tonight, the family in question having been picked by throwing a dart at the map of the town. How natural are the actors! They have no need to overcome the distance from their roles by stanislavskyian exercise, since they *are* what they play. Or "play". The author "ends" the play by fiat at eleven-ten (curtain), and has the after-theater party with friends at the West End Bar. No reviews, there was no audience, there was just one "performance." For all the "actors" know, it was an ordinary evening, pizza and television, hair put up in rollers, a wrong number and a tooth-ache. All that makes this slice of life an artwork is the declaration that it is so, plus the meta-artistic vocabulary: "actor," "dialogue," "natural," "beginning," "end." And perhaps the title, which may be as descriptive as you please, viz., "What a Family in Astoria Did . . .".

Titles are borne by artworks, interestingly enough, though not by things indiscernable from them which are *not* artworks, e.g., another period in the life of that or any family in Astoria or anywhere. Even "Untitled" is a kind of title: non-artworks are not entitled even to be untitled. Cézanne's hand-painted necktie may bear a label, say at the Cézanne House, along with other memorabilia, but "Cézanne's Necktie" is not its title ("Cézanne's Necktie" could be the title of Picasso's tie if it were painted in just the color of the Louvre's *Vase Bleu*). Noblemen have titles too. "Title" has the ring of status, of something which can be conferred. It has, indeed, enough of the ring of legality to suggest that "artwork"—perhaps like "person!"—is after all an ascriptive term rather than a descriptive—or exclusively descriptive—one.

Ascriptivity, as I understand it, is a property of predicates when they attach to objects in the light of certain conventions, and which apply less on the basis of certain necessary and sufficient conditions than of certain defeating conditions not holding. "Person" is defeasible, for example, through such avenues as minority, subcompetence, disenfranchisement, financial responsibility and liability, and the like. A corporation can consist of a single person, who is not identical with the corporation in question, and the distinction between that person and the corporation he belongs to is perhaps enough like the distinction between an artwork and the physical object it consists in but is not identical with that we can think of artworks in terms of privileges, exemptions, rights, and the like. Thus artworks, which happen to contain neckties, are entitled to hang in museums, in a way in which neckties indiscernible from the former are not. They have, again, a certain peer-group which their indiscernible but plebeian counterparts do not. The blue necktie which is an artwork belongs with the Cowper-Niccolini Madonna and the Cathedral of Laon, while the necktie just like it which is not an artwork belongs just with the collars and cufflinks of banal haberdashery, somewhat *abîmé* by blue-paint. The blue necktie, indeed, is in the museum and in the collection, but its counterparts, though they can be geometrically in the museum, are there only in the way sofas and palm-trees typically are. There is, in fact, a kind of *In-der-Pinakothek-sein* not so awfully different from the *In-der-Welt-sein* which pertains to persons in contrast with things. A necktie which is an artwork differs from one which is not like a person differs from a body: metaphysically, it takes two sets of predicates amazingly similar to the P- and M-predicates which *persons* take on a well-known theory of P. F. Strawson's: no accident, perhaps, if "person" too is an ascriptive predicate. The blue necktie, thus, which is an artwork, is *by* Picasso, whereas its counterpart is not *by* Cézanne even though he put the paint on it. And so forth. So let us try this out for a moment, stressing here the defeating conditions, less to strike a blow against Testamorbida than to see what kind of thing it is that can be subject to defeat of this order. I shall mention only two defeating conditions as enough for our purposes, though hardly exhausting the list. Indeed, were art to evolve, new defeating conditions would emerge.

(1) *Fakes.* If illusion were the aim after all of art, then there would be just exactly the same triumph in getting Stendhal to swoon at a fake Guido Reni as causing birds to peck at painted grapes. There is, I believe, no stigma attached to painting pictures of pictures: Burliuk once told me that, since artists paint the things they love and since *he* loved *pictures,* he saw no obstacle to painting pictures of pictures, viz., of Hogarth's *Shrimp Girl.* It *happens* that Burliuk remained himself, his picture of the *Shrimp Girl* deviating from the *Shrimp Girl* roughly as he differed from Hogarth. He was not, on the other hand, pretending the *Shrimp Girl* was *his* any more than he was pretending that Westhampton, which he also and in the same spirit painted pictures of, was *his*: what was *his* was the painting, a statement in paint which denoted the *Shrimp Girl* as his seascapes denoted glimpses of Westhampton: so we are distanced as much from the one motif as from the other, admiring in both cases the vehicle. Well, a man might love his own paintings as much as he loves those of others, so what was to have prevented Burliuk from painting, say, his *Portrait of Leda?* This is not a case of *copying* the latter, so that we have two copies of the same painting: it is explicitly a painting *of* a painting, a different thing altogether, though it might exactly enough resemble a copy. A copy is defective, for example, insofar as it deviates from the original, but the question of deviation is simply irrelevant if it is a painting of a painting: much as we do not expect the artist to use chlorophyl in depicting trees. Now, if deviation is irrelevant, so is non-deviation. A copy is, indeed, just like a quotation, showing what we are to respond to rather than being what we are to respond to: whereas a painting of a painting is something *to* which we respond. Artists who repeat themselves, the Pierre Menard phenomenon notwithstanding, raise some remarkable questions. Schumann's last composition was based on a theme he claimed was dictated to him by angels in his sleep, but was *in fact* the slow movement of his own recently published Violin Concerto. (Is it an accident that Schumann was working on a book of quotations at the time of his *Zusammenbruch?*) Robert Desnos's *Dernier Poème à Youki* ("*J'ai tant rêvé de toi que tu perds ta réalité . . .*") is simply, according to Mary Ann Caws, "a retranslation into French of the rough and truncated translation into Czech" of his earlier and famous poem addressed to the actress Yvonne George: but was Desnos delirious when he addressed this poem, at his death, to Youki (or did he confuse Youki and Yvonne) or think it was a new poem or what? (I mention Schumann and Desnos in case someone thinks Goodman's distinction of one- and two-stage arts has any bearing.) Repetitions are maddening.

A fake pretends to be a statement but is not one. It lacks the required relation to the artist. That we should mistake a fake for a real work (or *vice versa*) does not matter. Once we discover that it is a fake, it loses its stature as an artwork because it loses its structure as a statement. It at best retains a certain interest as a decorative object. Insofar as being a fake is a defeating condition, it is analytical to the concept of an artwork that it be "original." Which does not entail that it need or cannot be derivative, imitative, influenced, "in the manner of," or whatever. We are not required to invent a language in order to make a statement. Being an original means that the work must in a deep sense originate with the artist we believe to have done it.

(2) *Non-artistic provenance.* It is analytically true that artworks can only be *by* artists, so that an object, however much (or exactly) it may resemble an artwork is not *by* whoever is responsible for its existence, unless he is an artist. But "artist" is as ascriptive a term as "artwork," and in fact "by" is as ascriptive as either. Since, after all, not everything whose existence we owe to artists are *by* him. Consider the customs inspector who bears the stings of past and recent *gaffes* by his peers and decides to take no chances: a certain piece of polished brass—in fact the bushing for a submarine—is declared an artwork. But *his* so calling it that no more makes it an artwork than someone in the same métier calling an object near of morphic kin to it *not* an artwork made the latter *not* be one. What injustice, then, if an artist decides to exhibit the bushing as a found object.

Douaniers, children, chimpanzees, counterfeiters: tracing an object to any of these defeats it as an artwork, demotes it to the status of a mere real object. Hence the logical irrelevance of the claim that a child, a chimpanzee, a forger or, *à la rigueur*, a customs inspector could *do* any of them. The mere object perhaps does not lie outside their powers. But as an artwork it does. Much in the way in which not everyone who can say the words "I pronounce you man and wife" can marry people, nor who can pronounce the words "Thirty days or thirty dollars" can *sentence* a man. So the question of whether an object is *by* someone, and how one is qualified to make artworks out of real things, are of a piece with the question of whether it is an artwork.

The moment something is considered an artwork, it becomes subject to an *interpretation*. It owes its existence as an artwork to this, and when its claim to art is defeated, it loses its interpretation and becomes a mere thing. The interpretation is in some measure a function of the artistic context of the work: it means something different depending upon its art-historical location, its antecedents, and the like. And as an artwork, finally, it acquires a structure which an object photographically similar to it is simply disqualified from sustaining if it is a real thing. Art exists in an atmosphere of interpretation and an artwork is thus a vehicle of interpretation. The space between art and reality is like the space between language and reality partly because art *is* a language of sorts, in the sense at least that an artwork says something, and so presupposes a body of sayers and interpreters who are in position, who define what being in position is, to interpret an object. There is no art without those who speak the language of the artworld, and who know enough of the difference between artworks and real things to recognize that calling an artwork a real thing *is* an interpretation of it, and one which depends for its point and appreciation on the contrast between the artworld and the real-world. And it is exactly with reference to this that the defeating conditions for ascription of "artwork" are to be understood. If this is so, then ontological promotion of art is hardly to be looked for. It is a logical impossibility. Or nearly so: for there is one further move to reckon with.

IV

Much as philosophy has come to be increasingly its own subject, has turned reflexively inward onto itself, so art has done, having become increasingly its own (and only) subject: like the Absolute of Hegel, which finally achieved congruence with itself by becoming self-contemplative in the respect that *what* it contemplates is itself in contemplation. Rosenberg thus reads the canvas as an arena in which a real action occurs when an artist (but *nota bene: only* when an *artist*) makes a wipe of paint upon it: a stroke. To appreciate that the boundaries have been crossed, we must read the stroke as saying, in effect, about itself, that it *is* a stroke and not a representation of anything. Which the indiscernable strokes made by housepainters cannot *begin* to say, though it is true that they are strokes and not representations. In perhaps the subtlest suite of paintings in our time, such strokes—fat, ropy, expressionist—have been read with a deadly literalness of their makers' or the latter's ideologues intention as (mere) real things, and made the subject of paintings as much as if they were apples, by Roy Lichtenstein. These are paintings *of* brush strokes. And Lichtenstein's paintings say, about themselves, at least this: that they *are* not but only represent brush strokes, and yet they are art. The boundaries between reality and art as much inform these works as they did the initial impulses of the Abstract Expressionists they impale. The boundaries between art and reality, indeed, become *internal* to art itself. And this is a revolution. For when one is able to bring within oneself what separates oneself from the world, viz., as when Berkeley brings the brain into the mind, the distinction between mind and brain now standing as a distinction within the mind itself, everything is profoundly altered. And in a curious way, the Platonic challenge has been met. Not by promoting art but by demoting reality, conquering it in the sense that when a line is engulfed, what lies on both sides of that line is engulfed as well. To incorporate ones own boundaries in an act of spiritual topology is to transcend those boundaries, like turning oneself inside out and taking ones external environment in as now part of oneself.

I would like briefly to note two consequences of this. The first is that it has been a profoundly disorienting maneuver, increasingly felt as the categories which pertain to art suddenly pertain to what we always believed contrasted essentially with art. Politics becomes a form of theater, clothing a kind of costume, human relations a kind of role, life a game. We interpret ourselves and our gestures as we once interpreted artworks. We look for meanings and unities, we become players in a play.

The other consequence is more interesting. The relationship between reality and art has traditionally been the province of philosophy, since the latter is analytically concerned with relations between the world and its representations, the space between representation and life. By bringing within itself what it had traditionally been regarded as logically apart from, art transforms itself into philosophy, in effect. The distinction between philosophy of art and art itself is no longer tenable, and by a curious, astounding magic we have been made over into contributors to a field we had always believed it our task merely to analyze from without.

On Defining Art

W E NOTED IN THE INTRODUCTION to this section that, when one asks "What is art?" and propounds the sort of theory represented by the foregoing selections, he is apparently trying to give a formal definition of art. Assuming that this *is* what Tolstoy and the others are doing, let us first ask ourselves whether the definitions they give, and whether some of the reasons they offer for giving them, are adequate.

By my count Tolstoy gives six conditions that are severally necessary and jointly sufficient for something's being a work of art. Now suppose that someone were to wonder whether a certain piece of music, for example, Mozart's *Quintet in G Minor*, K. 516, is a genuine work of art as opposed to a "counterfeit," "an unsuccessful attempt at art." How alone, given Tolstoy's view, could he resolve his doubt? He would have to ascertain (1) whether the music was composed by someone; (2) whether at some time prior to his composing the music the composer experienced a certain feeling or emotion; (3) whether at some time prior to his composing but after his having had the feeling or emotion in question, the composer evoked the feeling or emotion in himself; (4) whether the composer "consciously" employed his composition to transmit the feeling or emotion in question to others; (5) whether someone other than the composer has heard his composition; and (6) whether as a result of hearing the composition the hearer was "infected" by the feeling or emotion in question. This is surely a large order! It would be easy enough to settle 1 and 5. But must one really settle 2, 3, 4, and 6 in order to determine whether something is a genuine work of art? Don't we (can't we) *know* that Mozart's *Quintet in G Minor*, K. 516, is a genuine work of art without knowing the answer to any of these four questions?

Suppose that a painter does succeed in "transmitting" a feeling of his to Peter but fails to "infect" Mary with it, Peter and Mary both being equally intelligent and sensitive viewers of his picture. Does this mean that his work both is and is not a genuine work of art? How can that be? You may be inclined to say that it is a genuine work of art for (or to) Peter but not for (or to) Mary. But what could this mean? It might mean that Peter believes the picture is a geunine work of art whereas Mary does not. But isn't it possible, everything remaining the same, that Peter does not believe the picure is a genuine work of art whereas Mary does?

Of course, art, as Tolstoy sees it, is a means of communication, and this may give us another approach to our question. If someone says something to me in Russian and I do not understand Russian, then he has failed to "transmit" his thought to me. But what follows from this? That Russian is not a genuine language? That the sentence in question is not a genuine sentence? Or that uttering the sentence is not a genuine means of communication? In the case given, yes, you may say in answer to the last question. But, from the fact that a means fails to achieve its end on occasion, does it follow that it is not a genuine means to that end—even on those occasions on which it fails to achieve its end? Using a screwdriver is a means for setting and removing screws. If you try to remove a screw with a screwdriver and fail, does that mean that your using the screw-driver was not a means to the end of removing the screw? Is an unsuccess-ful means no means at all? Or a "counterfeit" means?

In connection with this point, note that Tolstoy assumes that art (as an activity) has, like eating (his analogue), or farming, or practicing medicine, a definitive end, aim, or purpose. Of course, it may serve a variety of other purposes incidentally, for example, giving pleasure to people, but it is essentially a means to one end, the "transmission" of feel-ing or emotion. Leaving aside the question of whether *the* aim of art is the one Tolstoy cites, does, or must, art, as an activity, have a single, definitive end, aim, or purpose?

Croce's claim that art is a mode of knowledge raises some interesting questions.[1] Clearly not all thoughts framed in concepts are instances of "logical knowledge," that is, are *true* thoughts. If I think that the square constructed on the diagonal of a given square is more, or less, than twice the area of the given square, what I think is false and is therefore not knowledge. But if it is possible for a thought, an expression of putative logical knowledge, to be false, is it similarly possible for an "image," an expression of putative intuitive knowledge, to be false, that is, to mis-represent what it purports to represent or to represent nothing at all? In the case of sensuous images, for example, hallucinatory ones, Croce is willing to say yes. But what about those images expressive of impressions that constitute at least putative works of art: can *they* fail to be knowl-edge, that is, expressions of genuine *intuitions* (an intuition being by definition a mode of knowledge), and thereby fail to be works of art at all? A scale drawing can misrepresent what it is a drawing of, and we can tell whether it does by comparing the drawing with what it purports to represent. But if I have what I think is an image expressive of an in-tuition of certain impressions, is there, or can there be, any similar way of telling whether it actually represents the impressions it purports to represent, that is, whether it really expresses an intuition, and hence whether it is really a work of art? Can I compare the image with the impressions to see whether it does express knowledge of them? It would seem not; for until the impressions are intuited/expressed, I don't know what they are.[2] But if artistic expressions (images) are in principle immune to failure, if they *cannot* go wrong in a way at least analogous to the way in which a (conceptual) thought *can* be false, does it make any sense to speak of them as expressing knowledge at all? Does it make sense to speak of knowledge where there *cannot* be error?

Perhaps the greatest anomaly in Croce's position stems from his claim that works of art—expressed intuitions—can exist independent of their embodiment in some publicly apprehensible medium. It follows from this that the world could contain countless works of art without containing a single painting, statue, building, musical score or performance, text of a poem or novel, and so on. But is this really possible? To be sure, a poet might compose a poem "in his head" and never write it down, and we might allow that something similar could occur in the case of other arts, but could *all* poems, novels, musical compositions, paintings, and the like exist only in artists' imaginations? If they did, how *could* anyone ever imagine a painting, a building, or a statue? Isn't our ability to imagine such things dependent on the physical existence of such things? In other words, is Wollheim not right when he says, "there could not be Crocean 'intuitions' unless there were, first, physical works of art"?[3]

One way in which a formal definition can go wrong is by being viciously circular. For example, if one were to define art as that which is created by artists, having previously defined an artist as one who creates art, his definition would be viciously circular. Now Bell tells us that "we have no other means of recognizing a work of art than our feeling for it." And the feeling in question is what he calls "the aesthetic emotion." Of this emotion he says, "if we can discover some quality common and peculiar to all objects that provoke it, we shall have solved what I call the central problem of aesthetics." We shall have found a correct definition of art. Well, what is the quality common and peculiar to all objects that provoke the aesthetic emotion? Significant form. But, says Bell, "when I speak of significant form, I mean a combination of lines and colors . . . that moves me aesthetically," that is, that provokes the aesthetic emotion. Is Bell's definition not, then, viciously circular?[4]

According to Tolstoy, we use language to transmit our thoughts; art, to transmit our feelings. According to Croce, there are two distinct kinds of knowledge, logical and intuitive, each with its proper topic and each with its proper mode of expression, and art is a species of intuitive knowledge. In a somewhat similar vein, Langer holds that there are two different kinds of fact that call for different kinds of symbols for their expression or articulation: discursive and nondiscursive or "presentational" symbols.

Again, rather like Tolstoy and Croce, she identifies what art is "about" with feelings (felt life, vital experience, etc.). But unlike at least Croce, who holds that feelings *can* be understood either conceptually or intuitively, Langer holds that feelings (or, strictly speaking, *forms* of feeling) *cannot* be expressed in or symbolized by discursive symbols, for example, language, prose discourse; or at least they cannot be adequately or precisely so expressed or symbolized. On this claim her whole view of art rests: a work of art is "a non-discursive symbol that articulates what is verbally ineffable—the logic of consciousness itself."

First, what reason does Langer give for supposing that feelings (to stick with just one of the expressions she uses to designate the essential topic of art) are such that they, or our knowledge of or insight into them, cannot be expressed in discursive symbolism or language? In *Philosophy in a New Key*, she says, "Everybody knows that language is a very poor medium for expressing our emotional nature. It merely names certain vaguely and crudely conceived states . . .". And in *Problems of Art* she repeats the charge: "Verbal statement . . . is almost useless for conveying knowledge about the precise character of the affective life. Crude designations like 'joy,' 'sorrow,' 'fear' tell us as little about vital experience as general words like 'thing,' 'being,' or 'place' tell us about the world of perceptions." But does everybody know this? Is it so?

"I was afraid" may tell you very little about how I felt, just as "Paris is a place" or "The Eiffel Tower is a thing" tells you very little indeed about Paris or the Eiffel Tower. But in expressing or articulating or even describing our feelings, are we linguistically any more restricted than we are in talking about persons, places, and things? *Are* feelings any more or less verbally ineffable than anything else?

To come at the problem from another direction, consider Langer's central claim that feelings cannot be adequately expressed in discourse, that "the forms of feeling and the forms of discursive expression are logically incommensurate." What sort of claim is this? Is it like the claim that no one can run the mile in three minutes or less? Or is it like the claim that no one can run in opposite directions at one and the same time? It is a matter of empirical fact that no one can run the mile in three minutes or less, and perhaps no one ever will run it in that time. But we can easily imagine someone running it in that time. We cannot, however, imagine someone running in opposite directions at one and the same time; for it is logically, and not merely, physically impossible, for someone to be running due north, say, and at the same time running due south, that is, not due north. Now if the impossibility of expression that Langer has in mind is like our first one, we could imagine someone's adequately or precisely expressing his feelings in discourse; but if it is like our second one, we would in principle be unable to do so. But are we not in fact able to do so?

If you are told that something is impossible, ask "What's the obstacle?"

Langer sometimes suggests that the obstacle to our ability adequately to express our feelings in discourse is that the linguistic devices available to us are insufficient for the purpose; for example, we don't have precise enough names for our feelings—the ones we have are vague, crude, too general. But if this is the burden of her complaint, then aren't the defects in question remediable? Couldn't we easily introduce into language less vague, less crude, less general terms to do the job? And if we could, would that mean, as Langer clearly suggests, that art would become superfluous, that there would be nothing left for it to do? At other times, however, Langer suggests that the obstacle in question is in principle unremovable, like the obstacle to one's running in opposite directions at one and the same time. But if that were the case, then the very notion of discourse adequately expressing feeling would have to be incoherent. But is it?[5]

Dickie's definition of art, like Bell's, is dogged by the threat of vicious circularity, as he realizes. What threatens his definition in this way is the appearance in it of the parenthesis "(the artworld)." The parenthesis is either superfluous or it isn't. If it is, then it is eliminable from the definition without harm. But remove it and see what happens. On the other hand, if the definition requires the parenthesis, as it seems to, then it becomes circular. But not viciously so, Dickie claims, because "the whole account in which the definition is embedded contains a great deal of information about the artworld." But will this really get Dickie off the hook? Consider the example of vicious circularity given earlier: An artist is anyone who creates works of art, and a work of art is anything created by an artist. If this were embedded in an account that gave you a lot of information about artists (Vermeer, Jane Austen, Mozart, et al.), would that redeem it? "The artworld" is a rather unusual expression, and what we want to know is what it means. Can we be told what it means without invoking the concept of art somewhere along the line?

That the notion of the artworld is unclear may be dramatized by asking yourself who belongs to it or how you know whether someone does. Do you belong to it? Does a professor of aesthetics belong to it? Do regular museum visitors belong to it? Does the custodian of an art museum belong to it? Or the director's secretary? Or the director's assistant? You can obviously go on and on in this vein. It might be said that it is unimportant whether we know just who belongs to the artworld; the important thing is knowing whether someone is *acting on behalf of* the artworld in the way required by the definition. But is it any easier to determine who is doing this than it is to determine whether someone belongs to the artworld?

A master's degree can be conferred on someone by a person acting on behalf of a university. But it can also be denied or withdrawn; the conferral can, as it were, be negated, undone. Suppose that someone, A, acting on behalf of the artworld confers on a set of the aspects of an artifact the status of candidate for appreciation, while another person, B, acting on behalf of the artworld denies it that status. Is the artifact in question a work of art or isn't it?

Finally, suppose that someone said, "Raphael's *The School of Athens* in the Vatican is a work of art, but, although it is an artifact, no one acting on behalf of the artworld ever conferred upon a set of its aspects the status of a candidate for appreciation." What he says might in fact be false, but is it incoherent, does it imply a contradiction, in the way that "Peter is Paul's natural father, but, although Peter is a male, he is not and never has been a parent" is incoherent? If it is not, then can Dickie's definition be an adequate or true definition of art?

One reason why some people seem to feel a need for a formal definition of art is to enable them to tell what "the real thing" is from what isn't art at all or what is only "counterfeit" art. Recent developments in art, especially in the visual arts, have served only to magnify this felt need. As Rosenberg notes, "the nature of art has become uncertain" in a way in which, perhaps, it never was.

Consider the following possibility. A person already known as an artist (sculptor) buys 120 bricks and, on the floor of what advertises itself as an art gallery, arranges them in a rectangular pile, two bricks high, six across, and ten lengthwise.[6] He entitles it "Bricks." Across town a bricklayer's assistant at a building site takes 120 bricks of the very same kind and arranges them in the very same way. Is the first pile of bricks a work of art, the second not?

According to a prevalent view cited by Rosenberg, the answer is yes: "whatever an artist does is a work of art," and *ex hypothesi* the first pile of bricks was made by an artist. Rosenberg is unhappy with this, because, as he rightly notes, it leaves us with the "crucial question: 'What makes one an artist?.'" Artists don't exist simply by "self-declaration." "An artist is a product of art."

Danto allows for the possibility of there being "pairs of indiscernible objects, one an artwork and the other not," for example, our two piles of bricks, which implies that you can't tell simply by looking at an object whether it is a work of art. (Well, can you tell *simply* by looking at an orange whether it is an orange?) Something prevents the one pile of bricks "from entering the artworld," and, at least at first, Danto seems to agree with Rosenberg: it is not that the maker of the first pile of bricks "happens to be an *artist* that makes the difference." What, then, *does* make the difference?

First, it would appear that, other things being equal, a pile of bricks is a work of art only if it is "used to make a statement." About what? About art, or about "art and reality." Another way of saying the same thing, I gather, is that to be a work of art something must be "subject to an *interpretation*." But doesn't this merely move the difficulty to new ground? How do we tell whether something is being used to make a state-

ment, whether it is subject to interpretation? Second, for an object to be
an artwork, "the artworld must be ready for it"; certain historical pre-
conditions must be satisfied. But, again, how can we tell whether this
condition has been satisfied? Is the artworld ready for our first pile of
bricks when many critics and artists, to say nothing of the general public,
dismiss it as not being art at all? Third, again other things being equal,
something is an artwork only if it has (or could appropriately have) a title.
Well, our first pile of bricks has a title, our second does not. But how
important is this really? Finally, the predicate ". . . is an artwork" is
defeasible. Its ascription to an object can be defeated or shown to be improperly applicable in at least two ways. (1) If something is not "original"
—if it is a copy or a fake—then it is not an artwork; for then it is not a
genuine "statement" but at best only pretends to be one. So we are back
with the statement-requirement. (2) "It is analytically true that artworks
can only be *by* artists . . .". So something is an artwork only if it is *by*
an artist. This is indeed analytic but leaves us again with the problem
of determining who is an artist. The predicate ". . . is an artist" is
defeasible; its ascription to someone can be shown to be misplaced if, for
example, that someone is a child or a forger. But does this mean that we
can determine who is an artist only by some elaborate process of elimination? If so, what would the principle of elimination be? Why, for example,
are children excluded?

In the last section of his essay, Danto suggests that the boundaries
between art and nonart have now disappeared: "the categories which
pertain to art suddenly pertain to what we always believed contrasted
essentially with art." But *if* this contrast has disappeared, hasn't the
whole notion of art thereby become vacuous? Isn't to say that something
is an artwork to say as little about it as to say that it is something?[7]

So far we have been operating on the assumption that when someone
answers the question "What is art?" he is purporting to give us a formal
definition of art. But why should anyone want a formal definition of art?
And what good would it do him if he had one?

A powerful assumption operative in philosophy since at least the time
of Socrates seems to make the search for formal definitions compelling:
we can know what something is only if we can say what it is, that is, give
a correct formal definition of it. But in St. Augustine's *Confessions*, XI,
14, we find the following interesting passage:

> What, then, is time? There can be no quick and easy answer, for it is no
> simple matter to understand what it is, let alone find words to explain it.
> Yet, in our conversation, no word is more familiarly used or more easily
> recognized than "time." We certainly understand what is meant by the
> word when we use it ourselves and when we hear it used by others.
>
> What, then, is time? I know well enough what it is, provided that nobody
> asks me; but if I am asked what it is and try to explain I am baffled.[8]

Although Augustine goes on to try to define time, thinking that he *must* be able to do so if he knows what it is, his words suggest the interesting possibility that we *can* know what something is without being able to say what it is, formally define it. Don't you know what art is? (In fact, if you didn't know what it is, would you be able to understand the material in this section?) But can you give a correct formal definition of art?

Closely allied to the assumption that if we know what something is we must be able to define it is another, namely, that if we use a single word (univocally), for example, "cat," "chair," "tree," "art," to refer to a number of different individual things, there *must* be a set of properties common and peculiar to those things, by virtue of which we apply the same name to them.[9] This seems to be the only explanation of our ability to learn the application of general names as opposed to proper names. For giving someone clear examples of the sort of thing to which the general term applies apparently won't do; as, after having had a number of examples pointed out to one, each of which is referred to by the same word, how could he then go on to apply that word to other things except by recognizing some distinctive feature(s) common to the examples?

Despite its initial plausibility, this assumption often leads to anomalous results in the practice of those who make it. For if a general term applies to things only by virtue of their having some distinctive set of properties, those who know how to apply it must already know what that set is. How, then, can they spend time *searching* for that set, or think that finding it would be a *discovery*? And how can they disagree with one another as to what that set is, as the body of this section shows that they do, although they can equally well apply the term whose meaning the set is supposed to be?

Must all things univocally referred to by the same general term have a set of definitive properties? Or do we not rather call things by the same name for other reasons as well, for example, because they resemble one another in different ways without there being a single set of properties common to all to mark the boundaries of correct use?[10] And doesn't the history of the development of its meaning, as sketched by Kristeller, indicate that "art" has come to be applied to different things for this alternative reason?[11]

In view of the difficulties suggested so far, some philosophers have concluded that art cannot be formally defined, or have doubted whether it can be. If they have in mind the way "art" is used in common parlance, they may be right. But can't a formal definition of art be *stipulated* or, as it were, legislated for certain special purposes, for example, by Congress for the purpose of imposing customs duties on imported goods? But if what Tolstoy, Croce, et al., are doing is simply stipulating a definition of art, why should we be at all interested in what they have to say? And is there anything to keep their definitions from being simply arbitrary, as there is in the case of at least many legal definitions?

An alternative explanation of what they are doing is that, instead of offering us alternative definitions of art, alternative analyses of the *concept* of art, they are presenting alternative *conceptions* of art.[12] Roughly, a conception of something (man, God; philosophy, science; religion, art) is a more or less systematic way of looking at it, or, rather, of thinking and talking about it. It is usually expressible in a sentence that looks like a formal definition. It has to do with something that we think of as important. And it is usually defended by argument rather than by an appeal to a dictionary or to empirical evidence. How we talk about things is continuous with how we behave toward them; what we call them often reflects and determines our attitudes and reactions to them. Thus, "Homosexuality is a disease" is not part of the lexical definition of homosexuality, nor is it an ordinary empirical truth. It expresses a conception of homosexuality. An alternative conception is that homosexuality is a sin. Still another, that it is just one of a variety of natural modes of sexual preference or conduct. Persuading someone to adopt one of these conceptions would obviously affect the way in which he responds to homosexuals, for example, to look on them as sick and in need of treatment or to look on them as wicked and deserving of censure or punishment.[13]

Now when Clive Bell wrote *Art,* in 1913, the taste of his contemporaries was confined largely to what is called "academic" painting, "realistic" painting in which subject matter is of prime importance. Bell had seen paintings of Cézanne, Matisse, and other post-Impressionists, and he noticed that subject matter was not of prime importance in them, that their value did not rest on realism or sentimental associations but on what he called "significant form": lines, colors, and patterns that are exciting in themselves. He found also that he could look at earlier paintings, and at vases, carpets, and sculptures in much the same way as he looked at the paintings of Matisse, and with the same reward. But when he turned to the pictures of the academicians, the thrill disappeared. He announced his discovery by saying, "Art is significant form." What he discovered was not the essence or distinctive trait of art, as he may have supposed, but a fresh way of looking at works of visual art; one which, if generally adopted, would lead people, as it led him, to refer to academic pictures as "not art," or "not *really* art," and would lead art collectors, museum directors, and others to act in keeping with this new way of speaking—surely something of no negligible consequence.

The suggestion that what an art theorist is doing is spelling out and arguing for a conception of art is not irresistible, but it may have the virtue of accounting for certain features of theories of art that would otherwise be mysterious. Adopting it, if only for the sake of trying it on, what changes, if any, in our way of looking at art are being urged by Tolstoy, Croce, Langer, and Dickie? And what difference, if any, would adopting any of these theories make in our responses to art and artists?

Notes

1. Because Croce's theory is stated in an idiom that modern readers find difficult to comprehend, a brief statement of its principal theses may be of some use to the reader.

Croce's theory is a cognitive one: art is a mode of knowledge. Knowledge is of two kinds—intuitive and logical. The "faculty" of intuitive knowledge is the imagination (the ability to frame and entertain images); that of logical knowledge is the intellect (the ability to form and apply concepts). Intuitive knowledge is knowledge of the particular, the individual, the "concrete," whereas logical knowledge is knowledge of the general, the universal, the "abstract." Intuitive knowledge is embodied or "expressed" in images; logical knowledge, in concepts. Concepts may be used to form, frame, or articulate an image, and images may be used to form, or to illustrate or teach, concepts; that is, concepts may have a place in the expression of an intuition, and images may have a place in logical knowledge. Sense-perception (which is not the same as mere sensation) is intuitive knowledge embodied or expressed in sensuous images (what Kant called "sensuous representations"), but not all sensuous images embody or express knowledge, for example, hallucinatory ones. So there may be images that do not embody or express intuitions. But there are no unexpressed intuitions (or unexpressed thoughts): all knowledge, insight, or understanding requires expression or articulation. (In his *Vico and Herder: Two Studies in the History of Ideas*, New York, 1976, pp. 165-66, Isaiah Berlin attributes to the eighteenth century thinkers Hamann and Herder the notion that "words and ideas are one. Men do not think, as it were, in thoughts and ideas and then look for words in which to 'clothe' them, as one looks for a glove to fit a fully formed hand." Croce would agree.) What is intuited is identical with what is expressed. Some intuitions—those the expression of which are works of art—are intuitions of what are variously described as "impressions and feelings," "impressions, sensations, feelings, impulses, emotions," "what is felt and suffered . . . the flux or wave of sensation," "sensations and impressions," and so on. (Because the word "impressions" occurs most often, we will stick with that.) To have an impression is not the same as to "know" it, to understand or comprehend it; as merely "had" or suffered an impression is, as it were, mute. A mute impression may be understood or "known" in one of two ways, intuitively or logically. To understand it logically is to find concepts that fit it, for example, to describe it; to understand it intuitively is to frame or articulate an image that expresses or embodies it. Art is the expression of intuitions of otherwise mute impressions. (There are nonartistic intuitions of this kind, but the difference between these and works of art is merely "quantitative," that is, one of extensiveness and/or degree of complexity.) But art is not, Tolstoy to the contrary, essentially *communication*—except perhaps to oneself; it need not be addressed to anyone. Hence no physical object (e.g., painting, score or performance, text, etc.) is required; no such thing need exist for art to exist. The expressed intuition that constitutes a work of art *can* exist only in the artist's imagination.

2. See R. G. Collingwood, *The Principles of Art*, Oxford, 1938, p. 111: "Until a man has expressed his emotion, he does not yet know what emotion it is." Collingwood's theory of art is so close to Croce's that the two are often referred to simply as "the Croce-Collingwood theory."

3. Richard Wollheim, *Art and Its Objects*, New York, 1968, p. 37.

4. The vicious circularity occurs not strictly in the definition of art but in that of the *definiens,* be it the aesthetic emotion or significant form.

5. John Searle categorically denies Langer's claim that there are meanings that are in principle discursively ineffable. In his *Speech Acts: An Essay in the Philosophy of Language,* New York, 1969, pp. 19-20, he enunciates what he calls the "principle of expressibility": "whatever can be meant can be said," or "for any meaning X and any speaker S whenever S means (intends to convey, wishes to communicate in an utterance, etc.) X then it is possible that there is some expression E such that E is an exact expression of or formulation of X." By an "expression" Searle means a verbal expression, a bit of discourse. Can you think of any reason for not accepting Searle's principle?

6. This is not a fictitious case. See Robert B. Semple, Jr.'s article "Tate Gallery Buys Pile of Bricks—Or Is It Art?," *The New York Times,* Friday, February 20, 1976, p. 31.

7. Berkeley's view that all sensible objects, including the brain, are ideas *is* vacuous, because Berkeley makes it clear that there is and can be nothing with which "ideas" can contrast. So "All sensible objects are ideas" is no more informative than "All sensible objects are sensible objects."

8. Saint Augustine, *Confessions,* trans. by R. S. Pine-Coffin, Harmondsworth, England, 1961, pp. 263-64.

9. This assumption is explicitly enunciated by Bell: "either all works of visual art have some common quality, or when we speak of 'works of art' we gibber. Everyone speaks of 'art,' making a mental classification by which he distinguishes 'works of art' from all other classes. What is the justification for this classification? What is the quality common and peculiar to all members of this class? Whatever it be, no doubt it is often found in company with other qualities; but they are adventitious—it is essential."

10. Ludwig Wittgenstein refers metaphorically to such resemblances as "family resemblances." See his *Philosophical Investigations,* trans. by G. E. M. Anscombe, Oxford, 1953, #65-67. Wittgenstein was a vigorous and persistent opponent of the view that "there must be something common" to everything univocally referred to by the same name. He cites "games" as evidence to the contrary.

11. If the assumption here in question were true, you would expect formal definition to be ubiquitous. But "the kind of definition that consists in giving the connotation of a term in the form of a necessary and sufficient condition determining a class, far from being normal or customary, is something exceptional and remarkable." Max Black, "Definition, Presupposition, and Assertion," *Problems of Analysis,* Ithaca, N.Y., 1954, p. 25. Black's counterexample is "dachshund." The natural habitat of formal definition is mathematics.

12. On the contrast between concept and conception, see Wilson Follett, *Modern American Usage,* New York, 1966, p. 102.

13. A few other examples: "Now faith is the substance of things hoped for, the evidence of things not seen" (St. Paul, *Hebrews,* 11:1). This is how the Authorized Version reads. In *The New English Bible* we find, "And what is faith? Faith gives substance [or assurance] to our hopes, and makes us certain of realities we do not see."

"What is a poet? An unhappy man who in his heart harbors a deep anguish, but whose lips are so fashioned that the moans and cries which pass over them are transformed into ravishing music." Søren Kierkegaard, *Either/Or,* trans. by David F. Swenson and Lillian Marvin Swenson, Princeton, 1959, Vol. I, p. 19.

"Philosophy is a battle against the bewitchment of our intelligence by means of language." Ludwig Wittgenstein, *op. cit.,* #109.

Note that statements like these would commonly be referred to as definitions.

Suggestions for Additional Reading

Commentaries on, and criticisms of, theories presented in this section:

On Tolstoy: R. W. Beardsmore, *Art and Morality* (London, 1971); C. J. Ducasse, *The Philosophy of Art* (New York, 1929), Ch. 2; H. W. Garrod, *Tolstoy's Theory of Art* (Oxford, 1935); Gary R. Jahn, "The Aesthetic Theory of Leo Tolstoy's *What is Art?*," *J.A.A.C.*, 34 (1975), 59-65; I. Knox, "Tolstoy's Esthetic Definition of Art," *J. Phil.*, 27 (1930), 65-70; Theodore Redpath, *Tolstoy* (London, 1958). On Croce: B. Bosanquet, "Croce's Aesthetic," *P.B.A.*, 9 (1919-20), 261-288; Merle E. Brown, "Croce's Early Aesthetics: 1894-1912," *J.A.A.C.*, 22 (1963), 29-41, and *Neo-Idealistic Aesthetics: Croce-Gentile-Collingwood* (Detroit, 1966); E. F. Carritt, "Croce and His Aesthetic," *Mind*, 62 (1953), 452-465; C. J. Ducasse, *The Philosophy of Art* (New York, 1929), Ch. 3; John Hospers, "The Croce-Collingwood Theory of Art," *Phil.*, 31 (1956), 291-308; Bernard Mayo, "Art, Language, and Philosophy in Croce," *Phil. Quart.*, 5 (1955), 245-260; G. N. G. Orsini, *Benedetto Croce: Philosopher of Art and Literary Critic* (Carbondale, Ill., 1961); P. B. Patankar, "What Does Croce Mean by 'Expression'?," *B.J.A.*, 2 (1962), 112-125; Richard Wollheim, *Art and Its Objects* (New York, 1968), #22, 23, 50. On Bell: George Dickie, *Aesthetics: An Introduction* (Indianapolis, 1971), pp. 70-78, and "Clive Bell and the Method of *Principia Ethica*," *B.J.A.*, 5 (1965), 139-143; Rosalind Ekman, "The Paradoxes of Formalism," *B.J.A.*, 10 (1970), 350-358; R. K. Elliott, "Clive Bell's Aesthetic Theories and His Critical Purpose," *B.J.A.*, 5 (1965), 111-122; Thomas M. McLaughlin, "Clive Bell's Aesthetic: Tradition and Significant Form," *J.A.A.C.*, 35 (1977), 433-443; R. Meager, "Clive Bell and Aesthetic Emotion," *B.J.A.*, 5 (1965), 123-131; Herbert Read, "Clive Bell," *B.J.A.*, 5 (1965), 107-110; Jerome Stolnitz, *Aesthetics and Philosophy of Art Criticism* (Boston, 1960), pp. 134-156; Morris Weitz, *Philosophy of the Arts* (Cambridge, Mass., 1950), pp. 1-34. On Langer: Timothy Binkley, "Langer's Logical and Ontological Modes," *J.A.A.C.*, 28 (1970), 455-464; Samuel Bufford, "Susanne Langer's Two Philosophies of Art," *J.A.A.C.*, 31 (1972), 9-20; George Dickie, *Aesthetics* (Indianapolis, 1971), pp. 78-84; Forest Hansen, "Langer's Expressive Form: An Interpretation," *J.A.A.C.*, 27 (1968), 165-170, and "The Adequacy of Verbal Articulation of Emotions," *J.A.A.C.*, 31 (1972), 249-253; W. E. Kennick, "Art and the Ineffable," *J. Phil.*, 58 (1961), 309-320; B. F. Scholz, "Discourse and Intuition in Susanne Langer's Aesthetics,'" *J.A.A.C.*, 31 (1972), 215-226; C. L. Stevenson, "Symbolism in the Non-representational Arts," *Language, Thought, and Culture*, Paul Henle, ed. (Ann Arbor, 1958), pp. 196-225; Paul Welsh, "Discursive and Presentational Symbols," *Mind*, 64 (1955), 181-199. *On Dickie and the Institutional*

Theory: W. L. Blizek, "An Institutional Theory of Art," *B.J.A.*, 14 (1974), 142-150; Ted Cohen, "The Possibility of Art," *Phil. Rev.*, 82 (1973), 69-82; Melvin Rader, "Dickie and Socrates on Definition," *J.A.A.C.*, 32 (1974), 423-424; R. J. Sclafani, "Art as a Social Institution: Dickie's New Definition," *J.A.A.C.*, 32 (1973), 111-114; Anita Silvers, "The Artworld Discarded," *J.A.A.C.*, 34 (1976), 441-454. *On Rosenberg*: Morris Weitz, "Art and Nonart," *Partisan Review*, 40 (1973), 126-130. *On Danto*: R. J. Sclafani, "Artworks, Art Theory, and the Artworld ," *Theoria*, 39 (1973), 18-34. *On the challenge of modernism*: Stanley Cavell, *Must We Mean What We Say?* (New York, 1969), "Music Discomposed," pp. 180-212, and "A Matter of Meaning It," pp. 213-237.

Other theories of art:

Ernst Cassirer, *An Essay on Man* (New Haven, 1944), Ch. 9; R. G. Collingwood, *The Principles of Art* (Oxford, 1938); John Dewey, *Art as Experience* (New York, 1934); T. J. Diffey, "The Republic of Art," *B.J.A.*, 9 (1969), 145-156; C. J. Ducasse, *The Philosophy of Art* (New York, 1929), Ch. 8; Roger Fry, "An Essay in Aesthetics," *Vision and Design* (London, 1920; New York, 1956)—a view similar to Bell's; Nelson Goodman, *Languages of Art* (Indianapolis and New York, 1968); and "When Is Art?," *The Arts and Cognition*, David Perkins and Barbara Leondar, eds. (Baltimore, 1977), pp. 11-19; Joseph Margolis, *The Language of Art and Art Criticism* (Detroit, 1965), Ch. 3; Jacques Maritain, *Creative Intuition in Art and Poetry* (London and New York, 1953); Stefan Morawski, *Inquiries into the Fundamentals of Aesthetics* (Cambridge, Mass., 1974), pp. 88-124; DeWitt H. Parker, "The Nature of Art," *Révue Internationale de Philosophie*, 1 (1939), 684-702; Wladyslaw Tartarkiewicz, "What is Art?: The Problem of Definition Today," *B.J.A.*, 11 (1971), 134-153.

On the problem of defining art:

M. H. Abrams, "What's the Use of Theorizing About the Arts?," *In Search of Literary Theory*, M. W. Bloomfield, ed. (Ithaca, N.Y., 1972), pp. 3-54; M. W. Beal, "Essentialism and Closed Concepts," *Ratio*, 16 (1974), 190-205; Monroe C. Beardsley, Douglas N. Morgan, and Mary Mothersill, "On Art and the Definitions of Arts: A Symposium," *J.A.A.C.*, 20 (1961), 175-198; Lee R. Brown, "Definitions and Art Theory," *J.A.A.C.*, 28 (1969), 409-415; James D. Carney, "Defining Art," *B.J.A.*, 15 (1975), 191-206; T. J. Diffey, "Essentialism and the Definition of Art," *B.J.A.*, 13 (1973), 103-120; W. B. Gallie, "Essentially Contested Concepts," *P.A.S.*, 56 (1955-56), 169-198; and "Art as an Essentially Contested Concept," *Phil. Quart.*, 6 (1956), 97-114; W. E. Kennick, "Does Traditional Aesthetics Rest on a Mistake?," *Mind*, 67 (1958), 317-334; Haig Khatchadourian, "Family Resemblances and the Classification of Works of Art," *J.A.A.C.*, 28 (1969), 79-90; Berel Lang, " 'What Is Art?': Questions (and

Answers) About the Question," *Phil. and Phen.*, 33 (1973), 524-530; Maurice Mandelbaum, "Family Resemblances and Generalizations Concerning the Arts," *Am. Phil. Quart.*, 2 (1965), 219-228; R. J. Sclafani, in "Art, Wittgenstein, and Open-Textured Concepts," *J.A.A.C.*, 29 (1971), 333-342 and in " 'Art' and Artifactuality," *Southwest. J. Phil.*, 1 (1970), 103-110, claims that artifactuality is a necessary condition of art; Guy Sircello, "Arguing about 'Art'," *Language and Aesthetics*, B. R. Tilghman, ed. (Lawrence, Kan., 1973), pp. 65-86 is a reply to Kennick; B. R. Tilghman, "Wittgenstein, Games, and Art," *J.A.A.C.*, 31 (1973), 517-524; Morris Weitz, "The Role of Theory in Aesthetics," *J.A.A.C.*, 15 (1956), 27-35 is a seminal view, opposed by Abrams, Beal, Brown, Mandelbaum, and others; and *The Opening Mind: a Philosophical Study of Humanistic Concepts* (Chicago, 1977), Ch. 3, "Art" is a reply to Abrams, Mandelbaum, and Dickie; Paul Ziff, "The Task of Defining a Work of Art," *Phil. Rev.*, 62 (1953), 58-78.

II

Artistic Creativity

Introduction

ABOUT THE CONCEPT OF CREATIVITY, the art historian H. W. Janson has written:

> Empirically, I should say "creativity" is a mythic concept that claims an analogy between God, the paradigm of the true creator, and the artist, even though God, by definition, creates *ex nihilo* while the artist does no such thing. The concept was first applied in the 16th century, to and by artists who accepted this quasi-divine status, such as Michelangelo and Dürer. Since then, it has been so cheapened by overuse (we hear not only of new lipsticks "created" by cosmetics experts but of the "creativity" evidenced by children's drawings and even by those of chimpanzees) that the only thing to do is to leave it alone.[1]

By "leave it alone," I take it, Janson means drop it, forget it, don't use it at all, except in connection with God. But whether some choose to follow Janson's advice, we seem to be stuck with the concept; and it would appear only reasonable to take cognizance of what we are doing with it when we use it in talking about art.

The most memorable occurrence of the verb "to create" is in the English translation (Authorized Version) of the opening sentence of *Genesis*: "In the beginning God created the heaven and the earth."[2] According to reliable scholarly commentaries, the original Hebrew verb translated as "created" is *br'* or *bara*, a word that is applied solely to God's activity of effecting something or bringing it about. But the Greek translation of *Genesis* (the Septuagint) uses a form of the verb *poiein* (from which we get "poetry"), whereas the Latin (the Vulgate) uses a form of *creare* (*In principio creavit Deus* . . .), from which we get our verb "to create." But neither *poiein* nor *creare* was used exclusively of divine causality: they are ordinary verbs meaning to make, fashion, or produce.[3] Be that as it may, the English word was first used of God's work only; later it acquired a legal use, for example, to create (legally establish) a peerage or a corporation; and still later it was extended to the activities of artists (and others), perhaps by analogy to God's work.

Whether it was because of its religious associations or for some other reason, the notion of creation has retained an aura of mystery that does not surround that of making something, for example, of making a dress or a sand castle; and this is especially true of artistic creation.[4] How is it done?, What is the secret?, we wonder (especially if we are not competent or great artists ourselves); and we are inclined to start talking about Talent, Genius, Inspiration, Madness, the Unconscious, and the like, as if this will remove the mystery rather than simply give it a name.

For philosophers of art the so-called problem of creativity has, at least roughly, been defined by the following questions: What is it to create a work of art?; What is the creative process?; What goes on, especially in the mind, when one creates a work of art?; and What is it for something to be a creative work of art? The first three questions have often been taken to be synonymous, and the answer to the fourth has often been thought to imply an answer to one or more of the first three.

Tomas, for example, is basically interested in the fourth question, but he holds that when we speak of creative art we have in mind certain general facts about the activity of artistic creation, or the creative process, and he tries to spell out what these facts are. Beardsley's basic interest is not so much in the fourth question as in the second (or is it in the first three construed as one?). He is interested in "the creative process" as "that stretch of mental and physical activity between the incept [the "initial element of what later becomes the work of art"] and the final touch": "My problem is about what goes on in this interval—how the work of art itself comes into existence and takes on its character through the stages or phases of this process." Although in the last section of his paper his emphasis shifts from "how the artist's mind works" to "the experience of the beholder" of the work of art, which is, he says, "the true locus of creativity." Finally, I am interested in the first question (which, I argue, is not the same as the second or third) and in the fourth (which, I hold, can be answered without answering the second or third). Artistic creation is not a process, at least not a psychological one; and to say that a work of art is creative implies nothing about *how* it was created.

Notes

1. *Perspectives in Education, Religion, and the Arts*, Howard E. Kiefer and Milton K. Munitz, eds., Albany, N.Y., 1970, p. 302. The situation is even more bizarre than Janson allows. In *Books in Print 1977-1978*, we find such titles as *Creative Administration in Physical Education and Athletics*, *Creative Approach to Controlling Photography*, *Creative Bible Activities for Children*, *Creative Brooding*, *Creative Citizenship*, *Creative Control of Building Costs*, *Creative Cookery With Aluminum Foil*, *Creative Divorce*, *Creative Dreaming*, *Creative Finger Fun*, *Creative Fishing*, *Creative Food Experiences for Children*, *Creative*

Horsemanship, Creative Intimacy, Creative Loneliness, Creative Markdown Practices for Profit, Creative Retirement, and Creative Selling.

2. *The New English Bible* (New York, 1971) has God *making* heaven and earth.

3. Latin (and the same is true of Greek) has a number of verbs, roughly synonymous, that might have been used instead of *creare* to translate the opening sentence of *Genesis;* for example, *condere, fabricare, facere, fingere,* and *generare.* Thus, the Latin translation might easily have been: *In principio fecit Deus* . . . ; and Janson would perhaps have been spared his annoyance.

4. In Plato, as his dialogues *Ion* and *Phaedrus* show, an aura of mystery surrounds the making (*poiesis*) of *poems,* but not of paintings, statues, buildings, pieces of instrumental music, or prose writings.

VINCENT TOMAS

Creativity in Art

WHEN A RIFLEMAN AIMS at his target, he knows what he wants to do. He wants to hit the bull's-eye. Before he shoots, he knows what the target is; he knows that the black circle in the center of it is the bull's-eye; and he knows that hitting the bull's-eye consists in causing a bullet to pass through that black circle. He also knows, before he has squeezed the trigger, that if, after he has squeezed it, a hole appears in the black circle, he will have succeeded in doing what he wanted to do; and that if there isn't a hole there, he will have failed.

Furthermore, the rifleman knows what he ought to do to hit the bull's-eye. He knows what position he ought to assume, how he ought to adjust the sling, where exactly he ought to place his left hand, where he ought to place the butt so that it fits his shoulder and cheek, what the sight picture ought to be, how he ought to exhale a little and then hold his breath when the sight picture is correct, and how he ought to squeeze off the shot without knowing exactly when the explosion will come, so that he won't flinch until after it is too late to spoil his aim.

If, after the rifleman has attempted to obey all these rules, he fails to hit the bull's-eye, any sergeant can tell him, and the rifleman will agree, that he did fail; and that, since he did, he had not obeyed all the rules. For, if he had obeyed them, there necessarily would have been a hole in the bull's-eye. If, on the other hand, he does hit the bull's-eye, the white disc is displayed and the rifleman is congratulated. He is congratulated, whether the people who congratulate him realize it or not, for having been able to learn and obey all the rules.

When we congratulate an artist for being creative, however, it is not because he was able to obey rules that were known before he painted his picture or wrote his novel or poem, so that thereby he succeeded in doing what had been done before. We congratulate him because he embodied in colors or in language something the like of which did not exist before,

Reprinted from *The Philosophical Review*, Vol. LXVII (1958).

and because he was the originator of the rules he implicitly followed while he was painting or writing. Afterwards, others may *explicitly* follow the same rules and thereby achieve similar successes. But the academic painter or writer is like the rifleman. He, too, aims at a known target, and he hits his bull's-eye by obeying known rules. As Sir Joshua Reynolds wrote:

> By studying carefully the works of great masters, this advantage is obtained; we find that certain niceties of expression are capable of being executed, which otherwise we might suppose beyond the reach of art. This gives us a confidence in ourselves; and we are thus incited to endeavor at not only the same happiness of execution, but also at other congenial excellencies. Study indeed consists in learning to see nature, and may be called the art of using other men's minds.[1]

Unlike either the rifleman or the academic painter or writer, the creative artist does not initially know what his target is. Although he seems to himself to be "aiming" at something, it is not until just before he affixes his signature or seal of approval to his work that he finds out that *this* was the way to bring it into being. Creative activity in art, that is to say, is not a paradigm of purposive activity, that is, of activity engaged in and consciously controlled so as to produce a desired result. In the paradigmatic case, the agent envisages the result he desires to produce and has it consciously in view, and he believes that if he acts in a certain way the result desired will be produced. Although we may say that his activity is "teleologically controlled," to explain it we do not appeal to a final cause, but only to an efficient cause, namely, to his desire for the result he envisages and his beliefs. But when he is impelled to engage in creative activity, the artist, as has been said, does not already envisage the final result. He does not therefore already have an idea or image of it. And his activity therefore is not "controlled," as in the paradigm case, by a desire for an envisaged result and beliefs about how to obtain it.

If, however, creative activity differs from clear-cut cases of purposive activity in the ways mentioned, it resembles purposive activity in other ways. As has been said, the creative artist has a sense that his activity is directed—that it is heading somewhere. Now the cash value of the statement that the artist has a sense of being engaged in a directed activity, of going somewhere despite the fact that he cannot say precisely where he is going while he is still on the way, is that he *can* say that certain directions are not right. After writing a couplet or drawing a line, he will erase it because it is "wrong" and try again. If there were in him no tendency to go in a certain direction, he would not resist being pulled in just any direction. This element of conscious resistance to the lure of beckoning side paths, or the exercise of critical judgment, is what sets creative activity apart from the activity that is acquiescent to the leadership of revery. In the latter, anything goes and nothing is rejected. Here we ought not to say that nothing is rejected because everything that the imagination suggests is consented to as "right," but only that all is accepted without criticism. Coleridge and the idealists were correct, therefore, in so far as they distinguished creative activity from the exercise of passive imagination, or fancy. Essential to the former, while absent from the latter, are critical judgment and fastidiousness.

Creative activity in art, then, is activity subject to critical control by the artist, although not by virtue of the fact that he foresees the final result of the activity. That this way of construing creativity reflects part of what we have in mind when we speak of creative art can be shown if we contrast what results from creative activity so construed with what results from other activities that we do not call creative.

Thus we do not judge a painting, poem, or other work to be a work of creative art unless we believe it to be original. If it strikes us as being a repetition of other paintings or poems, if it seems to be the result of a mechanical application of a borrowed technique or style to novel subject matter, to the degree that we apprehend it as such, to the same degree we deny that it is creative. There are men who have trained themselves to paint in the manner of Rembrandt, and some have become so good at it that even an expert aided by X-rays may find it hard to decide that their pictures were *not* painted by Rembrandt. Whatever other merits we attribute to such a painter or to his work, we do not judge him to be creative. He is like the rifleman. He knows what his bull's-eye is, and he knows how to hit it. Even in the case of a painter who has created a style of his own, we do not say that he is creating his style when he is painting his thirtieth or fortieth picture in that style. We may judge the style to be a good one, and the painting as a whole to be good. Yet we will grant that with respect to style the painter is no longer creative but is only repeating himself. To create is to originate. And it follows from this that prior to creation the creator does not foresee what will result from it. As T. E. Hulme put it, "to predict it would be to produce it before it was produced."[2]

Hulme's remark may sound odd, but it really isn't. To predict the result of his creative activity, the artist would have to envisage that result. He would have to have the idea of it in mind. But if he already had the idea in mind, all that would remain to be done is to objectify the idea in paint or in stone, and this would be a matter of skill, or work. That is why sculptors who do not need to work their material before they can envisage the determinate statue they want to make, but who can describe exactly what it should be like before the first blow of the mallet is struck, often hire stone-cutters to execute their plan. By the time they have the idea, the creative act, which in this case is the production of the idea, is finished. But to produce that original idea, the sculptor does not first have to produce an idea of it.

Although we do not judge a work to be a work of creative art unless we believe it to be original, it is not enough that we should judge it to be merely different or novel. In discourse about art, we use "creative" in an honorific sense, in a sense in which creative activity always issues in something that is different in an interesting, important, fruitful, or other *valuable* way. If what the artist produces is a novelty, yet indifferent or bad, we do not regard him as a creator. It is granted that, as R. G. Collingwood points out, there is a sense of the word in which we say that a man creates a nuisance or a disturbance. Yet if we believe, for example, that all that the Dadaists "created" was a nuisance and a disturbance, we will not judge them to have been creative artists.

Since "creative" as applied to art has this honorific sense, we will tend not to apply the term to any activity which does not result in a product having positive aesthetic or artistic value. To the degree that a work lacks coherence and lucidity, to the degree that it is not a unified whole the relations between whose parts are felt by aesthetic intuition as necessary, not fortuitous, connections, to that degree will it fail to be a work of creative art. Now a reason or ground for a judgment that something is not a work of creative art, I suggest, is not merely that the work as we see it lacks coherence and lucidity. Rather, this lack in the work is taken as evidence of a lack of control by the artist over the activity to which the work owes its origin, or of coherence and lucidity in him. And if this were so, then what he produced would not be a work of creative art. This is why, I suggest, we distinguish works of creative art from products of passive imagination on the one hand, and from the art of the insane on the other.

To illustrate the sort of works that we can expect to be produced under the guidance of passive imagination, I will use two extreme examples. These were deliberately chosen because of their bearing on a theory of artistic creativity, one thesis of which is that "Poetic creation, like the dream, is governed by strict psychic laws."[3]

In 1823, Ludwig Börne published an essay entitled "The Art of Becoming an Original Writer in Three Days." According to Ernest Jones, it was his reading of this essay that gave Sigmund Freud his "trust in the validity of free associations."[4] Börne writes:

> Here follows the practical prescription I promised. Take a few sheets of paper and for three days in succession write down, without any falsification or hypocrisy, everything that comes into your head. Write what you think of yourself, of your women, of the Turkish war, of Goethe, of the Fonk criminal case, of the Last Judgment, of those senior to you in authority— and when the three days are over you will be amazed at what novel and startling thoughts have welled up in you. This is the art of becoming an original writer in three days.[5]

No doubt someone who follows this prescription will, when the three days are over, be amazed when he reads what novel and startling things he has written. And it is not impossible that some of the statements will be judged by him to be adequate formulations of what he thinks—of himself, of his women, of Goethe, or of the Last Judgment, difficult subjects every one of them about which most of us don't know what we think unless, by a creative act, as distinguished from free association, we have found out. But it is much more probable that what was so written would be rejected by the writer as an inadequate expression of his thought. In any case, if everything were left exactly as it was just because it happened to come into the writer's head, we would not take it seriously as creative literature. Rather, to borrow another quotation from Reynolds, we would say, "When [the] desire of novelty has proceeded from mere idleness or caprice, it is not worth the trouble of criticism."[6]

The second horrible example is drawn from an essay in many ways similar to the one by Ludwig Börne. It is by Alva Johnson, and the title is "How to Become a Great Writer."[7] Virtually all of this essay is the biography of a great writer. Johnson tells of a young man who, as Freud says of the artist, like other men longed "to attain honor, power, riches, fame, and the love of women,"[8] but to whom reality denied all these things. After graduating from a university, full of ambition, he accepted a job which he soon gave up in favor of another, paying less money but' offering better prospects. The prospects proved to be illusory, so he changed jobs again, drawn by further illusory prospects. This was repeated several times. After some years he found himself burdened with a family, and with an income smaller than his allowance as a student had been. Goaded by frustration, he did not take to drink but instead indulged in ritualistic daydreaming. For some years he devoted an hour each day to spinning castles in the air, and by inhabiting them in the role of hero he achieved a make-believe gratification of his desires. One day, when he was returning home, he bought a pulp magazine and read one of the stories. This opened his eyes. That evening, instead of daydreaming, he sat down with some sheets of paper and began to write one of his phantasies down. What he wrote was rejected by an extraordinary number of publishers. They gave such reasons as that the setting lacked authenticity, the style was atrocious, and the plot was infantile. But at length the manuscript was accepted and published, and the book proved to be a tremendous commercial success. By 1935 it and its sequels had sold twenty-five million copies and had been translated into fifty-six languages; and the author was living in a luxurious mansion in the Southwest. Thus he has won, as Freud says, "through his phantasy—what before he could win only in phantasy: honor, power, and the love of women."[9] The name of the writer is Edgar Rice Burroughs, and the title of his first book is *Tarzan of the Apes*.[10]

Its being subject to critical control sets creative art apart not only from the sort of thing just described, but from the art of the insane. There is an ancient tradition that the creative artist is a man possessed. To give once more the familiar quotations from Plato:

For the poet is a light and winged and holy thing, and there is no invention in him until he has been inspired and is out of his senses, and the mind is no longer with him: when he has not attained to this state, he is powerless and is unable to utter his oracles. [*Ion,* 534].

But he who, having no touch of the Muses' madness in his soul, comes to the door and thinks that he will get into the temple by art—he, I say, and his poetry are not admitted; the sane man disappears and is nowhere when he enters into rivalry with the madman [*Phaedrus,* 245].

Shakespeare says:

> The lunatic, the lover, and the poet
> Are of imagination all compact.
> [*Midsummer Night's Dream, V, i.*]

Despite this impressive tradition, we cannot accept the view that creative artists must literally be madmen. The pictures they paint and the poetry they write make sense, whereas this is not true of the art of the insane. When we gaze in succession upon a series of pictures by psychotics, we see that in them all there is a note of nightmare, delirium, or mania which is not present in, for instance, da Vinci's drawings of monsters or even in surrealist paintings. The difference may be described by saying that in surrealist painting, delusion or nightmare is portrayed or objectified, whereas no matter what an insane man portrays or objectifies —be it "Mother" or "God"—his psychosis is revealed. If the art of the insane makes sense to us, it is in the manner of a sign or symptom of psychosis, not in the manner of an expression of it.

Here it may occur to the reader to raise the question of Van Gogh, whose later works, we may suppose, are works of creative art, but in which there is a kind of stridency signifying madness. The answer, I suggest, is that it is only in so far as there is more in them than a stridency signifying madness that we regard them as products of creative art. Those paintings were not done, that is to say, in the complete absence of conscious control and criticism. In psychiatric language, which I borrow from Ernst Kris, those paintings were not completely tied to Van Gogh's delusional system. As Kris says, in Van Gogh

the disorder manifests itself in a change of style, but even though the style has changed, the connections with the artistic tendencies of the individual and his environment are preserved.[11]

Creativity and madness have traditionally been associated mainly though not entirely because of the phenomenon of inspiration. In the creative process, two moments may be distinguished, the moment of inspiration, when the new suggestion appears in consciousness, and the mo-

ment of development or elaboration. The moment of inspiration is sometimes accompanied by exalted feelings, and this is why, according to
Charles Lamb, it is confused with madness. According to Lamb,

> men, finding in the raptures of the higher poetry a condition of exaltation,
> to which they have no parallel in their own experience, besides the
> spurious resemblance of it in dreams and fevers, impute a state of dreami-
> ness and fever to the poet. But the true poet dreams being awake. He is
> not possessed by his subject but has dominion over it.[12]

The "moment" of development may last a long time, of course, even
years. During that more or less long moment the artist is striving to find
out what his inspiration is. As in the cases of Flaubert and Hemingway,
he may write and rewrite and hone and polish until at last he can look
upon what he has done and say, "There! That's what I wanted to say,
just as I wanted to say it." Before that, he knew only that what he had so
far done was *not* quite what he wanted to say, or quite how he wanted to
say it. It seems obvious that Flaubert, during that long moment of elaboration during which he fashioned *Madame Bovary,* was critically controlling what he was doing. He was neither mad nor free-associating nor
spinning daydreams. However, as Plato reminds us, if Flaubert had had
no touch of the Muses' madness in his soul, there would have been no
invention in him. He would have had no inspiration and therefore nothing to elaborate. In that case, however long he wrote and rewrote, honed
and polished, nothing would have come of it.

Now inspiration, as far as we know, is not subject to our will. We cannot decide to have an inspiration, nor can we by reasoning conclude our
way into it. And if by "art" we mean, as Plato did, skill—an activity consciously controlled so as to produce an already envisaged result—then art
is not enough to produce an inspiration. When, therefore, Plato says that
"there is no invention in him until he has become inspired and is out of
his senses, and the mind is no longer in him"; or when he says, "he who,
having no touch of the Muses' madness in his soul, comes to the door and
thinks that he will get into the temple by the help of art—he, I say, and
his poetry are not admitted," he may mean what I have just said, though
he says it in a less prosaic way. If he does mean that inspiration is necessary for creative art, and that it is not by reasoning or by the exercise of
skill that artists become inspired, we may agree. At the same time we
should observe that this does not entail that when an artist has been inspired he becomes incapable of exercising skill in developing his inspiration, or that reason in the sense of a capacity for critical control "is no
longer in him," or that the artist is literally a "madman."

Here it may be objected that cases of dramatically sudden and apparently fully determinate inspiration are being left out of the account, cases
such as the one Nietzsche describes in *Ecce Homo* in the following words:

something profoundly convulsive and disturbing suddenly becomes visible
and audible with indescribable definiteness and exactness. One hears—one
does not seek; one takes—one does not ask who gives. . . .There is the
feeling that one is utterly out of hand. . . .Everything occurs without
volition. . . .The spontaneity of the images and similes is most remarkable. . . .If I may borrow a phrase of Zarathustra's it actually seems as if the
things themselves came to one, and offered themselves as similes.[13]

In such cases, the two moments of inspiration and elaboration collapse
into one, and the poem issues forth in the complete absence of critical
control. Or so it would seem. It is such cases that lend support to such
truth as there is in the view that the creative artist is out of his mind, and
in the Romanticist theory that art is the spontaneous overflow of powerful feelings. But was the manner in which Nietzsche wrote *Thus Spake
Zarathustra* completely blind and automatic, or was there after all some
critical control? I submit that there probably was. My reasons for thinking that there probably was may perhaps not have very much weight; but
I am inclined to think that they have some weight—the weight of common
sense.

C. S. Peirce refers to a man, who, when he was asked what he thought
of the fact that the sun obeyed Joshua's command to stand still, replied,
"Well, I'll bet that the sun wiggled just a bit when no one was looking."
Similarly, I'll bet that Nietzsche edited just a bit while he wrote down
Thus Spake Zarathustra. Should we accept reports of fully determinate
inspiration at their face value as being about cases in which the moving
finger writes, and, having writ, moves on? Is it absurd to suspect that such
cases are in fact more like the parody of Omar's famous line?

> The moving finger writes, and having writ
> Moves on. But lo! It stops a bit.
> Moves back to cross a T, insert a word.
> The moving finger's acting quite absurd.

Even if Nietzsche didn't deliberately change a thing, even if all came
out just right from the very first line, was there not a relatively cool hour
when Nietzsche (and the same goes for Coleridge and "Kubla Khan")
read what he had written and judged it to be an adequate expression of
his thought? Haven't we all had the experience of being seized by the
Muse in the middle of the night and writing as if possessed, only to read
what we had written the next morning and to consign it not to a publisher but to the wastebasket?

If there was such a cool hour and such a critical judgment in Nietzsche's case, this is all that is needed to have made him create *Zarathustra*
on the view of creation presented above. C. J. Ducasse has stated the point
precisely in his *The Philosophy of Art*. Ducasse writes:

To say that art is conscious . . . or . . . critically controlled . . . does not mean that it need be conscious or so controlled either antecedently to or contemporaneously with the expressive act. . . . .But it does mean that a *critical judgment is an intrinsic, essential constituent of the productive activity called art*; and indeed, not merely a critical judgment, but a *favorable* one. . . . .One must be able to acknowledge the product as an adequate statement of oneself. . . . .The telic character, which truly belongs to art since a critical moment is an intrinsic part of it, may be said to accrue to the expressive activity which is its first moment ex post fact. That activity is telically construed and criticized *after* it has occurred. And the work of art is not the product of that activity simply, but of that activity telically construed and criticized, and if need be repeated until correction of the product results, i.e., until objectivity of the expression is obtained.[14]

Given the concepts of conscious critical control and inspiration, we are in a position, I think, to set aside certain theories about creativity in art. Whether this can be done, by the way, should be of interest not only to philosophers of art but to metaphysicians and others as well.

Eliseo Vivas, in *Creation and Discovery*, finds in artistic creativity a difficulty for any "naturalistic" theory of mind. According to Vivas, what a naturalistic theory has to explain, but so far cannot explain, is

The control that the new whole, which from the standpoint of consciousness has not yet been fully born, exercises over the artist's mind as he proceeds to bring it to birth . . . [We need to explain] the purposive thrust of the mind, the mind's ability to follow the lead of something which is not pushing it from behind, so to speak, since it is not-yet-there. It is this fact, the control of the not-yet-there total situation over the present, that leads the idealist to insist that a factor is here at work of an essentially teleological nature.[15]

When the problem is formulated in this way, we are asked to explain how artistic creation is guided or controlled by an object that is "not-yet-there," that is, by something that does not exist, since it has not yet been created. And we may be tempted to say that, since it exercises an influence, the to-be-created object *is*, somehow, "there." It is an ideal or subsistent object which, perhaps in the manner of Aristotle's prime mover, does not push the artist's mind from behind, but attracts it from in front. It is, that is to say, not a kick, but a carrot, which the artist follows until the subsistent object stands revealed to him. Hence, creation is discovery.

But what needs to be explained is not, as Vivas formulates it, "the control that the new whole exercises over the artist's mind as he proceeds to bring it to birth." What needs to be explained is the fact that creative activity is controlled, but not by virtue of the fact that the artist already envisages the result he will create. That the artist's choices are controlled by a whole that is not-yet-there is not a fact but a theory. On the alternative theory that has been presented in this paper, what control consists in is the making of critical judgments about what has so far been done. There may be a great many of these judgments, or, in the limiting cases, just one.

But how, when he makes his critical judgments, does the artist know what is right and what is wrong? On the alternative theory, he knows because there is something pushing him from behind. Whenever the artist goes wrong, he feels himself being kicked, and he tries another way which, he surmises, trusts, or hopes, will not be followed by a kick. What is kicking him is "inspiration," which is already there. What he makes must be adequate to his inspiration. If it isn't, he feels a kick. We have all felt similar kicks when we have tried to put into words something we mean that we have not formulated before. On many such occasions, and they are always occasions on which we are *listening* to what we are saying as well as talking, we have uttered a sentence and then withdrawn it because it did not express what we meant, and we have sought to substitute for it another sentence which did.

Admittedly, the concept of inspiration we have been making use of is in need of clarification. Fortunately, it is not essential to our present purpose to attempt this task, since no matter whether the inspiration that appears on the threshold of the artist's reflexive consciousness is an impression, an emotion, a phantasy, an unclear idea, or whatnot, it is something that is "already there" in the creative process. That it should be already there is, for our purpose, the essential point.

In conclusion, let us consider briefly the view that when the moment of inspiration is distinct from the more or less long moment of its development or elaboration, during this second moment the mind of the artist is directed by his apprehension of "aesthetic necessity."

According to Brand Blanshard,

> Invention turns on a surrender to the workings of necessity in one's mind. [There is in the artist] a surrender of the will to an order whose structure is quite independent of it and whose affirmation through the mind is very largely so.[16]

In writing the last act of *Othello*, Blanshard continues, Shakespeare wrote what he did

> for the same reason that we, in reading or hearing it, find it satisfying, namely that with the given dramatic situation in mind "he could no other". . . .Given the character of Othello, his prevailing mood, his habits of speech, the situation in which he was placed, and given the need to round out the whole in accordance with the implicit demands of the aesthetic ideal, there was only one course for the Moor to take; and that he did.[17]

On this view, when an artist is inspired, what is given to him is analogous to a set of postulates and definitions in logic or mathematics; and what he does when he develops his inspiration is analogous to what a logician does when he deduces theorems from the postulates. Another analogy which is sometimes used is that inspiration is like an acorn. If the artist is inspired by an acorn, he can nurture it properly and develop an oak; or he may nurture it improperly and develop a stunted oak; but he can by no means develop an elm.

Such analogies, while they express how it feels to the artist when he is creating, can I believe be very misleading, especially when they lead us to postulate an ideal order of aesthetic necessity. Granted that we intuit "aesthetic necessity" in works of art, a lot of missing premises must be supplied before we can conclude that artistic creation is in important respects similar to logical deduction. When searching for these premises, we do well to tread warily.

For instance, from the fact that we feel (assuming that we do so feel) that the last act of Othello perfectly coheres with the preceding acts, it does not follow that a different last act, in which the Moor takes a different course, would not also be felt to cohere with them. With a different last act, we should have a different play, to be sure; but it might be an equally coherent one. Someone acquainted with it, and not with the play that we have, might well say about it that given the preceding acts, there was in the last act "only one course for the Moor to take; and that he did."

If this possibility is denied, what is the reason for the denial? The reason cannot be, "Aesthetic necessity is like logical necessity," since that is the thesis at issue.

Notes

1. From a fragment. Published in Elizabeth Gilmore Holt, *Literary Sources of Art History*, (Princeton, 1947), p. 504.

2. "Speculations," in *The Problems of Aesthetics*, ed. by Eliseo Vivas and Murray Krieger (New York, 1953), p. 126.

3. A. Bronson Feldman, "Reik and the Interpretation of Literature," *Explorations in Psychoanalysis*, ed. by Robert Lindner and Clement Staff (New York, 1953), p. 103.

4. *The Life and Works of Sigmund Freud*, I (New York, 1953), 245. See also p. 246.

5. *Ibid.*, p. 246.

6. *Discourses*. In Holt, *op. cit.*, p. 510.

7. *Saturday Evening Post*, July 25, 1935.

8. *A General Introduction to Psychoanalysis*, tr. by Joan Riviere (New York, 1935), p. 327.

9. *Ibid*, p. 328.

10. Johnson, who was writing a popular article, makes no mention of Freud. But it is worth remarking that, if his account is accurate, Burroughs is a perfect case study in support of what Freud said about artists in "The Relation of the Poet to Daydreaming" (1908) and elsewhere. Ernst Kris is the only Freudian writer on art I have read who is not blind to the distinction between creative and noncreative art.

11. *Psychoanalytic Explorations in Art* (New York, 1952), p. 94.

12. "The Sanity of True Genius," *The Works of Charles and Mary Lamb,* ed. by E. V. Lucas, (New York, 1903), II, 187.

13. *The Philosophy of Nietzsche,* introduction by W. H. Wright, (New York, no date), pp. 896-897.

14. New York, 1929, pp. 115-116.

15. New York, 1955, pp. 151-152.

16. *The Nature of Thought* (New York, 1940), II, 139, 166.

17. *Ibid.,* p. 145.

MONROE C. BEARDSLEY

On the Creation of Art

FROM THE TIMES OF HOMER AND HESIOD, creative artists have wondered about the source of their power to summon into existence things hitherto unseen and even unthought. In our day, it has begun to seem feasible to solve this problem with something like conclusivness. Yet much of its mystery remains.

A number of distinct questions are involved here, only one of which I shall take up. For example, I shall not inquire why the artist creates in the first place—what obscure impulses compel him to make shapes or melodies, to dance or tell stories. This question has been given two sorts of answer. The first is in terms of conscious motives (the artist wants fame, money, love, power, etc.)—and here it seems pretty evident that there must be a vast variety of true answers, depending on the artist, the work at hand, and even the time of day or night. The second is in terms of unconscious needs and drives—and this I am not competent to pursue. Again, I shall not inquire how the creative process begins—what evokes the first stroke of the brush, the first words of the poem. In the creation of every work, no doubt something does come first, perhaps a single little fragment, perhaps a rush of ideas. This initial element of what later becomes the work has been referred to by various metaphors, some of them misleading, as we shall see—*germ, cell, seed, nucleus;* I will call it the *inceptive element,* or, for short, *incept.* The incept of the work may simply pop into the artist's mind—like Mozart's melodies or Housman's verses —or it may come from external sources, accidentally, like the notes struck by a cat on the keyboard or the pattern made by mud in the gutter. When it does come from within, it no doubt has preconscious causal conditions, though to trace them would surely be a difficult undertaking.

What I mean by the creative process is that stretch of mental and physical activity between the incept and the final touch—between the thought

From *Journal of Aesthetics and Art Criticism,* 23 (1965), pp. 291–304. Copyright 1965 by *Journal of Aesthetics and Art Criticism.* Reprinted by permission of the journal and the author.

"I may be on to something here" and the thought "It is finished." My problem is about what goes on in this interval—how the work of art itself comes into existence and takes on its character through the stages or phases of this process.

I

Many students of art have assumed, or expected to find, that there is such a thing as *the* process of art creation—that is, a pattern universally or characteristically discoverable whenever substantial works of art are produced. They would allow, of course, for many differences between one creative process and another, depending on the artist's habits and temperament, the medium in which he moves, and the demands of the particular work in progress. But they argue that beneath these differences there is what we might call the *normal creative pattern*, and that to understand this pattern would contribute much to our understanding of the finished product.

Nor is it unreasonable to suppose that there is such a creative pattern to be isolated and described. First, it might be said, the common character of works of art in all media—whatever it is that enables us to class them together—presents a prima-facie case for a creative pattern. For things that are alike may well have been produced in a similar way. Second, there is the analogy with aesthetic experience. For if there is a pattern of appreciation common to the arts, then why should there not be a pattern of creation, which would, in a sense, be its inverse? Third, there is the analogy with other kinds of creative activity. Dewey's classic description of the process of inquiry, or problem-solving, remains the standard one, though it has been refined and extended since its first appearance in *How We Think*. Practical and scientific problems differ considerably among themselves, just as works of art do, and if there is a common pattern of thought provoked by the former, there may be a common pattern of activity required for the latter.

It is true that the theory of a common character of the arts and the theory of a special aesthetic experience have been questioned in recent years.[1] I appreciate the force of the objections, which I won't go into here, but, like many others, I am not ready to abandon either of the theories. In any case, of course, the three arguments I have mentioned above are not conclusive; they are but suggestive analogies. If there is a common creative pattern, then it can be discovered only by direct study of creative processes. And we might expect to find three main sources of evidence: the artist, the psychologist, and the philosopher.

Our first inclination, of course, it to turn to the creative artist himself, for he ought to know, if anyone does, what is going on in his mind during that mysterious interval between the first pin-fall or brick-fall of an idea and the final laying down of pen or brush. And it is true that much of our best and most useful information about creative processes does come from artists. The trouble is that, for reasons of their own, they are often inclined to the most whimsical and bizarre statements, and seem to enjoy being deliberately misleading. For example, Christian Zervos tells us that Picasso once said to him:

> I take a walk in the forest of Fontainbleau. There I get an indigestion of greenness. I must empty this sensation into a picture. Green dominates it. The painter paints as if in urgent need to discharge himself of his sensations and his visions.[2]

But this is a most curious description of the creative process. If the painter suffers from a surfeit of green, does he avoid looking at green any more for a while? No, he goes to his studio, squeezes out the green pigment, and proceeds to cover a canvas with it. This is like drinking grapefruit juice to cure an acid stomach. To make the indigestion theory of artistic creation plausible, the green-surfeited painter would surely go off to paint a *red* painting—red being the chromatic analogue of sodium bicarbonate.

We have had, by the way, many other metaphorical models of the creative process or the mind during creation—though perhaps none more colorful than Picasso's heartburn. The famous treatise of John Livingston Lowes, *The Road to Xanadu,* is full of them—the "hooked atoms" jumbled about, the "deep well" of the unconscious into which the poet dips, the imagination as "loom." Once we read of Shelley's "fading coal." Now it is the digital computer that furnishes the most tempting figure.

Or consider a famous statement by Henry James, in his preface to *The Spoils of Poynton.*[3] He begins by saying that the "germ" of his novel, as he called it, lay in a story told at a dinner party in London. James dilates upon "the sublime economy of art," which starts with such a "prick of inoculation," when the virus is communicated, and then goes on to build a work out of itself. The lady who told the story began by mentioning a woman at odds with her son over the furniture in an old house bequeathed to the son by his father. James remarked "There had been but ten words, yet I had recognized in them, as in a flash, all the possibilities of the little drama of my *Spoils,* which glimmered then and there into life." James says he didn't want to hear any more of the story, because the germ was complete in itself; the seed had been "transplanted to richer soil." This claim has often been repeated and taken as a text. But, as S. P. Rosenbaum has shown, if we look in James's *Notebooks,* where he tells a good deal about the process of writing *The Spoils of Poynton,* we find that in fact, on the day after the party (December 24, 1893), James wrote down not only the germ but the whole story, as it was told him, and that in fact many other germs came into the picture before very long, as well.[4]

Probably the greatest contributions made by creative artists to the solution of our problem are not their own theories about what they do, but the records they leave us in the form of sketches and early drafts. We cherish, for example, the notebooks of Beethoven, the sketches and studies in which Picasso worked out his ideas for *Guernica,* and the rich materials contributed to the special collection at the University of Buffalo by living poets who are willing to allow scholars to study their methods of work, their ventures, erasures, substitutions, corrections, and revisions. I shall have occasion to make use of these materials later.

As for the psychologists, despite the considerable effort (or at least speculation) that has gone into the study of the artist's unconscious, not much is available by way of well-established conclusions about the way the poet's or painter's mind is actually working when he is on the job.[5] Some of the most interesting contributions have been made by gestalt psychologists, for example, Rudolf Arnheim, in his psychological study of some materials in the Buffalo collection, and in his recent study of *Guernica.*[6]

Among the most valuable of the psychological investigations are those undertaken nearly thirty years ago by Catharine Patrick.[7] She first secured a group of 55 poets (with 58 "non-poets" as a suitable control group), and, after putting them at ease, confronted them with a certain picture and made them write a poem about it. She asked them to talk aloud as they thought, and took down their words in shorthand. Then she went to the painters, and, tit for tat, presented them with a part of a poem by Milton, which they were to illustrate in some way—while again, she took down their vocal musings, and also kept note of what they were drawing, as time passed. Every encounter was carefully timed. And the results were supplemented by questionnaires.

These interviews resulted in a good deal of very interesting material. Professor Patrick set out to determine whether the typical process of artistic creation passes through the four stages classically distinguished by Graham Wallas in his book on *The Art of Thought*—the stages of preparation, incubation, inspiration, and elaboration. And she concluded that these stages can indeed be distinguished. But the most remarkable feature of her material, it seems to me, is precisely the opposite. All four of these activities are mixed together; they are constantly (or alternately) going on throughout the whole process.

When we turn to the philosophers, we find a few who have tried to bring together into something of a general theory the insights of artists and psychologists. They, too, of course, have their own occupational hazards, or professional vices, and are too readily drawn away from contact with actual works of art into theorizing about what might ideally be true. For one who has a metaphysical axe to grind, it is easy enough to find a congenial formula to describe the creative process. Depending on the angle of approach, the artist will be said to be converting sensations into intuitions, receiving divine inspiration, reshuffling the atoms of immediate experience, embodying the ideal in sensuous form, working out the consequences of an initial postulate, or affirming the authenticity of existence. But I am looking for less ambitious theories than these.

II

Philosophic reflection on the available empirical data has given us two widely-held accounts of the creative process. When we consider any artistic work of major proportions, whose creation we know something about, we are often struck by the gap between the final achievement and its humble incept. Clearly, the process between can be said to have moved in a desirable direction. Now in the usual case, although lucky accidents may make an important contribution, this process appears to be at least partly controlled. The problem for the aesthetician is, then: What is the nature of this control?

The earliest people who raised this question—Homer, Hesiod, and Pindar—were inclined to give it a supernatural answer, attributing their own feats to the intervention of the Muses. And the theory of divine inspiration, often in a pantheistic version, remains with us. But if we insist upon a naturalistic theory of artistic creation, we find two main ones. And these are distinguished in a way familiar to other branches of philosophy.

According to what I shall call the Propulsive Theory, the controlling agent is something that exists prior to the creative process, and presides over it throughout. According to the Finalistic Theory, the controlling agent is the final goal toward which the process aims. No doubt the two theories run into each other in the minds of some philosophers, and perhaps we need not strain to keep them wholly distinct. But even if there are not two theories, there are at least two errors—and this is what I am most concerned to note.

The theory of art as expression is probably the most popular form of the Propulsive Theory of the creative process. And I shall take R. G. Collingwood as representative of expressionism at its best.

> When a man is said to express emotion, what is being said about him comes to this. At first, he is conscious of having an emotion, but not conscious of what this emotion is. All he is conscious of is a perturbation or excitement, which he feels going on within him, but of whose nature he is ignorant.[8]

Before the emotion is expressed, the artist is oppressed by it; he works so his mind will become "lightened and eased." His aim is to make his emotion clear to himself—indeed, to discover what the emtion is. Thus Collingwood postulates a single emotion that preserves its identity through-

out the process of creation—if the work is to be genuine—and determines
the main course of that process.

The first difficulty with this theory is that no principle of identity can
be provided for this emotion.

> If artists only find out what their emotions are in the course of finding out
> how to express them, they cannot begin the work of expression by deciding
> what emotion to express.

Well said. But, on the other hand, after the artist has expressed his emotion, and come to experience it clearly, how does he know it is the same
emotion he started with? He cannot compare them, since the other was
unknown to him. How does he know that the emotion he feels now is not
a new and different emotion—an emotion that is perhaps felt as the *effect*
of the finished work, rather than its cause? As far as I can see, Collingwood
has no answer to this. And, moreover, in order to preserve his theory he
has to say some rather surprising things. For example,

> No artist, therefore, so far as he is an artist proper, can set out to write a
> comedy, a tragedy, an elegy, or the like. So far as he is an artist proper, he
> is just as likely to write any one of these as any other.

I am sure that statement would have startled Sophocles or Shakespeare—
not to mention Racine and Molière. According to Collingwood, the
genuine artist says, "I feel an emotion coming on; no telling what it is
until I write something (or paint it, or compose it); how will I know what
I've felt until I see what I've done?" If he insists from the start on writing
a tragedy, he will be forcing his emotion into some channel, and the
result cannot be art.

The whole concept of *clarifying* an emotion is itself very obscure. I have
a suspicion that when Bruckner finished one of his enormous symphonies,
his emotions were no more clear to him than they were at the start. At
least, they are no more clear to me. They are big emotions; anyone can
see that. But clarity is hardly the word for them. On the other hand,
nothing could be more clear than the special quality of the opening of
Mozart's *G Minor Symphony*; but what reason do we have for thinking
that Mozart's composition of this symphony began with some obscure
or indescribable emotion, rather than with the subject of the first four
bars? And what about artists who have spent years on a single work—
are we to say that the very same emotion was there throughout, striving
to clarify itself?

An interesting and well-worked-out version of the Finalistic or goal-
directed theory of art creation has recently been presented by David
Ecker.[9] He describes the creative process as "qualitative problem-solving,"
borrowing the concept from John Dewey. The stages of the process, he
says, consist of a series of problems and solutions: if I use this cool green

here I can get this plane to recede; "this jagged shape contrasts sharply with those open volumes." Now he makes it clear that the problems posed are within the work itself: "Artistic problem solving takes place in the artist's medium." The problem need not be verbally formulated, and various logical terms that might be applied to the process (such as "verification" and "hypothesis") are "grossly misleading." But the process is to be analyzed in terms of the categories of means and end; the choices involved, and the general direction, are controlled by the previsioned goal. (It is plain that Ecker's account would be strongly repudiated by Collingwood; according to Ecker the poet *must* begin by intending to write a tragedy, or comedy, or something—for otherwise he has no problem to solve.) Ecker quotes a very illuminating passage from the sculptor Henry Moore:

> . . . I sometimes begin a drawing with no preconceived problem to solve, with only the desire to use pencil on paper, and make lines, tones and shapes with no conscious aim; but as my mind takes in what is so produced a point arrives where some idea becomes conscious and crystallizes, and then a control and ordering begins to take place.
>
> Or sometimes I start with a set subject; or to solve, in a block of stone of known dimensions, a sculptural problem I've given myself, and then consciously attempt to build an ordered relationship of forms . . .[10]

The first part of this statement is very clear, and restricts one side of Ecker's theory. There may be, says Moore, no "preconceived problem to solve"—the only problem, if there is any, arises after the occurrence of the incept, the first lines of the drawing. The "control and ordering" begins with the elements of the work itself. The second part of the statement can be understood, it seems to me, in a similar way. Sometimes, says Moore, he starts with a subject—say, he is to make a reclining figure. Or a set of outside dimensions, within which to work. But basically this is the same sort of thing; the incept can be some lines randomly drawn on paper, or the subject, or the block of untouched marble, with its own particular size and shape.

The trouble appears when this is called a *problem*. What is the problem? It might be: "How can I make a good drawing using these lines I've already drawn?" Or "How can I make a good sculpture of a reclining figure?" Or "How can I make a good sculpture out of this block of marble?" But these are queer things to call *problems*: they are really *tasks*, the terms of which are voluntarily accepted by the artist. The main question involved in each of them is simply: "What do I do next?" A problem arises out of a conflict of some kind—a goad that the sculptor does not require. And it calls for a specific and determinate solution or set of solutions—which is not what the sculptor achieves.

Elsewhere I have stated my objections to the end-means terminology in art.[11] Actually, when Ecker gives his examples of ends and means, it

is clear that he is not really talking about these at all, but about the relation between what I call regional qualities and their perceptual conditions. The cool green is not a means to the receding plane; it is one of
the localized features of the visual design that help to make the plane
recede. The recession of the plane, to put it another way, is a comparatively large-scale property of the work, which depends (in part) upon
a comparatively small-scale property, the cool green. Now, if we ask
which the artist first intended and has as an "end-in-view," it is tempting
to say, with Ecker, that the artist

> arranges qualitative *means* such as lines, colors, planes, and textures, to
> achieve his qualitative *end*, which we might name "cubist," "impressionist,"
> or "expressionist".

But Ecker has already conceded that the end-in-view may be "some intended order" as well as a "pervasive quality." It may often be the case
that what the artist is consciously after is a certain arrangement of lines,
colors, planes, and textures, and the resulting regional quality is unexpected. It is odd to speak of the color as a "means" when it is chosen
for no ulterior motive.

The error here is a subtle one, but a very crucial one in talking about
art. It consists in jumping from the fact that regional qualities depend
upon their perceptual conditions to the conclusion that the former are
therefore always ends-in-view and the latter means, in the process of
creation. Perhaps no great harm would usually be done, but this way of
speaking leads to an impasse, which is fully exhibited in a sentence
quoted from John Dewey by Ecker:

> The doing or making is artistic when the perceived result is of such a
> nature that *its* qualities *as perceived* have controlled the question of pro-
> duction.[12]

Take the finished painting; note its quality. Now suppose we have photographs of various stages of the work, taken at daily or hourly intervals,
let us say, while the painter was working. None of these, of course, has
the *specific* quality of the finished painting. But Dewey says this quality
was all along controlling the artist's work. Since the quality did not exist
until the painting was finished, it could only have been in the artist's mind.
Does that mean that from the earliest stages of a painting, from the incept
onward, the painter has definitely in mind some regional quality that he
is trying to bring into existence on the canvas? It is conceivable that this
is sometimes the case, but most of the experience of artists goes against it:
it would be remarkable if the exact regional quality of the final painting
were that plain to the painter from the start.

Now, Dewey's statement can be interpreted in a somewhat more plausible way, if we introduce the notion of degrees of intensity for these

regional qualities. The final painting, let us say, is characterized by a firm semi-geometrical solidity and rigidity, with decisive lines and interlocking forms. We look at the first tentative strokes put down by the painter, in the earliest photograph, and we see that somehow, dimly but unmistakably, this final quality is foreshadowed in the early draft—a touch of it is already there, though nothing like the way it is there at the end. So the process of creation lying between these stages could be described, at least in part, as one in which a regional quality hit upon early in the game is gradually intensified with the complication of new lines and colors. So in this sense, it could be that the final quality has been at work throughout—not as a foreseen goal to which the process is heading teleologically, but as a present quality whose immediately perceivable value suggests to the painter that it would be even more valuable if there were, so to speak, more of it.

There is no doubt that something like this does often happen. Sometimes, we can see in the earliest stages of a great work that the quality we value so highly in the finished product has begun to emerge. But this is not always the case, by any means. Sometimes the quality that appears most definitely at the start turns out not to be fruitful; the artist's attempt to intensify it leads to radical formal rearrangements that end by destroying the original quality and substituting a very different one. The melody that was first tried out as a quick rondo theme becomes the subject of a slow movement—almost unrecognizably altered. The poem that started out as a few ironic lines about a current political issue transforms itself, almost against the poet's will, into a moving meditation on the human condition. Nor is such a process—contrary to what Dewey implies—any the less artistic because not the same, but different, qualities have been active in generating the process at different stages.

Vincent Tomas has effectively criticized the finalistic view that artistic creation is "a paradigm of purposive activity."[13] There is a sense of "heading somewhere," though without a given goal in terms of which success or failure can be defined as it can when the torpedo is launched towards a target. Yet, paradoxically, "the artist *can* say that certain directions are not right." And Tomas' solution, sound so far as it goes, is to emphasize the critical ingredient in creation. His theory is that creation is a self-correcting process, in which the artist constantly redirects its aims. Tomas does not show in detail how the artist does this. But I believe that he is right, and I will try to develop and defend this theory.

III

The real nature of the artist's control over the creative process will elude anyone who looks for a single guiding factor, whether a need or an end. It is internal to the process itself. I do not plan to argue for a single creative pattern, but to show how, in the absence of any such general pattern, each individual process that eventuates in a work of art *generates* its own direction and momentum. For the crucial controlling power at every point is the particular stage or condition of the unfinished work itself, the possibilities it presents, and the developments it permits. There are three things to discuss here, and I will say something about each— the incept, the development, and the completion of the work.

The first control over the artistic process is set up by the incept itself. And I want to emphasize, as I have said before, that the incept may be any sort of thing: the first sentence of a story or the last, a simple plot situation, a character, theme, scene, figure of speech, or tone or style. Paul Valéry has told us, instructively:

> My poem *Le Cimetière marin* began in me by a rhythm, that of a French line . . . of ten syllables, divided into four and six. I had as yet no idea with which to fill out this form. Gradually a few hovering words settled in it, little by little determining the subject, and my labor (a very long labor) was before me.[14]

Elsewhere, Valéry adds that his playing around with possibilities of this rhythm led to a certain kind of stanza, then—

> Between the stanzas, contrasts or correspondences would be set up. This last condition soon required the potential poem to be a monologue of "self," in which the simplest and most enduring themes of my affective and intellectual life, as they had imposed themselves upon my adolescence, associated with the sea and the light of a particular spot on the Mediterranean coast, were called up, woven together, opposed . . . All this led to the theme of death and suggested the theme of pure thought.[15]

This is exactly opposite to the usual idea that the poet must begin with his theme, or thesis, and that he characteristically then devises a suitable subject or set of images, and finally settles on the appropriate stanzaic form and meter. Now, I'll have to confess at this point that I am wide open to one kind of skeptical criticism. Considering that this particular poem is one of the most obscure poems in the French language, it might be said, we can draw no general conclusions from Valéry's method of composing it—what can you expect from a poet who begins with rhythms and ends with themes? Still, Valéry's account shows there is no one, privileged, order in which a poem has to get written. And even in the composition of more conventional poems, many different items (including metrical patterns) actually come first. Stephen Spender, for example, tells us in an essay that one of his poems began with a vision of the sea, and that another time, the words "A language of flesh and roses" came into his head as the incept of a possible poem while he was standing in the corridor of a train looking at a landscape of pits and pitheads— though at the time he was writing his essay, the words had not yet grown into an actual poem.[16] From a famous essay by Allen Tate, we gather that two elements of his "Ode to the Confederate Dead" were present from the start—the idea he calls *solipsism* and the idea of the dead—though it took ten years to fuse them together.[17] And according to Muriel Rukeyser, her poem "Orpheus" began with a sudden terrifying image of disintegration that came to her as she walked along a crowded street in New York.[18]

One of the most important questions about the role of the incept in the creative process is this: Does it exercise a pervasive influence throughout? If the Propulsive Theory is correct, one would expect to find the incept dominating the whole process, for whatever appears first would presumably be closely related to the original emotion. On second thought, I am not sure this really follows; it is hard to say what can be predicted from Collingwood's unknown and unknowable emotion. Again, if the Finalist Theory is correct, one would also expect the incept to dominate, for it would presumably embody the original problem or goal which directs the process to the end.

Now, one thing is evident: once an element is chosen, it sets up demands and suggestions as to what may come next, and also places limits upon it. Draw a single line on a piece of paper. If you do not think what you have there is worth much attention, the question is what you can do next to improve upon it. You can balance it, cross or oppose it by other lines, thicken and emphasize it, transform it into a more complex line or shape, etc. Or, of course, you can erase it—but then you are rejecting it as an incept and putting an end to that particular creative process. That every stage of the process powerfully affects the succeeding stage is plain; but our present question is whether the first stage is somehow dominant over all. Artists have spoken rather differently about this. For instance, Picasso once said that "Basically a picture doesn't change, that the first 'vision' remains almost intact, in spite of appearances."[19] But he also said that a picture cannot be thought out ahead of time, and "changes as one's thoughts change." The sketches for *Guernica* do have a notable continuity despite all the changes. The bull and the horse were there in the first sketch, and a woman appeared in one of the later sketches done the same day.

Another example is provided by Beethoven's long series of sketches for the spacious melody that he used for the variations in the slow movement of his string quartet in E flat, *Op. 127*. These have been studied by Victor Zuckerkandl.[20] When they are placed side by side, they illustrate the force of the incept very clearly. The first full bar of the final melody, with its stepwise motion upward from A flat to F, is there almost complete from the very first sketch, though with a slightly different rhythm; and the rest of the story is a struggle, resumed from time to time over a long period, to find an adequate continuation and completion of that incept. Beethoven tries various ways of carrying on the melody, and abandons them; he tries the initial bar in the key of C, in duple tempo, with turns and rhythmic alterations, to see if it can be made to move into the long flowing line that the incept seems to call for. The whole keeps changing its regional character as it grows, yet some of its outstanding final qualities can be described as intensifications of qualities that were there in the first sketch. But this is by no means true of all of Beethoven's work; Allen Forte, a careful student of the piano sonata, *Op. 109,* has remarked that "in many instances one can hardly recognize the final version from the initial sketches."[21]

Indeed, an incept that initiates a successful creative process may become almost lost in it. Of course there must be some continuity from incept to final work, otherwise we could not say that the incept was the start of that particular work. But there is a wide range of deviation from the straight line of development. An ingredient that has one quality as it first appears to the artist may later find a context that alters its quality completely. Dostoyevsky's novel *The Idiot* is an interesting case in point. We have a large collection of manuscript notes and drafts to tell us the agonizing story of Dostoyevsky's working out of that novel. In the very early stages, the Idiot (as he is called from the beginning) is

> described as a powerful, proud, and passionate individual. There is something Byronic about him, and he resembles those criminal, self-willed creations Valkovski and Svidrigailov. He is sensual, performs extravagant actions, and perhaps his most marked trait is egoism.[22]

Could anything be farther from the Idiot of the final novel? For two months, through eight detailed plans for the novel, Dostoyevsky worked toward the deadline for the first installment (published January 1868). As the plans succeed each other, we see certain characters take on the Christlike characteristics of Prince Myshkin as we now have him, and we see the Idiot developing a double nature that prepares the way, in the eighth plan, for his reversal of personality. Even so, the novel was still significantly changing between the first installment and the later ones.

Once the work is under way, with a tentative commitment to some incept, the creative process is kept going by tensions between what has been done and what might have been done. At each stage there must be a perception of deficiencies in what now *exists,* plus the sense of unrealized possibilities of improvement. The motivating force, as Tomas says, is a negative critical judgment. And this same point has been made by Valéry. To understand poetry, he remarks, we must study

> word combinations, not so much through the conformity of the meanings of these groups to an idea or thought that one thinks should be *expressed,* as, on the contrary through their effects once they are formed, from which one chooses.[23]

In other words, as the poet moves from stage to stage, it is not that he is looking to see whether he is saying what he already meant, but that he is looking to see whether he wants to mean what he is saying. Thus, according to Valéry, "Every true poet is necessarily a first rate critic"—not necessarily of others' work, but of his own.[24]

Each time the artist—whether poet, or painter, or composer—takes a step, he adds something to what is already there (A), and makes another and different object (B). If he judges B worse than A, he must go back. If B is better than A, the question is whether it is good enough to stand alone as a work of art. If not, the question is whether B can be transformed into still another and better object C. If this is impossible, if every attempt to improve it only makes it worse, then the whole project is left unfinished, for it is unfinishable.

One of the most puzzling questions about the creative process is how the artist knows when to stop. If the Propulsion Theory is correct, the answer is that he stops when his original impulse has exhausted itself. If the Finalistic Theory is correct, then the artist compares his work at every stage with the intact memory of his original vision of his goal, and when they match the work is done. But without these theories, it becomes more difficult to explain what it means to come to an end of a creative process.[25]

There are really two questions here: how the artist knows when *he* is finished, and how he knows when the *work* is finished. The first question is no doubt the easier. The artist comes to a point when he can no longer think of any way to improve his work. This becomes more and more difficult as the work progresses. In the early stages, lines and colors, stanzas and melodic fragments, can be added quite freely to see whether they can be assimilated. But in the later stages, as the work becomes more complex, the effect of every addition or alteration is more serious; a wrong line or color, a wrong word or melodic figure, can throw the whole thing badly off. Of course, the artist can never be certain he has done all he can. Happy is the painter, who can say, with Matisse,

> Then a moment comes when every part has found its definite relationship and from then on it would be impossible for me to add a stroke to my picture without having to paint it all over again.[26]

Many a painter has been notorious for a never-say-die determination to hang on to his paintings in the hope that he will think of a way of bettering them—unless extreme poverty or a wily dealer induces him to part with them. (Valéry, by the way, says he wouldn't have published *Le Cimetière marin* when he did, had it not been snatched from him. "Nothing is more decisive than the mind of an editor of a review," he remarks—though perhaps he could have put up more of a fight.)[27]

The artist generally knows, then, pretty well whether *he* is finished—

but that is not the same as saying that the *work* is finished. For when the artist has done all he can, the question remains whether the work has enough to it, whether it is worthy of standing by itself, as an object of aesthetic enjoyment. If he judges so, the artist says it is done. If he judges not, the artist says it is unfinished. And of course the threshold of contentment varies enormously from artist to artist.

These points are illustrated by the famous puzzle of Schubert's unfinished symphony. Unlike most great unfinished works, it was not cut short by death (Schubert had six more years to live), but simply abandoned by the composer after he had completed two magnificent movements. Hans Gál has proposed an interesting solution.[28] Schubert began a scherzo in B minor, which would have been the third movement. In the manuscript, the parts are at first quite fully indicated, then they drop out, as the composer loses interest, and the movement trails off in the trio. The trouble is that the opening subject is one of startling emptiness and dullness—and yet it is a compulsive theme, hard to get away from once it is started, especially if the scherzo must be in the conventional key. "Those obstrusive four bars," as Gál calls them, get a grip on the composer; he cannot shake them off, or, apparently, find a way of starting anew so long as every time he picks up the manuscript they stare him in the face. If we agree with Gál's hypothesis, the scherzo is a formidable example of a composition that cannot be well finished—even by a master. It must have required a powerful force indeed to make a composer leave off a symphony so excellently begun.[29]

In one respect, the foregoing account diverges from a remark by Rudolf Arnheim in his study of Picasso's *Guernica*. Arnheim speaks of the creative process as being "goal-directed throughout"[30]—a view I challenged earlier. And summing up the whole process, he says,

> A germinal idea, precise in its general tenor but unsettled in its aspects, acquired its final character by being tested against a variety of possible visual realizations. When at the end, the artist was willing to rest his case on what his eyes and hands had arrived at, he had become able to see what he meant.[31]

I would not put such stress upon the words, if these two sentences had not been so exact and eloquent up to the final clause. But the words "become able to see what he meant" seem to imply that what Picasso ended with was an expression, an explication, an embodiment, a realization, or whatever, of what was already in his mind at the start. Better, I think, to say that he had become able to mean something much better than he was able to mean a few months before, and that what he now was able to mean— that is, to make—was enough.

To draw together these remarks and examples, perhaps we can decide how far to generalize. Though there are no universal *stages* of the creative process, there are two clearly marked *phases,* which constantly alternate throughout. They involve an interplay between conscious and preconscious activities. There is the *inventive* phase, traditionally called *inspiration,* in which new ideas are formed in the preconscious and appear in consciousness. And there is the *selective* phase, which is nothing more than criticism, in which the conscious chooses or rejects the new idea after perceiving its relationships to what has already tentatively been adopted.

The problem of what goes on in the preconscious is apparently still unsolved. We would like to know how it is that a composer, having sung two bars to himself, suddenly thinks of a way to continue it—or that a painter, having outlined a figure, thinks of certain colors that might be added—or that a poet may look at a line he has just written and think of possible substitute words. To take a few examples from R. P. Blackmur,[32] suppose the poet has written "breathless tiptoeing," and it occurs to him that "flowering tiptoeing" might be better; or suppose he has written "chance deepening to choice" and substitutes "chance flowering to choice." Whether the new words are better than the old is the question to be decided by his conscious mind; but why one set of words rather than another comes to consciousness is the more mysterious question.

The psychological dispute seems to be formulable this way: to what extent are the preconscious processes associative; to what extent do they involve closure or strengthening of gestalts?[33] As far as I can make out both of these processes seem necessary to account for what the preconscious presents to the conscious. If, for example, "flowering" replaces "deepening" because of some meaningful connection of this figure with other images earlier in the poem, then we can say that the unconscious has found some degree of closure. On the other hand, the substitution may have only a very remote relationship to other words already set down, but it may serve to break down an existing gestalt, to introduce a more unstable cluster of meanings, which may lead to a more inclusive synthesis later. In this case, the word *flowering* would be described as due to free— or at least freer—association. It seems evident, in any case, that unless the preconscious can produce both kinds of ideas—those that close a gestalt and those that break one—poems could not get composed, nor could paintings or musical works.

IV

It is no doubt high time to face up to the question that is bound to arise after all these reflections and speculations about the creative process: what is the point of them? Or, in other words: what difference does it make to our relationship with the arts that we understand the creative process in one way or another? And here my answer is brief and unequivocal. It makes no difference at all. I think it is interesting in itself to know, if we can, how the artist's mind works, but I do not see that this has any bearing upon the value of what he produces. For that value is independent of the manner of production, even of whether the work was produced by an animal or by a computer or by a volcano or by a falling slop-bucket.[34]

This statement would be vigorously repudiated by some who have studied the creative process: they claim that their studies throw light on the "meaning" and "beauty" of poems, to use the words of Donald Stauffer, writing on "Genesis, or the Poet as Maker."[35] If we knew, says Stauffer, the genesis of a poem by Housman, it would "enable us to interpret this particular work with more precision." But his method puts the enterprise in none too favorable a light, it seems to me. Digging through the early stages of the composition of Marianne Moore's poem, "The Four Songs," he finds a typescript in which the poem is entitled "Poet to Lover (Admitting Limitations)." Moreover, he turns up other titles that the poet considered and rejected: "Poet to Plain-Reader," "Poet to Ordinary Man," and, oddly, "Asphodel." (This poem has as many titles as the White Knight's song "A-sitting on a Gate.") All these titles, says Mr. Stauffer, "should prove of value in interpreting the complete poem,"[36] and he proceeds to put them to use. But think of the implications. The poet discards the titles, and the genetic interpreter plucks them out of the wastebasket and uses them as though they had not been discarded. This is a pretty high-handed way to treat Marianne Moore. The logic of the situation is clear. Either the title of a poem makes a difference to the way it is read, or it does not. If not, then knowing the discarded titles has no effect on our interpretation. If so, then each title makes a slightly different poem, and Mr. Stauffer is simply refusing to read the poem that Miss Moore wanted us to read. Granted that her choice does not have to be final; some of the titles she threw away could conceivably be better than the one she kept. (After all, remember the time she was commissioned to suggest names for a brand-new car that the Ford Motor Company was planning to bring out. She came up with some lovely ones, but in the end they called it the Edsel.) But if you do not accept her title, then at least do not pretend that you are interpreting her final poem.

The informed observer will, of course, detect in these genetic maneuvers a particularly persuasive form of that vulgar error which William Wimsatt, Jr. and I stigmatized some years ago as the Intentional Fallacy. I do not know whether it is in good taste for me to rake over these old coals, but whenever a fallacy gets to be so old-fashioned and so familiar as this one, it is always heartening to find new instances of it, so that you know you are not beating a dead horse—even if he is not exactly the picture of health. What we attacked under a single name (intentionalism) were in fact two closely related forms of unsound argument: that which attributes a certain meaning to a work on the ground that the artist intended the work to have that meaning, and that which appraises the work at a certain value on the ground that it does or does not fulfill the artist's intention. If we took to interpreting poems in terms of what they were like before they were finished, we would be turning the whole creative process upside down, by refusing to consider the final product on its own terms. Let this method become popular, and you can expect poets, painters, and musicians to keep their wastebaskets emptied, by burning their early sketches just as soon as possible.

Is this our final conclusion, then—that questions about creativity are irrelevant to questions about actual works of art? Somehow it does not seem enough. From the beginning of thought about art, though in many different forms, the creativity of art has been noted and pondered. Associationists, intuitionists, romantics, and idealists have offered explanations. In the making of such works, something very special seems to be happening; something fresh is added to the world; something like a miracle occurs. All this is true. There is such a thing as creativity in art, and it is a very important thing. What I want to say is that the true locus of creativity is not the genetic process prior to the work but the work itself as it lives in the experience of the beholder. Let me explain—all too briefly and puzzlingly, no doubt—what I mean.

To begin with, what is a melody? It is, as we all know, a gestalt, something distinct from the notes that make it up, yet dependent upon them for its existence. And it has its own quality, which cannot be a quality of any particular note or little set of notes. Recall that melody from Beethoven's *E Flat Quartet*—grave, serene, soaring, affirmative, yet in a way resigned. Now when we hear a melody, however simple, we hear two levels of things at once: the individual notes and the regionally qualified melody that emerges from them. We hear the melody being born out of the elements that sustain it; or we hear the elements, the tones and intervals, coming together in an order that calls into existence an entity distinct from them, and superior to them. In the experience of a melody, creation occurs before our very ears. And the more intense the created qualities, the more complex the sets of cooperating elements, the tighter their mutual relations, the more fully we can participate in that basic aesthetic experience.

I need not argue in detail that the same holds for works of fine art. The essential feature of such a work—I am tempted to say, but recognizing that I am likely to sound dogmatic—the essential feature is not merely that certain visual elements (lines, shapes, colors) are assembled together, but that as we concentrate on their natures and relations, we become aware, suddenly or gradually, of what they add up to as a whole. For what they add up to is not an addition at all, but the projection of a new pattern, a new quality of grace or power.

When we consider a poem in this perspective, we see again that the important creativity is in the operation of the work itself. The sound-qualities such as meter and rhyme patterns, are one sort of emergent; more importantly, the interactions and interinanimations of words, in figurative or unusual language, create hitherto unmeant meanings; and more importantly, the objects and events of the poem mysteriously are made to accumulate symbolic reverberations, by which they seem to have a significance far beyond themselves. And this takes place in the act of reading; the excitement of seeing it happen is precisely the peculiar excitement of reading poetry.

The British literary critic, L. C. Knights, has made some comments that seem to me very similar to what I want to say, in a special issue of *The Times Literary Supplement*, on "The Critical Moment."[37] His example is from Wordsworth's famous sonnet,

> Dull would he be of soul, who could pass by
> A sight so touching in its majesty.

That is a strange combination of ideas—"touching" and "majesty." Knights says this:

> The peculiar pleasure of that last line—though the pleasure is independent of conscious recognition of the source—comes from the movement of mind by which we bring together in one apprehension 'touching' and 'majesty': feelings and attitudes springing from our experience of what is young and vulnerable, that we should like to protect, fuse with our sense of things towards which we feel awe, in respect of which it is we who are young, inexperienced or powerless.

The "movement of mind" of which he speaks, in bringing these two opposed feelings into a fusion, through the words of the poem, is an act of creation, for out of that fusion comes a new, complex, vital feeling that has elements of both and yet is reducible to neither. So, says Knights, the creative use of words "energizes" the mind—"new powers of vision and apprehension come into being."

It may seem that this way of looking at artistic creativity demeans the artist by making not him, but the work itself, the creative thing. But I do not think so. I do not forget that man is the maker—of nearly all the great works we have, or are likely to have. But the finest qualities of a work of art cannot be imposed on it directly and by fiat; the artist can, after all, only manipulate the elements of the medium so that *they* will make the quality emerge. He can only create a solemn melody by finding a sequence of notes that will have that quality. The powers he works with are, in the end, not his own but those of nature. And the miracle he makes is a miracle that celebrates the creative potentialities inherent in nature itself. But when in this way the artist makes plain to us over and over the marvellous richness of nature's potentialities, he also presents us with a model of man's hope for control over nature, and over himself. Artistic creation is nothing more than the production of a self-creative object. It is our intelligent use of what we are given to work with, both in the laws of the universe and in the psychological propensities of man, that we show our mastery, and our worthiness to inhabit the earth. In this broad sense, we are all elected, or perhaps condemned, to be artists. And what keeps us going in the roughest times is the reminder that not all the forms and qualities and meanings that are to emerge in the fullness of time have already appeared under the sun—that we do not know the limits of what the universe can provide or of what can be accomplished with its materials.

Notes

1. The former by Paul Ziff and Morris Weitz, whose views I have discussed in "Art and the Definitions of the Arts," *JAAC*, XX (1961), 175-87; the latter by George Dickie, in "Is Psychology Relevant to Aesthetics?" *Philosophical Review*, LXXI (1962), 285-302, "The Myth of the Aesthetic Attitude," *American Philosophical Quarterly* I (January, 1964), 56-65, and "Beardsley's Phantom Aesthetic Experience, *Journal of Philosophy*, LXII (1965), 129-36.

2. Brewster Ghiselin, ed., *The Creative Process: A Symposium* (U. of California, 1952), p. 51.

3. Henry James, *The Art of the Novel*, ed. R. P. Blackmur (New York, 1934), pp. 119-24.

4. *Notebooks*, ed. F. O. Matthiessen and Kenneth Murdock (New York, 1947), pp. 136-137. For further stages in the development of this novel (tentatively entitled *The House Beautiful*) see the references on p. 138. See also S. P. Rosenbaum, "Henry James and Creativity: 'The Logic of the Particular Case,'" *Criticism* VIII (Winter 1966), 44-52.

5. Douglas Morgan, "Creativity Today," *JAAC*, XII (1953), 1-24; and Stuart E. Golann, "Psychological Study of Creativity," *Psychological Bulletin*, LX (1963), 548-565.

6. *Poets at Work* (New York, 1948), by various authors, and *Picasso's Guernica: the Genesis of a Painting* (U. of California, 1962).

7. *Creative Thought in Poets, Archives of Psychology*, No. 178 (1935); "Creative Thought in Artists," *J. of Psychology*, IV (1937), 37-73.

8. R. G. Collingwood, *The Principles of Art* (Oxford, 1938), p. 109. See also Alan Donagan, *The Later Philosophy of R. G. Collingwood* (Oxford, 1962), ch. 5, §3.

9. "The Artistic Process as Qualitative Problem Solving," *JAAC*, XXI (1963), 283-.

10. Ghiselin, *op. cit.*, p. 77.

11. *Aesthetics: Problems in the Philosophy of Criticism* (New York, 1958), pp. 78-80.

12. *Art as Experience* (New York, 1934), p. 48.

13. "Creativity in Art," *Philosophical Review*, LXVII (1958), 1-155; "A Note on Creation in Art," *Journal of Philosophy*, LIX (1962), 464-69. The former is reprinted in Tomas, ed., *Creativity in the Arts* (Englewood Cliffs, N.J., 1964).

14. "Poetry and Abstract Thought," *The Art of Poetry*, trans. Denise Folliot (New York, 1961), p. 80.

15. "Concerning *'Le Cimetière marin,'* " *ibid.,* p. 148.

16. "The Making of a Poem," *Partisan Review,* XIII (1946), 294-308 (also in Tomas, *op. cit.*).

17. "Narcissus as Narcissus," *On the Limits of Poetry* (New York, 1948).

18. Frank Barron, *Creativity and Psychological Health* (Princeton, 1963), p. 229n. For examples of fiction incepts see Malcolm Cowley, ed., *Writers at Work* (New York, 1959), esp. pp. 7-8.

19. Arnheim, *op. cit.,* p. 30.

20. I am referring to a lecture given in the spring of 1963 at Swarthmore College.

21. *The Compositional Matrix* (Baldwin, N.Y., Music Teachers National Association Monographs, 1961), p. 4 Cf. Ernst Krenek's analysis of the sketches for the false entry of the subject in the *Eroica:* "The Problem of Creative Thinking in Music," in *The Nature of Creative Thinking,* a symposium published for the Industrial Research Institute, Inc. (New York U., 1952), pp. 54-57.

22. Ernest J. Simmons, *Dostoyevsky* (Oxford U., 1950), p. 202. See his whole book for very illuminating accounts of Dostoyevsky's creative processes.

23. "A Poet's Notebook," *op. cit.,* p. 178. Compare John Dryden's dedication of *The Rival Ladies* (in Ghiselin, *op. cit.,* p. 77): "When the fancy was yet in its first work, moving the sleeping images of things toward the light, there to be distinguished, and then either chosen or rejected by the judgment." The drafts of Yeats's "Sailing to Byzantium," written on looseleaf pages over several years, show how fertile he was in alternative possibilities for lines we now know so well, and that his problem was to select and combine; see Curtis Bradford, "Yeat's Byzantium Poems: A Study of Their Development," *PMLA,* LXXV (1960), 110-125 (I am indebted to Professor Robert Daniel, of Kenyon College, for this example). Cf. Martin K. Nurmi, "Blake's Revisions of *The Tyger,*" *PMLA,* LXXI (1956); 669-685.

24. "Poetry and Abstract Thought," *ibid.,* p. 76. This is echoed by Richard Wilbur in *The Nature of Creative Thinking,* p. 59, and by Ben Shahn, in *The Shape of Content* (see selection in Tomas, *op. cit.,* p. 20).

25. I. A. Richards, "How Does a Poem Know When It Is Finished?" in Daniel Lerner, ed., *Parts and Wholes* (New York, 1963).

26. "Notes of a Painter," in Eliseo Vivas and Murray Krieger, eds., *The Problems of Aesthetics* (New York, 1953), p. 259.

27. *Op. cit.,* p. 144.

28. "The Riddle of Schubert's Unfinished Symphony," *The Music Review,* II (1941), 63-67.

29. It is harder to understand what distractions led Mozart to abandon the more than 100 unfinished compositions (not counting the *Requiem*) that his widow preserved for us. See Erich Hertzmann, "Mosart's Creative Process," *Musical Quarterly,* XLIII (1957), 187-200.

30. *Op. cit.,* p. 134.

31. *Op. cit.,* p. 135.

32. *Poets at Work,* p. 48.

33. This is the point at issue, for example, between Lawrence S. Kubie, *Neurotic Distortion of the Creative Process* (U. of Kansas, 1948), esp. pp. 53-61, and Arnheim, *Picasso's Guernica,* p. 70.

34. For a decisive argument along this line, see John Hospers, "The Concept of Artistic Expression," *Proceedings of the Aristotelian Society,* LV (1955), 313-344.

35. In *Poets at Work,* p. 43.

36. *Ibid.,* p. 63.

37. July 26, 1963, p. 569.

W. E. KENNICK

Creative Acts

> There is a kind of general disease of thinking which
> always looks for (and finds) what would be called a
> mental state from which all our acts spring as from
> a reservoir.
>
> (Wittgenstein, The Brown Book)

IN JAMES JOYCE'S *Portrait of the Artist as a Young Man,* Stephen
Dedalus tells his friend Lynch that he has a book at home in which he
writes down questions and that in finding answers to them he has found
"the theory of the esthetic," which he is trying to explain to Lynch.
Among these is the question: "If a man hacking in fury at a block of
wood make there an image of a cow, is that image a work of art? If not,
why not?" ("That's a lovely one—said Lynch, laughing again.—That has
the true scholastic stink.") The scholastic stink notwithstanding, I propose to begin my inquiry into some features of the concept of creativity
in art with Stephen's question.

Just what is the puzzle expressed by this question? As I see it, there
are two points from which doubt might stem. The first concerns the
image: Can an image of a cow be a work of art? This question can easily
be answered in the affirmative: there is no reason why an image of a cow
cannot be a work of art. That something is an image of a cow does not
entail that it is a work of art, of course, but that something is a work
of art also does not entail that it is not an image of a cow. The second
point from which doubt might arise has to do not with the image but
with the manner of its production, with the man's making it by or as a
result of hacking in fury at a block of wood. To obviate the first difficulty
and dramatize the second let us change Stephen's question to read: If a
man—say, Michelangelo—hacking in fury at a block of marble make
there an image of four persons—say, the *Pietà* now in Santa Maria del
Fiore, Florence—is that image a work of art?[1] Now what is the problem?

The problem, I take it, has to do with some putative, or at least

From *Perspectives in Education, Religion, and the Arts,* edited by Howard E.
Kiefer and Milton Munitz, pp. 238-261. Copyright © 1970 State University of
New York Press. Reprinted by permission. Revised by the author.

problematic, incompatibility between hacking in fury at a block of marble and making a work of art, or, to put it the other way around, between an object's being a work of art and its being produced in the way described. But is there any such incompatibility?

The interest of aestheticians in the problem of creativity, by which I mean in part the problem of *how* works of art are produced, what might be called their mode of genesis, has hardly any parallels in other areas of philosophy. But the literature of aesthetics is replete with speculations about the nature of the creative process, as it is usually called, about what "goes on" when an artist carves a statue, writes a poem, or paints a picture. And these speculations are most often of a psychological (or apparently psychological) nature. But they appear to presuppose that there is a conceptual connection (like the connection between being a mother and having given birth to at least one child), rather than just a factual or empirical connection (like the connection between being a mother and being over the age of twelve), between being a work of art and being the result of a specifiable creative process. And yet is there such a connection? To put the matter schematically, Does a proposition of the form "*x* is a work of art"—or "*x* is a creative work of art"—entail a proposition, perhaps one referring to the psychology of the artist, about *x*'s mode of genesis?

Some aestheticians have claimed that to identify something as a work of (fine) art logically commits one to the view that it was produced in a certain way. Jerome Stolnitz is one of them. Although he warns us against committing the genetic fallacy ("the genesis of *x* is one thing, *x* itself is something else. Once *x* has been brought into being, it has, so to speak, a life of its own"),[2] nevertheless he holds—and not inconsistently—that "art-objects of any sort are set off from non-artistic objects such as rocks, trees, and yawns because of the way in which they are created. Hence, any definition of 'art' as an *object* must make reference to its origins."[3]

On the other side of the fence from Stolnitz, however, we find philosophers who hold that art objects are not set off from objects of nonart by their mode of genesis. Morris Weitz, for example, says, "Mostly, when we describe something as a work of art we do so under the conditions of there being some sort of artifact, made by human skill, ingenuity, and imagination . . .". But " 'X is a work of art and . . . was made by no one,' or . . . 'was made when he spilled the paint on the canvas,' . . . are sensible and capable of being true in certain circumstances." That something must in principle be a product of human creation is neither a necessary nor a sufficient condition of its being a work of art. "Consider: 'This piece of driftwood is a lovely piece of sculpture' "[4]—an utterance which Weitz takes as quite unproblematic.

If wind and water acting on a piece of stone make there an image of a man, is that image a work of art? As I understand it, Stolnitz would say, No; it is not a work of art, and if anybody took it for a work of art he would be making a mistake; whereas Weitz would say that at least it *could* be a work of art, that in identifying or describing it as a work of art one *need* not be making a mistake. Here we have an interesting opposition. How is it to be resolved?

If the question is simply which of these views is more closely consonant with our actual concept of art, my own sense of the matter is that Stolnitz is nearer to the truth than is Weitz. In the words of Ruby Meager,

> If we know for a fact that an object was the result of erosion and not of Barbara Hepworth, or of a chimpanzee and not Joan Miro, this would disqualify it altogether from the work-of-art stakes . . .[5]

Whatever its aesthetic merits may be, the Great Stone Face, unlike the sculptures on Mt. Rushmore, simply is not a work of art—not even a bad work of art. It is simply what Richard Wollheim nicely calls "a piece of uncontrived nature." "This piece of driftwood is a lovely piece of sculpture," said with a straight face and in a situation in which we are speaking about what is simply a piece of driftwood—and not, say, about a piece of driftwood that has been incorporated into a piece of sculpture or about a piece of sculpture that represents a piece of drift-wood—is as paradoxical, as *literally* senseless as "This dog [referring to a real live dog] is a lovely piece of sculpture."

Doubtless the concept of art is what Stuart Hampshire calls an "essentially disputed" concept or what Weitz calls an "open" concept,[6] and borderline cases are not difficult to conceive. But, however unclearly it may be marked, there is a border. The concept of art, like other descriptive concepts, is not *wide* open. The appeal to "family resemblances" among objects to justify our classification of otherwise disparate and heterogeneous things under the same genus or our extension of the concept to cover novel and unanticipated cases, is a game that, as things stand now—and have stood for some time—cannot even begin until the area of play has been circumscribed so as to include only products of human—or sufficiently humanlike—fabrication.[7] Surely an ear not dulled to all nuances of linguistic usage still recognizes a live metaphor in such phrases as "the art of chimpanzees." What we *would* say were chimpanzees to commence turning out objects on an aesthetic par with the sculptures of Donatello or the paintings of Titian has no bearing on the present point. J. L. Austin has remarked somewhere that we can easily imagine situations in which we would not know *what* to say, but this does not mean that we do not know what to say as things stand now. One might guess, or even predict, that were chimpanzees (or the processes of erosion, etc.) to begin behaving in the way indicated we would call their "works" works of art, but that would be to guess at, or predict, a linguistic or conceptual *innovation*.

The invention of the computer, of course, has brought us closer to the borderline of the concept of art, as it has brought us closer to the borderline of other concepts, the most important of which is the concept of thought. Can computers write poems or compose symphonies? The question is essentially a conceptual one, concerned not with what words *will* mean, or *can* mean, but with what they now *do* mean; and my own sense of the present situation is reflected in Douglas Morgan's remark that it is "possible that a piece of electronically composed music could fool me into thinking that a musical man, and not a musical machine, had done the work . . . [But] if I were to hear some machine-made music which I esteemed highly, I would tend to attribute its 'creativity' to the man who coded the machine, rather than to the machine itself."[8]

The point I have been trying to make is that a logically *necessary* condition of something's being a work of art is that it has been created by a person.[9] The question that concerns me has to do with the meaning of the word "created" in this formula: Does the word "created," as Stolnitz appears to hold, designate some specific psychological process or mental act or happening such that if that process or act or happening does not occur the object in question cannot be a work of art?

To begin with, we must distinguish between creative acts and creative processes. Most writers on creativity speak of "the creative process," usually meaning by that what happens or "goes on" in the artist's mind when he creates a work of art. But processes are not acts, although such processes as that of the refining of aluminum from bauxite may involve, or even consist of, a series of acts. Words naming or describing processes (e.g., "growth," "gestation," "digestion," "fermentation") tell us what happens in or to something rather than what is being, or has been, done.[10] But "to create," used with a personal subject and taking as direct object a name, description, or demonstrative that designates a work of art, is generically what Anthony Kenny calls "a verb of action," i.e., "a verb which may occur as the main verb in answer to a question of the form 'What did A do?' "[11] Specifically, it is what Kenny calls a "performance-verb" (one that signifies a performance), as opposed to a "static-verb" (one that signifies a state) or an "activity-verb" (one that signifies an activity). Two of the distinctive features of performance-verbs are that (1) they have continuous tenses—which separates them from static-verbs, and (2) where "Ø" stands for a performance-verb "A is Øing" implies that "A has not Ød"—which separates them from activity-verbs, which are such that "As is Øing" implies "A has Ød."[12]

"To create," however, is only the most general performance-verb that can be used in this connection with works of art—and, as I shall try to show below, it or some similar performance-verb is required; but its direct use is not very frequent. More often we use such performance-verbs as "write a poem," "paint a picture," "carve a statue," "design a building," and so on. Writing poems, painting pictures, composing music, and the like, are, of course, not inherently artistic acts or performances, by which I mean that "A wrote (painted) x" does not entail "x is a work of art," or, variously, "A wrote a poem (painted a picture)" does not entail "A created a work of art." (Think of the vast mass of so-called "commercial art" that appears in television, newspaper, magazine, and billboard advertisements. Songs, drawings, paintings, dramatic sketches, yes; but works of (fine) art, no.) But these acts or performances *are* such that in doing one or more of them one *may* be creating a work of art; and I propose to call them *creative acts* if they are such that in performing (having performed) one or more of them one is creating (has created) a work of art.[13]

If someone is painting, it may not be clear that he is performing a creative act, until he has finished (or ceased), i.e., until as a result of his painting he has brought a work of art (even an "unfinished" work of art, like Schubert's famous *Unfinished Symphony* or Lucretius's *De Rerum Natura* or perhaps Michelangelo's Florence *Pietà*) into existence. But then again it might be clear from the context of his performance, or he might truly describe his act in such a way, that we could say (truly) that the intended object of his act is a work of art and that, hence, his act is a creative act.[14] It is not requisite, for an act to be a creative act, that a work of art be the actual result of it, i.e., that a work of art be brought into existence by it: an artist might destroy his work before it is, or could be, clear from the *work* that it is a work of art. But neither is it requisite for an act to be a creative act that the intended object of the act be a work of art. Something can be a work of art and also an idol, and it can be an idol and not be a work of art. But, from the fact that the intended object of a man's carving is an idol, together with the fact that the idol he is carving is (or will be) also a work of art, it does not follow that the intended object of his act is a work of art. In this way, works of art can be created unintentionally or incidentally. It is at least doubtful that the sculptors of those great Egyptian statues of gods intended to produce works of art as well as idols; but that they did intend to produce idols is hardly a matter of doubt, and that they did produce works of art is certain.[15]

To return to Stephen Dedalus's question, or our emended version of it, If a man hacking in fury at a block of marble make there a pietà, is that image a work of art? That the man has made (created) an image of a certain description, is granted *ex hypothesi*; and that something may be an image and also a work of art is certain. The puzzle, therefore, would seem to be concerned with whether one can make (create), in the way described, what is at least, other things being equal, a possible work of art. Well, suppose that the purpose or objective of the man's hacking—which is an activity, by the way, and not a performance—is not to create a work of art, or even to produce an image, but is rather to work off a burden of anger or rage, can he not also be creating a work of art? As far as I can see, he can. He can be purposively or intentionally doing one thing (working off his rage) and incidentally doing another (creating a work of art).[16] And the converse is also true: he can be purposively or intentionally creating a work of art and incidentally working off his rage or vicariously satisfying some repressed wish (Freud).

Parenthetically, another interpretation is possible of the sentence "Hacking in fury at a block of marble, he made there an image." The hacking in fury . . ." clause may be seen as having merely adverbial force, as describing the *manner* of the making. Read in this way "hacking in fury at a block of marble" would contrast with something like "chipping calmly away at a block of marble." This reading raises no difficulties at all.

"There is not necessarily one, and only one, correct description of a given act," says Eric D'Arcy.[17] To put the point another way, one can be doing two or more things—even doing them purposively or intentionally—at the same time; not in the way that I may deliver a lecture, write on the blackboard, and jingle my keys at the same time, but in the way that I may write my name, sign a check, pay a bill, and discharge a financial obligation at the same time. It was his realization of this phenomenon as it operates in the area of speech that led J. L. Austin to draw his now well-known distinction between locutionary, illocutionary, and perlocutionary acts; and perhaps a parallel set of distinctions will be of some use in aesthetics. To perform a locutionary act is to say something, in the "full normal sense" of "say something," and such an act is normally what is reported when we quote directly what someone said. The performance of a locutionary act is thus the performance of an act *of* saying something. To perform a locutionary act, however, is usually also to perform an illocutionary act, i.e., to do something *in* saying something (e.g., to ask a question, issue an order, announce a verdict, make an appointment, etc.); and one may use the same locution (perform the same locutionary act) in performing different illocutionary acts. But in performing a locutionary act, and at the same time performing some illocutionary act, one may also be performing an act of yet another kind: "Saying something will often, or even normally, produce certain consequential effects upon the feelings, thoughts, or actions of the audience, of the speaker, or of other persons: and it may be done with the design, intention or purpose of producing them." To do this is to perform a perlocutionary act, i.e., to do something *by* saying something; and by performing the same illocutionary act one may perform different perlocutionary acts.[18]

Now there is at least a partial analogy between, on the one hand, painting pictures, composing music, or carving statues and, on the other hand, speaking; indeed, so-called "semiotic" theories of the nature of art would have it that there is at least a partial identity. Painting a picture, to put it loosely, resembles uttering a sentence, performing a locutionary act. But *in* painting a picture one may be creating a work of art, and thereby doing something analogous to performing an illocutionary act. And just as to perform the same locutionary act may be to perform different illocutionary acts, so also in painting a picture one may

be doing something as well as or in addition to creating a work of art:
e.g., making a likeness of someone (Valasquez's portrait of Pope Innocent X), celebrating or commenting on an event (Goya's *The Third of
May, 1808*), or illustrating a religious text (*Christ Washing the Feet of
Peter* from the Gospel Book of Otto III). I say "doing something as well
as or in addition to creating a work of art" for the reason that one may
create a work of art without doing any of the things mentioned—or anything else of the same kind—and he may do any of the things mentioned
without creating a work of art; so that where any of the things mentioned
is being done, in painting a picture a man is doing *two* things—creating
a work of art and illustrating a text, or whatever.[19] In writing my name
I may be signing a check *and* paying a bill *and* overdrawing my account.
Doing the one is not the same as doing the others, though all may be
done at the same time, i.e., *in* doing one and the same thing, namely,
writing my name; and it is possible that I am consciously or purposively
doing one of them while being unaware that I am also doing the others.
Further, painting a picture or writing a sonnet "will often, or even
normally, produce certain consequential effects upon the feelings,
thoughts, or actions" of the painter or writer or of others; "and it may be
done with the design, intention or purpose of producing them." Hence,
by painting a picture or writing verse one may be doing something
analogous to performing a perlocutionary act: vicariously satisfying some
unfulfilled repressed wish of his own, calling our attention to certain
evils of the social system, reminding us of our mortality, amusing us,
instructing us, shocking us, or, as Plato complained of Homer and the
tragedians in *Republic* II and X, leading us astray theologically and
corrupting us morally.

I have characterized creative acts as acts or performances that are such
that *in* doing (having done) one or more of them one is creating (has
created) a work of art. This means that creating a work of art is an act
analogous to an illocutionary, not a perlocutionary, act.[20] There are
theories of art—for example, Tolstoy's—that "define" art by reference to
the performance of a perlocutionary-like act.[21] As interesting and important as such theories may be, they cannot be taken as adequate definitions of art: Given any perlocutionary-like act, *a*, it is in principle possible for someone to create a work of art without doing *a*, which is to
say that the connection between creating a work of art and producing
effects of some kind is not necessary or conceptual, but contingent. But
the connection between creating a work of art and performing some
locutionary-like act is necessary or conceptual, not contingent, in that if
a person created a work of art he must have painted, or drawn, or composed, or written, or . . . . I know of no way of circumscribing or de-
limiting this list of potentially creative acts, i.e., acts that are such that
in doing one or more of them a person may be creating a work of art.
The number of things one can do, the number of locutionary-like acts
one can perform—fastening together the detached seat and handlebar

of a bicycle (Picasso's *Head of a Bull*), pasting bits of paper together, pro-
gramming a computer, arranging stones, and what not—that may result
in a work of art is indefinitely large; all we can say with certainty is that
a work of art must be the result of *some* act(s) or performance(s).

Nor can we *identify* creative acts with some one independently specifiable illocutionary-like act. R. G. Collingwood, as I understand him, uses
the notion of expressing an emotion as a performance-concept[22] and as
one applicable to illocutionary-like acts: in painting a picture or carving
a statue a man need not be creating a work of art, for he may be working
magic or attempting to amuse someone, but he is creating a work of art
if and only if in painting a picture or carving a statue he is expressing an
emotion. To express an emotion and to create a work of art are, thus, to
do the same thing. Yet the fact remains that the notions of expressing an
emotion and creating a work of art are not *logically* related in the way
Collingwood says they are, for no paradox or logical incoherence results
from asserting that a man has created a work of art and denying that he
has expressed an emotion (in Collingwood's sense). Hence, even if it were
true that whenever one creates a work of art he expresses an emotion, and
conversely, it would not follow that creating a work of art and expressing
an emotion are one and the same act. The connection between them,
again, would be contingent and not necessary. And this argument, as
far as I can see, applies *mutatis mutandis* to any other independently
identifiable illocutionary-like act (e.g., "imitating" or representing some
object or action, presentationally symbolizing forms of feeling, or portraying the "contradictions" of social life of a given historical epoch—
assuming that we know what it would be to do any of these things).

To return briefly to "the creative process": the same simple argument
that I have used against attempts to define art in terms of the performance
of some perlocutionary-like act as well as against efforts to identify "the"
creative act with some independently specifiable illocutionary-like act
can, I think, be used to counteract the tendency—not always easy to
detect amid the vagaries of speculation about what happens in the artist's
mind when he creates a work of art—to define works of art as products
of some specifiable *process*. To put it schematically: There is no psychological process, P, conscious or unconscious, such that "x is a work of art"
entails that P has occurred. Or, as F. E. Sparshott puts it:

> even if it were to be found to be true that some describable process did
> always occur in the production of works of art, the discovery would be of
> marginal interest to aesthetics; for the concept of a work of art is not a
> psychological concept, and it would remain possible that a work of art
> should appear without the process. What possible reason, then, can we
> have for postulating such a process?[23]

We can go even farther than Sparshott: "To create," unlike "to think,"
"to deliberate," "to dream," "to imagine," and the like, is not the name

of a mental act, activity, or process, any more than "to drive a car" or "to proram a computer" is. That only persons can create works of art and that whatever is a person has a mind does not imply that "to create" is a psychological verb, as philosophical idealists such as Croce and Collingwood have apparently supposed.

I turn now to the justification of my use of the verb "to create"—as opposed to, say, "to make" or "to produce"—in the formula: a logically necessary condition of something's being a work of art is that it has been created by a person. We need some such distinction as that between making and creating because we have committed ourselves, in talking about some kinds of art, to such distinctions as those between copy and original, and between design and execution.

The latter distinction, that between design and execution, can readily be illustrated by just about every work of architecture. The church of San Giorgio Maggiore in Venice—a work of art if ever there was one—was designed or created by Palladio, but it was executed, made, or built by unnamed masons. Numerous examples from painting and sculpture can also be adduced—for one, the late sculptures of René Magritte, all of which were executed by persons other than Magritte from drawings made by Magritte himself. Here, again, Magritte is the creator, although not the maker, of these works.

More troublesome, and more instructive, for our purposes is the distinction between copy and original. Many works of art exist in replica; some exist only in replica. For example, the work of Wu Tao-tzu, whom Sherman Lee describes as "certainly the greatest name of the T'ang Dynasty, if not the greatest name in Chinese painting," is "known to us only from copies."[24] Let us suppose that these copies are faithful replicas of their originals. Are they works of art separate from and additional to the works of Wu that are now lost? The correct answer, I think, is given by Meager: "We treat copies, when not mechanically produced, as also works of art, but not additional works of art."[25] What we possess in possessing a faithful copy of a painting by Wu is not a new work of art but simply a painting by Wu—in replica. The *creator* of the work of art in question was Wu, although the person who executed, produced, or made the object that we have was not Wu. But how is a faithful copy or replica to be distinguished from its (the) original? Two criteria immediately suggest themselves: C is an exact copy of O (1) if C is qualitatively indistinguishable from O (or is qualitatively similar to O within such limits as are tolerable for, say, a double or a stand-in) and (2) if C was produced later in time than O. But these criteria will not do. This point is dramatized by Meager's ingenious imaginary case:

> Imagine Joyce Cary's Mister Johnson when young, pupil at a native school in Darkest Africa, whose Eng. Lit. syllabus had consisted entirely of the Bible and Basic English, and who had had no other contact with

the tongue of Shakespeare; whose girlfriend's name was Pippa, and who
one year for his school magazine threw off 'Pippa Passes,' word for word
the replica of Browning's poem.[26]

An even more amusing example is provided by a George Price cartoon
that shows an archeologist, who has just opened an ancient Egyptian
tomb, aiming his flashlight at a wall that, in addition to the expected
paraphernalia of hieroglyphs and depictions of gods, holds an exact
duplicate of Whistler's famous *Arrangement in Gray and Black, No. 1*
(popularly known as *Whistler's Mother*)! The question raised for me
by these imaginary cases is not the same as that raised for Meager,
namely whether *if* two persons independently produced qualitatively
indistinguishable works, their products would be two poems, two paintings, or just one. My question is whether Mister Johnson's "Pippa Passes"
would be a *copy* of Browning's or Whistler's picture a *copy* of the ancient
Egyptian painter's; and I take it that it would not be, despite the fact
that *ex hypothesi* it is qualitatively indistinguishable from Browning's
poem or the Egyptian's picture and was produced at a later date. If this
is correct, then the criteria given will not serve to distinguish copy from
original, or creative artist from copyist. What is needed is some reference
to what Meager calls "original activity":

> We may take 'original activity' here to mean an activity not wholly
> determined in detail by its being mere obedience to specifications already
> laid down; and by 'mere obedience to specifications' we can mean the
> execution of specifications without reflective choice between possible ways
> of carrying them out resulting in different possible manifestations.[27]

That is, original activity must be—or must be like—what Plato (*Laws*
X) called "self-initiated motion"; its agent, what Aristotle (*Physics VIII*
and elsewhere) called a "prime mover." This definition of "original
activity" (which I would prefer to call an original act or performance) is,
for our purposes, a reasonably adequate, though negative, definition of
one notion constitutent of that of *creating,* and it will serve to remove
the taint of circularity from my original characterization of "creative
acts." Creative acts, now, are acts such that in performing (having performed) one or more of them one is performing (has performed) an
original act of producing a work of art. And if we understand creative
acts in this way, then Browning's act of writing "Pippa Passes" and
Mister Johnson's act of writing "Pippa Passes" are both creative acts,
even if we choose to say that Mr. Johnson implausibly—or miraculously
—produced the *same* work of art as Robert Browning. And the same
will hold for Whistler and Price's imaginary Egyptian painter. (Incidentally, we allow that two persons can independently make the same discovery or invent the same thing. Is there anything in the concept of

creation or in that of art that disallows the *possibility* of two persons independently creating the same work of art?)

A work of art has necessarily at least one creator, but it does not follow from this that whoever created it necessarily created it. "Regarded as a sentence about the Mona Lisa," says Anthony Kenny, " 'Leonardo painted the Mona Lisa' seems to be a necessary proposition, since the Mona Lisa is essentially a painting of Leonardo; regarded as a sentence about Leonardo, 'Leonardo painted the Mona Lisa' is contingent, since Leonardo, while remaining Leonardo, might never have painted anything."[28] But this is surely wrong. For if this were the case, it would be logically impossible for the Mona Lisa to turn out to have been painted by anyone other than Leonardo; but that the Mona Lisa *might* have been painted by someone other than Leonardo is at least a possible art-historical hypothesis. Furthermore, if it is argued that what we *mean* by the *Mona Lisa* is a painting by Leonardo, then by parity of reasoning it can be argued that what we mean by "Leonardo" is the man who, among other things, painted the *Mona Lisa*—in which case, regarded as a sentence about Leonardo, "Leonardo painted the Mona Lisa" would express a necessary proposition. In point of fact, the name "Leonardo" and the expression "the Mona Lisa" are not used in such a way that there is a necessary or logical connection between them.

Products of original acts, and *a fortiori* of creative acts, need not be original in the sense that they are qualitatively unlike the products of unoriginal acts or of other original acts. Consider speech acts, that is, locutionary acts. It is possible for me to repeat or copy what someone else has said ("Repeat after me: I, John, take thee, Mary . . . ," "I, John, take thee, Mary . . ."); but it is also possible for me to say, on my own, the same thing as someone else, in which case his speech act and my speech act are both original acts. The sentences we produce are tokens of the same type, differing from one another *solo numero*. And if what I say on my own is said later than what he says on his own, what I say is nothing new or novel in the sense that it is unlike something already said. Should we both say the same thing at the same time, what each of us says, that is, what both of us say, might be new or novel in that it is quite unlike anything anyone has already said. Speech (locutionary) acts are among the most familiar and conspicuous examples of original acts, many, if not most, of the products of which are original. Surely, much of what each of us says in the course of his life is in some way unlike anything anyone else has said, i.e., not exactly what someone else has said.[29] The same is true in art.

To tell whether an act is an original act, it is not enough to consider the product of that act, i.e., to determine whether it is a token of the same type as the token product of another act. One must consider how the act is performed, for example, whether it is an act of repeating or copying something already said or done. But because it is a matter of empirical or contingent fact that different *creative* acts (A's act as opposed to B's) never, or rarely, issue in the same product (tokens of the same type), if we know that something (a work of art) is the token product of a creative act, we can be reasonably confident that it is something new or original, that it differs qualitatively in some way, however insignificantly or unimportantly, from any other work of art yet produced. This judgment, however, that it does differ qualitatively from any work of art yet produced, does not depend on our knowing that it is the product of a creative act but upon a comparison of products of acts, creative or uncreative. But the fact that products of creative acts are usually, or even always, qualitatively new or original has apparently led some theorists of art to propound what might be called a paradox of creativity.

H. W. Janson puts it this way:

> the making of a work of art has little in common with what we ordinarily mean by 'making.' It is a strange and risky business in which the maker never quite knows what he is making until he has actually made it; or, to put it another way, it is a game of find-and-seek in which the seeker is not sure what he is looking for until he has found it.[30]

And Vincent Tomas puts it this way:

> To create is to originate. And it follows from this that prior to creation the creator does not foresee what will result from it.[31]

This is an interesting claim about which we might ask, where did Janson and Tomas get this information? To which the answer is, I gather, not from an empirical study of the lives of artists, but from reflection on the meaning of the operative verb, "to make, or to create, a work of art." In other words, it is true of Milton (A) that at some time he had not yet written or composed (created) *Il Penseroso*, although he was writing or composing *Il Penseroso*. But (B) until he had written or composed *Il Penseroso*, he did not know what he was writing or composing, did not foresee what would result from his act of writing or composing. How we know whether A is true of Milton is unproblematic; the question is how we know whether B is true. And the claim in question, I take it, is that if A is true, then B is true; in short, A implies B, in which case the claim is actually stronger than it is stated: it is not that one *does* now know or foresee what will result from his own creative acts, but that he *cannot* know or foresee this. For if A entails or logically implies B, then it is *impossible* for A to be true and B to be false.

First, is it *ever* possible to know or foresee what one is going to accomplish, as opposed to what one is accomplishing or has accomplished? Some philosophers would say no: knowledge or foresight of the future is in principle impossible. In their case, then, creative acts are on all fours with other acts; there is nothing special about them. Hence, there can be no paradox of creativity. But Janson and Tomas think there is something *special* about creative acts; hence, they must assume that one can know or foresee what will result from what he is doing in cases other than those of creating or originating.

Second, the claim that prior to creation the creator cannot know or foresee what will result from his creative act cannot be accepted in its present unrestricted form. For surely, assuming—rightly—that it is possible in at least some cases for one to know what he is going to do, one *can* know that he is going to paint a picture, say, and not write a poem or compose a symphony; *can* know that he is going to paint a seascape, say, and not a portrait or a still-life; *can* know that he is going to paint a seascape of Honfleur, say, and not one of Antibes or Monhegan Island —and all this before he has actually painted it. But, it will be replied, although he can know *in general* what he is going to do (create) before he has actually done it (created it), he cannot *quite* know, *fully* know, know *exactly*, know *to the minutest detail* what he is making until he has actually made it.

Two replies: first, we could continue to specify to any assignable degree of specificity the description of what our painter is going to do, and I do not see that we must in principle arrive at a point beyond which it is logically impossible for him to know what he is going to do. The burden of specifying that point is on those who claim that there is one. (The idea that creativity is incompatible with foreknowledge is rather like the old idea that God's foreknowledge is incompatible with human liberty or free will. But just as St. Augustine and others have shown that there is no incompatibility between foreknowledge and liberty, so there is none between foreknowledge and creativity.) Second, even if there is some point of specificity beyond which one could not know in principle what he is going to do, this will apply to acts other than to creative acts; indeed, to all acts. Richard Wollheim allows that a painter can know in advance that he is going to paint a picture of his model, say, but cannot know "to the minutest detail what he will do." Perhaps. But "the craftsman's [e.g., the shoemaker's] foreknowledge will often be no fuller."[32] That is, Janson and Tomas to the contrary, there is nothing *special* about art. Whatever lack of foreknowledge there may be *there* is reduplicated elsewhere, and the presence of it elsewhere is reduplicated there.

If we separate inner or mental acts from overt or physical acts, one may, of course, allow that a person can fully know in advance what he is overtly going to do because he has already thought out and decided just what to do, in which case the creative act would probably be said to have been performed in the mind of the creator—which is where some philosophers (e.g., Croce) would urge that it is always and necessarily performed. I do not wish to deny that creative acts can be performed in the mind, for clearly one can compose a poem "in his head." The question is whether creative acts must be performed in the mind (and not merely by using one's mind), i.e., whether overt creative acts must be preceded by inward or mental creative acts, and whether only where they are can one be said to know in advance just what he is overtly going to do.

Knowing what one is going to do overtly is not already to have done it inwardly. A: "What were you just about to say before you were interrupted?" B: "I was about to say . . .". To know what he was about to say, must B already have said inwardly what he was about to say? Suppose I ask myself, "What was I about to say? Oh, yes. . .". To know what I was about to say, must I here be recalling something I have already rehearsed inwardly? The answer to these questions, I take it, is No.[33] But speech acts, as we have noted, are among the more conspicuous of original acts, and their results—what is said, e.g., the sentences produced—are among the more conspicuous of original products. But if one can know just what he is going to *say* without already having said it inwardly (inwardly rehearsed it, worked it out in his head), and where what he says is something new, novel, or original in that it differs in some way from anything that has already been said, then I do not see what logical obstacle stands in the way of someone's knowing just what he is going to *create* without having already done it inwardly (e.g., worked it out in detail in his head) and where what he is going to create is an original work of art. If a poet or a painter were to tell us that before he had finished his poem or his picture he knew just what he was going to do, i.e., just what he was going to write or to paint, although he had not already composed the poem or worked out the picture in detail in his head, would his statement be paradoxical, senseless, logically incoherent? As far as I can see, it would not be. And if it would not be, then although to create *is* to originate, this does *not* imply that prior to creation the creator cannot know or foresee what will result from his creative act—a point perhaps supported by the logical coherence or intelligibility of the old theological doctrine that God knew from eternity just what He would create when He came to create the world. It may be the case, as I presume it is the case in at least some kinds of creative performances, e.g., automatic writing and action painting, that the artist does not know just what he is doing until he has done it, where what he is doing is described *after the fact* by a statement to the effect that he was creating this picture or that poem, but I do not see that there is anything in the concept of creation that necessitates this.

That one can know in advance what he is going to create does not imply, however, that one can know in advance (1) that what he is going to create is something original or (2) just how original it will be or wherein its originality will lie, i.e., in just what respects it will be original, even where what he is going to create *is* something original. And this may actually be the point of the paradox of creativity we have been considering. Those who say that the artist does not, or cannot, know or foresee what he is creating until he has created it may have it in mind that he does not, or cannot, know in advance (1) that his work will be original or (2) just wherein its originality will lie. Clearly, one may know what he is doing without knowing all there is to know about what he is doing and that one is doing something original, or doing something original in a particular way, may be things that it is reasonable to say one does not, or cannot, know about what he is doing until he has done it.

Consider first the knowledge *that* one's work will be original. I have already pointed out that it is a matter of empirical fact that different creative acts never issue in qualitatively identical products. There was nothing surprising in Ludwig Richter's discovery that if you set four persons to paint the same landscape, "all four firmly resolved not to deviate from nature by a hair's breadth," the result will be "four totally different pictures, as different from each other as the personalities of the four painters."[34] Given any creative act, it is highly probable—one might say that it is inductively certain—that the product of that act will be something original, something that differs qualitatively in some way from the products of all other creative acts. Cases like our imaginary cases of Browning and Mister Johnson, the Egyptian tomb painter and Whistler just do not arise—a fact that is no more mysterious or surprising than the fact that no two finger prints are the same. Given this fact, one *can* know in advance that what he will create will be something original.

Consider now the knowledge of how original one's work will be or wherein its originality will lie. Here, it seems to me, we can plausibly say that one cannot know in advance how original his work will be or just wherein its originality will lie. Just as one can know in advance that the product of his creative act will in *some* way be unlike the products of all other creative acts, so he might know in advance (assuming that he does know what he is going to create) *whether* what he is going to create will be similar to something already created and wherein it will be similar, namely, by finding the relevantly similar work. Had Mister Johnson known what he was going to write before he wrote it—and without having worked it out in his head in advance—chanced upon Browning's poem as he was about to write, he could have seen at once that what he was about to write was the same as what Browning had already written. (Compare speech acts again: "I was just about to say the same thing myself.") But just *how* original a person's work will be or wherein its originality will lie is something that he cannot similarly foresee. The class of works of art, like the class of utterances and unlike the class of words on this page, is indefinitely large; we have no criterion for knowing when we would have completed the enumeration of the class. Hence, we can easily tell whether, and how, a given work of art, even a projected work of art, is similar to a work already produced, namely, by finding the relevant work, but we cannot similarly tell how or to what degree a given work of art will be *unlike* any work of art yet produced. For, as Stuart Hampshire puts it, "the power and quality of the work [and here he is talking about its originality] is only known and understood in retrospect, often after many years."[35] An artist may know in advance what he wants to do or what he is going to do, but just how and to what degree what he is going to do will be original or creative awaits the doing of it and the indefinitely prolongable comparison of what he has done with what has been done already. The determination of the originality or creativity of the *work*, as opposed to that of the *act*, comes only after the completion of the creative act.

Closely associated with this point is another, namely, that if it is the case that "voluntary action is action which can be commanded; one can Ø voluntarily only if one can Ø when one is told to,"[36] then doing something original, especially something distinctively or markedly original, and *a fortiori* creating a distinctively original work of art, is, *qua* doing something *original*, nonvoluntary—and this even though there is an inductive certainty that, if one performs a creative act, the product of that act will be something that is somehow original. One can sensibly be commanded to paint a landscape, write a novel, or compose a sonata, but not to paint a masterpiece, write the great Amercian novel, or be the Mozart of our time. One can be commanded, in other words, to perform an original act but not to produce as a result of that act something distinctively original. One can, of course, *try* to do something original, creative, inventive, imaginative, and to enjoin this attempt is the point of such injunctions as "Be original," "Use your imagination"; but whether he *succeeds* must wait upon the outcome of what he has done. The difference between performing an original, and *a fortiori* a creative, act and producing as a result of that act something original is like the difference between looking for something and finding it. As Aristotle might put it, the creation of an original work of art may be an object of *boulesis* (wish) but not of *proairesis* (choice). One can choose to paint or not to paint, and he can choose what to paint, but he can only wish or hope that what he chooses to paint will turn out to be something distinctively, and not just trivially, original. (Compare the commands: "Say something"; "Now say something original, something unlike anything that has ever been said before." Except in special circumstances, I do not *try* to obey the first command; but I can only try to obey the second and hope that I will succeed.)

So far, I have, for the most part, been using the word "original," as applied to works of art, in a somewhat technical sense to mean different in some qualitative way from any other work of art. If we now restrict our attention to original products of creative acts, in this sense of "original," we find that we have a fairly rich vocabulary for describing the nature or character of the originality in any given case: "novel," "odd," "experimental," "new," "fresh," "eccentric," "unique," "bizarre," "outlandish," "avant-garde," "creative," "imaginative," "inventive," "inspired," and so on, terms that in various ways contrast with such terms as "uninspired," "imitative," "unimaginative," "mere hack-work," "old hat," "traditional," "academic," and the like. But of the terms used to mark kinds of originality, aestheticians have concentrated on "creative," "imaginative," and "inspired," terms applicable both to artists and to their works. Whether we wish to say that such terms are honorific or evaluative—they strike me as being like "kind," "generous," "intelligent," and so on, as applied to a person or to his acts or deeds, which are not always honorific or evaluative as opposed to merely descriptive—the fact remains that "creative," in that sense, is different from "creative" in the phrase "creative act," or "creative process." "Creative" in "creative act" is simply an adjective formed from the verb "to create." It is like "creative" in the phrase "creative writing course": in a creative writing course, a work might be produced, i.e., created, which is not creative; indeed, I presume that most work produced in creative writing courses is not (very) creative. The product of an original act which is also a creative act, in short, must be created but need not be creative. To merit the judgment that it is creative (imaginative, inspired), a work of art must not only be different from other works of art but, as Tomas puts it, "different in an interesting, important, fruitful, or other valuable way."[37] This means that the assessment of the creativity of a work of art requires aesthetic judgment; that is, it requires an exercise of taste, of aesthetic sensibility or discrimination. Anyone can tell at a glance whether two paintings or two poems are different, but not just anyone can tell at a glance which of two paintings or poems is the more creative. To tell this, one must be acquainted with properly comparable works of art and be able to appreciate the aesthetic significance of any artistic innovation, see how it enlarges the range of viable artistic alternatives and thereby "places" what has already been done by putting it, so to speak, in a new light.[38] If Cézanne was a creative artist, and not merely a creator of works of art, it was because he painted portraits, landscapes, and still-lifes that were markedly and distinctively different, in perceivable and specifiable ways, from any hitherto painted and such that they were artistically or aesthetically successful.

It would appear that one reason why some aesthetic theorists have been interested in the so-called creative process is that they believe that (1) in judging a work of art to be creative we are implicitly or by implication saying something about the psychology of the creator, and/or (2) that we can explain the difference between creative and noncreative art only by reference to the psychology of the creator.

First, it has been held—for example, by Tomas *(loc. cit.)*—that "what we have in mind when we speak of creative art" is something about the way it came into being; in particular, we "have in mind" that it was inspired (where "being inspired" is taken as the name of a psychological event) and that in the production of it the artist exercised critical control. But as far as I can see, we have nothing of the sort in mind. We tell whether a work of art is creative by looking at the work and by comparing it with previously produced works of art in the same or in the nearest comparable medium or genre. If the concept of a work of art is not a psychological concept, and therefore implies no reference to any specifiable process or mental happening, neither is the concept of creativity as applied to works of art a psychological concept. That a work of art is creative implies nothing about the psychology of the artist. To be sure, if a work of art is creative, then its artist is creative. But this is an empty or uniformative tautology. If Jones's swimming is graceful, then Jones is a graceful swimmer. Antecedent and consequent say the same thing.

And, second, the same difficulty bedevils any philosophical attempt to *explain* why certain works of art are creative while others are not. His famous distinction between the Fancy and the Secondary Imagination or Esemplastic Power came to him, Coleridge tells us, as a result of his discovery of Wordsworth's poetry.[39] The question he sought to answer was, "To what is Wordsworth's superiority as a poet *due?*" His answer, "To an exercise of Imagination as opposed to Fancy." And the same will explain Milton's superiority to Cowley: "Milton had a highly *imaginative*, Cowley a very *fanciful*, mind." What Coleridge attempted to do with the notion of Imagination, others before him and since have tried to do with such notions as those of inspiration or divine possession (Plato) and creative intuition (Maritain). The trouble with all such attempts, however, is that they are otiose: like the old explanation of the phenomena of heat and combustion by reference to the presence of the substance caloric, they give us bogus explanations, statements that have the mere appearance of an explanation. For no test or criterion of the exercise of esemplastic power or of creative intuition or of the occurrence of divine possession is provided, independent of the imaginativeness, creativity, or inspired quality of the works of art in question. To say that a certain piece of wood will burn because it contains caloric is merely to say that it will burn because it will burn; for the criterion of its containing caloric is that it will burn. Similarly, to say that Milton was superior to Cowley as a poet because Milton had the esemplastic power that Cowley lacked is to say no more than that Milton's *poetry* is imaginative whereas Cowley's is merely fanciful; for the sole criterion of Milton's possession of the esemplastic power is the imaginativeness of his verse. There is here no contingent connection between the imaginative or inspired quality of the work and the artist's exercise of some psychological power or faculty, his performance of some independently specifiable mental act; there is merely a logical connection between two statements, one of which only appears to be a psychological statement, a report of a mental act. "Milton's *Paradise Lost* is an imaginative poem" *entails* that Milton was an imaginative poet. To tell whether someone is an artist, i.e., has created a work of art, we must look to him as well as to what he has produced; to tell whether a work of art is creative, imaginative, or inspired, we must look to the work of art as it compares with other works of art; and to tell whether someone is a creative artist, we must do both—the first to determine whether he is an artist, the second to determine whether he is creative.

In Plato's *Euthyphro* (10), Socrates points out that it is not because something is seen that someone sees it, but because someone sees it that it is seen; not because something is led that someone leads it, but because someone leads it that it is led; and so on. To be sure, "*x* is seen" entails that someone or something sees *x*, and, conversely; the two propositions are equivalent. Still, we say that the first is true *because* the second is true, not that the second is true because the first is true. Similarly, although "A is a creative artist" entails that A's work is creative, and conversely; we say that the first is true *because* the second is true, and not that the second is true because the first is true. The artist may be the "cause" of his work, but it is because of the nature of his work that he is a creative artist.

I do not wish to deny that it is possible to establish genuine explanatory correlations between independently specifiable psychological characteristics, processes, or events on the one hand and the creation of imaginative or inspired works of art on the other. My claim is simply that we can know whether a work of art is creative, imaginative, or inspired while knowing nothing about the psychology of creation generally or about the psychology of a given creative artist specifically. Indeed, if we could not ascertain the originality or creativity of artistic work *independent of* our knowing anything about the psychology of creation, a psychology of creation would be impossible. Which is to say again what I have, in a way, been arguing throughout this paper: the concept of creativity is not a psychological concept.

Notes

1. A Frenchman, Blaise de Vigenère, saw Michelangelo at work on the Florence *Pietà* and wrote about his experience as follows: "I saw Michelangelo at work. He had passed his sixtieth year, and although he was not very strong, yet in a quarter of an hour he caused more splinters to fall from the very hard block of marble than three young masons in twice or thrice the time. No one can believe it who has not seen it with his own eyes. And he attacked the work with such energy and fire that I thought it would fly into pieces. With one blow he brought down fragments three or four fingers in breadth, and so exactly at the point marked, that if only a tiny piece of marble more had fallen, he would have been in danger of ruining the whole work." Quoted by Ludwig Goldscheider in his *The Sculptures of Michelangelo* (New York, 1940), pp. 20-21. The work de Vigenère describes was partially destroyed by Michelangelo himself around 1555 but was restored and "finished"—indeed, almost finished off—by Tiberio Calcagni. Goldscheider comments: ". . . Calcagni

died in 1565. When we see what he did to the work before he died, we must confess that his death was a piece of good fortune."

The Florence *Pietà* is not an exact analogue of Stephen Dedalus's cow, but a little imagination could easily make it so; and in philosophy imaginary cases will usually do as well as real ones.

2. Jerome Stolnitz, *Aesthetics and the Philosophy of Criticism* (Boston, 1960), p. 88.

3. *Ibid.*, p. 93. By an "art-object" Stolnitz means any object produced by art, i.e., by "the skilled, deliberate manipulation of a medium for the achievement of some purpose"—which would appear to make most man-made objects "art-objects."

4. Morris Weitz, "The Role of Theory in Aesthetics," *JAAC*, 15 (1956), pp. 33-34.

5. Ruby Meager, "The Uniqueness of a Work of Art," *Collected Papers in Aesthetics*, Cyril Barrett, ed. (Oxford, 1965), pp. 32-33. See also Arthur Danto, "Artworks and Real Things," *Theoria*, 39 (1973), 14: "Douaniers, children, chimpanzees, counterfeiters; tracing an object to any of these defeats it as an artwork, demotes it to the status of a mere real object."

6. Stuart Hampshire, *Thought and Action* (New York, 1959), pp. 230-231. And Weitz, *op. cit.*, p. 31: "A concept is open if its conditions of application are emendable and corrigible; i.e., if a situation or case can be imagined or secured which would call for some sort of *decision* on our part to extend the use of the concept to cover this, or to close the concept and invent a new one to deal with the new case and its new property." Weitz is correct in saying that under this definition of an open concept all empirical or descriptive concepts are open. But it does not follow from this definition, as Weitz seems to think it does, that there are or can be no necessary or sufficient conditions for the application of an open concept. The concept "bachelor" is an empirical-descriptive concept, but a necessary condition of its application is that the person to whom it is truly applied be unmarried. And it is a sufficient condition of a person's being married that he have a valid license to be married from the Commonwealth of Massachusetts and that he has been joined in wedlock to a member of the opposite sex by a clergyman licensed by the Commonwealth to perform marriages.

7. I say "sufficiently humanlike" to cover such imaginary, and therefore conceivable or logically possible, cases as Mickey Mouse and "men" from Mars.

8. Douglas N. Morgan, "Creativity Today," *JAAC*, 12 (1953), 8-9.

9. Below I try to justify the use of the word "created" as opposed to "made," "produced," or "fabricated."

That it be created by a person may not be the only necessary condition of something's being a work of art. For other possible necessary conditions, see Richard Wollheim, *Art and Its Objects, An Introduction to Aesthetics* (New York, 1968), p. 95.

10. See F. E. Sparshott, *The Structure of Aesthetics* (Toronto, 1963), p. 227: "To speak of 'the creative process' implies that the production of art is involuntary and unconscious—something that happens to one, not something one does." The production of art may at times be involuntary and unconscious, but it is still something one does and not something that happens to one.

11. Anthony Kenny, *Action, Emotion and Will* (New York, 1963), p. 154. Actually, the verb "to create" is not merely the name of an action but of an act: "As a general rule an action is called an act only when it can be described in a proposition with a personal subject; the actions of signing a check or killing a rival are acts, for one can say, "I signed the check," or "He killed his rival"; but the beating of the heart and the working of the liver [the heart's

action, the liver's action] are not acts: one cannot say, 'I beat my heart,' or 'I worked my liver' . . . . Every act, then (whether voluntary or involuntary), is an action; but not every action is an act." Eric D'Arcy, *Human Acts* (Oxford, 1963), pp. 6-7.

12. Kenny, *op. cit.*, pp. 171 ff. Not all performance verbs take a direct object, for example, "to grow up"; but when they do the accusative may be read as part of the verb, for example, "to paint a picture" as against "to paint." "To paint," "to write," and so on have a use as activity-verbs in addition to their use as performance-verbs: "Monet was painting all day in his studio" (activity-verb); "Valasquez painted the portrait of Pope Innocent X" (performance-verb). This is true also of the general verb "to create". Compare "He has been creating a nuisance all morning" with "Mozart created the quartet in a single day." "I was (still) writing the sonnet when you came in" (performance-verb) implies "I had not (yet) written the sonnet when you came in."

13. I am here artificially restricting the scope of the phrase "creative act"; I am not defining it. Clearly, one can create things other than work of art, for example disturbances, situations that are difficult to handle, uproars, impasses, and the like.

14. By the object of an act such as writing I mean that which is written (e.g., the sonnet); of painting, that which is painted (e.g., the portrait); and, in general, of creating, that which is created (the work of art). An intended object is not the same as an intentional object. If I set out to write a sonnet, the sonnet is the intended object of my writing; but if I fear that I shall never write a good sonnet, that I shall never write a good sonnet is the intentional object of my fear. See Kenny, *op. cit.*, Ch. 9.

15. In his *On Art and the Mind* (Cambridge, Mass., 1974), pp. 113-114, Richard Wollheim says, "From the fact that art is something that we do, it follows that art is, in some further and perhaps philosophically more technical sense, intentional. And this further sense is best brought out in the claim that in the making of art a concept enters into, and plays a crucial role in, the determination of what is made: or, to put it another way, that when we make a work of art, we make it under a certain description—though, of course, unless our attention is drawn to the question, we may not be in a position to give the description. . . . It is not simply that in describing a work of art after the event, as it were, we use concepts to characterize them or catch their characteristics: but the concepts have already been at work in the artist's mind in the determination of these characteristics. Indeed, one criterion of a description's adequacy is that in it the concepts that have helped fashion the work reappear. Thus, the description of the work is parasitic upon the description under which it was made."

It is not clear from this whether Wollheim is saying that one cannot in principle create a work of art unless he possesses the concept of art and unless that concept is "at work" in the artist's mind, "enters into, and plays a crucial role in, the determination of what is made." But this appears to be the burden of his account. If it is, he is surely wrong. The concept of making an idol or a stained glass window may enter into the determination of what a person is doing, in the sense that, were we to ask him what he is doing, he might truthfully reply, "Making an idol," or "Making a stained glass window." But he need not reply, or even be capable of replying, "Making a work of art," even if what he is in fact doing is making a work of art. According to Monroe Beardsley's *Aesthetics from Classical Greece to the Present* (New York, 1966), pp. 22-23, the Egyptians did not even have a word for "art" or "artist"; in which case no Egyptian could have spoken of himself as making a work of art. Does this mean that no Egyptian ever made a work of art? Of course not.

16. Related questions worth exploring: Can one create a work of art (write a poem, paint a picture, compose a quartet) in his sleep (as Coleridge is supposed to have composed *Kubla Khan*), under hypnosis, under the influence of drugs, or, in general, in situations in which he might be said not to know what he is doing, i.e., not know that he is writing a poem, painting a picture, or whatever?

Stolnitz (*op. cit.*, p. 95) tells us that his definition of art "implies that the artist is in conscious control of the process" of creation. In defense of this against artists who claim that creation (in their case) is involuntary or unconscious—like gestation—he says, "And yet we must remember that neither 'involuntariness' nor 'gestation' is reported in *all* instances of creation. They are widespread, but not universal. Hence they cannot be used to define the activity of 'art'" (p. 97). But by parity of reasoning, neither can deliberation or conscious control be so used; not *all* artists report this.

17. *Op. cit.*, p. 10.

18. See J. L. Austin, *How to do Things with Words* (Cambridge, Mass., 1962), pp. 94 ff. Report of locutionary act: "He said to me, 'You shouldn't do that.'" Report of illocutionary act: "He protested against (disapproved of) my doing that." Report of perlocutionary act: "He checked me (prevented my doing that, stopped me before it was too late, brought me to my senses, annoyed me, embarrassed me)." These are all ways of *saying what he did*.

19. For this reason portraits, illustrations, and so forth are not species of art in the way that cats, dogs, and the like are species of animal. "C is a cat" entails "C is an animal," but "P is a portrait" does not entail "P is a work of art."

20. It is important to note that even composing a poem or writing a novel is only *analogous* to performing an illocutionary act. See Austin, *op. cit.*, p. 104. A poem or a story, of course, consists of locutions, and in performing the locutionary acts in question the writer may be performing one or more illocutionary acts; but writing a poem is not one of them. For more on this matter, see Marcia M. Eaton, "Liars, Ranters, and Dramatic Speakers," p. 356.

21. Even Clive Bell's theory does this at times: "*Paddington Station* is not a work of art; it is an interesting and amusing document. In it line and color are used to recount anecdotes, suggest ideas, and indicate the manners and customs of an age [all illocutionary-like acts]: they are not used to provoke aesthetic emotion [a perlocutionary-like act]." *Art* (New York, 1958), p. 23 and *supra*, p. 65. The suggestion is that only if a painter uses line and color to provoke aesthetic emotion is his painting a work of art.

22. For Collingwood, that is, "to express an emotion" is a performance-verb. It has continuous tenses, and "A is expressing an emotion" implies "A has not (yet) expressed that emotion." See *The Principles of Art* (Oxford, 1938), *passim*, but esp. Ch. 6.

23. *Op. cit.*, pp. 227-228.

24. Sherman E. Lee, *A History of Far Eastern Art* (Englewood Cliffs, N.J., 1964), p. 265.

25. Meager, *op. cit.*, p. 26. I am concerned with only "exact" or "faithful" copies or replicas here; so-called "free" or "creative" copies (e.g., Dürer's drawing *Battle of the Sea Gods* after Mantegna's engraving) raise issues of another sort that are touched on in the last paragraphs of this essay.

26. *Ibid.*, pp. 31-32.

27. *Ibid.*, p. 31. The term "manifestation" is used in a technical sense: "Let us call the spatio-temporal phenomena [e.g., two or more bronze castings of the same statue, two or more performances of the same symphony] so related to a work of art that when a person sees or hears them he is seeing or hearing the work, *manifestations* of the work" (*ibid.*, pp. 25-26).

On my understanding of Meager's notion of original activity, it does not follow that an original act entails an exercise of "reflective choice." Briefly, if an act is an original act (*O*), then it is not an act of mere obedience to specifications already laid down (not-*M*); if it is an act of mere obedience to specifications already laid down (*M*), then it is not an act involving reflective choice (not-*R*). But "(*O* → not-*M*) and (*M* → not-*R*)" does not imply "(*O* → *R*)."

See also Arthur Danto, *op. cit.*, p. 14: ". . . it is analytical to the concept of an artwork that it be 'original' . . . . Being an original means that the work must in a deep sense originate with the artist we believe to have done it."

28. *Op. cit.*, p. 168.

29. See John Lyons, *Noam Chomsky* (New York, 1970), p. 21: a "general property of human language . . . is its *creativity* (or 'open-endedness'). By this is meant the capacity that all native speakers of a language have to produce and understand an indefinitely large number of sentences that they have never heard before and that may indeed never have been uttered before by anyone."

30. H. W. Janson, *History of Art* (Englewood Cliffs, N.J., 1962), p. 11.

31. Vincent Tomas, "Creativity in Art," *The Philosophical Review*, 67 (1958), p. 4; and *supra* p. 131. See also Stuart Hampshire, *op. cit.*, pp. 246-247.

32. *Art and Its Objects*, pp. 33-34.

33. See Ludwig Wittgenstein, *Zettel* (Oxford, 1967), #1, 2, 38, 44, 45, 57, 137.

34. Heinrich Wölfflin, *Principles of Art History*, M. D. Hottinger, trans. (New York, n.d.), p. 1.

35. *Op. cit.*, p. 247.

36. Kenny, *op. cit.*, p. 183.

37. *Op. cit.*, p. 4; and *supra*, p. 134. See Poincaré on mathematical creativity; "What is mathematical creation? It does not consist in making new combinations with mathematical entities already known. Anyone could do that, but the combinations so made would be infinite in number and most of them absolutely without interest. To create consists precisely in not making useless combinations and in making those which are useful . . .". Henri Poincaré, *The Foundations of Science*, Halsted, trans. (Lancaster, Pa., 1946), p. 386.

38. See Douglas Morgan, *op. cit.*, p. 19: "In rough, oversimplified terms . . . a painting . . . counts as 'creative' if it gives us a new way of seeing, as a Picasso or a Turner does . . .". But seeing what? Other paintings, I trust. Every creative innovation in an art, for example, Surrealism, gives us a new way of seeing at least some other products of that art, for example, the paintings of Jerome Bosch, and thereby provides us with a basis for a (possible) reassessment of the artistic or aesthetic significance of those other works. Whether, as Morgan suggests, this is a conceptual truth, having to do with the meaning of "creative," is difficult to determine, although I am inclined to agree with Morgan that it is one; that we would (tend to) withhold the predicate "creative" from a work that did not have this propensity. A judgment of creativity is in this way retrospective: it directs our attention not only to the work so judged, but to previous comparable works as well. "Inventive" or "innovative," on the other hand, has prospective force: an artist is inventive or innovative, but not necessarily creative, if he devises new ways of doing things that affect the practices of artists who come after him. Thus, Cézanne was both a creative and an inventive or innovative painter.

39. Samuel Taylor Coleridge, *Biographia Literaria*, Chs. 4 and 13. And see Basil Willey, *Nineteenth Century Studies* (New York, 1949), Ch. I, esp. sec. III.

On Creating Art

THE PHRASE "CREATIVE PROCESS" trips so easily off the tongue that we take for granted we know what we are talking about. But do we? Is playing a game of tennis or writing a letter to a friend a process? It sounds as odd to say it is as to say that sleeping is a process. But if writing a letter to a friend is not a process, why should anyone think that writing a poem, even writing *Paradise Lost*, is one? Is it perhaps because the ability to do the one is somehow more mysterious or puzzling than the ability to do the other that we are inclined to think that something special must "go on" in the latter case that does not go on in the former? But *is* the ability to do the one any more mysterious or puzzling than the ability to do the other? To be sure, very few people can write poems of the stature of *Paradise Lost*, whereas many people can write letters. But then very few people can play championship tennis or write prose of the stature of Tacitus's or Gibbon's; but, apart from supposing, indeed acknowledging, that these people are of superior *ability*, we are not inclined to suppose that there must be some peculiar process at work when they do what they do well. Why then suppose that there must be some peculiar process at work when Poussin paints a picture or Beethoven composes a symphony?

Vincent Tomas supposes that "what we have in mind when we speak of creative art" is something about the way it came into being. To be creative, Tomas argues, a work of art must satisfy six conditions: it must be (1) something "the like of which did not exist before"; (2) different in "an interesting, important, fruitful, or other *valuable* way"; (3) produced according to rules originated by the artist and implicitly followed by him during the process of production; (4) something the artist did not know he was "aiming at" until he was finished; (5) inspired; and (6) a result of exercised critical control.

These are presumably *necessary* conditions of something's being a creative work of art, but are they also supposed to be *sufficient* conditions? Still, if they are necessary conditions, then in knowing that something is a creative work of art, in addition to knowing two things about the work we also know four things about the artist: that he originated the rules that he followed in making it; that he did not know *this* is what he was aiming at until he was finished; that he was inspired; and that he exercised critical control over his work. But need we know any of these things to know whether the *work* is *creative*? I say the answer is no, but do you find my reasons for saying so persuasive?

Let us look at condition 3 a little more closely. That an artist follows rules while creating (and I assume that the rules in question are not merely such rules as those of grammar, punctuation, and spelling in the case of writing) is suggested to Tomas by his analogy of the rifleman. If a rifleman tries to hit the bull's-eye and fails, he has not obeyed all the rules (presumably of marksmanship): "If he had obeyed them, there necessarily would have been a hole in the bull's-eye." So we congratulate a marksman not for hitting the bull's-eye, as one might suppose, but for obeying the rules.

But if you try to hit the bull's-eye and fail, *must* you have failed to obey at least one of the rules of marksmanship? Can't one hit the bull's-eye by chance (have good luck, e.g., beginner's luck)? If so, can't he fail to hit it by mischance (have bad luck)? You stand properly, hold the gun properly, aim properly, your form is perfect—but just as you pull the trigger, someone bumps you, or the wind blows in your eyes and distracts you. *Ex hypothesi* you have obeyed all the rules, but you have failed to hit the bull's-eye. So can there be anything paradoxical in saying, "I obeyed all the rules, but I failed to hit the bull's eye"?

Like a marksman, a painter or a composer can, at least sometimes, be said to have a goal or objective—he's commissioned to paint a fresco of *The Last Supper* for a convent's refectory wall, say, or compose a quartet with a relatively easy cello part for the King of Prussia. In painting or composing must he be devising rules and implicitly—or explicitly— following them? There may be ccratin conditions that he has to meet, for example, those imposed by a patron, but must his every move be one of following a rule? What sort of rule? The sort we might formulate *after* he has done his work—first he did this, then he did that; so first one does this, then one does that? But if this is the sort of rule in question, could one do *anything* without following a rule of one's own or of someone else's devising? If not, wouldn't the distinction between rule-following or rule-obeying actions and other actions collapse? Is it necessary that all actions performed in creating a work of art be rule following? Isn't it possible for an artist, by doing something spontaneously, or even accidentally, mistakenly, or inadvertently, to produce a work of art, just as one might stumble on a discovery or hit the bull's-eye by chance?

Now let us look at condition 4: a creative work of art must be something that the artist did not know he was "aiming at" until he is finished. I have commented on one aspect of this claim in my essay, to what effect you may judge for yourself. Here I want to explore the notion of *finishing* a work of art, a notion that Beardsley too finds puzzling: "One of the most puzzling questions about the creative process is how the artist knows when to stop." According to Beardsley, "there are really two questions here: how the artist knows when *he* is finished, and how he knows when the work is finished." Tomas's question, I gather, is the former; and he holds that the artist is finished when he attains what he was "aiming at" all along, even though he does not know what he was aiming at until he attains it. In connection with Flaubert and Hemingway he says, "he may write and rewrite and hone and polish until at last he can look upon what he has done and say, 'There! That's what I wanted to say, just as I wanted to say it.' Before that, he knew only that what he had so far done was *not* quite what he wanted to say, or quite how he wanted to say it."

But, perhaps because this smacks too much of "intentionalism," Beardsley takes another view of the matter: "as the poet moves from stage to stage, it is not that he is looking to see whether he is saying [or has said] what he already meant [wanted or intended to say], but that he is looking to see whether he wants to mean what he is saying." If he does, then surely he's finished.

Did you mean what you said? Did you say what you meant? These are not the same questions. The first, for example, may question whether I am exaggerating ("You do that again, and I'll kill you!"), whether I am being sincere ("I love you"), or whether I am being ironic ("Warren G. Harding was surely one of the greatest presidents of the United States"). But it may also question whether I have uttered the right words for what I wanted to say. To take an extreme example, Sheridan's Mrs. Malaprop says to Sir Anthony Absolute (*The Rivals*, Act IV, Scene II), "my affluence over my niece is very small," but what she obviously means is that her influence is very small. The second question queries whether one has said what he wanted or intended to say. It too could be addressed to a Mrs. Malaprop; but it could also be addressed to a shy lover, say, who intended to declare his love but spent the occasion indulging in small talk.

The question to which Tomas's writer addresses himself, it seems, is the second one as it might be addressed to a Mrs. Malaprop: Is this the word I really want?, and so on. But what are we to make of the question Beardsley's poet addresses to himself? It is neither the first nor the second but "Do I *want to* mean what I have said?" Does this make any sense at all? Perhaps the question his poet really has in mind is this: "Does what I have written say something worthwhile, for example, is it amusing, provocative, illuminating, moving, profound?"

Although the questions we have been looking at have to do with writing, they can be generalized to cover other artistic acts: Did you mean to do what you did? Did you do what you meant to do? Is what you have done in some way worthwhile? I take it that an artist might ask himself any or all of these questions. Although Beardsley and Tomas seem to think that only one of these questions is the decisive question with respect to whether the artist has finished his work, might not any, or all, or none of them be?

As for when the *work* is finished, Beardsley holds that "The artist is finished" does not imply "The work is finished": "For when the artist has done all he can, the question remains whether the work has enough to it, whether it is worthy of standing by itself, as an object of aesthetic enjoyment." But is this how one tells whether a work of art is finished? If an artist has finished a work, and not merely stopped working on it, isn't the work thereby finished regardless of whether the work is worthy of standing by itself as an object of aesthetic enjoyment?

The question of whether a work of art is finished is closely connected in both Tomas's and Beardsley's mind with the question of "critical control"—Tomas's condition 6. According to Tomas, being subject to critical control sets creative art apart not only from works like *Tarzan of the Apes* but also from the art of the insane.[1] But does it? Suppose that Alva Johnson's story, or one like it, were not about Edgar Rice Burroughs but about Tolstoy or Jane Austen. Are we prepared to say that this is inconceivable?

The late paintings of Van Gogh may not have been executed "in the complete absence of conscious control and criticism," but how do we know? Is this an empirical inference based on biographical data or psychological theory; or is it a logical inference? Can we infer from the nature of Van Gogh's late paintings that he exercised critical control over them just as we can infer from Kant's being a bachelor that he was unmarried? That Tomas is unsure in what sense he means that critical control is a necessary condition of creativity is reflected in his response to Nietzsche's description of the composition of *Zarathustra*: he thinks it *probable*, he *bets*, that Nietzsche edited a bit. Yet almost immediately he cites with approval Ducasse's remark that "*critical judgment is an intrinsic, essential constituent of the productive activity we call art.*" But if critical control or judgment is intrinsic and essential, why assess probabilities or bet? Do you bet that a mother has at least one child?

But the Tomas-Ducasse position is even stronger than this. It is not just that a critical judgment on the part of the artist is intrinsic to art but that "a *favorable* one" is. And Beardsley seems to agree.

> The creative process is kept going by tensions between what has been done and what might have been done. At each stage there must be a perception of *deficiencies* in what now exists, plus the sense of unrealized possibilities of *improvement*. The motivating force, as Tomas says, is a negative critical judgment. (Italics mine.)

And

> Each time the artist . . . takes a step, he adds something to what is already there (A) and makes another and different object (B). If he judges B worse than A, the question is whether it is good enough to stand alone as a work of art.

But *must* there be at each "stage" or "step" anything of the sort? Think of speaking, for example, of conversing with a friend or telling him about a recent camping trip. In the first place, are there, or must there be, "stages" or "steps"? And even if there are, must there be constant criticism? If not, why must there be in art? Why can't Milton have written *On His Blindness* with as little self-criticism, namely none, as one frequently exercises in speaking? And must there be a final "favorable" judgment on the part of the artist to guarantee that he, or his work, is finished? Can't we easily imagine an artist, even a great artist, who is chronically dissatisfied with what he produces—nothing he does ever satisfies him—and yet he turns out masterpiece after masterpiece?

Closely connected with this point is Tomas's joint assertion that "if what the artist produces is . . . indifferent or bad, we do not regard him as a creator"; and if a work "lacks coherence and lucidity . . . this lack in the work is taken as evidence of a lack of control by the artist over the activity to which the work owes its origin." But do we not regard even bad artists as creators (what else could they be?), even though their work is not creative? And is the absence of coherence and lucidity (or whatever) in a work taken as evidence of a lack of control on the part of the artist? Might not an artist exercise as much control as it is possible to exercise without his work having coherence and lucidity (or whatever)? In short, might he not be just a poor artist?

In the last section of his essay, Beardsley raises the question, "What difference does it make to our relationship with the arts that we understand the creative process in one way or another?" And his "brief and unequivocal" answer is, "It makes no difference at all." But is his answer as unequivocal as it appears? For isn't his question really twofold: (1) Does it make any difference to us whether an object was produced by a human being rather than "by an animal or by a computer or by a volcano or by a falling slop-bucket?" And (2) Is its value "independent of the manner of production?" Beardsley, I take it, would say no to 1, yes to 2.

But if something is produced by an erupting volcano, can it be a work of art at all? Can it "say" anything, "mean" anything, be understood in the way a poem or a picture can be understood as opposed to the way in which an earthquake can be understood? And if it has any value at all, can it be the kind of value, positive or negative, that works of art possess? If not, isn't there all the difference in the world between our relationship to it and our relationship to works created by artists?

Because of his antipathy to "intentionalism," his desire to treat works of art apart from any consideration of how they came into being, Beardsley is led to the puzzling view that "the true locus of creativity is not the genetic process prior to the work but the work itself as it lives in the experience of the beholder." But how are we to understand this? Earlier we were told, "What I mean by the creative process is that stretch of mental [which would seem to rule out volcanos, by the way] and physical activity between incept and the final touch . . .". But if this *is* what Beardsley means by "the creative process," then how can "the true locus of creativity" now be where he says it is? Be this as it may, is it really true, or even intelligible, that "in the experience of a melody, creation occurs before our very ears"? In listening to the *Missa Solemnis* is it *I* who create the work of art? But the work of art is the *Missa Solemnis* and that was created by Beethoven long before I ever listened to it. Or is it the *Missa Solemnis* that creates the work of art in me? When I listen to it, it has, to be sure, certain effects on me, but those are by no stretch of the imagination a work of art—except according to some Pickwickian use of the phrase perhaps. Again, when I listen to it, there's lots of "movement of mind," but is this movement "an act of creation" (of what?) simply because the music "energizes" my mind, because "new powers of vision and apprehension come into being"? A positive answer would surely involve a bizarre use of "creation."

One final query: Does anything that Tomas or Beardsley, or even I, has to say about artistic creation really peculiar to the creation of *art*? We use examples of art again and again, but couldn't what we say be applied (the proper changes being made) to the writing of an ordinary term paper, say, or an article for a newspaper? If so, is there really any distinctive problem of *artistic* creation at all?

Notes

1. "The art of the insane" is an ambiguous phrase. It may mean either (1) the art of people who are insane or (2) insane art, art that does not "make sense," art that is of symptomatic interest alone, a kind of art usually produced by insane people. Van Gogh's late pictures may be the art of an insane man, but they are not insane art. We tell whether something is insane art by studying it, not by inquiring into the psychology of its maker. But we tell whether something is the art of an insane person only by inquiring into the psychology of its maker.

Suggestions for Additional Reading

S. Alexander, *Beauty and Other Forms of Value* (London, 1933), Ch. 4; John Beloff, "Creative Thinking in Art and Science," *B.J.A.*, 10 (1970), 58-70: Rhys Carpenter et al., *The Bases of Artistic Creation* (New Brunswick, N.J., 1942); R. G. Collingwood, *The Principles of Art* (Oxford, 1938), Chs. 6-11; June Downey, *Creative Imagination* (London, 1929); David W. Ecker, "The Artistic Process as Qualitative Problem Solving," *J.A.A.C.*, 21 (1963), 283-290; Brewster Ghiselin, ed., *The Creative Process*

(New York, 1955); Jack Glickman, "Creativity in the Arts," *Culture and Art*, L. Aagard-Mogensen, ed. (New York, 1976). 130-146 and "On Creating," *Perspectives in Education, Religion, and the Arts,* Howard E. Kiefer and Milton K. Munitz, eds. (Albany, N.Y., 1970), 262-265: a response to Kennick; Carl R. Hausman, *A Discourse on Novelty and Creation* (The Hague, 1975); Donald F. Hense, "Creativity and Prediction," *B.J.A.,* 6 (1966), 230-245 and "Logic, Creativity and Art," *Aust. J. Phil.,* 40 (1962), 24-34; Industrial Research Institute, Inc., *The Nature of Creative Thinking* (New York, 1952); Arthur Koestler, *The Act of Creation* (New York, 1964); Jeffrey Maitland, "Creativity," *J.A.A.C.,* 34 (1976), 397-409; Jacques Maritain, *Creative Intuition in Art and Poetry* (New York, 1953); Douglas Morgan, "Creativity Today," *J.A.A.C.,* 12 (1953), 1-24; Milton C. Nahm, *The Artist as Creator* (Baltimore, 1956), reprinted as *Genius and Creativity* (New York ,1965); E. Neumann, *Art and the Creative Unconscious*, R. Manheim, trans. (New York, 1966); Anthony Palmer and Andrew Harrison, "Creativity and Understanding," *P.A.S.,* Suppl. Vol. 45 (1971), 73-121; Julius Portnoy, *The Psychology of Art Creation* (Philadelphia, 1942); Henry R. Raleigh, "More on the Creation of Art," *J.A.A.C.,* 25 (1966), 159-165; H. E. Rees, *The Psychology of Artistic Creation* (New York, 1942); Mary Carmen Rose, "Artistic Creativity and Aesthetic Theory," *B.J.A.,* 12 (1972), 344-353; Albert Rothenberg and Carl R. Hausman, eds., *The Creativity Question* (Durham, N.C., 1976), an especially rich anthology of work by philosophers and psychologists; I. A. Taylor and J. W. Getzels, eds., *Perspectives in Creativity* (Chicago, 1975); Vincent Tomas, "A Note on Creation in Art," *J. Phil.,* 59 (1962), 464-469; Vincent Tomas, ed., *Creativity in the Arts* (Englewood Cliffs, N. J., 1964); Eliseo Vivas, *Creation and Discovery* (New York, 1955); Gordon Westland, "The Investigation of Creativity," *J.A.A.C.,* 28 (1969), 127-131.

III

Understanding
Works of Art

Introduction

ONE CAN UNDERSTAND, or fail to understand, a work of art in a way, or in ways, in which he cannot understand, or fail to understand, a tree, say, or a planet, or a chair. What constitutes understanding a work of art will typically differ from art to art, or even from work to work. Understanding a work of architecture or of music—how it "works," how it "goes," how its elements fit together, what's "going on" in it—is not the same as understanding a poem; nor is that the same as understanding a painting. And understanding one (kind of) painting, for example, Massacio's *The Tribute Money* (1427), is not the same as understanding another, for example, Morris Louis's *Aleph Series IV* (1960). The tests of understanding and the kinds of questions we pose are not the same from case to case, although they may overlap. But, although specific problems of understanding are legion and potentially raise a host of issues for philosophical scrutiny and debate, some general issues, for whatever reason, have been of special interest to philosophers, at least of late. Five of these have been chosen as the topics of the present section: the "logic" of critical interpretation; the concept of expression in art; the nature of artistic representation; the nature of metaphor and the so-called "paraphrastic heresy"; and finally the nature of fictional discourse.

Criticism of the arts consists largely of two related, indeed interrelated, activities: interpretation and evaluation. Although the term "criticism," which comes from the Greek verb meaning to judge or pass sentence upon, is often restricted to the latter (and is so restricted for the purposes of this book), we find that art critics devote much of their time and effort to interpretation. For before one can reasonably judge or evaluate a work of art, he must at least try to understand it, and the effort to understand often, perhaps invariably, involves interpretation.

In the first essay in this section Stuart Hampshire examines "the typical circumstances in which we put this word ['interpretation'] to a serious use" in order to see what force it carries—or, better, doesn't carry—when used in connection with works of art. One of the "negative conclusions" he arrives at is that, although "many works of art require interpretation," they also "require that the interpretation should be uncertain and not exclusive of different interpretations." An interpretation of a work of art need not claim "correctness," even tacitly. Indeed, "if correctness is taken to imply finality," then Hampshire sees "no reason to accept this as the right epithet of praise for a critical interpretation." The right epithet is more likely to be something like "plausible."

That "the same work of art can support alternative and even incompatible interpretations," which Annette Barnes calls the "Tolerance Principle," is an ambiguous claim. She sorts out various versions of it and does a "step-by-step analysis" of each, being particularly intent upon showing that the idea that "incompatible accounts [interpretations] of a given work can in principle be jointly defended as plausible," not to say true, "generates insurmountable difficulties."

Whether one accepts the so-called *expression theory* of art, namely, that in creating a work of art an artist is invariably expressing his feelings, emotions, or attitudes and that a work of art is essentially an expression of such states,[1] still he might hold that to understand a work of art is, in part at least, to understand what feelings or emotions it expresses or are expressed in it—assuming that some are. For example, Charles Rosen writes of the slow movement of the *Hammerklavier* sonata that its "deep expression of grief is one of Beethoven's most moving achievements";[2] and surely anyone who missed the grief here would to that extent have failed to comprehend the music. This raises an interesting problem of what it is to say that a piece of music, or any other work of art, expresses grief or joy, and how we tell whether it does.

Alan Tormey offers a general analysis of the concept of expression according to which only the "intentional states" of a person (or animal), states directed toward an object, be it real or imaginary, can be expressed, and according to which "sad expression" and "expression of sadness" are logically asymmetrical, in that to say that someone's face has a sad expression is merely descriptive of his face, whereas to say that someone's face expresses sadness "warrants" the inference that he's sad. He then applies points of his general analysis to an understanding of what he calls the "expressive properties" of works of art—their gaity, sadness, and the like—trying to show that the sadness of a poem, for example, does not automatically warrant an inference to the poet's sadness.

Guy Sircello's essay is about what he calls "anthropomorphic" predicates, properties, or qualities. Both people and works of art are often characterized as sad, humorless, witty, austere, aloof, ironic, and so on. When works of art, or parts of them, are so characterized, just what is being said about them? According to what Sircello calls the *canonical position*, anthropomorphic predicates are not essentially different from color terms—"sad melody" is logically on all fours with "red carnation"—

and as far as such predicates are concerned works of art are no different from natural objects. Sircello endeavors to show that both these claims are false. In doing so he offers what he takes to be a more adequate account of such predicates, central to which is his notion of an "artistic act," what an artist *does* in his work.

Understanding paintings, drawings, photographs, and sculptures typically involves knowing *whether* they represent anything and, if so, *what* they represent. We are all familiar with the puzzlement expressed by "What's that supposed to be?" uttered by the baffled viewer of a cubist-period Picasso, say. If the question is taken as symptomatic of a lack of sophistication or knowledge—and we are inclined so to take it—then the further and more interesting question arises: What does one have to know to know whether a painting, for example, represents anything or what it represents? This leads to the problem of the nature of representation, specifically of pictorial representation; a problem that was given new life (if it ever had much of one before then) by the appearance in 1960 of the art historian E. H. Gombrich's *Art and Illusion: A Study in the Psychology of Pictorial Representation.*

When a painting or photograph, P, is a painting or photograph *of* something, S, then Max Black wants to say that P *depicts* S or stands in a *depicting relation* to S. The question he addresses is, What is it for P to depict S? Some theorists of representation or depiction have offered what they take to be necessary, or necessary and sufficient conditions, of depiction. Black examines "the credentials of plausible candidates for the role of [at least] a necessary condition for the holding of the relation of 'depiction'" and finds them all wanting. He concludes that, although they will not serve to *define* depiction, they are not for that reason irrelevant to the application of the concept. "Depicting" is, as Black sees it, a "range" or "cluster concept," in that one or more of several criteria may, in different contexts, justify the claim that a given picture depicts a certain subject.

Kendall Walton does not give up so easily on trying to find at least necessary conditions of depiction, and he offers us an ingenious theory of depiction that, he holds, will explain the difference between describing and depicting something (and thereby show why, although we generally *read* literature and hence use our eyes, literature is not a visual art) and will also explain the persistent urge to suppose that pictures must resemble or look like what they depict, even though resemblance will do neither as a necessary nor as a sufficient condition of pictorial representation. Briefly, Walton argues that what makes something a depiction of a person or a vase of flowers, say, is the existence of a "game of make-believe" of a certain kind, "played" in a manner defined by certain conditions.

Although metaphors frequently appear in daily discourse, they are, we might say (metaphorically), the heart and soul of poetry. Most, if not all,

poetry contains metaphor. Understanding a poem, then, involves understanding metaphors. But what is it to do this? As one answer goes,
understanding a metaphor involves the ability to paraphrase it. And as
Stanley Cavell puts it, if I am unable to paraphrase a metaphor, "then
that is a very good reason, a perfect reason, for supposing that I do not
know what it means." But some critics and philosophers have denied that
metaphors are paraphrasable, or at least *fully* paraphrasable; and the
question is, How so?——a question that naturally raises issues about the
very nature of metaphor.

Max Black canvasses three views of the nature of metaphor: the "substitution" view, the "comparison" view (a special case of the first one),
and the "interaction" view. Although he appears to settle on a variant
of the "interaction" view, his final position is that there are three kinds of
metaphors, each of which can be accounted for by or will fit one of the
three views. The most interesting and important metaphors, however, are
the "interaction" ones that, according to Black, cannot be adequately
paraphrased or "replaced by literal translations."

In a famous essay, "The Heresy of Paraphrase," the literary critic
Cleanth Brooks raises the following question:

> is it not possible to frame a proposition, a statement, which will adequately
> represent the total meaning of [a] poem; that is, is it not possible to
> elaborate a summarizing proposition which will "say," briefly and in the
> form of a proposition, what the poem "says" as a poem, a proposition which
> will say it fully and will say it exactly, no more and no less? Could not the
> poet, if he had chosen, have framed such a proposition? Cannot we as
> readers and critics frame such a proposition?[3]

Brooks's answer is no; and the chief stumbling block appears to be
metaphor. But Stanley Cavell takes issue with Brooks's position. He
argues that "metaphors are paraphrasable. (And if that is true, it is
tautologous.)" And he concludes that "Brooks is wrong to say that poems
cannot in principle be fully paraphrased," although he concedes that
Brooks is "right to be worried about the relation between paraphrase and
poem."

In Act V, Scene II of Shakespeare's *Othello*, Othello smothers Desde-
mona and she dies. If someone witnessing this scene, perhaps Edward
Bullough's "proverbial unsophisticated yokel" who chivalrously inter-
feres "in the play on behalf of the hapless heroine,"[4] were to leap up
and shout "Stop! She's innocent!" just as Othello was about to kill his
wife, we would say that he had failed to understand what was going on.
Not that he failed to understand that Othello was about to kill Desde-
mona, for his behavior would be inexplicable if he didn't understand
that, but that he had failed to appreciate the fact that he was witnessing a
play and not a real-life event. This raises in a pointed way the question
of the difference between fact and fiction, or, to put it another way, the

nature of fiction and what it is to understand it as fiction. This is the problem addressed by Margaret Macdonald and Marcia Eaton. Macdonald says she is interested in "how an author uses words and sentences in fiction," in "the logic of fictional language"; Eaton says that she is interested in elucidating the "basic aesthetic concept" of "a literary work as a linguistic object."

Some philosophers hold that in writing fiction an author says what is true. A variant of this view is given by Kendall Walton in his "Pictures and Make-Believe." More often, they contend that what he says is false. Macdonald holds that a clarification of the concept of fiction leads to the view that fictional statements are neither true nor false: "in fiction language is used to create." Removing the issue from one of truth and falsity, Eaton explores the nature of this "creative" use of language by exploring the kinds of speech-acts that may be performed by an author when he writes fiction. What our "proverbial yokel" has failed to appreciate, as she sees it, is the nature of the speech acts performed by Shakespeare and by the actor playing Othello.

Notes

1. Tormey characterizes the *expression theory* more narrowly. Schematically, "if art object O has expressive quality Q, then there was a prior activity C of the artist A such that in doing C, A expressed his F for X by imparting Q to O (where F is a feeling state and Q is the qualitative analogue of F)."

2. Charles Rosen, *The Classical Style: Haydn, Mozart, Beethoven* (New York, 1971), p. 426.

3. Cleanth Brooks, *The Well Wrought Urn: Studies in the Structure of Poetry* (New York, 1947), pp. 205-206.

4. Edward Bullough, *Aesthetics: Lectures and Essays,* Elizabeth M. Wilkinson, ed. (London, 1957), p. 98.

STUART HAMPSHIRE

Types of Interpretation

I AGREE WITH Mr. Beardsley[1] that we cannot interpret the critic's role as an interpreter without raising an underlying question of how art is to be approached. I agree also that this is in part a pedagogical question and a question of desirability (sometimes called a question of value). How are people best introduced to the enjoyment of art? Secondly, why is it to the highest degree desirable that they should be? We are today postponing these larger questions. We are also leaving on one side the doubts that might be felt about the wide, inclusive use of the term "work of art." Are we justified in assuming a unity here? What is the interest that is distinctively an interest in things as works of art, an interest that is the same whether we are concerned with novels, quartets, the Bible, or the Parthenon?

Postponing these larger questions, I shall be concerned only with interpretation. Mr. Beardsley says two things about interpretation: (1) "that it is essentially connected with meaning, in a broad sense"; (2) that he who offers an interpretation "tacitly claims correctness for it." I shall examine these two statements.

What do we understand by the word "interpretation"? For we are, I think, concerned here with a word rather than with a distinct concept. Our starting point must in such a case be the typical circumstances in which we put this word to a serious use. I shall therefore give a few selected examples of types of interpretation, which I hope will not be taken to be different senses of the word interpretation. Since we have no defined concept of interpretation, we are not justified in speaking here of different senses of the word. We would be justified in speaking of different senses of the word if we had provided some rules for its correct applications. So far we have no such rules. But the word is not a homonym in the different employments now to be cited.

1. "What is your interpretation of the recent events in Russia?" A contemporary interpreter of the news might be asked this. He offers the type of interpretation that a historian would offer of political events in the past. Mr. Beardsley's word "meaning" is not out of place here. But of course our problem is to distinguish as specifically as we can the different kinds of meaning. What does the deposition of Khrushchev "mean"? This is the "mean" of "the clouds mean, or are a sign of, rain." What does Khrushchev's fall indicate or portend as likely to happen? Of what is it a symptom (or sign)? For symptoms are interpreted.

The historian puts the facts together and he offers his interpretation of an event in British eighteenth-century politics. Distinguish this kind of interpretation from the interpretation that a Marxist is committed to offer of British eighteenth-century politics. Distinguish also "The Whig Interpretation of History," the title of a once famous book. These last two are systematic interpretations, which find a meaning behind the events in accordance with some principles or guidelines. The news interpreter need not go as far as this. He puts the facts together in an arrangement which indicates the dependence of one event, or state of affairs, on another. Why should history, the whole sequence of political events, have a meaning (or direction or sense), as Marxists and some theists and Macaulay might be thought to have thought?

The news interpreter and the historian's interpretations can be assessed as "wild," "perverse," "unplausible," "does not fit the facts," and even as "correct." So far Mr. Beardsley has not erred. But the "meaning" that we have here, uncovered by interpretation, is not the type of meaning that the Significance-Theorist is interested in.[2] He is not interested in natural signs, nor in weak causal dependencies.

The word that might be substituted in some of these contexts, without too great a change of sense, is explanation. But in none of these cases *is* interpretation explanation, except for the Marxist, when he is a strict historical determinist.

2. In the above examples, or in some of them, to interpret entails filling in more of the story. So we think of an ordinary case of imputing motives to a person as a case of interpreting what he does. Here interpreting again comes near to explaining: but not for all types of motive. Some typical epithets of assessment here are "far-fetched," "strained." When we find *ulterior* motives, then we interpret, and we hope that it is a *possible* interpretation. But we will usually admit that it is not the *only* possible, the only plausible, interpretation; if it were, the motive would not be ulterior.

3. An interpretation is something that a psychoanalyst gives of the imagery that occurs in free association, or of parapraxes, or, above all, of a dream. A psychoanalyst is par excellence an interpreter. He interprets people to themselves. He therefore exhibits one part of a person trying to communicate with another. A dream is singled out among all natural

phcnomena as something that is taken to have a meaning, an ulterior meaning, a deeper meaning. It has always seemed to men, long before psychoanalysis existed, that dreams call for interpretation. As soon as one remembers a dream one almost unavoidably wonders what it could possibly mean. Remembering a dream even seems a way of asking oneself this question. The interpretation of a dream is an interpretation of symbols, which are neither exactly natural signs nor the conventional symbols of a language. ("The sea is *usually* a symbol of libido, but perhaps not in *this* dream.") What is the meaning beneath the surface, masked by the manifest content recalled? There is also the interpretation which a psychoanalyst offers of a passage of free association and of the patient's conduct during analysis, and of features of his conduct generally. This kind of interpretation agains comes near to explanation; but it is a special kind of explanation. He finds meaning (motive, purpose) in behavior and in words that seem insignificant or that seem to have some different significance. He even interprets acts as having a symbolic significance, and thereby explains them. He finds a deeper theme in details, which the ordinary observer, attending only to the plot, would have overlooked. "What was I really saying when I made that absurd mistake?" "What was he really doing when he did that otherwise inexplicable thing?" I shall recur to the interpretation of dreams. It is a plausible candidate for a possibly illuminating analogy.

4. "How do you interpret this passage in Aristotle's *Metaphysics*?" Here interpretation comes nearer to "read" and to "translate." Questions of interpretation are sometimes left open when all questions of translations, strictly speaking, are settled. But the interpretation and the translation can also be fused. In the latter case "interpret" nearly, or entirely, coincides with "read"; but it is a strong, artificially reinforced sense of "read." An interpretation is something that a passage in Aristotle may *bear*, or permit. Here we are evidently concerned with meaning; but sometimes with ulterior meaning, the meaning beyond or between the lines. It is a failure of Aristotle's, the failure to be clear, if the reader has too often to read between the lines. But it might be—and has been—held that all imaginative writing requires the reader to read between the lines, that the writing must, if it is imaginative, suggest more (mean more) than appears in the print. The Significance-Theorist will be satisfied with this type of meaning.

It is worth noticing that he who translates spoken, but not written, words is an interpreter. Is this because one interprets a person? He who interprets not a passage in Aristotle, but Aristotle the philosopher, or has his own interpretation of Aristotle, is not someone who finds the meaning of Aristotle, at least in the plain and satisfying sense of "meaning" just mentioned. Of any great writer, who is also a philosopher, there can be several interpretations. There is the phenomenalist Kant and the empiricist Aristotle. These interpretations differ from the usual ones in laying the stress on one of the philosopher's doctrines rather than on another. They say, "This is what he was really interested in." They do uncover a moving face behind a fixed mask of prose. They purport to discover something ulterior. The bland surface of, e.g., Spinoza's writing calls for an interpretation. Where would he have placed the stress? Which of these propositions would he have been least willing to doubt? Interpretation requires skill of a peculiar kind, namely, an attention to that which does not lie evident on the surface. He who translates must stay on the surface. He who reads carefully is often intermediate between these two positions.

5. Oracles are things that have to be interpreted. More even than dreams they demand interpretation. They exhibit proudly a gap between manifest content and real meaning. A fortune teller, I think, has a choice between interpreting the cards and just reading them. An astrologer reads my horoscope; for he has signs with allotted meanings, a dictionary. A palmist reads the lines of my hands, though he may also interpret some features of them. The archetypal interpreter was Hermes who brought messages to and fro as a go-between between gods and men. The gods often speak in riddles, or at least with grand obscurity. One interprets the Old Testament and the prophets.

I hope that no Significance-Theorist would claim that the interpretation which is in question in the criticism of art is interpretation guided by a rule, least of all, a rule that allows one to infer the deeper meaning from the manifest content. The interpreter of a work of art, who is a critic, is not a cryptographer, who *translates* the work. The work is not an oracle or a riddle. This would be a theory of literature, and of art generally, as essentially allegory. Yet critical interpretations that come nearer to allegorical interpretations have been sometimes enlightening; e.g., Mr. Wilson Knight seems driven to find concealed meanings, usually morals, in Shakespeare or in Byron; and he is often a critic who tells us what we hope to learn from critics; but one may subtract the criticism and keep it as a by-product of the discovered allegory. Poems, novels, and works of art generally do not covertly convey propositions, and novelists and poets are incidentally, not essentially, prophets. The works do not typically constitute messages; and if the critic finds *the* message, we expect that another critic will find a different message in the same work.

6. An actor interprets a role or part. A pianist or violinist interprets the piece of music that he plays. Apart from criticizing his competence and technique, we may criticize his interpretation. Once again, the work will not permit or bear this or that interpretation. The piece of music is susceptible of being interpreted in more than one different way. For some types of music one might intelligibly and truthfully say that it is of their nature to be susceptible of a great variety of different interpretations. Even the best interpretation of these romantic works might not be counted as a perfect and final interpretation, leaving nothing for any future performer other than exact reproduction. Some operas are in this way particularly indeterminate. Interpretation of this kind closely re-

sembles the interpretation, not of a specific passage in Aristotle or in Kant, but rather the interpretation of Aristotle or Kant. We assume that music and doctrines are, as far as accuracy is concerned, correctly reproduced. But a role in a play, or in an opera, a song, a whole philosophy, require an interpreter; there is a penumbra of uncertainty about where the stress should be laid, about which elements in the whole should be made to stand out prominently, and where there is a connection and where there is a disconnection.

We have now, I think, the two most plausible candidates for an illuminating analogy to critical interpretation. They are the interpretation of dreams and, secondly, the interpretation that an actor or musician gives. They are widely different types of interpretation, and different types of criticism will show an analogy with one rather than the other. It is plainly not an accident that art and dreams have commonly in history been assimilated. He who interprets a dream knows that he looks for a meaning which was not intended and which was not purposefully put there. Yet he attributes the meaning to the dreamer, who, in a sense, had these thoughts and wishes, and found a way at once to communicate them and to communicate them with a disturbing indefiniteness. Many works of art do have a mysterious power to disturb. Many do convey, without the intention to state, a wish for an ideal and impossible form of life, and a sense of loss that has to be discovered. Many works of art therefore require interpretation, and require that the interpretation should be uncertain and not exclusive of different interpretations. The critic, like the analyst interpreting a dream, cannot altogether disregard his subject's intentions and conscious purposes—what he thought he meant—as a sign that itself needs to be interpreted, and a critic may hope that his interpretation will be accepted by the artist as (for him) a surprising discovery; but a strong denial of the interpretation may sometimes not be a refutation.

He who interprets a role or a piece of music has narrow limits within which he must move. He must stay as close as he can to the text, and only then can he find different shades of emphasis, different phrasings, which he may choose, or which come naturally to his temperament. There are several kinds of art, and several kinds of works of art, which allow very little space for the interpreter to move. But a shade of emphasis may make all the difference in bringing out what is there in the text. The critic as parodist comes near to the actor in his role. In delineating a style, and making it visible, and in all questions of pure aesthetic quality, the critic has to be minutely exact. He makes one see (hear, notice, while reading) the exact calculation of intervals, the pauses, transitions, juxtapositions, omissions.

These observations about serious uses of the word "interpretation" only indicate negative conclusions. First, that we must not too simply say that interpreting is a weak kind of explaining. It sometimes is, and sometimes it isn't. In any case, there are many very different types of explanation. Secondly, we must not say that interpretation "is essentially connected with meaning in a broad sense." It usually is, but not always and necessarily. More important, the sense of "meaning" is not only broad, but too broad. It would be easier to discover why we use the word "interpretation" in the great variety of different contexts in which it occurs than it would be to discover why we use the word "meaning" as broadly as we do. The verb of activity is usually more easily understood, in a philosophical sense, than the undifferentiated noun; for we can usually delineate the purposes and the social setting which are normal for the activity. The third negative conclusion is: critical interpretation does not always "tacitly claim correctness," and usually it does not claim to be guided by a rule. If correctness is taken to imply finality, then I see no reason to accept this as the right epithet of praise for a critical interpretation. Some interpretations are impossible, absurd, unplausible, farfetched, strained, inappropriate, and the object does not permit many of the interpretations that have been suggested. But the epithet of praise is more likely to be "illuminating," "plausible," even "original," also "interesting." "True interpretation" is an unusual form of words in the context of criticism. "Correct interpretation" does sometimes occur in these contexts; but it isn't standard and even less is it universal. In general aesthetics it has sometimes been remarked that it is typical of works of art that they should normally be susceptible of some interpretation and not susceptible of just one interpretation. They are open, and they are published, exhibited, or left about, for scrutiny. Works of art typically *require*, or at least invite, criticism. To look at something with great care, and attentively, is already to be on the verge of appraising it. The critics may be parasites on the body of literature and of art; but there are creatures which can only remain alive as long as they have their appropriate parasites. Perhaps there are types of art, and types of works of art, which do not *require* interpretation, in the way which music requires to be interpreted or in the way in which dreams require to be interpreted. But even they do need to be read, or seen, intensely and carefully, and one kind of interpreting critic sets himself to make this possible.

Notes

1. Hampshire's essay is a response to Monroe C. Beardsley's "The Limits of Critical Interpretation," *Art and Philosophy: a Symposium*, Sidney Hook, ed. (New York, 1966), pp. 61-87. Ed.
2. By the Significance-Theory Beardsley means the view that all works of art have a meaning, in some broad sense, "and therefore all works require to be interpreted—or at least are capable of being interpreted . . ." . *Op. cit.*, pp. 62-63. Ed.

ANNETTE BARNES

Half an Hour Before Breakfast

LITERARY CRITICS say a good many things about literature, about each others' sayings about literature, about the nature and function of criticism. A random sampling of criticism's theories and practices leaves one feeling a bit like the White Queen, who, for practice, believed the impossible for half an hour before breakfast.

Whatever else literary critics may be, individually and collectively, they have been prolific. Under critical scrutiny literary works spawn innumerable interpretations. What to do when confronted by divergent interpretations of the same work is a problem which continues to baffle and frustrate both literary and philosophical critics, as well as the living authors whose work is being criticized.[1] No one denies that divergent interpretations are offered. Should one argue, as Monroe Beardsley does, that if one keeps at the recalcitrant text, in most cases the correct interpretation will surface?[2] Or should one allow, as Joseph Margolis does, that the same work can support alternative and even incompatible interpretations, and try to remove the puzzlement by explicating the logic of interpretive discourse and the ontic status of the artwork?

In this paper I focus on the account of interpretive criticism which Margolis gives in his book *The Language of Art and Art Criticism*[3] and develops further in later articles.[4] I am particularly concerned with his suggestion that if we examine the way critics talk about artworks we shall find that "the philosophically most interesting feature of critical interpretation is its tolerance of alternative and seemingly contrary hypotheses."[5] He believes that this alleged tolerance has radical consequences for the way works of art are individuated and for the model of confirmation appropriate to interpretive claims.

That we do not individuate works of art as we do physical objects is clear not only from the fact that we speak of the same work performed in

From *Journal of Aesthetics and Art Criticism*, 34 (1976), pp. 261–271. Copyright 1976 by *Journal of Aesthetics and Art Criticism*. Reprinted by permission of the journal and the author.

substantially different ways but also from the fact that we allow seemingly incompatible accounts of a given work (the counterpart of the description of a physical object) to stand as confirmed.

... If contrary descriptions of an ordinary natural object, an oak tree, for instance, were regarded as confirmed, we should then be obliged to insist that the descriptions were true of two different objects. Evidently, we do not speak of works of art in this way. The only shift possible appears to be to provide a model of confirmation other than that of simple truth and falsity.[6]

The model of confirmation which Margolis provides in his book and believes to be the appropriate model in the domain of the interpretive critic is the model of plausibility and implausibility: "where his effort is interpretive, we cannot judge the critic's remarks to be simply true or false, accurate or inaccurate, but only that his interpretation, . . . , is 'plausible,' 'reasonable,' 'admissible,' 'indefensible,' 'not impossible,' and the like."[7]

Though acknowledging that considerations of plausibility are relevant in other areas—in science, hypotheses are discussed in terms of plausibility when there is a "technical inability" to obtain the requisite information for deciding truth—Margolis believes that considerations of plausibility "are always marginal to the main effort of science."[8] He finds them "more nearly central to aesthetic criticism."[9] For critical interpretations "are, in principle, logically weak."[10] "[G]iven the goal of interpretation, we do not understand that an admissible account necessarily precludes all others incompatible with itself."[11] Interpretations tolerate each other even when they are incompatible. In light of this relative weakness of interpretive statements, compared with statements of fact, he claims that "the sort of rigor associated with determining matters of fact is flatly inappropriate in the circumstances in which interpretations are provided."[12] Faced with two conflicting interpretations, an occurrence which he believes cannot in principle be ruled out, Margolis claims that both may be acceptable, i.e., both may be plausible.

Two things must be noted. First, Margolis does not deny that sometimes one speaks of the correct interpretation in literature. He claims, however, that this occurs only after "significant, further restrictions such as holding to canons of historical accuracy, or the artist's intentions or the like,"[13] have been imposed. He allows that sometimes critics might want to find, for example, the most historically accurate interpretation. He denies, however, that it makes sense to say that that (or any other) interpretation is the correct one simpliciter. In "Critics and Literature," he argues that competing ways of interpreting the work are available given different critical interests and tastes. He claims that "there is no straightforward sense in which competing classificatory schemes may be shown to be truer or more correct or fitting for the *purpose* critics share,"[14] on the grounds that there is no one purpose critics share.

Second, Margolis does not deny that "simply true" has some place in literary criticism. There are certain features of works of art which can be described. Descriptions in art, like descriptions of ordinary physical objects, are true and false. For example, Margolis believes that "in the literary and dramatic arts, plot, action, characters, vocabulary, rhythm, rhyme, style of language, and the like are said to be described."[15] Contrasting with descriptions are interpretive proposals, e.g., "[a] Freudian reading of *Alice in Wonderland*, a Marxist reading of the *Oresteia*."[16] "Criticism then is methodologically treated as interpretive, in the sense that any account will be viewed as plausible more than as true, once what is indisputably descriptive has been provided—and always with a caution that the work may be construed in alternative ways."[17]

Though Margolis believes that interpretations and descriptions are distinct in many regards, the tolerance for incompatibles is central.[18] For convenience I shall refer to his claim[19] as the tolerance principle:

We Allow Seemingly Incompatible Accounts of a Given Work . . . to Stand as Confirmed. In the passage quoted earlier,[20] he takes the tolerance principle as providing support for the following controversial theses:

A. We do not individuate works of art as we do physical objects.

B. The model of confirmation applicable to interpretive accounts of art works is not the model of confirmation used with regard to descriptions of physical objects.

I shall argue that the tolerance principle is either true and not interesting, or else interesting and false. In either case the tolerance principle does not support A or B. I do not in this paper directly address the question of how works of art are individuated, although I do show why Margolis can't use the tolerance principle to support his contention that we do not individuate any works of art as we do physical objects. I shall also show why a major argument, which Margolis uses to demonstrate the necessity of a new model of confirmation for interpretations in literature, does not work.

The first task is to see exactly what the tolerance principle implies. Although in the statement of the principle quoted above, Margolis uses the term "seemingly" with respect to incompatible interpretations, elsewhere he makes it clear that he believes that it is in principle possible to defend plural and actually incompatible critical hypotheses as interpretations: "it is logically possible to identify one and the same work under alternative and incompatible interpretations."[21] For the moment I shall omit the term "seemingly" and take the principle to refer to an alleged curious tolerance in literary criticism of genuinely incompatible interpretations.

There are several possible versions of the principle, though we shall be interested in the following four:

I. Incompatible accounts[22] of a given work can in principle be jointly defended as true

II. Incompatible accounts of a given work can in principle be jointly defended as plausible

III. Incompatible accounts of a given work can in principle be separately defended as true

IV. Incompatible accounts of a given work can in principle be separately defended as plausible

In order to eliminate those versions of the tolerance principle which clearly are not what Margolis had in mind, it is helpful to look at some examples of incompatible interpretations. Margolis is not prolific with examples, but he does indicate how they might arise. There are various points of view, various imaginative schemes that a critic can use when she or he engages in the interpretive process. They range from elaborate and large scale visions—Freudian, Marxist, Christian, Jungian, Existentialist—to more limited or less clearly formulated ones. Margolis suggests that readings generated from different large scale frameworks, from incompatible points of view, can be incompatible. For the moment, I shall use examples of incompatible interpretations where the frameworks of the opposing critics are not clearly incompatible. Since I am making claims about any pair of incompatible interpretations, how the interpretations are generated does not make a difference here.

Consider the following two examples taken from the critical literature. In his essay on *King Lear*, Stanley Cavell notes that there are interpretations of the play which characterize Lear as senile. Cavell responds, "Lear senile? But the man who speaks Lear's words is in possession, if not fully in command, of a powerful, ranging mind."[23] A critic commenting on another critic's interpretation of *A Doll's House* notes that "Nora is usually interpreted as a narcissistic and infantile woman in the beginning of the play; Hardwick sees her as free, whole and intelligent right from the start."[24] I take it these are cases where Margolis would agree that more than a description of the characters is needed, viz., the account depends upon a way of reading the text.

In each case, if both of the two interpretations were true of the same art work, if the art work is an entity and "true" is used in its ordinary way, it would follow that contrary characteristics were being attributed to the work. For Margolis it is not logically tolerable for contrary characteristics to be defended as jointly true of the same work. If it is true to say that Lear is senile, then it cannot simultaneously be true to say that Lear is in possession of a powerful, ranging mind. "Senile" and "being in possession of a powerful, ranging mind" are incompatible expressions— they cannot be true of the same subject at once, at least not at the same time, in the same respect, and so on. Nora cannot truly be said to be free, whole and intelligent *and* narcissistic and infantile at the start of the play, if "free, whole . . ." is meant to exclude "narcissistic and infantile."

For on no view of the characterization of an *entity* are we going to hold
that incompatible characterizations may be rendered of the same entity and
jointly defended as admissible characterizations *of* that entity.[25]

It is extremely important to understand what Margolis means here.
The crucial expressions are "incompatible" and "jointly defended as admissible." The conflict Margolis is interested in is a logical conflict. The
joint defense of incompatible characterizations of an entity involves one
in logical inconsistency. Any rational person would feel the force of
the inconsistency.

The following two characterizations are incompatible characterizations
if they are offered as characterizations of one and the same oak tree (and
if we are counting leaves in the same way, at the same time, and so on).

1. The oak tree has less than 100 leaves.
2. The oak tree has more than 300 leaves.

If the two statements are incompatible, if 1 and 2 cannot both be true,
then the truth of one of the statements entails the denial of the other.
To jointly defend these incompatible characterizations one would have
to defend their conjunction:

3. The oak tree has less than 100 leaves and the oak tree has more than
300 leaves. (The oak tree has less than 100 leaves and more than 300
leaves.)

Turning to two incompatible characterizations of an art work, one
would be involved in the same kind of logical inconsistency if one asserted:

4. Lear is senile and Lear is in command of his faculties. If we take
"admissible" in "jointly defended as admissible" to mean "admissible as
true" then a statement like 4 would involve us in an inconsistency if the
work of art were an ordinary entity, i.e., a physical object like an oak tree.

It may seem that version I of the tolerance principle must be false, and
thus can be eliminated. Incompatible accounts of a given work cannot in
principle be jointly defended as true. However, in Margolis's statement
quoted earlier, the denial of joint ascription was conditional upon the
work of art being an entity. It is clear that Margolis believes that no artwork is an ordinary entity, if ordinary entities are physical objects like
trees. In his latest published article, they are physically embodied and
culturally emergent *entities.* In "On Disputes About the Ontological
Status of a Work of Art," he writes as if he wants to deny completely that
a work of art is an entity. I have reconciled these two moves by assuming
that he denies works of art entity status if "entity" is to be understood as
"ordinary physical object."

Could an artwork's failure to be an ordinary entity like a physical object account for its jointly tolerating incompatible interpretations without logical inconsistency? That is, do we have to rule out I if the artwork is not an ordinary entity? It doesn't appear that Margolis wants to defend I along these lines, even if he could. Margolis does imply that art works, whatever their ontological status, cannot jointly tolerate incompatible accounts if the model of confirmation is simple truth and simple falsehood. The implication resides in his shift to plausibility to avoid logical inconsistency, so he must really want to rule I out.

Would the shift to plausibility help in the above examples to remove logical inconsistency? That is, can we jointly defend as admissible incompatible accounts of an art work if we understand "admissible" to mean "admissible as plausible" (in the spirit of II incompatible accounts of a given work can in principle be jointly defended as plausible)?

A shift to plausibility would not help here. Joint admission on either model of confirmation (truth or plausibility) generates insurmountable difficulties. We may escape logical inconsistency, but what we do get is equally unacceptable. Consider the following examples:

3a. It is true that the oak tree has less than 100 leaves and more than 300 leaves.

3b. It is plausible that the oak tree has less than 100 leaves and more than 300 leaves.

4a. It is true that Lear is senile and is in command of his faculties.

4b. It is plausible that Lear is senile and is in command of his faculties.

One is seriously confused whichever of the above one says. In fact it would be extremely odd to talk about the plausibility or implausibility of 3 or 4, (i.e., to assert 3b or 4b), since if 3 and 4 are logically impossible how can 3 or 4 be plausible?

Though one might be tempted to say of 3b and 4b that they involve *logical* inconsistency, as do 3a and 4a, there are difficulties with such a claim. For the purpose of this paper it is sufficient to say that anyone claiming 3b or 4b would be in unacceptable trouble. He would be involved in what we might call conceptual inconsistency. 3b and 4b are false, though perhaps someone might think that he believed them. (Plausibility is tied to a statement's power to persuade and someone might think himself persuaded.) I would argue that anyone who believed that he held either 3b or 4b would not understand what he allegedly believed he held. If one understands the concepts "less than 100" and "more than 300," or "senile" and "in command of one's faculties," then one cannot jointly ascribe both members of either pair to one entity at the same time, in the same respect, and so on.

Another version of the tolerance principle, version II, looks as if it can be eliminated. Incompatible accounts of a given art work cannot in principle be *jointly* defended as plausible. Once again the term "entity" might be thought relevant. Incompatible accounts of an artwork cannot be jointly defended as plausible if the work is an ordinary entity. Margolis, we noted, believes that artworks are not ordinary entities. Perhaps the non-ordinary entity status of an artwork is sufficient to remove the difficulties about 4b and II. But it would seem that if not being an ordinary entity were enough to remove the difficulties about 4b and II, it should be able to do likewise for 4a and I as well. Though plausibility and truth do not amount to the same thing, if the difficulty of 4b could be removed, it is hard to see why the difficulty in 4a couldn't be removed as well. If the difficulty in 4a and I were removed, then there would be no need to introduce II.

We are left with version III and IV of the tolerance principle. Margolis has said that the model of simple truth and falsity was not applicable to the interpretive domain so we know he will rule out III leaving us with IV.

There are statements closely related to 3a and 3b, and 4a and 4b, such that the switch from truth and falsity to plausibility and implausibility can make a difference in the truth status of the respective claims. Margolis, in his discussion of plausibility, does suggest that these other statements are what he has in mind.

3aa. It is true that the oak tree has less than 100 leaves and it is true that the oak tree has more than 300 leaves.

3bb. It is plausible that the oak tree has less than 100 leaves and it is plausible that the oak tree has more than 300 leaves.

4aa. It is true that Lear is senile and it is true that Lear is in command of his faculties.

4bb. It is plausible that Lear is senile and it is plausible that Lear is in command of his faculties.

In talking about the difference between plausibility and truth, Margolis notes that when "P is true" and "Q is true" are contraries, "P is plausible" and "Q is plausible" are not.[26] 3aa and 4aa are each statements of contrariety, 3bb and 4bb are not.

In the realm of plausibility, the defense of two interpretations or two descriptions as *separately* plausible, does not commit one to their *joint* defense, viz., to the defense of their conjunction as plausible. It might be permissible to defend two interpretations—for example, two incompatible interpretations—as separately plausible, when it is not permissible to defend them as jointly plausible. When 3b or 4b is false, 3bb and 4bb can be true.

The interpretive critic who defends 4bb is not committed to 4b. If literary critics defend the plausibility of both incompatible interpretations in the manner of 4bb, they are not committed to defending them jointly, viz., defending their conjunction as in 4b. Rather they are committed to defending them both only in the sense that they defend each of the two incompatible interpretations as separately plausible (4bb).

In the realm of truth, the defense of two descriptions or two interpretations as separately true does commit one to their joint defense. If critics defend the truth of both incompatible interpretations in 4aa, then they are logically committed to (a) defending each of them separately as true, *and* (b) defending their conjunction as true. The truth values of 3a and 3aa, and 4a and 4aa, will always be the same.

III is ruled out as a version of the tolerance principle since a separate defense of true claims, as we saw, does commit one to a joint defense as well. We are left with IV. Since a separate defense of plausible accounts does not commit one to their joint defense, IV is not false, even though II is false.

(IV) Incompatible Accounts of a Given Work can in Principle be Separately Defended as Plausible. Throughout the preceding discussion I have spoken as if it made sense for Margolis to talk of genuinely incompatible interpretations. As I shall now show, given Margolis's positive position, he has effectively blocked himself from using that terminology.

Margolis's motive for shifting from talk of truth to talk of plausibility was to account for the tolerance in criticism of incompatible interpretations, a tolerance he found significant. Two plausible interpretations were not contraries if they both were defended as separately plausible.

Logical incompatibility is a relation between statements[27] such that the truth of one statement entails the denial of the other. Margolis tells us that interpretive statements are not simply true or false, they are rather plausible and implausible. What, therefore, does incompatibility mean in the realm of the merely plausible? What does it mean for Margolis to say that two interpretations are incompatible?

Margolis does say that "neither plausible nor implausible statements are logically precluded from being judged true or false."[28] But with regard to interpretive statements this claim is at best misleading. Margolis does not believe that technological developments in interpretive criticism will generate procedures for determining simple truth. We talk in terms of plausibility, he says "only when we cannot actually determine truth."[29] But, I take it, Margolis means *with regard to interpretive criticism* that the "cannot" in "cannot actually determine truth," refers to a *logical* and not a technical inability. I assume that there is no activity which critics simply happen to be unable to perform here which, if performed, would change the situation, for it is not critics' ineptitude that confines critical interpretations to the domain of the plausible. Although plausibility does not preclude simple truth—for example, plausible statements in science can later be confirmed as true—in interpretive criticism the "simply true" accorded to statements of fact is precluded in principle. This is an implication of his claim that interpretive statements are logically weak. Plausible interpretive claims are logically precluded from being judged simply true or simply false.

Since Margolis believes that interpretations are never simply true or false but are only plausible and implausible, interpretations are never logically incompatible. If the model of truth and falsity were an appropriate model for interpretations, then interpretations could be incompatible, but since, on Margolis's account, interpretations are not and cannot be true, they are not and cannot be incompatible. They are not contraries since they are not true or false.

Margolis, in his statement of what we have called the tolerance principle, did use the qualifier "seemingly." It now appears that for Margolis that qualifier is essential. When he drops that qualifier, as he does in many places, he is in error.

Are we then to understand tolerance principle IV to read: "Seemingly incompatible accounts of a given work can in principle be defended as separately plausible?" Although Margolis, if he is to be consistent, must reinstate the term "seemingly" in the principle, I shall continue to use the stronger version of the tolerance principle. Incompatible accounts of a given work can in principle be defended as separately plausible. I use the stronger principle since in its weaker version it is hard to see why the principle is philosophically interesting. Moreover, I believe Margolis does in fact use the stronger version of the principle. Not only does he frequently say that incompatible interpretations can in principle be tolerated (and not seemingly incompatible interpretations), he uses the tolerance principle to provide support for two controversial theses, A and B. If interpretations were not incompatible, but only seemingly incompatible, it is difficult to understand why the tolerance of non-incompatible interpretations would have significant consequences. I shall show that even if the model of truth and falsity were applicable to interpretations, and thus talking about incompatible interpretations was not idle, the tolerance principle, version IV, would have no radical consequences.[30]

I believe that the tolerance principle, version IV, is true. But that, as it will turn out, is not to admit much. For it is true and non-controversial. I shall argue:

1. The tolerance principle in this formulation can be accepted by any critic.

2. The tolerance principle in this formulation will not do the work Margolis requires it to do. The tolerance principle IV will not support A, nor will it support B.

Tolerance Principle (IV) is True and Non-Controversial. If Margolis's claim were simply that it is in principle possible to defend as separately plausible incompatible interpretations, then critics need not deny IV. I see no reason why critics could not agree with statements like 4bb.

Beardsley—who introduces what he says might be called "the principle of 'the Intolerability of Incompatibles,' i.e., if two of them are logically incompatible, they cannot both be true,"[31]—could accept IV. Since Beardsley does not "wish to deny that there are cases of ambiguity where *no* interpretation can be established over its rivals,"[32] nor does he "wish to deny that there are many cases where we cannot be sure that we have the correct interpretation,"[33] he could agree that it is in principle possible to defend as separately plausible incompatible accounts of some works.

But does IV commit us to its possibility with regard to all works? In unambiguous texts two incompatible interpretations could gain initial plausibility though one believed, as Beardsley, for example, does, that ultimately one interpretation would have to be given up. One might say that though Beardsley need not deny the truth of IV, he thinks the principle in this form has relatively little relevance to literary practice. If the principle says only that for any given text, we can't rule out *a priori* the possibility of its being able to support contradictory readings, then Beardsley could agree. In practice, he would argue, precious few works actually sustain two such readings.

The tolerance principle, version IV, and statements like 4bb do not provide the central point of contention among philosophers writing about literary criticism. For example, John Hospers notes:

> A frustating and at the same time fascinating aspect of complex works of literature is their resistance to a single interpretation, in that many propositions seem to be implied, some of them contradicting others. . . . Nor need any of the conflicting interpretations be wrong; both of two contradictory propositions may really be suggested by a work of literature, and though of course they cannot both be true, they may both really be implied, . . .[34]

Using our model, Hospers would agree that statements like 4bb can well be true, though he would hold that 4a could not be true. (If I am correct in what I have been claiming, the falsity of 4a insures the falsity of 4b as well.)

We have argued that the tolerance principle, version IV, is not controversial. Margolis believes that this principle supports a far more controversial thesis, the thesis that interpretations of literary works are never simply true or correct but are merely plausible and implausible. Though philosophers like Beardsley might be prepared to acknowledge that contrary readings may gain initial plausibility, Beardsley believes that it is possible to go beyond plausibility in most cases and establish truth or correctness. Once one talks about correctness, contrary readings cannot of course be true. Let us, therefore, turn to Margolis's belief that this tolerance principle has more radical consequences.

Tolerance Principle (IV) will not Support A (A—We do not Individuate Works of Art as we do Physical Objects.) If interpretive critics are only defending separately plausible interpretations (4bb) and are, therefore, not involved in the inconsistency of 4b, then not all art works need be individuated differently from physical objects. Or to be more specific, to allow that incompatible interpretations can in principle be defended as separately plausible, doesn't commit one to believing A, that all works of art are individuated differently from ordinary physical objects. To see why this is so consider the following:

Prior to space flights incompatible characterizations of the moon's condition were accepted as plausible.

5bb. It is plausible that there are lava flows on the moon and it is plausible that there are no lava flows on the moon.

The acceptance of 5bb did not lead scientists to believe that the moon was individuated differently from other physical objects. It is only if they accepted

5. There are lava flows on the moon and there are no lava flows on the moon.

that they would be faced with logical inconsistency if they assumed the moon was an ordinary physical object.

Consider the oak tree and Lear examples. If 3bb were true—one hadn't done any counting yet, but was making rough estimates—this would not lead us to suppose oak trees weren't ordinary physical objects since on 3bb we are not committed to both these characterizations being *jointly* defended as in 3b. Similarly, if 4bb were true—there was textual support for each—why should we suppose that *King Lear* is at best a very queer entity since, when we support analogous claims with regard to other objects, we are not led to suppose them queer.

Let us see what the force of the argument is. We looked at incompatible accounts of both physical objects and works of art. If they were both entities and the model of confirmation were truth, then the joint ascription of such accounts would result in logical inconsistency. To escape logical inconsistency (given that incompatible accounts of art works are in principle to be tolerated) we shifted to talk of plausibility. The critics are only defending their claims as plausible, not true. If we shift to a model of plausibility and say with regard to incompatible interpretations, that they are both plausible (individually plausible) critics will not be logically inconsistent. The shift to plausibility allows critical practice to be rational and tolerant. It is only if they regard their claims as true that they get into difficulty (4a or 4aa). Since 4aa does commit one to 4a, the statement of either involves logical inconsistency.

But we saw that in order to avoid serious confusion we needed to understand that critics only defend their incompatible accounts as separately plausible. If they defended them as jointly plausible, they would still be in unacceptable difficulty (4b is not defensible). But if critics only separately defend as plausible incompatible accounts, then they are not doing anything that the scientist couldn't do. Scientists, as Margolis points out, do defend as plausible incompatible accounts of physical objects (5bb). If critics are only defending 4bb, then it seems hard to see why the acceptance of incompatible interpretations leads one to individuate art works in a way unlike that in which we individuate physical objects.

This is not to deny that we might individuate artworks in different ways, or some artworks in different ways—there might well be evidence of a different sort for such individuation—for example, the existence of the performing arts—but Margolis thought that the fact that critics allow incompatible accounts of an artwork to stand confirmed gave independent support for their different individuation.[35] I have argued that it does not give such independent support.

Tolerance Principle (IV) will not Support B (B—The Model of Confirmation Applicable to Interpretive Accounts of Art Works is not the Model of Confirmation used with regard to Descriptions of Physical Objects). If what I have argued above is correct and literary critics can do what in principle scientists can do—that is, they can defend incompatible accounts as plausible, i.e., separately plausible—then it seems that the model of confirmation applicable to incompatible accounts of artworks is the same model of confirmation as is applicable to incompatible accounts of physical objects, that is, the model of plausibility and implausibility. In science, incompatible accounts can be defended as separately plausible. In literature, interpretations which, if the model of confirmation were truth, would be incompatible, can be defended as separately plausible. What is the difference between what the scientist and critic can in principle do here which warrants the introduction of the model of plausibility and implausibility for *all* interpretations?

The scientist uses plausibility and implausibility for incompatibles when there is difficulty establishing correctness. This does not prevent the use of the model of truth and falsity for descriptions. In the critical realm incompatible interpretations could be defended as separately plausible without any logical difficulty. The tolerance principle IV doesn't show us why critics could not use the model of truth and falsity with regard to compatible interpretations.

Margolis, as we mentioned earlier, does believe that there are other reasons why the model of confirmation applicable to interpretive accounts of artworks cannot be the model of confirmation used with regard to descriptions of physical objects. All I have done here is to indicate why the tolerance principle IV doesn't give us a reason for believing this.

I have sorted out versions of the tolerance principle and done a step by step analysis of the various versions in an attempt to get exactly the version Margolis intended. Given what he tells us about plausibility, the tolerance principle was to be understood as IV. I then claimed that, so understood, the tolerance principle did not do what he thought it did. Is there perhaps a version of the tolerance principle that could do what he wants, that could support A and B? I shall argue that in order to understand one of Margolis's arguments, one has to understand the tolerance principle in some other sense than IV. But if one does that the difficulties are compounded.

What I suspect has happened is that Margolis illegitimately shifts from version IV of the tolerance principle to version II, without realizing what he has done. For example, I believe that in "On Disputes About the Ontological Status of a Work of Art," Margolis does use tolerance principle II rather than IV in an argument designed to support thesis A, that is, to show that we do not individuate any works of art as we do ordinary physical objects.[36] In this paper I have argued that Margolis is entitled only to tolerance principle IV, a principle which allows separate rather than joint defense of incompatible interpretive accounts.

If, for the sake of argument, we allowed that version II (Incompatible accounts of a given work can in principle be jointly defended as plausible) of the tolerance principle *might* be defensible, if, for example, the ontological status of any artwork were unlike that of a physical object and II were not, as we argued previously, thus patently false, Margolis, using II, still would not be able to establish the conclusions that he wants. Tolerance principle II cannot be used to show that we do not individuate works of art as we do physical objects (A). If we try to modify II to avoid conceptual inconsistency, and assume that the artwork is not an ordinary entity, then its use as a premise in an argument to show that we do not individuate works of art as we do physical objects is question begging. Nor can Tolerance Principle II be used to show that a new model of confirmation is needed for interpretive accounts of artworks (B). If the ontological status of an artwork could in some way make it possible to *jointly* ascribe *plausible* and incompatible intepretations without inconsistency, then why couldn't this status make it possible to jointly ascribe *true* and incompatible interpretations without inconsistency? If the artwork were an entity unlike an ordinary physical object, then there is no reason to think that the shift to joint plausibility rather than joint truth would make any difference.

I have allowed for the sake of argument that version II of the tolerance principle might be defensible if the ontological status of any artwork were unlike that of a physical object. But, I contend, if one looks at interpretive criticism, one finds that whatever way artworks are in fact individuated, they are not jointly allowed to be either contrary or inconsistent ways, although they are allowed to be alternative ways given alternative frames of reference. One can in principle rule out the joint defense of incompatible and inconsistent interpretations in the way one can in principle rule out the joint defense of incompatible or inconsistent descriptions. For, unlike the White Queen, one has difficulty believing that one believes the impossible.[37]

Notes

1. Joyce Carol Oates, in a letter to *The New York Times Book Review* (April 22, 1973), pp. 30, 32, expresses both an author's and critic's discontent.

2. Monroe Beardsley, *Aesthetics* (New York, 1958), p. 145; Monroe Beardsley, *The Possibility of Criticism* (Detroit, 1970), p. 26. Hereafter, I shall refer to this text as *TPC*.

3. Joseph Margolis, *The Language of Art and Art Criticism* (Detroit, 1965), pp. 85-94. Hereafter, I shall refer to this text as *TLA*.

4. Joseph Margolis, "Three Problems in Aesthetics," *Art and Philosophy*, ed. by Sidney Hook (New York, 1966); Joseph Margolis, "On Disputes About the Ontological Status of a Work of Art," *The British Journal of Aesthetics* Vol. 8, (1968); Joseph Margolis, "Critics and Literature," *The British Journal of Aesthetics* Vol. 11 No. 4, (Autumn 1971); Joseph Margolis, "Works of Art as Physically Embodied and Culturally Emergent Entities," *The British Journal of Aesthetics* Vol. 14 No. 3, (1974).

5. *TLA*, p. 91.

6. *TLA*, p. 50.

7. *TLA*, p. 76. Cf. also pp. 50, 89, 91-2.

8. *TLA*, p. 93.

9. Ibid.

10. Ibid.

11. Ibid., p. 92.

12. Ibid., p. 94.

13. Ibid., p. 94.

14. Margolis, "Critics and Literature," p. 378.

15. *TLA*, p. 82.

16. Ibid.

17. Ibid.

18. *TLA*, p. 76. "The difference between a critic's interpretation and description centers then, . . . on the virtuoso, performing aspect of the former; on the absence of any object prior to interpretation that may pass as the full work of art, in the sense proper to the performing art; and on our familiar willingness, in the context of appreciation, to attend to alternative and even incompatible interpretations of a work of art, whether of the sort a critic might supply or of the sort a performing artist might supply."

19. *TLA*, p. 50.

20. Pages 206-207 of this text.

21. Margolis, "Works of Art as Physically Embodied and Culturally Emergent Entities," p. 194. Cf. also *TLA*, pp. 76, 89.

22. I have used the word "accounts" to accord with Margolis's usage. However, "accounts" must be understood to refer only to *interpretive accounts* and not to descriptive ones.

23. Stanley Cavell, "The Avoidance of Love," *Must We Mean What We Say?* (New York, 1969), p. 288.

24. Barbara Probst Solomon, "Seduction and Betrayal," *The New York Times Book Review* (May 5, 1974), p. 4.

25. Margolis, "On Disputes About the Ontological Status of a Work of Art," p. 153.

26. *TLA*, p. 93.

27. I use the term "statement." I wish to avoid discussing here the issues involved in deciding whether the logical relation is a relation between propositions or sentences rather than statements.

28. *TLA*, p. 93.

29. Ibid.

30. In the tolerance principle, as I use it, the assumption is that if the model were truth, and truth is an appropriate model, then the principle, in its only true version, is uninteresting. If we leave it open whether truth is an appropriate

model, or if we reinterpret the principle in terms of conceptually inconsistent accounts, the arguments I advance in this paper would go through.

31. *TPC*, pp. 44. Beardsley's principle is true by definition.

32. Ibid.

33. Ibid.

34. John Hospers, "Implied Truths in Literature," *Philosophy Looks at the Arts*, ed. by Joseph Margolis (New York, 1962), p. 212.

35. In the quotation, pages 206–207 of this text, he says that artworks are individuated differently from physical objects is clear "also from the fact. . . ."

36. Margolis, "On Disputes . . . ," pp. 153-4. If what has been said about the interpretation of a work of art holds—that, in principle, incompatible interpretations may be defended critically and that often, because of the puzzling nature of particular works, we cannot characterize a work of art as such without reference to some defensible interpretation by means of which its structure as a work of art may be exhibited—then the properties or features that interpretations impute or ascribe to works of art cannot, for logical reasons, be construed as the native, *describable* properties or features of such works. And if they cannot and if nevertheless we are characterizing (and often must thus characterize) particular works of art by so speaking, we cannot speak of such works as *entities* in any way that bears a close resemblance to the way in which we speak of physical entities and the like.

If I understand Margolis, the argument in the above passage would go roughly like the following:

1. In principle, incompatible intrepretations of artworks may be defended critically.
2. Artworks must often be interpreted before one can give an adequate account of their properties. (What properties the artwork is said to have is thus dependent upon an interpretation, that is, those properties over and above the minimally describable ones.)
3. The properties that are ascribed to the artwork under incompatible interpretations cannot (logically) be native, describable properties.
4. Physical objects have only native describable properties.
5. Therefore, artworks are unlike physical objects.

Although premise 4 is not stated in the passage quoted, I take it that 4 explains (part of) what entityhood as a physical object implies, and would account for the fact that incompatible descriptions of physical objects may not in principle be defended crtically, a principle he often explicitly states. That Margolis means something like this is supported by claims that he makes in a recent paper, "Works of Art as Physically Embodied . . . Entities," esp. pp. 189, 194.

To see that 1 in the argument must be interpreted as a defense of joint plausibility (the tolerance principle understood as II) suppose that 1 is not so taken. Suppose we understand 1 to mean "defended as separately but not jointly plausible" (tolerance principle IV). Leaving all the other premises the same we could construct an argument, analogous to this changed argument, using as subject a physical object.

In order to give an adequate account of a planet which we have no direct access to, we have to hypothesize about its nature. Incompatible hypotheses may be offered, in principle, can be offered and critically defended as separately plausible. The properties that are ascribed to the planet under incompatible hypotheses cannot be the native describable properties of the planet. Premise 4 remains the same. Therefore, a planet is unlike a physical object. Clearly this won't do.

If 1 in the original argument is taken to mean that incompatible interpretations can in principle be defended as jointly plausible (tolerance principle II) then we cannot construct an analogous argument to the original using as subject a physical object.

37. I wish to thank Gerald Barnes and Alan Tormey for their helpful comments on an earlier version of this paper.

ALAN TORMEY

The Concept of Expression

I. Behavior and Expression

WE EXPRESS, both in our speech and our nonlinguistic behavior, a prodigious variety of things, from beliefs and attitudes to moods, intentions, and emotions, from hope, hostility, and anger to pity, doubt, and elation. It is clear, however, that neither behavior nor language is expressive of everything that could be said to be a state of a person. We do not, for example, express our blood count, our temperature, our weight, or our age. Our first task then will be to distinguish those states of a person that are expressed, or expressible in language and behavior from those that are not, and to isolate if possible some condition or criterion for marking that distinction.

It is tempting to think that a criterion may already be available; and a glance at the random list above might suggest that whatever—and only whatever—shall count as a "psychological" or "mental" state of a person may be expressed in his behavior. But it may be plausibly objected that sensations and perceptions are more properly regarded as psychological or mental than as merely physical states of a person, and that it is not clear that we *express*, in any way, either our sensations or our perceptions. If this is the case then, the rough-hewn distinction between the mental and the physical will fail to provide an adequate criterion for marking the difference between expressible and nonexpressible states of a person. But this also suggests that a study of the differences between sensation (or perception) and such expressible states of a person as his attitudes and emotions may reveal the criterion we are seeking.

Let us explore then the possibility of locating some condition common to the occurrences of expression that will explain the exclusion of sensation from the list of states which are normally expressed in our behavior. . . .

Beliefs, attitudes, and emotions have objects, while sensations do not. We can describe this difference by noting that sensations, unlike beliefs, attitudes and emotions have no *intentional objects*. . . . I propose to define an intentional object as whatever is designated by the *prepositional* object of a particular mental act, state, or attitude. (More precisely, an intentional object is whatever is designated by a prepositional object occurring in a sentence used to ascribe some such state to a person. The ellipsis, once this is understood, should cause no confusion.)

If I am fascinated *by* centaurs, apprehensive *over* money, angry *with* the cook, or afraid *of* the dark, then centaurs, money, the cook, and the dark are the intentional objects of these states. Two points should be noted about the status of an intentional object as the concept will be employed here. First, there may or may not be anything in the world to which an intentional object corresponds. If I am greatly interested in the Hippogriff, it does not follow that there is or that there is not some creature that answers to the description of the Hippogriff, though it remains true to say that the Hippogriff is the (intentional) object of my interest. More generally, the truth of an intentional ascription such as '*A* is interested in witches' does not entail the truth of another statement asserting the existence of witches, as the truth of the nonintentional statement '*A* is walking in the garden' requires that there *be* a garden for *A* to walk in.[1] And, secondly, the description of an intentional object is a function of what the person himself *takes* to be the attributes of whatever he admires, wishes, fears, or is angry with. If I am angered by your insolence and deceit, it does not follow that you have in fact been insolent and deceitful, but only that I believe that you have and that I have taken or mistaken your actions in that light. . . .

And at this point we may introduce an ancillary definition. To say of a person that *he* is in an *intentional state* is to say that some sentence radical of this logical type may be truly predicated of him. Thus, if 'is hoping for salvation' is true of Gemma, then Gemma is in a particular intentional state.

These definitions are intended to ensure a measure of epistemological neutrality among competing analyses of mental or psychological states; and it is just such difficulties that I want to obviate at the outset since they are not immediately relevant to the analysis of expression.

At the very least then, there appears to be some point in speaking of beliefs, attitudes, and emotions as having intentional objects and no point whatever in speaking of the objects of sensations. Admiration for Bartok, approval of socialism, affection for owls, and interest in archaeology are intentional states that are, truly or falsely, predicated of persons. But sensations are not about, for, or toward anything, and consequently, they are not intentional.

This may escape attention since sensations are *of* something and 'of' is a preposition. We speak of a sensation of dizziness just as we would speak of a feeling of anger or an attitude of hostility. But the 'of' is systematically ambiguous. Anger is not the object of my feeling, nor is hostility the object of my attitude, and dizziness is not the object of my sensation.

In each case we could omit the preposition and rephrase the expression. We could have spoken with equal propriety of a dizzy sensation, an angry feeling, and a hostile attitude. But while hostile attitudes and angry feelings are directed toward 'objects' from which they are logically distinguishable, a sensation cannot be directed at anything. In the case of dizziness the sensation is not logically separable from the dizziness; it is a sensation-of-dizziness. A sensation has its logical terminus in the mere awareness of its presence, in simply being had. Compare, e.g., (1) "sensation of heat" with (2) "fear of darkness." The "of" is transitive in (2), but not in (1). Heat is not the object of the sensation as darkness is the object of fear.[2]

We are now in a position to explain why sensations are nonintentional in spite of the occurrence of the preposition in such expressions as "sensation of cold" or "sensation of dizziness." "Sensation" functions, logically, at the same level as "emotion" or "attitude" and not at the level of, say, "fear" or "hostility." Thus, "sensation of cold," "emotion (or feeling) of fear," and "attitude of hostility" are logically similar constructions. The "of" is intransitive in all three, and there are no intentional objects in these expressions. However, it would be possible to go on, in the latter two instances, to ask "fear *of* what?" and "hostility *toward* what?" Here the prepositions are transitive, and an answer to these questions will denote the intentional objects of the fear and the hostility. In contrast, we cannot go on to ask in the first case "cold of what?" or "dizziness of what?"

The locution "sensation of . . ." is used to specify the *kind* of sensation that is meant, just as to talk of a feeling of anger is to say what sort of feeling it is, and not to name an object of the feeling. It is the *particular* feeling or attitude that has an object, and it is just here, with respect to particular sensations, that we cannot pursue the parallel question. Here there is no possibility for the occurrence of a transitive preposition and thus no possibility that sensations have intentional objects. . . .

Finally, we can distinguish between the causes and the objects of such states as hatred, fear, and faith.[3] The child believes *in* Santa Claus *because* her father has assured her he exists. Sensations have causes, but no objects. . . .

The tentative conclusion that may be extracted from the foregoing discussion is that intentionality is characteristic of those states of a person that are expressible and absent from those that are not. . . .

I have argued that intentionality is at least a necessary condition for expression. It remains now to explore some of the consequences of this position.

The concept of expression is associated in a primitive way with the image of "pressing out."[4] There is something "inside" which is ex-pressed, forced out, and which in turn reveals what remains inside. But human expression is revealing in a dual sense. If we hear an outburst of nervous laughter *as* an expression of embarrassment we are aware both that something is occurring "inside" the person, and that there is some event or situation, real or imagined, by which he is embarrassed. Thus an expression points simultaneously in two directions, back toward the person and outward toward the object.[5] It is a characteristic of the concept of expression to make implicit allusion to both these features of a total situation; and for this reason it is logically incomplete to speak, for example, of the "expression of fear," or the "expression of desire." Until the object of the fear or the desire is disclosed, the description is either vacuous or chronically vague. Expression of the fear of spiders may have little in common with expression of the fear of Communism; and expression of a desire for recognition little in common with expression of a desire for oblivion.

Consequently it would be misleading to analyse expression as a simple two-term relation, implying that X expresses Y if X is, say, some pattern of behavior and Y some mental state or process characteristically manifested in behavior of the type of which X is a member. This suggests that the analysis is complete when it has shown how the expressive behavior reveals or refers back to the condition of the person himself. And this is equivalent to assuming, a priori, that all expressions of fear (or desire or belief) *must* have something in common and that we are sufficiently enlightened when we know that something is an expression of fear *simpliciter*. Knowing the object of the fear would then be an interesting, though inessential addition to our knowledge. But this would be to rest content with a logically incomplete description. We cannot make sense of the notion of an expression unless we are willing to fuse this reflexive revelation with the indication of intentional objects in our analysis of the meaning of expressive behavior. An adequate analysis of the logic of "expression" then must include a reference to the intentional character of the expressed condition. . . .

II. Inference and Expression

Having established a criterion for determining which states of a person are expressible in behavior, we may now consider the logical relations that link behavioral expressions and those states of a person that are said to be expressed. Before undertaking a discussion of these relations, however, we must note an important distinction marked by a difference in syntactic form.

Consider the following sentences:

S_1 A sad expression is a mark of the thoroughbred beagle.

S_2 An expression of sadness crossed her face as she watched him close the gate.

"Sad expression" does not mean "expression of sadness"; but this is easily overlooked wherever they can be interchanged without apparent loss or alteration of meaning as in S_2 above. The difference is more evident if we attempt the substitution in sentences whose subjects denote insensate objects. Noh masks and cypress trees may *have* sad expressions, but their expressions are not expressions *of* sadness. Sad expressions are to the expression of sadness as anger-like behavior is to the expression of anger. Anger-like behavior may occur in the absence of anger, but an expression of anger cannot (*logically* cannot); and analogously, sad expressions may occur without sadness (the beagle and the Noh mask), while the expression of sadness cannot.

Moreover, the syntactic arrangement cannot in many cases be shuffled at all. There are sneering expressions, but there are no expressions of sneer. A sneering expression may well *be* expressive of something—contempt or disdain perhaps—but we cannot discover what it expresses by a simple syntactic maneuver, translating "ϕ expression" into "expression of ϕ"; and even where there are symmetrical syntactic possibilities—that is, where "ϕ expression" and "expression of ϕ" are both available—a particular occurrence of a ϕ expression need not be an expression *of* ϕ. We shall see on reflection that constructions which exemplify these two syntactic forms are logically independent.

The outlines of this distinction can be sketched briefly. Wherever the qualifier appears before the noun ("ϕ expression") the phrase (*A*) is a *description* of certain observable features of a situation; and whenever the form "expression of ϕ" (*B*) occurs, it may commonly be taken to be an inference warranting expression, relating some intentional state of a person to particular aspects of his observable behavior. Since the larger part of this study is concerned with an analysis of expressions which exemplify syntactic form *B*, the possibility of confusion or inconsistency can be lessened if this distinction is kept in mind. An analysis of syntactic form *A* presents no problems apart from those of any systematic study of descriptive discourse, and that is not the present objective.

Still, there is one point that remains unsettled. There must be some connection, it would seem, between sad expressions and the expression of sadness, even if sneering expressions are not so related to expressions of sneer(ness). It cannot be mere coincidence that some objectively discernible features of the world also happen to be connected with the expression of certain states of mind and character. This much may be admitted, but I would argue that the connection is genetic and not logical.[6] Innumerable expressions of human sadness have deposited a calcified and conventional image of sadness—the human figure, heavy, bent, and slow, with slackened mouth and downcast eyes. And around this conventional image the descriptive content of "sad expression" has crystallized.

Without such conventions no consistent descriptive meaning could be attached to any instance of a ϕ expression, and the existence of accessible conventions of this sort explains, in part, our ability to "project" sadness, anger, and despair into the nonhuman world. But we must be careful to notice the dissociation of the two syntactic forms at just this point. The convention enables us to describe a set of features as a "ϕ expression" *without implication*. A malformed face may bear an unmistakably cruel expression; but, having perceived this, nothing further can be inferred about its owner's inclination to cruelty. By contrast, to speak of an expression *of* cruelty in a face *is* to license such implications.

Conventional expectations are not as binding for instances of B as they are for instances of A, and we may evolve novel or even bizarre ways of expressing some of our intentional states. (One need only recall some of the classical examples of aberrant behavior in psychoanalytic literature.) The very possibility of novel expressions depends on the absence of restrictive conventions, or, more commonly, on the open-textured character of existing conventions. Such possibilities are not open equally to instances of A. The descriptive content of "sad expression" must remain relatively fixed within a given linguistic and cultural setting, or risk distortion which would deprive it of any useful function.

Because of these asymmetries there is no logically binding link between A and B such that one is inferrible from the other. Membership in A neither entails nor rules out membership in B; they are logically independent. If it is an error to believe that the presence of a sad expression invariably betrays an expression of sadness, then it is equally erroneous to think that an expession of sadness will invariably present us with something describable as a sad expression. Sad expressions do not entail, nor are they entailed by expressions of sadness, though they are related in other ways; and there are numerous instances of both A and B which cannot be transformed into meaningful or parallel instances of the other (e.g., sneering expressions and expressions of intention). . . . Accordingly, the logic of expression (B) may be outlined schematically as follows:

If A's behavior B is an *expression of* X, then there is a warrantable inference from B to an intentional state of A, such that it would be true to say that A has (or is in state) S; and where S and X are identical . . .

Behavior, as Carnap has observed,[7] is expressive if it discloses something about the *person* exhibiting the behavior. A mincing walk, a timorous voice, a seductive gesture are expressive when they reveal something of the person himself, and the conclusions of the previous chapter suggest that what is revealed in expressive behavior are intentional states of the person.[8] . . .

We may now go on to explore the relation between expressive behavior and those intentional states of a person that are revealed, displayed, or, in some way shown forth in his behavior; and I shall argue that there is no descriptively distinct class of performances or bodily movements that constitutes expressive behavior. The concept of an expression implies the warranting of certain inferential structures, and it cannot be located by scrutiny of the descriptions of behavior alone, unless those descriptions include among their truth conditions the relevant inferential moves. Explosive laughter, a facial grimace, a shudder, or a periodic tic are, in themselves, neither expressive nor nonexpressive, and only if we have reason to connect the behavior inferentially with some desire, belief, intent, or conflict are we entitled to treat it as an expression. . . .

Consider, for example, the following descriptions of a person at a particular time, t-1:

D_1 A has a red face.
D_2 A's face is flushed.
D_3 A is blushing.

To describe A as having a red face does not necessarily imply a relation between the color of his face and a correlated psychological state. There are people who have naturally ruddy complexions, and there is nothing in D_1 which suggests that A is not such a case. D_2, on the other hand, would seem to imply that at least a change in A's complexion has occurred, but it is still neutral as to its cause. D_3, however, would be out of place if we were not willing to admit a connection between the color of A's face and some psychological state such as embarrassment or shame.

There are descriptions then which can be used correctly only where a relation between observed appearance and a psychological state of the person is thought to exist. To use D_3 rather than D_1 or D_2 is to imply that the appearance of a red face can be linked inferentially to some psychological state and thus may constitute an expression of that state.

The truth conditions for saying that A is blushing are logically related to the truth conditions for saying that A's appearance is an expression of his embarrassment or shame. Consider how such a description might be falsified. If we were to discover that A had been eating hot peppers or drinking heavily, for example, we might be led to retract D_3 and replace it with a more neutral description such as D_1 or D_2. Descriptions such as D_3 carry with them *intentional implications*, i.e., they provide conceptual linkages between observable features of the world and intentional states of persons.

The suggestion that there are conceptual as well as causal linkages to be considered here leads us to the next, and more significant point. There is a (now familiar) argument in philosophy that psychological predicates occupy a crucial and pivotal position in our language. They range, according to this view,[9] over both public and private domains, and they refer not to the covert mental life alone but to a complex of inner agitation and outer show. "Anger," "jealousy," and "depression" acquire their meanings from a coalescence of the public and the private. Thus jealous behavior is not merely *evidence* for the presence of jealousy but, in an important sense, a constituent part of the complex referent of the predicate "jealous" . . . [10]

This position is by now well entrenched and widely accepted. It is reviewed here, without further defense, to bring out the implications for our analysis of expression. Behavior that is expressive of jealousy (or anger or depression) is a *constituent part* of that state on this view, and consequently, I would argue, the inference which proceeds from the behavior to the expressed state is not a causal inference but one which moves from a part of a conceptual complex to another part, or to the whole of it. We are close here to the grammarian's category of *synecdoche*. A mast is not merely evidence of the presence of an approaching ship; it is a part of the ship. It "stands for" the ship as part to whole, not as effect to cause or sign to significandum. And so with expressive behavior. Jealous behavior is not *merely* evidence of the presence of jealousy; it is a part of the complex pattern which comprises the full significance of "jealousy." There may be jealousy without jealous behavior, of course, just as there may be ships without masts, but this does not mean that the behavior, when present, is not a proper and logical constituent of the jealousy, any more than it means that masts, when present, are not proper parts of the ship. . . .

It might be argued that the propriety of inference is challenged if behavior alone can justify the ascription of such predicates as "jealous" or "depressed," since there should then be no room for an inference from the behavior to something else. But even assuming we are entitled to *predicate* "jealous" on the basis of overt behavior alone, we invariably *intend* more than a summary description of the observable behavior in making such predications. We intend to attribute to the person, in addition to his behavior, some associated set of attitudes, tendencies, beliefs, feelings, or motives, conscious or otherwise. (We need to be reminded here that the meaning of a term and the criteria for its application need not be identical.). . . .

When we speak of the "expression of jealousy" then, we imply the validity of an inferential move from one segment of the conceptual matrix which comprises the meaning of "jealousy" to another segment of that matrix, or to the whole of it. . . .

To speak of an expression then, is not to refer to a special class of observably discriminable movements, but to imply that some particular inferential pattern is warranted. . . .

V. Art and Expression: A Proposal

Philosophical concern with the expressive dimension of art has taken many directions, and it would serve no clear purpose to attempt to survey or assess them all, even if that were an attainable goal. Rather, the aim of the present chapter is limited to an extension of some of my earlier arguments and conclusions to the structuring of a proposal for comprehending and describing the expressive character of art works.

It is transparently evident that it would make no sense to assert that a work of art literally *had*, e.g., the property anguish or longing or sadness— that it *was* anguished or sad (or else, as E. F. Carritt once remarked, we should have to cheer the poor thing up); and yet it is common enough to claim that an art work is *expressive of* anguish or longing or sadness. And we have seen in the preceding chapter that there are good reasons for taking "is expressive of————," not as a relational predicate linking an art work to something external to it, but as an incomplete one-place predicate which, properly completed, is descriptive of some feature of the art work. It will be convenient to refer to the properties denoted by predicates of this sort as *expressive properties*. Thus, a work expressive of anguish will be said to have the *expressive* property anguish rather than simply the property anguish, the modification serving both to indicate affinities with instances where 'anguish' has unqualified application and to obviate absurdities engendered by taking art to exhibit full-blooded sentient states. The question then becomes one of establishing the connection between a property γ and the expressive property γ and explaining the apparent fact that expressive properties are not merely garden variety properties belonging to special classes of objects.

The analysis developed in earlier parts of this study suggests the following proposal: expressive properties are those properties of art works (or natural objects) whose names also designate intentional states of persons. Thus "tenderness," "sadness," "anguish," and "nostalgia" may denote expressive properties of art works because they also denote states of persons that are intentional, and thus expressible in the fullest and clearest sense. This proposal imposes limitations on what shall be counted as an expressive property, and to that extent is to be regarded as a stipulation. But it is a stipulation that I believe can be defended and shown to have important advantages over alternative ways of understanding the expressive dimension of art.

Restricting our attention to art works then, an expressive property γ will be understood to be any property of an art work denoted by a predicate which also denotes intentional states of persons. Nonexpressive properties will constitute a complementary class defined merely by exclusion. . . .

The relation between the expressive and the nonexpressive properties of an art work is obviously an intimate one. Ravel's *Pavane pour une infante défunte* is often characterized as tender or nostalgic, and these expressive properties are dependent, in some way, upon such nonexpressive properties of the piece as the contour of the melodic line, the quasi-modal harmonic structure, the moderate tempo, and the limited dynamic range.

Similarly, the animated opening bars of "Parade" from Benjamin Britten's *Les Illuminations*, though not expressive *of* animation, can be heard as expressive of apprehension, and apprehension would be an expressive property of the piece.

It is this relation between expressive and nonexpressive properties that I intend to explore, and in virtue of which I shall suggest that art works can be thought of as autonomously self-expressive objects, viz., that the complex of relations among the properties of an art work is such that it can be seen as presenting some of its properties and revealing others; those properties which are its expressive properties themselves being revealed through the presentation of varying sets of nonexpressive properties.[11]

All this of course demands both clarification and defense; and we have first to justify the retention of an expression vocabulary to characterize the relation. The choice results in part from the elimination of alternatives. The relation between expressive and nonexpressive properties is more intimate than would be implied by reference to necessary conditions, critical warrants, or rule-governed regularities, all of which leave open the possibility that the relata are logically independent. But more positive reasons can be derived from arguments presented earlier for taking the behavioral and linguistic expressions of a person to be *partially constitutive* of his intentional states. It was argued there that certain observable aspects of behavior are logically proper parts of the complex referents of such predicates as "anger," "jealousy," "joy," and "fear," and thus partially constitutive of the intentional states denoted by predicates of this sort. And since we have already stipulated that expressive properties of art works are the aesthetic correlates of intentional states of persons, it follows that the relation between nonexpressive and expressive properties of art works is analogous to the relation between human (or animal) behavior and the intentional states of which the behavior is partially constitutive.

The aesthetic situation is analogous, however, with the important difference that the nonexpressive properties of an art work are *wholly* constitutive of its expressive properties, there being no "inner" aspects of art comparable to the ostensibly private states of persons. And since there is nothing "hidden" from us in an art work, there is no room for the construction of inferences from some of its properties to others. . . . To recall an example, the tempo, dynamics, harmonic texture, melodic contour of Ravel's *Pavane* are not merely the grounds, warrants or criteria for asserting that the work is tender, they are the *constituents* of its tenderness. This relation of constituency is the aesthetic analogue of the expression of full-blooded intentional states of persons, and furnishes, I believe, at least provisional justification for describing art works as self-expressive objects ("*self*-expressive" to prevent relapse into the language of the Expression theory with the attendant implications that what is expressed belongs to something, or someone, other than the work itself).

The tenderness of the *Pavane* and the apprehensiveness of "Parade" are properties of the works themselves expressed in, or through, the differing complexes of tempo, texture, and structure.

A serious difficulty may appear to arise here, for if a given set [c] of nonexpressive properties is wholly constitutive of an expressive property γ it might appear that [c] is equivalent to a set of necessary and sufficient conditions for γ. And it would follow from this that we should need only to establish the presence of [c] in a particular work to conclude that it was necessarily expressive of γ, since [c] would entail γ. . . .

However, it would be a mistake to assume that the present argument implies an equivalence of [c] with a set of necessary and sufficient conditions for γ. For such an equivalence to hold, [c] must be unambiguously correlated with γ. But the relation between sets of nonexpressive properties and the expressive properties of art works is such that a given set of nonexpressive properties may be compatible with, and constitutive of, any one of a *range* of expressive properties, just as a given set of gestures or movements may be compatible with (and partially constitutive of) more than one intentional state of a person. That is, [c] will not be uniquely constitutive of γ; and thus, while the nonexpressive properties of an art work are wholly constitutive of its expressive properties they are *ambiguously* constitutive. And this ambiguity is the source of our inability to determine decisively whether, for example, the Ravel *Pavane* is more truly expressive of tenderness or of yearning or of nostalgia, since all of these may fall within the compatibility range of the work's nonexpressive properties. Moreover, the ambiguity is symmetrical. Not only will [c] be compatible with more than one expressive property, but more than one work may be justifiably described as tender without it following that they possess identical sets of nonexpressive properties. In consequence, the relation is not one of necessary and sufficient conditions nor of sufficient conditions alone, and no encouragement is lent to the fear (or the hope) that rule books and check lists will replace the exercise of "taste" and herald the triumph of the philistine. . . .

I have argued that the relation between the nonexpressive and the expressive properties of an art work is one of ambiguous constituency. There are good reasons, moreover, for believing that the resultant expressive ambiguity is essentially uneliminable and that, consequently, critical disagreements of at least one sort are, of necessity, irresoluble.

There are no uniquely decisive procedures for adjudicating between critical judgments that a work *W* displaying the set [c] of nonexpressive properties is expressive of γ rather than δ, or δ rather than θ, so long as the relevant grounds for such claims are recognized to lie in the work itself, and as long as [c] remains compatible with a range of expressive properties which includes γ, δ, and θ.[12]

Moreover we cannot confirm, or disconfirm, claims about the expressive properties of art works in the same way we frequently confirm claims that a *person* is expressing a particular intentional state. There is no access to independent evidence comparable to a person's avowals of his feelings or his subsequent behavior. Paintings, unlike people, remain silent in the face of our persistent misjudgments of them; and the possibility of disagreement over the expressive properties of art works remains essentially and necessarily open.

It may be suggested that there are, after all, means available to us for eliminating or accommodating critical disputes resting on the expressive ambiguity of art works. We may be tempted, for example, to resolve the issue by conceding that a work has *all* the expressive properties falling within the relevant compatibility range. But this is an excessively generous concession, and it is open to the objection that *some* of the expressive properties falling within a particular compatibility range may be psychologically or aesthetically incongruent. It might be extremely difficult to say, for instance, of a particular drawing by Käthe Kollwitz whether it was expressive of despair, anxiety, resignation, or fear. But to attempt to resolve the difficulty by attributing to the work a conjunction of such properties, or predicating of it some complex property (despair-anxiety-resignation-fear) would not only be to abandon all efforts at critical discrimination, it would do violence to our common understanding of these qualities. The converse alternative would be to assign members of the compatibility range of expressive properties disjunctively to the work. This, however, while logically inoffensive, is also aesthetically pointless. One must make critical choices *within* the range of available predicates, and it could hardly be thought aesthetically enlightening to be told that the Kollwitz drawing was actually expressive of (despair or anxiety or resignation or fear). Expressive ambiguity can neither be eliminated nor accommodated by such critical strategy, and resort to either conjunctive or disjunctive descriptions of the expressive properties of art works is an evasion and not a resolution of the critical problem.

There is a further and perhaps more decisive reason for believing the expressive ambiguity of many art works to be essentially uneliminable. The expressive "gestures" of art often occur in an aesthetic space devoid of explicit context and intentional objects. And it is the absence or the elusiveness of intentional objects that impedes our critical attempts to dissolve the ambiguity and disclose an unequivocal expressive quality in the art work. It may be true that we cannot tell from a smile, isolated from its context, whether it is a smile of parental benevolence directed toward a sleeping child or a smile of sadistic satisfaction directed toward a suffering victim.[13] But these are uncertainties that could theoretically be resolved by uncovering the intentional context. In contrast, many art works are intentionally incomplete. There are no further contexts to be uncovered and no intentional objects to be disclosed. We are free of course to invent contexts, to wrap the art work in fictions that would yield intentional objects. But is one invention more accurate, one fiction closer to the truth than another? Is there any question of *justifying* our inventions? The resolution of expressive ambiguity would require that there were.

It is not a contingent failing of art or ourselves that we frequently cannot discover what the expressive gestures of a work are *about* (toward, for, against, etc.); it is a common and aesthetically relevant condition of much of our art. . . . There are innumerable works of art of which it would be pointless even to raise the question of intentional contexts or intentional objects—of Miro's *Painting, 1933* or the trio sonata from *The Musical Offering*, for example, and this should strengthen the suspicion that whatever expressive ambiguity such works display is not an aesthetic flaw but an inherent condition.

Now, in contrast with Baroque trio sonatas, abstract dance forms, and much contemporary visual art, many art works commonly classed as representational present us with intentional contexts (contexts in which intentional objects can be identified) as integral parts of their content. Most theatrical works exemplify this. In Euripides we are shown not only the tears of Medea; we are shown what the tears are about. In this respect Greek tragedy and Baroque instrumental music are worlds apart. The world of the drama encompasses intentional objects while the world of the trio sonata precludes them.

To the extent that intentional contexts are available then it might appear that expressive ambiguity can be circumscribed or decisively removed. But the appearance is chimerical. In works of representational art we can, and should, distinguish between the expressive properties *of* the work and contained or represented expressions *in* the work. Among the things a representational art work may represent are acts of expression, and failure to distinguish between represented acts of expression and expressive properties of the work itself will generate crucial confusions. It has been said, for example, of Bernini's *David* that it expresses a concentrated and intense determination. But this is misleading. The *work* does not express this, David does. The Bernini work *represents* David-expressing-intense-determination. And it does not follow from this that intense determination is an expressive property of the work itself. It does not follow that it is *not* an expressive property of the work either. Identical predicates *may* apply to work and represented content alike, but each predication is independent of the other, and false hopes for regenerating a corollary of classical expression theories may arise here if there is failure to notice the ellipsis when one goes on (incorrectly) to describe the work itself as expressing David's determination. . . .

In general, it is only the contained or represented expression whose ambiguity is dissolved by the availability of intentional contexts in the art work. We may, given the circumstances of the action of a drama, be justifiably certain that the cries of the protagonist are an expression of remorse, but this leaves unanswered the question of the expressive properties of the *play*. The drama itself may project pity, horror, or contempt toward the remorse of the protagonist. That is, it may have as one of *its* expressive properties pity, horror, or contempt, and thereby comment expressively on the represented acts of expression. Acts of expression cannot themselves be expressed in art, but they can be depicted, described, reflected upon, or judged, and all these possibilities lie within the province of one or several of the representational arts. The distinction we have been considering should in fact explain the capacity of representational arts, generally, to make expressive comments on their represented content. While the availability of intentional contexts may help to obviate ambiguity in the represented expressions then, it may do little or nothing to alleviate critical discord resting on the expressive ambiguity of an art work itself, even where the work is incontestably representational and contains intentional contexts as an integral part of its content.

Expressive ambiguity is an inherent feature of most if not all of our art. And it is a continuing dilemma of critical practice that we are faced with the necessity of making and defending choices from a range of available alternatives for describing the expressive character of particular art works—choices that must be made in the absence of any clearly decisive means for eliminating alternative and competing descriptions. This dilemma is, I believe, inescapable since it rests on the aesthetic need for making *some* critical choices conjoined with the impossibility of establishing the necessity for making just those choices that we do make. And it is this that makes the exercise of critical judgment so intriguing to those whose tolerance for indeterminacy is high and so frustrating to those for whom the quest for certainty is always paramount. . . .

Notes

1. See Chisholm, *Perceiving*, Ch. 11, for a further defense of this distinction.

2. For convenience, I shall use the terms "transitive" and "intransitive" to mark this distinction. Transitive and intransitive occurrences of "of" correspond closely to the grammatical distinction between subjective and objective genitive case functions. See, for example, Barbara M. H. Strang, *Modern English Structure* (London: Edward Arnold, 1962), Ch. VI.

3. Cf. Wittgenstein's remark: "We should distinguish between the object of fear and the cause of fear. . . . Thus a face which inspires fear or delight (the object of fear or delight), is not on that account its cause, . . .". [*Philosophical Investigations*, tr. G.E.M. Anscombe (New York: Macmillan, 1953), p. 135ᵉ].

4. The OED gives the following etymology for the verb "express": ". . . f. L. *ex*-out + *pressāre* to press. Taken as Eng. repr. of L. *exprimĕre* of which the chief senses were I. to press out. . . ." See also, definition 11, 7: "To manifest or reveal by external tokens. Of actions, appearances, etc.: Now almost exclusively with reference to feelings or personal qualities, the wider use being arch. or poet."

5. The object of course need not be immediately or observably present. But an expression implies the existence of some such object. I cannot be embarrassed

and not be embarrassed *by* something, real or imagined, present or absent, occurrent or past.

6. The relation discussed here is not that between *sadness* and the expression of sadness but the relation between sad expressions and the expression of sadness. The former *is* a logical relation, in the sense that it is noncontingent.

7. Rudolph Carnap, *Philosophy and Logical Syntax* (London: Kegan Paul, Trench, Trubner, 1935).

8. Here, and throughout this chapter, "expressive behavior" is to be understood to imply that the behavior is *an expression (B)* of something.

9. Differing versions of the position which I shall schematically outline above may be found in Kenny, *Action, Emotion and Will;* P. F. Strawson, *Individuals* Ch. III (New York: Doubleday, 1963); Austin, "Other Minds."

10. Cf. Strawson's remark that "*X*'s depression *is* something, one and the same thing, which is felt, but not observed, by *X*, and observed, but not felt, by others than *X*" (*Individuals*, p. 105) and Austin's observation that "It seems fair to say that 'being angry' is in many respects like 'having mumps.' It is a description of a whole pattern of events, including occasion, symptoms, feeling and manifestation, and possibly other factors besides. . . . Moreover, it is our confidence in the general pattern that makes us apt to say we 'know' another man is angry when we have only observed parts of the pattern: for the parts of the pattern are related to each other very much more intimately than, for example, newspaper men scurrying in Brighton are related to a fire in Fleet Street" (Austin, "Other Minds," pp. 77-78).

11. Guy Sircello, in an interesting article, "Perceptual Acts and Pictorial Art: A Defense of Expression Theory," *Journal of Philosophy,* LXII (1965), 669-77, reaches what seems to me a view similar to this, though it is stated and developed quite differently. There are limitations to Sircello's position, however, that I should not like to accept. Aside from the difficulty of conceiving of expressiveness as arising from "virtual acts of perception" which occur in the art work but which are admittedly performed by no one, acts of perception—virtual or otherwise—are not among the things that can sensibly be said to be *expressed.* Also, Sircello's claims are supported entirely by reference to representational art works, and it is doubtful whether the argument, even if sound, could be extrapolated to account for the expressiveness of nonrepresentational art works. Apparently, also, on Sircello's view an art work may express such things as truthfulness and frankness, though no justification is given for regarding these as specifically *expressive* (or expressible) properties. On my view, of course, they are not expressive properties since "truthfulness" and "frankness" do not denote intentional states of persons.

12. The membership of particular compatibility ranges is flexible and subject to continuous revision, as we can note from the commonplaces of art history and art criticism. We now "see" Bambara antelope figures in ways in which no one would have seen them before Cézanne and Modigliani, and we "hear" the Mahler symphonies quite differently after exposure to Schoenberg and Stockhausen. The actual membership of particular compatibility ranges must of course be determined by aesthetic or critical judgment and not by philosophical theory.

13. Cf. Wittgenstein, *Philosophical Investigations,* paragraph 539, p. 145^e.

GUY SIRCELLO

Expressive Properties of Art

ROMANTIC IDEAS ABOUT MIND and its relation to art did not receive their clearest expression until the twentieth century. Then philosophers like Croce, Collingwood, Cassirer, Dewey, and Langer tried to spell out exactly how it is that art can be expressive. But to many other twentieth-century philosophers, especially to those working in the various "analytical" styles whose intellectual ancestry was anything but Romantic, those philosophical discussions of expression in art were puzzling. This puzzlement can best be seen in the work of Monroe Beardsley and O. K. Bouwsma, philosophers who represent two distinct strains in recent analytical philosophy.

I think it is fair to understand the puzzlement of both Beardsley and Bouwsma in the following way. We understand relatively well what it is for a *person* to express such things as feelings, emotions, attitudes, moods, etc. But if we say that sonatas, poems, or paintings also express those sorts of things either we are saying something patently false or we are saying something true in an uninformative, misleading, and therefore pointless way. For to say of works of art that they express those sorts of things seems to imply that they are very much like persons. Therefore, unless we believe that philosophers who think of art as expression believe the unbelievable, that is, that art has feelings, attitudes, and moods and can express them, we must believe that such philosophers are trying, however inadequately, to come to grips with genuine truths about art.

Furthermore, there is such an obvious disparity between the nature of art and the thesis that art can express the same sorts of things that people do that we cannot understand that thesis as simply a clumsy and inept way of stating some truths about art. We must understand it, rather, as a kind of *theoretical* statement, that is, as a deliberately contrived and elaborated way of construing some simple facts about art. Both Beardsley and Bouwsma thus speak of the "Expression *Theory*" of art.

From *Mind and Art: An Essay on the Varieties of Expression* (Copyright © 1972 by Princeton University Press; Princeton Paperback 1978), pp. 16-46. Reprinted by permission of Princeton University Press.

What are the facts which the Expression Theory is meant to interpret? Although Beardsley and Bouwsma differ slightly in the way they put the point, they agree that works of art have "anthropomorphic" properties. That is, we may often properly characterize works of art as, for example, gay, sad, witty, pompous, austere, aloof, impersonal, sentimental, etc. A "theory" of art as expression, therefore, can say no more than that art works have properties designated by the same words which designate feelings, emotions, attitudes, moods, and personal characteristics of human beings.

The nature of these properties has not been probed very deeply by analytical critics of the Expression Theory. Beardsley calls them "qualities." Bouwsma prefers to call them "characters," pointing out their affinity with the "characters" of a number of things like sounds, words, numerals, and faces. In case this suggestion is unhelpful, Bouwsma further invites us to conceive the relation of the "character" to the art work in terms of the relation of redness to the apple in a red apple. At this point he is exactly in line with Beardsley, who mentions a red rose instead of a red apple.[1]

The Bouwsma-Beardsley position on the question of expression in art is currently rather widely accepted. Indeed, John Hospers, writing in the *Encyclopedia of Philosophy* has, in effect, canonized the view.[2] Accordingly, I shall refer to it henceforth as the Canonical Position. Now despite the fact that it has illuminated the concept of expression in art, the Canonical Position is false in some respects and inadequate in others. In this chapter and the next two I shall argue (1) that attributions of "characters," or "anthropomorphic qualities," to works of art come in a number of different varieties, (2) that the simple thing-property relation is not an adequate model for understanding any of those varieties, (3) that there are far better reasons for calling art "expressive" than are allowed by the Canonical interpretation of Expression Theory, (4) that the presence of "anthropomorphic qualities" in works of art is not the only fact about art which makes it expressive, and (5) that the features of art which make it expressive have precise parallels in non-artistic areas of culture such as philosophy, historiography and science.

The Canonical Position has two incorrect presuppositions. The first is that works of art are very much like such natural objects as roses and apples as well as, I suppose, such natural quasi- and non-objects as hills, brooks, winds, and skies. The second is that the anthropomorphic predicates of art are not essentially different from simple color terms like "red" and "yellow." No one has seriously argued, as far as I know, that any art work is *just* like some natural "object." Everyone admits that there are basic differences between art and nature, most of them related to the fact that art is made by human beings and natural things are not. What the first presupposition of the Canonical Position amounts to, therefore, is that as far as the anthropomorphic predicates are concerned works of art are not different from natural objects.[3]

It is fairly easy to show that this presupposition is false by the following strategy. Anthropomorphic predicates are applied to natural things in virtue of certain non-anthropomorphic properties of those things. Of course these properties vary, depending on the particular predicate as well as on the thing to which it is applied. Hills, for example, may be austere in virtue of their color, their vegetation (or lack of it), or their contours; an ocean may be angry in virtue of its sound and the force and size of its waves; a tree may be sad in virtue of the droop and shape of its branches. With respect to a number of art works to which anthropomorphic predicates are applied, I shall inquire what it is about those works in virtue of which the predicates are applicable. This strategy will yield categorial features of art which do not belong to natural things.

(1) Like most of Raphael's Madonna paintings, the one called *La Belle Jardinière* can be described as calm and serene. It is fairly clear what there is about this painting which makes it calm and serene: the regular composition based on an equilateral triangle, the gentle and loving expressions on the faces of the Mother, the Child, and the infant John the Baptist, the placid landscape, the delicate trees, the soft blue of the sky, the gentle ripples in the Mother's garments blown by a slight breeze, and, finally, the equanimity and quiet with which the artist views his subject and records the details of the scene.

(2) We might reasonably describe Hans Hofmann's *The Golden Wall* as an aggressive abstract painting. But in this painting there is no representational content in the usual sense and therefore nothing aggressive is depicted. What is aggressive is the color scheme, which is predominantly red and yellow. Blue and green are also used as contrasting colors, but even these colors, especially the blue, are made to look aggressive because of their intensity. Furthermore, by the way they are juxtaposed, the patches of color are made to appear as though they were rushing out towards the observer and even as though they were competing with one another in this rush towards the observer.

(3) We might say of Poussin's *The Rape of the Sabine Women* (either version, but especially the one in the Metropolitan Museum of Art in New York City) that it is calm and aloof. Yet it is quite clear that the depicted scene is *not* calm and that no one in it, with the possible exception of Romulus, who is directing the attack, is aloof. It is rather, as we say, that *Poussin* calmly observes the scene and paints it in an aloof, detached way.

(4) Breughel's painting called *Wedding Dance in the Open Air* can be aptly if superficially described as gay and happy. In this case however it is surely the occasion and the activities of the depicted peasants which are happy. Perhaps the prominent red used throughout the painting can be called "gay." The faces of the peasants however are neither happy nor gay. They are bland, stupid, and even brutal. It is this fact which makes the painting ironic rather than gay or happy. Yet there is certainly nothing about a peasant wedding, the dull peasants, or their heavy dance

which is ironic. The irony lies in the fact that the painter "views," "observes," or depicts the happy scene ironically.

(5) John Milton's "L'Allegro" is not only "about" high spirits, but it is surely a high-spirited, i.e., gay and joyful, poem. The gaiety and joy are evident in several ways. First, the scenes and images are gay and joyful: Zephir playing with Aurora, maids and youths dancing and dallying, the poet himself living a life of "unreproved" pleasure with Mirth. Second, the diction and rhythms are light-hearted: "Haste thee nymphs and bring with thee / Jest and youthful Jollity, / Quips and Cranks, and wanton Wiles, / Nods, and Becks and Wreathed Smiles."

(6) Another sort of example entirely is William Wordsworth's sentimental poem "We Are Seven." This poem is quite obviously not *about* sentimentality. It purports simply to record the conversation between the poet and a child. Neither the child nor the poet (that is, the "character" in the poem), moreover, is sentimental. The child matter-of-factly reports her firm conviction there are still seven members of her family despite the fact that two of them are dead. The poet is trying, in a rather obtuse and hard-headed sort of way, to get her to admit that there are only five. But the little girl is made to win the point by having the last word in the poem. She is thus made to seem "right" even though no explicit authorization is given to her point of view. By presenting the little girl's case so sympathetically, Wordsworth (the poet who wrote the poem, not the "character" in the poem) treats the attitude of the little girl, as well as the death of her siblings, sentimentally.

(7) The case of "The Dungeon" by Coleridge is different again. At least the first half of this poem is angry. But it is not about anger or angry persons. It is a diatribe in verse (and certainly not a poor poem on that account) against the cruelty, injustice, and wasteful ineffectiveness of prisons.

(8) T. S. Eliot's "The Lovesong of J. Alfred Prufrock" can, with considerable justice, be called a compassionate poem. In this case it is quite clear that the compassion exists in the way in which the character Prufrock is portrayed as a gentle and sensitive, if weak, victim of ugly and sordid surroundings.

(9) Suppose that we say that the second movement of Beethoven's *Eroica* symphony is sad with a dignified and noble sadness characteristic of Beethoven. In this case the sadness is in the slowness of the tempo, and the special quality of the sadness comes from the stateliness of the march rhythm, from the use of "heavy" instruments like horns and tympani and from the sheer length of the movement.

(10) A somewhat different case is presented by Mozart's music for Papageno, which is gay, carefree, light-headed and light-hearted like Papageno himself. What differenitates this case from (9), of course, is that the Mozart music is intended to suit a certain kind of character, whereas the Beethoven has no clear and explicit "representational" con-

tent. Despite this difference, however, the "anthropomorphic qualities" of the Mozart music are, like those of the Beethoven, audible in properties of the sound: in the simple harmonies, tripping rhythms, and lilting melodies of Papageno songs.

(11) A slightly different case from either (9) or (10) is that presented by the first movement of Vivaldi's "Spring" Concerto. The first lilting, happy theme represents the joyful advent of spring. This is followed by the gentle music of the winds and waters of spring. Next, this pleasantness is interrupted by the angry music representing a thunder shower, after which the happy, gentle music returns. In this music the "programmatic" content is clear and explicit because we know the poetry from which Vivaldi composed the music.

(12) Quite different from the three cases immediately preceding is the witty Grandfather theme from Prokoviev's *Peter and the Wolf.* Grandfather's music, played by a bassoon, is large, lumbering, and pompous like Grandfather himself. But what makes it witty is that it portrays a dignified old man as just a bit ridiculous. Through the music Prokoviev pokes gentle fun at the old man, fun which is well-motivated by the story itself. For in the end Peter turns out to be more than equal to the danger which Grandfather has ordered him to avoid.

(13) Finally, there is music like the utterly impersonal and detached music of John Cage, exemplified in *Variations II* played by David Tudor on (with) the piano. But where can we locate the "qualities" of impersonality and detachment in Cage's music? They do not seem to be "properties" of the sounds and sound sequences in the way that gaiety is a property of Papageno's music or sadness is a property of Beethoven's. Indeed, we feel that these "anthropomorphic qualities" of Cage's music depend on the very fact that the sounds themselves are completely lacking in "human" properties. They are as characterless as any of a thousand random noises we hear every day. In fact, *Variations II* does have the apparent randomness and disorganization of mere noise. But we would not be inclined to call *any* random sequences of noises "impersonal" and "detached," even if they sounded very much like the sounds of *Variations II.* The predicates "impersonal" and "detached" are not applied to Cage's music simply in virtue of some features of its sounds. These "qualities" of *Variations II* arise rather from the fact that the composer presents what sounds like mere noise as music. Cage offers this "noise" for us to attend to and concentrate upon. Moreover, he offers it to us without "comment," and with no intention that it evoke, represent, or suggest anything beyond itself. That is to say, Cage offers these noise-like sounds in a totally uninvolved, detached, impersonal way, seeking in no way to touch our emotional life.

From the preceding examples we can see that there are some respects in which anthropomorphic predicates are applied to works of art in virtue of features of those works which they share or could share with

some natural things. In the Raphael it is the composition of the painting which accounts in part for the "calm" of the painting. But "composition" here refers simply to the configuration of lines and shapes,
which sorts of features can of course be shared by natural objects.
Similarly, the aggressiveness of Hofmann's painting is due to its colors
and their arrangement. In the Beethoven and Mozart examples the
anthropomorphic qualities are traceable to features of sound which can
be present in natural phenomena. The ocean crashing on the shore, a
twig tapping against a windowpane, the gurgle of a stream—all of these
can have "tempi," "rhythms," and even "tone color." Natural "melodies"
are present in the rustle of trees and the howl of winds as well as in the
songs of birds. Even the anthropomorphic qualities of verbal art can be
like properties of natural things. For, as the example of "L'Allegro"
shows, such qualities can be attributed to poetry at least partly in virtue
of the tempo and rhythm of its verses.

Some of the above examples of anthropomorphic qualities applied to
art, however, show that such qualities sometimes belong to works of art
in virtue of what those works represent, describe, depict, or portray. Thus
the calm and serenity of the Raphael is due in part to the countryside,
the sky, the garments, and the faces depicted; the gaiety of the Breughel
comes from the gaiety of the depicted scene, and the high spirits of Milton's
poem are due to the gay, happy scenes and images described and presented. In cases of this sort, neither paintings nor poems are comparable
to natural things with respect to the way they bear their anthropomorphic
qualities. And the situation is similar with respect to all other forms of
representational art, whether prose fiction, drama, ballet, opera, or
sculpture. Only architecture and music are generally incapable of bearing
anthropomorphic qualities in this way. This is true, moreover, even for
music with a sort of representational content such as the Mozart music
mentioned in (10) above. For it is not due to the fact that Mozart's songs
are written for a gay, lighthearted character that they are properly described as gay and lighthearted. It is rather that the songs suit Papageno
precisely in virtue of the gaiety and lightheartedness of their "sound"
and are thereby capable of portraying him musically.

There is a second way in which anthropomorphic predicates may be
applied to art works which is unlike the ways in which such predicates
apply to natural things. In the discussion of (1) through (13) above we
discovered the following:

(a) *La Belle Jardinière* is calm and serene partly because Raphael
views his subject calmly and quietly.

(b) *The Rape of the Sabine Women* is aloof and detached because
Poussin calmly *observes* the violent scene and *paints* it in an aloof, detached way.

(c) *Wedding Dance in the Open Air* is an ironic painting because
Breughel *treats* the gaiety of the wedding scene ironically.

(d) "We Are Seven" is a sentimental poem because Wordsworth *treats* his subject matter sentimentally.

(e) "The Dungeon" is an angry poem because in it the poet angrily *inveighs* against the institution of imprisonment.

(f) "The Lovesong of J. Alfred Prufrock" is a compassionate poem because the poet compassionately *portrays* the plight of his "hero."

(g) Prokoviev's Grandfather theme is witty because the composer wittily *comments* on the character in his ballet.

(h) Cage's *Variations II* is impersonal because the composer *presents* his noise-like sounds in an impersonal, uninvolved way.

I have italicized the verbs in the above in order to point up the fact that the respective anthropomorphic predicate is applied to the work of art in virtue of what the artist *does* in that work. In order to have a convenient way of referring to this class of anthropomorphic predicates, I shall henceforth refer to what verbs of the sort italicized above designate as "artistic acts." I do not intend this bit of nomenclature to have any metaphysical import. That is, I do not mean that the viewings, observings, paintings, presentings, portrayings, and treatings covered by the term "artistic acts" all belong to a category properly called "acts." Nor do I mean that all activities properly called "artistic" are covered by my term "artistic act." As shall come out later, many artistic activities are neither identical with, constituents of, nor constituted by "artistic acts." Furthermore, I do not want to suggest that "artistic acts" have anything more in common than what I have already pointed out and what I shall go on to specify. To do a complete metaphysics of artistic acts might be an interesting philosophical job but one which would distract me from my main purposes in this book.

What the preceding discussion has shown is that the view of art presupposed by the Canonical Position ignores complexities in works of art which are essential in understanding how they can bear anthropomorphic predicates. Even more significant is the discovery that anthropomorphic predicates apply to art works in virtue of "artistic acts" in these works. For, as I shall argue presently at length, it is precisely this feature of art works which enables them to be *expressions* and which thereby shows that the Canonical Position has missed a great deal of truth in classical Expression Theory.

As far as I know, no adherent of the Canonical Position, with one exception to be noted below, has recognized the existence of what I call "artistic acts," much less seen their relevance to expression in art. But it is not difficult to anticipate the first defensive move a proponent of the Canonical Position would likely make against the threat posed by "artistic acts." It would go somewhat as follows. What the "discovery" of "artistic acts" shows is merely that not all applications of anthropomorphic predicates to art works attribute qualities to those works. They merely *seem* to do so because of their grammatical form. But in fact statements of this sort say nothing at all about the art work; they describe the artist. After all, "artistic acts" are acts of the artists, and they cannot possibly be acts of (i.e., performed by) the art works themselves.

However superficially plausible this objection is, it can be shown to have little force. First, the objection presupposes a false dichotomy: a statement must be descriptive either of a work of art *or* of its artist. On the contrary, there seems to be no reason why when we talk in the above examples of the painting's aloofness, the poem's sentimentality, etc., we cannot be talking *both* about the painting or poem and about how Poussin painted or how Wordsworth treated his subject. And it is in fact the case that we are talking about both. The best proof of this is that the *grounds* for the truth of the descriptions of artistic acts in (a) through (g) above can come from the art work in question. One knows by looking at Poussin's painting that he has painted the scene in an aloof, detached way. The cold light, the statuesque poses, the painstaking linearity are all visible in the work. Similarly, we recognize by reading Wordsworth's poem that he treats his subject sentimentally. That is just what it is to give the child, who believes that the dead are present among the living, the advantage over the matter-of-fact adult. We can also recognize the impersonality of *Variations II* by listening to its neutral, noise-like sounds. A test for statements describing art in anthropomorphic terms is always and quite naturally a scrutiny of the art, even when the terms are applied in virtue of "artistic acts."

Moreover it is not as if this sort of attention to the work of art were merely a second-best way of testing such statements. One does not look, listen, or read in order to *infer* something about the aloof way Poussin painted, the compassionate way Eliot portrayed his hero, etc. We must not imagine that had we actually been with the artist at work, we could *really*, i.e., immediately and indubitably, have seen his aloofness, compassion, sentimentality, etc. How absurd to think that when Poussin's way of painting is described as aloof, what is meant is that Poussin arched his eyebrows slightly, maintained an impassive expression on his face, and moved his arms slowly and deliberately while he painted the picture. Or that because Eliot portrays Prufrock compassionately, he penned the manuscript of his poem with tears in his eyes. Not only would such facts not be needed to support statements about Poussin's aloofness or Eliot's compassion, but they are totally irrelevant to such statements. For even if we knew the way Poussin looked and moved when he was painting the Sabine picture or the way Eliot's face looked when he penned "Prufrock," we could not infer that the painting and poem were, respectively, aloof and compassionate in the ways we are discussing.

The foregoing considerations do not mean that the "artistic acts" in question are not truly acts of the artists, that is, are not truly something which the artists have done. Nor do they imply that these artistic acts are phantom acts, airy nothings existing mysteriously in works of art and disembodied from any agents.[4] They simply mean that these acts are not identifiable or describable independently of the works "in" which they are done. Probably nothing makes this point clearer than the fact that descriptions of artistic acts of this sort can be known to be true even when little or nothing is known about the author, much less what he looked like and what his behavior was like at the precise time that he was making his art. It can be truly said, for example, that Homer describes with some sentimentality the meeting of the returned Odysseus and aged dog Argos. And yet it would be absurd to say that the truth of that statement waits upon some detailed knowledge about Homer, even the existence of whom is a matter of considerable dispute.

Artistic acts are peculiar in that descriptions of them are at once and necessarily descriptions of art works. They are in this way distinguishable from other sorts of acts of artists which contribute to the production of works of art, e.g., looking at the canvas, chiseling marble, penning words, applying paint, revising a manuscript, thinking to oneself, etc. But artistic acts, for all their peculiarity, are not entirely alone in the universe; there are other sorts of things which people do which are analogous to artistic acts in significant ways. Note the following: A person may scowl angrily, and thereby have an angry scowl on his face; he may smile sadly and thereby have a sad smile on his face; he may gesture impatiently and thus make an impatient gesture; he may shout defiantly and produce thereby a defiant shout; he may pout sullenly and a sullen pout will appear on his face; his eyes may gleam happily and there will be a happy gleam in his eyes; he may tug at his forelock shyly or give a shy tug at this forelock. What is interesting about these clauses is that they show how an anthropomorphic term can be applied either adverbially to "acts" or adjectivally to "things" without a difference in the sense of the term or of the sentences in which it is used. This sort of shift in the grammatical category of a term is clearly analogous to what is possible with respect to those anthropomorphic predicates applied to works of art in virtue of their artistic acts. Thus one may, without change of meaning, say either that Eliot's "Prufrock" is a compassionate poem or that Eliot portrays Prufrock compassionately in his poem; that Poussin paints his violent scene in an aloof, detached way or that the Sabine picture is an aloof, detached painting.[5]

This grammatical shift is possible in both sorts of cases because of the inseparability of the "act" and the "thing." One does not *infer* from a smile on a person's face that he is smiling any more than one *infers* that Eliot portrayed Prufrock compassionately from his compassionate poem, and for analogous reasons. The "acts" of smiling, pouting, shouting, tugging are not even describable without also and at once describing the smile, pout, shout, or tug. Smiling, after all, is not an act which produces or results in a smile so that something could interfere to prevent the smiling from bringing off the smile. "Smiling" and "smile," we are inclined to say, are simply two grammatically different ways of referring to the same "thing."[6]

Now the parallel I want to point out is not between smile-smiling, pout-pouting, tug-tugging, on the one hand, and poem-portraying, picture-(act of) painting, music-presenting, on the other. For clearly Poussin's Sabine painting is more than (is not simply identical with) Poussin's aloof way of painting the violent scene; Eliot's poem is more than his compassionate way of portraying its title character; Cage's music is more than his impersonal presentation of noise-like sounds. When we have described these artistic acts we have not by any means completely described the respective art works. The analogy rather is between smile-smiling and portrayal-portraying, presentation-presenting, treatment-treating, view-viewing, etc. Therefore, when we designate artistic acts by a noun term, those acts seem to be "parts" or "moments" of the works of art to which they pertain. We may then more properly understand the way in which an anthropomorphic adjective applies to an art work in virtue of such a "part" in something like the way in which a person's whole face is called sad in virtue merely of his sad smile or his sad gaze, or in which a person's behavior is generally angry in virtue (merely) of his quick movements and angry tone of voice. In these cases, too, it is not as if the terms "sad" and "angry" *completely* described the face or the behavior or even all parts and aspects of the face and behavior even though they can *generally* characterize the face and the behavior.

The foregoing comparison points out that not only is it the case that anthropomorphic predicates do not always apply to art works the way predicates, anthropomorphic or not, apply to natural objects, but that sometimes anthropomorphic predicates apply to works of art rather like the way that they apply to verbal, gestural, and facial *expressions*. For sad smiles are characteristic expressions of sadness in a person; angry scowls, of anger; shy tugs at forelocks, of diffidence; sullen pouts, of petulance. And this is an all-important point which the Canonical Position has missed in its interpretation of the Expression Theory of Art. Had proponents of the Canonical Position pursued their inquiry into anthropomorphic predicates further, they would have been forced to question whether such predicates apply to art in the way they apply to objects or in the way they apply to common human expressions.

Instead of pursuing this line of questioning, however, they were misled by the noun-adjective form of their favorite example—sad music—into their object-quality interpretation of Expression Theory, an interpretation which of course makes that "theory" seem very far removed indeed from the "facts" which were alleged to have motivated it. Small wonder that Beardsley's final judgment on Expression Theory is that it "renders itself obsolete" after it has reminded us that anthropomorphic predicates may reasonably be applied to art works. Even O. K. Bouwsma, who of all the proponents of the Canonical Position comes closest to the point I am maintaining, was not able to see quite where his comparison between sad music and sad faces leads. For instead of making a transition from sad faces to sad *expressions* on faces, he takes the (rather longer) way from sad faces to red apples.

There is more to the comparison between artistic acts and facial, vocal, and gestural expressions than the formal or grammatical similarities just noted. Even more important are the parallels between the "significance" of things like sad smiles and angry scowls and the "significance" of aloofness or irony in paintings, sentimentality or compassion in poems, and impersonality or wittiness in music. For there are parallels between what facial, gestural and vocal expressions, on the one hand, and artistic acts, on the other, can tell us about the persons responsible for them. In order to draw out these parallels explicitly I shall use the cases of an angry scowl and a compassionate portrayal in the mode of Eliot's "Prufrock."

First, it is obvious that an angry scowl on a person's face might well mean that the person is angry. It might be more than simply an expression of anger; it might be an expression of *his* anger. Now it should need very little argument to show that a compassionate poem like "Prufrock" might be an expression of the poet's own compassion. He might be a person with a generally sympathetic and pitying attitude towards modern man and his situation. In that case, a poem like "Prufrock," at least a poem with "Prufrock's" kind of compassion is precisely what one could expect from the poet, just as one could expect an angry man to scowl angrily. But just as we cannot reasonably expect that *every* time a person is angry he scowls angrily, we cannot expect that every man who is a poet and who has compassion towards his fellows will produce poetry with the compassion of "Prufrock." If a man can keep his anger from showing in his face, a poet can, with whatever greater difficulties and whatever more interesting implications for himself and his poetry, keep his compassion from showing in his poetry.

Moreover, just as there is no necessity that a man's anger show in his face, there is no necessity that an angry scowl betoken anger in the scowler. There is a looseness of connection between anger and angry expressions which is matched by a looseness between compassion and compassionate poems. One reason that a man might have an angry scowl on his face is that he is *affecting* anger, for any of a number of reasons. Now although the range of reasons for affecting compassion in his poetry might be different from the range of reasons for affecting anger in his face, it is nevertheless possible that a corpus of poetry with "Prufrock's" sort of compassion might betoken nothing more than an affectation of compassion. This might be the case if, for example, the poet is extremely "hard" and sarcastic but thinks of these traits as defects. He might then quite deliberately write "compassionate" poetry in order to mask his true self and present himself to the world as the man he believes he should be.

On the other hand, both angry scowls and compassionate poetry might be the result simply of a desire to imitate. Children especially will often imitate expressions on people's faces, but even adults sometimes have occasion to imitate such expressions, e.g., in relating an anecdote. A poet might write poems with Eliot's sort of compassion in them in imitation of Eliot's early attitude. This imitation might be executed by a clever teacher in order to show more vividly than by merely pointing them out the means Eliot used to convey his special sympathy in "Prufrock." Or Eliot might be imitated because his techniques and style, together with the attitudes they imply, have become fashionable among serious poets or because these attitudes strike a responsive chord among serious poets. The latter sorts of imitation are rather like the imitations which a child might make of a person whom he regards as a model. It is not unusual for a girl who admires a female teacher, say, to practice smiling in that teacher's kind, gentle way or for a very young boy at play to "get angry" in the same way he has seen his father get angry.

A poet might write poems with the compassion of "Prufrock," not because he is either affecting or imitating the attitude of that poem, but because he is *practicing* writing poetry in different styles and different "moods." This may be just something like a technical exercise for him, or it may be part of a search for a characteristic attitude or stance which seems to be truly "his own." He thus "tries on" a number of different poetic "masks," so to speak, to see how they fit him. In a similar way, an adolescent girl grimacing before her mirror might "try on" various facial expressions to see how they "look on her" and to discover which is her "best," or perhaps her most characteristic face: innocent, sullen, sultry, haughty, or even angry.

Finally, an angry scowl on a face might be there when the person is portraying an angry person on the stage. There is a similar sort of situation in which compassionate poetry might be written not as betokening a characteristic of the poem's real author but as betokening the traits of a *character* in a play or novel who is *represented* as having written the poem. No actual examples of such a character come immediately to mind; but we surely have no trouble imagining a master of stylistic imitation writing a novelized account of modern literature in which he exhibits examples of the "Prufrock"-like poetry of an Eliot-like figure.

What I have argued so far is not that all art is expression, nor even that all art works with artistic acts anthropomorphically qualified are expressions. My argument shows only that artistic acts in works of art are remarkably like common facial, vocal, and gestural expressions. It also demonstrates that precisely in virtue of their artistic acts and of the similarity they bear to common kinds of expressions, works of art may serve as expressions of those feelings, emotions, attitudes, moods, and/or personal characteristics of their creators which are designated by the anthropomorphic predicates applicable to the art works themselves. And it thereby demonstrates that one presupposition of the Canonical Position is clearly wrong: namely, that art works, insofar as they allow of anthropomorphic predicates, are essentially like natural things untouched by man.

But the second presupposition of the Canonical Position, to wit, that anthropomorphic predicates of art are like simple color words, is also false. It is false with respect to all of the three ways, distinguished earlier, that anthropomorphic predicates can be applied to works of art. And it is *a fortiori* false with respect to those predicates which are applied to art in two or three ways at once, as most of them are. The falsity of the presupposition can be brought out in an interesting way by showing how the three ways of applying anthropomorphic predicates to art bear a certain resemblance to color attributions which are rather unlike simply calling a (clearly) red rose red or an (indubitably) green hill green.

Suppose that a sign painter is painting a sign in three colors: yellow, red, and blue. Since the sign is large, he is required to move his equipment several times during the job. Suppose that he employs an assistant to attend to this business. Now we can imagine that the painter will have occasion to give directions to his assistant. He might say, "Bring me the red bucket, but leave the blue and yellow ones there, since I'll need them on that side later." Now if we suppose that the color of all the paint containers is black, when the painter calls for the "red bucket," he must mean "the bucket of red paint," and would surely be so understood by his assistant. In the context the phrase "red bucket" only *appears* to have the same grammatical form as "red rose." I suggest that to the extent that a painting or other representational work of art is called "gay" or "sad" solely in virtue of its subject matter or parts thereof, the latter terms function *more* like "red" in "red bucket" than in "red rose."

It is a common opinion that "sad" in "sad smile" and "gay" in "gay laughter" function metaphorically.[7] There may well be a use of "metaphor" such that the opinion is true. Whether there is such a use will not be determined until there exists a thorough philosophical study of metaphor; and I do not intend to offer one here. But even if it turns out to be true that such uses of anthropomorphic words are metaphorical, it cannot be very useful simply to say it. For such uses *appear* not to be metaphorical at all. After all, it is not as if calling a smile sad were representing the smile as, as it were, feeling sad, acting sad, weeping and dragging its feet. To see a smile's sadness is not to discern the tenuous and subtle "likeness" between the smile and a sad person. It is much more straightforward to think that a smile is sad because it is a smile *characteristic* of a sad person who smiles; that laughter is gay because such laughter is *characteristic* laughter of persons who are gay. In this respect "sad smile" is rather like "six-year-old behavior" or "Slavic cheekbones." These phrases do not indirectly point to unexpected similarities between a sort of behavior and six-year-old children or between cheekbones and persons. They designate, respectively, behavior which is *charac-teristic* of six-year-old children and cheekbones *characteristic* of Slavs. And there is no inclination at all to call these phrases "metaphorical."

Yet to say that a sad smile is a smile characteristic of sad people is not to deny what the Canonical Position affirms, namely, that "sad" d a "property" or "character" of the smile. Surely there is somethi, the smile which marks it as sad: its droopiness, its weakness, its ᴠ But the term "sad" still has a different import from "droopy," "weak," or "wan" when applied to smiles, even though all the latter terms are also characteristic smiles of sad persons. The difference is that the term "sad" *explicitly* relates the character of the smile to sadness of persons. A comparable sort of color term might be "cherry red." "Cherry red" is like the term "bright red with bluish undertones" in that they both designate roughly the same shade of red, which is characteristic of cherries. But the former term is unlike the latter in that it *explicitly* relates the color to cherries.

It might seem that the Canonical Position would be correct in its interpretation of anthropomorphic terms as they apply to those features of works of art which they can share with natural things. For the term "sad" applied to the second movement of the "Eroica" and to a weeping willow must surely denote some properties of the music and of the tree. And they do: drooping branches in the tree; slow rhythm and "heavy" sound in the Beethoven. But "sad" differs from "drooping," "slow," and "heavy" as in the preceding case; it immediately relates the properties of the sounds and the branches to properties of other things which are sad. In these cases "sad" does function metaphorically, harboring, as it were, a comparison within itself. To find an analogy among color words, this use of "sad" is like "reddish." Like "reddish," which quite self-consciously does not denote true redness, "sad" in "sad tree" does not denote true sadness but only a kind of likeness of it. This use of "sad" is also arguably analogous to the use of "red" in "His face turned red with shame." But whether "sad tree" and "sad rhythm" are closer to "reddish clay" or to "red face" is, if determinable at all, unimportant for my point. For "reddish clay" and "red face" are equally unlike "red rose" and "red apple" when the latter refer to a full-blown American Beauty and a ripe Washington Delicious.

In this section I have argued that anthropomorphic terms, when applied to art, are *more* like "red' in "red bucket (of paint)," "cherry red" in "cherry red silk," or "reddish" in "reddish clay" than like "red" in "red rose." But, in truth, anthropomorphic predicates of art are not *very* much like any of these. The reason is that what all anthropomorphic predicates ultimately relate to are human emotions, feelings, attitudes, moods, and personal traits, none of which are very much at all like colors. But there is point in drawing out the comparison between anthropomorphic predicates and color-terms more complicated than "red" in "red rose." The point is that "red" as applied to bucket, "cherry red," and "reddish" are all in some way relational terms in ways that "red" said of a rose is not. "Red bucket" means "bucket *of* red paint"; "cherry red" means "the red *characteristic* of cherries"; and "reddish" means "of a color *rather like* red." Had proponents of the Canonical Position troubled to refine their comparison between anthropomorphic predicates and color predicates, they might have been forced to recognize the relational aspects of the former. Eventually they might have been led to see that anthropomorphic terms finally relate to various forms of the "inner lives" of human beings. And *that* is where Expression Theory begins. The Canonical model of the red rose (or apple) ultimately fails to help us understand how anthropomorphic predicates apply to art because such predicates are not very much like simple quality-words and what they apply to are not very much like natural objects.

In spite of all of the above arguments, the Canonical Position is not left utterly defenseless. Although it is the notion of "artistic acts" which is most threatening to the Canonical Position, proponents of that position have been almost totally unaware of this threat. Not totally unaware, however. There is a brief passage in Monroe Beardsley's book *Aesthetics: Problems in the Philosophy of Criticism* in which he mentions an artist's "treatment" and "handling," two examples of what I have called "artistic acts." Beardsley does not relate them, however, to the analysis of anthropomorphic terms. He discusses them under the rubric "misleading idioms," and he suggests that all talk about art concerning "handling" and "treatment" not only can be but should be translated into talk which makes no mention of these sorts of acts.[8]

These are meager clues, but from them it is possible to excogitate an objection to my notion of "artistic arts" which a defender of the Canonical Position might raise. We should first note a remark which Beardsley makes elsewhere in his book when he is concluding his interpretation of Expression Theory. He states that all remarks about the expressiveness of an art work can be "translated" into statements about the anthropomorphic qualities either of the subject matter or of the "design," i.e., roughly the properties which the work could share with natural things.[9] A defense against the notion of "artistic acts" might thus run as follows: Any statement which describes an artistic act anthropomorphically can be "translated" into a statement which describes features of the work of art other than its artistic acts. So stated, however, the defense is ambiguous; it has two plausible and interesting interpretations. First, it might mean that any anthropomorphic description of an artistic act in a work can be replaced, without loss of meaning, by a description of the subject matter and/or design of the work in terms of the same anthropomorphic predicate. Or it might mean that there are descriptions, of whatever sort, of the subject matter and/or design of a work which, given any true anthropomorphic description of an artistic act in that work, entail that description.

The first interpretation of the objection is easily shown to be false. All that is required is that some examples of art be adduced in which anthropomorphic predicates are applicable with some plausibility to an "artistic act" but which are in on other way plausibly attributable to the work. Let us look again at the works of Poussin, Eliot, and Prokoviev discussed earlier in this chapter.

In the Poussin painting of *The Rape of the Sabines* there is nothing about the violent subject matter which could be called "aloof." Certainly the attackers and the attacked are not aloof. Romulus, the general in charge, is a relatively *calm* surveyor of the melee, but he cannot be called aloof, partly because we cannot see him well enough to tell what his attitude is. "Aloof" does not apply with regard to the formal elements of the Poussin painting either. It is difficult even to imagine what "aloof" lines, masses, colors, or an "aloof" arrangement thereof might be. The light in the painting is rather cold, and that feature does indeed contribute to the aloofness of the work. "Cold light" is not, however, the same as "aloof light," which does not even appear to be a sensible combination of words.

A similar analysis is possible with respect to Eliot's "Prufrock." If we consider first the "material" elements of the poem—its rhythm, meter, sound qualities, etc.—we realize that "compassionate" simply cannot apply to those features meaningfully. Moreover, there is nothing about the subject matter of "Prufrock" which is compassionate. Certainly Prufrock himself is not compassionate; he is simply confused, a victim of his own fears and anxieties, and of the meanness and triviality of his routinized life and soulless companions.

Finally, the wittiness of Prokoviev's Grandfather theme cannot be supposed to be a "property" of the music the way its comic qualities are. The music is amusing, or comic, because the wheeziness of the bassoon is funny and because the melody imitates the "structure" of a funny movement (one *must* move in an amusing way to that melody). Moreover, although Grandfather himself is funny, he is definitely not witty. What is comical, amusing, or funny is not always witty. To be witty is generally to make, say, or do something comical, amusing, or funny "on purpose." That is why Prokoviev's musical *portrayal* of a comical grandfather is witty. Similar analyses of the Breughel painting, the Wordsworth poem and the Cage music mentioned previously could obviously be carried out. But the point, I take it, is already sufficiently well made.

The second interpretation of the hypothetical attack on the importance of artistic acts borrows any initial plausibility it possesses from the fact that anthropomorphic descriptions of artistic acts can be "explained" or "justified" in terms which neither mention artistic acts nor use any of the terms which describe them. For example, one might point out the irony in the Breughel painting discussed above by noting the combination of the gay scene and the dull faces of its participants. Or one might justify the "aloofness" he sees in the Poussin by remarking on the cold light, clear lines, and statuesque poses in a scene of violence and turmoil. And in discussing the impersonality of *Variations II* it is necessary to mention that the Cage work sounds like accidentally produced noise, which is senseless and emotionally neutral, but that this noise-like sound is to all *other* appearances music, i.e., it is scored, it is performed on a musical instrument, it is even reproduced on recordings. From these facts about the way in which anthropomorphic descriptions are justified, it might seem plausible that the statements which figure in the justification *entail* the original description. But such is not the case, as the following will show.

It has been suggested that the reason that Breughel's peasant faces are dull and stupid-looking is that the painter was simply unable to paint faces which were happy. Whether the suggestion is true or well supported by the evidence is not an issue here. What is important is that were there any reason for believing Breughel to have been incompetent in that way, then there might be (not necessarily "would be") that much less reason for believing that there is irony in Breughel's *Wedding Dance*. That is because Breughel's incompetence and Breughel's irony *can* in this case function as mutually exclusive ways of accounting for a "discrepancy" in the picture. Of course, there are ways of admitting both the incompetence and the irony. It is possible to suppose, for example, that Breughel used his particular incompetence in making an ironic "statement" about peasant existence. Such a supposition would imply that Breughel was aware of his limitation and made use of it in his work. However, were it *known* that the *only* reason for the discrepancy in the painting was Breughel's incompetence, the "irony" would disappear. It makes no difference, incidentally, that such a thing could probably *never* be known. I am making a logical point regarding the way an attribution of a certain sort to an "artistic act" relates to other aspects of a painting like the Breughel. In short, certain facts about the painting's subject matter do indeed "ground" the attribution but by no means logically entail that attribution. And that is so for the good reason that the same facts about the subject matter are consistent with a supposition about Breughel which might be incompatible with the description of the painting as ironic.

A similar point can be illustrated in Poussin's Sabine painting. In that work there is a discrepancy between the violent scene, on the one hand, and the "still," clear figures, on the other. Two persons might agree about the character of the figures and the character of the depicted scene, however, and yet disagree whether these facts entail that Poussin painted the rape of the Sabines in an aloof, reserved way. One viewer might think simply that the work is incoherent, that Poussin's coldly classical means are not suited to the end he had in mind, namely, to depict the violence of the event. In this quite reasonable view, the discrepancy makes the painting "fall apart" rather than "add up" to an aloof and reserved point of view. Here then are two incompatible descriptions of a work which are equally well grounded on facts which allegedly "entail" one of the descriptions. I am mindful that it might be objected that there are other features of the Sabine painting than the ones mentioned which preclude the judgment of "incoherence" and necessitate the judgment of "aloofness." The best I can say is that there seem to me to be no such additional features contributing to the "aloofness" of the painting and that the burden of proof is upon those who disagree.[10]

Finally, let us suppose that a devoted listener of traditional Western music scoffs at the description of Cage's *Variations II* as "impersonal music." He insists that it is nothing but what it sounds like—meaningless noise. He charges that Cage is a fraud whose "music" is a gigantic hoax, a put-on, and that Cage is laughing up his sleeve at those who take him seriously, perform his "scores," record the performances, and listen gravely to his nonsense. He has, the traditional listener says, read some of Cage's "ideological" material relating to his "music" but he has noted how laden with irony it is. To him that shows that Cage is not to be taken seriously because he does not take himself seriously. Now such a doubter does not disagree with the description of *Variations II* which is used to justify calling it "impersonal." The disagreement concerns rather the way we are to assess John Cage. Are we to judge him to be a responsible and serious, albeit radically innovative, composer of music or not? It is only when Cage's seriousness is assumed that the term "impersonality" applies to his music. Otherwise, the aforementioned justification for calling it impersonal is equally justification for calling it nonsense.

What the above three cases demonstrate is that a true anthropomorphic description of an artistic act might presuppose conditions having nothing necessarily to do with the way the formal elements and/or subject matter are describable. The conditions mentioned are (1) the competence of the artist, (2) the coherence of the work, (3) the seriousness of the artist. But there are surely other examples which would bring light to other conditions of this sort. With sufficient ingenuity one could likely discover and/or construct examples of art in which anthropomorphic descriptions of artistic acts would or would not be applicable depending upon how one assessed the artist with respect to, say, his maturity, his sanity, his self-consciousness, his sensitivity, or his intelligence.

Now it is probably too rigid to regard "competence," "coherence," "seriousness," "maturity," "sanity," and the rest as denoting necessary *conditions* for the legitimate description of all artistic arts. It is probably not true that the artist *must* be serious, competent, sane, etc., and that the work *must* be coherent in order for any anthropomorphic description (of an artistic act) to apply to any work. What these terms should be taken as denoting are "parameters" according to which an artist or a work can be measured in whatever respect is relevant in a particular case. To do so would be to admit that there is probably not a single set of particular conditions of these sorts presupposed in *all* descriptions of artistic acts.

Naming these parameters simply points out the *sorts* of considerations which *might* be relevant in particular descriptions of artistic acts, leaving it an open question which of these parameters are relevant, and to what degree, in particular cases.

In any event, what the recognition of such parameters means is that any attempt to save the Canonical Position by "eliminating" descriptions of artistic acts in favor of "logically equivalent" descriptions of formal elements and/or represented subject matter is doomed to fail. For the description of artistic acts in anthropomorphic terms does presuppose something about the artist which cannot be known *simply* by attending to his art. A similar point holds with respect to common expressions. The look of a sullen pout on a person's face does not mean that the person is pouting sullenly if we discover that the look results from the natural lay of his face. And thus it is that no description simply of the configuration of the person's face can *entail* the statement that the person is pouting sullenly.

But it is equally true that the assertion that a person is pouting sullenly is incompatible with the claim that the person's face has the same configuration as it does when he is not pouting sullenly. The sullen pout *must* make a difference visible on the face. Analogously, for an anthropomorphic predicate of an artistic act to be applicable to a work of art there *must* be *some* features of the material elements and/or the subject of the work which *justify* the attribution of the term, even though they do not *entail* that attribution. One thing, however, is never presupposed or implied when an anthropomorphic predicate is truly applied to a work, namely, that the predicate is truly applicable to the *artist*. In this, too, works of art are like expressions.

Notes

1. Cf. Monroe Beardsley, *Aesthetics: Problems in the Philosophy of Criticism* (New York: Harcourt, Brace, 1958), pp. 321-332; and O. K. Bouwsma, "The Expression Theory of Art," in *Philosophical Analysis,* ed. Max Black (Ithaca: Cornell University Press, 1950), pp. 75-101.

2. *The Encyclopedia of Philosophy,* ed. Paul Edwards (New York: Macmillan and The Free Press, 1967), 1, 47.

3. I hope it is clear that throughout this discussion the emphasis is on "natural," not on "object." But I will, for convenience, use the terms "object" and "thing" to cover non-objects and non-things as well.

4. Nor are they "virtual," i.e. unreal, acts, as I have maintained in another place. Cf. my "Perceptual Acts and Pictorial Art: A Defense of Expression Theory," *Journal of Philosophy,* LXII (1965), 669-677. Giving these acts a separate and unusual metaphysical status not only complicates the universe needlessly, it is unfaithful to the commonsense facts of the situation. There are no good

reasons to deny what our ways of talking implicitly affirm, namely, that "artistic acts," perceptual and otherwise, are "acts" of the artist.

Of course it is true that sometimes when anthropomorphic terms are predicated of art works, they apply to subject matters and to "material" aspects of the work such as lines, colors, sounds, masses, etc., as well as to "artistic acts." My point above is only that anthropomorphic adjectives may be applied to a work only in virtue of an artistic act, in which case it is, without change of meaning, immediately applicable in adverbial form to that act.

6. It is no objection to this assertion that in virtue of the natural lay of their faces some people have perpetual "smiles," "smirks," "pouts," etc., on their faces even when they do not smile, smirk, or pout. Of course a "smile" of this sort is different from a smile; that is what the scare quotes signify. But even though a person with such a "smile" on his face is not thereby smiling, he is, significantly, "smiling."

7. Nelson Goodman's recent theory of expression seems to depend rather heavily on the opinion that such uses of anthropomorphic predicates are metaphorical. As far as I can tell, however, Goodman merely asserts and does not argue for this opinion. Nor does he offer anything more than the briefest sketch of a theory of metaphor, which could be used to support his assertion. See his *Languages of Art: An Approach to a Theory of Symbols* (Indianapolis: Bobbs-Merrill, 1968), pp. 50-51, 80-95.

8. Beardsley, *Aesthetics*, pp. 80 ff.

9. *Ibid.*, p. 332.

10. These statements commit me to the position that a positive judgment about the Poussin cannot be deduced from any descriptions of the painting of the sort which "ground" its aloofness. For arguments in favor of this general position see my "Subjectivity and Justification in Aesthetic Judgments," *Journal of Aesthetics and Art Criticism,* xxvii (1968), 3-12.

MAX BLACK

How Do Pictures Represent?

Some Questions

THERE ON THE WALL is a painting: it plainly shows some racehorse or other, with trees that might be beeches in the background and a stableboy doing something or other with a pail in the foreground. That the picture shows all these things, that all these things and more can be seen in the painting, is beyond doubt. But what makes that painting a picture of a horse, trees, and a man? More generally, what makes any "naturalistic" painting or photograph a representation of its subject? And how, if at all, does the situation change when we pass to such "conventional" representations as maps, diagrams, or models? To what extent do "convention" or "interpretation" help to constitute the relation between any representation and its subject?

These are the sorts of questions that I would like to consider (though not all of them in this essay), more in the hope of clarifying the questions themselves than in the hope of finding acceptable answers. For the main difficulties in the inquiry arise from lack of clarity in such words as "representation," "subject," and "convention" that spring naturally to mind and cannot be avoided without tiresome paraphrase.

Preliminary Qualms

Are questions as imprecise and confused as these worth raising? Or are they perhaps merely symptoms of the philosopher's itch to puzzle himself about what seems unproblematic to everybody else? Well, the itch is infectious, even to laymen. The disconcerting thing, as we shall soon see, is that the most plausible answers that suggest themselves are open

From Max Black, "How Do Pictures Represent," pp. 95–130 of E. H. Gombrich, Julian Hochberg, and Max Black, *Art, Perception, and Reality*, Copyright © 1972, the Johns Hopkins University Press and reprinted with their permission.

to grave and perhaps fatal objections. Yet even partial answers have consequences for such varied topics as perception, cognition, the structure of symbol systems, the relations between thought and feeling, and the aesthetics of the visual arts. To understand the reasons for the excessive discord produced by questions about representation would be sufficient reward for what threatens to be an arduous, even a somewhat tiresome, investigation.

Some Working Definitions

When a painting—or some other visual representation, such as a photograph—is a painting *of* something, *S*, I shall say that *P depicts S*; alternatively, that *P* stands in a *depicting relation* to *S*. There is, however, room for misunderstanding here.

Suppose *P* shows Washington crossing the Delaware. Then *P* is related to Washington's actual crossing of the Delaware, in 1776, in such a way that it can be judged to be a more or less faithful, or a more or less inaccurate, painting of that historical episode. I do not want to count that historical event as a special case of the subject, *S*, introduced in the last paragraph. Consider for contrast the case of another painting that shows Hitler crossing the Hudson in 1950: here there is no actual event to serve as a control of the painting's fidelity; yet we still want to say that the painting has a "subject" that is depicted by it.

Let us call Washington's crossing of the Delaware the *original scene* to which the painting refers; and for the sake of precision let us say that the painting does not merely depict that scene but rather *portrays* it. Then the painting of Hitler's imaginary river crossing will have no original scene to portrary; but it may be said to. *display* a certain subject. Thus portraying and displaying will count as special cases of depicting.

The displayed subject might be conceived of as the *content* of the visual representation.[1] I shall normally be concerned with depicting in the special sense of "displaying," and correspondingly with that "subject" of a painting that is its "content," not its "original scene." Where the context is suitable and no other indication is given, the reader may take "depict" and "display" henceforward as synonymous.

It should be borne in mind that I am not initially committed to there always being an irreducible difference between "subject" and "original scene." More importantly still, I am not committed—as talk about the relation between *P* and *S* might misleadingly suggest—to the existence of the "subject" *S* as an independent entity in its own right. It is compatible with everything that has so far been said that *displaying S* might turn out to be a unitary predicate, carrying no implication as to the existence or non-existence of *S*. Thus, the occurrence of *S* in depicting *S* might be "intensional," not "extensional."

In Search of Criteria

An ambitious investigator of our syllabus of questions might hope to discover an analytical definition of *displaying* or *displaying S,* that is to say, some formula having the structure:

P displays S if and only if R,

where *R* is to be replaced by some expression that is more detailed and more illuminating (whatever we take that to mean) than the unelaborated word, "displays." *R,* then, will constitute the necessary and sufficient condition for *P* to "display" *S.*

It is probably unrealistic to expect that we can find a set of necessary and sufficient conditions conforming to this pattern. But we need not be committed to this goal, for it would already be somewhat illuminating if we could only isolate some necessary conditions. A still more modest goal, difficult enough to attain, would be to exhibit some *criteria* for the application of expressions of the form "displays *S,*" that is to say conditions that count, in virtue of the relevant meaning of "displays" and nothing else, for or against its applicability to given instances. Such criteria need not be invariably or universally relevant, always in point whenever it makes sense to speak of something showing or displaying something else: the criteria of application might vary from case to case in some systematic and describable fashion. The goal would then be partial but explicit insight into the pattern of uses of 'depicts' and its paronyms, rather than a formal definition.[2] Nevertheless, although this is the program, I shall first adopt the plan of examining seriatim a number of plausibly necessary conditions for "displaying." Only after we have become convinced that none of these candidates separately—and not even all of them jointly—can serve as an analysis of our quaesitum shall I proceed to argue for a more flexible type of answer.

Somebody influenced by Wittgenstein's parallel investigations of fundamental concepts might regard our enterprise, even thus circumscribed, as reprehensibly quixotic, expecting to find the "patterns of use" too ravelled for reduction to any formula. Such pessimism might be countered by recalling that "creative power" of language, as important as it is truistic, in virtue of which we can understand what is meant by something of the form "*P* is a painting of *S*" even when asserted of some painting in a new, unfamiliar or recondite style. That we think we understand what is said in such contexts argues powerfully for the existence of an underlying pattern of application waiting to be exhibited. Even if this were an illusion, it would be one in need of explanation.

A Principled Objection

A search for analytical criteria of application for "displaying" naturally recalls the many abortive efforts that have been made to provide partial or complete analyses of verbal meaning. Indeed, there may be more than analogy here. Of a verbal text we can properly say, echoing some of our earlier formulations, that it is a description or representation *of* some scene, situation, or state of affairs, presented via the "content" of the text and possibly corresponding to some verifying fact (the analogue of our "original scene"). Thus questions arise that seem to parallel those about pictorial representation which I have emphasized. Some writers, indeed, try to assimilate the latter to the former, drawing their explanatory and analytical concepts from the domain of verbal semantics.

Now are there any good reasons to think that a search for a conceptual map of verbal meaning is bound to be abortive? The late John Austin seems to have thought so (Austin, 1961), for reasons that do not seem to have been discussed in print.

Austin contrasts a search for the meaning of a particular word or expression with what he takes to be the illegitimate search for meaning in general. He reminds us that the first kind of question is answered when we can "explain the syntactics" and "demonstrate the semantics" of the word or expression in question. That is to say, when we can state the grammatical constraints on the expression and its ostensive or quasi-ostensive links with non-verbal objects and situations (where this is appropriate). But then Austin objects that the supposedly more general question "What is the meaning of a word in general?" is a spurious one. "I can only answer a question of the form 'What is the meaning of "x"?' if 'x' is some particular word you are asking about. This supposed *general* question is really just a spurious question of a type which commonly arises in philosophy. We may call it the fallacy of asking about 'Nothing-in-particular' which is a practice decried by the plain man, but by the philosopher called 'generalizing' and regarded with some complacency".

If Austin were right, a similar absurdity should infect our main question about the meaning of "*P* is a painting of *S*," since we are not raising it about any given painting, but about no painting in particular. Austin's idea, so far as I have been able to follow it, seems to have been that the rejected general question about the meaning of a word in general is apt to be taken as a search for a single meaning, *common to all words*. And similarly, if he were right, our own problem would be the ridiculous one of trying to find a single common subject for all paintings. So conceived, the quest would indeed be spurious, not to say preposterously confused.

It is interesting to notice, however, that immediately after rejecting the "general question" about meaning, Austin admits as legitimate the general question "What is the 'square root' of a number?"—of any number, not any particular number. But if that is a legitimate way of looking for a definition of "square root", why should we not regard the "general question" about meaning, with equal justice, as a legitimate way of looking for a definition—or at least something relevant to the definition —of "meaning"?

Austin's reason for distinguishing the two cases apparently arises from his conviction (which I share) that " 'the meaning of *p*' is not a definite description of any entity", whereas "square root of *n*" is (when the variable is replaced by a constant). I cannot see why this should make a relevant difference. It would indeed be naive to think of the search for an analysis of "displaying *S*" as presupposing the existence of some entity indifferently displayed by all paintings. But this concession need not imply the rejection of any search for general criteria as spurious. Oddly enough, after Austin's characteristically energetic attack upon the "general" enterprise of delineating the concept of meaning, he proceeds to assign that same task an acceptable sense by taking it to be an attempt to answer the question "What-is-the-meaning-of (the phrase) 'the-meaning-of (the word) "x" '?". The corresponding question for us might be "What is the meaning of (the phrase) *displaying S*?". We can then proceed, as Austin recommends, to investigate the "syntactics and semantics" of that expression, without commitment to the existence of dubious entities and without nagging anxieties about the supposed spuriousness of the enterprise. It may prove impossible to reach our goal, but that remains to be seen.

How Does a Photograph Depict?

I shall now consider for a while the form taken by our basic question about the nature of depiction, when applied to the special case of photographs. For if any pictures stand in some "natural" relation to their displayed or portrayed subjects, unretouched photographs ought to provide prime examples. There, surely, we ought to be able to discern whatever complexities underlie the notion of faithful "copying" at its least problematic. Since photographs also provide minimal scope for the "expressive" intentions of their producers, we shall be able to bracket considerations connected with the expressive aspects of visual art (whose crucial importance in other contexts is, of course, undeniable).

What, then, is it about a given photograph, *P,* that entitles us to say that it is a photograph of a certain *S*? Here is a picture postcard labelled "Westminster Abbey." What justifies us and enables us to say that it is a photograph *of* a certain famous building in London—or, at least, for somebody who has never heard of the Abbey, of a certain building having certain presented properties (twin towers, an ornamented front, and so on)?[3]

Appeal to a Causal History

The first answer to be considered seeks to analyze the imputed depicting relation in terms of a certain causal sequence between some "original scene" (what the camera was originally pointed at) and the photograph, considered as an end-term in that sequence. The photograph, P, that is to say a certain piece of shiny paper, showing a distribution of light and dark patches, resulted—so the story goes—from a camera's being pointed upon a certain occasion at *Westminster Abbey*, thus allowing a certain sheaf of light rays to fall upon a photo-sensitive film, which was subsequently subjected to various chemical and optical processes ("developing" and "printing"), so that at last *this* object—the photograph in our hands—resulted. In short, the aetiology of the representing vehicle, P, is supposed to furnish our desired answer.

Reducing the causal narrative to essentials, we get the following account: P portrays S, in virtue of the fact that S was a salient cause-factor in the production of P; and P displays S', in virtue of the fact that S satisfied the description that might be inserted for "S'" (a building having towers, etc.). On this view, P might be regarded as a *trace*[4] of S, and the interpretation of P is a matter of inference to an earlier term in a certain causal sequence.

An immediate obstacle to the acceptability of this account is the difficulty in specifying the "portrayed subject," S, and that abstract of it which is the "displayed subject," S'. For an inference from P to the circumstances of its original generation will yield any number of facts about the camera's focal aperture, its distance from the nearest prominent physical object, perhaps the exposure time, and so on, which we should not want to count as part of the "subject" in either sense of that word. There must be some way of selecting, out of the set of possible inferences from the physical character of P, some smaller set of facts which are to count as relevant to P's content.

An associated difficulty lurks behind the lazy formula that identifies S', the displayed subject (and our main interest), with a certain "abstract" of the properties of S. At the moment the photograph was taken, the Abbey must have had any number of properties that might be inferred from the photograph, though irrelevant to that photograph's content. (If the picture showed the doors open, one might correctly infer that visitors were to be found in the Abbey's interior on that day.) Even to limit S' to a specification of visual properties will not serve: somebody might be able to infer correctly all manner of conclusions about the Abbey's visual appearance (e.g., that it looks as if it were leaning on the spectator) without such items being *shown* in the picture.

Some writers have thought that such objections might be overcome by considering the "information" about the Abbey's visual appearance at a certain moment, supposedly embodied in the final print. Such "information" is conceived to have been contained in the sheaf of light-rays originally impinging upon the camera's lens and to have remained "invariant" through all the subsequent chemical transformations. What makes anything, *A*, a "trace" of something else, *B*, is just that *A* in this way presents information about *B*. Examination of the imminent "information" contained in P would thus presumably allow us to distinguish between warranted and unwarranted inference to *P*'s aetiology and so to eliminate the uncertainties about the displayed and the portrayed subjects. I shall subject this conception to criticism below. But we might as well notice another difficulty at once.

Suppose the causal history of a certain photograph to be as outlined above (pointing at the Abbey, chemical changes in the photo-sensitive emulsion, and so on) while the final outcome consisted of nothing better than a uniform grey blur. Should we then, in order to be consistent, have to maintain that we did indeed end with a photograph of Westminster Abbey, though a highly uninformative one?[5] Notice that the Abbey might indeed present the appearance of a grey blur if seen through eyelids almost closed: perhaps the "uninformative" photograph should be regarded as yielding only an *unusual view* of the Abbey? But this is surely too paradoxical to be acceptable.

The moral of this counter-example is that reliance upon the photograph's history of production is insufficient to certify it as having the Abbey, or an abbey, as its subject. No genetic narrative of the photograph's provenance, no matter how detailed and accurate, can logically guarantee that photograph's fidelity. (Of course, if the "accuracy" of the causal account is to be determined by some other kind of test—say "invariance of information," construed as involving no reference to any causal history—the causal account is already shown to be insufficient.)

The causal account I have imagined, now seen to be insufficient as an analysis of the photograph's content, can also be shown not to be necessary either.

Suppose someone invents a new kind of photo-sensitive paper, a sheet of which, upon being "exposed" by simply being held up in front of the Abbey, immediately acquires and preserves the appearance of a conventional photograph. Would we then refuse to call it a photograph of the Abbey? We might perhaps not want to call it a *photograph,* but no matter: it would still surely count as a visual representation of the Abbey.

A defender of the causal approach might retort that the extraordinary paper I have imagined was at least printed at the Abbey, so that the "essentials" of the imputed causal history were preserved. After all, he might add, we are not even normally interested in the details of the particular chemical and physical processes used in producing the final print. Well, so long as we are indulging in fantasy, let us suppose that the extraordinary imprinting effect was producible only by pointing the sensitive paper *away* from the Abbey, while the result was still indistinguishable from the conventional photograph: would that disqualify the product as a visual representation and, for all we know, a highly faithful one?

Some philosophers might reply that if causal laws were violated in these or other extraordinary ways, we "should not know what to think or say." But that seems a lazy way with a conceptual difficulty. Perhaps a single odd example of the kind I have imagined would leave us hopelessly puzzled. But if the phenomenon were regularly reproducible by a standard procedure, I suppose we should be justified in saying that we had simply discovered some new, albeit puzzling, way of producing representations or "likenesses" of the Abbey and other objects. It would be easy to concoct any number of other counter-examples in which end-products indistinguishable from conventional photographs might arise from radically unorthodox procedures.

One might be inclined to draw the moral that the causal histories of photographs—or their fantastic surrogates—are wholly irrelevant to our warranted judgments that they are depictions of the Abbey. But to reject the causal view so drastically may be too hasty. Suppose we found some natural object that "looked like" a certain subject—say, a rock formation that from a certain standpoint looked for all the world like Napoleon: should we then say that the rock formation must be a representation of Napoleon? (Or suppose, for that matter, that objects, looking for all the world like photographs, simply rained down from the sky at certain times.) Surely not. It looks as if the background of a certain aetiology is at least relevant (without being either a necessary or a sufficient condition) in ways that need to be made clearer before we are through.

An obvious counter might be that in the case of the imagined sensitive paper, and in the other examples that we might be inclined to concoct, something must be deliberately *positioned* in order to create, if all goes well, a representation of the subject in question. To be sure, this would exclude the supposed counter-instances of the natural objects, or the objects of unknown provenance that were simply indistinguishable from conventional photographs. But in this imagined objection, there is plainly an appeal to a very different sort of criterion, the *intention* that launched the causal process. This deserves separate discussion. Let us first, however, look more closely at the suggestion that the notion of "information" provides the clue for which we are searching.

Appeal to Embodied "Information"

As I have already said, our puzzle about the blurred photograph would be regarded by some writers as explainable by the "absence of sufficient information" in the final print. More generally, the concept of "information," supposedly suggested by the notion thus designated in the mathematical theory of communication, is held to be useful in resolving the conceptual difficulties that we are trying to clarify.[6]

The current vogue for speaking about "information" contained in representations—and indeed, for bringing that notion into almost any kind of discussion—is certainly influenced by the supposed successes of the notion of "information" that is prominent in the sophisticated mathematical theories usually associated with the name of Shannon.[7] Yet it is easy to show that the two senses of "information" involved have very little to do with one another.

Let us recapitulate briefly what "information" means in the context of the mathematical theory. The first point to be made is that in that theory we are dealing with a *statistical* notion—let us call it "selective information"[8] henceforward to avoid confusion. The typical situation to which the mathematical theory applies is one in which some determinate stock of possible "messages," which may be conceived as alternative characters in an "alphabet" (letters, digits, or pulses of energy) *to which no meaning is necessarily attached,* are encoded into "signals" for transmission along a "communication channel" and ultimate reception, decoding and accurate reproduction of the original "message." Thus individual letters of the English alphabet are converted into electrical pulses along a telegraph wire, in order to produce at the other end a copy of the original string of letters composing the complex message sent.

A rough explanation of the notion of the "selective information" associated with such a communication system would identify it with the amount of "reduction of initial uncertainty" that such a system can achieve. Suppose the various possible messages m_i are known to occur with long-run frequencies or probabilities p_i. We might say that the "information" conveyed by the receipt of a particular message, m_i, varies inversely as its initial probability of occurrence, p_i, For, the higher the initial probability of transmission, the "less we learn" by receiving the message. If the message in question were, in the limiting case, certain to arrive, we should "learn nothing" by receiving it. The mathematical quantity called the (selective) information is the measure of the amount of a certain magnitude—roughly speaking, the reduction in the amount of initial uncertainty of reception, as I have suggested above. It is important to stress that this has nothing to do with the meaning, if any, of such a message, and nothing to do even with its specific content. If I seek an answer to a question by means of a telegram, the only two possible answers being either Yes or No, and both being antecedently equally likely to be sent, then either answer contains the same "(selective) information." Each answer transforms a probability of $\frac{1}{2}$ into certainty. An anxious suitor, awaiting an answer to his proposal of marriage, would of course say that the information received in the one case would be interestingly different from the information he would receive in the other. But that is because he is using "information" in the common or garden sense of what might be called *substantive* information. The theorists of the mathematical theory have no interest in substantive information —which is, of course, their privilege, and not a reproach. To think otherwise would be as misguided as to make it a reproach to a theory of measurement that it tells us nothing about the smell or taste of the masses discussed in that theory.

It would obviously be pointless to think of adapting this model to the case of representation. In place of the messages we should have to think of the original "scenes" corresponding to the representations, to which the long-term frequency of occurrence would have no sensible application. Even in some special case, say that in which male and female entrants to a college were photographed with stable long-range frequencies, the selective or statistical information attached to any photograph would tell us absolutely nothing about the photograph's subject or content—which is our present interest.

A few writers who have clearly seen the limited applicability of the statistical concept here called "selective information" have undertaken studies of what they call "semantic information," that might seem more useful for our purpose.[9] For it would seem that "semantic information," unlike selective (statistical) information, is concerned with the "content" or meaning of verbal representations (statements, texts). The theory of semantic information is presented as a rational reconstruction of what Hintikka calls "information in the most important sense of the word, viz., the sense in which it is used of whatever it is that meaningful sentences and other comparable combinations of symbols convey to one who understands them."[10] Now this seems to be just what we are looking for: the "displayed subject" of a photograph does seem close to what common sense would call the information that could be understood by a suitably competent receiver (viewer).[11] However, if we follow the constructions provided by Hintikka and other pioneers of "semantic information theory" we shall discover, to our disappointment, that they, too, provide something, of whatever interest, that will not help us in our present investigation. For it turns out that the "semantic information" of a given statement is roughly the same as the range of verifying situations associated with that statement—or, more accurately, some measure of the "breadth" of that range. And here, what is finally provided is a measure of extent and not of content.

"Semantic information" is a sophisticated refinement of the common sense notion of the *amount* of information in a statement. Just as a report of a body's mass tells us nothing about what stuff that body is composed of, so a report of semantic information would tell us nothing about what the statement in question is *about*. If we have two statements of parallel logical structure, say, "My name is Black" and "My name is White,"[12] any acceptable definition of semantic information will assign the *same* semantic information to each statement. If this concept (whose interest I do not wish to deny) were applicable to paintings,[13] we should have to count distinct paintings with roughly comparable subjects (say, two paintings of a flock of grazing sheep) as having and conveying the "same information." But of course the displayed subjects of two such paintings might be manifestly different.

We need a term to distinguish what Hintikka, as we have seen, called "the most important sense of information," i.e., what we mean by that word in ordinary life: let us call it *substantive* information. And let us stretch the word to apply to false statements as well as to true ones (so that what would ordinarily be called "misinformation" also counts as substantive, but incorrect, information). What then could we mean by talking about the (substantive) information contained in a given photograph?

On the assumption that we have a sufficiently firm grip upon the notion of the substantive information contained in a *statement,* one might think of replacing the given photograph, *P,* by some complex statement, *A,* such that a competent receiver might learn just as much from *A* as from *P,* if *P* were to be a faithful record of the corresponding original scene. But surely there is something fanciful about this suggestion. Suppose somebody were to be presented with such a statement, *A,* and asked then to retrieve the photograph, *P,* of which it is supposed to be in some sense a translation, from a large set of different photographs. Is there good reason to think that such a task must be performable in principle? It seems to me, on the contrary, that the notion of a complete verbal translation of a photograph (and still more, the notion of a verbal translation of a painting) is a chimaera. A picture shows more than can be said—and not simply because the verbal lexicon is short of corresponding equivalents: it is not just a matter of the nonavailability of verbal names for the thousands of colours and forms that we can distinguish. But if so, the notion of information that has its habitat in connection with verbal representations (statements) will still fail to apply to the case that interests us.[14] In the end, it seems that what is picturesquely expressed by means of the figure of the "information" contained in a photograph or a painting comes to nothing else than what we mean when we talk about the "content" of the painting or "what it shows" (its displayed subject). There would be no objection to the introduction of a metaphor or analogy based upon information, if that provided any illumination. It seems to me, however, that this is not the case, and that reliance upon "information" on the basis of a more or less plausible analogy amounts in the end only to the introduction of a synonym—and a misleading one at that—for "depicting" or "representing." It is not unfair to suggest that "the information conveyed by a painting" means nothing more than "what is shown (depicted, displayed) by that painting."

We may, nevertheless, draw a useful lesson from this abortive digression. One caution, stressed repeatedly by theorists of statistical and semantic information alike, is that the measures of information they discuss are always *relative* to a number of distinguishable factors in the relevant situations. In the case of statistical information, the amount of information is relative to the distribution of long-term frequencies of the system of possible messages transmissible in the communication channel in question; in the semantic case, the amount of information embodied in a statement is relative to the choice of a language and, on some treatments, to assumptions about given laws constituting an antecedent stock of given "information" to which any statement not inferrible from those laws makes an additional contribution. We might, therefore, be encouraged to draw a somewhat obvious moral: that however we come to identify or describe the substantive content of a painting or other visual representation, the answer will be relative to some postulated body of knowledge (concerning for instance the chosen schema of representation, the intentions of the painter or sign-producer, and so on). The idea that a painting or a photograph "contains" its content or subject as straightforwardly as a bucket contains water is too crude to deserve refutation. But ideas as crude as this have in the past controlled some of the discussions of our present topic.

Appeal to the Producer's Intentions

I shall now consider the suggestion that a way out of our difficulties might be found by invoking the intentions of the painter, photographer, or whoever it was that acted in such a way as to generate the visual representation whose "subject" we are canvassing. I do not know of any theorist who has based a full-fledged theory of representation on this idea, but corresponding theories of verbal representation are fairly common. Thus Professor Grice, in a well-known paper on "meaning,"[15] has urged that the meaning of an utterance can be analysed in terms of certain complex intentions to produce a certain effect in the hearer.[16] Again, Professor E. D. Hirsch, in a well-known book, has defined verbal meanings as "whatever someone has *willed* to convey by a particular sequence of linguistic signs and which can be conveyed (shared) by means of those linguistic signs."[17] There seems to be no reason in principle why this kind of approach should not be equally valid in connection with visual representation—or, indeed, in connection with any sort of representation at all.

The undeniable attraction of this kind of emphasis upon the producer's intention or "will" can be attributed to its tendency to remind us forcibly about the conceptual gap between the "interpretation" of some natural object (as when we infer from the characters of some trace to the properties of something that produced that trace), and the "interpretation" of a man-made object, intentionally created to have meaning or "content" of a sort that is accessible to a competent receiver. But to agree, in Grice's terminology, that the import of a painting is "non-natural" and not reducible to the termini of factual inferences from the vehicle is one thing; to suppose that the determinable subject of such a non-natural object can be defined in terms of features of the producer's intentions is something else that is far more problematic.

There is, to begin with, the immediate objection that the producer's intention, supposing it to have existed in some uncontroversial way, may misfire. Suppose I set out to draw a horse and, in my lack of skill, produce something that nobody could distinguish from a cow by simply looking; would it then necessarily be a drawing of a horse, just because that was what I had intended? Could I draw a horse by simply putting a dot on paper? If the answers were to be affirmative, we should have to regard the artist's intentions as having the peculiar character of infallibility: simply wanting a painting to be a painting of such-and-such would necessarily make it so. Surely this is too paradoxical to accept. Of a botched and un-recognizable drawing we should want to say "He intended to draw a horse, but failed" as we should say, in certain circumstances, of any failed intention. The notion of intention involves the notion of possible failure.

A still more serious difficulty and one, if I am not mistaken, that is fatal to this approach, is that there is no way of identifying the relevant intention except by invoking the very notion of a subject of a possible painting that such reference to intention is supposed to clarify. Let us take the envisaged analysis in its crudest and least defensible form. Suppose the proposed analysis of "P depicts S" were to be "M, the producer of P, intended P to be a depiction of S." In this form, the logical circularity is patent: we could not understand the proposed analysis of depicting without already having a clear notion of that relation at our disposal. Nor could the invoked producer properly have any explicit intention to produce P as a depiction of S unless *he* inde-pendently understood what it would be like for the resulting P in fact to be a painting of S: to refer back to the intention that he would have if he were to be trying to make P depict S would enmesh him in hopeless circularity.[18]

The situation would be less objectionable, if the proposed analysis were to take the form: "P depicts S if and only if M, the producer of P, intended E," where E is imagined replaced by some complex expression (and not a straightforward synonym of "P depicts S").[19] Then the cir-cularity noted above would be absent. Only in order for this kind of analysis to be acceptable, E must have the same extension as "P depicts S": we have captured the right intention only if what M intended to do was necessary and sufficient for P being a depiction of S (though not ex-pressed in those words). And if so, we can then dispense with the reference to M's intention altogether, since "P depicts S if and only if E" will, by itself, constitute the analysis we were seeking. This way of look-ing at the matter would also have the advantage of meeting the difficulty about the failed intention that we noticed above.[20]

I conclude that in spite of its attractions, the appeal to the producer's intention accomplishes nothing at all to our purpose.

Depiction as Illusion

We have now considered three types of answers to our prime questions as to the analysis of a statement of the form "P depicts S". Of these, one, the reliance upon the "information" supposedly embodied in the repre-sentation, P, seemed empty, and the two others, in appealing to a causal history and the producer's intention respectively, invoked temporal antecedents that seemed only contingently connected with the final out-come.[21] We still need, it seems, to isolate something about *the representa-tion itself* that will, in favorable circumstances, permit a qualified and competent viewer to perceive in the art object, without dubious in-ferences to antecedent provenance or partially fulfilled intentions,[22] something about P that makes it a painting of S and nothing else.

The reader may be surprised that I have waited until now to consider a famous answer that has behind it the authority of Aristotle and a thousand other theorists who have, in one form or another, endorsed his conception of art as mimesis. Let us try to formulate the conception of art as an "imitation of reality" in a way that will commit us to as little presupposed theory as possible.

Why not say that when I look at a naturalistic painting—say of a white poodle on a sofa—it is *as if*, looking through the picture frame, I actually saw an animal having a certain appearance, resting on a piece of furniture at a certain distance from me. Of course, I know all the time that there is no such poodle in the place where I seem to see it; and that is what makes the experience an illusion, but not a delusion.[23] We are not really deceived, but we have had enough visual experience to know that we see *what it would be like* if the poodle were really there. There is a suspension of disbelief on the viewer's part, as there is when reading fiction, which describes non-existent persons *as if* they really existed. We might therefore speak of "fictive" or "illusive" vision in such cases.

The expression "as if," which I have used in my proposed formula, with its obtrusive reminder of "The Philosophy of As If," may smack of hocus-pocus. But this can be held in check, I think, and the expression treated as a harmless shorthand. To say "A is as if B" is simply to say "If B were the case, then A; but also not B." In a case of illusion, the ob-server knows that not-B, in spite of appearances; in a case of deception or delusion, he believes that *B* is the case, contrary to fact. Thus the proposed analysis for our imagined case is: If there were a poodle of a certain sort and in a certain posture on a sofa at such and such a distance from me, I would see what I now see. Hence, I can see, here and now, what the subject of the picture is, without reference to the painting's aetiology, the artist's intentions, or anything else that is not immediately present. This account must certainly have some truth in it: a layman, in the presence of a painting by Claudio Bravo, will certainly report that it looks for all the world as if there were a parcel behind the surface, and a viewer, no matter how armored by theoretical commitments against the role of illusion, cannot avoid, if he is ingenuous, making a similar report for other cases of *trompe l'œil*. There is, of course, a serious question whether an account that seems to fit this special type of case can be extended, without distortion or eventual tautology, to fit all cases of response to visual representations that are partially naturalistic. I think, however, that there is no serious difficulty in stretching the view to cover cases in which the presented subject is unfamiliar. There is no particular puzzle, on this view, in accounting for the viewer's sight of a flying horse or a fleshy goddess floating in the air. And the account can even be held to fit certain "abstract" works: if I see in a Rothko painting a receding plane bounded by a contrasting strip, and so on, that sight is not unlike what I have learned to see by looking at clouds. Similarly for Mondrian's *Manhattan Boogie-Woogie* or other such abstractions.[24]

On this view, puzzles about how a *P* can depict a determinate *S* reduce to questions about normal perception of the form "How is it that a real poodle can look like a poodle?" I am not sure what useful sense can be ascribed to a question of this form;[25] at any rate, it would fall outside the scope of our present inquiry.

Let us now consider possible objections. The first type consists in effect of the objection that the "illusion" is not, and is not intended to be, complete. As we shift our position with respect to the canvas, we do not get the systematic changes in appearance that would occur if there really were a live poodle in the indicated position: a painted canvas does not even produce as much "illusion" as a mirror. Furthermore, the presented visual appearance is "frozen," does not show the slight but perceptible changes to be seen in even a "still life," and so on.[26]

The second type of objection draws our attention to the perceptible distortion to be noticed even in the most "realistic" paintings: in all but special cases, the sensitive viewer will see the brush strokes and will be aware, after all, that what he sees is not "very much like" the real thing.[27]

The undoubted presence of interfering and distorting features, even in the most "faithful" of paintings, is, up to a point, not serious for a defender of the theory that identifies depiction with illusion. Illusions need not be perfect and we have plenty of experience in genuine perception of discounting variations in appearance[28] and ignoring the effects of imperfections of the eye (floating specks, effects of myopia, and so on). Once we have learned *how* to look through the partially distorting medium of paintings and photographs, we shall simply see the depicted subjects as if they were really present.

But the real difficulties are concealed in the deceptive phrase, "once we have learned how things look," for this concedes in effect that in many cases there is a sense in which the subject does *not* look in the painting as it would if it were really present behind the canvas-plane— and such large deviations from ordinary vision cannot be written off by means of the retort we have just envisaged. If Picasso's women are to be seen *as* women (seen as if they were women behind the canvas) we shall have to learn a key of interpretation for which there is no analogue in normal perception. For instance, we shall have to learn to distinguish between a "faithful" painting of a green face and a green painting of a white face. But once we allow, as we must, for such prior induction into the "technique of representation," the equation of depiction with fictive representation or "illusion" loses its attraction. Instead of saying "P is a representation of S because seeing P is, with some reservations for incompleteness and distortion, like looking at S (seeing P is as if one were seeing S)," we now have to say something like: "In general, P is a representation of S, if P looks like S, according to the conventions embodied in the artist's style and technique." And now, one wonders how much work the surviving reference to "looking as if S were present" really does. Given a case of extreme distortion, is it still necessary to say that we see, and are required to see, something that looks as if it were behind the canvas? Is this not perhaps only a misleading way of making the obvious point that if we have learned how Picasso in his cubistic period painted a woman, we shall *know* that the painting is of a woman?[29] Is anything added by the insistence that we also "see the painting as if" it were something really there? I am inclined to think that by the time the theory has been stretched so far it has degenerated into useless mythology.

Finally, we might notice that the view under examination can be regarded as reducing "depicting" to "looking-like." For instead of saying that P is seen as if S were present, one might as well say that P "looks like S" (although we know that S is not present). Most defenders of an illusion theory have indeed supposed some view concerning resemblance between a picture and its subject to be at its foundation. But this deserves separate examination.

Depiction as Resemblance

We have seen that any tenable conception of depiction as involving a sort of illusion (seeing the painting's subject *as if* it were present) must provide room for the observable differences, ranging all the way from selection to outright distortion, between the subject as represented and as it would appear if actually present. Only when delusion or deception is the controlling aim of the artist, do we get even an approximation to total "imitation." Now a favored way of allowing for the element of unlikeness in even the most "faithful" visual picture is to invoke a notion of *resemblance*: the picture is not conceived now as "looking as if" the subject were present, but rather as looking as if something *like,* something resembling, the subject were present.

A typical statement of this standpoint is the following by Professor Beardsley: " 'The design X depicts an object Y' means 'X contains some area that is more similar to the visual appearance of Y's than to objects of any other class.' "[30]

On a certain rather simplistic conception of similarity or resemblance (which I take to be synonyms in the present context), it is easy to launch devastating objections to any attempt to make resemblance central to the relation of depiction. For one thing, a photograph or a painting, considered as physical objects, is really not at all like horses or trees or oceans, and there is something askew in supposing a "design" to be more "similar" to a tree than to an ocean. (Cf. asking whether a postage stamp is more similar to a person than to a piece of cheese.) But if we take Beardsley's formula as a careless way of saying that the *look* or appearance of the "design" has to be "more similar" to the *look* of a tree than to the look of an ocean, we are at once enmeshed in all the conceptual difficulties that attend any conception of comparisons between such dubious entities as "looks."[31]

We need not enter upon this controversial range of questions, since the superficial logical structure of the verb "to resemble" makes any resemblance view excessively implausible. To take only a single point: we tend to think of the relation of resemblance or similarity as symmetrical. If *A* resembles *B*, then necessarily *B* resembles *A,* and both resemble one another.[32] However, if we take this seriously, we shall find ourselves committed to saying that any tree is a representation of any naturalistic picture of a tree. And since nothing resembles a painting so much as a reproduction of it, the absurdity lurks close at hand of identifying the subject of any picture with its copy.[33]

Further Objections to a Resemblance Model

The well-known objections, restated above, to regarding resemblance as the basis of naturalistic depiction, might well leave us unsatisfied. We might have an uneasy feeling that appeal to the surface grammar of "resemblance" is too summary a way of disposing of a putative insight. To be sure, if we treat resemblance as symmetrical and transitive, we shall be saddled with paradoxical consequences; but is there not, after all, we might still think, *something* to the notion that a naturalistic photograph "resembles" or "looks like"[34] its subject? And if so, could we not modify the superficial implications to preserve this insight? If ordinary language commits us to saying, for instance, that in some sense of resemblance a painting resembles nothing as much as itself, is it beyond the wit of man to establish a more appropriate sense of the crucial expression? It will be worth our while to probe more deeply.

Our common, simplifying, conception of "resemblance" is controlled, I would like to suggest, by one or more "pictures"[35] or idealized prototypes of application. Consider the following simple examples of clear cases of "resemblance":

1. A writer is buying a new supply of typing paper in an unfamiliar shop. He *compares* a sheet that is offered him with one from his old and nearly exhausted stock. "That is *rather like* what I want; but that is better; perhaps that *resembles* what I need sufficiently closely."

2. A housewife goes to a shop to buy some extra material for a dress she is making: she compares the material *in imagination* with what she already has. "That *looks almost* like what I need; it *resembles* it very closely; I think it will do."

3. A film producer needs a stand-in for his principal actor in some dangerous sequence. He *compares* the two men, deciding whether the substitute sufficiently *resembles* the star, so that the audience will not detect the substitution.

4. A historian compares the career of Hitler and Stalin for *"points of resemblance."*

5. In trying to sway a judge, an advocate offers a previously decided case as a precedent, but is met with the objection, "I don't see sufficient resemblance between the cases."

Such examples and the many others that could easily be produced suggest the following reflections:

a. The notion of resemblance is closely connected with the **notions of** *comparison* and *matching* (also with that of *similarity*, which I shall here ignore). In some of the cases, but not in others, the ideal limit of the scale of relative resemblance is that of indistinguishability: if the writer could not tell the new paper apart from the old, he would surely be satisfied, though he would be willing to accept something less satisfactory. And similarly, *mutatis mutandis*, for cases 2 and 3.

b. In other cases, the degree of "resemblance" in the things compared turns upon point-to-point correspondences, so that there is an observed *analogy* between the things compared, while indistinguishability is not in question (cases 4 and 5).

c. What determines the choice of specific criteria of degree of resemblance in a particular case results from the overarching purpose of the particular process of matching or analogical comparison: sometimes it is a question of finding an acceptable *surrogate,* with respect to appearance, durability, or other properties; sometimes a matter of finding a justification for applying general concepts, dicta, maxims, or principles (cases 4 and 5). In short, what counts as a sufficient degree of resemblance, and the respects in which features of resemblance are treated as relevant, is strongly determined by the overall purpose of the process. To put the point negatively: in the absence of such a purpose, any proposed process of comparison is indeterminate and idle. If I am asked to compare *A* with *B,* or to say how much resemblance there is between them, in the absence of any indication of what the comparison is to be used for, I do not know how to proceed. Of course, if politeness requires me to make some response, I may invent some purposive context, trying to assimilate the task to some familiar case, and hence seeking for points of color resemblance, or similarity of function, or whatever else ingenuity may suggest.

Of the points I have singled out for emphasis, the first two serve mainly to remind us of the great variety of procedures that are covered by the umbrella term "resemblance": that compendious label covers a large variety of processes of matching and analogy-drawing, performed in indefinitely many ways and for indefinitely many purposes, with corresponding variety in what counts as appropriate and relevant to the comparison procedures. But the third point, stressing the relativity of comparision with relation to some controlling purpose, is the crucial one for the present inquiry. It is quite opposed in tendency to the picture we have of "resemblance" being constituted by the sharing of common properties, as if we could decide the question whether one thing were or were not similar to another *in vacuo,* without any reference to the aim of the exercise. (Cf. asking whether *A* is better than *B,* which also demands a comparison, in the absence of further determination of the question's sense.)

Let us now apply these elementary reflections to our prime case of the painting and its subject. The first obstacle to using either pattern of resemblance (the search for an approximate match or the search for an analogical structure) is, as we have already seen, that the "subject" is normally not available for independent scrutiny. When the painting is "fictive," there can be no question of placing it side-by-side with its subject in order to check off "points of resemblance." But let this pass, though the point is far from trivial: it remains that the determining purpose of the imputed comparison is left unstated. What is the *point* of my looking first at a portrait of Queen Elizabeth and then at the queen herself, in order to find points of resemblance? There can be no question here of the painting being a surrogate for the person, as in some of our exemplary cases. Nor can it be a matter of being able to make corresponding statements about the two, though that *might* be the point, if the portrait were to be preserved in some historical archive to supplement and amplify some verbal description. We are left with nothing better than the empty formula that the painting should "look like" the sitter. But that is merely to substitute the unanalyzed expression "looks like" for our problematic expression "resembles." Here again, the point about the absence of determination of purpose is relevant. Given that for some purposes and in some contexts the most naturalistic *trompe l'œil* portrait will look conspicuously unlike a person, what is to *count* as "looking like"? Whatever merits the resemblance view might have, it cannot provide answers to these questions.

My chief objection to the resemblance view, then, is that when pursued it turns out to be uninformative, offering a trivial verbal substitution in place of insight. (In this respect it is like the view of depiction as the expression of "information" previously discussed.) The objection to saying that some paintings resemble their subjects is not that they don't, but rather that so little is said when only this has been said.

"Looking Like"

I have agreed that stress upon "resemblance," however philosophically uninformative in the end, does at least serve the useful purpose of reminding us how the fact that a painting resembles something *in the sense of looking like it* may be relevant. It would be a willful violation of common sense to say, for instance, that whether a photograph "looks like" a tree, a man, or whatever the case may be, has *nothing* to do with its function as a picture. Certainly a picture may "look like" its subject, but the problem is to see whether we can say anything useful about what "looking like" amounts to. So it should be worth our while to examine somewhat more closely the notions connected with the expression "looking like" or its grammatical variants.

Here we shall immediately find, as in the case of the words connected with "resemblance," that there are paradigmatic uses that need to be distinguished. So let us begin again with some examples.

1. We are meeting somebody at the station. Pointing to someone approaching in the distance, you say, "That looks like him."
2. On meeting twin brothers, you say "Tom does look very much like Henry, doesn't he?"
3. Of a cloud: "Look at that: doesn't it look like a bird?"
4. We might say of a man: "He looks very much like a wolf."

The first type of case might be identified as one of *seeming*. It can sharply be distinguished from the others by the possibility of substituting the phrase "looks as if," with corresponding adjustment in the rest of the utterance. Thus, in case 1, little if any difference would result from saying "That looks *as if it* were him." Two other grammatical points may be made. If we try to insert adverbial qualification, as in "That looks *very much* like him," we may justifiably feel that we are shifting to another use: thus to the latter remark, but not to the original one I have imagined, it might be natural to reply, "I don't see the resemblance." A connected point is the difficulty of negating the original remark: If I want to disagree with "That looks like him," in the intended use, the best I can do is to say, "No, that does not look like him" or "I don't think so"—while "No, that looks unlike him" has, in context, the feel of playing on words. For present purposes, we may think of this first use of "looks like" as connected with qualified assertion: the whole utterance has the force of expressing a weak truth-claim, with the implication of lack of sufficient and conclusive reason. (Cf. the form "That might be him.") I note this use only to exclude it from further consideration, since it obviously has no application to our prime subject: there is normally no occasion to make qualified assertions about the subject of a painting or picture.[36]

The second type of case is the one already discussed, in which explicit and even point-by-point matching is present or in the offing. Here, reference to "resemblance," in uses close to some that we previously listed, is appropriate.

In the third case (the cloud "looking like a bird"), I should want to argue that the attempt to assimilate it with full-blooded matching would be a distortion. For one thing, we seem here to be engaged in some kind of indirect *attribution*, rather than in some implicit comparison. For instance, a supplementary question of the form "Like *which* bird?" would be rejected as stupid, unless taken to be a request for further specification of the attribute (an eagle, rather than merely a bird). Here, it is worth emphasizing that recourse to "points of resemblance" will seem particularly out of place; indeed, the form of words "Look at that cloud: doesn't it *resemble* a bird?" will feel like a shift to the previous type of use.[37] One might say that, in certain cases of this type, the speaker is more or less indirectly describing the situation *before* him. It is as if, given the task of describing the cloud in terms of an animal, he were to say "If I *had* to describe it as some kind of animal, the only one that would fit would be 'a bird'." There are some obvious analogies here to the use of metaphor, as contrasted with the use of simile: *looking-like* in the context of attribution, rather than comparison, is closer to metaphor than to simile.

Finally, there are cases like the last ("He looks like a wolf"), where the suggestion of comparison, which is admittedly still present, is so far suppressed as to have almost no effect. Saying of a man that "He looks like a wolf" or, alternatively, "He has a wolfish look" may be a way of recording an immediate impression, with no thought of being able to specify points of resemblance or, in some cases, of being able to specify *any* ground for description. In such cases we might be said to be dealing with *non-exponible* metaphor or catachresis. On being challenged as to the propriety of our description, perhaps the best we can say is that it seems to fit—which is, of course, saying very little.

The chief moral that I wish to draw from this brief examination of some related uses of "looks like" is that if we had to position in our schema the use of such a sentence as "That looks like a sheep" (said while pointing to a picture), we should do well to choose the last of our four types. If one says of a painting, or part of one, "That looks like a man," one is normally not saying that there is partial but incomplete evidence for its being a man (which would be preposterous), nor that there are exponible points of resemblance between that patch of painting and a man (which is highly implausible and, in the absence of any assignable point to the comparison, idle), nor attributing a property to that patch as one might, by way of simile, call a cloud bird-like, but rather saying something about that very thing before us, as we say of a man that he has a wolfish look, intending to say something directly about him—and not about a certain imputed relation to wolves. If so, the sense in which a realistic painting "looks like" its subject still resists analysis. One might even be inclined to say, indeed, that that expression ought to be avoided, as tending to have misleading suggestions.

If a child were to ask how one would learn to find out whether a canvas "looks like" a man, perhaps the best we could say is, "Watch a painter at work on his canvas and then, in the end, perhaps you will really *see* a man when you look at the painting." But if that is the best that we can say (as I believe), it looks as if the fruits of our analytical investigation are, after all, very meagre.

A Landing Place

I have now completed the task of examining the credentials of plausible candidates for the role of a necessary condition for the holding of the relation of "depiction." I have satisfied myself, and perhaps the reader also, that none of the criteria examined will supply a necessary condition.

Appeal to the "causal history" of a photograph or a naturalistic painting came to look like the invocation of contingent factual circumstances that may in fact be needed for the production of a terminal visual representation, but do not determine its character as a picture by virtue of logical or linguistic necessity. By considering extraordinary, but logically possible, cases in which deviant casual histories might produce pictures indistinguishable from our paradigms of faithful likenesses, we were able to eliminate appeal to a causal history of a special kind as a necessary or a sufficient condition. The same verdict, however disappointing, was all that emerged from our examination of the other criteria. Reference to the imputed intentions of the picture's producer seemed enmeshed in hopeless circularity, since the very specification of such an intention required independent specification of what would count as fulfilling the producer's intention. The seductive model of "information," factitiously borrowing prestige from an irrelevant mathematical theory, proved a will-o'-the-wisp, amounting in the end to no more than a linguistic rechristening of the problematic concept of "depiction." Finally, reliance upon the attractive notion of "resemblance" between a picture and its "subject" left us, once we had unravelled the skein of criteria concealed by the deceptive surface unity of the abstract label of "resemblance," with nothing more than our original problem, under the guise of questions as to what it really means to say that a picture "looks like" what it represents, in the crucial cases in which "looking like" cannot properly be assimilated to point-to-point matching with some independently given object of comparison.

Are we then left empty-handed? Should we confess that the investigation we undertook has been a complete failure with no hope of improvement? Such conclusions would, in my judgment, be too hasty. For the point needs to be made, and with emphasis, that the disqualification of some proposed condition as a necessary and sufficient criterion by no means shows that condition to be *irrelevant* to the application of the concept in question.

It would, for instance, be quite wrong to suppose that knowledge of how photographs are regularly produced, and of the perceptible changes that occur in the series: displayed scene, negative, and final positive, have *nothing* to do with our ultimate judgement of the photograph's representative content. On the contrary, our mastery of the skill of interpreting or "reading" photographs depends essentially upon our schematic knowledge of how such photographs are *in fact* normally produced.[38] It is through our knowledge of the photograph's provenance that we understand what the photograph "shows." In cases of mysterious provenance, as when a layman looks at an X-ray photograph, the absence of relevant factual knowledge of aetiology obnubilates comprehension. Indeed, in disputed or ambiguous cases, specific reference to the circumstances of production may be necessary in order to determine *what* the subject is.[39]

Similar remarks apply to the currently discredited appeal to the producer's intentions.[40] Although we cannot define "depiction" or "verbal representation" in terms of intention without vicious circularity, it may be altogether proper, indeed sometimes essential, to refer back to the producer's intentions in order to be able to read the very picture in which his intentions, to the extent that they were successful, were ultimately embodied. Here, as before, to pretend that we could ever learn to understand photographs or paintings without repeated reference to what photographers and painters were trying to achieve would be unrealistic.

Finally, similar points can be made about "resemblance" and "looking like." Our justified qualms about the capacity of these to provide defining conditions for the overall concept must not be allowed to obscure the utility, at times, of relying upon point to point comparisons or—to jump to something different—to the "way the picture looks" or simply to "what we inescapably see in the picture."

The proper moral to be drawn from the initially disconcerting outcome of our investigation is that the notion of "depicting" is what has been called a "range concept" or a "cluster concept."[41] The criteria we have considered—and perhaps others we have overlooked—form a skein, none of them being separately necessary or sufficient, but each of them relevant in the sense of potentially counting toward the proper application of the concept of depiction. In perfectly clear cases, all of the relevant criteria point together toward the same judgment, whether we rely upon what we know about the method of production, the intentions of the producer, or the sheer "look" of the picture as it appears to a competent viewer who sufficiently knows the tradition within which the picture is placed.[42]

A reader who might agree with this kind of moral might still perhaps wonder why, if "depicting" is properly to be viewed as a "range-" or "cluster-concept," just *these* criteria should have been "clustered" together. One answer might be to invite such a questioner to undertake the *Gedankenexperiment* of imagining conditions in which the criteria were disassociated.[43] The point of *our* concept of depiction— the "only" concept we have—might then become plainer. But such an answer, whatever its pedagogical merits, is somewhat evasive.

There is something of the first importance lacking from our account, namely all consideration of the purposes of the activities in the course of which, what we, in our culture, recognize as "pictures" are produced. And no account of the concept of depicting, or of the various related concepts bundled together under that label, could be adequate without some examination of such purposes.

This weakness in our discussion might even be felt in connection with our account of how photographs depict. Photographs have been talked about in this essay as if they were objects having no identifiable uses and consequently no intelligible interest. But we are ovbiously keenly interested in photographs, and for a variety of reasons. If we focus upon one such interest, say that of *identifying persons* (as in passport photographs), we shall not find it difficult to see why some of our criteria harmonize with that purpose. Of course, it is by no means easy to formulate, with any show of thoroughness, the many purposes that photographs serve in our culture; and when we pass to the more difficult realm of art objects, the difficulties multiply. But the moral to be drawn is that clarity about the basic notion of artistic representation cannot be expected to be reached by a process of logical analysis alone, however sophisticated in its apparatus of "cluster concepts" and "family resemblances," but will call for a less tidy and more exacting inquiry into the production and appreciation of art objects within "ways of life." But this is hardly the place for what is already too long a discussion.[44]

Notes

1. There is an obvious analogy here with the sense/reference distinction connected with verbal descriptions. In the case of such a description, the "original scene," if any, corresponds to the entity or event identified by the description. The displayed subject of the painting is analogous to the description's sense or meaning, which attaches to it whether or not it identifies any actual entity or event.

2. Cf. the corresponding analytical task for "the concept of cause," where, in my opinion, the best to be hoped for is a similar mapping of variations of sense, based upon an exhibition of the relevant criteria of application underlying such variation.

3. I am here deliberately ignoring, for the time being, the distinction previously introduced between the displayed and the portrayed subject. For to make this distinction at once might interfere with the plausibility of the first answer now to be considered.

4. "It will be helpful if we look at images as traces, natural or artificial ones. After all, a photograph is nothing but such a natural trace, a series of tracks left . . . on the emulsion of the film by the variously distributed lightwaves which produced chemical changes made visible and permanent through further chemical operations" (Gombrich 1969, p. 36).

5. Some members of my audience at the lecture on which this essay is based were willing to take this view, insisting that the aetiology had over-riding importance, no matter how disappointing the resulting "trace." This illustrates the grip that the causal model can have—to the point of its being accepted in the teeth of the most absurd consequences.

6. Gombrich, influenced by Professor J. J. Gibson's writings on perception, has suggested that instead of speaking about "interpretation" we speak instead about how "the sensory system picks up and processes the *information* present in the energy distribution of the environment" (Gombrich 1969, p. 47). He adds that he is "fully alive to the danger of new words, especially fashionable words, becoming new toys of little cash value" (*ibid.*). But he relies strongly upon what he takes to be "the concept of information [as] developed in the theory of communication" (p. 50) throughout his article.

7. See Shannon and Weaver (1949) and Cherry (1966) for explanations of the technical theory. It is ironic that experts in information theory have repeatedly protested, apparently without success, about the misleading consequences of identifying what is called "information" in the technical theory with the meaning of that word in ordinary language.

8. See Cherry (1966), p. 308.

9. See especially Bar-Hillel (1964), Chapters 15-17, and Hintikka (1970). Bar-Hillel says: "It must be perfectly clear that *there is no logical connection whatsoever between these two measures, i.e., the amount of (semantic) information conveyed by a statement and the measure of rarity of kinds of symbol sequences* [our "selective information"], even if these symbol sequences are typographically identical with this statement" (p. 286, italics in original). And again. "*The concept of semantic information has intrinsically nothing to do with communication*" (p. 287, original italics)—and hence it has nothing to do with the concept of information that is defined relative to communication systems. On the other hand, Hintikka says he has "become increasingly sceptical concerning the possibility of drawing a hard-and-fast boundary between statistical information theory and the theory of semantic information" (p. 263). His suggestion that

semantic information theory start with "the general idea that information equals elimination of uncertainty" (p. 264), a formula that would, as explained above, fit the case of selective (statistical) information, shows the link that Hintikka relies upon—in spite of Bar-Hillel's vigorous attempt to separate the two concepts.

10. Hintikka 1970, p. 3.

11. There is, to be sure, some violence done to ordinary language here. Common sense would reserve the use of "information" for what is conveyed by the photograph about the original scene. It would be paradoxical to think of the painting of an *imaginary* scene as providing information to anybody—just as paradoxical as supposing that *The Pickwick Papers* contains information about Mr. Pickwick.

12. On the plausible assumption that the two surnames occur with equal frequency in the populations in question.

13. I do not think that anybody has yet tried to apply the concept of semantic information to visual representations. One difficulty, and perhaps not the most serious one, would be that of "articulating" a given verbal representation in a way to correspond to the articulation of statements in a given language into an ordered array of phonemes. Unless we can regard a photograph or a painting, by analogy, as composed of atomic characters, corresponding to phonemes, the desired analogy will hardly find a handhold. Then, of course, there is the lurking difficulty behind any attempt to assimilate paintings or other verbal representations to assertions with potential truth-value. This might serve for blueprints, graphs, and other representations designed to convey purported facts ("information" in the ordinary sense), but would hardly fit, without inordinate distortion, our prime case of paintings.

14. Of course, I do not wish to deny that we can put into words some of the things that we can learn from a faithful photograph. If anybody wants to express this by saying that information can be gleaned from such a photograph, there can be no harm in it. But we shall never in this way be able to identify the subject of the photograph. One is at this point strongly inclined to say that in some sense the visual subject can *only* be shown.

15. See Grice (1957) and (1969) for the elaboration and modification of his position in reply to criticism.

16. The details do not concern us here. The novelty in Grice's account consists in differentiating between a primary intention on the speaker's part to produce a certain belief or action in the hearer, and a secondary intention that recognition of that primary intention shall function as a reason for the hearer to comply with the primary intention.

17. Hirsch (1967), p. 31. The reference to meaning as something that can be conveyed to and shared by others shows that Hirsch is not simplistically identifying the content of an utterance with the content of the speaker's intention. For elaboration of his views about this, see pp. 49-50 of his book. I have no quarrel with Hirsch's vigorous case for the need to refer to an author's intentions in providing adequate interpretations of a text.

18. A similar point has been well made by Miss Anscombe (see Anscombe 1969). "If thinking you are getting married is essential to getting married, then mention of thinking you are getting married belongs in an explanation of what getting married is; but then won't an explanation of what getting married is be required if we are to give the content of thought when one is getting married?" (p. 61). With intention replacing thought, this is the structure of my own argument above.

19. This is, in fact, the structure of Grice's analysis of non-natural meaning, which is therefore not open to the charge of immediate circularity.

20. It might be an interesting feature of the logical grammar of "depicts" if it were true that "*P* depicts *S*" entailed "The producer of *P* intended *P* to depict *S*." (Cf. "That counts as a move in the game only if the player intended to make that move"—which need not be circular and may indeed be informative.) Unfortunately, even that is not true: the photograph may show much that its producer did not intend and would not even retroactively assimilate to his intention. There is such a thing as unintentional showing—as there is such a thing as unintentional speaking.

21. This is not strictly true for the case of intention: what the artist successfully succeeded in achieving, in accordance with an embodied intention, does usually determine the intrinsic character of the product.

22. We might say that the only intention that is relevant is the intention that the artist succeeded in embodying in the painting. Of course, a knowledge of the background—the tradition within which the artist was working, the purpose he had in mind, and other things—may well help us to "read" his painting, but the satisfactory reading must in the end be based upon what is there to be found in the painting.

23. For views of this sort, see Gombrich (1961), passim. Given Professor Gombrich's illuminatingly rich and detailed discussions of "illusion" in his great book and elsewhere, I would hesitate to saddle him with any simple view about the role of illusion in art. That he seems to assign a central, though by no means exclusive, role to such illusion seems indicated by such references as "the illusion which a picture can give" (Gombrich 1969, p. 46). But he has always carefully distinguished, as I wish to do, "the difference between an illusion and a delusion" (*op. cit.,* p. 60).

24. I am not arguing that looking "through the surface" is a proper way of looking at all abstractions: in Mondrian's case, we know it would be contrary to his intentions. My point is only that the conception of depiction as illusion can cover a far wider range of cases than is sometimes assumed.

25. The undoubted interest of this type of question for psychologists such as Professor J. J. Gibson (see, for instance, his 1968 book) arises from the need to explain how a flux of radiant energy, reaching the eyes, can be so processed that the viewer can correctly see the poodle as solid, at a certain distance from him, and so on. But answers to this kind of question, important as they are, are not our concern here. Cases of veridical experience are sufficiently familiar to be used as explanations for the more problematic cases of seeing *as if*.

26. "As the eye passes over the picture, across the frame, to the wall on which it is placed, it cannot but become aware, however cunning the painting may be, of a discrepancy or discontinuity which is fatal to the illusion" (Wollheim 1963, p. 25). This assumes, without justification, that unless an illusion is total, it is not an illusion at all. Imagine an open aperture through which I could see an actual landscape outside: then what happened as my eye passed over the walls and so on would not prevent me from saying that I saw the landscape.

27. Cf. the reaction of Roy Campbell on first seeing snow, having seen only paintings of it before: "From paintings I had imagined it to be like wax, and snow flakes to be like shavings of candle grease" (quoted from Gombrich 1961, p. 221).

28. Cf. the famous "constancy phenomenon" (for which see, for instance, Hochberg 1964, p. 50). We see a poodle—indeed the same poodle, from different angles, at different distances, and in various lights. Then why should we not be able to see the poodle through whatever distortions are due to the artistic medium and the artist's handling of it? If we can recognize the poodle in moonlight, or even in a trick mirror, then why not when it is, as it were, seen through a painting darkly?

29. Even in a very distorted representation, we can sometimes analyze the particular elements that are operative, picking out one outline or color patch as the face, another as the arm, and so on (but it does not seem necessary that we should always be able to do this). Reliance upon such clues, if that is what they should be regarded as being, does not fit easily into the conception we are here examining.

30. Beardsley (1958), p. 270. I do not wish to saddle Beardsley with some version of the depicting-as-illusion view. An adherent of the conception that the essence of faithful naturalistic depiction is to be found in some relation of resemblance need not be committed to any opinions about the resulting "illusion," although the two conceptions fit well together.

31. The archetypical situation of our crudest conceptions of resemblance, as arising from comparisons of objects, is that of having the two objects side by side and looking at each in turn, in order to "perceive" relevant resemblances. But then the "comparison" of appearances would require a kind of second-order looking at looks. Perhaps this can sometimes be achieved. However, it seems remote from what happens when we see something in a painting as a horse. We do not in the mind's self-observing eye compare the look of what we now see with the look that we should see if we were faced with a horse. To say "That looks like a horse" refers surely to some more primitive operation.

32. It is important that these logical features are not always exemplified in the ordinary language uses of 'look like.' When *A* looks like *B*, *B* need not look like *A*, and the two need not look alike. It is this kind of point that makes any easy reference to resemblance or similarity (as a substitute for the less pretentious but more relevant notion of looking-like) so unsatisfactory.

33. This kind of objection has often been made before. "An object resembles itself to the maximum degree but rarely represents itself; resemblance, unlike representation [=depiction, in this context] is symmetric. . . . Plainly, resemblance in any degree is no sufficient condition for representation" (Goodman 1968, p. 4).

34. I do not mean to imply that these two expressions can always replace one another. Indeed, I shall soon argue that the associated patterns of use show important differences.

35. I am using this word here in somewhat the way that Wittgenstein often did in his later writings. Cf. such a characteristic remark as "The *picture* of a special atmosphere forced itself upon me" (Wittgenstein 1953, p. 158). Wittgenstein's notion of a "picture" deserves more attention than it has yet received. Many of our key words are associated with what might be called semantic myths, conceptions of exemplary and archetypical cases in which the use of an expression seems to be manifested in excelsis. Such an archetypical situation is not merely a paradigm but, as it were, a paradigm of paradigms, wherein we think we can grasp the essence of the expression's meaning in a single flash of insight. It is as if the extraordinary complexity of the expression's actual use were compressed into a dramatic and memorable fiction. To the extent that we are dominated by such a primeval myth, we are led to procrustean conceptualization —a cramping, because over-simplified, conception of the word's meaning. (Of course, Wittgenstein has said this far better.)

36. An exception might be a case in which we were trying to identify the sitter of some portrait or the actual scene of some landscape. In such special case we might say "It looks like Borgia" or "It looks like Salisbury Plain." That would imply the presence of some visual evidence for the identification in question.

37. An obstacle to making this kind of point persuasively is that uses of the words I am discussing are more elastic and variable than I may seem to be contending. I do not doubt that 'resembles' can sometimes and without im-

propriety or ambiguity be used as a contextual synonym for 'looks like.' Yet, if I am not mistaken, the differences in use that I am trying to emphasize really exist and could be fixed more sharply in a longer and more laborious investigation.

38. One might conjecture that a factor in the alleged inability of members of primitive cultures to understand photographs on first seeing them may be partly due to such ignorance of the mode of production. If these bewildered would-be interpreters were allowed to follow through the stages of production, with a chance to compare the negative with the external world, they might begin to have a clue to what Professor Stenius has called the "key" of the relevant system of representation (cf. Stenius 1960, p. 93, where the useful term "key" is however used in a somewhat more restricted sense). For reports of the inability of primitives to "understand" photographs, see for instance Segall et al. (1966), pp. 32-34.

39. Some interesting examples will be found in Gombrich (1969). We should, for example, not know what to make of his illustration of the "Tracks of an oyster catcher" without the accompanying commentary (pp. 35-36)—which explains, *inter alia,* that the bird shown was superimposed on a photograph by an artist. Our knowledge of this unusual causal history materially influences our "reading." Consider also the cases, discussed by Gombrich in the same paper, in which we need to "interpret" photographs of deliberately camouflaged objects (pp. 37 ff.). I agree with Gombrich that "knowledge, a well-stocked mind, is clearly the key to the practice of interpretation" (p. 37). But I think it is also *a* key to the mastery of the relevant *concept* of interpretation.

40. This is hardly the place to discuss the so-called "Intentional Fallacy" that has been memorably castigated in Wimsatt (1954). Professor Hirsch makes the useful and commonly overlooked point that Wimsatt (and his collaborator Monroe Beardsley) "carefully distinguished between three types of intentional evidence, acknowledging that two of them are proper and admissible" (Hirsch 1967, p. 11).

41. For the general methodology of handling such concepts, see Black (1954), chapter 2.

42. Hard cases of "interpretation" typically arise when there is a real or apparent conflict between the defining criteria. When, for instance, we have firm evidence of the producer's intentions and of the means for realizing his intentions within the tradition to which he adheres, but cannot yet "see" the desired embodiment in the picture itself and do not know whether to blame the artist or ourselves.

43. For instance, by imagining, *in full detail,* what the situation would be in a "tribe" (that convenient mental construct) whose members were keenly interested in "seen" likenesses, in total disregard of the intentions or modes of productions responsible for such objects.

44. One of the great merits of Professor Wollheim's stimulating little book on aesthetics (Wollheim 1968) is that he initiates such discussion.

References

Anscombe, G. E. M. "On promising and its justice, and whether it needs be respected *in foro interno.*" *Critica* 3 (April/May 1969).

Austin, John L. "The Meaning of a Word." In his *Philosophical Papers,* ed. J. O. Urmson and G. J. Warnock. Oxford: The Clarendon Press, 1961.

Bar-Hillel, Yehoshua, *Language and Information.* Reading, Mass.: Addison-Wesley Publishing Company, 1964.

Beardsley, Monroe C. *Aesthetics*. New York: Harcourt, Brace and Company, 1958.

Black, Max. *Problems of Analysis*. London: Routledge & Kegan Paul, 1954.

Cherry, Colin. *On Human Communication*. 2nd ed. Cambridge, Mass.: MIT Press, 1966.

Gibson, James J. *The Senses Considered as Perceptual Systems*. Boston: Houghton Mifflin Company, 1966.

Gombrich, E. H. *Art and Illusion*. Revised ed. Princeton: Princeton University Press, 1961.

―――. "The Evidence of Images." In *Interpretation, Theory and Practice*, ed. Charles Singleton. Baltimore: Johns Hopkins Press, 1969.

Goodman, Nelson. *Languages of Art*. Indianapolis and New York: The Bobbs-Merrill Company, 1968.

Grice, H. P. "Meaning." *The Philosophical Review* 66 (July 1957).

―――. "Utterer's Meaning and Intention." *The Philosophical Review* 78 (April 1969].

Hintikka, Jaakko. "On Semantic Information." In *Information and Inference*, ed. J. Hintikka and P. Suppes. Dordrecht: D. Reidel Publishing Company, 1970.

Hirsch, E. D. *Validity in Interpretation*. New Haven: Yale University Press, 1967.

Hochberg, Julian E. *Perception*. Englewood Cliffs, N. J.: Prentice-Hall, Inc., 1964.

Segall, Marshall H.; Campbell, Donald; and Herskovits, Melville J. *The Influence of Culture on Visual Perception*. Indianapolis and New York: The Bobbs-Merrill Company, 1966.

Shannon, Claude E., and Weaver, Warren, *The Mathematical Theory of Communication*. Urbana, Ill.: University of Illinois Press, 1949.

Stenius, Erik. *Wittgenstein's 'Tractatus'*. Oxford: Basil Blackwell, 1960.

Wimsatt, William K., Jr. *The Verbal Icon*. Lexington, Ky.: University of Kentucky Press, 1954.

Wittgenstein, Ludwig. *Philosophical Investigations*. Oxford: Basil Blackwell, 1953.

Wollheim, Richard. "Art and Illusion." *British Journal of Aesthetics* 3 (January 1963).

―――. *Art and Its Objects*. New York: Harper & Row, 1968.

KENDALL L. WALTON

Pictures and Make-Believe[1]

IN SOME RESPECTS I stand towards [a picture-face] as I do towards a
human face. I can study its expression, can react to it as to the expression of the human face. A child can talk to picture-men or picture-
animals, can treat them as it treats dolls.[2]

[R]epresentation is originally the creation of substitutes out of given
material.[3]

I. Introduction

People, objects, and events are *pictured*, or depicted, in *representational* paintings. In novels, by contrast, such things are *described*. Novels
employ "verbal" symbols, whereas paintings and other pictures use
"visual" ones. This difference is both obvious and elusive. That there is
a distinction of a fundamental sort between depicting and describing
seems beyond question. But the difference threatens to vanish when we
reach for it.

In reading a novel to ourselves we *look* at the print on the pages. We
examine a copy of *Brothers Karamazov* with our eyes in order to find out
about Alyosha, as we visually investigate the canvas in order to learn
about the peasants in Breughel's painting *Haymaking*. Why then don't
the marks on the pages of the novel count as "visual" symbols and the
novel as a "visual" art? Of course novels, unlike pictures, can be heard
as well as seen, when they are read aloud. Does that mean that the
novel is, indifferently, an aural or a visual art? The trouble is that
novels seem not to be perceptual at all, in some sense in which paintings
are perceptual, despite the fact that novels, or copies or readings of them,
are to be perceived.

A too easy explanation is that paintings, or parts of them, look like or

From *The Philosophical Review*, LXXXII (1973), pp. 283-319. Revised for this
book and reprinted by permission of *The Philosophical Review* and the author.

resemble what they picture—*Haymaking* looks like fields, peasants at work, haystacks, and so forth. But a copy of *Brothers Karamazov* does not look like the people and events it describes, nor does any of the print it contains. And neither do the sounds of an oral reading of the novel sound like what is described. There are serious difficulties in this proposal, some of which have been exposed by Ernst Gombrich. Nelson Goodman, and others.[4] The resemblance between *Haymaking* and any ordinary peasants, fields, and haystacks turns out on second thought to be exceedingly remote; the painting is a mere piece of canvas covered with paint, and that is what it looks like. A novel about a novel resembles much more significantly what it describes, but that does not make it any the less a novel or any more a picture.

Yet, whatever the ills of resemblance theories of depiction, we cannot afford simply to repress them. Their immense attractiveness strongly suggests that they proceed from some important truth, however murkily perceived and expressed. No theory of depiction can be fully convincing, I submit, unless it accommodates or explains the urge to suppose that pictures do, and must, look like what they picture.[5]

I shall propose a theory of depiction which does not itself postulate any resemblance between pictures and what they depict and so escapes the objections to theories which do; yet one which exposes and renders intelligible the motivations behind such theories. It will also, incidentally, throw some light on the obscure but intriguing notion of *"seeing as."* And it will explain why the novel does not qualify as a visual art along with painting.

We *see* the peasants and haystacks in *Haymaking*. We can also, if we wish, smile or scowl or stare or smirk at a picture-man; we can look deeply into his eyes or avert our eyes from his, look longingly or lovingly at him, or gaze at him absent-mindedly. We can point at picture-haystacks, and examine them methodically or haphazardly with our eyes.

But we do not see Alyosha or Ivan when we read *Brothers Karamazov*. And we cannot stare or smile or point or gaze at Alyosha or Ivan; we cannot, that is, unless the novel provides an illustration, a picture, of them. We might look or smile at (or toward) the print on the pages as we read, but this is not looking or smiling at Alyosha or Ivan.

Picture-men can, moreover, look at us, face toward or away from us, walk in our direction, and so forth, although ordinarily they do not notice or recognize viewers. But Ivan and Alyosha do not look at or away from the reader. They neither face us nor face in the opposite direction. The novel might describe a front view of Alyosha—that is, the features of Alyosha's front side but not those of his back side might be described, just as the front but not the back features of a peasant facing us are pictured. But this does not make Alyosha face us; perhaps he is facing the narrator or fictional reporter of the novel. The view that is described is not our view.

These observations provide a glimpse of the basic difference between pictures and novels, between picturing and describing. But only a fleeting glimpse. For we do not *really* see, or stare or smile at, any peasants when we confront *Haymaking*; there are no peasants there to be seen or stared or smiled at. And we know perfectly well that this is so. All we actually see or smile or stare at (or toward) while looking at a picture is a complex of symbols, and that we can do while reading a novel.[6]

Perhaps reformulation will rescue the distinction. Is it that we *imagine* seeing peasants when we look at *Haymaking*? There is no bar to imagining seeing what does not exist, what is only "imaginary" or "fictional." But we can also imagine seeing the Karamazovs. We can imagine doing just about anything.

A slightly better attempt locates the difference in what the works encourage or instruct us to imagine, what we are supposed to imagine on confronting them. We can, if we choose, imagine peasants' sipping martinis on the beach at Nice, when we see *Haymaking*. But what we are supposed to imagine, what the picture calls for us to imagine, is peasants' working in a field. *Brothers Karamazov* instructs us to imagine Smerdyakov's falling down a flight of stairs, among other things, though we could imagine instead his flying to the moon. (Perhaps there are implicit conventional rules for ascertaining from a work what we are supposed to imagine.) It may be proposed, then, that *Haymaking* instructs us to imagine not only peasants' working in a field but also our watching them work, whereas *Brothers Karamazov* instructs us to imagine Smerdyakov's falling but not our seeing him fall.

This suggestion leads to a dead end. A novel containing vivid visual descriptions encourages readers to have visual images of objects or events that are described; sometimes we can hardly help having such images. Having a visual image of something is not the same as imagining seeing it. But it is not implausible that a novel which encourages the former also encourages the latter. It is not at all clear, then, that a vividly written novel does not "instruct" us to imagine seeing things, in the way that pictures supposedly do. Furthermore, we could add to *Brothers Karamazov* explicit instructions of the relevant kind by inserting in the text the sentence, "Imagine yourself, dear reader, watching Smerdyakov as he tumbles down the stairs." But that addition in no way converts the passage of the novel into a picture. Perhaps it does not because no imagining, whether or not in response to "instructions" in a novel, constitutes *"seeing"* the book, or words, phrases, or paragraphs of it, *"as"* objects or events of the kinds described. Whatever "seeing as" is, it is not imagining. And imagining does not hold the key to the difference between pictures and novels.

It may have been noticed that when we, as we say, "see, or stare, or smile at the peasants" in the painting, we really do see, stare, or smile, though not at *peasants*. But when we imagine seeing, staring, or smiling at someone, Alyosha or anyone else, we need not be seeing, staring, or smiling at all. This is an important clue.

II. The Imaginary and the Make-Believe

In playing with mud pies children pronounce in assertive tone propositions such as the following:

There are three pies here.
I have already baked that pie.
There are raisins in this pie.
That idiot man stepped on one of our pies.
You got a bigger piece than I did.

Commonly these statements, taken literally, are false (or neither true nor false), and are known to be so by the children who make them. But we might regard them as being "fictionally true," or "true in the game of make-believe," in appropriate cases. Thus, I will say, it may be that *p*(F) (read: "It is fictionally true that *p*"), even if it is not true that *p*. A proposition can of course be fictionally false. If *there are three pies in the oven*(F), *it is false that there are only two pies in the oven*(F) (and also it is false that *there are only two pies in the oven* (F)).

Many contexts other than games of make-believe are conveniently construed as providing for statements having fictional truth values. Objects which do not exist and events which do not occur may nevertheless "exist in" or "occur in" dreams, daydreams, novels, paintings, films, plays, legends, and myths.[7]

The fictional truth value of a statement is always relative to some particular game of make-believe, daydream, or other suitable fictional context. It may be that *p*(F) relative to one such context, and *not-p*(F) relative to another one. When it is said that something is fictionally true, or fictionally false, it must always be clear relative to what context it is said to be so, although this does not always have to be made explicit.

It would be desirable to have a generalized account of how to tell whether something is fictionally true or fictionally false (or neither). But providing one would be enormously difficult, and it is not necessary for our present purposes to do so. We know well enough how to go about answering questions about what happened "in" a dream or a daydream, and about characters "in" paintings and novels. We do not need a theoretical basis for answering such questions any more than we need an analysis of the nature of (literal) truth to decide what is true and what is false. Of course there will be instances in which it is hard to decide whether or not a proposition is fictionally true, just as it is sometimes difficult to determine what is (literally) true.

But it is important to differentiate between two species of fictional truth, and to distinguish fictional truth in general from other varieties of what might be called non-literal truth. The former is the subject of this section, and the latter will occupy the next.

What determines the fictional truth value of a proposition relative to a given context varies with the proposition and with the context. In some cases fictional truths are linked to facts about the real world, to literal truths. If *there are three pies here*(F), that is so probably in virtue of the presence in a designated area of three globs of mud. It is understood that were it not for the globs it would be false that *there are three pies here*(F) (and true that *there are not three pies here*(F)). We can regard the game of make-believe as containing a rule to the effect that *there are three pies here*(F) if and only if there are in a certain area three globs of mud of a certain sort, or three of a specified set of globs of mud. Similarly, it may be because one glob is bigger than another one that *this pie is bigger than that one*(F); the fact that a glob contains pebbles may make it true that *this pie contains raisins*(F); and it may be true that *someone stepped on a pie*(F) in virtue of the fact that someone set his foot down on a glob of mud. In cases like these I will say that what is fictionally true is, more specifically, *make-believedly* true. If *p*(F) because of some fact about the real world in the way illustrated by these examples, then *p*(MB). (This will have to be made more precise.)

It may be that in some contexts what is fictionally true is so just because someone imagines, or pretends, or supposes that it is true. Perhaps all that is necessary for it to be true that *Jones is Emperor of China*(F), in the context of a daydream of Jones, is that he imagine on a certain occasion that he is Emperor of China.

But while daydreaming, Jones might deliberate as to whether to be Emperor of China or Emperor of Japan in his fantasy. Suppose that he finally decides on the former. It seems reasonable to count "*Jones is Emperor of China*(F)" true, and "*Jones is Emperor of Japan*(F)" false, relative to the daydream. But I am not prepared to deny that he *imagined* being Emperor of Japan while he was deliberating. So what makes it true in his daydream that *he is Emperor of China*(F) is his *decision* that that should be so; not, or not merely, his imagining being Emperor of China.

Several people may collaborate on a daydream—for example, a daydream about a flight to Pluto. If *the flight took forty-seven years*(F), that is so not because one or even all of the daydreamers imagined that it took forty-seven years, but because (roughly) the members of the group tacitly or explicitly decided or agreed that, in their collective daydream, *it took forty-seven years*(F).

The details of the several examples just given do not matter very much for our purposes. What is important is that, in any case in which "*p*(F)" is true merely because of the fact that one or more persons imagine that *p* (or pretend, or suppose, or make-believe, or dream that *p*), or decide or agree to imagine that *p*, or decide or agree to let it be true that *p*(F), or do any combination of these things, I will say that p is *imaginarily* true, that *p*(I).

We can now characterize what is *make-believedly* true as what is fictionally true in virtue of some fact *other than* anyone's imagining, or deciding or agreeing to imagine, that it is (really) true, or deciding or agreeing to make it fictionally true. I will allow that something is make-believedly true when what makes it fictionally true is *partly* the fact that someone imagines that it is true. But a proposition is not make-believedly true when someone's imagining that it is true by itself (given the "rules of the game of make-believe," or whatever "rules" are relevant) makes it fictionally true.[8]

Facts of the two sorts may separately, rather than jointly, make something fictionally true. When the two facts function independently—that is, when each is sufficient for the fictional truth of p even assuming the absence of the other—I will allow that p is both imaginarily and make-believedly true. But a restriction is needed to handle cases in which the two facts do not function independently. If *p*(F) because someone imagines that p, it may be (in some sense) because or in virtue of some other fact (for example, the fact that the person is in a certain neurological state, or that he confronts some stimulus) that that person imagines that p, and hence indirectly because or in virtue of that other fact that *p*(F). We will stipulate that the fact more directly responsible for the fictional truth of p, in cases like this, is what determines whether p is imaginarily or make-believedly true.[9] So in this example p is imaginarily true, and not make-believedly true.

Since I have explained imaginary and make-believe truth in terms of fictional truth, the explanations must be regarded as incomplete until more is said about the nature of fictional truth in the next section. I shall defer until then final formulations of the definitions of imaginary and make-believe truth. (See p. 297.)

A particular utterance of p may, depending on the context, be properly construed as the statement or assertion that it is literally true that p, or that it is imaginarily true that p, or that it is make-believedly true that p. I will speak accordingly of literal, imaginary, and make-believe statements or assertions of p.

Some propositions may be make-believedly true and others imaginarily true relative to the same context. Fictional truths concerning a game of mud pies are, for the most part, make-believe truths. But participants in a game of mud pies might decide just to decree that something is fictionally true in their game, without linking it to any other actual fact. They might decree, for example, that *Johnny once served a scrumptious pie to Napoleon*(F), in which case *Johnny once served a pie to Napoleon*(I) relative to the game of make-believe. (This might be a reason to assign Johnny the role of head waiter.) In another game, it might be that *Johnny served a pie to Napoleon*(MB), because Johnny placed a mud glob in front of a tree labeled "Napoleon." A game of make-believe may degenerate into a joint or solitary daydream if it acquires an excess of imaginary truths.

Care should be taken not to confuse decisions simply to make propositions fictionally and thus imaginarily true, with decisions to adopt certain rules of make-believe which have the foreseen consequence that certain propositions are make-believedly true. A decision to stipulate that *there is a pie here*(F) might be prompted by the discovery of a glob of mud. But if it is understood that the fictional truth does not depend on the presence of the glob except in so far as the glob encouraged the stipulation—that is, if it is understood that should the glob turn out to be a hallucination it would still be true that *there is a pie here*(F), then that is an imaginary truth. Alternatively, discovery of the glob may prompt a decision to establish the rule that *there is a pie at place P*(F), and thus that *there is a pie at place P*(MB), just in case that glob or one like it is at P. It may be obvious when this decision is made that it will result in the truth of "*there is a pie at P*(F)"; it may be, *in effect,* a decision to make that true. But the result is a make-believe rather than an imaginary truth. It may not always be easy to ascertain which kind of decision has been made, and hence whether something is imaginarily or make-believedly true.

The most significant feature of make-believe truths, as opposed to imaginary ones, is the independence they enjoy from what people take to be fictionally true. If it is a rule of make-believe that the sizes of make-believe pies are equivalent to the sizes of the corresponding globs of mud, and if a glob of mud in Sally's hands is in fact larger than one in Johnny's, then *Sally's pie is bigger than Johnny's pie*(MB) *no matter what* anyone thinks. It may be that Johnny and Sally and everyone concerned believe, mistakenly, that Johnny's glob is bigger than Sally's, and hence that *Johnny's pie is bigger*(MB). (Perhaps they also *imagine* that Johnny has a bigger pie.) Nevertheless, the fact of the matter is that *Sally's pie is the bigger one*(MB). And people may *discover* that this is so on discovering that Sally has the larger glob. We can be ignorant or mistaken about make-believe truths just as easily as we can about the literal truths they rest on; in both cases we are at the mercy of the same fallible verification procedures.

III. The Fictional and the Metaphorical

Make-believe truths have a kinship with metaphorical truths. If on a campaign trip to the Midwest a politician metaphorically started prairie fires (that is, if *the politician started prairie fires*(Met)), that is so in virtue of the success of his campaign activities. What is metaphorically true, like what is make-believedly true, depends on what is literally true.

But metaphorical truths (or at least many typical examples of them) differ in a crucial respect from what I want to call make-believe truths. In this respect imaginary and make-believe truths—that is, fictional truths—stand together.

The point of stating a metaphorical truth is, typically, to inform hearers of the literal truth it depends on. Saying "Jones's campaign started prairie fires in the Midwest" is (in an appropriate context) a way of telling someone something about the progress of the campaign, something that could have been put literally. But the purpose of asserting in a game of make-believe, "This is a raisin pie," typically is not to inform anyone of pebbles in a glob of mud. That assertion hardly functions as a way of saying that there are pebbles in the glob. Participants in the game of make-believe are probably interested in the pebbles only for what they render make-believedly true. It may well make no difference whether it is because of pebbles in the glob that *the pie contains raisins*(MB), or whether there are no pebbles in it, but the rules of the game are such that *the pie contains raisins*(MB) because of something else (because of the light color of the mud, for example). What matters is what is the case "in the game of make-believe," not what is the case in the real world, that is, whether or not *the pie contains raisins*(MB) rather than whether or not the glob contains pebbles.

The focus of interest in the metaphor example, by contrast, is the progress of Jones's political campaign. And that interest is independent of whether we choose literal or metaphorical means of describing the campaign, and if the former, of which metaphorical means we choose. Metaphors characteristically serve to describe, illuminate, clarify, or perhaps explain facts about the real world, but what is "true in a world of make-believe" is of interest in its own right.

The difference is best expressed as a difference in how make-believe and metaphorical statements can be paraphrased. One can reasonably report of someone who said, "Jones's campaign started prairie fires in the Midwest," that he said that Jones's campaign aroused great enthusiasm for his candidacy among Midwestern voters. This, or some such literal description of the progress of the campaign, constitutes a roughly adequate paraphrase of what was said. But what one asserts in saying, "This is a raisin pie," in the context of a game of make-believe is not that there are pebbles in a certain glob of mud. The speaker may "imply" that there are—hearers might learn from his statement that there are, and that he believes that there are—but he does not say that there are.[10] Similarly, if on seeing *Haymaking* someone says, "The peasants are working hard," it would be absurd to report him as having said that the painting contains lines, shapes, and colors of such and such sorts. And descriptions of Alyosha, Ivan, and Smerdyakov do not amount to descriptions of the sentences that occur in the novel, or of the marks that are to be found in a copy of it. In all of these cases there is a literal truth that makes what one says true (if it is true), but that literal truth is not a paraphrase of what one says.

Paraphrasing a metaphorical statement is of course not always a simple matter. Limits to the subtlety or richness of our literal vocabulary sometimes preclude any very adequate literal paraphrase; one reason for speaking metaphorically is to express what is difficult to express literally. But even so one can usually find a more or less approximate literal paraphrase. And one can await the necessary enrichment of his literal language. (On the death of the metaphor, the sentence in question may become a literal paraphrase of its own previous self.) Ambiguous metaphors, which abound in poetry, are particularly resistant to paraphrase. There may be several or many equally plausible candidates for paraphrases of a single ambiguous metaphorical statement, and no reasonable way to decide between them—that is, it may be that none of the candidates is *definitely* even an approximate paraphrase. But one can at least say what the various candidates are. And it is not impossible that there should be a literal statement with matching ambiguities, which would be definitely a paraphrase of the metaphorical statement.[11]

The impossibility of similarly paraphrasing make-believe statements is not due to any limitations of our literal language; it is an impossibility in principle. To say that *this is a raisin pie*(MB) is not to say anything whatever about mud or pebbles. It is hopeless to look for a literal paraphrase of the kind in question—even for an approximate paraphrase or a candidate for one.

Just what kind of paraphrase is it that metaphorical statements admit of but make-believe statements do not? The point is not that make-believe statements cannot be paraphrased, nor that they cannot be paraphrased literally. "*This is a dried grape pie*(MB)" and, more idiomatically, "This is a dried grape pie, in the game of make-believe" are both, when taken literally, paraphrases of "This is a raisin pie," uttered in the context of a game of make-believe. But these paraphrases, although literal themselves, are statements to the effect that something (namely, "This is a dried grape pie") which considered alone would be a literal paraphrase of "This is a raisin pie" taken literally, is make-believedly true.

Any literal paraphrase of a make-believe statement must be of this sort. In paraphrasing "This is a raisin pie," one may refer to, rather than use, the sentence "This is a dried grape pie." That sentence may be either mentioned, as in " 'This is a dried grape pie' is make-believedly true," or it may be referred to otherwise, as in "The last sentence inside quotation marks in the previous paragraph is make-believedly true." (There may be disagreement about whether these qualify as paraphrases.) But one cannot literally paraphrase a make-believe statement of p without *either* using or referring to a sentence which, taken literally and by itself, would be a paraphrase of p taken literally.[12] One cannot literally paraphrase such a statement without somehow expressing or referring to the proposition which *p*, taken literally, expresses. I take this to be an essential feature of make-believe statements, and what distinguishes them from metaphorical statements. "Jones started prairie fires in the Midwest," taken metaphorically, can (at least in principle) be paraphrased without using or referring to any literal paraphrase of that sentence taken literally (any sentence which, taken literally, would paraphrase "Jones started prairie fires in the Midwest" taken literally). Non-literal paraphrases of make-believe statements are of various kinds. "This is a raisin pie" asserted in a make-believe context may be paraphrased by (*a*) "This is a dried grape pie" in the same context. If "iron mine" is taken as a metaphore for "raisin pie," (*b*) "This is an iron mine" may also serve as a paraphrase. (*c*) "This is, metaphorically, an iron mine" in the make-believe context is a paraphrase which is not itself to be taken metaphorically. And (*d*) "This is an iron mine in the game of make-believe" (or "*This is an iron mine*(MB)") is a paraphrase when it is metaphorical but its assertion is not a make-believe assertion (when it is not the assertion that it is itself make-believedly true). In (*a*) and (*c*), but not in (*b*) and (*d*), literal paraphrases of "This is a raisin pie" taken literally are used. But in (*b*) and (*d*) a sentence ("This is an iron mine") is used which, taken *metaphorically*, is a paraphrase of "This is a raisin pie" taken literally. ("This is, metaphorically, an iron mine in the game of make-believe" is a literal paraphrase of the make-believe statement, and it uses a literal paraphrase of "This is a raisin pie" taken literally— namely, "This is, metaphoricallly, an iron mine.")

What one says in asserting "This is a raisin pie" in a game of mud pies thus involves *essentially* the notion of something's being a raisin pie (literally). What is said is of course not that that is literally the case, that it is true of the real world. But, rather than regarding the speaker simply as saying something *else* about the real world, it is natural to regard him as saying that something is a raisin pie in a "fictional world," a "world of make-believe." (Something is said about the real world—that it is true of the real world that in a "fictional world" a pie contains raisins.) There are, however, no "metaphorical worlds" which metaphorical statements are about. It is not true *in a fictional world* that the politician (literally) started prairie fires. To speak metaphorically is merely to speak in a special way about the real world.

Imaginary truths are also comfortably construed as truths about "fictional worlds" ("imaginary worlds"). And the restriction on paraphrases of make-believe statements applies to imaginary statements as well. "The flight to Pluto took forty-seven years," asserted in the context of a daydream about a flight to Pluto, can be literally paraphrased as "*The flight to Pluto took forty-seven years*(I)," or as "In the daydream the flight to Pluto took forty-seven years." I am not sure whether "Jones imagined that the flight took forty-seven years," or "Jones and Smith agreed to imagine that the flight took forty-seven years," or anything of the sort should count as a paraphrase. But all of these candidates for paraphrases, including the last ones, use or refer to something ("The flight to Pluto took forty-seven years") which, taken literally, is a paraphrase of "The flight to Pluto took forty-seven years" taken literally. And there seems to be no even plausible literal way of paraphrasing the imaginary statement of which this is not true.

Thus a statement must be literally paraphrasable only in this way in order to be either make-believe or imaginary, in order to be a *fictional* statement. This enables us to give both necessary and sufficient conditions for fictional truth. I shall assume that it is clear enough in what contexts a sentence is not to be taken literally. And I shall assume that it is clear enough when the assertion of a sentence in a context in which it is to be taken in some non-literal way is the assertion of something true.

p(F) relative to context *C* if and only if

(*i*) *p* is not literal in *C*
(*ii*) *p* is true in *C*
(*iii*) In order to paraphrase literally the statement of *p* in *C* one must either use or refer to a sentence which, taken literally and alone, would be a paraphrase of *p* taken literally.

Imaginary and make-believe truth can then be defined as follows:

p(I) relative to *C* if and only if

(*i*) *p*(F) relative to *C*
(*ii*) *p* is true in *C* in virtue of someone's (or several people's) imagining (pretending, supposing, dreaming) that *p*, or deciding or agreeing to do that, or deciding or agreeing to consider it true that *p*(F), or some combination of these; and this fact is more directly responsible for the truth of *p* in *C* than is any fact which is not of this sort.

p(MB) relative to *C* if and only if

(*i*) *p*(F) relative to *C*
(*ii*) *p* is true in *C* in virtue of some fact which is not the fact of anyone's imagining (pretending, supposing, dreaming) that *p*, or deciding or agreeing to do that, or deciding or agreeing to consider it true that *p*(F), or any combination of these; and this fact is more directly responsible for the truth of *p* in *C* than is any fact which is of that sort.

It should be emphasized that these definitions are not intended to capture the everyday senses of "fictional," "imaginary," and "make-believe." These terms are merely convenient labels for the notions the definitions do capture, although their convenience is probably enhanced by some connections with ordinary usage.

Metaphor has not been defined, and it need not be here since the notion of metaphor will play no part in the discussion that follows. But I have claimed that metaphorical statements are paraphrasable in the way that fictional statements are not, and that metaphorical truths are not fictional in my sense. This may not hold for some examples of what are customarily considered metaphorical truths, some varieties of what might be called "irreducible metaphors." But I recommend construing metaphor so that these examples do not count as metaphorical truths; they are better considered make-believe truths. Bending our usual terminology in this way will pay off in perspicuity. (I do not suggest that all non-literal truths which are not fictional be regarded as metaphorical truths.)

Musical compositions, or performances of them, are sometimes considered *metaphorically* gay, serene, anguished, melancholy, and so forth.[13] But to say that the "Funeral March" of Beethoven's *Eroica* is anguished surely is not to say something about what harmonies, pitches, rhythms it contains (unless merely that they are harmonies, pitches, and rhythms constituting music which is anguished). No technical description of the sounds is a paraphrase of the statement that the music is anguished. And there seems to be no literal way of paraphrasing it without using or referring to some literal paraphrase of "The music is anguished" taken literally. Thus, I suggest, the music is not metaphorically anguished, but rather make-believedly so.

This may not be quite right. It is not obvious that "The music is anguished" *can* be taken literally, that it would make sense to say that music is, *literally*, anguished. Perhaps what is make-believedly true is not that the music is anguished, but that the music expresses (someone's or something's) anguish. "The music is anguished," as that is ordinarily understood, is to be construed as elliptical for "The music expresses anguish," the latter to be taken make-believedly. In any case what is said in describing music as anguished essentially involves the notion of anguish; it cannot be paraphrased without using or referring to some literal paraphrase of "The music expresses anguish," if not "The music is anguished," taken literally. What is said is, if true, a make-believe rather than a metaphorical truth.

We have seen that make-believe truths are like both metaphorical and imaginary truths in different respects, and unlike both in the reverse respects. They share with metaphorical truths dependence on literal truths and the consequent independence of what people imagine or take to be non-literally true. But like imaginary truths, statements of them are not literally paraphrasable by statements of the literal truths they depend on, nor by anything else which does not make explicit their non-literal, their fictional status. They are truths about "worlds" which are distinct from the real world; yet which, like the real world, are not mere figments of people's imaginations.

Make-believe worlds have a unique combination of advantages. They are enough like the real world to be fun, permitting surprise, suspense, and the thrill of discovery. Yet they can be manipulated in ways that the real world cannot be, they often allow us to get away with doing ordinarily dangerous things (such as gobbling up all the pies at once, or splattering them on people's faces) without having to face the usual real world consequences, and they enable us to test our reactions to tragedy without tragedy actually befalling anyone.

The notion of the make-believe will help us to get at the basic difference between pictures and novels.

IV. Pictures and Novels

I propose regarding pictures as props in games of make-believe. "Truths" about picture-objects are fictional, and necessarily so. If statements about the peasants in *Haymaking* were construed merely as ways of describing the patterns of paint splotches on the canvas, rather than as descriptions of peasants in a "fictional world," *Haymaking* would not be for us a representational picture. And "truths" about picture-objects are make-believe rather than imaginary; they are fictionally true in virtue of configurations of paint on canvas. The colors and shapes on the surface of *Haymaking* make it the case that *the peasants are working hard*(MB).

It is equally reasonable to construe "truths" about characters in novels as make-believe ones. *Smerdyakov fell down the stairs*(F) in virtue of the presence of certain sentences in the novel; hence *Smerdyakov fell down the stairs *(MB).[14]

The difference lies in our earlier observation that we somehow see, stare, and smile at picture-objects in a way that we do not do those things to novel-objects. When I look at *Haymaking* *I see peasants*(MB), and perhaps also *I smile at peasants*(MB). It is fictionally true that I see peasants, on looking at the canvas, and that is so in virtue of what I do in front of the canvas, plus the fact that the shapes on the canvas are as they are (otherwise it would not be peasants that I am make-believedly seeing). When I read *Brothers Karamazov*, on the other hand, at most *I see, or smile, at Alyosha*(I), if *I see or smile at Alyosha*(F) at all. There is no provision for any action of mine or anything else (except, possibly, my imagining seeing or smiling at Alyosha), making it fictionally true that I see or smile at Alyosha.

But there is another hole to plug. If a novel is about both me (in the way *War and Peace* is about Napoleon) and Alyosha, and if it describes me as seeing Alyosha, it is true in virtue of sentences in the book that *I see Alyosha*(F). Hence *I see Alyosha*(MB). This of course is not comparable to what happens when it is make-believedly true that I see peasants while I am looking at the painting. It requires nothing of me, not even my reading the novel.

We might stipulate that when the subject expression of a fictionally true proposition refers to a real object, that object fictionally possesses the property attributed to it by the predicate of the proposition. If *O is P*(F), and we are willing to quantify over "O," then O *is P*(F). (This converts the sentence operator "* . . .*(F)" into a predicate operator.) Corresponding senses could be given to "O *is P*(I)" and "O *is P* (MB)." But this would not yet bring out a difference between pictures and novels. It would make *both* "I *see peasants*(MB)" and "I *see Alyosha*(MB)" true, if "*I see peasants*(MB)" and "*I see Alyosha* (MB)" are both true. We must specify further that "O *is P*(MB)" can be true only when *O is P*(MB) in virtue of some fact *about* O. On the reasonable ruling that the fact that certain sentences occur in a novel is not a fact about me, it is now not true that I *see Alyosha*(MB) if it says in a novel that I see Alyosha. But it remains true that when I look at *Haymaking* I *see peasants*(MB), for *I see peasants*(MB) in virtue (partly) of what I am doing when I look at the picture.

The notion of something's being a fact *about* a certain object is not unproblematical. But we need not rely on it here. Since the cases we will be concerned with are cases in which a person make-believedly performs a certain action, let us say that a (real) person, A, *X-es*(MB), where X is an action,[15] just in case it is true partly in virtue of A's (really) performing some action that *A X-es*(MB). Since it is because (roughly) I look at *Haymaking* in a certain way that *I look at peasants* (MB), I *look at peasants*(MB). It is in, or by, looking at the painting in the appropriate manner that I *look at peasants*(MB). But the reader does not *look at Alyosha*(MB), and would not even if he were a character in the novel described as looking at Alyosha. For nothing he actually does makes it true that *he looks at Alyosha*(MB).

Often to *X something*(MB) one must really X something. It is probably by cutting, or stepping on, a glob of mud that one *cuts a pie* (MB) or *steps on a pie*(MB). And one *looks at peasants*(MB) by looking at a picture. But this is not true of all make-believe actions. It is unlikely that in *baking a pie*(MB) one bakes anything, though he must do something (he may shape a glob of mud in a pan and place it in a cardboard box for a specified period of time). And one probably does not eat anything when he *eats a pie*(MB). *Looking through a bottle at objects behind it*(MB) while confronting a painting of a transparent bottle does not involve looking through anything, and *scowling at peasants*(MB), though it involves scowling in the direction of certain parts of a canvas, does not involve scowling at them.

The difference we have noted between *Haymaking* and *Brothers Karamazov* is typical of pictures and novels generally. I suggest that representational pictures are distinguished from novels mainly by their role in a game of make-believe of a certain kind—a game which allows for our performing various make-believe visual actions, for our *seeing, looking at, staring at, noticing, recognizing, visually examining things*(MB).

There is no non-arbitrary way to specify precisely which and how many make-believe visual actions must be provided for. Pictures we are familiar with accommodate a very wide range of them. I would suppose that elimination of any significant number of them would raise serious doubts about whether the canvases should count as representational *pictures*.

Novels also figure in games of make-believe. What is fictionally true of characters in novels is make-believedly true. Moreover, there are certain make-believe actions (or pseudo actions) that readers can perform vis-à-vis characters. One can *think about, sympathize with, root for, find out about, or put a hex on Alyosha or Smerdyakov*(MB), although some of these make-believe actions do not involve doing anything to or with the novel or a copy of it. What novel characters lack, if they do not happen to be pictured in illustrations, is the possibility of being objects of make-believe *visual* actions.

This provides the needed rationale for classifying (representational) painting, photography, and so forth as visual arts, while excluding the novel.

V. Pictures Pursued

Much remains to be said about what it is for something to be a representational picture.[16] Some of the additional conditions that must be met concern the nature of the rules of the games of make-believe in which pictures are involved. I will call games with rules of the requisite kind "pictorial" games. Other conditions concern how pictorial games must be "played" for objects involved in them to be pictures.

(*i*) The actions which count as *seeing, staring at, noticing objects* (MB) in a pictorial game of make-believe must be themselves instances of seeing or looking at something in some way. If what counts as *seeing an object*(MB) is cutting, drawing, kicking, eating, igniting, or blowing on something, what is cut, drawn, blown on, or whichever would hardly qualify as a picture of what is make-believedly seen.

(*ii*) The various actions of *seeing, staring, noticing, examining, and so forth*(MB) which fill one's contemplation of a painting are conscious cognitive activities. The viewer may or may not be aware of what he *actually* sees or stares at, but he is aware, typically, that he *sees or stares at objects of certain sorts*(MB), that he *notices that a peasant looks morose*(MB), and so forth. One who performs make-believe visual actions on confronting a picture is, in short, a knowing participant in the game of make-believe.

If stepping on a glob of mud counts as *stepping on a pie*(MB) in a game of mud pies, a further rule might specify that one *steps deliberately on a pie*(MB) only if he steps on a glob realizing that that constitutes *stepping on a pie*(MB). But the rule need not be so. It might be that any, or any deliberate, stepping on a glob of mud, or any parent's stepping on one, or stepping on a glob in such a way that one's shadow crosses it, counts as *stepping deliberately on a pie*(MB). (A black list might be kept of people who have *deliberately stepped on a pie*(MB).)

There could be a game of make-believe in which one *looks at a peasant*(MB) just in case he looks at appropriate splotches of paint on an appropriate canvas, whether or not he realizes that *there is a peasant*(MB) or that he *looks at a peasant*(MB). Or *noticing a peasant*(MB) might depend on uttering the word "peasant," for whatever reason, while looking in the direction of the canvas. But a game of make-believe cannot qualify as a pictorial one if it provides for the performance of make-believe visual actions only in ways such as these. In *seeing a peasant*(MB) or *noticing a peasant*(MB) merely by looking at paint splotches, or by saying "peasant" while looking at the canvas, one is not doing anything like "seeing" the canvas "as" a peasant.

The needed requirement is put most easily, I suggest, by specifying that the rules of a pictorial game of make-believe must insure that: A *knows that p*(MB) only if A knows that *p*(MB)— that is, in order make-believedly to know that p a person must really know that p is make-believedly true.

The performance of many visual actions—for example, noticing, recognizing, seeing (or at least seeing that), fixing one's attention on, examining closely—entails or is in some other way connected with knowing certain facts. Probably some of these actions cannot be performed without knowing that one is performing them; some require knowing, or coming to know, something about objects perceived; some involve hoping or expecting or attempting to come to know certain things. The performance of corresponding make-believe actions similarly entails or involves corresponding make-believe knowledge. If in order to notice a peasant one must know that there is a peasant before him, in order to *notice a peasant*(MB) one must *know that there is a peasant before him*(MB).[17] And if *noticing a peasant*(MB) requires *knowing that there is a peasant before one*(MB) it requires also, in pictorial games, knowing that *there is a peasant before one*(MB).

It should be evident that this requirement greatly restricts the range of cases in which it can be true that a person make-believedly performs a certain visual action. The details of the restrictions depend on what (real) actions involve in what ways what knowledge. Spelling this out is a spongy task which I will leave to others.

(*iii*) Mud pies and many other common games of make-believe seem not especially or primarily "visual" ones, in contrast to pictorial games. This may be partly because pictorial games provide for the performance of many make-believe visual actions, but few nonvisual ones. Even smiling, scowling, and pointing are either partly visual or closely connected with visual actions. Sculpture is a little less exclusively visual than painting is. One can *stroke the head of a man*(MB) by stroking a sculpture. But running one's hand over a canvas does not as readily count as *stroking a man's head*(MB). Puppets and dolls accommodate many more make-believe nonvisual actions. And although one can *look at, examine, and point at pies*(MB) in a game of mud pies, actions such as *baking, cutting, serving, eating pies*(MB) and *quarreling over who got the biggest piece*(MB) are usually more important in that game.

But this leaves unexplained a crucial difference between mud pies and pictures. One might well feel that we do not "see" a glob of mud "as" a pie in the way that we see lines on canvas as a man. What we call "seeing a mud glob as a pie" seems to be a less visual variety of "seeing as," to be merely *regarding* or *considering* a glob as a pie.

The explanation for this lies, I suggest, in differences between how we come to know make-believe facts in pictorial games (or how we are prepared to do so), and how this often happens in games of mud pies. Two observations are in order here.

(*a*) When we examine "Haymaking" we *discover* that *there are peasants working in a field*(MB), that *some of them are carrying loads on their heads*(MB), and so forth. But in a game of mud pies we sometimes come to know that propositions are make-believedly true by making them so, not by discovering that they already are. We establish their make-believe truth rather than learn of it. We do this by making certain decisions—not decisions *simply* to make something make-believedly true (that would be impossible owing to the nature of make-believe truths), but decisions to adopt rules of make-believe which have the foreseen result that something is make-believedly true. The rules may be devised *ad hoc* for the purpose of bringing about that result. For example, we may choose to let a glob of mud "be" a pie—that is, to adopt a rule such that, because of the presence of a glob of mud of which we are already aware, "*there is a pie here*(MB)" becomes true. This hardly amounts to *discovering* that *there is a pie here*(MB).

The rules of pictorial games are usually much more general than those of mud pies. They apply not just to a few pictures but to all pictures of a certain broad style or genre, and they are roughly constant through many years or centuries. The rules can change, of course, but they evolve gradually and are almost never established by explicit fiat.[18] Pictorial games do not need to be set up every time we "play," as games of mud pies may need to be. When we come to the painting the relevant rules are already in force, and we have already learned (acquired, internalized, mastered) them. We are prepared to *discover* that, for example, *there are peasants working in a field *(MB) on noticing or being exposed to the relevant characteristics of the canvas, not merely to make that so by establishing an appropriate rule. In general, it seems to me that an essential part of what it is for certain objects to function as representational pictures for a group of people is that, at least ordinarily, the people know (have mastery of, have internalized)[19] the rules of make-believe which make certain propositions make-believedly true in virtue of properties of those objects, and know them prior to acquiring the knowledge of those make-believe truths on noticing or being exposed to the relevant properties of the objects.

(*b*) Sometimes we do discover rather than establish make-believe facts in a game of mud pies, when the appropriate rules have been established previously. But these discoveries often differ significantly from those with respect to pictures. In order to discover that *there are three pies here* (MB), or that *this is a raisin pie*(MB), one may have to notice explicitly that there are three mud globs of the relevant kind in the specified area, or that a given glob contains pebbles, and one may have to recall more or less consciously the applicable rule of make-believe. But we need not attend especially to the details of line, color, or shading on a canvas nor call to mind rules of our pictorial game in discovering that *there are peasants working in a field*(MB), and so forth. Indeed, it is usually impossible for us to describe any but the most obvious features of a canvas which are responsible for make-believe truths that we have learned by examining it. And most laymen are largely ignorant of the pictorial rules—although this does not prevent them from "reading" paintings readily. The rules of pictorial games are more thoroughly "internalized" than are those of games of mud pies.

In many cases in which we discover make-believe facts in a game of mud pies, one might say, we do not see but *infer* what is make-believedly true, but we often simply recognize, notice, look and see, that certain things are make-believedly true when we confront a picture. When we examine *Haymaking*, for example, it *looks* to us as though *there are peasants before us*(MB).[20]

But the crucial difference is not this simple. One may well infer, consciously and explicitly, rather than simply see, that *there are twenty-four pillars and twenty-three arches on a building*(MB) while looking at a picture of such a building. This may be inferred from facts such as the fact that *there are seven pillars and seven arches visible on the west side*(MB), *one pillar on the west side is obscured by a cart*(MB), *most of the east side of the building is hidden, but it is apparently exactly like the west side*(MB), and so forth. Some of these facts will be ascertained by counting individual make-believe pillars and arches. In this case make-believe truths are inferred. But they are inferred from other make-believe truths that are discovered just by looking at the canvas; not from the facts about the physical characteristics of the canvas that they depend on. Inferences of *this* kind are entirely appropriate in a pictorial game of make-believe.

What is important for objects to be representational pictures for a group of people is that the people have "internalized" the rules of make-believe sufficiently to be able to discover make-believe facts on examining the objects without explicitly inferring them from the facts they depend on and the rules of make-believe. The people must be able to discover them either by simply noticing, recognizing, seeing that certain things are make-believedly true, or by inferring that they are from other make-believe truths that are recognized in that way. A person who on seeing *Haymaking* did go through the enormously complex process of investigating the forms on the canvas and figuring out from them with the help of memorized pictorial rules what is make-believedly true would not be "seeing" the picture "as" a scene of peasants haying. And I speculate that if we "internalized" sufficiently the rules for mud pies and were generally able to ascertain make-believe facts by looking at the globs without paying particular attention to their features or the rules of the game, we would be "seeing" the globs "as" pies, in a fully visual sense.

The points I have made under *(iii)* do not differentiate pictures from novels. One does not decide on rules of make-believe as he reads *Brothers Karamazov*; he *discovers* what kind of a person Alyosha is, that Smerdyakov fell down a flight of stairs, and so forth. And these discoveries are made without paying much attention to the relevant details of the shapes on the pages or bearing in mind the relevant rules of make-believe. But in the case of pictures, discovering that $*p*$(MB) in this way counts as $*$seeing, noticing, or recognizing (visually) that $p*$(MB), whereas in the case of novels discovering that $*p*$(MB) similarly, even though it involves using our eyes, does not count as $*$noticing, seeing that, etc. $p*$(MB), although it does count as $*$discovering that $p*$(MB) or $*$learning that $p*$(MB). This, perhaps, is why one does not see a novel as what it describes. The reason that in many instances we do not see globs of mud as pies, in a visual sense, lies rather in how we come to know make-believe facts in a game of mud pies.

VI. Analysis of P-depiction

The suggestions made so far need to be consolidated and to be put more precisely. This requires unraveling an ambiguity of "picture of."

There are pictures of unicorns, but there are no unicorns for them to be pictures of. Many pictures of men are such that there are no men whom they picture, although there are men; Paul Klee's *Old Man Calculating* is (presumably) not a picture of any *actual* man, but it is correctly describable as a "picture of a man" (there is a man "in the picture"). Statements of the form: "*D* is a picture of . . ." sometimes do, and sometimes do not, allow quantification over ". . . ." It is legitimate in some contexts to infer from the fact that "*D* is a picture of . . ." that there is something which is . . . of which *D* is a picture, and it is illegitimate to infer this in other contexts.

If a picture is a picture of some actual, existing man, I will say that it *depicts*$_q$ a man. And in general, if there is something which is . . . of which D is a picture, I will say that D *depicts*$_q$ . . . . If a picture is a "picture of a man" in the sense in which its being that does not depend on there being an actual man whom it pictures, I will call it a *man-depicting* picture. In general, when D is a "picture of . . ." in the sense in which it is not legitimate to infer from that that there is something which is . . . of which it is a picture, I will say that D is a . . . depicting picture. There are thus unicorn-depicting pictures, Zeus-depicting pictures, and Abominable Snowman-depicting pictures, as well as man-depicting pictures.[21]

A picture may of course both depict$_q$ a man and be a man-depicting picture. This will be so if it depicts an actual man *as* a man. If a man whom a picture depicts$_q$ happens to be a car salesman, the picture depicts$_q$ a car salesman—there is a car salesman whom it pictures. But if it does not depict him as a car salesman it is not a car-salesman-depicting picture; it would not have been a "picture of a car salesman" in any sense if the man it depicts$_q$ had not existed, or had not been a car salesman.

A parallel distinction holds for novels. *Brothers Karamazov* is a novel about (among other things) Alyosha and the murder of an old man, although Alyosha does not exist and there is no murder of an old man which it is about. It is an Alyosha-describing novel, and a murder-of-an-old-man-describing novel, but it does not describe$_q$ either Alyosha or a murder. *War and Peace* is war-describing and Napoleon-describing, and in addition it describes$_q$ a war and Napoleon. *War and Peace* also describes$_q$ a man whose grave Hitler visited, since Hitler visited the grave of a man whom it describes$_q$. But it is not a man-whose-grave-Hitler-visited-describing novel; it does not describe Napoleon as being such a man.

What is it for something to be a P-depicting picture for a society, S?[22] A P-depicting picture must be P-depicting. But many things besides pictures can also plausibly be called P-depictions. Obvious candidates are representational sculptures, plays (or performances of them, or actors and their actions), and program music (or performances thereof). All of these share with P-depicting pictures many of the characteristics that make them P-depicting; indeed the most interesting and significant ones. To bring out these similarities I will define first a notion of P-depiction in general.[23] The conditions of this definition can later be strengthened to provide an analysis of what it is to be a P-depicting *picture,* but the genus is of much more theoretical interest than are the distinctions among its species.

For a start, if D is a P-depiction (for S) there must be a game of make-believe (in S) such that "*There is a P^*(MB)" is true (relative to the context of that game) in virtue of D's possession of certain properties. And certain actions that might be performed, which are themselves instances of perceiving D, must count as *seeing a P^*(MB), *staring at a P^*(MB), *listening to a P^*(MB), or make-believedly performing some (indefinite) number of perceptual actions vis-à-vis a (make-believe) P.

These conditions need strengthening. The make-believe truth that there is a *P*—that is, that there exists *some* P *or other*—does not ensure the make-believe existence of any particular *P*. But properties of a man-depicting picture, or a man-depiction of any kind, make it make-believedly true not merely that there is some man or other, but that a particular, identifiable man exists. One can *distinguish that man [namely, the man whose make-believe existence depends on properties of the depiction] from others*(MB)—by *pointing at him* (MB) or by *describing him as the man who . . .*(MB). And one can *give him a name*(MB). (If *there is a P*(MB) it must be true, I suppose, that *there is an identi-fiable, namable P*(MB). But it need not be true that a spectator can *identify, or name, a P*(MB).)

So if *D* is a *P*-depiction, "*O* exists*(MB)" and "*O* is a P*(MB)" must be true in virtue of properties of *D,* where *"O" is a name or identifying description of something*(MB).

Moreover, it will not do to allow a man-depiction to be such that *one* man make-believedly exists in virtue of properties of the depiction, but people make-believedly see or otherwise perceive a *different* man by perceiving the depiction. The man whom people make-believedly perceive by perceiving the depiction must be the same one who owes his (make-believe) existence to properties of the depiction.

We can now state the complete analysis of *P*-depiction. The arguments on the preceding pages are designed to support the claim that conditions (1), (2), and (3) below are *necessary* for *D*'s being a *P*-depicting picture, and hence necessary for its being a *P*-depiction. I suggest that these con-ditions taken together are also *sufficient* for *D*'s being a *P*-depiction, though I have offered no proof of this.

D is a *P*-depiction for society *S* if and only if:

(1) There is in *S* a game of make-believe such that
(*a*) *O* exists*(MB) and *O* is a P*(MB), where *"O" is a name or identifying description of something*(MB).
(*b*) *O* exists*(MB) and *O* is a P*(MB) in virtue of the fact that *D* possesses certain properties (literally).
(*c*) Certain actions that members of *S* might perform count (would count) as their make-believedly performing various perceptual actions vis-à-vis *O*, such as (to give only visual examples) their *seeing O* (MB), *looking at O*(MB), *staring at O*(MB), *gazing at O*(MB), *recognizing that *O* is a P*(MB), *examining O's features*(MB).
(*d*) These actions are themselves instances of perceiving *D* in various ways.
(*e*) A *knows that p*(MB) only if *A* knows that *p*(MB).
(2) Members of *S* know (have mastery of, have internalized) the rules which make it true in virtue of properties of *D* that *O* exists*(MB) and *O* is a P*(MB), and if they acquire the knowledge that *O* exists* (MB) and *O* is a P*(MB) on noticing or being exposed to the relevant properties of *D* they knew these rules prior to doing so.

(3) Members of S have internalized the rules which make "*O exists*
(MB)" and "*O is a P*(MB)" true in virtue of properties of D sufficiently
so that they can ascertain those make-believe facts on examining D without explicitly inferring them from the relevant properties of D and the
rules.[24]

Representational *pictures* are distinguished from depictions of other
kinds largely by which of their properties are responsible for what they
depict. It is the markings on the surface of a man-depicting picture (the
color and/or brightness of various portions of the surface) that make
it *man*-depicting, rather than monkey- or skyscraper-depicting or some-
thing-else-depicting. A man-depicting sculpture, by contrast, is man-
depicting because of the shape of its surface. Combining this point with
a further restriction or two that seem called for yields a plausible
account of pictorial P-depiction. D is a P-depicting picture for S, I suggest,
if and only if D satisfies the conditions for being a P-depiction, strengthened by substituting (1′) for (1). (1′) is like (1) except that (1) (*b*) is replaced by

(1′) (*b′*) *O exists*(MB) and *O is a P*(MB) in virtue of the fact *that
there are certain markings on D's surface,*

(1) (*d*) is replaced by

(1′) (*d′*) These actions
are themselves instances of *seeing or looking at D* in various
ways,

and (perhaps)[25] (1) (*c*) is replaced by

(1′) (*c′*) Certain actions that members of S might perform count (would
count) as their make-believedly performing various *visual*
actions vis-à-vis O, such as . . . .

I will not attempt an analysis of *depiction*$_q$ here, but we are in a position to state one necessary condition. Let us say that something (a picture,
sculpture, or whatever) is *representational* (for S) if and only if there is
some property, P, such that it is a P-depiction (for S). Only things which
are representational can depict$_q$. Something can depict$_q$ a P without being a
P-depiction, as we have seen. (A depiction$_q$ of a salesman need not be
salesman-depicting.) I would suppose, moreover, that there is *no* particular property, P, such that something cannot in any conceivable circumstance depict$_q$ a given object unless it is P-depicting (see footnote 23).
But in no circumstances could something which is not a P-depiction, for
any P at all, depict$_q$ anything. This is a consequence of the fact that
something cannot depict$_q$ an object without depicting it *as* something or
other.

So D depicts$_q$ something for S only if there is some property, P, such
that (1), (2), and (3) are true (construing "P" as a variable rather than a
constant).

VII. Resemblance

It will be instructive to look again at the notion that representation is a matter of resemblance, in light of the conclusions arrived at so far. I will concentrate on the view that resemblance is connected with what it is for a picture to be *P*-depicting, which seems to me more plausible than the view that depiction$_q$ involves resemblance.[26]

If conditions (1'), (2), and (3) (or even just [1], [2], and [3]) are necessary for something to be a *P*-depicting picture, as I claim, it seems that resembling a *P* is at least not sufficient. The fact that something resembles or looks like a *P* does not guarantee that it is appropriately involved in a game of make-believe of the appropriate sort. Resemblances might encourage adoption of certain sorts of rules of make-believe, but they do not automatically establish any. No degree or kind of resemblance between an object and any man or men forces us to count anything we might do as *seeing a man*(MB) or *recognizing a man*(MB), nor does anyone's awareness of such a resemblance. If John looks like his twin brother Frank, we are not thereby obliged to count looking at John as *looking at Frank*(MB). And we can recognize that a particular toadstool resembles a mushroom (is mushroom-resembling—see below) without counting any perceiving of the toadstool as *looking at a mushroom* (MB).

Is resembling or looking like a *P* *necessary* for being a *P*-depicting picture? Clearly there does not have to be a *P* which a *P*-depicting picture resembles, since there need be no *P*'s at all for a picture to be *P*-depicting. But something can "resemble a *P*" or "look like a *P*" even if there is no *P* that it resembles or looks like, and even if there are no *P*'s at all. A skinny rhinoceros or a papier-mâché unicorn may quite properly be said to resemble or look like a unicorn, though there is no unicorn which it resembles. The statement that an erupting volcano looks like a gigantic monster breathing fire would not ordinarily imply that there is such a monster which it resembles. When quantification over ". . ." in statements of the form, "*X* resembles . . ." is illegitimate, we may speak of *X*'s being unicorn-resembling, gigantic-fire-breathing-monster-resembling, and so forth, analogously to something's being unicorn-depicting and so forth. The question thus arises whether something can be a *P*-depicting picture if it is not *P*-resembling.

It is unlikely that anyone would maintain that pictures *alone* among *P*-depictions must be *P*-resembling, so I will not restrict the issue to *P*-depticing *pictures*. Must something be *P*-resembling in order to be a *P*-depiction of any sort?

No significant[27] *P*-resemblance would seem to be necessary for *P*-depiction if, as I proposed, conditions (1), (2), and (3) are sufficient. For those conditions could be satisfied by virtually any object, no matter how lacking in *P*-resemblance it might be. Given just about any object, one could, with sufficient ingenuity (and perhaps perversity), devise a set of rules for a game of make-believe which satisfy condition (1). This seems obvious enough not to require demonstration. And I can see no reason in principle why those rules could not be established and internalized by members of a society in such a way that conditions (2) and (3) are met. This might in practice be difficult or even impossible, owing to limitations or peculiarities of the human psyche or nervous system. The rules might be too complex for human beings to learn or internalize, for example. If any object is such that *no* set of rules satisfying condition (1) could be learned or internalized in the way called for by (2) and (3), that object could not be a man-depiction, not at least for a society of humans like ourselves. But the impossibility, if it exists, is a contingent one and should not affect an analysis of the nature of *P*-depiction. The theoretical possibility of something's being man-depicting but not man-resembling remains in any case. And it is safe to say that the range of objects which are not barred even in this contingent way from being man-depictions is broad enough to include many which possess no noteworthy man-resemblance.

Someone might counter by simply denying that conditions (1), (2), and (3) are sufficient for *P*-depiction. I gave no proof of their sufficiency, and have none to offer. Several indirect considerations derived from the necessity of (1), (2), and (3) can, however, be brought against the view that *P*-depictions must be *P*-resembling. These considerations do not destroy that view. But they may deflate it enough so that it will no longer seem compelling.

In the first place, the supposition that *P*-resemblance is necessary for *P*-depiction is not needed to account for the distinction between pictures and novels. Nor is it needed to accommodate the intuition that painting, and also sculpture, and theater, are *visual* or *perceptual* arts in a way in which written literature is not. These jobs are done quite adequately by conditions (1) (*c*) and (1) (*d*).

Moreover, we are in a position to explain much of the preanalytic urge to think that *P*-resemblance is necessary for *P*-depiction even if it is not. One can point to a man-depicting canvas and say truly, "*That* looks like a man" ("That is man-resembling"), if this is interpreted as "*That looks like a man*(MB)" ("*That is man-resembling*(MB)"). Among the make-believe perceptual actions one performs in connection with a man-depiction is *recognizing, noticing a man*(MB), *seeing (or otherwise perceiving) that what one is looking at (perceiving) or pointing at is a man* (MB). And the real actions in virtue of which one does these things are instances of perceiving the depiction which involve coming to know that *what one is seeing (pointing at) is a man*(MB) ([1] [*e*])—that is, they are instances of recognizing, noticing, seeing that *what one is seeing (pointing at) is a man*(MB). So one make-believedly recognizes a man by really recognizing that make-believedly there is a man before one;

one make-believedly recognizes a man because it really looks as though make-believedly there is a man before him. We can understand if this, appreciated confusedly, comes out as, it really looks as though what one is seeing is (really) a man—that is, what one is seeing, the canvas, is man-resembling. The likelihood of this confusion increases, no doubt, the more thoroughly internalized the rules of make-believe are.

Another probable cause of the impression that *P*-depiction requires *P*-resemblance is the fact that *P*-depictions frequently are in fact notably *P*-resembling in certain respects, and we can reasonably expect them to be. Some rules of make-believe are more natural, simpler, easier to learn, remember, and internalize, and more likely to be adopted (explicitly or otherwise) than others are. And the reason some rules are more natural is often that they preserve certain sorts of resemblances. (Another reason may be that previously established rules constitute precedents for rules of certain kinds rather than others, and no doubt there are still other reasons.) The rule that *the pie contains raisins*(MB) just in case the glob contains pebbles is more natural than either a rule whereby *the pie contains raisins*(MB) just in case the glob does *not* contain pebbles, or a rule that whether or not *the pie contains raisins*(MB) depends on whether or not the mud of the glob is light-colored. No doubt this is mainly because a pebbled glob is more raisin-pie-resembling than a non-pebbled glob is, and more raisin-pie-resembling than non-raisin-pie-resembling; and a pebbled as opposed to a non-pebbled glob is more raisin-pie-resembling than is a light-colored glob as opposed to a dark-colored one. *P*-depictions are likely to be *P*-resembling for similar reasons.

But a more important reason for *P*-depictions to be *P*-resembling derives from the necessity of perceivings of a *P*-depiction counting as make-believe perceivings of a *P*. The more an object, *D*, looks like a *P* (the more it is visually *P*-resembling), the more *looking* at *D* will be *looking-at-a-P-resembling*. And the more looking-at-a-*P*-resembling looking at *D* is, the more natural it will be to count looking at *D* as *looking at a P*(MB). Likewise, seeing that *there is a P before one*(MB) by examining *D* is more likely to count as *seeing that there is a P before one*(MB) the more it looks to one as though there is a *P* before him when he examines *D*—that is (roughly), the more *P*-resembling *D* is.

None of this provides any legitimate reason to think that *P*-resemblance is part of what makes something *P*-depicting, or that a *P*-depiction *must* be (significantly) *P*-resembling. What makes something a *P*-depiction, if it is one, is the existence of a game of make-believe of the required kind and its being "played" in the manner conditions (2) and (3) demand. The *P*-resemblance of an object at most encourages establishment of such a game of make-believe, and facilitates "playing" it a appropriately.

VIII. Postscript

Since the original publication of "Pictures and Make-Believe" in 1973, I have come to realize that the expressions "fictionally true," "imaginarily true," and "make-believedly true" are misleading in suggesting that what we are dealing with are special varieties of truth, that to be fictionally true is to be *true*, although it is to possess a kind of truth different from the ordinary one. There is only one kind of truth, and it corresponds to what I called "literal truth." What is "fictionally true" is not thereby true, any more than "plastic flowers" are flowers or "toy trucks" trucks. To be "fictionally true" is to possess a property independent of truth, one which is better called that of being simply *fictional*.

The temptation to think of fictionality (and its species, imaginariness and make-believedness) as varieties of truth is deeply ingrained, however. And it is profoundly revealing of the fundamental nature of fiction, as I explain in two recent papers.[28] The insight gained by delving into the causes of this temptation underscore my claim in "Pictures and Make-Believe" that people make-believedly perform visual actions when they look at pictures, and it brings out the fundamental significance of this fact.

It should be mentioned also that I now prefer to construe fictionality ("fictional truth") as a property of propositions. Thus there is a category difference between the fictional and the metaphorical which is obscured in "Pictures and Make-Believe"; it is sentence tokens, or utterances, not propositions, which are metaphorical.

"Pictures and Make-Believe" would be different in still other ways if I were writing it now. But I have left it mainly as it was, in the belief that even my mistakes may be instructive.

Notes

1. This paper profited greatly from the comments of various people, especially Daniel Bayer, John G. Bennett, and G. Lee Bowie.
2. Ludwig Wittgenstein, *Philosophical Investigations* (New York, 1958), translated by G. E. M. Anscombe, p. 194.
3. Ernst Gombrich, "Meditations on a Hobby Horse," in *Meditations on a Hobby Horse and Other Essays on the Theory of Art* (London, 1963), p. 8.
4. Gombrich, *Art and Illusion* (New York, 1960); Goodman, *Languages of Art* (Indianapolis, 1968).
5. I find Goodman's positive account of depiction unsatisfying on this score. According to Goodman, the distinguishing mark of pictures, as contrasted to descriptions, is a purely syntactic property ("density") of the symbol schemes to which they belong (*op. cit.*, pp. 225-228). It seems at least initially implausible that an account of this sort should do justice to the intuitions underlying resemblance theories.

6. It will not help simply to declare that viewers of *Haymaking* "see" peasants in a sense in which that does not entail the peasants' existence. For it is far from obvious what the required sense of "see" is. "The viewers see peasants" cannot in this context mean "There appear to them to be peasants"; the latter is just false (except in rare instances of *trompe l'œil*). Little is to be gained, either, by saying that viewers see parts of the picture *as* peasants (or that they see peasants *in* the picture). The notions of "seeing as" and "seeing in" are as much in need of analysis as the notion of depiction itself, if not more so. And I believe that an adequate analysis of them would have to make use of central elements of the account of depiction I am about to propose. Cf. Richard Wollheim, *Art and Its Objects* (New York, 1968), secs. 11-13; and Robert Howell, "The Logical Structure of Pictorial Representation", *Theoria,* XL (1974), 76-109.

7. There is no need to recognize fictional *objects*, objects which have properties but lack existence. (Cf. Jaakko Hintikka, "*Cogito Ergo Sum*: Inference or Performance," *Philosophical Review* LXXI [1962], 6-8, 20-21.) It is not (literally) true that Hamlet thinks, any more than that he exists. "*Hamlet thinks**(F)" is true, but so is "*Hamlet exists**(F)."

8. If a fact is only *partly* responsible for the fictional truth of a proposition (given the relevant "rules") the proposition is not fictionally true "*in virtue of*" that fact, in the sense intended in the forthcoming definitions.

9. A fact, *f*, is more directly responsible for the fictional truth of *p* than another fact, *f'*, is just in case *p* is fictionally true in virtue of *f'* only because *p* is fictionally true in virtue of *f* and *f* is a fact in virtue of *f'*.

10. To say, "This is a raisin pie," *could,* in a suitable setting, be a metaphorical way of saying that a glob contains pebbles—even during a game of mud pies. When this is so the utterance is a metaphorical rather than a make-believe assertion. But typically that is not so when the sentence is uttered by participants in a game of mud pies.

11. On some theories of metaphor explicit similes are paraphrases of metaphorical statements. "Ambiguous" metaphors are paraphrased, perhaps, by similes which do not specify the respect of resemblance ("X is like Y, in some respect or other"), although if this is so the metaphor should not be called "ambiguous," since the simile is not ambiguous.

12. A separate requirement that a make-believe statement of *p* must not be the statement that *p* is literally true will guarantee that there must be something in the paraphrase to indicate that it is not a statement of the literal truth of the sentence which is thus used or referred to.

13. E.g., by Goodman, *op. cit.,* Ch. II.

14. It might be tempting to consider this an imaginary truth, on the ground that the relevant sentences in the novel function merely to record agreements or decisions about what is to be fictionally true, or to facilitate making them. (Compare a child's announcement, "Let's say that Johnny once served a pie to Napoleon.") But the presence of the relevant sentences makes it the case that *Smerdyakov fell down the stairs**(F), even if they resulted from a slip of the pen and were never read—i.e., if neither the author nor any reader intended or took it to be that *Smerdyakov fell down the stairs**(F). And if those sentences had been omitted, even inadvertently, it would have been false that *Smerdyakov fell down the stairs**(F). If the author's decision that something should be fictionally true is responsible for its being so, it is *less directly* responsible than are the sentences in the novel. (The question of whether myths, legends, and the like are imaginarily or make-believedly true is more difficult—and more interesting.)

15. I will include knowing, believing, intending, expecting, and other such "mental states" (or dispositions) under the rubric "actions" here. This gloss will do no harm in the present context.

16. The notion I am concerned with is that of being a representational picture *for a certain society*, though I will sometimes omit specifying the society. See n. 24.

17. There could be games of make-believe in which this is not so. Even "*p*(MB)" and "*not-p(MB)" might both be true in a suitable game. (Cf. *Alice in Wonderland*, and the graphics of M. C. Escher.) But it seems to me an essential feature of pictorial games of make-believe that the usual connections between performing visual actions and knowing certain things carry over to their make-believe counterparts. I will take this for granted in what follows.

18. An artist's affixing a title to a canvas might in some instances be construed as explicitly adopting a rule of make-believe, and one which applies only to that one painting. But it seems to me that titles are better regarded as being governed by rules concerning titles generally, rather than as establishing specific rules. One such general rule is that if a painting which contains lines and shapes of a certain sort is entitled, e.g., "Napoleon," "*Napoleon exists*(MB)" rather than merely "*A man exists*(MB)" is true.

19. This is not meant to imply that they must have gone through a process of learning or internalizing the rules. I leave open the possibility that some at least of the rules are innate. There may even be "pictorial universals."

20. Cf. Richard Wollheim, "On Drawing an Object," in Wollheim, *On Art and the Mind* (Cambridge, Mass., 1974), p. 25.

21. The terms "man-depicting picture," etc. are borrowed from Goodman, *op. cit.*, pp. 21-24. But I will not follow him in abbreviating, e.g., "man-depicting picture" as "man-picture."

22. For convenience I will consider only cases in which "*P*" is replaced by a (hyphenated) predicate, such as "man," or "man-with-a-pipe." The minor adjustments in what follows which would be necessary to accommodate cases in which "*P*" is replaced by a proper name or a definite description are obvious enough.

23. The slight discomfort that might be engendered by speaking of "depiction" in connection with program music, and perhaps theater and film, as well as pictures, can be easily tolerated in light of the need for a term to cover all of those cases.

24. I have not discussed the question of what it is for something to be a *P*-depiction not merely for a certain society, but absolutely. But I do not suggest that that is an improper or pointless question. If a cubist painting by Picasso which is a *P*-depiction for us should be considered by ancient Egyptians or a tribe of Martians construing it in terms of *their* pictorial game of make-believe not to be a *P*-depiction, we may well feel that they *misunderstand* the painting. And we may admit that it would be equally illegitimate to force our game of make-believe on ancient Egyptian or Martian works. Perhaps (very roughly) D is a *P*-depiction *simpliciter* if D is a product of a society, *S*, and is a *P*-depiction for *S*. More exactly, I think the criteria for determining whose game of make-believe is applicable to a given work, and hence what kind of a depiction it is absolutely, are essentially analogous to the criteria I have claimed to be relevant in deciding which "categories" a work is correctly "perceived in." Cf. my "Categories of Art," *Philosophical Review*, LXXIX (1970), 334-367.

25. I know of no clear examples in which the performance of visual actions counts as make-believedly performing aural or other nonvisual actions—i.e., cases in which (1) (*c*) and (1′) (*d′*), but not (1′) (*c′*), are satisfied. Whether in such a case D should count as a *P*-depicting picture if it qualifies otherwise is unclear.

26. It is relatively easy to show that resembling an object is neither necessary nor sufficient for depicting$_q$ it. If a portrait of John resembles or looks like him, it may look like John's twin brother just as much, or even more. Yet

it depicts$_q$ John and not his brother. Hence resemblance is not sufficient for depiction$_q$. Suppose that everyone believes that Jones once became a turtle for a period of twenty-four hours, or that everyone believes that everyone else believes that, or that there is a myth to that effect which everyone knows even if no one believes it or thinks anyone else does. In such circumstances an ordinary turtle-depicting picture, perhaps entitled "Jones," might depict$_q$ Jones, even if Jones has never, in fact, been a turtle. Depicting$_q$ Jones incorrectly as a turtle is nevertheless depicting$_q$ him. Similarly, there are pillar-of-salt-depicting pictures which depict$_q$ Lot's wife, whether or not she did become a pillar of salt as is supposed. In view of this it is hard to maintain that any significant resemblance to an object is necessary for depicting$_q$ it. Even if a *man*-depicting picture, which depicts$_q$ a man resembles him, a turtle-depicting or pillar-of-salt-depicting picture which depicts$_q$ him hardly does, if he has never been a turtle or a pillar of salt. (It is still arguable that a picture depicting$_q$ Jones must be Jones-resembling, in the sense explained below. But this is plausible only if a Jones-depicting picture must be Jones-resembling. Whether *that* is so will be discussed shortly.)

27. It is arguable that no object can fail to be P-resembling, for any P, to at least some slight extent and in some way. If so it is true, but trivially so, that some (slight) degree of P-resembling is necessary for P-depiction.

28. "How Remote Are Fictional Worlds From the Real World?", *The Journal of Aesthetics and Art Criticism*, XXXVII (1978), and "Fearing Fictions," *Journal of Philosophy*, LXXV (1978), 5-27. I pursue other issues connected with "Pictures and Make-Believe" in "Are Representations Symbols?", *The Monist*, LVIII (1974), 236-254, and in "Points of View in Narrative and Depictive Representation," *Nous*, X (1976), 49-61.

MAX BLACK

Metaphor

"Metaphors are no arguments, my pretty maiden."
(*The Fortunes of Nigel*, Book 2, Ch. 2.)

TO DRAW ATTENTION to a philosopher's metaphors is to belittle him—like praising a logician for his beautiful handwriting. Addiction to metaphor is held to be illicit, on the principle that whereof one can speak only metaphorically, thereof one ought not to speak at all. Yet the nature of the offence is unclear. I should like to do something to dispel the mystery that invests the topic; but since philosophers (for all their notorious interest in language) have so neglected the subject, I must get what help I can from the literary critics. They at least do not accept the commandment, "Thou shalt not commit metaphor," or assume that metaphor is incompatible with serious thought.

I

The questions I should like to see answered concern the "logical grammar" of "metaphor" and words having related meanings. It would be satisfactory to have convincing answers to the questions: "How do we recognize a case of metaphor?", "Are there any criteria for the detection of metaphors?", "Can metaphors be translated into literal expressions?", "Is metaphor properly regarded as a decoration upon 'plain sense'?", "What are the relations between metaphor and simile?", "In what sense, if any, is a metaphor 'creative'?", "What is the point of using a metaphor?". (Or, more briefly, "What do we *mean* by 'metaphor'?" The questions express attempts to become clearer about some uses of the word "metaphor"—or, if one prefers the material mode, to analyze the notion of metaphor.)

The list is not a tidy one, and several of the questions overlap in fairly

Reprinted from *Proceedings of the Aristotelian Society*, LV (1954-5) by courtesy of the Editor of the Aristotelian Society.

obvious ways. But I hope they will sufficiently illustrate the type of inquiry that is intended.

It would be helpful to start from some agreed list of "clear cases" of metaphor. Since the word "metaphor" has some intelligible uses, however vague or vacillating, it must be possible to construct such a list. Presumably, it should be easier to agree whether any given item should be included than to agree about any proposed analysis of the notion of metaphor.

Perhaps the following list of examples, chosen not altogether at random, might serve:

(i) "The chairman ploughed through the discussion."

(ii) "A smoke-screen of witnesses."

(iii) "An argumentative melody."

(iv) "Blotting-paper voices" (Henry James).

(v) "The poor are the negroes of Europe" (Baudelaire).

(vi) "Light is but the shadow of God" (Sir Thomas Browne).

(vii) "Oh dear white children, casual as birds,
Playing amid the ruined languages" (Auden).

I hope all these will be accepted as unmistakable *instances* of metaphor, whatever judgments may ultimately be made about the meaning of "metaphor." The examples are offered as clear cases of metaphor, but, with the possible exception of the first, they would be unsuitable as "paradigms." If we wanted to teach the meaning of "metaphor" to a child, we should need simpler examples, like "The clouds are crying" or "The branches are fighting with one another." (Is it significant that one hits upon examples of personification?) But I have tried to include some reminders of the possible complexities that even relatively straightforward metaphors may generate.

Consider the first example—"The chairman ploughed through the discussion." An obvious point to begin with is the contrast between the word "ploughed" and the remaining words by which it is accompanied. This would be commonly expressed by saying that "ploughed" has here a metaphorical sense, while the other words have literal senses. Though we point to the whole sentence as an instance (a "clear case") of metaphor, our attention quickly narrows to a single word, whose presence is the proximate reason for the attribution. And similar remarks can be made about the next four examples in the list, the crucial words being, respectively, "smoke-screen," "argumentative," "blotting-paper," and "negroes."

(But the situation is more complicated in the last two examples of the list. In the quotation from Sir Thomas Browne, "Light" must be supposed to have a symbolic sense, and certainly to mean far more than it would in the context of a text-book on optics. Here, the metaphorical sense of the expression, "the shadow of God" imposes a meaning richer than usual upon the subject of the sentence. Similar effects can be noticed in the passage from Auden [consider for instance the meaning of "white" in the first line]. I shall have to neglect such complexities in this paper.)

In general, when we speak of a relatively simple metaphor, we are referring to a sentence or another expression, in which *some* words are used metaphorically, while the remainder are used non-metaphorically. An attempt to construct an entire sentence of words that are used metaphorically results in a proverb, an allegory, or a riddle. No preliminary analysis of metaphor will satisfactorily cover even such trite examples as "In the night all cows are black." And cases of symbolism (in the sense in which Kafka's castle is a "symbol") also need separate treatment.

II

"The chairman ploughed through the discussion." In calling this sentence a case of metaphor, we are implying that at least one word (here, the word "ploughed") is being used metaphorically in the sentence, and that at least one of the remaining words is being used literally. Let us call the word "ploughed" the *focus* of the metaphor, and the remainder of the sentence in which that word occurs the *frame*. (Are *we* now using metaphors—and mixed ones at that? Does it matter?) One notion that needs to be clarified is that of the "metaphorical use" of the focus of a metaphor. Among other things, it would be good to understand how the presence of one frame can result in metaphorical use of the complementary word, while the presence of a different frame for the same word fails to result in metaphor.

If the sentence about the chairman's behaviour is translated word for word into any foreign language for which this is possible, we shall of course want to say that the translated sentence is a case of the *very same* metaphor. So, to call a sentence an instance of metaphor is to say something about its *meaning*, not about its orthography, its phonetic pattern, or its grammatical form.[1] (To use a well-known distinction, "metaphor" must be classified as a term belonging to "semantics" and not to "syntax"—or to any *physical* enquiry about language.)

Suppose somebody says, "I like to plough my memories regularly." Shall we say he is using the same metaphor as in the case already discussed, or not? Our answer will depend upon the degree of similarity we are prepared to affirm on comparing the two "frames" (for we have the same "focus" each time). Differences in the two frames will produce *some* differences in the interplay[2] between focus and frame in the two cases. Whether we regard the differences as sufficiently striking to warrant calling the sentences *two* metaphors is a matter for arbitrary decision. "Metaphor" is a loose word, at best, and we must beware of attributing to it stricter rules of usage than are actually found in practice.

So far, I have been treating "metaphor" as a predicate properly applicable to certain expressions, without attention to any occasions on which the expressions are used, or to the thoughts, acts, feelings, and intentions of speakers upon such occasions. And this is surely correct for *some* expressions. We recognise that to call a man a "cesspool" is to use a metaphor, without needing to know who uses the expression, or on what occasions, or with what intention. The rules of our language determine that some expressions must count as metaphors; and a speaker can no more change this than he can legislate that "cow" shall mean the same as "sheep." But we must also recognise that the established rules of language leave wide latitude for individual variation, initiative, and creation. There are indefinitely many contexts (including nearly all the interesting ones) where the meaning of a metaphorical expression has to be reconstructed from the speaker's intentions (and other clues) because the broad rules of standard usage are too general to supply the information needed. When Churchill, in a famous phrase, called Mussolini "that *utensil*," the tone of voice, the verbal setting, the historical background, helped to make clear *what* metaphor was being used. (Yet, even here, it is hard to see how the phrase "that utensil" could ever be applied to a man except as an insult. Here, as elsewhere, the general rules of usage function as limitations upon the speaker's freedom to mean whatever he pleases.) This is an example, though still a simple one, of how recognition and interpretation of a metaphor may require attention to the *particular circumstances* of its utterance.

It is especially noteworthy that there are, in general, no standard rules for the degree of *weight* or *emphasis* to be attached to a particular use of an expression. To know what the user of a metaphor means, we need to know how "seriously" he treats the metaphorical focus. (Would he be just as content to have some rough synonym, or would only *that* word serve? Are we to take the word lightly, attending only to its most obvious implications—or should we dwell upon its less immediate associations?) In speech we can use emphasis and phrasing as clues. But in written or printed discourse, even these rudimentary aids are absent. Yet this somewhat elusive "weight" of a (suspected or detected[3]) metaphor is of great practical importance in exegesis.

To take a philosophical example. Whether the expression "logical form" should be treated in a particular frame as having a metaphorical sense will depend upon the extent to which its user is taken to be conscious of some supposed analogy between arguments and other things (vases, clouds, battles, jokes) that are also said to have "form." Still more will it depend upon whether the writer wishes the analogy to be active in the minds of his readers; and how much his own thought depends upon and is nourished by the supposed analogy. We must not expect the "rules of language" to be of much help in such enquiries. (There is accordingly a sense of "metaphor" that belongs to "pragmatics," rather than to "semantics"—and this sense may be the one most deserving of attention.)

III

Let us try the simplest possible account that can be given of the meaning of "The Chairman ploughed through the discussion," to see how far it will take us. A plausible commentary (for those presumably too literal-minded to understand the original) might run somewhat as follows:—

"A speaker who uses the sentence in question is taken to want to say *something* about a chairman and his behaviour in some meeting. Instead of saying, plainly or *directly*, that the chairman dealt summarily with objections, or ruthlessly suppressed irrelevance, or something of the sort, the speaker chose to use a word ('ploughed') which, strictly speaking, means something else. But an intelligent hearer can easily guess what the speaker had in mind."[4]

This account treats the metaphorical expression (let us call it *"M"*) as a substitute for some other literal expression (*"L"*, say) which would have expressed the same meaning, had it been used instead. On this view, the meaning of *M*, and its metaphorical occurrence, is just the literal meaning of *L*. The metaphorical use of an expression consists, on this view, of the use of that expression in other than its proper or normal sense, in some context that allows the improper or abnormal sense to be detected and appropriately transformed. (The reasons adduced for so remarkable a performance will be discussed later.)

Any view which holds that a metaphorical expression is used in place of some equivalent *literal* expression, I shall call a *substitution view of metaphor*. (I should like this label to cover also any analysis which views the entire sentence that is the locus of the metaphor as replacing some set of literal sentences.) Until recently, one or another form of a substitution view has been accepted by most writers (usually literary critics or writers of books on rhetoric) who have had anything to say about metaphor.

To take a few examples. Whately defines a metaphor as "a word substituted for another on account of the Resemblance or Analogy between their significations."[5] Nor is the entry in the Oxford Dictionary (to jump to modern times) much different from this: "Metaphor: The figure of speech in which a name or descriptive term is transferred to some object different from, but analogous to, that to which it is properly applicable; an instance of this, a metaphorical expression."[6] So strongly entrenched is the view expressed by these definitions that a recent writer who is explicitly arguing for a different and more sophisticated view of metaphor, nevertheless slips into the old fashion by defining metaphor as "saying one thing and meaning another."[7]

According to a substitution view, the focus of a metaphor, the word or expression having a distinctively metaphorical use within a literal frame, is used to communicate a meaning that might have been expressed literally. The author substitutes M for L; it is the reader's task to invert the substitution, by using the literal meaning of M as a clue to the intended literal meaning of L. Understanding a metaphor is like deciphering a code or unravelling a riddle.

If we now ask why, on this view, the writer should set his reader the task of solving a puzzle, we shall be offered two types of answer. The first is that there may be, in fact, no literal equivalent, L, available in the language in question. Mathematicians spoke of the "leg" of an angle because there was no brief literal expression for a bounding line; we say "cherry lips," because there is no form of words half as convenient for saying quickly what the lips are like. Metaphor plugs the gaps in the literal vocabulary (or, at least, supplies the want of convenient abbreviations). So viewed, metaphor is a species of *catachresis*, which I shall define as the use of a word in some new sense in order to remedy a gap in the vocabulary. Catachresis is the putting of new senses into old words.[8] But if a catachresis serves a genuine need, the new sense introduced will quickly become part of the *literal* sense. "Orange" may originally have been applied to the colour by catachresis; but the word is now applied to the colour just as "properly" (and unmetaphorically) as to the fruit. "Osculating" curves don't kiss for long, and quickly revert to a more prosaic mathematical contact. And similarly for other cases. It is the fate of catachresis to disappear when it is successful.

There are, however, many metaphors where the virtues ascribed to catachresis cannot apply, because there is, or there is supposed to be, some readily available and equally compendious literal equivalent. Thus in the somewhat unfortunate example,[9] "Richard is a lion," which modern writers have discussed with boring insistence, the literal meaning is taken to be the same as that of the sentence "Richard is brave."[10] Here, the metaphor is not supposed to enrich the vocabulary.

When catachresis cannot be invoked, the reasons for substituting an indirect, metaphorical, expression are taken to be stylistic. We are told that the metaphorical expression may (in its literal use) refer to a more concrete object than would its literal equivalent; and this is supposed to give pleasure to the reader (the pleasure of having one's thoughts diverted from Richard to the irrelevant lion). Again, the reader is taken to enjoy problem-solving—or to delight in the author's skill at half-concealing, half-revealing his meaning. Or metaphors provide a shock of "agreeable surprise"—and so on. The principle behind these "explanations" seems to be: When in doubt about some peculiarity of language, attribute its existence to the pleasure it gives a reader. A principle that has the merit of working well in default of any evidence.[11]

Whatever the merits of such speculations about the reader's response, they agree in making metaphor a *decoration*. Except in cases where a metaphor is a catachresis that remedies some temporary imperfection of literal language, the purpose of metaphor is to entertain and divert. Its use, on this view, always constitutes a deviation from the "plain and strictly appropriate style" (Whately).[12] So, if philosophers have something more important to do than give pleasure to their readers, metaphor can have no serious place in philosophical discussion.

IV

The view that a metaphorical expression has a meaning that is some transform of its normal literal meaning is a special case of a more general view about "figurative" language. This holds that any figure of speech involving semantic change (and not merely syntactic change, like inversion of normal word order) consists in some transformation of a *literal* meaning. The author provides, not his intended meaning, m, but some function thereof, $f(m)$; the reader's task is to apply the inverse function, f^{-1}, and so to obtain $f^{-1}(f(m))$, i.e., m, the original meaning. When different functions are used, different tropes result. Thus, in irony, the author says the *opposite* of what he means; in hyperbole, he *exaggerates* his meaning; and so on.

What, then, is the characteristic transforming function involved in metaphor? To this the answer has been made: either *analogy* or *similarity*. M is either similar or analogous in meaning to its literal equivalent L. Once the reader has detected the ground of the intended analogy or simile (with the help of the frame, or clues drawn from the wider context) he can retrace the author's path and so reach the original literal meaning (the meaning of L.)

If a writer holds that a metaphor consists in the *presentation* of the underlying analogy or similarity, he will be taking what I shall call a *comparison view* of metaphor. When Schopenhauer called a geometrical proof a mousetrap, he was, according to such a view, *saying* (though not explicitly): "A geometrical proof is *like* a mousetrap, since both offer a delusive reward, entice their victims by degrees, lead to disagreeable surprise, etc." This is a view of metaphor as a condensed or elliptical *simile*. It will be noticed that a "comparison view" is a special case of a "substitution view." For it holds that the metaphorical statement might be replaced by an equivalent literal *comparison*.

Whately says: "The Simile or Comparison may be considered as differing in form only from a Metaphor; the resemblance being in that case *stated*, which in the Metaphor is implied."[13] Bain says that: "The metaphor is a comparison implied in the mere use of a term" and adds, "It is in the circumstance of being confined to a word, or at most to a phrase, that we are to look for the peculiarities of the metaphor—its advantages on the one hand, and its dangers and abuses on the other."[14] This view of the metaphor, as condensed simile or comparison, has been very popular.

The chief difference between a substitution view (of the sort previously considered) and the special form of it that I have called a comparison view may be illustrated by the stock example of "Richard is a lion." On the first view, the sentence means approximately the same as "Richard is brave"; on the second, approximately the same as "Richard is *like* a lion (in being brave)," the added words in brackets being understood but not explicitly stated. In the second translation, as in the first, the metaphorical statement is taken to be standing in place of some *literal* equivalent. But the comparison view provides a more elaborate paraphrase, inasmuch as the original statement is interpreted as being about lions as well as about Richard.[15]

The main objection against a comparison view is that it suffers from a vagueness that borders on vacuity. We are supposed to be puzzled as to how some expression (M), used metaphorically, can function in place of some literal expression (L) that is held to be an approximate synonym; and the answer offered is that what M stands for (in its literal use) is *similar* to what L stands for. But how informative is this? There is some temptation to think of similarities as "objectively given," so that a question of the form, "Is A like B in respect of P?" has a definite and pre-determined answer. If this were so, similes might be governed by rules as strict as those controlling the statements of physics. But likeness always admits of degrees, so that a truly "objective" question would need to take some such forms as "Is A more like B than like C in respect of P?"—or, perhaps, "Is A closer to B than to C on such and such a scale of degrees of P?" Yet, in proportion as we approach such forms, metaphorical statements lose their effectiveness and their point. We need the metaphors in just the cases when there can be no question as yet of the precision of scientific statement. Metaphorical statement is not a substitute for a formal comparison or any other kind of literal statement, but has its own *distinctive* capacities and achievements. Often we say, "X is M," evoking some imputed connexion between M and an imputed L (or, rather, to an indefinite system, L_1, L_2, L_3, . . .) in cases where, prior to the construction of the metaphor, we would have been hard put to find any *literal* resemblance between M and L. It would be more illuminating in some of these cases to say that the metaphor *creates* the similarity than to say that it formulates some similarity antecedently existing.[16]

V

I turn now to consider a type of analysis which I shall call an *interaction view* of metaphor. This seems to me to be free from the main defects of substitution and comparison views and to offer some important insight into the uses and limitations of metaphor.[17]

Let us begin with the following statement: "In the simplest formulation, when we use a metaphor we have two thoughts of different things active together and supported by a single word, or phrase, whose meaning is a resultant of their interaction."[18]

We may discover what is here intended by applying Richards' remark to our earlier example, "The poor are the negroes of Europe." The substitution view, at its crudest, tells us that something is being *indirectly* said about the poor of Europe. (But what? That they are an oppressed class, a standing reproach to the community's official ideals, that poverty is inherited and indelible?) The comparison view claims that the epigram *presents* some comparison between the poor and the negroes. In opposition to both, Richards says that our "thoughts" about European poor and (American) negroes are "active together" and "interact" to produce a meaning that is a resultant of that interaction.

I think this must mean that in the given context the focal word "negroes" obtains a *new* meaning, which is *not* quite its meaning in literal uses, nor quite the meaning which any literal substitute would have. The new context (the "frame" of the metaphor, in my terminology) imposes *extension* of meaning upon the focal word. And I take Richards to be saying that for the metaphor to work the reader must remain aware of the extension of meaning—must attend to both the old and the new meanings together.[19]

But how is this extension or change of meaning brought about? At one point, Richards speaks of the "common characteristics" of the two terms (the poor and negroes) as "the ground of the metaphor" (*op. cit.*, p. 177), so that in its metaphorical use a word or expression must connote only a *selection* from the characteristics connoted in its literal uses. This, however, seems a rare lapse into the older and less sophisticated analyses he is trying to supersede.[20] He is on firmer ground when he says that the reader is forced to "connect" the two ideas (p. 125). In this "connexion" resides the secret and the mystery of metaphor. To speak of the "interaction" of two thoughts "active together" (or, again, of their "interillumination" or "co-operation") is to *use* a metaphor emphasizing the dynamic aspects of a good reader's response to a nontrivial metaphor. I have no quarrel with the use of metaphors (if they are good ones) in talking about metaphor. But it may be as well to use several, lest we are misled by the adventitious charms of our favourites.

Let us try, for instance, to think of a metaphor as a *filter*. Consider the statement, "Man is a wolf." Here, we may say, are *two* subjects—the *principal subject*, Man (or: men) and the *subsidiary subject*, Wolf (or: wolves). Now the metaphorical sentence in question will not convey its intended meaning to a reader sufficiently ignorant about wolves. What is needed is not so much that the reader shall know the standard dictionary meaning of "wolf"—or be able to use that word in literal senses—as that he shall know what I will call the *system of associated commonplaces*. Imagine some layman required to say, without taking special thought, those things he held to be true about wolves; the set of statements resulting would approximate to what I am here calling the system of commonplaces associated with the word "wolf." I am assuming that in any given culture the responses made by different persons to the test suggested would agree rather closely, and that even the occasional expert, who might have unusual knowledge of the subject, would still know "what the man in the street thinks about the matter." From the expert's standpoint, the system of commonplaces may include half-truths or downright mistakes (as when a whale is classified as a fish); but the important things for the metaphor's effectiveness is not that the commonplaces shall be true, but that they should be readily and freely evoked. (Because this is so, a metaphor that works in one society may seem preposterous in another. Men who take wolves to be reincarnations of dead humans will give the statement "Man is a wolf" an interpretation different from the one I have been assuming.)

To put the matter in another way: Literal uses of the word "wolf" are governed by syntactical and semantical rules, violation of which produces nonsense or self-contradiction. In addition, I am suggesting, literal uses of the word normally commit the speaker to acceptance of a set of standard beliefs about wolves (current platitudes) that are the common possession of the members of some speech community. To deny any such piece of accepted commonplace (*e.g.*, by saying that wolves are vegetarians—or easily domesticated) is to produce an effect of paradox and provoke a demand for justification. A speaker who says "wolf" is normally taken to be implying in some sense of that word that he is referring to something fierce, carnivorous, treacherous, and so on. The idea of a wolf is part of a system of ideas, not sharply delineated, and yet sufficiently definite to admit of detailed enumeration.

The effect, then, of (metaphorically) calling a man a "wolf" is to evoke the wolf-system of related commonplaces. If the man is a wolf, he preys upon other animals, is fierce, hungry, engaged in constant struggle, a scavenger, and so on. Each of these implied assertions has now to be made to fit the principal subject (the man) either in normal or abnormal senses. If the metaphor is at all appropriate, this can be done—up to a point at least. A suitable hearer will be led by the wolf-system of implications to construct a corresponding system of implications about the principal subject. But these implications will *not* be those comprised in the commonplaces *normally* implied by literal uses of "man." The new implications must be determined by the pattern of implications associated with literal uses of the word "wolf." Any human traits that can without undue strain be talked about in "wolf-language" will be rendered prominent, and any that cannot will be pushed into the background. The wolf-metaphor suppresses some details, emphasizes others—in short, *organizes* our view of man.

Suppose I look at the night sky through a piece of heavily smoked glass on which certain lines have been left clear. Then I shall see only the stars that can be made to lie on the lines previously prepared upon the screen, and the stars I do see will be seen as organised by the screen's structure. We can think of a metaphor as such a screen, and the system of "associated commonplaces" of the focal word as the network of lines upon the screen. We can say that the principal subject is "seen through" the metaphorical expression—or, if we prefer, that the principal subject is "projected upon" the field of the subsidiary subject. (In the latter analogy, the implication-system of the focal expression must be taken to determine the "law of projection.")

Or take another example. Suppose I am set the task of describing a battle in words drawn as largely as possible from the vocabulary of chess. These latter terms determine a system of implications which will proceed to control my description of the battle. The enforced choice of the chess vocabulary will lead some aspects of the battle to be emphasized, others to be neglected, and all to be organised in a way that would cause much more strain in other modes of description. The chess vocabulary filters and transforms: it not only selects, it brings forward aspects of the battle that might not be seen at all through another medium. (Stars that cannot be seen at all, except through telescopes.)

Nor must we neglect the shifts in attitude that regularly result from the use of metaphorical language. A wolf is (conventionally) a hateful and alarming object; so, to call a man a wolf is to imply that he too is hateful and alarming (and thus to support and reinforce dislogistic attitudes). Again, the vocabulary of chess has its primary uses in a highly artificial setting, where all expression of feeling is formally excluded: to describe a battle as if it were a game of chess is accordingly to exclude, by the choice of language, all the more emotionally disturbing aspects of warfare. (Similar by-products are not rare in philosophical uses of metaphor.)

A fairly obvious objection to the foregoing sketch of the "interaction view" is that it has to hold that some of the "associated commonplaces" themselves suffer metaphorical change of meaning in the process of transfer from the subsidiary to the principal subject. And *these* changes, if they occur, can hardly be explained by the account given. The primary metaphor, it might be said, has been analyzed into a set of subordinate metaphors, so the account given is either circular or leads to an infinite regress.

This might be met by denying that *all* changes of meaning in the "associated commonplaces" must be counted as metaphorical shifts. Many of them are best described as *extensions* of meaning, because they do not involve apprehended connexions between two systems of concepts. I have not undertaken to explain how such extensions or shifts occur in general, and I do not think any simple account will fit all cases. (It is easy enough to mutter "analogy," but closer examination soon shows all kinds of "grounds" for shifts of meaning with context—and even no ground at all, sometimes.)

Secondly, I would not deny that a metaphor may involve a number of subordinate metaphors among its implications. But these subordinate metaphors are, I think, usually intended to be taken less "emphatically," *i.e.*, with less stress upon *their* implications. (The implications of a metaphor are like the overtones of a musical chord; to attach too much "weight" to them is like trying to make the overtones sound as loud as the main notes—and just as pointless.) In any case, primary and subordinate metaphors will normally belong to the same field of discourse, so that they mutually reinforce one and the same system of implications. Conversely, where substantially new metaphors appear as the primary metaphor is unravelled, there is serious risk of confusion of thought (*cf.* the customary prohibition against "mixed metaphors").

But the preceding account of metaphor needs correction, if it is to be reasonably adequate. Reference to "associated commonplaces" will fit the commonest cases where the author simply plays upon the stock of common knowledge (and common misinformation) presumably shared by the reader and himself. But in a poem, or a piece of sustained prose, the writer can establish a novel pattern of implications for the literal uses of the key expressions, prior to using them as vehicles for his metaphors. (An author can do much to suppress unwanted implications of the word "contract," by explicit discussion of its intended meaning, before he proceeds to develop a contract theory of sovereignty. Or a naturalist who really knows wolves may tell us so much about them that *his* description of man as a wolf diverges quite markedly from the stock uses of that figure.) Metaphors can be supported by specially constructed systems of implications, as well as by accepted commonplaces; they can be made to measure and need not be reach-me-downs.

It was a simplification, again, to speak as if the implication-system of the metaphorical expression remains unaltered by the metaphorical statement. The nature of the intended application helps to determine the character of the system to be applied (as though the stars could partly determine the character of the observation-screen by which we looked at them). If to call a man a wolf is to put him in a special light, we must not forget that the metaphor makes the wolf seem more human than he otherwise would.

I hope such complications as these can be accommodated within the outline of an "interaction view" that I have tried to present.

VI

Since I have been making so much use of example and illustration, it may be as well to state explicitly (and by way of summary) some of the chief respects in which the "interaction" view recommended differs from a "substitution" or a "comparison" view.

In the form in which I have been expounding it, the "interaction view" is committed to the following seven claims:

(1) A metaphorical statement has *two* distinct subjects—a "principal" subject and a "subsidiary" one.[21]

(2) These subjects are often best regarded as *systems* of things," rather than "things."

(3) The metaphor works by applying to the principal subject a system of "associated implications" characteristic of the subsidiary subject.

(4) These implications usually consist of "commonplaces" about the subsidiary subject, but may, in suitable cases, consist of deviant implications established *ad hoc* by the writer.

(5) The metaphor selects, emphasizes, suppresses, and organizes features of the principal subject by *implying* statements about it that normally apply to the subsidiary subject.

(6) This involves shifts in meaning of words belonging to the same family or system as the metaphorical expression; and some of the shifts, though not all, may be metaphorical transfers. (The subordinate metaphors are, however, to be read less "emphatically.")

(7) There is, in general, no simple "ground" for the necessary shifts of meaning—no blanket reason why some metaphors work and others fail.

It will be found, upon consideration, that point (1) is incompatible with the simplest forms of a "substitution view," point (7) is formally incompatible with a "comparison view"; while the remaining points elaborate reasons for regarding "comparison views" as inadequate.

But it is easy to overstate the conflicts between these three views. If we were to insist that only examples satisfying all seven of the claims listed above should be allowed to count as "genuine" metaphors, we should restrict the correct uses of the word "metaphor" to a very small number of cases. This would be to advocate a persuasive definition of "metaphor" that would tend to make all metaphors interestingly complex.[22] And such a deviation from current uses of the word "metaphor" would leave us without a convenient label for the more trivial cases. Now it is in just such trivial cases that "substitution" and "comparison" views sometimes seem nearer the mark than "interaction" views. The point might be met by classifying metaphors as instances of substitution, comparison, or interaction. Only the last kind are of importance in philosophy.

For substitution-metaphors and comparison-metaphors can be replaced by literal translations (with possible exception for the case of catachresis) —by sacrificing some of the charm, vivacity, or wit of the original, but with no loss of *cognitive* content. But "interaction-metaphors" are not expendable. Their mode of operation requires the reader to use a system of implications (a system of "commonplaces"—or a special system established for the purpose in hand) as a means for selecting, emphasizing, and organizing relations in a different field. This use of a "subsidiary subject" to foster insight into a "principal subject" is a distinctive *intellectual* operation (though one familiar enough through our experiences of learning anything whatever), demanding simultaneous awareness of both subjects but not reducible to any *comparison* between the two.

Suppose we try to state the cognitive content of an interaction-metaphor in "plain language." Up to a point, we may succeed in stating a number of the relevant relations between the two subjects (though in view of the extension of meaning accompanying the shift in the subsidiary subject's implication system, too much must not be expected of the literal paraphrase). But the set of literal statements so obtained will not have the same power to inform and enlighten as the original. For one thing, the implications, previously left for a suitable reader to educe for himself, with a nice feeling for their relative priorities and degrees of importance, are now presented explicitly as though having equal weight. The literal paraphrase inevitably says too much—and with the wrong emphasis. One of the points I most wish to stress is that the loss in such cases is a loss in *cognitive* content; the relevant weakness of the literal paraphrase is not that it may be tiresomely prolix or boringly explicit— or deficient in qualities of style; it fails to be a translation because it fails to give the *insight* that the metaphor did.

But "explication," or elaboration of the metaphor's grounds, if not regarded as an adequate cognitive substitute for the original, may be extremely valuable. A powerful metaphor will no more be harmed by such probing than a musical masterpiece by analysis of its harmonic and melodic structure. No doubt metaphors are dangerous—and perhaps especially so in philosophy. But a prohibition against their use would be a wilful and harmful restriction upon our powers of inquiry.[23]

Notes

1. *Any* part of speech can be used metaphorically (though the results are meagre and uninteresting in the case of conjunctions); any form of verbal expression may contain a metaphorical focus.

2. Here I am using language appropriate to the "interaction view" of metaphor that is discussed later in this paper.

3. Here I wish these words to be read with as little "weight" as possible!

4. Notice how this type of paraphrase naturally conveys some implication of *fault* on the part of the metaphor's author. There is a strong suggestion that he ought to have made up his mind as to what he really wanted to say—the metaphor is depicted as a way of glossing over unclarity and vagueness.

5. Richard Whately, *Elements of Rhetoric* (7th revised ed., London, 1846), p. 280.

6. Under "Figure" we find: "Any of the various 'forms' of expression, deviating from the normal arrangement or use of words, which are adopted in order to give beauty, variety, or force to a composition; *e.g.* Aposiopesis, Hyperbole, Metaphor, etc." If we took this strictly we might be led to say that a transfer of a word not adopted for the sake of introducing "beauty, variety, or force" must necessarily fail to be a case of metaphor. Or will "variety" automatically cover *every* transfer? It will be noticed that the O.E.D.'s definition is no improvement upon Whately's. Where he speaks of a "word" being substituted, the O.E.D. prefers "name or descriptive term." If this is meant to restrict metaphors to nouns (and adjectives?) it is demonstrably mistaken. But, if not, what *is* "descriptive term" supposed to mean? And why has Whately's reference to "Resemblance or Analogy" been trimmed into a reference to analogy alone?

7. Owen Barfield, "Poetic Diction and Legal Fiction" in *Essays Presented to Charles Williams* (Oxford, 1947), pp. 106-127. The definition of metaphor occurs on p. 111, where metaphor is treated as a special case of what Barfield calls "tarning." The whole essay deserves to be read.

8. The O.E.D. defines catachresis as: "Improper use of words; application of a term to a thing which it does not properly denote; abuse or perversion of a trope or metaphor." I wish to exclude the pejorative suggestions. There is nothing perverse or abusive in stretching old words to fit new situations. Catachresis is merely a striking case of the transformation of meaning that is constantly occurring in any living language.

9. Can we imagine anybody saying this nowadays and seriously meaning anything? I find it hard to do so. But in default of an authentic context of use, any analysis is liable to be thin, obvious and unprofitable.

10. A full discussion of this example, complete with diagrams, will be found in Gustaf Stern's *Meaning and Change of Meaning* (Göteborgs Högskolas Arsakrift, vol. 38, 1932, part I) pp. 300 ff. Stern's account tries to show how the reader is led by the context to *select* from the connotation of "lion" the attribute (bravery) that will fit Richard the man. I take him to be defending a form of the substitution view.

11. Aristotle ascribed the use of metaphor to delight in learning; Cicero traces delight in metaphor to the enjoyment of the author's ingenuity in overpassing the immediate, or in the vivid presentation of the principal subject. For references to these and other traditional views, see E. M. Cope, *An Introduction to Aristotle's Rhetoric* (London, 1867), "Appendix B to Book III, Ch. II: *On Metaphor.*"

12. Thus Stern (*op. cit.*) says of all figures of speech that "they are intended to serve the expressive and purposive functions of speech better than the 'plain statement'" (p. 296). A metaphor produces an "enhancement"

(*Steigerung*) of the subject, but the factors leading to its use "involve the expressive and effective (purposive) functions of speech, not the symbolic and communicative functions" (p. 290). That is to say, metaphors may evince feelings or predispose others to act and feel in various ways—but they don't typically *say* anything.

13. Whately, *loc. cit.* He proceeds to draw a distinction between "Resemblance, strictly so called, *i.e. direct* resemblance between the objects themselves in question (as when we speak of '*table*-land,' or compare great waves to *mountains*)" and "Analogy, which is the resemblance of Ratios—a similarity of the relations they bear to certain other objects; as when we speak of the '*light* of reason,' or of 'revelation'; or compare a wounded and captive warrior to a stranded ship."

14. Alexander Bain, *English Composition and Rhetoric* (Enlarged edition, London, 1887) p. 159.

15. Comparison views probably derive from Aristotle's brief statement in the *Poetics*: "Metaphor consists in giving the thing a name that belongs to something else; the transference being either from genus to species, or from species to genus, or from species to species, or on grounds of analogy" (1457*b*). I have no space to give Aristotle's discussion the detailed examination it deserves. An able defence of a view based on Aristotle will be found in S. J. Brown's *The World of Imagery* (London, 1927, especially pp. 67 ff).

16. Much more would need to be said in a thorough examination of the comparison view. It would be revealing, for instance, to consider the contrasting types of case in which a formal comparison is preferred to a metaphor. A comparison is often a prelude to an explicit statement of the grounds of resemblance; whereas we do not expect a metaphor to explain itself. (Cf. the difference between *comparing* a man's face with a wolf mask, by looking for points of resemblance—and seeing the human face *as* vulpine.) But no doubt the line between *some* metaphors and *some* similes is not a sharp one.

17. The best sources are the writings of I. A. Richards, especially Chapter 5 ("Metaphor") and Chapter 6 ("Command of Metaphor") of his *The Philosophy of Rhetoric* (Oxford, 1936). Chapters 7 and 8 of his *Interpretation in Teaching* (London, 1938) cover much the same ground. W. Bedell Stanford's *Greek Metaphor* (Oxford, 1936) defends what he calls an "integration theory" (see especially pp. 101 ff) with much learning and skill. Unfortunately, both writers have great trouble in making clear the nature of the positions they are defending. Chapter 18 of W. Empson's *The Structure of Complex Words* (London, 1951) is a useful discussion of Richards' views on metaphor.

18. *The Philosophy of Rhetoric*, p. 93. Richards also says that metaphor is "fundamentally a borrowing between and intercourse of *thoughts*, a transaction between contexts" (p. 94). Metaphor, he says, requires two ideas "which co-operate in an inclusive meaning" (p. 119).

19. It is this, perhaps, that leads Richards to say that "talk about the identification or fusion that a metaphor effects is nearly always misleading and pernicious" (*op. cit.*, p. 127).

20. Usually, Richards tries to show that similarity between the two terms is at best *part* of the basis for the interaction of meanings in a metaphor.

21. This point has often been made. *E.g.*:—"As to metaphorical expression, that is a great excellence in style, when it is used with propriety, for it gives you two ideas for one." (Samuel Johnson, quoted by Richards, *op. cit.*, p. 93).

The choice of labels for the "subjects" is troublesome. See the "Note on terminology" appended to this paper.

22. I can sympathize with Empson's contention that "The term ['metaphor'] had better correspond to what the speakers themselves feel to be a rich or suggestive or persuasive use of a word, rather than include uses like the *leg*

of a table" (*The Structure of Complex Words*, p. 333). But there is the opposite danger, also, of making metaphors too important by definition, and so narrowing our view of the subject excessively.

23. (*A note on terminology:*) For metaphors that fit a substitution or comparison view, the factors needing to be distinguished are: (i) some word or expression E; (ii) occurring in some verbal "frame" F; so that (iii) $F(E)$ is the metaphorical statement in question; (iv) the meaning $m'(E)$ which E has in $F(E)$; (v) which is the same as the literal meaning $m(X)$, of some literal synonym, X. A sufficient technical vocabulary would be: "metaphorical expression" (for E) "metaphorical statement" (for $F(E)$), "metaphorical meaning" (for m') and "literal meaning" (for m).

Where the interaction view is appropriate, the situation is more complicated. We may also need to refer (vi) to the principal subject of $F(E)$, say P (roughly, what the statement is "really" about), (vii) the subsidiary subject, S (what $F(E)$ would be about if read literally); (viii) the relevant system of implications, I, connected with S; and (ix) the resulting system of attributions, A, asserted of P. We must accept at least so much complexity if we agree that the meaning of E in its setting F depends upon the transformation of I into A by using language, normally applied to S, to apply to P instead.

Richards has suggested using the words "tenor" and "vehicle" for the two "*thoughts*" which, in his view, are "active together" (for "the two *ideas* that metaphor, at its simplest, gives us," *Op. cit.*, p. 96, my italics) and urges that we reserve "the word 'metaphor' for the whole double unit" (*ib.*) But this picture of two *ideas* working upon each other is an inconvenient fiction. And it is significant that Richards himself soon lapses into speaking of "tenor" and "vehicle" as "things" (*e.g.* on p. 118). Richards' "vehicle" vacillates in reference between the metaphorical expression (E), the subsidiary subject (S) and the connected implication system (I). It is less clear what his "tenor" means: sometimes it stands for the principal subject (P), sometimes for the implications connected with that subject (which I have not symbolized above), sometimes, in spite of Richards' own intentions, for the *resultant* meaning (or as we might say the "full import") of E in its context, $F(E)$.

There is probably no hope of getting an accepted terminology so long as writers upon the subject are still so much at variance with one another.

STANLEY CAVELL

Aesthetic Problems
of Modern Philosophy

THE SPIRIT OF THE AGE is not easy to place, ontologically or empirically; and it is idle to suggest that creative effort must express its age, either because that cannot fail to happen, or because a new effort can create a new age. Still, one knows what it means when an art historian says, thinking of the succession of plastic styles, "not everything is possible in every period."[1] And that is equally true for every person and every philosophy. But then one is never sure what is possible until it happens; and when it happens it may produce a sense of revolution, of the past escaped and our problems solved—even when we also know that one man's solution is another man's problem.

Wittgenstein expressed his sense both of the revolutionary break his later methods descry in philosophy, and of their relation to methods in aesthetics and ethics.[2] I have tried, in what follows, to suggest ways in which such feelings or claims can be understood, believing them to be essential in understanding Wittgenstein's later philosophy as a whole. The opening section outlines two problems in aesthetics each of which seems to yield to the possibilities of Wittgensteinian procedures and, in turn, to illuminate them. The concluding section suggests resemblances between one kind of judgment recognizable as aesthetic and the characteristic claim of Wittgenstein—and of ordinary language philosophers generally—to voice "what we should ordinarily say."

What I have written, and I suppose the way I have written, grows from a sense that philosophy is in one of its periodic crises of method, heightened by a worry I am sure is not mine alone, that method dictates to content; that, for example, an intellectual commitment to analytical philosophy trains concern away from the wider, traditional problems of human culture which may have brought one to philosophy in the first place. Yet one can find oneself unable to relinquish either the method or the alien concern.

A free eclecticism of method is one obvious solution to such a problem. Another solution may be to discover further freedoms or possibilities within the method one finds closest to oneself. I lean here towards the latter of these alternatives, hoping to make philosophy yet another kind of problem for itself; in particular, to make the medium of philosophy— that is, of Wittgensteinian and, more generally, of ordinary language philosophy—a significant problem for aesthetics.

Two Problems of Aesthetics

Let us begin with a sheer matter of words—the controversy about whether a poem, or more modestly, a metaphor, can be paraphrased. Cleanth Brooks, in his *Well Wrought Urn*,[3] provided a convenient title for it in the expression "The Heresy of Paraphrase," the heresy, namely, of supposing that a "poem constitutes a 'statement' of some sort" (p. 179); a heresy in which "most of our difficulties in criticism are rooted" (p. 184).

> The truth of the matter is that all such formulations (of what a poem says) lead away from the center of the poem—not toward it; that the "prose sense" of the poem is not a rack on which the stuff of the poem is hung; that it does not represent the "inner" structure or the "essential" structure or the "real" structure of the poem (p. 182). We can very properly use paraphrases as pointers and as shorthand references provided that we know what we are doing. But it is highly important that we know what we are doing and that we see plainly that the paraphrase is not the real core of meaning which constitutes the essence of the poem (p. 180).

We may have some trouble in seeing plainly that the paraphrase is *not* the real core, or essence, or essential structure or inner or real structure of a poem; the same trouble we should have in understanding what *is* any or all of these things, since it takes so much philosophy just to state them. It is hard to imagine that someone has just flatly given it out that the essence, core, structure, and rest of a poem is its paraphrase. Probably somebody has been saying that poetry uses ornaments of style, or requires special poetic words, or has been saying what a poem means or what it ought to mean—doing something that makes someone else, in a fit of philosophy, say that this is distorting a poem's essence. Now the person who is accused in Brooks writ is probably going to deny guilt, feel that words are being put into his mouth, and answer that he knows perfectly well that a "paraphrase, of course, is not the equivalent of a poem; a poem is more than its paraphrasable content." Those are the words of Yvor Winters, whose work Professor Brooks uses as "[furnishing] perhaps the most respectable example of the paraphrastic heresy" (p. 183).[4] And so the argument goes, and goes. It has the gait of a false issue—by which I do not mean that it will be easy to straighten out.

One clear symptom of this is Brooks's recurrent concessions that, of course, a paraphrase is all right—if you know what you're doing. Which is about like saying that of course criticism is all right, in its place; which is true enough. But how, in particular, are we to assess a critic's reading the opening stanza of Wordsworth's "Intimations" Ode and writing: ". . . the poet begins by saying that he has lost something" (Brooks, p. 116)? We can ransack that stanza and never find the expression "lost something" in it. Then the critic will be offended—rightly—and he may reply, Well, it does not actually say this, but it means it, it implies it; do you suggest that it does not mean that? And of course we do not. But then the critic has a *theory* about what he is doing when he says what a poem means, and so he will have to add some appendices to his readings of the poetry explaining that when he says what a poem means he does not say exactly quite just what the poem means; that is, he only points to its meaning, or rather "points to the area in which the meaning lies." But even this last does not seem to him humility enough, and he may be moved to a footnote in which he says that his own analyses are "at best crude approximations of the poem" (p. 189). By this time someone is likely to burst out with: But *of course* a paraphrase says what the poem says, and an *approximate paraphrase* is merely a bad paraphrase; with greater effort or sensibility you could have got it exactly right. To which one response would be: "Oh, I can tell you exactly what the Ode means," and then read the Ode aloud.

Is there no real way out of this air of self-defeat, no way to get *satisfying* answers? Can we discover what, in such an exchange, is causing that uneasy sense that the speakers are talking past one another? Surely each knows exactly what the other means; neither is pointing to the smallest fact that the other fails to see.

For one suggestion, look again at Brooks' temptation to say that his readings *approximate* to (the meaning of) the poem. He is not there confessing his personal ineptitude; he means that any paraphrase, the best, will be only an approximation. So he is not saying, what he was accused of saying, that his own paraphrase was, in some more or less definite way, inexact or faulty: he denies the ordinary contrast between "approximate" and "exact." And can he not do that if he wants to? Well, if I am right, he *did* do it. Although it is not clear what he *wanted* to. Perhaps he was *led* to it; and did he realize that, and would his realizing it make any difference? It may help to say: In speaking of the paraphrase as approximating to the poem (the meaning of the poem?) he himself furthers the suggestion that paraphrase and poem operate, as it were, at the same level, are the same kind of thing. (One shade of color approximates to another shade, it does not approximate, nor does it fail to approximate, to the object of which it is the color. An arrow pointing

approximately north is exactly pointing somewhere. One paraphrase may
be approximately the same, have approximately the same meaning, as
another paraphrase.) And then he has to do everything at his philosophical disposal to keep paraphrase and poem from coinciding; in particular,
speak of cores and essences and structures of the poem that are not
reached by the paraphrase. It is as if someone got it into his head that
really pointing to an object would require actually touching it, and then,
realizing that this would make life very inconvenient, reconciled himself
to common sense by saying: Of course we *can* point to objects, but we
must realize what we are doing, and that most of the time this is only
approximately pointing to them.

This is the sort of thing that happens with astonishing frequency in
philosophy. We impose a demand for absoluteness (typically of some
simple physical kind) upon a concept, and then, finding that our ordinary
use of this concept does not meet our demand, we accommodate this discrepancy as nearly as possible. Take these familiar patterns: we do not
really see material objects, but only see them indirectly; we cannot be
certain of any empirical proposition, but only practically certain; we
cannot really know what another person is feeling, but only infer it. One
of Wittgenstein's greatest services, to my mind, is to show how constant a
feature of philosophy this pattern is: this is something that his diagnoses
are meant to explain ("We have a certain picture of how something must
be"; "Language is idling; not doing work; being used apart from its
ordinary language games"). Whether his diagnoses are themselves satisfying is another question. It is not very likely, because if the phenomenon
is as common as he seems to have shown, its explanation will evidently
have to be very much clearer and more complete than his sketches
provide.

This much, however, is true: If you put such phrases as "giving the
meaning," "giving a paraphrase," "saying exactly what something means
(or what somebody said)," and so on, into the ordinary contexts (the
"language games") in which they are used, you will not find that you are
worried that you have not really *done* these things. We could say: *That* is
what doing them really is. Only that serenity will last just so long as
someone does not start philosophizing about it. Not that I want to stop
him; only I want to know what it is he is then doing, and why he follows
just those particular tracks.

We owe it to Winters to make it clear that he does not say any of the
philosophical things Brooks attributes to him. His thesis, having expressed his total acquiescence in the fact that paraphrases are not poems,
is that *some* poems cannot be paraphrased—in particular, poems of the
chief poetic talent of the United States during the second and third
decades of the twentieth century; that poems which are unparaphrasable
are, in that specific way, defective; and that therefore this poetic talent
was led in regrettable directions. The merit of this argument for us,

whether we agree with its animus or not, and trying to keep special theories about poetic discourse at arm's length, is its recognition that paraphrasability is one definite characteristic of uses of language, a characteristic that some expressions have and some do not have. It suggests itself that uses of language can be distinguished according to whether or not they possess this characteristic, and further distinguished by the kind of paraphrase they demand. Let us pursue this suggestion with a few examples, following Wittgenstein's idea that we can find out what kind of object anything (grammatically) is (for example, a meaning) by investigat..ng expressions which show the kind of thing said about it (for example, "explaining the meaning").

It is worth saying that the clearest case of a use of language having no paraphrase is its literal use. If I tell you, "Juliet [the girl next door] is not yet fourteen years old," and you ask me what I mean, I might do many things—ask you what *you* mean, or perhaps try to teach you the meaning of some expression you cannot yet use (which, as Wittgenstein goes to extraordinary lengths to show, is not the same thing as *telling* you what it means). Or again, if I say, "Sufficient unto the day is the evil thereof," which I take to be the literal truth, then if I need to explain my meaning to you I shall need to do other things: I shall perhaps not be surprised that you do not get my meaning and so I shall hardly ask you, in my former spirit, what you mean in asking me for it; nor shall I, unless my disappointment pricks me into offense, offer to teach you the meaning of an English expression. What I might do is to try to *put my thought another way*, and perhaps refer you, depending upon who you are, to a range of similar or identical thoughts expressed by others. What I cannot (logically) do in either the first or the second case is to *paraphrase* what I said.

Now suppose I am asked what someone means who says, "Juliet is the sun." Again my options are different, and specific. Again I am not, not in the same way, surprised that you ask; but I shall *not* try to put the thought another way—which seems to be the whole truth in the view that metaphors are unparaphrasable, that their meaning is bound up in the very words they employ. (The addition adds nothing: Where else is it imagined, in that context, that meanings are bound, or found?) I may say something like: Romeo means that Juliet is the warmth of his world; that his day begins with her; that only in her nourishment can he grow. And his declaration suggests that the moon, which other lovers use as emblems of their love, is merely her reflected light, and dead in comparison; and so on. In a word, I paraphrase it. Moreover, if I could not provide an explanation of this form, then that is a very good reason, a perfect reason, for supposing that I do not know what it means. Metaphors are paraphrasable. (And if that is true, it is tautologous.) When Croce denied the possibility of paraphrase, he at least had the grace to assert that there were no metaphors.

Two points now emerge: (1) The "and so on" which ends my example of paraphrase is significant. It registers what William Empson calls the "pregnancy" of metaphors, the burgeoning of meaning in them. Call it what you like; in this feature metaphors differ from some, but perhaps not all, literal discourse. And differ from the similar device of simile: the inclusion of "like" in an expression changes the rhetoric. If you say "Juliet is like the sun," two alterations at least seem obvious: the drive of it leads me to expect you to continue by saying in what definite respects they are like (similes are just a little bit pregnant); and, in complement, I *wait* for you to tell me what you mean, to deliver your meaning, so to speak. It is not up to me to find as much as I can in your words. The over-reading of metaphors so often complained of, no doubt justly, is a hazard they must run for their high interest.[5] (2) To give the paraphrase, to understand the metaphor, I must understand the ordinary or dictionary meaning of the words it contains, *and* understand that they are not there being used in their ordinary way, that the meanings they invite are not to be found opposite them in a dictionary. In this respect the words in metaphors function as they do in idioms. But idioms are, again, specifically different. "I fell flat on my face" seems an appropriate case. To explain its meaning is simply to *tell* it—one might say you don't *explain* it at all; either you know what it means or you don't; there is no richer and poorer among its explanations; you need imagine nothing special in the mind of the person using it. And you will find it in a dictionary, though in special locations; which suggests that, unlike metaphors, the number of idioms in a language is finite. In some, though not all, of these respects the procedure of "giving the meaning" of an idiom is like that in translating: one might think of it as translating from a given language into itself. Then how is it different from defining, or giving a synonym?

One final remark about the difference between idioms and metaphors. Any theory concerned to account for peculiarities of metaphor of the sort I have listed will wonder over the literal meaning its words, in that combination, have. This is a response, I take it, to the fact that a metaphorical expression (in the "*A* is *B*" form at least) sounds like an ordinary assertion, though perhaps not made by an ordinary mind. Theory aside, I want to look at the suggestion, often made, that what metaphors literally say is *false*. (This is a response to the well-marked characteristic of "psychic tension" set up in metaphors. The mark is used by Empson; I do not know the patent.) But to say that Juliet is the sun is not to say something false; it is, at best, wildly false, and that is not being just false. This is part of the fact that if we are to suggest that what the metaphor says is true, we shall have to say it is wildly true—mythically or magically or primitively true. (Romeo just may be young enough, or crazed or heretic enough, to have meant his words literally.) About some idioms, however, it is fair to say that their words literally say something that is quite false; something, that is, which could easily, though maybe comically, be imagined to be true. Someone might actually fall flat on his face, have a thorn in his side, a bee in his bonnet, a bug in his ear, or a fly in his ointment—even all at once. Then what are we to say about the literal meaning of a metaphor? That it has none? And that what it literally says is not false, *and* not true? And that it is not an assertion? But it sounds like one; and people do think it is true and people do think it is false. I am suggesting that it is such facts that will need investigating if we are to satisfy ourselves about metaphors; that we are going to keep getting philosophical theories about metaphor until such facts are investigated; and that this is not an occasion for adjudication, for the only thing we could offer now in that line would be: all the theories are right in what they say. And that seems to imply that all are wrong as well.

At this point we might be able to give more content to the idea that some modes of figurative language are such that in them what an expression means cannot be said at all, at least not in any of the more or less familiar, conventionalized ways so far noticed. Not because these modes are flatly literal—there is, as it were, room for an explanation, but we cannot enter it. About such an expression it may be right to say: I know what it means but I can't say what it means. And this would no longer suggest, as it would if said about a metaphor, that you really do not know what it means—or: it might suggest it, but you couldn't be sure.

Examples of such uses of language would, I think, characteristically occur in specific kinds of poetry, for example, Symbolist, Surrealist, or Imagist. Such a use seems to me present in a line like Hart Crane's "The mind is brushed by sparrow wings" (cited, among others, in the Winters essay), and in Wallace Stevens's "as a calm darkens among water-lights," from "Sunday Morning." Paraphrasing the lines, or explaining their meaning, or telling it, or putting the thought another way—all these are out of the question. One may be able to say nothing except that a feeling has been voiced by a kindred spirit and that, if someone does not get it, he is not in one's world, or not of one's flesh. The lines may, that is, be left as touchstones of intimacy. Or one might try *describing* more or less elaborately a particular day or evening, a certain place and mood and gesture, in whose presence the line in question comes to seem a natural expression, the only expression.

This seems to be what Winters, who profitably distinguishes several varieties of such uses of language, distrusts and dislikes in his defense of reason, as he also seems prepared for the reply that this is not a *failing* of language but a feature of a specific approach of language. At least I think it is a reply of this sort, which I believe to be right, that he wishes to repudiate by appealing to "the fallacy of expressive (or imitative) form," instanced by him at one point as "Whitman trying to express a loose America by writing loose poetry," or "Mr. Joyce [endeavoring] to express disintegration by breaking down his form." It is useful to have a name for this fallacy, which no doubt some people commit. But his remarks seem a bit quick in their notation of what Whitman and Joyce were trying to express, and in their explanation of why they had to express themselves as they did; too sure that a break with the past of the order represented in modern art was not itself necessary in order to defend reason; too sure that convention can still be attacked in conventional ways. And they suggest scorn for the position that a high task of art has become, in our bombardment of sound, to create silence. (*Being* silent for that purpose might be a good example of the fallacy of imitative form. But that would depend on the context.) The fact is that I feel I would have to forgo too much of modern art were I to take his view of it.

Before we leave him, we owe it to Brooks to acknowledge a feature of Winters's position which may be causing his antipathy to it. Having wished to save Winters from a misconstruction of paraphrase, we gave back to that notion a specificity which, it now emerges, opens him to further objection. For his claim that poems that cannot be paraphrased— or, as he also puts it, do not "rest on a formulable logic"—are therefore defective now means or implies that all poems not made essentially of metaphorical language (and/or similes, idioms, literal statements) are defective. It is certainly to be hoped that all *criticism* be rational, to be demanded that it form coherent propositions about its art. But to suppose that this requires all poetry to be "formulable," in the sense that it must, whatever its form and pressure, yield to paraphrase, the way single metaphors specifically do, is not only unreasonable past defense but incurs what we might call the fallacy of expressive criticism.

In summary: Brooks is wrong to say that poems cannot in principle be fully paraphrased, but right to be worried about the relation between paraphrase and poem; Winters is right in his perception that some poetry is "formulable" and some not, but wrong in the assurance he draws from that fact; both respond to, but fail to follow, the relation between criticism and its object. And now, I think, we can be brought more unprotectedly to face the whole question that motivates such a conflict, namely, what it is we are doing when we describe or explain a work of art; what function criticism serves; whether different arts, or forms of art, require different forms of criticism; what we may expect to learn from criticism, both about a particular piece of art and about the nature of art generally. . . .[6]

Notes

1. Heinrich Wolfflin, *Principles of Art History*, foreword to the 7th German edition. Quoted by E. H. Gombrich, *Art and Illusion* (New York: The Bollingen Series, Pantheon Press, 1960), p. 4.

2. Reported by G. E. Moore, "Wittgenstein's Lectures in 1930-33," reprinted in Moore's *Philosophical Papers* (London: George Allen and Unwin, 1959), p. 315.

3. *The Well Wrought Urn* (New York: Harcourt, Brace & Co., 1947). All page references to Brooks are to this edition. "The Heresy of Paraphrase" is the title of the concluding chapter.

4. For Winters's position, I have relied solely on his central essay, "The Experimental School in American Poetry," from *Primitivism and Decadence,* itself republished, together with earlier of his critical works, under the title *In Defense of Reason* (Denver: Alan Swallow, 1947).

5. Added 1968. I should have made it more explicit that throughout this essay I am using "paraphrase" to name solely that specific form of account which suits metaphors (marked, for example, by its concluding sense of "and so on"). So when I say that stretches of literal prose "cannot be paraphrased," I mean to imply the specification ". . . in *that* way." Certainly an exercise useful in the teaching of reading can be given as "Paraphrase the following passage," where what is wanted is a resumé of the passage which shows a grasp of the difficult words and constructions in it and of its over-all sense. But in *that* context, paraphrase is explicitly not a candidate for anything likely to be taken as a *competitor* of the passage in question.

6. The second problem of aesthetics discussed by Cavell—"Is such music as is called 'atonal' . . . really without tonality?"—is here omitted as not germane to the present topic. The last part of Cavell's essay, "Aesthetic Judgment and a Philosophical Claim," is also omitted. Ed.

MARGARET MACDONALD

The Language of Fiction

I

"EMMA WOODHOUSE, handsome, clever and rich, with a comfortable home and happy disposition seemed to unite some of the best blessings of existence and had lived nearly twenty-one years in the world with very little to distress or vex her."

The opening sentence of Jane Austen's novel *Emma* is a sentence from fiction. *Emma* is a work in which the author tells a story of characters, places and incidents almost all of which she has invented. I shall mean by "fiction" any similar work. For unless a work is largely, if not wholly, composed of what is invented, it will not correctly be called "fiction." One which contains nothing imaginary may be history, science, detection, biography, but not fiction. I want to ask some questions about how an author uses words and sentences in fiction. But my interest is logical, not literary. I shall not discuss the style or artistic skill of any storyteller. Mine is the duller task of trying to understand some of the logic of fictional language; to determine the logical character of its expressions. How do they resemble and differ from those in other contexts? What are they understood to convey? Are they, e.g. true or false statements? If so, of or about what are they true or false? If not, what other function do they perform? How are they connected? These are the questions I shall chiefly discuss.

First of all, "fiction" is often used ambiguously both for what is fictitious and for that by which the fictitious is expressed. Thus "fiction" is opposed to "fact" as what is imaginary to what is real. But one must emphasize that a work of fiction itself is not imaginary, fictitious or unreal. What is fictitious does not exist. There are no dragons in the Zoo. But the novels of Jane Austen do exist. The world, fortunately, contains them just as it contained Jane Austen. They occupy many bookshelves. Works

Reprinted from *Proceedings of the Aristotelian Society,* Supplementary Vol. XXVIII (1954) by courtesy of the Editor of the Aristotelian Society.

of fiction, stories, novels are additions to the universe. Any unreality attaches only to their subject matter.[1]

Secondly, everyone understands the expressions of fiction. Or, if they do not, the reason is technical, not logical. One may find it hard to understand some of the expressions of Gertrude Stein or *Finnegan's Wake* but this is due to the peculiar obscurity of their style and not to the fact that they occur in works of fiction. No one who knows English could fail to understand the sentence quoted from *Emma*. That Emma Woodhouse was handsome, clever and rich is understood just as easily as that Charlotte Brontë was plain, sickly and poor. Both are indicative sentences which appear to inform about their subjects. But while the sentence containing "Charlotte Brontë" expresses a true statement of which Charlotte Brontë is the subject, that containing "Emma Woodhouse" cannot work similarly, since Jane Austen's Emma did not exist and so cannot be the logical subject of any statement. "Emma Woodhouse" does not and cannot designate a girl of that name of whom Jane Austen wrote. This has puzzled philosophers.[2] If apparent statements about Emma Woodhouse are about no one, of what is Jane Austen writing and how is she to be understood? Perhaps a subsistent wraith in a logical limbo is her subject? This will not do; or, at least, not in this form. Jane Austen is certainly "pretending" that there was a girl called Emma Woodhouse who had certain qualities and adventures. According to one view she is understood because we understand from non-fictional contexts the use of proper names and the general terms in which she describes Emma Woodhouse and her adventures. There is no Emma Woodhouse, so Jane Austen is not writing about her; rather she is writing about a number of properties, signified by the general terms she uses, and asserting that they belonged to someone. Since they did not "Emma Woodhouse" is a pseudo-designation and the propositions are false, though significant. Readers of *Emma* need not, and usually do not, believe falsely that its propositions are true. A work of fiction is, or is about, "one big composite predicate" and is so understood by readers who need neither to know nor believe that any subject was characterized by it. If, however, there had been, by chance, and unknown to Jane Austen, a girl called Emma Woodhouse who conformed faithfully to all the descriptions of the novel, its propositions would have been about and true of her and Jane Austen would have "accidentally" written biography and not fiction.[3]

This seems a somewhat strained account of a story. As Moore says,[4] it does not seem false to deny that Jane Austen wrote about Emma Woodhouse, even though she did not exist. There are many senses of "about." The common reader would be mystified to be told that *Emma* is not about Emma Woodhouse, Harriet Smith, Miss Bates, Mr. George Knightley and the rest, but is, instead, about such a peculiar object as a "composite predicate." He would, surely, find this quite unintelligible. It is also false to say that a work of fiction may be "accidentally" history or biography. For if there were ten girls called "Emma Woodhouse" of whom all that Jane Austen wrote were true, they are not the subject of *Emma,* for Jane Austen is not telling a story of any of them, but of a subject of her own invention. Moreover, it would not only be necessary that Emma Woodhouse should have a real counterpart but that such counterparts should exist for every other element of her novel. You cannot separate Emma from Highbury, her companions and the ball at the Crown. They all belong to the story. Such a coincidence would be almost miraculous. So Moore seems to be right when he says:[5]

"I think that what he [Dickens] meant by 'Mr. Pickwick,' and what we all understand is: 'There was only one man of whom it is true both that *I am going to tell you about him* and that he was called "Pickwick" *and* that, etc.' In other words, he is saying from the beginning, that he has one and only one man in his mind's eye, about whom he is going to tell you a story. That he has is, of course, false: it is part of the fiction. It is this which gives unique reference to all subsequent uses of 'Mr. Pickwick.' And it is for this reason that Mr. Ryle's view that if, by coincidence, there happened to be a real man of whom everything related of Mr. Pickwick in the novel were true then 'we could say that Dickens' propositions were true of somebody' is to be rejected . . . *since Dickens was not telling us of him*: and that this is what is meant by saying that it is only 'by coincidence' that there happened to be such a man."

I think this can be seen to be true even in circumstances which might appear to support Ryle's view. *Jane Eyre* and *Villette* are known to contain much biographical material. Charlotte Brontë knew her original as Dickens did not know of a "coincidental" Mr. Pickwick. Yet *Jane Eyre* and *Villette* are still works of fiction, not biography. They are no substitute for Mrs. Gaskell's *Life of Charlotte Brontë.* For although she may be *using* the facts of her own life, Charlotte Brontë is not writing "about" herself, but "about" Jane Eyre, Helen Burns, Mr. Rochester, Lucy Snowe, Paul Emmanuel and the rest. Or, she is writing about herself in a very different sense from that in which she is writing about the subject matter of her novels.

Ryle and Moore agree, with many others, that the sentences of fiction express false statements and Moore adds, I think rightly, that, so far, at least, as these are fictional, they could not be true. But there is a more radical view for which there is also some excuse. If a storyteller tells what he knows to be false, is he not a deceiver and his work a "tissue of lies"? That storytelling is akin to, if not a form of, lying is a very common view. "To make up a tale," "to tell a yarn" are common euphemisms for "to tell a lie." A liar knows what is true, but deliberately says what is false. What else does the storyteller who pretends that there was a girl called "Emma Woodhouse," etc., when she knows this is false? A liar intends to, and does, deceive a hearer. Does not a storyteller do likewise? "Poets themselves," says Hume, "though liars by profession, always endeavour to give an air of truth to their fictions."[6] Hume is contrasting all other expressions as indifferently lies or fiction, with those which are true of matter of fact. Hume is quite wrong to classify all poetry with fiction, though some stories may be told in verse. But no one could correctly call, e.g. Shakespeare's Sonnets, Keats' Odes or Eliot's Four Quartets, works of fiction. Nor are they statements of fact, but their analysis is not my task here. I wish only to protest against a common tendency to consign to one dustbin all expressions which do not conform to the type of statement found in factual studies. Even though they are not factual statements, expressions in literature may be of many different logical types. It is clear, however, that for Hume storytelling is a form of lying. And, indeed, a storyteller not only says what he knows to be false but uses every device of art to induce his audience to accept his fancies. For what else are the ancient incantatory openings, "Once upon a time . . . ," "Not yesterday, not yesterday, but long ago . . . ," and their modern equivalents, but to put a spell upon an audience so that the critical faculties of its members are numbed and they willingly suspend disbelief to enter the state which Coleridge called "illusion" and likened to dreaming?[7] All this is true. Everyone must sometimes be informed, instructed, exhorted by others. There are facts to learn and attitudes to adopt. However dull, these processes must be endured. But no one is obliged to attend to another's fancies. Unless, therefore, a storyteller can convince, he will not hold an audience. So, among other devices, he "endeavours to give an air of truth to his fictions." It does not follow that what he says *is* true, nor that he is a deceiver. One must distinguish "trying to convince" from "seeking to mislead." To convince is a merit in a work of fiction. To induce someone to accept a fiction, however, is not necessarily to seduce him into a belief that is real. It is true that some people may be deceived by fiction. They fail to distinguish conviction from deception. Such are those who write to the B.B.C. about Mrs. Dale and the Archers as if they believe themselves to be hearing the life histories of real families in these programmes. But this does not show that the B.B.C. has deliberately beguiled these innocents. Finally, a liar may be "found out" in his lie. He is then discredited and his lie is useless. Nor is he easily believed again. But it would be absurd for someone to complain that since *Emma* was fiction he had "found out" Jane Austen and could never trust her again. The conviction induced by a story is the result of a mutual conspiracy, freely entered into, between author and audience. A storyteller does not lie, nor is a normal auditor deceived. Yet there are affinities between fiction and lying which excuse the comparison. Conviction, without belief or disbelief, as in art, is like, but also very different from, unwitting deception. And a liar, too, pretends but not all pretending is lying.

A fictional sentence does not, then, express a lying statement. Does it express a false statement which is not a lie? False statements are normally asserted from total or partial ignorance of the facts. Those who assert them mistakenly believe they are true. This is not true of the storyteller. Neither he nor his auditor normally believes that his statements are true. Moreover, though a proposition may be false, it must make sense to say that it might be true. It is false that Jane Austen wrote *Pickwick Papers* but it is not nonsense to suggest that it might have been true. As already seen, however, no factual discovery can verify a fictional statement. It can then never be true. So it would seem to be necessarily false or logically impossible. But the expressions of fiction are neither self-contradictory nor nonsensical. Most of them are perfectly intelligible. Those which are not are so for reasons quite unconnected with truth and falsity. It is not because James Joyce's statements are all false that they are unintelligible. For those of Jane Austen and Dickens are equally false, but not obscure.

Alternatively, it might be said that the propositions of fiction are false, but neither believed nor asserted. Their fictional character consists in the fact that they are merely proposed for consideration, like hypotheses. "Let us suppose there was a girl called Emma Woodhouse, who . . . etc." For a proposition may be entertained, but yet be false. So an author puts forward and his audience considers, but neither affirm, the false propositions of fiction.[8] Now, a storyteller does invite his audience to "Imagine that . . . ," "Pretend that . . ." and even "Suppose that . . ." or "Let it be granted that . . ." He does not often preface his story with just these remarks, but he issues a general invitation to exercise imagination. So far one may liken his attitude to that of someone proposing an hypothesis in other fields. An hypothesis, like a lie or a story, requires some invention; it is not a report of observed fact. But these suggested fictional hypotheses are also very different from all others. Non-fictional hypotheses are proposed to explain some fact or set of facts. "If the picture is by Van Dyck, then . . ."; "Suppose that malaria is transmitted by mosquitoes, then. . . ." They suggest, e.g., the origin of a painting or the cause of a disease. But a story is not told to solve any such problem. Moreover, a non-fictional hypothesis must be testable or be mere speculation without explanatory value. But, obviously, nothing can count as evidence in favour of a fictional story. And what no fact can confirm none can disconfirm either. So, if a story consists of propositions entertained for consideration, the purpose of such entertainment must be for ever frustrated since they can never be asserted as true, false, probable or improbable. I conclude, therefore, that the expressions of fiction do not function either as propositions or hypotheses.

Nevertheless, as I have said, one can easily understand why people are tempted to identify fictional expressions with lies, falsehoods, unverifiable hypotheses. For what it is worth, the English dictionary appears to support this view. "Fiction," it says, "the act of feigning, inventing or imagining: that which is feigned, i.e. a fictitious story, fable, fabrication, falsehood." If the last four terms are intended as synonyms, this certainly suggests that all fiction is falsehood. Both rationalist and religious parents have forbidden children to read fairy stories and novels lest they be led astray into false and immoral beliefs. Yet its logical difference from these seems to show that fiction is not false, lying, or hypothetical statement. It is clear that "S pretends that p" cannot entail p. This is, again, the point of saying that the truth of p must be "coincidental." When discovered, no future S (or storyteller) could pretend that p, for one cannot pretend that a proposition is true when it is, and is known to be, true. But neither, in fiction, can "S pretends that p" entail "not-p," or even "Perhaps-p." So, fictional expressions must be of a different type from statements.

An alternative is the familiar emotive answer. This is associated chiefly with the name of I. A. Richards. I can mention it only briefly. According to it, sentences in fiction, as in all non-informative contexts, express an emotional state of their author and seek to induce a similar state in his audience. A work is judged better or worse according to the amount of harmonious mental adjustment by which it was caused and which it effects. This view is difficult to estimate because of its vague use of the word "express." It tends to suggest that the expressions of fiction are disguised exclamations such as "Hurrah!" or "Alas!" Or that these could be substituted for them. This, of course, is impossible. No one could tell the story of *Emma* in a series of smiles, sighs, tears, shouts or the limited vocabulary which represents such emotive expressions. Most stories, one must reiterate, are told in normal English sentences which are common to fact and fiction and appropriately understood. This is, indeed, just the problem. If the expressions of Jane Austen were as easily distinguishable from factual statement as exclamation from articulate utterance no one would be puzzled. "Emotive expression" must, therefore, be compatible with understood sense.[9] It is true that emotional relationships play a large part in most fiction, but so does much else. Nor need these subjects coincide with the experience of either author or audience. No story, even though told in the first person, can be completely autobiographical without ceasing to be fiction. And whether or not a work of fiction uses autobiographical material, the actual, or suspected, direct intrusion of personal feeling by the author is liable to be fatal to the work.

"I opened it at chapter twelve and my eye was caught by the phrase 'Anybody may blame me who likes.' What were they blaming Charlotte Brontë for, I wondered? And I read how Jane Eyre used to go up on the roof when Mrs. Fairfax was making jellies and look over the fields at the distant view. And then she longed—and it was for this that they blamed her—that 'then I longed for a power of vision which might overpass that limit . . . I desired more of practical experience . . . more of intercourse with my kind. . . . I believed in the existence of other and more vivid kinds of goodness and what I believed in I wished to behold. . . . Who blames me? Many no doubt and I shall be called discontented. . . . When thus alone I not infrequently heard Grace Poole's laugh.'

"That is an awkward break, I thought. It is upsetting to come upon

Grace Poole all of a sudden. The continuity is disturbed. One might say, I continued, . . . that the woman who wrote these pages had genius . . . but if one reads them over and marks that jerk in them, that indignation, one sees . . . that her books will be deformed and twisted." (Virginia Woolf; *A Room of One's Own*, p. 104.)

In short, Charlotte Brontë will, or will appear to, express her own feelings too nakedly through her heroine, in order to induce a sympathetic emotional response in her readers, instead of telling her story. Someone may protest that this amounts to *describing*, not expressing, her emotions. But this is not ostensibly so. The passage is still a soliloquy by Jane Eyre, not an introspective report by Charlotte Brontë. Virginia Woolf is giving an interpretation of the passage, but this would not be necessary if it were a simple description of Charlotte Brontë's feelings. If her critic is right and if, nevertheless, the passage is not what is meant by an expression of the author's emotion by fiction, this cannot be because it is a straightforward description of fact. Another objection might be that this is a crude example of expression and does not prove that the task of fiction is not to express emotion. Skilful expression is impersonal, almost anonymous. One cannot tell from their works what Shakespeare or Jane Austen felt. Hence the floods of speculation by critics. One knows only too well from her novels what Charlotte Brontë felt, so she is not truly expressing, but merely venting, her emotions. But then, if one so often cannot tell whose, or even what, emotion is being expressed, what is the point of saying that all fictional expressions are emotive? Should the criterion be solely the effect on their audience? Certainly, a tale may amuse, sadden, anger, or otherwise move a hearer. But is the fact that *Emma* may cause one to laugh or sigh what distinguishes it as a work of fiction from a statement of fact? This must be false for much that is not fiction has the same effect. The answer of the theory is that a work of fiction, like any work of literary art, causes a very special emotional effect, an harmonious adjustment of impulses, a personal attitude, not otherwise obtainable. But no independent evidence of any such pervasive effect is offered, nor can I, for one, provide it from experience of reading fiction. So, if one cannot distinguish fiction from fact by the normal emotional effects which fiction sometimes causes, nor by the pervasive changes it is alleged to cause, the theory only reformulates and does not explain this distinction.

But the theory does emphasize that language has less pedestrian uses than those of the laboratory, record office, police court and daily discourse. Also, that to create and appreciate fiction requires more than intellectual qualities. Most fiction would be incomprehensible to a being without emotions. One must be able to enter imaginatively into its emotional situations though its emotions need not be felt. One need not *feel* jealousy either to construct or understand Mr. Knightley's censorious attitude to Frank Churchill, but someone who had never felt this might find an account of it unconvincing. Authors differ, too, in what may be vaguely called "climate" or "atmosphere," which is emotional and moral as well as intellectual. The "worlds" of Jane Austen and Henry James, e.g., differ considerably from those of Emily Brontë and D. H. Lawrence. Also, much of the language of fiction is emotionally charged. For it depicts emotional situations which are part of its story. But none of these -facts is positively illuminated by a theory which limits the language of fiction to the expression of an emotion transferred from author to auditor even if such a transaction were fully understood. It does not seem to be the feeling which generates them nor that which they cause which wholly differentiates the ironies of Gibbon from those of I. Compton Burnett. Nor is it either Tolstoy or ourselves in whom we are primarily interested when reading *War and Peace*. Rather it is the presentation of characters, actions and situations. The vast panorama of the novel shrinks into triviality as the instrument of the emotional adjustments of Tolstoy and his readers. I conclude, therefore, that the characteristic which differentiates fictional sentences from those which state facts is not that the former exclusively express anybody's emotions, though many of them have a very vital connection with emotion.

II

When someone reports a fact he may choose the language or symbolism of his report. He may choose to use this carefully or carelessly. But there is a sense in which he cannot choose what he will say. No one could report truly that Charlotte Brontë died in 1890; that she wrote *Villette* before *Jane Eyre*; that she was tall, handsome and a celebrated London hostess. No biography of Charlotte Brontë could contain such statements and remain a biography. For what is truly said of Charlotte Brontë must be controlled by what she was and what happened to her. But Jane Austen was under no such restraints with Emma Woodhouse. For Emma Woodhouse was her own invention. So she may have any qualities and undergo any adventures her author pleases. It is not even certain that these must be logically possible, i.e. not self-contradictory. For some stories, and not the worst, are extremely wild. There is *Finnegans Wake* as well as *Emma*. A storyteller chooses not only the words and style but also, and I suggest with them, provides the material of a fictional story. I want to stress this fact that in fiction language is used to *create*. For it is this which chiefly differentiates it from factual statement. A storyteller performs; he does not—or not primarily—inform or misinform. To tell a story is to originate, not to report. Like the contents of dreams, the objects of fiction may presuppose, but do not compete with, those of ordinary life. Unlike those of dreams, however, they are deliberately contrived. Hence, they differ too from lunatic frenzies. A lunatic unintentionally offends against fact and logic. He intends to respect them. He thinks he is right, however wild his fancies, when he is always wrong. But a storyteller, though equally wild, is never deluded. He invents by choice, not accident.

As I have already said, most of a storyteller's words and sentences are understood to have the same meanings as the same words and grammatical forms in non-fictional contexts. For all who communicate use the same language, composed mainly of general terms. But language may be used differently to obtain different results. When a storyteller "pretends" he simulates factual description. He puts on an innocent air of informing. This is part of the pretence. But when he pretends, e.g. that there was a Becky Sharp, an adventuress, who finally came to grief, he does not inform or misinform about a real person called "Becky Sharp" or anyone else: he is creating Becky Sharp. And this is what a normal audience understands him to be doing. Of course, he does not thereby add to the population of the world. Becky Sharp is not registered at Somerset House. But this, too, is shown by language. A storyteller, like a dramatist, is not said to create persons, human beings, but *characters*. Characters, together with their settings and situations, are parts of a story. According to Ryle, although "it is correct to say that Charles Dickens created a story, it is wholly erroneous to speak as if Dickens created Mr. Pickwick."[10] But Dickens *did* create Mr. Pickwick and this is not equivalent to saying, as Ryle does, that what Dickens created was a "complex predicate." No one would ever say this. But it is perfectly ordinary and proper to say that an author has created certain characters and all that is required for them to function. "In Caliban," said Dryden, "Shakespeare seems to have *created* a being which was not in nature."[11] He was not in nature because he was part of *The Tempest*. To create a story is to use language to create the contents of that story. To write "about" Emma Woodhouse, Becky Sharp, Mr. Pickwick, Caliban, and the rest is to "bring about" these characters and their worlds. Human beings are not normally called "characters." If they are, it is by analogy with art. One might say, "I met a queer character the other day; he might have been created by Dickens." This does not show that Dickens wrote or tried to write about such a person, but that his readers now view their fellows through Dickens' works. So may one now see Constable and Cézanne pictures in natural landscapes, which would not have been seen without these artists. A character, like all else in pure fiction, is confined to its rôle in a story. Not even the longest biography exhausts what could be told of any human person, but what Jane Austen tells of Emma Woodhouse exhausts Emma Woodhouse. A character may be completely understood, but the simplest human being, if any human being is simple, is somewhere opaque to others. A character has no secrets but what are contained within five acts or between the covers of a book or the interval from supper to bedtime.[12] A story may, indeed, have a sequel, but this is a new invention, not a report of what was omitted from the original.

This may be challenged. Surely, it will be said, many characters in fiction are as complex as human beings? Do not critics still dispute about the motives of Iago and the sex of Albertine? But to say that a character is limited to what is related of it in a story does not imply that this must always be indisputably obvious. All it implies is that the only way to find out about a character is to consult the author's text. This contains all there is to discover. No one can ever find independent evidence which the author has missed. Not even Dr. Ernest Jones for the alleged "complexes" of Hamlet. Assuming that the text is complete and authentic, there may be different interpretations of it and thus of a character but no new evidence such as may render out of date a biography. No one will find a diary or a cache of letters from Hamlet to his mother which will throw light upon his mental state. Nor must this be for ever secret in the absence of such evidence. For Hamlet is what Shakespeare tells and what we understand from the text, and nothing more.

What is true of characters is true also of other fictional elements of a story. "Barchester" does not name a geographical place. It is the setting or scene of a number of Trollope's characters. So is his magic island for Prospero and his companions. The words used to "set the scene" of a story paint as it were the backcloth to its incidents. "Scene" is a term of art, a word from the language of the theatre. One would naturally say "The scene of Archdeacon Grantly's activities is laid in Barchester," but not, unless affecting histrionics, "The scene of this Conference is laid in Oxford." It would be more normal to say "This Conference is being held in Oxford." "Scene" is used of natural situations only when these are being treated artificially. Finally, the situation and incidents of a story form its plot. They conform to a contrived sequence of beginning, middle and end—or have some modern variety of this shape. But human life and natural events do not have, or conform to, a plot. They have no contrived shape.

It is thus, then, that we talk of works of fiction and their fictional contents. They are contrivances, artefacts. A story is more like a picture or a symphony than a theory or report. Characters, e.g. might, for a change, be compared with musical "themes" rather than with human flesh and blood. A composer creates a symphony, but he also creates all its several parts. So does a storyteller, but his parts are the characters, settings and incidents which constitute his story. The similarity is obscure just because the storyteller does, and must, use common speech with its general terms, so that he appears to assert propositions about an independent reality in a manner similar to that of one who does or fails to report what is true. So, philosophers conclude, since pure fiction cannot be about physical objects, it must be about wraith-like simulacra of real objects or equally attenuated "predicates." I do not, however, want to claim a special mode of existence for fictional objects as the contents of fiction. And though it is obvious that fiction writers use our common tongue I do not think that what they do is illuminated by saying that they write about predicates or properties. It is agreed that a storyteller both creates a story, a verbal construction, and the contents of that story. I want to say that these activities are inseparable. Certainly, no one could create pure fiction without also creating the contents which are its parts. One cannot separate Emma

Woodhouse from *Emma* as one can separate Napoleon from his biography. I do not say that Emma is simply identical with the words by which she is created. Emma is a "character." As such she can, in appropriate senses, be called charming, generous, foolish, and even "lifelike." No one could sensibly use these epithets of words. Nevertheless, a character is that of which it makes no sense to talk except in terms of the story in which he or she is a character. Just as, I think, it would make no sense to say that a flock of birds was carolling "by chance" the first movement of a symphony. For birds do not observe musical conventions. What is true of characters applies to the settings and incidents of pure fiction. To the questions "Where will they be found?"; "Where do they exist?," the answer is "In such and such a story," and that is all. For they are the elements or parts of stories and this is shown by our language about them.

But the content of very little fiction is wholly fictitious. London also forms part of the setting of *Emma* as it does of many of Dickens' novels; Russia of *War and Peace* and India of *A Passage to India*. Historical persons and events also seem to invade fiction. They are indeed the very stuff of "historical" novels. Do not the sentences in which the designations or descriptions of such places, persons and incidents occur express true or false statements? It is true that these real objects and events are mentioned in such fictional expressions. Nevertheless, they certainly do not function wholly as in a typographical or historical record. They are still part of a story. A storyteller is not discredited as a reporter by rearranging London's squares or adding an unknown street to serve his purpose. Nor by crediting an historical personage with speeches and adventures unknown to historians. An historical novel is not judged by the same standards as a history book. Inaccuracies are condemned, if they are, not because they are bad history or geography, but because they are bad art. A story which introduces Napoleon or Cromwell but which departs wildly from historical accuracy will not have the verisimilitude which appears to be its object and will be unplausible and tedious. Or if, nevertheless, interesting will provoke the question, "But why call this character Oliver Cromwell, Lord Protector of England?" Similarly, for places. If somewhere called "London" is quite unrecognizable, its name will have no point.

So I am inclined to say that a storyteller is not making informative assertions about real persons, places and incidents even when these are mentioned in fictional sentences. But rather that these also function like purely fictional elements, with which they are always mingled in a story. Russia as the setting for the Rostovs differs from the Russia which Napoleon invaded which did not contain the Rostovs. There was a battle of Waterloo, but George Osborne was not one of the casualties, except in Thackeray's novel. Tolstoy did not create Russia, nor Thackeray the battle of Waterloo. Yet one might say that Tolstoy did create Russia-as-the-background-of-the-Rostovs and that Thackeray created Waterloo-as-the-scene-of-George-Osborne's-death. One might say that the mention of realities plays a dual role in fiction; to refer to a real object and to contribute to the development of a story. But I cannot pursue this, except to say that this situation differs from that in which, e.g. Charlotte Brontë uses the real events in her life in *Jane Eyre*. For she does not *mention* herself nor the real places and incidents upon which her story is modelled.

I have tried to say how the expressions of fiction operate and to show that they differ both from statements and emotive expressions. I also began by asking how they are connected. It is clear that their order need not be dictated by that of any matter of fact. Nor are they always even bound by the principles of logic. Do their connections, then, follow any rule or procedure? Is there a conception by which their transitions may be described? Since a work of fiction is a creative performance, however, it may be thought senseless to ask for such rules or such a conception. Is not the creation of that which is new and original, independent of logic and existence, just that to which no rules are appropriate and no conception adequate? But the creation of a work of fiction, however remarkable, is not a miracle. Nor is its author's use of language entirely lawless and vagabond but is directed by some purpose. Certainly, no set of rules will enable anyone to write a good novel or produce a good scientific hypothesis. But a scientist employs his ingenuity to invent a hypothesis to connect certain facts and predict others. He provides an organizing concept related to the facts to be organized and governed by the probability that it provides the correct explanation. As already emphasized, the situation of the storyteller is different.

In his Preface to *The Portrait of a Lady*, Henry James recalls that in organizing his "ado" about Isobel Archer, having conceived the character, he asked, "And now what will she *do*?" and the reply came immediately, "Why, the first thing she will do will be to come to Europe." He did not have to infer, guess, or wait upon observation and evidence; he *knew*. He knew because he had thus decided. He so decided, no doubt, for a variety of artistic reasons; to develop his conception of a certain character in relation to others, against a particular background, in accordance with his plot. His aim was to produce a particular, perhaps a unique, story; a self-contained system having its own internal coherence. There is certainly a sense in which every work of fiction is a law unto itself. Nevertheless, I think there is a general notion which governs these constructions though its application may give very different results. This is the Aristotelian notion which is usually translated "probability" but which I prefer to call "artistic plausibility." This is not an ideal phrase but is preferable to "probability" which suggests an evidential relation between premises and conclusion and "possibility" which suggests a restriction to logical conceivability which might exclude some rare, strange, and fantastic works. It is, moreover, a notion which applies only to what is verbal. Though some comparable notion may apply to them, one does not normally talk of "plausible" pictures, statues and symphonies, but does talk of "plausible stories." A plausible story is one which convinces; which induces acceptance. But since the plausibility is artistic plausibility, the conviction induced will not be the belief appropriate to factual statement. Nevertheless, one drawback to the notion is that it may suggest that all fiction is, or should be, realistic or naturalistic. It is true that although fiction does not consist of statements about life and natural events, yet much fiction does take lived experience as a model for its own connections. Sometimes, as with Charlotte Brontë's novels, using autobiographical material. Such stories convince by being "lifelike." But by no means all fiction is thus naturalistic. Nor is a story allegedly founded on fact necessarily fictionally convincing. To repeat the Aristotelian tag, "a convincing impossibility is better than an unconvincing possibility." There is, in fact, a range of plausible connections in fiction, varying from the purest naturalism to the wildest fantasy. If any convinces then it is justified. Much should obviously be said about who is convinced and whether he is a reliable judge, but I can do little more here than indicate the type of connection which differentiates works of fiction from descriptions of fact. It is the task of the literary critic to analyse the different types of plausibility exemplified by, e.g. *Emma, War and Peace, The Portrait of a Lady, Wuthering Heights, Moby-Dick, Alice in Wonderland* and *Grimm's Fairy Stories*. And though, perhaps, no rules can be given for attaining any particular type of plausibility, yet it is sometimes possible to say what does or would make a work unplausible. A mixture of elements from different plausible systems would, e.g., have this result. It is quite plausible that Alice should change her size by drinking from magic bottles, but it would be absurd that Emma Woodhouse or Fanny Price should do so. Or, to make such an incident plausible, Jane Austen's novels would need to be very different. For it would have needed explanation in quite different terms from the conventions she uses. This also applies to more important plausibilities. Emma Woodhouse could not suddenly murder Miss Bates after the ball, or develop a Russian sense of sin, without either destroying the plausibility of the novel or bringing about a complete revolution in its shape, though these incidents are in themselves more likely than that which befell Alice. But such examples raise questions about fiction and fact, art and life which I cannot now discuss.

Notes

1. Cf. also "Art and Imagination," *Proc. Aris. Soc.,* 1952-53, p. 219.
2. See earlier Symposium on "Imaginary Objects," *Proc. Aris. Soc.,* Supp. Vol. 12, 1933, by G. Ryle, R. B. Braithwaite and G. E. Moore.
3. *Loc. cit.,* G. Ryle, pp. 18-43.
4. *Ibid.,* p. 59.

5. *Loc. cit.,* p. 68.

6. *Treatise of Human Nature,* Bk. 1, Pt. 3, Sec. 10.

7. Cf. Notes on *The Tempest* from *Lectures on Shakespeare.*

8. I understood Professor Moore to hold such a view in a discussion in 1952. I do not, however, claim his authority for this version. Nor do I know if he is still of the same opinion.

9. Cf. also Empson, *The Structure of Complex Words,* London, 1951, ch. 1.

10. *Loc. cit.,* p. 32.

11. Quoted by Logan Pearsall Smith. S. P. E. Tract XVII, 1924.

12. See also *Aspects of the Novel,* E. M. Forster, chs. 3 and 4.

MARCIA M. EATON

Liars, Ranters, and Dramatic Speakers

> They [critics] will call upon Shakespeare—they always do—and will quote that hackneyed passage about Art holding the mirror up to Nature, forgetting that this unfortunate aphorism is deliberately said by Hamlet in order to convince the bystanders of his absolute insanity in all art-matters. . . . My dear fellow, whatever you may say, it is merely a dramatic utterance, and no more represents Shakespeare's real views upon art than the speeches of Iago represent his real views upon morals.
>
> (Oscar Wilde, *The Decay of Lying*)

ONE OF THE OUTSTANDING SHORTCOMINGS of arguments offered on both sides of many controversial issues in aesthetics has been a failure to clarify many of the basic concepts that are employed. Frequently one meets with skepticism with regard to such clarification. However, success is the best proof against skepticism, and in this paper I hope to show that elucidation of at least one basic aesthetic concept is, at least in some degree, possible. I shall herein be concerned with one aspect of the nature of a literary work—a literary work as a linguistic object.

I

Elsewhere I have introduced some machinery for dealing with this notion, but for the sake of the self-containment of this paper I shall repeat and enlarge upon it here.[1] Very simply, a linguistic object is a word or group of words. A linguistic action is a conscious action in

From *Language and Aesthetics, Contributions to the Philosophy of Art*, edited by Benjamin R. Tilghman, pp. 43-63. Reprinted by permission of the Regents Press of Kansas.

which a person uses a linguistic object in any of various ways. One possible classification of these various ways in which linguistic objects are used is that which Austin provides in *How to Do Things with Words*. First, there are actions that are "locutionary," in which a person says or writes certain words and in so doing means to refer to certain things. Second, there are "illocutionary" acts, in which the locution is put to such uses as asserting, questioning, commanding, expressing a wish, and so forth. Third, there are "perlocutionary" acts, in which the locution has certain consequences such as persuading, convincing, deceiving, evoking, and so forth.

These classes of linguistic actions (or speech acts, as they are often called) can easily be applied to the actions of writers of literature. When a writer writes down words, sentences, and so forth, he is performing a locutionary act. When he makes assertions, commands, asks questions, and so forth, he is performing illocutionary acts. And, lastly, when a writer produces certain effects on the part of his readers—for example, informing, persuading, or arousing—he is performing perlocutionary acts.

How does a work of literature fit into this scheme? Let us first consider the sentence "Today is Monday." When someone consciously utters this sentence, he is performing a linguistic action, usually that action known as asserting. Likewise when someone writes down that sentence, he is making an assertion, and the written sentence that results is the record or product of his linguistic act of asserting. This product is a linguistic object—a group of written words.

One class of linguistic actions performed by most literary writers is very unusual, that is, quite different from the kind of action ordinarily performed in everyday discourse, both spoken and written. The locutionary and perlocutionary actions of an author are much the same as those of the average language user. But the illocutionary acts that a writer performs vary a great deal from those of the average speaker. The most commonly discussed illocutions are assertions, questions, and commands; so let us consider them. Writers may perform these actions; but often they do not. Rather they are responsible for attributing assertions, questions, commands, and so forth, to others, namely, to *dramatic speakers*. Writing literature may in fact be viewed as putting words into the mouths of dramatic speakers and thus causing *them* to perform certain illocutionary acts.

The notion of a dramatic speaker is not new, though it is often referred to by other terms, for example, "the protagonist." Wellek and Warren discuss a similar notion in their section on author psychology in *Theory of Literature*. Wimsatt and Beardsley characterize such a speaker in the following way: "Even a short lyric poem is dramatic, the response of a speaker (no matter how abstractly conceived) to a situation (no matter how universalized). We ought to impute the thoughts and attitudes of the poem immediately to the dramatic *speaker*, and if to the author at

all, only by an act of biographical inference."[2] I am in partial agreement with Wimsatt and Beardsley here. In essence, I take the dramatic
speaker to be the person who is saying the words that constitute a literary
work.

But who is that person? In drama, the answer to this question is fairly
simple. The dramatic speakers are the characters in the play to whom
the playwright has attributed the lines. It is not the actor actually saying
those lines. For example, in *Hamlet* one dramatic speaker is Hamlet
(not Sir Laurence Olivier, Richard Burton, Sir John Gielgud, and so
forth), another is Claudius, and so on through the list of characters. No
matter who appears in these roles, the dramatic speaker remains constant, as long as the text remains constant.

In novels or short stories the "person" is a bit harder to tie down.
Consider the following excerpt, typical of a novel.

> "It's a miracle he has recovered consciousness," the doctor whispered to
> Raskolnikov.
> "What's your opinion?" Raskolnikov asked.
> "He won't live long."
> "Isn't there any hope at all?"
> "Not the slightest. He's at the last gasp. His head's badly injured, too.
> I could bleed him, I suppose, but it won't be of any use. Sure to die in five
> or ten minutes."
> "In that case, why not bleed him?"
> "I might, but I warn you it's absolutely useless!"
> Just then more footsteps were heard, the crowd on the landing parted,
> and a priest, a little grey-haired old man, appeared on the threshold with
> the Sacrament. A policeman had gone to fetch him soon after the ac-
> cident. . . .

There are two basic ways of handling such examples. One can treat the
statements within quotation marks as statements by various dramatic
speakers (Raskolnikov; the doctor), and the remarks not in quotation
marks as made by yet another dramatic speaker, namely, the narrator.
Or a whole novel may be treated as one long statement by a story teller,
parts of whose remarks are reports of other peoples' utterances. At this
point, I see no reason for preferring one of these methods to the other.

The "person" becomes much more difficult to identify when we come
to poetry. A poem can, and I believe should, be viewed as a statement or
a series of statements in various grammatical moods. To put the matter
quite simply, the dramatic speaker is the person making those statements.
In poetry such as *Spoon River Anthology*, the speakers are the various
people to whom Masters attributes the lines, for example, Fiddler Jones,
the village atheist, Carl Hamblin, and so forth. In such a case, the
dramatic speaker is akin to those of drama. In other poems, such as
Longfellow's "Hiawatha," the dramatic speaker is like the storytelling

dramatic speaker of novels. Usually in poetry, however, the dramatic speaker is just an unidentified someone—a person we imagine to be making the statements constituting the poem. As Wimsatt and Beardsley say, we do sometimes by biographical inference equate the writer with the dramatic speaker, but this is by no means necessarily, nor even most frequently, the case.

Any literary work may be the linguistic object that is the record or product of an author's actually asserting, questioning, commanding, wishing, and so forth. But usually it is not. Herein lies one of the characteristics of literature which distinguishes it from other linguistic entities. An author attributes linguistic actions to others; he does not (usually) perform those actions himself. No one would deny that when Shakespeare wrote the words "Get thee to a nunnery," he was performing a linguistic action. But it would be false to say that he, Shakespeare, was himself making a command or a request. Nor do we want to say that when he wrote in one of his sonnets "Why didst thou promise such a beauteous day," he was asking a question.

I call this extraordinary activity, whereby an author attributes linguistic actions to others, namely, dramatic speakers, *translocuting*. A fairly detailed description of this activity of translocuting follows:

L = the act of locuting
l = the act of illocuting
P = the act of perlocuting
T = the act of translocuting
TI = the act of transillocution
TP = the act of transperlocution
TT = the act of transtranslocution
S = an ordinary, nonliterary speaker or writer
A = a literary writer
DS = dramatic speaker

Then,

$$S \xrightarrow[\text{thereby producing}]{\text{locutes}} I \,\&\, (\text{sometimes } P)$$

Sometimes

$$A \xrightarrow[\text{thereby producing}]{\text{locutes}} I \,\&\, (\text{sometimes } P)$$

But usually,

$$A \xrightarrow[\text{thereby producing}]{\text{translocutes}} TI \,\&\, (\text{sometimes } TP \lor TT)$$

Or, equivalently,

$$A \xrightarrow[\text{thereby producing}]{\text{translocutes}} [DS \xrightarrow[\text{thereby producing}]{\text{locutes}} I_{DS} \,\&\, (\text{sometimes } P_{DS} \lor TT_{DS})]$$

I have included this schema only for the purists among my readers. It sounds and looks much more complicated than it is. In plain language, the above stipulates this: Ordinary (nonliterary) speakers and writers locute, thereby producing illocutions and sometimes perlocutions. Authors and poets and dramatists locute and occasionally thereby produce illocutions and sometimes perlocutions. However, authors, poets, and dramatists more often translocute, thereby producing transillocutions and sometimes transperlocutions and/or transtranslocutions.[3] Or, equivalently, an author, poet, or dramatist translocutes, thereby producing a dramatic speaker who locutes, thereby producing an illocution and sometimes perlocutions and translocutions. Shakespeare translocuted when he wrote "to be or not to be," thereby producing a transillocution, which is equivalent to an illocution on the part of a dramatic speaker.

In passing, it is important to note that literature is not unique in having dramatic speakers as a central element. Advertisements, both visual and audio, have them. For example, when I see a billboard with the words "Winston tastes good like a cigarette should" written on it, I deal with it as I would deal with any linguistic object. Something is being said, and thus it is easy to infer that there is someone doing the saying. We are not apt to treat all advertising speeches as serious remarks made by the adman who wrote them, any more than we attribute all poetic remarks to the poet who made them. Admen translocute most of the time.

It is obvious that central to my analysis of a work of literature is the concept of a dramatic speaker. The concept is vulnerable in the following ways. Adding translocution to Austin's schema would be needlessly multiplying entities if the concept of dramatic speaker were empty. Further, if the concept of a dramatic speaker is beyond unmuddling, then it not only fails to help clarify the notion of a literary work, but does serious harm to that notion in making it more confused and mysterious than it already is. Further, even if unmuddled, it may be useless and/or unnecessary.

Let me begin by defending myself against the accusation of unnecessarily multiplying entities. If such multiplication has taken place, it began long before I put my pen to paper. As I mentioned earlier, it is not my invention. The work of literary critics is full of talk about dramatic speakers, usually referred to in different terms, for example, "the protagonist," "the hero," "the main character," "the title role," and so forth.

But the mere fact that others have used the notion is certainly not grounds, by itself, for continuing that use. There must be positive reasons for the belief in the utility or necessity of such an entity.

Whenever we confront a literary work, we necessarily are aware of the fact that we are dealing with a syntactically and semantically ordered subject. Habits of ordinary discourse cause us to ask, "What is being said here?" and related questions. Further, we know that if something is being said, then there must be someone saying it. We do not always, or even most often, want to assert that the author is the speaker. To do so would be to attribute irrationality, inconsistency, insanity, dishonesty, stupidity, and so forth, to many authors and poets.

Shakespeare is not contemplating suicide when Hamlet says "To be or not to be." This accounts for the introduction of the concept of protagonist, hero, and so forth, in the past. The concept of translocutions further allows us to attribute acts not to writers (thereby avoiding the necessity of making liars or kooks of them) but to the characters whom they create. Thus we are able to put the explanation and interpretation of literature on a par with everyday discourse.

The various problems that the concept of translocution is introduced to elucidate and solve have been dealt with by other philosophers in different ways. Strawson, Austin, and Nowell-Smith, for example, take the line that literature is somehow secondary—parasitic on ordinary discourse. They believe that the statements made in a literary work are "pretend" statements, in some ways underdeveloped or not full-fledged. I shall discuss my reasons for rejecting such a tack below.

Monroe Beardsley has independently arrived at a concept very close to translocutions. He suggests that literature can be dealt with as linguistic works in which illocutions are imitated: "A poem, I suggest, is an imitation of a complex illocutionary act."[4] Obviously, I have great sympathy for his program. But I am put off by the term "imitation." I find its relation to "parasitic" and "secondary" too close for comfort. Again my reasons for this discomfort will become clear later.

This completes my apology for using dramatic speakers and for adding "translocution" to the already overpopulated philosophic vocabulary. The time has come to put them to use, and with the success or failure of this application lies the existence or nonexistence of justification for such an addition.

II

Consider an ordinary, garden-variety speech act. Here a speaker utters (writes) something that is heard (read) and interpreted by a hearer (reader). The literary speech act is very similar to this. Here a writer writes something (namely, the literary work) which is read and interpreted by a reader. However, this literary speech act depends for its existence upon a different, or subspeech, act. This subspeech act consists in a dramatic speaker or group of dramatic speakers making statements which are then read (or heard) and interpreted by a reader.

For practical reasons, the number of things one can do with the utterance made in an ordinary speech act is restricted. However, literary utterances (works) lend themselves to a great variety of activities. One can read a literary work in order to escape, to glean information, to have vicarious experiences, to become sexually aroused, and so on. The list is practically endless. One may read to create, that is, may use the words already written down by someone else, give them a new interpretation, and thus create a new work.[5] However, I am interested only in one general type of activity, which is the act of reading, ordinarily so-called. It is difficult to characterize this activity in any simple way; but essentially it consists of reading some work, X, by some writer, A, because one feels that something interesting is being said in an interesting or aesthetically pleasing way, without any ulterior purpose.

This last kind of activity can itself be subdivided into any number of subactivities. I shall divide it into two main subactivities. (a) A reader, R, may read because he wants to know what A has to say, in the sense of the perlocutions that A is attempting to perform. Here R uses the work, W, to go beyond W; that is, R is interested in W at least in part because he wishes to find out something about A. (b) A reader, R_ϕ, reads W because he wants to know what the dramatic speaker is saying. He may do this (1) in light of the work itself or (2) in light of the work plus the larger context of the work, such as historic period, author biography, literary traditions, and so forth. This latter activity approaches the activity described in (a). I have nothing other than intuitions concerning which of these activities or subactivities is the one in which most people most commonly engage. In spite of this I believe that (b:1) is the most aesthetically interesting and relevant of the above.

Thus I shall assume that there are times, and I believe they are frequent, when we want to interpret the actions of a dramatic speaker or group of dramatic speakers. There are problems associated with this activity which the concept of dramatic speakers and translocution can clear up.

I mentioned above that some philosophers have wished to treat the language of literature as "play" language, as language that for some reason or other is secondary to language in its primary use, namely, ordinary, everyday discourse. The motivation behind such a treatment is not difficult to explain. One way of getting at the reasons for relegating literary language to a secondary position is to consider literary language as it is connected to the problem, or cluster of problems, surrounding intention. In general, certain broad types of intentions can be attributed to certain kinds of illocutions. Questions are asked with the intention of someone giving an answer. Commands are given with the intention of someone carrying them out. Assertions are uttered with the intention of informing. In literature, however, this correspondence breaks down. Consider the following examples: In one of Shakespeare's sonnets the dramatic speaker asks the sun this question:

> Why didst thou promise such a beauteous day,
> And make me travel forth without my cloak,

> To let base clouds o'ertake me in my way,
> Hiding thy bravery in their rotten smoke?

No one would believe that the question is meant to be answered, unless he believed that the speaker was insane. In Milton's poem "On Time" the dramatic speaker makes this command:

> Fly envious *Time*, till thou run out thy race,
> Call on the lazy, leaden-stepping hours,
> Whose speed is but the heavy Plummets pace;
> And glut thy self with what thy womb devours . . .

Certainly the speaker here does not expect his command to be carried out.

Is it possible to make any sense at all out of calling something a command when we know it is not intended to be carried out? Or a question if it is not meant to be answered? It has appeared obvious to some persons that these questions must be given negative replies; and from a negative reply it follows quite naturally that literary commands and questions no longer have the full-fledged quality of ordinary, nonliterary questions and commands. Thus some philosophers have agreed in viewing the use of language in literature as secondary, though their arguments do not necessarily make use of the concept of intention in the manner that I have used it above. In "On Referring" Strawson calls a failure to mention anything or anyone by using a sentence (a frequent occurrence in literature) a "spurious" use of language.[6] Later he changed "spurious" to "secondary." Austin believes that language is used in literature in a "parasitic," "not serious" way. It is not put to its "full normal use."[7] Nowell-Smith gives as Rule 1 of contextual implication the following:

> When a speaker uses a sentence to make a statement, it is contextually implied that he believes it to be true. And, similarly, when he uses it to perform any of the other jobs for which sentences are used, it is contextually implied that he is using it for one of the jobs that it normally does.[8]

This rule, he says, is often broken. But when it is broken, as in literature, language is being put to a secondary or parasitic use.

By calling language as it is used in literature secondary or parasitic, all of these men imply that it is necessary to understand a command, for example, in ordinary conversation (that is, in its primary use) before one can understand its secondary use. None of the men discusses the issue in detail. However, the view that they are getting at is, I believe, something like the following. In language we have the imperative mood, the interrogative mood, and the indicative mood. The primary uses of these moods respectively are commanding, questioning, and asserting. All other uses of these moods are secondary or parasitic—depending in some way upon the primary uses. Similarly, our understanding of the secondary use is dependent upon our understanding of the primary use.

I believe that this view is incorrect. To say that the *primary* uses of the imperative, the interrogative, and the indicative moods are commanding, questioning, and asserting implies that these are their most common uses. This is an empirical claim which no one of the above philosophers proves. And I think there are reasons to believe that such a proof is not forthcoming. Certain conditions must be fulfilled in order for someone to succeed in making a command or assertion or in asking a question. In order for someone to issue a full-fledged command (as opposed to a request, for example), he must have the authority needed and also must intend to be obeyed. In order for someone to make an assertion, he must intend to inform someone of his belief concerning some matter. In order for someone to ask a question, he must intend that someone answer him.[9] A person can command someone to do something without using the imperative mood, assert without using the indicative mood, and question without using the interrogative mood; but ordinarily these linguistic actions are carried out by using the corresponding mood. However, it is probably not the case that these moods are most commonly used for questioning, asserting, or commanding.

Consider the imperative mood. Very rarely does a person have the proper authority needed for the sentence in imperatival form to constitute a command when it is uttered. The imperative mood is more commonly used to voice requests, wishes, and desires or to express feelings. ("Shut the door"; "Turn left at the corner"; "Don't miss the movie at the Orpheum"; and so forth.) Commands are very loosely tied to the imperative mood.

Similarly, although sentences in the indicative mood are tied with greater strength, it is a mistake to say that the primary use of the indicative mood is to assert. The indicative mood is probably used most frequently in polite conversation in which the intention to inform is often, if not usually, absent, or at least in the background. ("It is a nice day"; "My parents are fine"; "I've been very busy lately"; and so forth.)

Questions are more strongly tied to the interrogative mood; that is, the necessary intention of getting someone to give an answer is usually present when someone utters a sentence in this mood. But frequently speakers ask "rhetorical questions" in which such an intention is missing. This is very prevalent in literature.

My reasons for not calling statements in poetry secondary are different from those for not calling statements in novels or plays secondary. Thus I shall first discuss poetry. Some statements that appear in poetry are like commands, assertions, and questions. But the only way in which they are like them is in their mood. Here the similarity ends. It is for this reason that they are not to be called secondary uses at all. They are rather uses of the various grammatical moods that are not unlike uses to which those moods are put in ordinary discourse. For example, "Fly envious Time" is in the imperative mood, but it is certainly not a command. It is nonetheless a perfectly serious, nonparasitic use of the imperative mood. I may go to the window and shout, "Stop raining!" This is one way of expressing my desire that the rain stop. No one would say I was making even a secondary command. Similarly, the imperatival form can be used in poetry to express some wish, desire, or feeling. This is, in fact, how "Fly envious Time" is used. In interpreting this poem, no one would say that the dramatic speaker was commanding time to fly. Rather one would say that the dramatic speaker was expressing his wish that time pass more quickly. The same kind of thing can be said about questions and assertions.

In novels and plays the situation is different. Characters in novels and plays do use the imperative mood to command, the indicative mood to assert, the interrogative mood to question. (This is possible in poetry, but much rarer than in novels and plays.) It is undoubtedly the fictional, "pretend," nature of these media that has led some people to feel the pull toward calling such uses non-serious. When interpreting the action of a novel or a play, we say such things as, "He commanded the troops to retreat"; "He asked the butler where his master was"; "He said (asserted) that the police were outside"; just as we say such things as "He left the room"; "He married the boss's daughter"; "He lived on the moon." The question "Did he really leave the room?" is ambiguous in the same way that "Did he really make a command?" is ambiguous. If we understand the question to assume "in the play or novel," then the answer is yes. But in so far as we are talking about a fictional occurrence the answer is, of course, no. A character in a play or novel who makes a command makes a full-fledged command. It is wrong to talk about secondary or nonserious commands, just as it is wrong to talk about secondary or nonserious marriages.

The important distinction to bear in mind here is the difference between pretending to use and using to pretend. An actor pretends to be someone commanding. Usually he is not someone pretending to command nor is he pretending to be someone pretending to command, although he can do these things too, if the script calls for it. "Is he really commanding?" is a misleading question. Everything an actor does in one sense is a pretense, just as the whole play is a pretense. But questions about particular actions assume the framework of the play. To the question "Did he really tell her to go to a nunnery?" the answer is yes. The phrase "in the play" or "in *Hamlet*" is understood. Similarly, the phrase "in the book" is understood in connection with novels, and the phrase "in the poem" is understood in connection with some types of poetry.

Perhaps a word should be said about pretending. While the following three criteria probably do not constitute necessary and sufficient conditions for "pretending to x," they may nonetheless serve as an approximation of such conditions for the purposes here:

1. A does something, s, which, when he actually does x, can be correctly described as a part of x.

2. s is an important part of x, that is, one of the features of x that distinguishes x from all other acts; but s is not equal to x.

3. A is intentionally refraining from doing some further part of x, which, when added to the distinguishing part, s, will result in success of x, or in A's actually x-ing.

In order to understand these criteria it will be helpful to consider some examples. Suppose A pretends to eat. He chews and swallows. This satisfies 1 and 2. If he chews and swallows air, this also satisfies 3. If A has food in his mouth, he chews, but—by 3—does not swallow. Or A pretends to hit B. He swings his arm in the direction of B (1 and 2) but intentionally fails to make contact with B (3). When an actor is pretending, his pretending consists in pretending to be someone doing something. Most often (that is, in most conventional, as opposed to "happening," dramas) he actually does that thing; what is left out is his really being that person.

In attempting to give an interpretation of a work of literature, reference to the intentions of the dramatic speaker or character is often of help. "Why did he leave the room?" "He wanted to get a revolver." "Why did the captain command his men to go up the hill?" "He wanted to surprise the enemy." "Why did he tell time to fly?" "He wanted to express his desire that time pass more quickly." But employing the notion of dramatic speaker, we are no longer faced with the need to refer to authorial intentions in order to explain at least a great deal of the action, both linguistic and nonlinguistic, of a literary work, and we do this without sacrificing the full-fledged nature of literary language. Relying on material external to a work for the explanation or evaluation of that work has long been a process looked upon unfavorably by various schools of aesthetics. Translocuting and dramatic speakers provide a rationale for doing away with overdependence on referring to things outside of a work.

Thus one of the most fruitful applications of the notions of dramatic speaker and translocution is in connection with the problem of intention. I have elsewhere utilized these concepts in this connection.[10] However, I shall add to my previous treatment of the issue(s) in the section below.

III

In everyday conversation we must know the intentions of the person with whom we are conversing if we are to understand or correctly interpret what he says. Assuming that my views concerning the nature of a literary object are not altogether false, it seems a natural step to say that we must know the intentions of the dramatic speaker if we are to correctly interpret what he says. Surely it is true that we misinterpret a work if we misidentify the dramatic speaker. This misinterpretation could assume gigantic proportions if, for example, we took the lines

> I shall be telling this with a sigh
> Somewhere ages and ages hence:
> Two roads diverged in a wood, and I—
> I took the one less traveled by,
> And that has made all the difference.[11]

to be said by the village prostitute. We also misinterpret a work if we misconstrue that speaker's intentions, for example, interpret the dramatic speaker above to be recommending conformity at all cost.

Change the dramatic speaker and you change the interpretation of that work. Change the intentions of the dramatic speaker and you likewise change the interpretation of the work, just as the interpretation often alters when we misconstrue the intention of a speaker in nonliterary discourse. Of course, we are not always conscious of the fact that we are positing a dramatic speaker and his intentions when we read a literary work. However, it seems to me that the notion does serve as machinery for getting a clearer picture of the nature of a literary work and the interpretation thereof, without being required to involve the writer as a speaker (asserter, questioner, and so forth).

I spoke earlier of the fictional, pretense character of literature which has led persons to deal with literary language as secondary. Plato felt the pull of this feature of literature when he spoke of poets as craftsmen whose end product is "twice-removed" from reality. But one can agree that literature is removed from reality without concluding, as Plato and others have, that poets are liars. The *trans-ing* process, if I may call it that for simplicity's sake, whereby a writer transfers illocutions to dramatic speakers allows for exactly such a stand. As Wilde says, Iago's speeches in no way force us to be critical of Shakespeare's morals. Dramatic speeches are not lies uttered by poets.

Further, just as attention to the trans-ing aspect of literary writing prevents us (without biographical evidence) from identifying the beliefs and moral standards of poets with those of the dramatic speakers whom they create, so it should keep us from some of the pitfalls of some of the doctrines of expressionistic theories of the Collingwood ilk. Consider the following passage:

> It does not, of course, follow that a dramatic writer may not rant in character. The tremendous rant at the end of *The Ascent of F6*, like the Shakespearian ranting on which it is modelled, is done with tongue in cheek. It is not the author who is ranting, but the unbalanced character he depicts; the emotion the author is expressing is the emotion with which

he contemplates that character; or rather, the emotion he has towards that
secret and disowned part of himself for which the character stands.¹²

Here Collingwood is discussing the theory, T, that x expresses y if and
only if P feels y when he writes x. The various shortcomings of this
theory have been discussed at length by many philosophers. I wish to
show here how the concepts of dramatic speaker and translocution prevent one from ever feeling drawn to such a view.

Collingwood speaks of "ranting in character" and then of "ranting
with tongue in cheek" as if they were the same. He goes on to say that
it is not the author who is ranting, but the character (dramatic speaker)
who is ranting, which is, of course, my view. However, Collingwood
then goes on to qualify that position to such an extent that it becomes
impossible for me to agree with him. He says that while the author does
not express, for example, the anger that Hamlet feels upon seeing his
mother and uncle together, he does express the emotion (pity?) that he,
Shakespeare, feels upon viewing Hamlet in such a situation. Collingwood then goes the full circle to T, or a revised version of T, by adopting a more or less Freudian view of the artistic process, wherein the
writer expresses his neuroses in his work.

What in fact happens, to repeat myself, is that when we read a literary
work, we are given a set of translocutions or a set of illocutions made by
a dramatic speaker. "Transexpressions," to coin the obvious phrase, are
quite different from ordinary expressions of emotion. "Get thee to a
nunnery" written by Shakespeare may express Hamlet's anger, but surely
it is a mistake to demand the emotions expressed by a dramatic speaker
(through his linguistic and nonlinguistic actions) to be felt, even watered-
down or controlled, by the author. The trans-ing process removes responsibility for emotions from the author, just as it removes responsibility
for beliefs and morals from him. Responsibility can only be established by
biographical investigation, which is surely external to a discussion of any
given work qua work.

But are the intentions of an author to be left out completely when we
read one of his works? Or can those intentions affect the interpretation
of his work? There are many different sorts of intentions that an author
may have. All linguistic actions are in part the result of certain intentions
that the person performing those actions has. Thus far we have spoken
of four possible types of actions an author may perform: locutions, illocutions, translocutions, and perlocutions. With each of these classes of
linguistic actions a corresponding class of linguistic intentions may be
posited. Further, authors have all sorts of intentions to perform nonlinguistic actions. (By a nonlinguistic action I understand an action that
could be performed without an explicit use of language.) One kind of
nonlinguistic action that an author may intend to perform is a practical
action, such as making money, praising one's country, winning the love

of a woman, and so forth. Another kind of nonlinguistic action that an author might want to perform is that of expressing his feelings, an act that can be carried out nonlinguistically (by crying or vomiting) as well as linguistically.

As I am in this paper dealing with literature as a linguistic object, I shall limit my discussion to the linguistic intentions of an author. I shall not discuss in detail nonlinguistic intentions. (Suffice it to say that failure to discuss them does not imply belief in their irrelevance or unimportance, but rather a desire to limit the scope of this discussion. Briefly, I believe that the relation between linguistic and nonlinguistic intentions in an author corresponds to the relation of those types of intentions in ordinary speakers and writers.)

How, then, is the author related to a dramatic speaker? The transillocutions that an author performs result in the illocutions of a dramatic speaker. All that we can know about a dramatic speaker comes through the work (or perhaps works) of a writer, so a writer is responsible for the very existence of the dramatic speaker. He is also, of course, responsible for the speeches of a dramatic speaker.

It seems only natural, then, when we are confronted with a problem of interpreting the actions of the dramatic speaker, to seek aid from the person who is responsible for those actions. This is not to say that the intentions of the author are identical with those of the dramatic speaker. Milton did not necessarily intend to express a desire of *his* that time pass more quickly, although there was undoubtedly some thought or feeling that he did want to express, or some feeling that he wished to evoke in his readers when he wrote "Time." The transillocutionary intentions that a writer has result in the illocutions of his dramatic speakers, so we may at times wish to consult the cause to help interpret the effect.

Other linguistic intentions also affect the work. In the first place these directly affect the intentions of the dramatic speaker, that is, are among the causal determinants of the dramatic speaker's intentions. For this reason, knowledge of a poet's intentions may help us to get at the meaning of a poem. Suppose we cannot discover the intentions of the dramatic speaker from the poem itself; for example, there is some ambiguity that even careful reading does not clear up. The intentions of the poet may provide evidence for determining the probable intentions of the dramatic speaker. For example, if the dramatic speaker mentions a dove, I may not be sure whether or not he intends it to have its customary symbolic meaning. If I find out that the poet intended to use religious symbolism, then I have good reason for deciding to interpret the dove as such a symbol.

The objection may be made that the poem is a failure if we cannot know what the intentions of the dramatic speaker are without going outside the poem itself. It is perhaps hard to imagine a work in which we do not have any idea about whether or not a particular symbol is

religious without referring to the intentions of the poet. Some persons
may feel that a poem is not worth interpreting if the dramatic speaker's
intentions are not clear from the work itself. But often we do feel that
a poem is worthwhile even if everything, the speaker's intentions included, is not immediately clear;[13] and in such cases knowing the poet's
intentions may help us to discover the intentions of the dramatic speaker,
thereby placing us in a better position for interpreting the work.

But now let us look at the author's linguistic intentions apart from the
dramatic speaker. The locutionary, illocutionary, and perlocutionary intentions of an author are all to be treated as the intentions of a regular
speaker using language in a special, though certainly nonsecondary, way.
In ordinary conversation it is taken for granted that a speaker's or writer's
locutionary intentions are carried out when he utters or writes a sentence.
That is, we assume that he has said the words he wanted to say and that
those words mean what he thinks they mean. Admittedly, this is sometimes not the case, as with slips of the tongue and typographical errors.
But mistakes such as these are generally easily cleared up—usually by
asking the speaker what his intentions (locutionary) were. The same
holds true for an author. When we are faced with a literary work, we
assume that the locutionary intentions of the author have been carried
out, for example, that there are not printing errors.

When an author is illocuting himself (rather than transillocuting), his
illocutionary intentions affect his action just as do those of the ordinary
speaker when he is asserting, commanding, questioning, and so forth. In
puzzling cases his illocutionary action can be interpreted by discovering
what he intended to do, that is, what kind of illocutionary act he intended to perform—assert, joke, request, and so forth. It is true that an
answer to the question "What illocution did you plan to perform?" is
more readily available in the case of a regular speaker than it is in the
case of an author. But difficulty in obtaining evidence is not to be confused with the uselessness of that evidence.

The same type of thing is to be said concerning the perlocutionary intentions of an author. It must be admitted that simply knowing what
consequences an author intended does not insure that those consequences will in fact occur. Suppose a writer is most interested in
convincing his readers of something. Will it help to know this? That is,
if I know this, will I be convinced? Ordinarily not. Suppose Gerard
Manley Hopkins intended to convince me that one should love God
when he wrote "Pied Beauty." If I do not believe in God, then no
matter how much Hopkins intends that I love Him, I will not be convinced to do so.

Nonetheless, knowing what consequences were intended may help
one to understand a work. Knowing the perlocutionary intentions of a
writer may, for example, help me to decide whether a particular poem
is narrative, didactic, rhetorical, and so forth. I may be able to tell when

language is that of exaggeration with the end of persuasion. That is, I may get a grip on the poem as a whole, and certainly that is one facet of interpretation.

Some critics have carried the use of authorial intentions to an extreme. However, as long as one bears in mind the omnipresence of dramatic speakers and the primacy of translocuting in the activity of writing literature, this use will necessarily be limited. Without authors, there are no dramatic speakers. But once given life, dramatic speakers stand, and speak, by themselves.

Notes

1. See Marcia Eaton, "Art, Artifacts and Intentions," *American Philosophical Quarterly*, April 1969, and "Good and Correct Interpretations of Literature," *Journal of Aesthetics and Art Criticism*, Winter 1970.

2. W. K. Wimsatt and Monroe C. Beardsley, "The Intentional Fallacy," in *The Verbal Icon* (Lexington, Ky.: University of Kentucky Press, 1954), p. 5.

3. The notion of transtranslocution is simply a device for handling the actions of dramatic speakers when they are poets, authors, and dramatists. For example, in a novel about a novelist, the fictional novelist may translocute due to transtranslocutions on the part of the real novelist.

4. This is from an unpublished article by Monroe C. Beardsley, "The Testability of Interpretation."

5. See Eaton, "Good and Correct Interpretations of Literature," for a discussion of this type of activity.

6. P. F. Strawson, "On Referring," in *Essays in Conceptual Analysis*, ed. Anthony Flew (London: Macmillan & Co., 1956), p. 35.

7. J. L. Austin, *How to Do Things with Words*, ed. J. O. Urmson (Cambridge, Mass.: Harvard University Press, 1962), p. 104.

8. P. H. Nowell-Smith, *Ethics* (Penguin Books, 1954), p. 81.

9. See Austin, *How to Do Things with Words*, for a full treatment of this matter.

10. See Eaton, "Good and Correct Interpretations of Literature."

11. Robert Frost, "The Road Not Taken," from *Mountain Interval* (New York: Henry Holt & Co., 1916).

12. R. G. Collingwood, "Expression in Art," in *Problems in Aesthetics*, ed. Morris Weitz (New York: Macmillan Co., 1959), p. 192.

13. David Nivison has suggested to me an interesting example of a poem (one of Edward Arlington Robinson's), which is widely admired even though its admirers are all rather puzzled about its meaning. It is discussed in Ronald Moran's "Meaning and Value in 'Take Havergal,'" *Colby Library Quarterly*, March 1967.

On Understanding Art

ALTHOUGH THE TWO may sometimes overlap, there would appear to be a difference between *describing* a work of art and *interpreting* it. To say that Manet's *Olympia* contains a nude woman is to describe that picture, in part, but not to interpret it. So also for saying that the atmosphere of a Dutch interior, for example, a typical Pieter de Hooch, is quiet and peaceful. Anyone can see this at a glance, which suggests that statements about the obvious in a work of art, for example, that the first phrase of Herrick's "Corinna's Going A-Maying" is "Get up," are to be classified as descriptions and not as interpretations. Of course, what is obvious to you might not be obvious to me; so the borderline between description and interpretation is indefinite. Still, to the extent to which a work, or something in a work, calls for explanation, it calls for interpretation; and interpretation—or at least one kind of interpretation— would seem to be a species of explanation whose function is to aid understanding and appreciation.[1]

It is obvious to anyone with eyes to see that Piero della Francesca's *Madonna and Saints*—the so-called Montefeltro Altarpiece in the Brera Museum, Milan—contains an egg suspended by a chain. At first glance it may appear, indeed it may seem obvious, that the egg is a hen's egg; but in a famous essay on this picture,[2] Millard Meiss argues that it is an ostrich egg, and he endeavors to explain what it is doing there, what it symbolizes. His essay gives us a brilliant interpretation of Piero's picture.

Suppose, however, that Piero himself had told someone that the egg is an ostrich egg and what it symbolizes. Would he be interpreting his own picture? Consider an analogue. In the *Gospel According to Matthew*, xiii, Jesus relates the Parable of the Tares or, as *The New English Bible* has it, the Parable of the Darnel.[3]

> The kingdom of Heaven is like this. A man sowed his field with good seed;
> but while everyone was asleep his enemy came, sowed darnel among the
> wheat, and made off. When the corn [grain] sprouted and began to fill out,

the darnel could be seen among it. The farmer's men went to their master and said, "Sir, was it not good seed that you sowed in your field? Then where has the darnel come from?" "This is an enemy's doing," he replied. "Well then," they said, "shall we go and gather the darnel?" "No," he answered; "in gathering it you might pull up the wheat at the same time. Let them both grow together till harvest; and at harvest-time I will tell the reapers, 'Gather the darnel first, and tie it in bundles for burning; then collect the wheat into my barn.' "

Jesus' disciples come to him and say, "Explain to us the parable of the darnel in the field." And Jesus replies, "The sower of the good seed is the Son of Man. The field is the world; the good seed stands for the children of the kingdom, the darnel for the children of the evil one . . .".

When Jesus answers the disciples, are his words an *interpretation* of the parable? Were one of the disciples to have uttered the very same words in answer to a request from another for an explanation of the parable, it seems clear that his words would have been an interpretation of it. Why not Jesus' words, then? Can the same words, although uttered by different persons, both be and not be an interpretation? If so, are Jesus' words not an interpretation of the parable because he could not have been mistaken about what it meant, or about what he meant by it; could not have got it wrong? (We assume, of course, that he was not lying about what he meant and was not trying to deceive or mislead the disciples.)

A similar situation can obviously obtain in art, although it rarely does. If it does, two questions arise: (1) Are the artist's words an interpretation of his work? (2) Are the artist's words unimpeachably authoritative about what his work means, about what he meant, or about what he meant by it?[4]

Hampshire holds that the interpretation of dreams is a plausible candidate for an illuminating analogy to the interpretation of art. Let us invoke the analogy. Someone relates a dream he had. You ask, "What do you think it means?" He tells you. (He's read Freud, of course.) Is he interpreting his own dream? Here the answer seems to be, yes. Is this perhaps because "he who interprets a dream [whether he is the dreamer or not] knows that he looks for a meaning which was not intended and which was not purposefully put there"? Will this make the difference between Jesus' explaining his parable and the dreamer's explaining his dream?

Works of art too might have "a meaning which was not intended and was not purposefully put there," and to the extent to which they have, interpretations of them might well resemble the interpretation of dreams. But then they might (also) have a meaning that was intended and was purposefully put there. In that case is the only other plausible candidate for an illuminating analogy to critical interpretation the work of the actor or musician?[5] Are there not other equally illuminating analogues, for example, the kind of interpreting we (sometimes) do of remarks made by other people in the normal course of a day?

That alternative interpretations of a work of art are possible is obvious. But among alternative interpretations we must distinguish between logically complementary and logically incompatible ones. Logically complementary ones are such that, although different, they could all be true at once. Thus it could be that both a Freudian and a Marxist interpretation of *Madame Bovary* are true—along with others. But Hampshire objects to speaking of interpretations as being true at all and concedes that only in nonstandard cases can they even be said to be correct. Is he right about this? When Meiss says that the egg in the Montefeltro Altarpiece is an ostrich egg, that it symbolizes "the miraculous conception and the birth of Christ," and "may perhaps allude to the exceptional, and in the eyes of contemporaries, not wholly natural birth" of Federico da Montefeltro's son, isn't it possible that what he says is true? Hampshire allows that an interpretation may be plausible, but if plausible why not true? Does it make sense to characterize a statement as plausible if it *could* not (in principle) be true or correct?

Assuming an affirmative answer to this question, Barnes argues that logically incompatible interpretations of a work of art cannot be *jointly* true, or even plausible. Of course, you can offer one interpretation of a work and I can offer another that is logically incompatible with it, and each can be as plausible as the other. But here they are *separately* plausible. What Barnes rules out is their joint plausibility, and can there be any objection to that?

One might try to avoid Barnes's strictures in one of two ways. First, he might hold with Margaret MacDonald that "the work of art is what it is interpreted to be," that there is "no work of art apart from *some* interpretation," that "there is no object which is 'the real' play or sonata which exists independently of any interpretation."[6] But is this acceptable? Doesn't it imply that before a work is interpreted there is no work to interpret? Doesn't it also imply that there can in principle be no different or alternative, let alone incompatible, interpretations *of the same work*; that the person who interprets Lear as senile and the person who interprets Lear as in full possession of his faculties cannot be talking about the same play, let alone disagreeing?

Second, he might hold that, grammatical appearances to the contrary, interpretive remarks are not really statements, but injunctions, instructions, implicit imperatives; they tell us how we are to read, look at, or listen to a work. Thus "Lear is senile" is not a statement about a character in Shakespeare's play and, hence, is neither true nor false; it is an implicit imperative and says, in effect, "Read (play) *King Lear* as a play about a senile man." Although this might avoid the kind of logical incompatibility Barnes is strictly talking about (assuming that only *statements* can be logically incompatible), doesn't it still leave us with something closely resembling it? For if "Lear is senile" is an implicit imperative, so is "Lear is in full possession of his faculties," in which case, is the joint imperative, "Read *Lear* as a play about a senile man, but at the same time don't read it that way, rather read it as a play about a man in full possession of his faculties," any better off than the joint statement, "Lear is senile but also in full possession of his faculties"? Further, if instructions are to be more than arbitrary, must they not be grounded on features, or putative features, of the work?, in which case aren't we then right back with the problem we were trying to avoid?

Both Tormey and Sircello are interested in the fact that there is a range of predicates applicable both to persons and to works of art, predicates that designate something that might be said to be "expressed" either by a person or in a work of art. According to Tormey such predicates signify what he calls "expressive properties" when applied to works of art, and, in keeping with his basic claim that "intentionality is a necessary condition for expression," he characterizes "expressive properties" as those whose names also designate intentional states of persons. According to Sircello the predicates in question signify "anthropomorphic properties," which are presumably the same as the "expressive properties" mentioned in his title. But if you look at some of Sircello's examples—"gay, sad, witty, pompous, austere, aloof, impersonal, sentimental"—the question arises whether his "expressive properties" are the same as Tormey's or whether they constitute a much wider range of properties. For do "impersonal" and "austere," for example, designate intentional states of persons? Further, Sircello says that "works of art may serve as expressions of those feelings, emotions, attitudes, moods, and/or personal characteristics of their creators that are designated by the anthropomorphic predicates applicable to the art works themselves," which appears to imply that intentionality is *not* a necessary condition for expression. For consider moods and personal characteristics. A person may be calm, tranquil, gloomy, modest, depressed, manic, phlegmatic, sanguine, bold, intelligent, mature, witty, bad tempered, perceptive, happy-go-lucky, dull witted, or shallow; and, in at least some of these cases so may a work of art or part of one. But are any of these—and the list can be extended—intentional states of a person? If not, can any of these features of persons be said to be *expressed* (as opposed to manifested or exhibited) in or by a work of art, or even by persons themselves? Does one, or can one, express a choleric disposition or intelligence or maturity? In short, is the range of anthropomorphic properties not considerably greater than that of expressive properties, rather than equivalent to it as Sircello seems to hold? Or is Tormey perhaps mistaken in thinking that only intentional states can be expressed?

Turning to Tormey's account of the expressive properties of art, we are confronted with the question of whether he has one, or really two, views of their nature. On the one hand, he holds that such a statement as "This poem is expressive of anguish" is not a relational or two-place predicate statement such as "Washington crossed the Delaware in 1776" but, rather is, a one-place predicate statement such as "The carnation she wore was red," which brings Tormey's position close to, or makes it identical with, what Sircello calls the Canonical Position.[7] On the other hand, when Tormey turns to a discussion of the relation between the expressive and nonexpressive properties of a work of art he holds that works of art are to be thought of as "autonomously self-expressive objects," meaning, I take it, that a poem expressive of anguish is autonomously self-expressive of anguish. But is the term "expressive" here "expressive A" or "expressive B"? It would appear to be the latter, for the relation between nonexpressive and expressive properties, Tormey tells us, is "analogous to the relation between human (or animal) behavior and the intentional states of which the behavior is partially constitutive." The big difference is that "the nonexpressive properties are *wholly* constitutive" of an art work's expressive properties, thereby leaving no room for an inference to some "inner" intentional state. Still, the constitutiveness here "is the aesthetic analogue of the expression of full-blooded intentional states of persons." But again, in what sense of "expressive" are works of art self-expressive of anguish and the like? It would seem that it must be, and yet cannot be (because no inference to intentional state is warranted), "expressive B." In sum, can a coherent reading be given to Tormey's account of the expressive properties of art?

Although the nonexpressive properties of an art work are wholly constitutive of its expressive properties, they are, according to Tormey, "ambiguously constitutive," and the ambiguity is uneliminable. In virtue of the very same nonexpressive properties, a Kollwitz drawing may be expressive of "despair, anxiety, resignation, or fear." But it would be senseless to say that it is expressive of all of them at once, and "aesthetically pointless" to say that it is expressive of despair *or* anxiety *or* resignation *or* fear. One has to make a choice. But the choice of one has exactly the same basis as the choice of another, the nonexpressive properties being the same; so on what basis is one to choose? Is the choice inherently arbitrary? Does it make no difference how we choose? It may be unreasonable to ask for "a clearly decisive means" for choosing between one expressive epithet and another within a given range, but is it unreasonable to ask for *some* means? And does Tormey so much as suggest what this means might be?

In building his case against the Canonical Position's claim that anthropomorphic predicates are applicable to works of art in the same way they are applicable to natural things, Sircello gives thirteen numbered examples, some of which show that anthropomorphic predicates "sometimes belong to works of art in virtue of what those works represent, describe, depict, or portray," and in this they are incomparable to such predicates as they may apply to natural things. To demonstrate a second way in which anthropomorphic predicates apply differently to works of art and natural things, Sircello gives eight lettered examples, each of which corresponds to one of the numbered ones. For example, 3, "Poussin's *The Rape of the Sabine Women . . .* is calm and aloof," corresponds to b, "*The Rape of the Sabine Women* is aloof and detached because Poussin calmly *observes* the violent scene and *paints* it in an aloof, detached way." These examples are meant to show that there are reasons why works of art have the anthropomorphic properties they do, which have no analogues in the case of natural things. Sircello refers to what the italicized verbs designate as "artistic acts," and of these he says, "anthropomorphic predicates apply to art works in virtue of 'artistic acts' in these works" and "it is precisely this feature of art works which enables them to be *expressions.*"

But note that there are no *lettered* examples corresponding to *numbered* examples 2, 5, 9, 10, and 11. If, however, anthropomorphic predicates do indeed apply to art works in virtue of the artistic acts in these works and if it is precisely this that enables art works to be expressions, then we should be able to supply the missing lettered examples. But consider example 2: "Hans Hofmann's *The Golden Wall* [is] an aggressive abstract painting." The proper correspondent should be a statement about Hofmann's doing something aggressively. But what can he sensibly be supposed to have done aggressively to make his picture aggressive? All Sircello says is, "What is aggressive is the color scheme . . ." Did Hofmann then arrange or combine the colors aggressively? That seems to make no sense.

Again, consider example 5: "John Milton's 'L'Allegro' . . . is surely a high-spirited, i.e., gay and joyful, poem." But what is Milton supposed to have *done* high-spiritedly, that is, gaily and joyfully? We are told only that the poem is high-spirited because "the scenes and images [in it] are gay and joyful" and "the diction and rhythms are light-hearted." And the same considerations apply to examples 9, 10, and 11. Does Sircello perhaps mean that only *some* anthropomorphic predicates apply to art works in virtue of the artistic acts in these works and that this enables only *some* of them to be expressive? If so, then what account is to be given of the others?

Let us return to 3 and b—although actually b alone will serve. We have two statements: "Poussin's *Sabine Women* is an aloof, detached painting" and "Poussin painted the *Sabine Women* in an aloof, detached way." The first is said to be true *because* the second is true. But aren't the two, according to Sircello, actually equivalent? He tells us that "an anthropomorphic term can be applied either adverbially to "acts" or adjectivally to "things" without a difference in the sense of the term or of the sentences in which it is used. . . . Thus one may, without change of meaning, say either . . . that Poussin paints his violent scene in an aloof, detached way or that the Sabine picture is an aloof, detached painting." This makes the two statements in question equivalent in meaning, that is, such that one cannot be true and the other false. In that case, what kind of *explanation* of the aloofness and detachment of Poussin's picture can the artistic act in question be? Doesn't "Poussin's picture is aloof and detached because he painted it in an aloof and detached way" reduce to "Poussin's picture is aloof and detached because it is aloof and detached"?

More serious than this is the question whether Sircello does not end up contradicting himself. He anticipates that the proponent of the Canonical Position will try to eliminate talk about artistic acts as "misleading" by holding that statements about such acts can be "translated" into statements about features of a work of art other than such acts—specifically, that a statement of the latter sort can in principle always be found which will *entail* a statement of the former sort. Sircello denies this, and in support of his denial he cites the example of Breughel's *Wedding Dance in the Open Air*, which he has earlier characterized as ironic. The irony of Breughel's painting rests on a discrepancy between the happy occasion of the wedding with its lusty dancing and the "bland, stupid, and even brutal" faces of the peasants depicted. But suppose the discrepancy responsible for the irony were solely the result of incompetence on Breughel's part, were due solely to the fact that he was incapable of painting any other kind of face. The irony would then disappear; the painting would not be ironic after all.

But doesn't this mean that "Breughel's painting is ironic (for the reasons given)" implies a fact about Breughel, namely, that he was not incompetent, that he could paint bright, happy faces as well as dull, stupid-looking ones? It would certainly seem so. But how can this square with Sircello's earlier claim that artistic acts "are not identifiable or describable independently of the works 'in' which they are done" and that "probably nothing makes this point clearer than the fact that descriptions of artistic acts . . . can be known to be true even when little or nothing is known about the author"? If Breughel can be known to have treated the gaiety of the wedding scene ironically from looking at his picture and without knowing *anything* about Breughel, for example, whether he was competent to paint happy faces, then how can the claim that he treated the scene ironically be defeated by citing his incompetence?

In connection with the attribution of expressive or anthropomorphic properties to works of art, consider the following simple experiment. You are given the following two lines:

You are then asked to name one of them "iron" and the other "gold" and are not permitted to use any other names. If you named the left one "iron" and the right one "gold" you belong to the significantly large majority (in the neighborhood of 80 percent) who have done likewise. How do you account for this phenomenon? And does it suggest an explanation of how a piece of music might be described as sad or joyful?[8]

In "Pictures and Make-Believe," Kendall Walton, as you have seen, gives still another account of the expressive properties of art. Do you find it more, or less, convincing than either Tormey's or Sircello's?

While arguing against certain theories of representation, Max Black makes several points that may strike the reader as more controversial than he takes them to be. For example, in his discussion of the embodied-information theory (the "substantive" information variant), he says,

> Suppose somebody were to be presented with . . . a statement, A, [e.g., a description of a person or a building] and asked then to retrieve the photograph, P, of which it is supposed to be in some sense a translation, from a large set of different photographs. Is there good reason to suppose that such a task must be performable in principle?

His answer is, no—the reason being that the notion of a "complete verbal translation" of a picture is "a chimaera," because "a picture shows more than *can* be said" (italics mine). But does *every* picture always show more than can be said, for example, a rough sketch of a house? Or do only some pictures do this? And if so, how do we tell the one from the other? Black is willing to allow that "we can put into words some of the things that we can learn from a faithful photograph." But if some, then why not, at least in principle, all? It would seem that a detailed verbal description of a person wanted by the police, say, might actually contain or provide *more* information about its subject than a not very good black-and-white photograph of the same subject. But if this is the case, then not *every* picture shows more than can be said.

Earlier, in his discussion of the causal history view, Black says,

> Suppose we found some natural object that "looked like" a certain subject—say, a rock formation that from a certain standpoint looked for all the world like Napoleon: should we then say that the rock formation must be a representation of Napoleon?

His answer, surely not. Of course, it might not be that the rock formation *must* be a representation of Napoleon; but the more interesting question is, *could* it be? It is not entirely clear what Black's answer to this is, but it seems to be the same. But why can't the rock formation in question be a representation of Napoleon? If the conditions Kendall Walton lays down for "*P*-depiction" are indeed sufficient, as he says they are, can't the rock formation in question count as a *P*-depiction of Napoleon?

Again, in connection with the producer's intentions view, Black asks, "Could I draw a horse by simply putting a dot on paper?" The question is rhetorical; the answer is, no. But why can't one draw a horse simply by putting a dot on paper? And could the dot in question not be a *P*-depiction of a horse according to Walton's criteria?

In the same connection Black holds that the idea that "simply wanting a painting to be a painting of such-and-such would necessarily make it so" is "too paradoxical to accept." Perhaps. But consider an interesting case from the history of painting. In 1572 the Venetian master Veronese was commissioned by the monks of SS. Giovanni e Paolo to paint a picture for their refectory to replace a *Last Supper* by Titian that had been destroyed by fire. When the picture was completed about a year later Veronese was summoned before the Inquisition to explain the presence in the picture of certain elements that appeared to be doctrinally offensive. Veronese's answers to the inquisitors' questions were, it seems, evasive, enigmatic, and disingenuous. For example, on being asked what the subject of the picture was, he replied "The Last Supper that Jesus took with his disciples in the house of Simon." But this would seem to give the picture two different and incompatible subjects: the Last Supper and the Feast in the House of Simon. The inquisitors were unhappy and asked that the picture be changed to their satisfaction. But all Veronese did was to give it the title it now bears: "Feast in the House of Levi"! The inquisitors were satisfied.[9]

This is not quite the kind of case Black has in mind, but it is close enough to raise the question, "Given that a picture can (for whatever reasons) depict several possible subjects, for example, the Last Supper, the Feast in the House of Simon, or the Feast in the House of Levi, can a painter make it depict one of them simply by saying that it does?" Or "Can he make it depict one subject today and another subject tomorrow simply by saying that it does?" Veronese's inquisitors seem to have thought so. Were they being simple-minded? And what would Walton's answer to the question have to be?

One of the first problems raised by Kendall Walton's theory of depiction is one he himself has come to appreciate, namely, the introduction of fictional truth values. Is he not multiplying truth values, or kinds of them, beyond necessity and thereby turning his theory into something of a philosophical Rube Goldberg machine? Clearly, to make-believe, to imagine, to dream, and to pretend that something is the case are not the same. But is there any reason for supposing that when someone relates a dream, say, his statements have a different kind of truth value from those he might make in relating what happened to him on a certain occasion when he was a child? In relating a dream one says such things as "I was running down a long, empty street when suddenly a lion appeared in front of me, and when I tried to turn back I found I couldn't." But isn't this really elliptical for the *literal* truth "I *dreamt* I was running, etc."? Of course, we don't prefix "I dreamt" to every statement we make in the course of relating a dream, but in the appropriate context is it not understood to be there?

And is this not also the case with make-believe? The child says, "There are three pies here," but is this not an ellipsis for "I am (we are) making-believe that there are three pies here" or, more simply, "There are three make-believe pies here"—both of which may be literally true in the appropriate context?

It is not clear from Walton's "Postscript" whether he would go along with this, but can't every statement he offers as fictionally true, that is, either make-believedly true or imaginarily true, be rewritten in suitable fashion as a (possible) literal truth? If so, will this in any way affect the substance of his theory?

And is there not a further difficulty with the notion of fictional truth —or, if he prefers, of fictionality—as it is defined by Walton. Consider the necessary and sufficient conditions he gives for fictional truth: A statement, p, is fictionally true relative to context C if and only if three conditions are satisfied. Condition (i) is that "p is not literal in C." Since "literal" contrasts with *both* "metaphorical" and "fictional" (used generically to cover both "make-believe" and "imaginary"), condition (i) allows p to be metaphorical, for example, "I had them rolling in the aisles,' said in the course of relating a dream. Condition (ii), "p is true in C," seems not to be problematic; "I had them rolling in the aisles" could be true whether it appears in the report of a dream or in the account of an afterdinner speech I actually gave. But now we come to condition (iii): "In order to paraphrase literally the statement of p in C, one must either use or refer to a sentence that, taken literally and alone, would be a paraphrase of p taken literally." Suppose someone says, "What do you mean you 'had them rolling in the aisles'?," and I reply, "I mean I had them laughing frequently and heartily," this is a paraphrase of the metaphorical statement "I had them rolling in the aisles." But for "I had them rolling in the aisles" to be true of what I dreamt (a clear case of fictional truth), must I use or refer to a sentence that, taken literally and alone, would be a paraphrase of "I had them rolling in the aisles" taken *literally*? Surely, "I had them laughing frequently and heartily" will not do as a paraphrase of "I had them rolling in the aisles" taken *literally*.

The only way I can see to avoid this difficulty is to go back to condition (i) and to gloss "not literal" as "fictional." But wouldn't that make the definition of fictional truth viciously circular? Or is there another way out?

Finally, Walton admits that he has given no proof that the necessary conditions stipulated for *P*-depiction are also sufficient conditions, although he holds they are. Can you imagine something that satisfies these conditions but is clearly not a case of *P*-depiction? If you can, you will have shown that they are *not* sufficient.

The most controversial part of Black's essay on metaphor comes at the end, where he holds that although "substitution-metaphors and comparison-metaphors can be replaced by literal translations . . . with no loss of *cognitive* content," interaction-metaphors cannot. If "we try to state the cognitive content of an interaction metaphor in 'plain language,' " try to provide a "literal paraphrase" of it, the statement in plain language, the paraphrase, "will not have the same power to inform and enlighten as the original." Although Black does not make clear what he means by "cognitive content," presumably it is, or is something like, information. In any case, why must a paraphrase *inevitably* miss the mark in the way that Black says it must? Given a paraphrase of a metaphor that is as complete as we can make it, suppose we ask Black *what* cognitive content has been omitted. Either the question can be answered or it can't. If it can, then can't the answer be added to the paraphrase given so that it now suffers from no loss of cognitive content? But if it can't (and this would seem to follow from what Black says), then how does he or anyone else know that some cognitive content has been left out? Suppose *we* say that nothing has been left out; *he* says that something has. Is there any conceivable way of resolving this disagreement?[10]

Consider a related issue. Black allows that "up to a point, we may succeed" in paraphrasing an interaction metaphor; but we can't *fully* succeed. Isn't this like Brooks's claim that a paraphrase can at best be only approximate? If so, isn't it subject to Cavell's retort that here such contrasts as those between "partly" and "fully," "some" and "all," "approximate" and "exact" have been implicitly denied, in which case to say that only up to a point can an interaction metaphor be paraphrased is uninformative? If the notion of a full, complete, or exact paraphrase of a metaphor is robbed of any sense, has in principle no application, isn't the notion of a partial, incomplete, or merely approximate paraphrase thereby rendered nugatory?

One thing that may trouble Black, and that certainly troubles Brooks and Winters, is the idea of paraphrase's being a *replacement* or *substitute* for the statement paraphrased. In Shakespeare's *Antony and Cleopatra* (Act II, Scene II), Agrippa says to Enobarbus about Julius Caesar and Cleopatra, "He plough'd her, and she cropp'd." One might say that what this means is that Caesar had sexual intercourse with Cleopatra and that she conceived and bore him a child. Of course, the *tone* of the original—its wit, its irreverence, and its ribaldry (however you wish to describe it)—is lost in such a lifeless paraphrase; so the paraphrase cannot replace or substitute for the original. As Wittgenstein says,

> It may be that if it is to achieve its effect a particular word cannot be replaced by any other; just as it may be that a gesture cannot be replaced by any other. (The word has a *soul* and not just a meaning.) No one would believe that a poem remained *essentially unaltered* if its words were replaced by others in accordance with an appropriate convention.[11]

But to say that one word, or set of words, cannot always *replace* another without loss is not to say, or to imply, that a form of words can never be paraphrased without loss of cognitive content, is it?[12]

In saying the "Brooks is wrong to say that poems cannot in principle be fully paraphrased" Cavell seems to admit that metaphors can in principle be fully paraphrased. But is this consonant with what he says about paraphrase? He uses the word "paraphrase" in a restricted way "to name solely that specific form of account that suits metaphors (marked, for example, by its concluding sense of 'and so on')." What this seems to say is that the paraphrase of a metaphor can never explicitly be completed; that no matter what I say by way of paraphrasing a metaphor, I must always add "and so on." But is this logically compatible with the claim that metaphors can in principle be fully paraphrased?

What is at issue is what it means to say of a metaphor that it is endlessly paraphrasable. Suppose someone asks me what the even numbers are, and I reply, "2, 4, 6, 8, 10, and so on." Here I cannot in principle give "all" the even numbers (which is not to say that no matter how many I give, I have given *only* some of them), because it is *a priori* true that the series of even integers is infinite or endless. Any attempt to give the series of even integers must end with "and so on." Is this the kind of "and so on" that is involved in Cavell's account? If it is, can his claim that poems, and *a fortiori* metaphors, are in principle fully paraphrasable be consistent with his claim that they are endlessly paraphrasable?

Marcia Eaton distinguishes between two ways of handling works of fiction, especially those that attribute remarks to characters and do so in direct discourse:

> One can treat the statements within quotation marks as statements by various dramatic speakers . . . , and the remarks not in quotation marks as made by yet another dramatic speaker, namely, the narrator. Or the whole novel may be treated as one long statement by a storyteller, parts of whose remarks are reports of other peoples' utterances.

Margaret Macdonald appears to adopt the second view of fiction: "fictional sentences" are about imaginary persons, places, things, and events. But do fictional sentences express propositions that are either true or false? Although she pays almost no attention to the view that they say what is in some sense true, she rejects the fairly widespread idea that what they say is false.

First, fictional sentences do not express lies. To lie is to say what is false (or at least what one believes to be false) with intent to deceive. But although storytellers try to make their stories "plausible"—and by a plausible story Macdonald means "one which convinces, which induces acceptance"—they do not intend to deceive and, hence, do not lie. The conclusion may be acceptable, but the argument raises problems about the concept of plausibility. Of *what* does the storyteller try to convince us; *what* does he induce us to accept, if not the truth or probability of what he says?

Do fictional sentences express false statements that are not lies? It might appear that they do. For the sentence, "Emma Woodhouse . . . had lived nearly twenty-one years in the world with very little to distress or vex her," says in effect (according to at least a widely held view of such sentences), "There was a person named 'Emma Woodhouse' and she had lived nearly twenty-one years in the world . . . etc." And since the first part of this statement is false, the whole is false.[13]

Macdonald rejects this: "no factual discovery can verify a fictional statement. It can never be true." But if it can never be true, then it must be (1) necessarily false, (2) contingently false, or (3) neither true nor false. It can't be necessarily false, for a fictional statement does not, as such, imply a contradiction. It can't be contingently false, for "what no fact can confirm none can disconfirm either." Thus, it must be neither true nor false. But why can no factual discovery verify or disconfirm a fictional statement—a premise central to Macdonald's argument? Because it is false? That view is rejected. Because fictional statements are, by virtue of the fact that they are fictional, neither true nor false? If so, does this not beg the question?[14]

Apart from this argument, it might still be the case that fictional sentences are neither true nor false. But if they are not, how do we know this? Does it follow from the meaning of "fictional"? If it does, how are we to explain the fact that such philosophers as Hume and Moore and Ryle, all of whom knew very well what "fictional" means, held that fictional statements are false? Were they unwittingly contradicting themselves?

On the positive side, Macdonald holds a view of fiction that runs counter to that of Kendall Walton. She holds that a storyteller "invites his audience to 'Imagine that . . . ,' 'Pretend that . . ,' and even 'Suppose that . . .' or 'Let it be granted that . . .' He does not often preface his stories with just these remarks, but he issues a general invitation to exercise imagination." In Walton's terms, Macdonald holds that fictional statements are *"imaginarily* true" or are, more simply, imaginary. But he holds that they are *make-believe.* He holds that "if **p**(F) because of some fact about the real world . . . , then **p**(MB);" whereas if " '**p**(F)' is true merely because of the fact that one or more persons imagine that *p* (or pretend, or suppose, or make-believe, or dream that *p*), or decide or agree that *p*, or decide or agree to let it be true that **p**(F), or do any combination of these things, I will say that *p* is *imaginarily* true, that **p**(I)." Specifically, he holds that "Smerdyakov fell down the stairs" is *make-believedly* true "in virtue of the presence of certain sentences in the novel [*The Brothers Karamazov*]."

Suppose someone says, "Let us imagine that long ago there was a huge dark forest in the center of which stood a small cottage . . . ," and you do as you are invited to do; then "Long ago there was a huge dark forest . . . etc." is said by Walton to be *imaginarily* true, even though what you do is done in virtue of the invitation in question. But if Macdonald is right about what storytellers do, namely, that they implicitly invite us to imagine certain things, is there any significant difference between Dostoveysky or Jane Austen and my imaginary someone? In short, when we read the appropriate sentences in *The Brothers Karamazov*, do we—even given Walton's specifications—imagine or make-believe that Smerdyakov is falling down the stairs?

As Eaton sees it, understanding fiction is not a question of imagination or make-believe but simply one of understanding a dramatic speaker. On who this dramatic speaker is, she takes a moderate line; the dramatic speaker may be a fictional person or he may be the author. The narrower view, held by some philosophers, is that the dramatic speaker is *always* a fictional person, albeit he may at times closely resemble the author. Is Eaton not right to take the approach she does? In the Preface to his *Poems of the Past and the Present*, Thomas Hardy says that some of his poems are "dramatic or impersonative" whereas others are "individual," that is, ones in which he, Hardy, is speaking *in propria persona*.[15] Are we not to believe Hardy? Are we to disregard what he says? On what grounds? Those who advocate the narrower view sometimes do so in order to obviate all appeals to the intentions of the author. But can this be done? Can a dramatic speaker, as Eaton says in effect, mean more, or less, than the author means him to mean?

Notes

1. For what it is worth, the word "interpretation" is of Latin derivation. The verb *interpretari* means to explain, expound, translate; to understand, appreciate, comprehend; to decide, determine. The noun *interpretatio* means an explanation or exposition; a translation or version, significance or meaning. And the noun *interpres* means an agent, mediator, or go-between, a broker, a ngotiator, an explainer or expounder, a translator.

2. Millard Meiss, "*Ovum Struthionis*: Symbol and Allusion in Piero della Francesca's Montefeltro Altarpiece," and "Once Again Piero della Francesca's Montefeltro Altarpiece," *The Painter's Choice: Problems in the Interpretation of Renaissance Art* (New York, 1976), pp. 105-141.

3. Darnel is a poisonous weed resembling rye, sometimes called "rye grass." The translation given is that of *The New English Bible*.

4. The questions "What does that mean?," "What do you mean?," and "What do you mean by that?" are not (always) the same. Consider a simple example of where they differ. During the intermission at a performance of *Don Giovanni* you overhear someone say, "He had a little talent, that fellow." You speak English, so there's no question about what the utterance means, as there might be in the case of someone who speaks only a little English, if any. But who is he talking about? Mozart, it turns out. So what he means is that Mozart had a little talent. But what does he mean by that? Well, he's not being patronizing; on the contrary, he's speaking ironically and intends a compliment. By his words he means that Mozart had a *great* talent.

5. The kind of interpretive work done by an actor or a musician might, especially in a didactic situation, be taken as implicitly statemental, as saying in

effect, "This is how it goes (is meant to go, should go)"; in which case alternative interpretations would be subject to the logic of statemental interpretations.

6. Margaret Macdonald, "Some Distinctive Features of Arguments Used in Criticism of the Arts," *Aesthetics and Language,* William Elton, ed. (New York, 1954), pp. 126-127. This essay originally appeared in *P.A.S.,* Suppl. Vol. 23 (1949). There the corresponding sentences are weaker in force.

7. On pp. 121-122 of *The Concept of Expression* (omitted from the Tormey selection in this book) Tormey says, "statements of the form, 'The music expresses ϕ,' or 'The music is expressive of ϕ' must, if we are to understand them as making relevant remarks about the music and not as making elliptical remarks about the composer, be interpreted as intensionally equivalent to syntactic form A; that is, they are to be understood as propositions containing 'expression' or 'expressive' as syntactic parts of a one-place predicate denoting some perceptible quality, aspect, or *gestalt* [sic] of the work itself. . . . 'The *music* expresses ϕ' cannot be interpreted as an instance of the use of 'expression' (B) since it would make no sense to ask for the *intentional object* of the music."

8. It does to Charles L. Stevenson from whom the example is borrowed. See his "Symbolism in the Nonrepresentational Arts," *Language, Thought, and Culture,* Paul Henle, ed. (Ann Arbor, Mich., 1958), esp. pp. 210 ff. Stevenson borrows the example from Heinz Werner, *Comparative Psychology of Mental Development* (New York, 1948), p. 70.

9. See P. H. Osmond, *Paolo Veronese, His Career and Work* (London, 1927), pp. 68-70. And for accounts of the feast in the house of Levi (the Apostle Matthew), see *Matthew* ix, *Mark* ii, *Luke* v; for that in the house of Simon the Pharisee, *Luke* ii; for the Last Supper, *Matthew* xxvi, *Mark* xiv, *Luke* xxi, *John* xiii.

10. Black might be construed as *defining* an interaction metaphor as one that cannot be paraphrased without loss of cognitive content, but then the question would be whether there are any interaction metaphors as defined.

11. Ludwig Wittgenstein, *Philosophical Grammar,* Rush Rhees, ed., Anthony Kenny, trans. (Oxford, 1974), p. 69.

12. For more on two sentences having the same meaning or sense but not being interchangeable, see A. G. Pleydell-Pearce, "Sense, Reference, and Fiction," *B.J.A.,* 7 (1967), 225-236.

13. It has been objected to this view that if, for example, "Emma Woodhouse was rich" is false, so also is "Emma Woodhouse was not rich," and for the same reason. But the two statements are contradictory; hence, if one of them is false, the other must be true. (See Monroe C. Beardsley, *Aesthetics,* New York, 1958, p. 413.) According to the view under discussion, however, the two statements are *not* contradictory. For each is analyzable into a conjunction, and "*p* and *q*" and "*p* and not-*q*" are not contradictories but contraries: both cannot be true, but both can be false.

14. The claim that a fictional, or even a false, statement cannot be verified (shown to be true) is ambiguous, and her neglect of this ambiguity may be responsible for Macdonald's difficulty here. "If a statement is fictional (or false), it can't be verified" may mean either (1) that "It is logically impossible for a statement to be both fictional (or false) and verified" or (2) that "If a statement is fictional (or false), it is logically impossible for it to be verified." Macdonald apparently takes the sentence to mean 2. But 2 is a nonsequitur, unless we *mean* by a fictional statement one that cannot be verified. (But do we?) For even if *p* is false, it does not follow that it cannot be verified, that the calim that *p* has been verified implies a contradiction, although it is necessarily the case that *p* cannot be both false and verified at the same time. That is, "If Boots is a dog, he can't be a cat." This doesn't mean that if Boots is a dog, then it's

logically impossible for him to be a cat. What is logically impossible is that Boots be both a dog and a cat at the same time.

15. *The Complete Poems of Thomas Hardy,* James Gibson, ed. (New York, 1976), p. 84.

Suggestions for Additional Reading

On interpretation:

Henry D. Aiken, "The Aesthetic Relevance of Artists' Intentions," *J. Phil.,* 52 (1955), 742-753; Monroe C. Beardsley, *Aesthetics* (New York, 1958), 17-29, 114-147, 267-309, 318-352, 400-419, "The Limits of Critical Interpretation," *Art and Philosophy: A Symposium,* Sidney Hook, ed. (New York, 1966), 61-87, and *The Possibility of Criticism* (Detroit, 1970), 16-61; Frank Cioffi, "Intention and Interpretation in Literature," *P.A.S.,* 64 (1963-1964), 85-106, reprinted in *Collected Papers on Aesthetics,* Cyril Barrett, ed. (Oxford, 1965), 161-183; Dennis Dutton, "Plausibility and Aesthetic Interpretation," *Can. J. Phil.,* 7 (1977), 327-340; A. J. Ellis, "Intention and Interpretation in Literature," *B.J.A.,* 14 (1974), 315-325; Solomon Fishman, *The Interpretation of Art* (Berkeley, 1963); E. D. Hirsch, Jr., *The Aims of Interpretation* (Chicago, 1976) and *Validity in Interpretation* (New Haven, 1967); John Hospers, *Meaning and Truth in the Arts* (Chapel Hill, N.C., 1946), Pt. I; Arnold Isenberg, "Some Problems of Interpretation," *Aesthetics and the Theory of Criticism* (Chicago, 1973), 199-215; Peter Jones, "Understanding a Work of Art," *B.J.A.,* 9 (1969), 128-144; John Kemp, "The Work of Art and the Artist's Intentions," *B.J.A.,* 4 (1964), 146-154; Ernst Kris and Abraham Kaplan, "Esthetic Ambiguity," *Psychoanalytic Explorations in Art* (New York, 1952); Richard W. Lind, "Must the Critic Be Correct?," *J.A.A.C.,* 35 (1977), 445-456; Joseph Margolis, "Critics and Literature," *B.J.A.,* 11 (1971), 369-384 and *The Language of Art and Art Criticism* (Detroit, 1965), Pt. III; T. Redpath, "The Meaning of a Poem," *British Philosophy in the Mid-Century,* C. Mace, ed. (London, 1957), 361-375, reprinted in *Collected Papers on Aesthetics,* Cyril Barrett, ed. (Oxford, 1965), 145-159; John F. Reichert, "Description and Interpretation in Literary Criticism," *J.A.A.C.,* 27 (1969), 281-292; Paul Ricoeur, *Interpretation Theory: Discourse and the Surplus of Meaning* (Fort Worth, Tex., 1976); Gary Shapiro, "Intention and Interpretation in Art: A Semiotic Analysis," *J.A.A.C.,* 33 (1974), 33-42; Charles S. Singleton, ed., *Interpretation: Theory and Practice* (Baltimore, 1969); Charles L. Stevenson, "Interpretation and Evaluation in Aesthetics," *Philosophical Analysis,* Max Black, ed. (Ithaca, N.Y., 1950), 341-383; Richard Wollheim, *Art and Its Objects* (New York, 1968), #37-39.

On expression:

O. K. Bouwsma, "The Expression Theory of Art," *Philosophical Analysis,* Max Black, ed. (Ithaca, N.Y., 1950), 75-101; Nelson Goodman, *Languages of Art* (Indianapolis and New York, 1968), Ch. II; O. H. Green, "The Expression of Emotion," *Mind,* 79 (1970), 551-568; Stuart Hampshire, *Feeling and Expression* (London, 1961); R. W. Hepburn, "Emotions and Emotional Qualities: Some Attempts at Analysis," *B.J.A.,* 4 (1964), 225-265; John Hospers, "The Concept of Artistic Expression," *P.A.S.,* 53 (1954-1955), 313-344; V. A. Howard, "On Musical Expression," *B.J.A.,* 11 (1971), 268-280; Peter Mew, "Projection and Expression," *B.J.A.,* 12 (1972), 354-358; Douglas N. Morgan, "The Concept of Expression in Art," *Science, Language, and Human Rights* (Philadelphia, 1952), 145-165; Vincent Tomas, "The Concept of Expression in Art," *Science, Language, and Human Rights* (Philadelphia, 1952), 127-144; B. R. Tilghman, *The Expression of Emotion in the Visual Arts: A Philosophical Inquiry* (The Hague, 1970); Richard Wollheim, "Expression," *On Art and the Mind* (Cambridge, Mass., 1974), 84-100.

On representation and symbolism in the visual arts:

Virgil C. Aldrich, "Pictures and Persons—An Analogy," *Rev. Met.,* 28 (1974-1975), 599-610; Rudolf Arnheim, *Art and Visual Perception* (Berkeley, 1954), and *Visual Thinking,* (Berkeley, 1969); Kent Bach, "Part of What a Picture Is," *B.J.A.,* 10 (1970), 119-137; Monroe C. Beardsley, *Aesthetics* (New York, 1958), Ch. VI; Errol Bedford, "Seeing Paintings," *P.A.S.,* Suppl. Vol. 40 (1966), 47-62; John G. Bennett, "Depiction and Convention," *The Monist,* 58 (1974), 255-268; Richard Bernheimer, *The Nature of Representation* (New York, 1961); B. Falk, "Portraits and Persons," *P.A.S.,* 75 (1974-1975), 181-200; J. J. Gibson, "The Information Available in Pictures," *Leonardo,* 4 (1971), 27-35, "Pictures, Perspective and Perception," *Daedalus,* 89 (1960), 216-227, "A Theory of Pictorial Perception," *Audio-Visual Communications Review,* 1 (1954), 3-23; E. H. Gombrich, *Art and Illusion,* 2nd ed., (London, 1962), "The Evidence of Images," *Interpretation: Theory and Practice,* Charles S. Singleton, ed. (Baltimore, 1969), "The Mask and the Face: the Perception of Physiognomic Likeness in Life and in Art," *Art, Perception, and Reality* (Baltimore, 1972), 1-46, *Meditations on a Hobby Horse and Other Essays on the Theory of Art* (London, 1963), and "The What and the How: Perspectival Representation and the Phenomenal World," *Logic and Art: Essays in Honor of Nelson Goodman,* R. Rudner and I. Scheffler, eds. (Indianapolis and New York, 1972); Nelson Goodman, *Languages of Art* (Indianapolis and New York, 1968), Chs. I, IV, V, VI; R. L. Gregory, *The Intelligent Eye* (London, 1970); M. R. Haight, "Picturing Unreality," *Analysis,* 32 (1971-1972), 65-67 and "Who's Who in Pictures," *B.J.A.,* 16 (1976), 13-23; N. G. E. Harris, "Goodman's Account of Representation," *J.A.A.C.*, 31 (1973), 323-327; Andrew Harrison, "Representation and Conceptual Change," *Philosophy and the Arts*, Royal Institute of Philosophy Lectures, 6, (1971-1972), 106-131; Göran Hermerén, *Representation and Meaning in the Visual Arts* (Lund, Sweden, 1969), Ch. II; Marcus B. Hester, "Are Paintings and Photographs Inherently Interpretative?," *J.A.A.C.*, 31 (1972), 235-247; Julian Hochberg, "The Representation of Things and People," *Art, Perception, and Reality* (Baltimore, 1972), 47-94; Robert Howell, "The Logical Structure of Pictorial Representation," *Theoria*, 40 (1974), 76-109; John M. Kennedy, *A Psychology of Picture Perception* (San Francisco, 1974); G. Kepes, *Language and Vision* (Chicago, 1944); Paul A. Kolers, "Reading Pictures and Reading Texts," *The Arts and Cognition*, D. Perkins and B. Leondar, eds. (Baltimore, 1977), 136-164; Diana Korzenik, "Saying It with Pictures," *The Arts and Cognition*, D. Perkins and B. Leondar, eds. (Baltimore, 1977), 192-207; James W. Manns, "Representation, Relativism and Resemblance," *B.J.A.*, 11 (1971), 281-287; Ruby Meager, "Seeing Paintings," *P.A.S.*, Suppl. vol. 4 (1966), 63-84; Maurice Merleau-Ponty, "Eye and Mind," *The Primacy of Perception*, James Edie, ed. (Evanston, Ill., 1964); Douglas N. Morgan, "Icon, Index, and Symbol in the Visual Arts," *Phil. Studs.*, 6 (1955), 49-54; David Novitz, "Picturing," *J.A.A.C.*, 34 (1975), 145-155; Erwin Panofsky, *Meaning in the Visual Arts* (New York, 1955); Risto Pitkänen, "The Resemblance View of Pictorial Representation," *B.J.A.*, 16 (1976), 313-323; Michael Polanyi, "What Is a Painting?," *B.J.A.*, 10 (1970), 225-236; Norvin Richards, "Depicting and Visualizing," *Mind*, 82 (1973), 218-225; L. R. Rogers, "Representation and Schemata," *B.J.A.*, 5 (1965), 159-178; Mark Roskill, "On the Recognition and Identification of Objects in Paintings," *Crit. Inq.*, 3 (1977), 677-707; T. G. Roupas, "Information and Pictorial Representation," *The Arts and Cognition*, D. Perkins and B. Leondar, eds. (Baltimore, 1977), 48-79; Joel Snyder and Neil W. Allen, "Photography, Vision, and Representation," *Crit. Inq.*, 2 (1975), 143-169; Roger Squires, "Depicting," *Phil.*, 44 (1969), 193-204; G. F. Todd, "On Visual Representation," *B.J.A.*, 15 (1975), 347-357; Kendall L. Walton, "Are Representations Symbols?," *The Monist*, 58 (1974), 236-254; Richard Wollheim, *Art and Its Objects* (New York, 1968), #11-13, 26-27, "Nelson Goodman's *Languages of Art*," *On Art and the Mind* (Cambridge, Mass., 1974), 290-314, "On Drawing an Object," *ibid.*, 3-30, "Reflections on *Art and Illusion*," *ibid.*, 261-289, and "Representation: the Philosophical Contribution to Psychology," *Crit. Inq.*, 2 (1977), 709-723; E. M. Zemach, "Description and Depiction," *Mind*, 84 (1975), 567-578.

On metaphor:

Terrence F. Ackerman, "The Literal, the Metaphorical, and the Real," *Ratio*, 17 (1975), 191-205; William P. Alston, *Philosophy of Language* (Englewood Cliffs, N.J., 1964), 96-106; Monroe C. Beardsley, *Aesthetics*

(New York, 1958), Ch. III, "Metaphor," *The Encyclopedia of Philosophy* (New York, 1967), Vol. 5, 284-289, and "The Metaphorical Twist," *Phil. and Phen.*, 22 (1962), 293-307; Ralph Berry, "The Frontier of Metaphor and Symbol," *B.J.A.*, 7 (1967), 76-83; Timothy Binkley, "On the Truth and Probity of Metaphor," *J.A.A.C.*, 33 (1974), 171-180; Ted Cohen, "Figurative Speech and Figurative Acts," *J. Phil.*, 72 (1975), 669-684, and "Notes on Metaphor," *J.A.A.C.*, 34 (1976), 249-259—one of the best discussions of metaphor available; Martin Foss, *Symbol and Metaphor in Human Experience* (Princeton, 1949): Paul Henle, "Metaphor," *Language, Thought, and Culture,* Paul Henle, ed. (Ann Arbor, 1958), 173-195; Marcus B. Hester, "Metaphor and Aspect Seeing," *J.A.A.C.*, 25 (1966), 205-212; Arnold Isenberg, "On Defining Metaphor," *Aesthetics and the Theory of Criticism* (Chicago, 1973), 105-121; Haig Khatchadourian, "Metaphor," *B.J.A.*, 8 (1968), 227-243; James W. Manns, "Metaphor and Paraphrase," *B.J.A.*, 15 (1975), 358-366; M. A. McCloskey, "Metaphors," *Mind*, 73 (1964), 215-233; Peter Mew, "Metaphor and Truth," *B.J.A.*, 11 (1971), 189-195; Paul J. Olscamp, "How Some Metaphors May Be True or False," *J.A.A.C.*, 29 (1970), 77-86; I. A. Richards, *The Philosophy of Rhetoric* (New York, 1936), Chs. 5, 6; Edith Watson Schipper, "A Note on Metaphor," *J.A.A.C.*, 28 (1968), 199-201; J. Srzednicki, "On Metaphor," *Phil. Quart.*, 10 (1960), 228-237; Gustav Stern, *Meaning and Change of Meaning* (Göteborg, 1931); Donald Stewart, "Metaphor, Truth, and Definition," *J.A.A.C.*, 32 (1973), 205-218; C. M. Turbayne, *The Myth of Metaphor* (Columbia, S. C., 1970); Martin Warner, "Black's Metaphors," *B.J.A.*, 13 (1973), 367-372; René Welleck and Austin Warren, *Theory of Literature* (New York, 1949), Ch. 15; Paul Welsh, "On Explicating Metaphors," *J. Phil.*, 60 (1963), 622-624; Philip Wheelwright, *Metaphor and Reality* (Bloomington, Ind., 1962).

On fictional discourse:

Karl Aschenbrenner, "Implications of Frege's Philosophy of Language for Literature," *B.J.A.*, 8 (1968), 319-334; Ann Banfield, "Narrative Style and the Grammar of Direct and Indirect Speech," *Foundations of Language,* 10 (1973), 1-39; Monroe C. Beardsley, *Aesthetics* (New York, 1958), Chs. III, VIII, IX; Arnold Berleant, "The Verbal Presence: An Aesthetics of Literary Performance," *J.A.A.C.*, 21 (1973), 339-346; H. G. Blocker, "The Truth About Fictional Entities," *Phil. Quart.*, 24 (1974), 27-36; Wayne C. Booth, *The Rhetoric of Fiction* (Chicago, 1961); Jerry S. Clegg, "Some Artistic Uses of Truths and Lies," *J.A.A.C.*, 31 (1972), 43-47; Francis X. J. Coleman, "A Few Observations on Fictional Discourse," *Language and Aesthetics,* Benjamin R. Tilghman, ed. (Lawrence, Ka., 1973), 31-42; Marcia M. Eaton, "On Being a Character," *B.J.A.*, 16 (1976), 24-31 and "The Truth Value of Literary Statements," *B.J.A.*, 12 (1972), 163-174; R. K. Elliott, "The Aesthetic and the Semantic: A Reply to Mr. Playdell-Pearce," *B.J.A.*, 8 (1968), 35-48 and "Poetry and Truth," *Analysis,*

27 (1966-1967), 77-85; Richard M. Gale, "The Fictive Use of Language," *Philosophy*, 46 (1971), 324-339; Käthe Hamburger, *The Logic of Literature,* Marilynn J. Rose, trans. (Bloomington, Ind., 1973); Colin Lyas, "The Semantic Definition of Literature," *J. Phil.*, 66 (1969), 81-95; D. H. Mellor, "On Literary Truth," *Ratio*, 10 (1968), 150-168; Peter Mew, "Facts in Fiction," *J.A.A.C.*, 31 (1973), 329-337; Earl Miner, "That Literature is a Kind of Knowledge," *Crit. Inq.*, 2 (1976), 487-518; Joseph Margolis, "Psychological and Logical Distinctions Respecting Fiction," *J.A.A.C.*, 27 (1969), 257-260; Thomas G. Pavel, "Possible Worlds in Literary Semantics," *J.A.A.C.*, 34 (1975), 165-176; D. Z. Phillips, "Allegiance and Change in Morality: A Study in Contrasts," *Philosophy and the Arts*, Royal Institute of Philosophy Lectures, 6, 1971-1972, 47-64; A. G. Pleydell-Pearce, "Sense, Reference and Fiction," *B.J.A.*, 7 (1967), 225-236, and "A 'No Reference' Theory of Aesthetics," *B.J.A.*, 8 (1968), 407-409—a reply to Elliott; D. E. B. Pollard, "Fiction and Semantics," *Ratio,* 15 (1973), 57-73; Allan Rodway, "Life, Time and the 'Art' of Fiction," *B.J.A.*, 7 (1967), 374-384; Donald J. Schneider, "Techniques of Cognition in Modern Fiction," *J.A.A.C.*, 26 (1968), 317-328; Mary Sirridge, "J. R. Tolkein and Fairy Tale Truth," *B.J.A.*, 15 (1974), 81-92; F. E. Sparshott, "Truth in Fiction," *J.A.A.C.*, 26 (1967), 3-7; Kendall L. Walton, "Fearing Fictions," *J. Phil.*, 75 (1978), 5-27 and "How Remote Are Fictional Worlds From the Real World?," *J.A.A.C.,* 37 (1978); Morris Weitz, "Truth in Literature," *Révue Internationale de Philosophie*, 9 (1955), 116-129; John Woods, *The Logic of Fiction* (The Hague, 1974).

IV

Aesthetic Experience

Introduction

THE MATERIAL OF THIS SECTION is only rather arbitrarily dissociable from that of the next one, or even the next two, as the reader will discover. Still, because people insist on talking about "the aesthetic experience" as if that were a single topic of discussion, it seemed advisable, if only for heuristic reasons, to give it a run for its money.

Although the term "aesthetic" once belonged to a quite small realm of discourse, namely, discourse about sense perception, the boundaries of its use are now so extensive that it is difficult to say whether it has a variety of distinct meanings, of related meanings, or of overlapping meanings (and dictionaries are most unhelpful here), with the consequence that on many occasions of its use it is often difficult, if not impossible, to gloss its meaning. Often it means "of or pertaining to art," but not always. And where it does not mean that, even the context in which it appears is frequently unhelpful in determining just what it does mean.

Conjoin "aesthetic" with "experience" and you compound the difficulty. For what does "experience" mean? The term seems to be elastic enough to cover almost any, or any kind of, thing one does consciously or consciously has happen to him. Thus one who performs a surgical operation is having the experience of performing a surgical operation; one who does or undergoes something pleasant is having a pleasant experience, or even an experience of pleasure; one who looks at or sees something has a visual experience; one who has been psychoanalyzed has had the experience of being psychoanalyzed; one who has seen and talked with a lot of drug addicts has had a lot of experience with drug addicts; one who has taught mathematics for many years has had a lot of experience in teaching mathematics; and so on. It is difficult to think of a sentence about what someone has done or endured that cannot be translated into the idiom of "experience."

This being the case, one should be on guard when one encounters talk about "aesthetic experience," especially about "*the* aesthetic experience."

It is not that such talk is irredeemably condemned to vagueness, imprecision, or vacuity, but rather that, the linguistic situation being what it is, the opportunities for confusion and misunderstanding are greater in this area than in that of organic chemistry, say.

J. O. Urmson's title contains a misnomer: it is not really what makes *situations* aesthetic that interests him, but what makes *reactions* (or reactions and judgments) aesthetic. By a reaction he means something like (an experience of) satisfaction or dissatisfaction, pleasure or displeasure, boredom, excitement, outrage, approval, or even indifference. He rightly notes that the adjective "aesthetic" is used in contrast with such adjectives as "moral," "personal," "economic," "intellectual," "religious," and "erotic." And he wants to determine what makes a reaction aesthetic as opposed, or in addition, to moral, say. He rejects the view that an aesthetic reaction is essentially a reaction to a special kind of object, for example, a work of art, or to some special property, for example, beauty. He holds that we determine whether a reaction is aesthetic by the kind of explanation one gives, or would give, of the reaction.

When he comes to look for some common denominator of explanations that marks a reaction as aesthetic, Urmson finds that, in at least the simpler cases, the common denominator is how an object looks, tastes, smells, feels, sounds—not only whether it is pleasantly sweet or a rich dark red, but also whether, for example, it looks powerful or swift: "if a thing looks to have a characteristic which is a desirable one from another point of view [e.g., the horse-trainer's point of view in the case of swiftness], its looking so is a proper ground of aesthetic appreciation. What makes the appreciation aesthetic is that it is concerned with a thing's looking somehow without concern for whether it really is like that."

This last sentence has been taken by some aestheticians as definitive not of aesthetic appreciation, but of aesthetic *vision*. To perceive (have a perceptual experience of) an object aesthetically is to attend solely to how it appears, or, more radically, to attend solely to appearances, regardless of whether there is even anything "there" that appears. Peter Kivy subjects this view to criticism, arguing that it will not do. He then turns to another and recently rather popular variant of the view that aesthetic perception is a special species of perception or way of perceiving, namely, that it is essentially "aspect-perceiving" or "seeing-as," for example, perceiving (hearing) a series of notes as a melody or seeing certain lines, shapes, and colors "as hanging together in a coherent design." He tries to show that one version of this view is confused and thereby hopes to cast doubt on the view in general.

Still on the subject of aesthetic perception, Nelson Goodman addresses the fascinating question of whether there is any "aesthetic difference" between an original painting and, say, a faithful copy or forgery of it, one so faithful that not even an expert can tell "merely by looking" which is which. Although many people are inclined to say that there would be no aesthetic difference between the two in such a case, Goodman argues ingeniously that there is actually a world of aesthetic difference between them.

The aesthetic experience has been held to consist in that experience we have of an object when and only when we adopt a special attitude—"the aesthetic attitude"—toward it. Historically there have been two important and influential theories of the aesthetic attitude: (1) that adoping the aesthetic attitude towards an object consists in performing a special action, namely, "distancing" or "psychically distancing" it, a view introduced by the British psychologist and aesthetician Edward Bullough in 1912; (2) that adopting the aesthetic attitude toward something does not consist in performing a special action but in performing an ordinary action, such as attending, in a special way, namely, disinterestedly—a view older and more widespread than the first. George Dickie argues that the aesthetic attitude, in either version, is a myth, that there is no such thing. He claims further that the disinterested attention view is misleading: it distorts the notion of aesthetic relevance; it misrepresents the relation between critic and art work by making the critic's attitude inevitably nonaesthetic; and it misrepresents the relation of morality to aesthetic merit.

Although some aestheticians have doubted whether there is any such thing as aesthetic experience in the sense of a type of experience comprehensively definable, Monroe Beardsley disagrees. In the face of such skepticism he engages in what he calls "a conceptual rescue operation." There is such a thing as aesthetic experience, and it can be distinguished from nonaesthetic experience "in terms of its own internal properites." Chief among these properties are unity, coherence, and completeness. But are these properties really properties of an *experience,* or just properties of an object experienced? Beardsley's answer is that a coherent experience, say, is something more than just an experience of something coherent, and he tries to show how it is.

As Beardsley sees it "the greatest philosophical significance" of rescuing the concept of aesthetic experience is that this concept alone supplies us with a "persuasive analysis of artistic goodness," for the goodness of a work of art is a direct function of its capacity to provide aesthetic experience.

J. O. URMSON

What Makes a Situation Aesthetic?

PHILOSOPHERS HAVE HOED OVER the plot of aesthetics often enough, but the plants that they have raised thereby are pitifully weak and straggling objects. The time has therefore not yet come for tidying up some corner of the plot; it needs digging over afresh in the hope that some sturdier and more durable produce may arise, even if its health be rather rude. I therefore make no excuse for reopening what seems to me to be the central problem of aesthetics: I hope that by a somewhat new approach I may succeed in making a contribution, if but a small one, towards its solution.

We may refer to a person as, in a given situation, getting an aesthetic thrill or aesthetic satisfaction from something, or of his finding something aesthetically tolerable, or aesthetically dissatisfying, or even aesthetically hateful. In a suitable context the adjective "aesthetic" and the adverb "aesthetically" may well be superfluous, but it is sometimes necessary to introduce one of these words in order to make it clear that when we refer, say, to a person's satisfaction we are not thinking of moral satisfaction, economic satisfaction, personal satisfaction, intellectual satisfaction, or any satisfaction other than aesthetic satisfaction. If we merely know that someone gained satisfaction from a play we do not know for sure that we are in the aesthetic field. Thus a play may give me moral satisfaction because I think it likely to have improving effects on the audience; economic satisfaction because it is playing to full houses and I am financing it; personal satisfaction because I wrote it and it is highly praised by the critics; intellectual satisfaction because it solves a number of difficult technical problems of the theatre very cleverly. But the question will still be open whether I found the play aesthetically satisfying. Though these various types of satisfaction are not mutually exclusive, it is clear that when we call a satisfaction aesthetic the purpose must be to mark it off from the other types.

Reprinted from *Proceedings of the Aristotelian Society,* Supplementary Vol. XXXI (1957) by courtesy of the Editor of the Aristotelian Society.

The philosophical task to be tackled in this paper is therefore this: to make explicit what it is that distinguishes aesthetic thrills, satisfactions, toleration, disgust, etc., from thrills, satisfactions, etc., that would properly be called moral, intellectual, economic, etc. I put the question in this form because I think that it is tempting to consider the aesthetic as an isolated matter and within the field of the aesthetic to concentrate unduly upon the most sublime and intense of our experiences; but I am convinced that it is important to ensure that our account of the aesthetic should be as applicable to toleration as to our most significant experiences and should make it clear that in characterising a reaction or judgment as aesthetic the point is to distinguish it from other reactions and judgments that are moral, economic, and so on. Only thus can we hope to bring out the full forces of the term "aesthetic."

This is not intended to be a problem especially about the appreciation of works of art. No doubt many of our most intense aesthetic satisfactions are derived from plays, poems, musical works, pictures and other works of art. But to me it seems obvious that we also derive aesthetic satisfaction from artifacts that are not primarily works of art, from scenery, from natural objects and even from formal logic; it is at least reasonable also to allow an aesthetic satisfaction to the connoisseur of wines and to the gourmet. I shall therefore assume that there is no special set of objects which are the sole and proper objects of aesthetic reactions and judgments, and which are never the objects of an economic, intellectual, moral, religious or personal reaction or judgment. We may judge a power-station aesthetically and find economic satisfaction in a work of art that we own. We may take it, then, that we are not exclusively concerned with the philosophy of art, and that whatever the criteria of the aesthetic may be they cannot be found by trying to delimit a special class of objects.

If the aesthetic cannot be identified by its being directed to a special class of objects, it might be more plausibly suggested that the criteria of the aesthetic are to be sought by looking for some special features of objects which are attended to when our reaction or judgment is aesthetic; beauty and ugliness have often been adduced as the features in question. Alternatively it has often been suggested that aesthetic reactions and judgments contain or refer to some unique constituent of the emotions of the observer, either a special "aesthetic emotion" or an "aesthetic tinge" of some other emotion. I think that most commonly theories elicited by our problem have been variations on one or other of these two themes, a variation on the first theme being called an objectivist theory and a variation on the second being called subjectivist. I propose to give some reasons in this paper for finding both these theories unsatisfactory as answers to our problem, even if neither is wholly false as a mere assertion; in their place, I shall suggest that the correct answer is to be given in terms of the explanation of the reaction or the grounds of the judgment. I shall make some tentative remarks about what sort of grounds for a judgment make that judgment aesthetic, but cannot even begin the systematic treatment of the subject.

Let us revert to an illustration already casually used, and suppose that we observe a man in the audience at a play who is obviously beaming with delight and satisfaction. If I now maintain that his delight is purely economic, what have I to do in order to establish this contention? If the question at issue were whether he was delighted or merely contented it would no doubt be necessary to ascertain fairly accurately his emotional state; but if it be agreed that he is delighted and the only issue is whether his delight is properly to be called economic, it is surely clear that phenomenological study of his emotions is not necessary. If, however, we find him to be the impresario, and he agrees that the complete explanation of his delight is that there is a full house, and the reaction of his audience indicates a long run, what more could possibly be needed to justify us in describing his delight as economic? It seems hard to dispute that in the case of economic delight, satisfaction, disappointment and the like the criterion of the reaction's being economic lies in the nature of the explanation of that reaction. Similarly it would be beyond dispute that a man's delight was wholly personal if it were conceded that its explanation was entirely the fact that his daughter was acquitting herself well in her first part as a leading lady; again his delight will be moral if wholly explained by the belief that the play will have a good effect on the conduct of the audience. It would, I suggest, be very surprising if the way of establishing that delight, satisfaction and other reactions were aesthetic turned out to be quite different from the way in which we establish them to be moral, personal, economic, intellectual, etc. Nor would it be surprising merely as a novelty; it would be logically disturbing to find that one had suddenly to depart from a single *fundamentum divisionis*, which had sufficed for all the other types, when one came to the aesthetic.

We must now note a further point about the logical relation between the concepts of the moral, the aesthetic, the economic, the intellectual, and the personal, as applied to reactions, both because it is of some logical interest and because a misunderstanding of it has led to some silly theories. *Triangular, square* and *pentagonal,* as applied to surfaces, are clearly species of a single genus and as such are mutually exclusive; there is a single *fundamentum divisionis* which is the number of sides that the rectilinear surface has. The same applies, *mutatis mutandis,* to *bachelor, married* and *widowed* as applied to men. On the other hand *triangular, red* and *large* are three logically unconnected predicates of surfaces, and *bachelor, bald* and *wealthy* are similarly unconnected predicates of men. What then are we to say about the predicates *moral, economic* and *aesthetic* as applied to, say, satisfactions? Clearly they are not technically species of a genus for they are not mutually exclusive as are species of a single genus; I may be simultaneously satisfied by a single object aestheti-

cally, morally and economically, just as well as a man may be simultaneously bald, wealthy and a widower. But on the other hand to ask whether
a satisfaction is moral or aesthetic makes as good sense as to ask whether
a surface is square or triangular, whereas only in a very odd context can
one ask whether a man is bald or a widower; furthermore, if a satisfaction
is wholly moral it is not at all aesthetic; whereas being wholly bald does
not prevent a man from being a widower. Thus moral, aesthetic and economic satisfactions seem neither to be logically disconnected nor to be
true species of a genus.

Aesthetic and moral satisfactions thus seem to be related as are business
and sporting associates. A man may be both a business and a sporting
associate, yet the point of calling a man a business associate is to distinguish his status from that of a sporting or other type of associate, as it
does not distinguish him from, say, an associate first met at Yarmouth. In
the same way, to call a satisfaction aesthetic has the point of distinguishing its status from that of being a moral or economic satisfaction, though
a satisfaction may be both aesthetic and moral. It surely follows that the
criteria for a reaction's being aesthetic cannot be wholly unrelated to the
criteria for its being moral or economic—they must be connected in such
a way that we can see how being wholly one excludes being also another
and yet how a single reaction can be both moral and aesthetic.

If we find the criterion for distinguishing aesthetic from kindred reactions in the nature of the explanation of the reactions we can readily
account for this logical situation. To say that a satisfaction is wholly aesthetic, for example, will be to say that the explanation or grounds of the
satisfaction are wholly of one sort, which will necessitate that the satisfaction cannot rest also on moral grounds; on the other hand there is
clearly nothing to prevent our satisfaction from being multiply-grounded
and thus simultaneously aesthetic and moral, aesthetic and economic, and
so on.

But if we were to accept different kinds of criteria of the aesthetic, the
moral and the economic we should be in difficulties here. Thus if a philosopher were to hold (and some apparently do) that a moral judgment
is one that asserts an object to have a certain character and an aesthetic
judgment to be one that announces or expresses the special emotional
state of the speaker he would be maintaining views which, however plausible when consistently adhered to in isolation, are poor bed-fellows. For
one would expect a wholly moral judgment interpreted as ascribing a
moral character, to deny implicitly the presence of a special aesthetic or
special economic character; similarly a wholly aesthetic judgment, interpreted as expressing a special aesthetic emotion, should deny implicitly
the presence of a special moral or economic emotion. Consistency is required here.

So much for the logical point of being clear on the relation between
the aesthetic, the moral, the economic, etc. Unclarity on the point can

lead to other less philosophical confusions. Thus the belief that moral considerations are relevant to a thing's aesthetic rank seems to stem from an awareness that appreciation may be simultaneously based on aesthetic and moral considerations coupled with a blindness to the fact that to call an appreciation aesthetic has as part of its point the effect of ruling out the moral as irrelevant. At the opposite extreme those who rage at any moral comment on a work of art are so conscious that the moral is irrelevant to the aesthetic that they suppose some error in allowing one's general satisfaction to have both a moral and an aesthetic component.

I have illustrated sufficiently the dangers of considering aesthetic reactions and judgments in abstraction from moral, economic and other kindred reactions and judgments. Similarly we must not concentrate on aesthetic delight and neglect other aesthetic reactions. The view that delight is aesthetic when that emotion has some special aesthetic tinge is not unplausible in isolation; we can no doubt bring aesthetic disgust under the same theory easily enough. But what if I am asked for an aesthetic judgment on what seems to me a very ordinary building and I reply truthfully that I find it merely tolerable? Am I reporting an emotion of toleration which has an aesthetic tinge, or perhaps an absolute tinge with no emotion to be tinged? But if I be taken to report merely the absence of any emotion or tinge by what criterion can we say that I am making an aesthetic judgment at all? It is surely important that we should be able to distinguish an aesthetic judgment of toleration from merely refraining from any aesthetic judgment at all; to regard a thing with mere aesthetic toleration is quite different from not considering it in an aesthetic light at all.

Thus the view that what distinguishes the aesthetic reaction and judgment is the presence of a special emotion or a special emotional tinge has already proved unsatisfactory on two counts. First, we have seen that we require a similar type of criterion of the aesthetic, the moral, the intellectual and the economic reaction, whereas the emotional criterion is very unplausible in some of these cases. Secondly, we have seen that however plausible with regard to strong emotional reactions, the emotional view is most unplausible when we consider such cool aesthetic reactions as that of bare toleration. Even if these difficulties were overcome, it is perhaps worth noticing that on this view a single reaction which involved, say, simultaneous economic, moral, aesthetic and intellectual satisfaction might well be required to involve an emotion having a quite kaleidoscopic variety of tinges.

But apart from these more logical points it is surely clear that when we experience emotions that we should wish to call aesthetic they are often very different from each other. Thus Tovey (*Essays in Musical Analysis*, Vol. I, p. 200) speaks of a theme "which gives Mozart's most inimitable sense of physical well-being" precisely because most of even the most delightful musical themes are so different in emotional effect.

Or again, is it so clear that aesthetic emotions are different in kind from others? Tovey, we have seen, compares a Mozart theme to a quite non-aesthetic delight, and Housman can be adduced as a still more striking, since unwilling, witness. Enumerating three types of "symptoms" of poetical delight in his lecture, "The Name and Nature of Poetry," he says, "One of these symptoms was described in connexion with another object by Eliphaz the Temanite: 'A spirit passed before my face; the hair of my flesh stood up' "; another he describes by using Keats's words about his feelings for Fanny Brawne, "everything that reminds me of her goes through me like a spear"; the third, he says, "consists in a constriction of the throat and a precipitation of water to the eyes," an experience which is surely common to many emotional situations, and not confined to the aesthetic.

The objection to the view that what distinguishes the aesthetic judgment or reaction from others is that it alone involves the recognition or awareness of beauty and ugliness, if offered as a solution to our problem, is rather different. As a minor objection it is worth pointing out that we should hesitate to call many things for which we have a great aesthetic admiration "beautiful," that "beautiful" is a relatively specialised word of aesthetic appraisal, though this will inevitably elicit the answer that here "beauty" is being used with a wider meaning than is currently assigned to it. But granted that "beauty" and "ugliness" are being used with a wide enough significance, the trouble with this answer to our problem is not that it is false but that it is futile. Of course if I admire a thing aesthetically I must be aware of its beauty, or of its charm, or of its prettiness or some other "aesthetic characteristic"; this is true in the same way as it is platitudinously true that moral admiration must involve awareness of a thing's moral goodness or rectitude or of some other "moral characteristic." But the trouble is that we have no independent way of telling whether we are aware of beauty or ugliness on the one hand or rightness or wrongness on the other; to know this we must know whether our admiration is aesthetic or moral, or, more accurately, to try to discover whether our admiration is aesthetic or moral and to try to discover whether we are aware of beauty or rightness are not two distinct enquiries but a single enquiry described in two ways neither of which is more luminous than the other. To identify the aesthetic judgment by the aesthetic characters of which it involves awareness is therefore not helpful.

Let me now set out more generally and completely the view that I wish to urge. The terms, "good," "bad" and "indifferent" are, I take it, among the widest terms of appraisal that we possess, and we do appraise things on the basis of criteria, criteria to be formulated in terms of the "natural" features of the things appraised. But usually we wish at any time to appraise a thing only from a restricted point of view. We may, for instance, wish to appraise a career from the restricted point of view of its worth as a means of earning a livelihood; to do so we restrict our attention to a special set of the criteria of a good career, all others being for the purpose irrelevant. I wish to suggest that the moral, the aesthetic, the economic, the intellectual, the religious and other special appraisals should all be understood as being appraisals distinguished by their concentration on some special sub-set of criteria of value. To say that something is good as a means is not to say that it is good in some special sense distinct from that of "good as an end" but to appraise it from a special point of view; similarly to judge a thing aesthetically good or first-rate is not to call it good in a sense different from that in which we call a thing morally good, but to judge it in the light of a different sub-set of criteria. We may if we wish choose to invent a special meaning for "beautiful" in which it becomes shorthand for "good from the aesthetic point of view," but that is only a dubious convenience of no theoretical significance. The central task of the philosopher of aesthetics is, I take it, to clarify the principles on which we select the special set of criteria of value that are properly to be counted as relevant to aesthetic judgment or appraisal. We may recognise an aesthetic reaction by its being due to features of the thing contemplated that are relevant criteria of the aesthetic judgment, and the aesthetic judgment is one founded on a special sub-set of the criteria of value of a certain sort of thing.

It may justly be said that so far I have done little more than to assert this view dogmatically, though I should wish to claim that I have given it some *a priori* probability by showing that it is a view which will enable us to deal with some of the difficulties that other views cannot surmount. Certainly, I have as yet done nothing to indicate on what principles the criteria of value relevant to the aesthetic judgment are selected.

This lacuna can only be properly filled by field-work, and then only filled completely by a full-scale work on aesthetics. By doing field-work I mean studying examples of people actually trying to decide whether a certain judgment is or is not aesthetic and observing how they most convincingly argue the matter. Unfortunately to do this on an elaborate scale in one paper of a symposium is hardly possible; I can but ask you to believe that this paper has been written only after a considerable amount of such work, and produce one or two examples of it to show more clearly what I have in mind.

In his more philosophical moments A. E. Housman tried to account for the peculiar nature of the aesthetic in terms of emotional, and even physical, reactions; but here is an example of what he has to say at a more literary and less philosophical level: "Again, there existed in the last century a great body of Wordsworthians, as they were called. It is now much smaller; but true appreciation of Wordsworth's poetry has not diminished in proportion: I suspect that it has much increased. The Wordsworthians, as Matthew Arnold told them, were apt to praise their poet for the wrong things. They were most attracted by what may be called his philosophy;

they accepted his belief in the morality of the universe and the tendency of events to good; they were even willing to entertain his conception of nature as a living and sentient and benignant being; a conception as purely mythological as the Dryads and the Naiads. To that thrilling utterance which pierces the heart and brings tears to the eyes of thousands who care nothing for his opinions and beliefs they were not noticeably sensitive; and however justly they admired the depth of his insight into human nature and the nobility of his moral ideas, these things, with which his poetry was in close and harmonious alliance, are distinct from poetry itself."

It does not matter whether we agree with Housman about Wordsworth; but I do hope that all will agree that this is the right sort of way to set about showing that an appreciation is not aesthetic. Clearly Housman does not deny that what the nineteenth century admired in Wordsworth was admirable; but he says that if your admiration of Wordsworth is based on certain grounds (the philosophical truth and moral loftiness of the content of the poetry) it is not aesthetic admiration, whereas if it is based on what Housman calls the "thrilling utterance," by which the surrounding paragraphs abundantly show him to mean the sound, rhythm and imagery of the words used, then it is aesthetic admiration. Whether Housman is right about Wordsworth or not, whether he has selected the most important criteria of poetical merit or not, this is the type of argument to be expected in a competent discussion; but to have argued the case by adducing the claim that Wordsworthians tended to concentrate rather on traits other than beauty would in fact have been to have restated the case rather than to have argued it. Moreover, if some Wordsworthian had maintained that Wordsworth's pantheism did bring tears to his eyes it would clearly have made no difference to the argument; it is concentration on the utterance, rather than having tears in your eyes, that makes you truly appreciative of the poetry.

Housman's *The Name and Nature of Poetry* is a mine of similar examples. Though he says in a theoretical moment: "I am convinced that most readers, when they think that they are admiring poetry, are deceived by inability to analyse their sensations, and that they are really admiring, not the poetry of the passage before them, but something else in it, which they like better than poetry," in fact all the concrete examples are in accordance with my theory and not his own. Thus the later seventeenth century writers are said by Housman to have but rarely true poetic merit not on the basis of any analysis of sensations but because, for example, they aimed to startle by novelty and amuse by ingenuity whereas their verse is inharmonious.

If, then, Housman's practice is sound it vindicates my view and stultifies his; nor is the obvious fact that we would not rate highly poetry that did not move us, relevant to the question how we are to distinguish a high aesthetic rating from another type of high rating. If field work and reflection in general vindicate my contention as do these examples from Housman I cannot see what else can be relevant; but I freely own that it is the cumulative weight of a large collection of examples from a variety of fields that is necessary, and these I have not supplied; nor could we ever attain a strict proof.

But all this being granted we are still only on the periphery of our subject and the most difficult question remains to be dealt with. It is comparatively easy to see that there must be general principles of selection of evaluative criteria which determine whether our evaluation is to be counted as aesthetic, moral, intellectual or of some other kind; nor is it at all difficult to give examples of what anyone, who is prepared to accept this way of looking at the matter, can easily recognise as being a criterion falling under one or another principle. It would be a very odd person who denied that the sound of the words of a poem was one of the criteria of the aesthetic merit of a poem, or who maintained that being scientifically accurate and up to date was another; similarly it is clear that the honesty of a policy is a criterion of its moral goodness whereas, even if honesty is the best policy, honesty is not a direct criterion of economic merit. But it is by no means easy to formulate these general principles.

This difficulty is by no means peculiar to aesthetics. Part of the general view of which the aesthetic doctrine given here is a fragment is that what determines whether a judgment is moral is what reasons are relevant to it; but everyone knows the difficulty of answering the question what makes a judgment a moral judgment. (In my terminology Kant's answer would be that the reasons must refer to the rationality or otherwise of consistently acting in a certain way.) Certainly it would be over-optimistic to expect to find very precise principles; probably there will be some overlap of criteria between the various spheres of evaluation in anybody's practice; certainly there are some overt border-line disputes whether this or that criterion is relevant to, say, aesthetic evaluation.

I think, however, that there is one peculiar difficulty in trying to find the principle, however vague, that determines what sort of reasons are relevant to a judgment if it is to be counted as aesthetic. When we think of giving reasons for an aesthetic judgment we tend at once to call to mind what we would give as reasons for our appreciation of some very complex works of art; rightly considering, for example, that the plays of Shakespeare are things intended especially for consideration from the aesthetic point of view (I believe that a work of art can most usefully be considered as an artifact primarily intended for aesthetic consideration), we tend to think that we can most usefully tackle our problem by examining what would be relevant to an appreciation of, say, *Hamlet,* merely leaving aside obvious irrelevancies like cost of production. But this is most unfortunate, because, dealing with things intended primarily for aesthetic appreciation, we are inclined to treat as relevant to aesthetic appreciation very much more than we would in the case of things not so officially dedicated to aesthetic purposes; for practical purposes it would be pedantic to do otherwise. Moreover it is obviously very difficult to get straight our grounds for appreciating anything so complex. I am inclined to think that if *Hamlet* were rewritten to give the essential plot and characterisation in the jargon of the professional psychologist there could still be a lot to admire that we at present mention in our aesthetic appreciations, but we would no longer regard it as aesthetic appreciation but rather as intellectual appreciation of psychological penetration and the like.

For these and other reasons, it seems to me hopeless to start an enquiry into the nature of aesthetic grounds by concentrating our attention on great and complex works of art. Among other reasons is that in evaluating great works of art the reasons proximately given will almost inevitably already be at a high level of generality and themselves evaluative —we will refer to masterly style, subtle characterization, inevitability of the action and so on. If we are to have any hope of success we must first set our sights less high and commence with the simplest cases of aesthetic appreciation; in this paper, at least, I shall try to look no further.

If we examine, then, some very simple cases of aesthetic evaluation it seems to me that the grounds given are frequently the way the object appraised looks (shape and colour), the way it sounds, smells, tastes or feels. I may value a rose bush because it is hardy, prolific, disease-resistant and the like, but if I value the rose aesthetically the most obvious relevant grounds will be the way it looks, both in colour and in shape, and the way it smells; the same grounds may be a basis for aesthetic dislike. Though I might, for example, attempt to describe the shape to make you understand what I see in it these grounds seem to me to be really basic; if I admire a rose because of its scent and you then ask me why I admire its scent I should not in a normal context know what you want. These grounds are also those that we should expect to be basic in aesthetics from an etymological point of view, and while one can prove nothing philosophically from etymologies, etymological support is not to be despised. Things, then, may have sensible qualities which affect us favourably or unfavourably with no ulterior grounds. Surely there is no need to illustrate further these most simple cases of aesthetic evaluation.

But there are some slightly more sophisticated cases which need closer inspection. I have in mind occasions when we admire a building not only for its colour and shape but because it looks strong or spacious, or admire a horse because it looks swift as well as for its gleaming coat. These looks are not sensible qualities in the simple way in which colour and shape are. It is clear that in this sort of context to look strong or spacious or swift is not to seem very likely to be strong or spacious or swift. I might condemn a building for looking top-heavy when I knew very well it was built on principles and with materials which ensured effectively that it would not be top-heavy. It is no doubt a plausible speculation that if a building looks top-heavy in the sense relevant to aesthetics it would probably seem really to be top-heavy in the untutored eye; but if an architect, who knows technically that a building is not top-heavy, judges it to look top-heavy when he considers it aesthetically he is in no way estimating the chances of its being blown over.

We are now considering the facts which, exclusively emphasized, lead to the functional view of aesthetics. The element of truth in that view I take to be that if a thing looks to have a characteristic which is a desirable one from another point of view, its looking so is a proper ground of aesthetic appreciation. What makes the appreciation aesthetic is that it is concerned with a thing's looking somehow without concern for whether it really is like that; beauty we may say, to emphasize the point, is not even skin-deep.

We have, then, isolated two types of aesthetic criteria, both of which are cases of looking (sounding, *etc.*) somehow; in the simpler type it is the sensible qualities, in the narrowest sense, that are relevant; in the slightly more complex type it is looking to possess some quality which is non-aesthetically desirable that matters. We like our motor-cars in attractive tones and we like them to look fast (which does not involve peering under the bonnet) ; we like, perhaps, the timbre of a bird's note and we like it also for its cheerful or nobly mournful character, but would not be pleased if it sounded irritable or querulous; the smell of a flower may be seductive in itself but it will be better still if it is, say, a clean smell. Both these elementary types of criteria go hand in hand and are constantly employed.

The most obvious criticism of these suggestions is not that they are wrong but that they are incapable of extension to the more complicated situations in which we appraise a work of art. I cannot try now to deal with this sort of objection in any full way. But I should like to make two small points. First, I would repeat my suggestion that we are inclined to allow in non-aesthetic criteria "by courtesy" when we are evaluating a work of art, so that we may even include intellectual merit. Secondly, the fact that such things as intellectual understanding are essential to an aesthetic appreciation of a work of art does not in itself establish the criticism. If, for example, we enjoy listening to a fugue it is likely that a part of our appreciation will be intellectual; no doubt intellectual understanding of what is going on is also necessary to aesthetic appreciation; but the fact that I cannot enjoy the sound of a theme being continually employed, sometimes inverted or in augmentation or in diminution, unless I have the theoretical training to recognise this, does not prevent my aesthetic appreciation from being of the sound. I am still appreciating the way a thing sounds or looks even when my intellect must be employed if I am to be aware of the fact that the thing does look or sound this way.

There remain many difficulties; above all the notion of "looking in a certain way," especially in such cases as when we say something looks strong or swift, needs more elaboration. But to carry out this task is beyond the scope of this paper. Apart from a short appendix, I shall now close with a brief summary, a summary of a paper which is intended to do no more than to distinguish the aesthetic judgment and reaction from others and perhaps to indicate the best way in which to proceed to the further problems of the philosophy of aesthetics.

Summary

1. The problem raised is how an aesthetic judgment, reaction or evaluation is to be distinguished from others.

2. We should expect to find a criterion which allows us to distinguish the aesthetic, the moral, the economic, the intellectual and other evaluations by a single *fundamentum divisionis*.

3. All evaluations are made on the basis of criteria for the merit of the kind of thing in question.

4. An aesthetic evaluation is one which is made on the basis of a selection from the total body of relevant criteria of merit.

5. In at least the simpler cases of aesthetic evaluation the relevant criteria appear to be those which are concerned with the way the object in question looks or presents itself to the other senses.

6. It is impossible to distinguish the aesthetic by a special object, by a special characteristic attended to, or by a special emotion.

Appendix

It may appear to some that too little importance has been accorded to the emotions in this paper. To avoid misunderstanding I will mention one or two ways in which I recognise the importance of considering the emotions in aesthetics.

First, I recognise that we would be very little interested in the aesthetic aspect of things but for their emotional effect upon us.

Secondly, I acknowledge that if we experience an emotional thrill when we look at a picture or hear a piece of music we do not normally have to examine our grounds and reasons to know that we are reacting aesthetically in a favourable way. But I do want to maintain that it is the nature of the grounds that makes our appreciation aesthetic and that if on an examination of our grounds we find, as sometimes happens, that our reasons are appropriate rather to moral evaluation or are erotic, or what you will, we will, if we are honest, recognise that our reaction was not after all aesthetic. Of course we have trained ourselves to a great extent to approach pictures and music from the aesthetic angle so that we shall not in general be mistaken if we rely on an unanalysed impression.

Thirdly, there are a great number of terms that we use in aesthetic evaluation—*pleasant, moving, pretty, beautiful, impressive, admirable* and *exciting* among others. I do not know what makes one more appropriate than another in a given context; partly, perhaps, they are more or less laudatory, or are based on a still more restricted selection of criteria than a mere judgment of goodness or badness; but I suspect that the choice of word is at least in part determined by the precise character of the emotion experienced.

For these and other reasons I do not wish to belittle the importance of the emotions in the philosophy of aesthetics; but I do wish to deny most emphatically that the aesthetic field can be distinguished from others by an attempt to analyse the emotions involved therein: and that is all that the thesis of this paper requires.

PETER KIVY

Aesthetic Perception

The Doctrine of Aesthetic Vision

SINCE THE END OF THE EIGHTEENTH CENTURY, there has been a view widely held by thinkers of varying other persuasions that aesthetic perception is not ordinary perception of some special species of quality, but, rather, a special species of perception of ordinary qualities. This view, which has sometimes been called the doctrine of "aesthetic disinterestedness," had its beginnings at the outset of the eighteenth century—at the time, in fact, when aesthetics as we now think of it was first being practiced.[1] The crux of the doctrine is that what is distinctive about aesthetic perception arises from a particular attitude which we assume when we contemplate anything aesthetically.

The many convolutions of the doctrine as it passed through eighteenth-century British psychology and nineteenth-century German metaphysics led always away from the "reality" of the perceptual object. Early in the eighteenth century Francis Hutcheson emphasized the irrelevance, even the necessary absence of self-interest in the aesthetic attitude. The "Pleasure of Beauty," he wrote, ". . . is distinct from that Joy which arises from Self-love upon prospect of Advantage."[2] From the notion that aesthetic contemplation ignores the personal utility of the object contemplated comes the related notion that the aesthetic attitude is one of complete indifference to *possession* of the object. For what one need not use "upon prospect of Advantage," one need not bring home and lock away. And it is this aspect of aesthetic contemplation that Edmund Burke dwelt upon at mid-century:

> By beauty I mean, that quality or those qualities in bodies by which they cause love, or some passion similar to it. . . . I likewise distinguish love, by which I mean that satisfaction which arises to the mind upon contemplating anything beautiful, of whatsoever nature it may be, from desire

or lust; which is an energy of the mind, that hurries us on to the *possession* of certain objects that do not affect us as they are beautiful, but by means altogether different.[3]

Utility, and desire for the possession of the object having been declared irrelevant to the aesthetic attitude, it is but a step to the Kantian dictum that in aesthetic contemplation the *actual existence* of the object is a matter of complete indifference. Thus:

> The delight which we connect with the representation of the real existence of an object is called interest. . . . Now where the question is whether something is beautiful, we do not want to know, whether we, or any one else, are, or even could be, concerned in the real existence of the thing, but rather what estimate we form of it on mere contemplation (intuition or reflection).[4]

We need trace the doctrine no further to extract the general argument with which we must deal; all of the necessary materials are in Kant's formulation. Kant, of course, like Hutcheson and Burke, is speaking here only of the beautiful. But if we generalize for aesthetic perception as a whole, we see that the reality of the object of aesthetic perception suffers the same fate: complete irrelevance. Hence it follows that when we describe an object aesthetically, our description need not be accurate: the object need not actually exist as described or indeed exist at all. When we describe an object aesthetically, we will describe it as *p, q,* and *r* if it appears *p, q,* and *r,* whether or not it is *p, q,* and *r* at all, or whether there is even an object appearing. In other words, it is sufficient for something being aesthetically *p, q,* and *r* that I am having *p*-ish, *q*-ish, and *r*-ish perceptions. So the distinction between being or only seeming aesthetically *p, q,* and *r* cannot arise; for something will be aesthetically *p, q,* and *r* when there are *p*-ish, *q*-ish, and *r*-ish appearances, irrespective of whether anything is *p, q,* and *r* at all. And if this is the case, then the condition-governed model of aesthetic terms cannot be correct: for one of its consequences is that it does indeed make sense to distinguish in an aesthetic description between being *p, q,* and *r,* and only appearing *p, q,* and *r.* If, therefore, we are to sustain the condition-governed model, we must dispatch, or at least disarm this well-entrenched adversary. And as the purpose here is not historical, it will be well to tangle rather with a contemporary embodiment, the most recent and most interesting being that of Vincent Tomas in a widely discussed article called "Aesthetic Vision."[5]

It is Tomas' aim to formulate a distinction between "ordinary vision" and "aesthetic vision," between seeing things in "the common way" and seeing things aesthetically. Roughly, the distinction is as follows:

> (1) When we see things in "the common way," our attention is directed toward the stimulus objects that appear to us, or toward what they signify,

and we do not particularly notice the ways in which these objects appear. . . .

(2) When we see things aesthetically, our attention is directed toward appearances, and we do not particularly notice the thing that presents the appearance, nor do we care what, if anything, it is that appears.[6]

Tomas illustrates the distinction with numerous examples, not, one suspects, all really illustrative of the same distinction, but one of which, at least for our purposes, can be taken as about typical.

Commonly, when we see a penny, we are about to pay a bill or count our change, and it makes no difference to us how the penny looks . . . our attention is directed toward the stimulus object—as it "really is"—not toward its appearance. . . . And if, for some reason, we are then asked, "How did it look?" we would probably reply, "Why—like a penny." But a penny may look dull or look shiny. Under some conditions it will look round, and under most conditions it will look elliptical. . . . The reply, "It looks like a penny," is an indication that the penny was seen in the common way—that the perceiver did not notice the way the penny looked.[7]

The key concepts here, fraught with long-standing difficulties, are "appearance" and "stimulus object," which Tomas elsewhere calls "phenomenological object" and "ontological object."[8] It would be well to consider briefly the manner in which these troublesome notions are put forward in the present instance. We are asked to entertain the following "experiment in the imagination".

It is the seventeenth century and we are somewhere in the Vatican, in a room where there are also two other men, a picture, and a mirror. One of the men is Velasquez and the other is Pope Innocent X. The picture is the one referred to in art catalogues as *Pope Innocent X* (National Gallery Gallery of Art, Washington). The visual apparatus of each man, the lighting conditions, and everything else are "normal."[9]

Consider now these six cases:

(1) Velasquez looks at the Pope and we say "He sees a man."
(2) Velasquez looks at *Pope Innocent X* and we say "He sees a picture."
(3) Velasquez looks at the Pope's reflection in the mirror and we say "He sees a mirror."
(4) Velasquez looks at the Pope and he says "I see a man."
(5) Velasquez looks at *Pope Innocent X* and he says "I see a man."
(6) Velasquez looks at the Pope's reflection in the mirror and he says "I see a man."

On the undoubtedly true assumption that our descriptions in (1), (2), and (3) of what Velasquez saw are correct, Velasquez' description of what he saw in (5) and (6) would seem to be incorrect. For in (5) Velasquez did not see a man at all but a picture; and in (6) he did not see a man either but a reflection in a mirror. But (5) and (6) are not incorrect if we assume Velasquez to be describing what Tomas calls the "ontological" or "stimulus object": "if he was describing not the picture but a way in which the picture appeared to him, his description, so far as it went, was not inaccurate and need not be misleading."[10] Because "In principle, the appearance of a man and the appearance of a portrait of a man could be identical, in which case the accurate descriptions of each appearance would be identical." (The same argument, of course, applies *pari passu* to the reflection in the mirror.)

What Tomas means by an "ontological" or "stimulus object," then, is an "object" of the kind we refer to when we say that Velasquez sees a man in (1), that Velasquez sees a picture in (2), and that Velasquez sees a mirror in (3); and what Tomas means by "appearance" or "phenomenological object" is what Velasquez refers to in (5) and (6) when he says that he sees a man. And in this sense of "appearance," Tomas concludes that "In every case of aesthetic vision, what is attended to is an appearance, and the question of what actual object—a picture, a mirror, or a man—presents that appearance does not arise."[11] In other words, "the question of reality does not arise in *any* case of aesthetic vision. . . ."

Animadversions on the "Doctrine"

Tomas' position has been very capably criticized in recent years by Frank Sibley and by Marshall Cohen in a symposium devoted to the aesthetic relevance of the being-seeming distinction.[12] Sibley was prepared to defend a rather drastic revision of Tomas' position whereas Cohen rejected it almost entirely. I have studied both with great profit, and have been influenced by many of their examples. However, I intend to take a rather different tack here; and although I want to acknowledge my debt, I do not want to suggest that either Sibley or Cohen would agree with what I am about to say.

There is, to begin with, very good reason to doubt that in all aesthetic perception we are always attending to what Tomas calls the "appearance" and never to the "stimulus object," assuming we can really make the distinction clear. So if it were indeed the case that all aesthetic seeing is as Tomas describes it, there would remain a vast territory of aesthetic perception in which his strictures would not apply and in which there would be no reason to doubt the relevance of the seems-is distinction. With regard to aesthetic seeing there may be some prima facie plausibility to Tomas' analysis; but with aesthetic hearing one already begins to squirm, and at (say) the experience of reading *David Copperfield,* the mind boggles. In what sense am I attending to an "appearance" when listening to a symphony and a "stimulus object" when a fire engine goes by? Whatever I hear, it is the same kind of thing in both cases, and I am at a loss really whether to call it "appearance" or "stimulus object." But I certainly know how to describe what I hear: a siren, concert A, the screech of tires, an oboe, a bell, a diminished seventh. Which is the "appearance" and which the "stimulus object"?

Thus Tomas' argument gives us no reason to believe that the being-appearing distinction is irrelevant anywhere but in visual aesthetic perception (which is, indeed, the only kind he claims to examine). But does it lend support to the contention even here? I want to grant, for the sake of argument, that in every case of aesthetic vision, that is, of aesthetic seeing, we are, as Tomas maintains, attending to the "appearance," never the "stimulus object." I want to argue that even so it is false that "the question of reality does not arise in *any* case of aesthetic vision." There is, it seems to me, a kind of Platonic fallacy at work here which is worth ferreting out.

Once it was fashionable for scientists to give popular lectures in which they revealed that a piece of wood only appears solid but really is made up of a great many tiny particles, in violent motion, and a great deal of "empty space." The line that Wittgenstein, and others, have taken with regard to this rather perplexing statement of the scientist is to claim he is misusing language—misusing the distinction between being solid and only appearing so. Wittgenstein says in the *Blue Book*:

> We have been told by popular scientists that the floor on which we stand is not solid, as it appears to common sense, as it has been discovered that the wood consists of particles filling space so thinly that it can almost be called empty. This is liable to perplex us, for in a way of course we know that the floor is solid, or that, if it isn't solid, this may be due to the wood being rotten but not to its being composed of electrons. To say, on this latter ground, that the floor is not solid is to misuse language.[13]

The term "real" does not take some ultimate Platonic object which the scientist has grasped and the rest of us have not. We do not have to wait for the physicist's final word on the ultimate constituents of matter before we determine that the piece of wood we are contemplating is really solid. Oak is solid; balsa wood and rotten logs look solid enough but really are not. And we all know how to find out which is what.

What makes the physicist's statement so seductively plausible in its implausibility? Partly it is the mistaken Platonic conviction which many of us consciously or unconsciously share with the physicist that the word "real" has its meaning in virtue of reference to some hidden reality which we have gradually been getting closer to and which the physicist has at long last started from its lair. But that is not all: it is partly, too, that the physicist has behaved in a way quite like in some respects the way we behave when we make the determination "really is" or "only appears." The distinction between appearance and reality in ordinary usage is spelled out by familiar sets of routines: by operations commonly accepted. To find out if the wood is really solid or only appears so we kick it, or push it, or scrutinize it: we do something to it. To find out if a swatch of fabric is one color or another we compare it to something, or bring it out into the daylight, or hold it at a different angle: we go through some accepted routine. The physicist too, when he discovers that the wood is not really solid but a conjury of particles and spaces, goes through a routine: a particularly elaborate and fantastically sophisticated one; and *there* is where the trouble lies. For having gone through his routine as we have gone through ours, we feel that he has fulfilled the requirements which license one to conclude "only seems, really isn't." But not every routine will do. The ordinary meaning of "really solid" is limned in by a range of routines and operations to which the physicist's does not belong. This range is, one supposes, in some state of flux, and, no doubt, science has contributed to it over the centuries. However, until such time as this range expands to accommodate the procedures whereby the atomic physicist determines that the wood really isn't solid, he is indeed, as Wittgenstein says, misusing language, although he is misusing it in a way that is forever putting snares at our feet because of its parallel with ordinary linguistic usage.

Tomas makes the scientist's mistake of assuming that "real" does indeed name some ultimate object: in his case the "stimulus object." If he were correct, then anyone who is not dealing with the "stimulus object" cannot be dealing with the "real" but only the "appearance," and hence the question of reality cannot arise for him. But this is simply not the case. There are contexts in which the real is indeed the "stimulus object." There are, however, contexts in which the real is something else again, as in the following example. Suppose we are looking at a picture of a dress in the rotogravure section of the Sunday paper. I claim that the dress is fuchsia and you claim that it is violet, and we both agree on settling the matter through the commonly accepted routine of taking the picture out of doors and looking at it in direct sunlight. We do so and decide that it "really is" violet although it "looks" fuchsia in artificial light. But now along comes a third party who knows a little bit about printing and says: "You are both mistaken; the picture is neither fuchsia *nor* violet. It *looks* fuchsia in artificial light and violet in sunlight, if you scan it at a distance of a few inches; but if you examine it very closely you will see that it is *really* a mass of red and blue dots." Now you and I were truly discussing whether the dress is fuchsia or violet; but neither of us was talking about what Tomas calls the "stimulus object." We were talking about whether what Tomas calls the "appearance" really is fuchsia, or only appears so. And we settled the argument in a perfectly straightforward way without ever talking about the "stimulus object." It was only the third party, the printing expert, who was using "real" to refer to the "stimulus object" and "only seems" to refer to the "appearance," although he too made his determination through a common routine: "looking closely." Further, you and I and the third party were all using "really is" and "only seems" quite correctly; you and I were correct in concluding that the dress "really is" violet, and the third party was also correct when he concluded that the picture is neither fuchsia nor violet but "really" red and blue.

When the context and "routine" are such that the real is taken to be what Tomas calls the "stimulus object," then the dress cannot possibly be "really" fuchsia *or* violet; but in another context, and relative to another "routine," we may ask if the dress "really is" violet, and the answer may truthfully be "Yes." For the "stimulus object" is not the only "reality," the printer's scrutiny not the only "routine." Thus, even if the aesthetic object in aesthetic vision were never the "stimulus object" but always the "appearance," this would not *of itself* preclude our distinguishing in the aesthetic object between "really being" and "only appearing"; it would not *of itself* make the question of reality irrelevant.

However, this is not the whole story. For it may very well be sometimes true that the distinction between "really is" and "only appears" is indeed irrelevant in a given context or from a certain point of view. Attending to the "appearance" rather than the "stimulus object," I have argued, does not render the distinction irrelevant. But there are other conditions, perhaps, that might. So it might be argued that these conditions—whatever they may be—always obtain when we are contemplating something aesthetically. The best way to deal with this argument, I think, is to find some context (not necessarily aesthetic) in which the distinction between being and appearing *is* irrelevant. For as it stands, the claim is a vague one and requires exemplification. Having done this, we can ask ourselves whether this context—and its relevant conditions—characterize all aesthetic preception.

Consider the old dispute about whether or not the pitcher's "curve ball" really curves or only appears to. Suppose it were determined by means of some photographic apparatus or other that Dizzy's curve ball really does curve but that Daffy's doesn't, being only an extremely convincing optical illusion. Suppose further that even after all of the batters are convinced by the photographic evidence, when Daffy throws his "curve ball" to the batter at the plate it still appears to the batter to curve, and no matter how he fights against them, his reflexes always react as if it really does curve, forcing him to swing where it isn't. From the batter's point of view Daffy's curve looks exactly like Dizzy's and is just as hard to hit, no matter how much the batter squints or tells himself "It doesn't really curve at all." Surely we could say that from the batter's point of view, the distinction between appearance and reality—between seeming to curve and really curving—is irrelevant. Dizzy can hardly ask for a higher salary than Daffy because his curve ball "really curves" and Daffy's does not—nor can the batters take any consolation in it. So here is a case in which from a certain point of view it is quite irrelevant whether something appears so-and-so or really is.

Is this the kind of situation we are *always* in when we contemplate things from the aesthetic point of view? It may very well be that it is sometimes irrelevant from the aesthetic point of view whether an object appears *p* or really is *p*. That there is no need to contest. But is it *always* irrelevant, from the aesthetic point of view? Of course knowing exactly *what the* aesthetic point of view is would, we justifiably feel, help considerably in answering this question. The trouble is, as we have seen, that the question "What is the aesthetic point of view?" often has had as its answer "The point of view from which it is irrelevant whether X is *p* or only appears *p*." So the thesis that the being-appearing distinction is always irrelevant in aesthetic perception becomes true by virtue of the irrelevance of the distinction becoming the defining property of aesthetic perception. Yet, without essaying our own answer to this much-vexed (and perhaps over-worked) question "What is the aesthetic point of view?" we can certainly point out that there seem to be cases in which we would (intuitively, at least) want to say: "Here is an instance of the aesthetic point of view in which the being-appearing distinction is relevant."

Let me illustrate with one kind of example where the distinction between being and appearing seems to play an essential role in an aesthetic context. The example is provided by Joshua Reynolds in the fourteenth of the *Discourses*:

> it is certain that all those odd scratches and marks, which, on close ex-amination, are so observable in Gainsborough's pictures, and which even to experienced painters appear rather the effect of accident than design: this chaos, this uncouth and shapeless appearance, by a kind of magic, at a certain distance assumes form, and all the parts seem to drop into their proper places, so that we can hardly refuse acknowledging the full effect of diligence, under the appearance of chance and hasty negligence. That Gainsborough himself considered this peculiarity in his manner, and the power it possesses of exciting surprise, as a beauty in his works, I think may be inferred from the eager desire which we know he always expressed, that his pictures, at Exhibition, should be seen near, as well as at a dis-ance.[14]

Notice that Reynolds distinguishes between appearance and reality here in what we might think of as a reversal of Tomas' usage. For it is "the odd scratches and marks" which, one would think, are Tomas' "stimulus object," and *they* are Reynold's "appearance," "this uncouth and shape-less appearance," whereas the "reality" is Tomas' "appearance," which only emerges at a distance, where "all the parts drop into their proper places, so that we can hardly refuse acknowledging the full effect of diligence, under the appearance of chance and hasty negligence." Or, to use Tomas' alternate terminology, the "ontological object" is Tomas' reality and Reynold's appearance, the "phenomenological object" Tomas' appearance and Reynold's reality. We have, then, not only a case in which the being-appearing distinction is aesthetically relevant, but a case in which the term "real" has reference to what Tomas would claim it cannot refer—the latter circumstance perhaps indicating what a slippery pair of customers "appearance" and "reality" really are.

But let us now turn Reynolds upside down and conform ourselves to Tomas' terminology. For certainly there are a great many features that will "drop into their places" when we step back from a Gainsborough and that we might want to call "appearances" which the "stimulus object" ("those odd scratches and marks") presents: a mass of red and yellow scratches will become a smooth orange patch, aesthetic qualities such as "tension," "delicacy," "balance," and the rest, will emerge. We can thus say that the Gainsborough, from a certain distance, appears p, q, and r, where p, q, and r are a mixed bag of aesthetic and nonaesthetic qualities, but that when we examine the picture closely we find that it is not p, q, or r at all. Not only is this a perfectly correct way of using "is" and "appears," it is a vital part of the way we describe the Gainsborough aesthetically. It is not the case that all we are interested in here is how the Gainsborough appears from the viewing distance at which p, q, and r jump into place; we are interested too in the fact that it really isn't p, q, or r at all but only a collection of "scratches." Part of our aesthetic experience, of course, involves perceiving p, q, and r, but part of it too involves closer scrutiny of Gainsborough's jagged brush-strokes: "what we enjoy," writes E. H. Gombrich, "is not so much seeing these works from a distance as the very act of stepping back, as it were, and watching our imagination come into play, transforming the medley of color into a finished image."[15] This is a description of an aesthetic experience. Unlike the batter's point of view, the aesthetic point of view in this experience is not confined to a certain circumscribed place. Our aesthetic vantage point, in contemplating the Gainsborough, is not restricted to the viewing distance at which the "medley of colors" transforms itself into the "finished image." We are meant to step closer to a Gainsborough, just as we are meant to walk around a Rodin.

Consider, though, the following comment: "Those little colored scratches of the Gainsborough only appear to be solid little masses of color; if you look at them under a microscope you will see that they are *really* bits of pigment imbedded in drab blobs of linseed oil." The critic might here reply: "We are not interested, when we contemplate the Gainsborough aesthetically, in what the scratches really are—only in how they appear." So, it might be argued, when we view the Gainsborough from one foot away, and then from fifteen, we are not seeing first how things are and then how they appear; we are seeing how they appear from one foot away and how they appear from fifteen; only the microscope reveals what *really* is, and *that* is aesthetically irrelevant. Thus (the argument continues) we *are* only attending, in aesthetic contemplation, to how the Gainsborough appears, not what it really is.

How we reply to this argument depends upon whether or not we want to accept unchallenged the statement that the scratches of the Gainsborough only appear solid but (under the microscope) are revealed really to be grey blobs with color-flecks. Is this statement like the physicist's—that the wood really isn't solid but tiny particles and a lot of space? If so, then we can reply simply: it is a misuse of language and hence false to say that the scratches are not really solid masses of color. But if we want to accept the statement at face value, we must concede that there is nothing wrong with representing matters in this way. We must insist, however, that it is not the only correct way of representing them. What we see through the microscope has no monopoly on reality here: to claim that would be to commit the Platonic fallacy of thinking the "real" is some special object. There may be nothing wrong in saying that the Gainsborough appears *p, q,* and *r* from fifteen feet away, appears a medley of scratches from one foot away, and really is a collection of bits of pigment imbedded in grey linseed oil. But there is nothing wrong, either, in the critic saying that the Gainsborough appears *p, q,* and *r* from fifteen feet away, but when you get up close you discover that it really is a medley of color scratches. That this latter description is equally correct is adequate for the present purposes.

What might the upholder of "aesthetic vision" reply? Suppose that he insists the "aesthetic point of view" is only the point of view from which the Gainsborough *appears p, q,* and *r.* In a way, the phrase "aesthetic point of view," taken quite literally, suggests a certain place. And what is *the* aesthetic point of view—*the* specific place from which we view the Gainsborough aesthetically? (The batter's point of view, after all, is specifically given to be a marked off square in which he must stand.) It cannot be *both* fifteen feet away and one foot away if there is only *one* aesthetic point of view *literally.* Well, if it must be one or the other, what more reasonable conclusion than that the aesthetic point of view is the point fifteen feet from the picture where everything "falls into place," where the picture appears *p, q,* and *r?*

First, I think, we must resist taking the phrase "aesthetic point of view" literally. Second, we must ask why we should place the aesthetic point of view where the upholder of the doctrine of aesthetic vision would wish us to place it. If we insist that the aesthetic point of view must be the point of view from which the painting appears *p, q,* and *r,* then it merely becomes true by fiat—by stipulative definition—that from the aesthetic point of view only the appearance is attended to. But is the philosopher to legislate the aesthetic point of view solely for the protection of his pet theory? Gainsborough, Reynolds tells us, expressed "the eager desire that his pictures, at Exhibition, should be seen near, as well as at a distance." Was Gainsborough *not,* then, expressing his wishes as to the aesthetic point of view his viewers should take? Is there a better way of describing what Gainsborough was expressing than to say that he was expressing his views about the aesthetic point of view proper to his pictures? If we give up this way of describing it, we should have compelling reasons for doing so; for if "aesthetic point of view" has any ordinary linguistic use at all, outside of aesthetic theories, here is that use—to characterize the way a painter thinks his pictures should be looked at.

If then, we substitute "aesthetic attitude" (say) for "aesthetic point of view," or if we take "aesthetic point of view" in other than a strictly literal sense, we can safely say that the aesthetic attitude, or aesthetic point of view, whatever else it may be, is an attitude or point of view which includes seeing the Gainsborough close up, far away, stepping back, and, in Gombrich's words "watching our imagination come into play, transforming the medley of color into a finished image." The aesthetic point of view is not one vantage point—like the batter's point of view, or a seat on the fifty-yard line. I may be taking the aesthetic point of view all the while I am walking forward and back, looking at the Gainsborough now from here, now from there. And from this complex "point of view" the distinction between what is and what appears is very relevant indeed.

There is, to be sure, a good deal more to the question than can be illustrated with this single example. It might rather be the subject of another book. For the present one, however, we must let the matter drop with the tentative conclusion that the irrelevance of the being-appearing distinction in *all* aesthetic contexts is, at least, very doubtful, and therefore must be given a Scotch verdict. . . .

Aspects or Qualities?

Since quite early in the eighteenth century, perhaps even before, judgments of the form "X is beautiful" have seemed to many to occupy some kind of middle-ground between the "objective" and the "subjective"— the defensible and the merely idiosyncratic. One of its most interesting and little commented upon expressions occurs in Francis Hutcheson's first *Inquiry* (1725) where he writes in one place:

by *Absolute* or *Original* Beauty, is not understood any Quality suppos'd to be in the Object, which should of itself be beautiful, without relation to any Mind which perceives it: For Beauty, like other Names of sensible Ideas, properly denotes the *Perception* of some Mind; so *Cold, Hot, Sweet, Bitter*, denote the Sensations in our Minds, to which perhaps there is no resemblance in the Objects, which excite these Ideas in us, however we generally imagine that there is something in the Object just like our Perception. The Ideas of Beauty and Harmony being excited upon our *Perception* of some *primary Quality*, and having relation to *Figure* and *Time*, may indeed have a nearer resemblance to Objects, than these Sensations, which seem not so much any *Pictures* of Objects, as *Modifica-*

tions of the perceiving Mind; and yet were there no mind with a *Sense* of Beauty to contemplate Objects, I see not how they could be call'd beautiful.[16]

Couched in terms of a derivative Lockean empiricism, we have here recognition on Hutcheson's part that there is something peculiarly "between the cracks" about judgments of the beautiful. The notorious "resemblance" theory of perception, which Locke's immediate followers and critics extracted, perhaps mistakenly, from the *Essay Concerning Human Understanding,* had it that such "sensations" as those of coldness, hotness, bitterness, sweetness, were mental entities taken (wrongly) as pictures or representations of qualities in the external world; whereas such "sensations" as those of shape, motion, and so on—the so-called "primary qualities"—*were* indeed "resemblances" of external qualities. If "X is square" be taken, then, as the paradigm case of an "objective" judgment, and "X is bitter" of a subjective one, what are we to say of a judgment that predicates p of X, where p names a "sensation" which bears "a nearer resemblance" to an external quality than the sensations of bitterness or sweetness do, but nevertheless names only a sensation— "properly denotes the *Perception* of some Mind"—just as "bitter" and "sweet"? It cannot be an "objective" judgment; for then p would name something in addition to a sensation, that is, a quality which the appropriate sensation resembles. Nor can it be a "subjective" judgment either; for then there could not be that "near" resemblance of the sensation to the quality: there could be no resemblance at all. Thus, albeit in an awkward theory, Hutcheson has expressed what to a host of aestheticians since has been an important truth about aesthetic value judgment: that it wavers between the subjective and the objective.[17]

It is this kind of hermaphroditic existence that has also seemed to many to characterize the terms we use to describe (rather than evaluate) works of art. And that, I suspect, is one of the reasons why the phenomenon known as "aspect-perceiving" has figured so prominently in recent discussions of aesthetic perception. I shall begin, where such discussions usually do, with a picture called the "Duck-Rabbit," which Wittgenstein was mainly responsible for projecting into philosophy in general, and, indirectly, into aesthetics in particular.

The figure can be "seen as" either a duck's or a rabbit's head.
Consider now, the following three "disagreements":

(1) Mr. A says the artichoke is bitter and Mr. B says it is sweet.
(2) Mr. A says the rose is red and Mr. B says it is blue.
(3) Mr. A says "It's a duck" and Mr. B says "It's a rabbit."

It would seem that (3) falls somewhere between (1) and (2). For (3) is something like (1) in that the figure is both a duck and a rabbit, duck to Mr. A, rabbit to Mr. B, as the artichoke is both bitter and sweet, bitter to Mr. A and sweet to Mr. B; whereas it is unlike (2) in that the rose is not—cannot be—both red and blue. And (3) is, on the other hand, something like (2) and unlike (1) in that we feel being duck-like or rabbit-like are somehow "qualities" of the "object," as red or blue might be: that Mr. A and Mr. B are perceiving a different quality "in" the "object" when Mr. A sees it as a duck and Mr. B sees it as a rabbit; whereas they are not when the artichoke tastes bitter to Mr. A and sweet to Mr. B. Aspect-perceiving, if we mean by it the kind of thing the Duck-Rabbit represents, seems somehow to mediate between the subjective and the objective—much as Hutcheson conceived of the aesthetic value judgment —"between the cracks." Or, as Wittgenstein characteristically puts the matter: " 'But this isn't seeing!'—'But this is seeing!'—It must be possible to give both remarks a conceptual justification." . . .[18]

Aspect-Perceiving and Aesthetic Perceiving

We spoke in the chapter preceding of a long-standing program in aesthetics, namely, the attempt to understand aesthetic perceiving not as ordinary perceiving of extraordinary qualities but, rather, as a special way of perceiving ordinary qualities. That program is being perpetuated still in the recent attempts to construe aesthetic perceiving as aspect-perceiving. There has been more than one such attempt: the thing is definitely in the air. It would be impossible, within the confines of the present study, however, to canvas the field. I shall therefore concentrate on one formulation of the view, that of B. R. Tilghman in a recent essay called "Aesthetic Perception and the Problem of the 'Aesthetic Object'." This places a severe but, I am afraid, a necessary . . . limitation on my argument here. Establishing that one particular view of aesthetic aspect-perceiving is mistaken will not establish that all such views are mistaken. . . . All that I can hope to do here is cast some doubt on the view that aesthetic perceiving is aspect-perceiving by refuting the view in one of its formulations. . . .

Tilghman takes his departure, as I have, from Wittgenstein's discussion of the Duck-Rabbit. And he points out, as Wittgenstein did, that when we have come to see the ambiguous nature of the figure, we have come to see something in quite a different way than a person who as yet only sees "a duck" or "a rabbit." To begin with, a person who only sees "a duck," or "a rabbit," would not think of saying "I am seeing it *as* a duck," or "I am seeing it *as* a rabbit": only, "It's a duck," or "It's a rabbit." "It would make no sense for the man who had seen only the rabbit-aspect to say 'I am seeing it as a rabbit.' " But when one comes to see both the duck- and the rabbit-aspect of the Duck-Rabbit,

> he may also realize that in both instances he was seeing the same object and that in reality the figure is neither a duck nor a rabbit, but a duck-rabbit that can be seen now as the one and now as the other. He may even notice the change taking place, as it were, before his eyes and he can say "Now it is a duck and now it is a rabbit."[19]

What are the significant characteristics of this new way of seeing not just a duck or a rabbit but a duck-rabbit, now *as* a duck, now *as* a rabbit? Tilghman writes:

> I take it that to report a perception is to report that an object of a certain sort is seen. Thus, I report seeing a rabbit-figure, the duck-rabbit figure, or, not being aware of the visually ambiguous character of the duck-rabbit, that I see another rabbit-figure. But when I notice the ambiguous character of the duck-rabbit and see it now as a duck and then as a rabbit and say "Now it's a rabbit" I am not reporting a perception. That is, I am not reporting that I am seeing a different object. The object remains the same, I see it is the same and has not changed, but yet I see it in a different way.[20]

Thus, when we have come to see the Duck-Rabbit now as a duck, now as a rabbit, we have come to see "something" which changes and yet does not change. Were we reporting a "perception" when we said first "Now it's a duck," and then "Now it's a rabbit," we would be reporting that something had changed from a duck into a rabbit (or a duck had been replaced by a rabbit). But when we report "Now I see it as a duck," and then "Now I see it as a rabbit," we are clearly not reporting a change in the figure: "it is a report that I have seen the object in a new way."

Seeing now the duck, now the rabbit, requires, of couse, that one have a normally functioning perceptual apparatus; but it requires too achieving a certain technique: a perceptual skill of a distinctive sort. "The logic of seeing-as necessarily involves the notion of the mastery of techniques in addition to any possibly necessary physiological conditions."[21] One must, to begin with, be acquainted with ducks and rabbits—which, to be sure, is a prerequisite also for recognizing non-ambiguous pictures of ducks and rabbits. Beyond that, though, "Seeing the figure as a duck involves the ability to do such things as describe the figure as one would a real duck, e.g., point out the relevant features of the head, show which way it is looking, etc.; match the figure with a picture of a real duck, and the like."[22] The same kind of ability is involved, of course, in seeing the figure as a rabbit. And, one presumes, being able to see the figure as a duck *or* a rabbit requires both the duck-skills, the rabbit-skills, as well as the achievement of seeing the figure now as one, now as the other—an achievement which cannot simply be the sum of the other two.

At this point Tilghman is prepared to apply the notion of aspect-perceiving to aesthetic perception. But before we follow him in this it would be well to pause for a moment and meditate on the strategy that must be employed in taking the step from the Duck-Rabbit to the work of art.

J. L. Austin has pointed out that there are many ways of describing "seeing" in ordinary language, "different ways of saying what is seen," which can be described too in terms of "seeing as."[23] Thus, to say that aesthetic perception is a case of "seeing as" may be to say nothing more than that aesthetic perception is a case of perception, since "seeing as" may simply be another way to describe perfectly ordinary ways of perceiving. In order for the statement "Aethetic perception is a case of 'seeing as'" to be made informative and non-trivial, we must unpack the notion of "seeing as" embodied in it. There is nothing trivial in the statement "Seeing the Duck-Rabbit now as a duck, now as a rabbit, is a case of 'seeing as.'" But that is because one has spelled out how this particular kind of "seeing as" differs from ordinary seeing. The same must be done for the former statement; and this, as we shall see, leads to difficulties.

The transition from perceiving the Duck-Rabbit to perceiving a work of art aesthetically is made by Tilghman with the following example.

> Imagine someone looking at the shop drawings of a piece of machinery To a layman or an engineer unfamiliar with that particular mechanism the drawings might appear to be a confused jumble of lines. The trained engineer, however, may come to see the drawing as a certain piece of machinery. The lines now fall into their proper relationships and he recognizes the various parts of the mechanism and how they fit together.[24]

Perceiving a painting, for example, like perceiving the blueprint, is a case of either seeing or not seeing things "fall into their proper relationships"; seeing or not seeing "how they fit together." To see things "in their proper place," to see "how they fit together" in a painting is to see the painting aesthetically. "When we appreciate a painting we come to see the elements of line, shape, and colour as hanging together in a coherent design and we come to see the human and emotional significance of the scenes represented." Thus we now have our required analysis of aesthetic "seeing as": it is a kind of *appreciation* in which we perceive things as hanging together, as coherent; and we see "human and emotional significance."

Now there are, it seems to me, two very obvious and fatal kinds of counterexample that can be adduced here. First, let us imagine someone listening rather dreamily, and perhaps not too intently, to the lilting and seductive strains of Weber's *Invitation to the Dance*. He seems to be having a pleasant enough experience. But along comes a musician to disturb his revery and educate his perception. "Notice," the musician says, "that this is not merely a string of waltzes. It is a *rondo* in which one of the waltzes recurs, setting up a pattern of repetition. (Weber in fact subtitled it *Rondeau brillant*.) Further, the work is introduced by a seemingly diffuse section which, however, has a definite program:

> First approach of the dancer to whom the lady gives an evasive answer. His more pressing invitation; her acceptance of his request. Now they converse in greater detail; he begins; she answers; he with heightened expression; she responds more warmly; now for the dance! His remarks concerning it; her answer; their coming together; their going forward; expectation of the beginning of the dance.[25]

And it ends with a coda, also programatic, which utilizes the same thematic material as the introduction. A perfectly rounded musical form!" At once the piece is seen by the previously casual listener to "hang together"; he comes to see, too, "the human and emotional significance represented."

But now a problem arises. We would all agree that before the muscian came along to instruct him, our listener was not having a particularly deep or rich experience; but he was having an *aesthetic* experience, albeit a shallow and undistinguished one. Yet the work was not seen by him to "hang together," nor did he see its emotional and human significance. It would certainly be odd to insist that his experience of *Invitation to the Dance* was, prior to instruction, not an aesthetic experience. If that wasn't an aesthetic experience, what was it? Nevertheless, it was an experience, in which what was being perceived was *not* perceived as "hanging together," was *not* perceived as emotionally and humanly significant. So it couldn't, according to Tilghman, be a case of aesthetic perception; it couldn't be an aesthetic experience.

Of course one can always stubbornly insist that the work does *really* seem to the listener to "hang together" and is *really* perceived as emotionally and humanly significant even before the musician happens along, but "hangs together" in a *different* way and has *different* emotive and human significance before the listener has been enlightened. But this sounds very much like bending the facts to fit the theory. If "hanging together" and "seeing emotional and human significance" mean what they ordinarily do, then, I submit, our example is a very clear case of coming to see something "hanging together," and coming to see it as emotionally and humanly significant when previously it was not seen so. Conversely, one can stubbornly insist that the pre-instruction perception is not *really* aesthetic, but, again, at the cost of subjecting the facts to the theory, in the manner of the man who insists "This couldn't be pudding because I like it—and I don't like pudding."

The second counterexample arises from Tilghman's apparent identification of aesthetic perception with a kind of *appreciation*. For consider the following case. Mr. A is reading a novel. He neither likes the novel nor does he think it is a good novel; in fact he finds it a bore and thinks it is trash. Can he correctly be described as "appreciating" the novel? Such a description would be strange in this context. Someone might be said to "appreciate" a novel that he was enjoying but thought was bad; and might be said to "appreciate" a novel that he did not like but thought was good.[26] He could hardly be said to "appreciate" a novel he neither liked nor thought was good. If he is not appreciating it, however, he cannot, according to Tilghman, be perceiving it aesthetically; for aesthetic perception, according to him, is a species of appreciating, and Mr. A is not appreciating the novel. So it follows from Tilghman's position that a person who is perceiving a work of art that he does not like and thinks is bad cannot be perceiving it aesthetically. But how, one wonders, can one find out if he enjoys a work of art and if it is a bad work of art except by perceiving it aesthetically? In a word, Tilghman's view simply cannot accommodate unpleasant experiences of bad works of art, at least it cannot accommodate them as "aesthetic" experiences—which seems to me to be an absolutely fatal flaw.

Tilghman's use of "appreciation" might, perhaps, be defended along the following lines.[27] Since we can say, for example, "He does not appreciate Hume's argument," meaning "He does not understand Hume's argument," we might sometimes mean "He does not understand Goethe's *Faust*" when we say "He does not appreciate Goethe's *Faust*." And if "appreciate" is taken in this way, then, presumably, it would make sense to say "He does not like Goethe's *Faust* and thinks it is a bad work of art, but he *appreciates* it." The trouble with this line of argument is that what we mean when we say "He does not understand Hume's argument" is not the same kind of thing we mean when we say "He does not understand Goethe's *Faust*"; and what we mean when we say "He does not appreciate Hume's argument" is not the same kind of thing we mean when we say "He does not appreciate Goethe's *Faust*." The following illustration may be helpful here:

MR. A. I don't understand Beethoven's *Grosse Fuge*.
MR. B. There is nothing to *understand*: you can understand an argument in Hume's *Treatise* but you can't understand the *Grosse Fuge;* it doesn't *say* anything.
MR. A. You are taking "understand" in too literal a sense: when someone says they don't *understand* a work of art they don't mean it in the same way as when they say they don't understand a philosophical argument; they mean something like—well—*appreciate*.

In other words, in aesthetic contexts, "understand" is a somewhat figurative term which is more literally rendered by "appreciate"; and in (say) a philosophical context "appreciate" is a somewhat figurative term which is more literally rendered by "understand." To say "I understand

Goethe's *Faust* but don't like it and think it is a bad work of art" is indeed an odd statement, in need of some kind of explanation, such as: "I don't mean *understand* in its usual aesthetic sense but, rather, in the sense in which I would say I don't *understand* Hume's arguments in the *Treatise.*"

Thus our conclusion regarding Tilghman's identification of aesthetic perception with appreciation still stands. On Tilghman's view, unpleasant experiences of bad works of art cannot properly be called "aesthetic" experiences—sufficient grounds, one would think, for rejecting the view out of hand.

An interesting point emerges, I think, from Tilghman's attempt to understand aesthetic perception as a kind of aspect-perceiving; and to bring it out more effectively I would like to sketch, very briefly, another possible approach to the same problem, an approach *suggested* by some remarks of Virgil Aldrich. I underscore the word "suggested" because the approach is one that I suspect Professor Aldrich would disavow, although the remarks I have in mind have served me as a springboard to it. Aldrich writes, in partial explanation of his claim that aspect-perceiving provides the key to aesthetic perception:

> Let us call "observation" the perceptual mode in which material things are realized in physical space. Then the very looking at things will be an incipient awareness of their space properties as fixed by metrical standards and measuring operations. Things seen this way will have a different structural cast from that of the same things in the aesthetic perception of them. Let us call the latter mode "prehension." The aesthetic space of things perceived thus is determined by such characteristics as intensities of values of colors and sounds, which . . . comprise the medium presented by the material things in question. . . . Thus prehension is, if you like, an "impressionistic" way of looking, but still a mode of perception, with the impressions objectively animating the material things—there to be prehended.[28]

When we *observe,* in Aldrich's sense, "the characteristics of the material thing are realized as 'qualities' that 'qualify' it . . ."; but when we *prehend,* we are either "getting aesthetic space-values of the thing as structured simply by color and sound . . . ," or "seeing the thing as something that it is not thought really to be. . . ."

What catches the eye, here, are such contrasts as that between "metrical standards," "measuring operations," and "intensities or values of colors and sounds"; between " 'qualities' that 'qualify' " and "seeing the thing as something it is not thought really to be," "an 'impressionistic' way of looking." To the reader coming fresh from (say) Tomas' article on "Aesthetic Vision," or any of the other traditional "appearance" theories of aesthetic perception, this sounds very like the contrast between cases of seeing in which the question of reality is relevant and cases in which it is not. And the possibility then presents itself of understanding aspect-perceiving in aesthetics in terms of seeing things merely *as* appearances. Thus the view suggested by—but not, I repeat, imputed to—Aldrich is that aesthetic perceiving is aspect-perceiving of the kind in which only the appearance is attended to.

Now as this view is merely a reexpression of the old view that aesthetic perception involves attending not to things "as they really are" but "merely to the way things appear," it is open to all of the objections raised previously against the earlier view; and they need not be repeated here. What I wish to bring out, however, is that a seemingly new path has turned out to lead right back into a familiar and well-trodden dead end. And if we look at Tilghman's position with this in mind we will see the very same thing. For one of the major operators there is the notion of "hanging together"—the notion that what distinguishes aesthetic perception is a kind of "organic unity" or "wholeness" not met with in ordinary ways of perceiving the world. It turns out, then, to be a reexpression in part of the well-known "organicist" theory, against which a serious objection can be brought.

It has long been apparent that not merely aesthetic perception but *all* perception tends to exhibit "wholeness" or "unity" which meets the organicist's aesthetic requirements. Strawson, among others, has pointed this out in a review of Harold Osborne's recent venture into the organic theory of aesthetic perception. He writes: "when one recognizes a person's face or a locality or any individual thing, for which aesthetic excellence is not claimed, one may well be noticing something that passes Mr. Osborne's test for organic wholeness: *i.e.* one sees it as a single individual, and the parts might look different away from the whole."[29] To which we might add, Mr. Osborne's requirements for organic unity are met not only by perceptions for which no aesthetic *excellence* is claimed but for which no *aesthetic* quality of any kind is claimed: that is, for which "nonaesthetic" is the proper description. Mr. Osborne replies that aesthetic unity is "different in kind" from the unity of ordinary perception;[30] and that may very well be so. But it is in itself an admission that the concept of unity alone cannot distinguish the perception of aesthetic excellence from other kinds of perception in which aesthetic excellence is not claimed; and the argument will show too that the concept of unity alone cannot distinguish aesthetic from nonaesthetic perception unless one is willing to say—as some indeed have said—that *all* perception is aesthetic. It is unity "plus". . . . And what the extra magic ingredient is the notion of unity alone cannot tell us.

The organicist then appears to be caught between Scylla and Charybdis. If he construes "coherence," or its ilk, in anything like the ordinary way, there seem to be cases (as in our example of Weber's *Invitation to the Dance*) where we want to say something is an instance of the aesthetic, but is not "coherent." If, on the other hand, he construes "coherence" in a sense wide enough to include everything we would want to call aesthetic, he ends up by having to include literally *everything*, the nonaesthetic as well as the aesthetic. Thus, again, the "new way" of aspect-perceiving has led us back to a very old, and, I think, unacceptable way of dealing with the problem of aesthetic perception.

Nor can we console ourselves on this regard with anything like "well begun, half done." There might be a temptation to think that identifying aesthetic perception with aspect-perceiving—i.e. "seeing as"—is a major insight, and the failure of two attempts at distinguishing *aesthetic* aspect-perceiving from other possible kinds a minor setback in comparison. But this is a mistake. To say that aesthetic seeing is "seeing as" means next to nothing unless we can explain aesthetic "seeing as" into the bargain. We must realize here the force of Austin's observation that "seeing as" can be the name for some perfectly ordinary kinds of seeing. To say "I see the Duck-Rabbit as a duck" may be to describe a different kind of seeing than the kind described by the boy at the Zoo who stands in front of the Gorilla's cage and says "I see a Gorilla." But the man who says "I see *Death of a Salesman* as a tragedy" or "I see *The Origin of Species* as the most important book of the nineteenth century" is seeing *Death of a Salesman* or *The Origin of Species* in exactly the same way as the man who says simply "*Death of a Salesman* is a tragedy" or "*The Origin of Species* is the most important book of the nineteenth century." It is a philosophical task to distinguish aesthetic perceiving from other kinds. It may very well be the *same* task to distinguish aesthetic "seeing as" from other possible kinds since "seeing as" need not necessarily be anything but ordinary seeing. And that is why the contention that aesthetic seeing is "seeing as" may very well be trivial, and the failure to distinguish aesthetic "seeing as" from ordinary kinds as profound a failure as the continued failure of philosophers to distinguish aesthetic perception from perception in general.

Notes

1. The story of aesthetic disinterestedness in the eighteenth century has been admirably told by Jerome Stolnitz in "On the Origins of 'Aesthetic Disinterestedness,'" *Journal of Aesthetics and Art Criticism,* XX (1961).

2. Francis Hutcheson, *An Inquiry into the Original of our Ideas of Beauty and Virtue* (2nd ed.; London, 1726), p. 12.

3. Edmund Burke, *A Philosophical Enquiry into the Origin of our Ideas of the Sublime and Beautiful,* ed. J. T. Boulton (New York: Columbia University Press, 1958), p. 91. My italics.

4. Immanuel Kant, *Critique of Aesthetic Judgment,* trans. J. C. Meredith (London: Oxford University Press, 1911), pp. 42-43.

5. Vincent Tomas, "Aesthetic Vision," *The Philosophical Review,* LXVIII (1959).

6. *Ibid.*, p. 53.

7. *Ibid.*, pp. 54-55.

8. "The Concept of Expression in Art," reprinted in *Philosophy Looks at the Arts*, pp. 30-44, *passim*.

9. "Aesthetic Vision," p. 55.

10. *Ibid.*, p. 57.

11. *Ibid.*, p. 58.

12. Frank Sibley, "Aesthetics and the Looks of Things"; Marshall Cohen, "Appearance and the Aesthetic Attitude," *The Journal of Philosophy*, LVI (1959), pp. 905-26.

13. Ludwig Wittgenstein, *The Blue and Brown Books* (New York: Harper Torchbooks, 1965), p. 45. The "argument" between the scientist and the common man is set out in what has become a classic analysis: L. Susan Stebbing, *Philosophy and the Physicist* (New York: Dover Publications, 1958), ch. 3.

14. Sir Joshua Reynolds, *Discourses,* ed. Edmund Gosse (London: Kegan Paul, Trench and Co., 1883), p. 263. Cf. E. H. Gombrich, *Art and Illusion* (2nd ed.; New York: Pantheon Books, 1965), pp. 191-202.

15. *Art and Illusion,* p. 199.

16. Hutcheson, *Inquiry*, pp. 14-15.

17. In Kant's more familiar formulation, "the judgment of taste is . . . one resting on subjective grounds . . . which yet, for all that, is objective . . . ," *Critique of Aesthetic Judgment,* p. 70.

18. Ludwig Wittgenstein, *Philosophical Investigations,* trans. G. E. M. Anscombe (New York: Macmillan, 1953), p. 203e.

19. B. R. Tilghman, "Aesthetic Perception and the Problem of the 'Aesthetic Object,'" *Mind,* New Series, LXXV (1966), p. 359.

20. *Ibid.*, p. 360.

21. *Ibid.*, p. 362.

22. *Ibid.*, p. 361.

23. J. L. Austin, *Sense and Sensibilia,* ed. G. J. Warnock (New York: Oxford University Press, 1964), p. 101.

24. Tilghman, *op. cit.*, pp. 362-63.

25. John Warrack, *Carl Maria von Weber* (New York: Macmillan, 1968), p. 191.

26. I am assuming that it makes sense to say of a novel (or other work of art) "It's good but I don't like it" or "It's bad but I like it."

27. This objection was raised by Elmer H. Duncan.

28. Virgil C. Aldrich, *Philosophy of Art* (Englewood Cliffs, N.J.: Prentice-Hall, 1963), p. 22.

29. P. F. Strawson (in a review of H. Osborne's *Theory of Beauty*), *Mind,* New Series, LXIII (1954), p. 415.

30. Harold Osborne, "Artistic Unity and Gestalt," *The Philosophical Quarterly,* XIV (1964), p. 225.

NELSON GOODMAN

Art and Authenticity

> . . . the most tantalizing question of all: If a fake is so expert that even after the most thorough and trustworthy examination its authenticity is still open to doubt, is it or is it not as satisfactory a work of art as if it were unequivocally genuine?
>
> *Aline B. Saarinen*

1. The Perfect Fake

FORGERIES OF WORKS OF ART present a nasty practical problem to the collector, the curator, and the art historian, who must often expend taxing amounts of time and energy in determining whether or not particular objects are genuine. But the theoretical problem raised is even more acute. The hardheaded question why there is any aesthetic difference between a deceptive forgery and an original work challenges a basic premiss on which the very functions of collector, museum, and art historian depend. A philosopher of art caught without an answer to this question is at least as badly off as a curator of paintings caught taking a Van Meegeren for a Vermeer.

The question is most strikingly illustrated by the case of a given work and a forgery or copy or reproduction of it. Suppose we have before us, on the left, Rembrandt's original painting *Lucretia* and, on the right, a superlative imitation of it. We know from a fully documented history that the painting on the left is the original; and we know from X-ray photographs and microscopic examination and chemical analysis that the painting on the right is a recent fake. Although there are many differences between the two—e.g., in authorship, age, physical and chemical characteristics, and market value—we cannot see any difference between them; and if they are moved while we sleep, we cannot then tell which is which by merely looking at them. Now we are pressed with the question whether there can be any aesthetic difference between the two pictures;

From *Languages of Art: An Approach to a Theory of Symbols* (2nd Ed., 1976) by Nelson Goodman, pp. 99-112. Reprinted by permission of Hackett Publishing Company, Inc., Indianapolis, Indiana.

and the questioner's tone often intimates that the answer is plainly *no,* that the only differences here are aesthetically irrelevant.

We must begin by inquiring whether the distinction between what can and what cannot be seen in the pictures by "merely looking at them" is entirely clear. We are looking at the pictures, but presumably not "merely looking" at them, when we examine them under a microscope or fluoroscope. Does merely looking, then, mean looking without the use of any instrument? This seems a little unfair to the man who needs glasses to tell a painting from a hippopotamus. But if glasses are permitted at all, how strong may they be, and can we consistently exclude the magnifying glass and the microscope? Again, if incandescent light is permitted, can violet-ray light be ruled out? And even with incandescent light, must it be of medium intensity and from a normal angle, or is a strong raking light permitted? All these cases might be covered by saying that "merely looking" is looking at the pictures without any use of instruments other than those customarily used in looking at things in general. This will cause trouble when we turn, say, to certain miniature illuminations or Assyrian cylinder seals that we can hardly distinguish from the crudest copies without using a strong glass. Furthermore, even in our case of the two pictures, subtle differences of drawing or painting discoverable only with a magnifying glass may still, quite obviously, be aesthetic differences between the pictures. If a powerful microscope is used instead, this is no longer the case; but just how much magnification is permitted? To specify what is meant by merely looking at the pictures is thus far from easy; but for the sake of argument,[1] let us suppose that all these difficulties have been resolved and the notion of "merely looking" made clear enough.

Then we must ask who is assumed to be doing the looking. Our questioner does not, I take it, mean to suggest that there is no aesthetic difference between two pictures if at least one person, say a cross-eyed wrestler, can see no difference. The more pertinent question is whether there can be any aesthetic difference if nobody, not even the most skilled expert, can ever tell the pictures apart by merely looking at them. *But notice now that no one can ever ascertain by merely looking at the pictures that no one ever has been or will be able to tell them apart by merely looking at them.* In other words, the question in its present form concedes that no one can ascertain by merely looking at the pictures that there is no aesthetic difference between them. This seems repugnant to our questioner's whole motivation. For if merely looking can never establish that two pictures are aesthetically the same, something that is beyond the reach of any given looking is admitted as constituting an aesthetic difference. And in that case, the reason for not admitting documents and the results of scientific tests becomes very obscure.

The real issue may be more accurately formulated as the question whether there is any aesthetic difference between the two pictures *for me* (or for *x*) if I (or *x*) cannot tell them apart by merely looking at them. But this is not quite right either. For I can never ascertain merely by looking at the pictures that even I shall never be able to see any difference between them. And to concede that something beyond any given looking at the pictures by me may constitute an aesthetic difference between them *for me* is, again, quite at odds with the tacit conviction or suspicion that activates the questioner.

Thus the critical question amounts finally to this: Is there any aesthetic difference between the two pictures for *x* at *t*, where *t* is a suitable period of time, if *x* cannot tell them apart by merely looking at them at *t*? Or in other words, can anything that *x* does not discern by merely looking at the pictures at *t* constitute an aesthetic difference between them for *x* at *t*?

2. The Answer

In setting out to answer this question, we must bear clearly in mind that what one can distinguish at any given moment by merely looking depends not only upon native visual acuity but upon practice and training.[2] Americans look pretty much alike to a Chinese who has never looked at many of them. Twins may be indistinguishable to all but their closest relatives and acquaintances. Moreover, only through looking at them when someone has named them for us can we learn to tell Joe from Jim upon merely looking at them. Looking at people or things attentively, with the knowledge of certain presently invisible respects in which they differ, increases our ability to discriminate between them—and between other things or other people—upon merely looking at them. Thus pictures that look just alike to the newsboy come to look quite unlike to him by the time he has become a museum director.

Although I see no difference now between the two pictures in question, I may learn to see a difference between them. I cannot determine now by merely looking at them, or in any other way, that I *shall* be able to learn. But the information that they are very different, that the one is the original and the other the forgery, argues against any inference to the conclusion that I *shall* not be able to learn. And the fact that I may later be able to make a perceptual distinction between the pictures that I cannot make now constitutes an aesthetic difference between them that is important to me now.

Furthermore, to look at the pictures now with the knowledge that the left one is the original and the other the forgery may help develop the ability to tell which is which later by merely looking at them. Thus, with information not derived from the present or any past looking at the pictures, the present looking may have a quite different bearing upon future lookings from what it would otherwise have. The way the pictures in fact differ constitutes an aesthetic difference between them for me now because my knowledge of the way they differ bears upon the role of the present looking in training my perceptions to discriminate between these pictures, and between others.

But that is not all. My knowledge of the difference between the two pictures, just because it affects the relationship of the present to future lookings, informs the very character of my present looking. This knowledge instructs me to look at the two pictures differently now, even if what I see is the same. Beyond testifying that I may learn to see a difference, it also indicates to some extent the kind of scrutiny to be applied now, the comparisons and contrasts to be made in imagination, and the relevant associations to be brought to bear. It thereby guides the selection, from my past experience, of items and aspects for use in my present looking. Thus not only later but right now, the unperceived difference between the two pictures is a consideration pertinent to my visual experience with them.

In short, although I cannot tell the pictures apart merely by looking at them now, the fact that the left-hand one is the original and the right-hand one a forgery constitutes an aesthetic difference between them for me now because knowledge of this fact (1) stands as evidence that there may be a difference between them that I can learn to perceive, (2) assigns the present looking a role as training toward such a perceptual discrimination, and (3) makes consequent demands that modify and differentiate my present experience in looking at the two pictures.[3]

Nothing depends here upon my ever actually perceiving or being able to perceive a difference between the two pictures. What informs the nature and use of my present visual experience is not the fact or the assurance that such a perceptual discrimination is within my reach, but evidence that it may be; and such evidence is provided by the known factual differences between the pictures. Thus the pictures differ aesthetically for me now even if no one will ever be able to tell them apart merely by looking at them.

But suppose it could be *proved* that no one ever will be able to see any difference? This is about as reasonable as asking whether, if it can be proved that the market value and yield of a given U.S. bond and one of a certain nearly bankrupt company will always be the same, there is any financial difference between the two bonds. For what sort of proof could be given? One might suppose that if nobody—not even the most skilled expert—has ever been able to see any difference between the pictures, then the conclusion that I shall never be able to is quite safe; but, as in the case of the Van Meegeren forgeries[4] (of which, more later), distinctions not visible to the expert up to a given time may later become manifest even to the observant layman. Or one might think of some delicate scanning device that compares the color of two pictures at every point and registers the slightest discrepancy. What, though, is meant here by "at every point"? At no mathematical point, of course, is there any color at all; and even some physical particles are too small to have color. The scanning device must thus cover at each instant a region big enough to have color but at least as small as any perceptible region. Just how to manage this is puzzling since "perceptible" in the present context means "discernible by merely looking," and thus the line between perceptible and nonperceptible regions seems to depend on the arbitrary line between a magnifying glass and a microscope. If some such line is drawn, we can never be sure that the delicacy of our instruments is superior to the maximal attainable acuity of unaided perception. Indeed, some experimental psychologists are inclined to conclude that every measurable difference in light can sometimes be detected by the naked eye.[5] And there is a further difficulty. Our scanning device will examine color—that is, reflected light. Since reflected light depends partly upon incident light, illumination of every quality, of every intensity, and from every direction must be tried. And for each case, especially since the paintings do not have a plane surface, a complete scanning must be made from every angle. But of course we cannot cover every variation, or even determine a single absolute correspondence, in even one respect. Thus the search for a proof that I shall never be able to see any difference between the two pictures is futile for more than technological reasons.

Yet suppose we are nevertheless pressed with the question whether, if proof *were* given, there would then be any aesthetic difference for me between the pictures. And suppose we answer this farfetched question in the negative. This will still give our questioner no comfort. For the net result would be that if no difference between the pictures can in fact be perceived, then the existence of an aesthetic difference between them will rest entirely upon what is or is not proved by means other than merely looking at them. This hardly supports the contention that there can be no aesthetic difference without a perceptual difference.

Returning from the realm of the ultra-hypothetical, we may be faced with the protest that the vast aesthetic difference thought to obtain between the Rembrandt and the forgery cannot be accounted for in terms of the search for, or even the discovery of, perceptual differences so slight that they can be made out, if at all, only after much experience and long practice. This objection can be dismissed at once; for minute perceptual differences can bear enormous weight. The clues that tell me whether I have caught the eye of someone across the room are almost indiscernible. The actual differences in sound that distinguish a fine from a mediocre performance can be picked out only by the well-trained ear. Extremely subtle changes can alter the whole design, feeling, or expression of a painting. Indeed, the slightest perceptual differences sometimes matter the most aesthetically; gross physical damage to a fresco may be less consequential than slight but smug retouching.

All I have attempted to show, of course, is that the two pictures can differ aesthetically, not that the original is better than the forgery. In our example, the original probably is much the better picture, since Rembrandt paintings are in general much better than copies by unknown painters. But a copy of a Lastman by Rembrandt may well be better than the original. We are not called upon here to make such particular comparative judgements or to formulate canons of aesthetic evaluation. We have fully met the demands of our problem by showing that the fact that we cannot tell our two pictures apart merely by looking at them does not imply that they are aesthetically the same—and thus does not force us to conclude that the forgery is as good as the original.

The example we have been using throughout illustrates a special case of a more general question concerning the aesthetic significance of authenticity. Quite aside from the occurrence of forged duplication, does it matter whether an original work is the product of one or another artist or school or period? Suppose that I can easily tell two pictures apart but cannot tell who painted either except by using some device like X-ray photography. Does the fact that the picture is or is not by Rembrandt make any aesthetic difference? What is involved here is the discrimination not of one picture from another but of the class of Rembrandt paintings from the class of other paintings. My chance of learning to make this discrimination correctly—of discovering projectible characteristics that differentiate Rembrandts in general from non-Rembrandts—depends heavily upon the set of examples available as a basis. Thus the fact that the given picture belongs to the one class or the other is important for me to know in learning how to tell Rembrandt paintings from others. In other words, my present (or future) inability to determine the authorship of the given picture without use of scientific apparatus does not imply that the authorship makes no aesthetic difference to me; for knowledge of the authorship, no matter how obtained, can contribute materially toward developing my ability to determine without such apparatus whether or not any picture, including this one on another occasion, is by Rembrandt.

Incidentally, one rather striking puzzle is readily solved in these terms. When Van Meegeren sold his pictures as Vermeers, he deceived most of the best-qualified experts; and only by his confession was the fraud revealed.[6] Nowadays even the fairly knowing layman is astonished that any competent judge could have taken a Van Meegeren for a Vermeer, so obvious are the differences. What has happened? The general level of aesthetic sensibility has hardly risen so fast that the layman of today sees more acutely than the expert of twenty years ago. Rather, the better information now at hand makes the discrimination easier. Presented with a single unfamiliar picture at a time, the expert had to decide whether it was enough like known Vermeers to be by the same artist. And every time a Van Meegeren was added to the corpus of pictures accepted as Vermeers, the criteria for acceptance were modified thereby; and the mistaking of further Van Meegerens for Vermeers became inevitable. Now, however, not only have the Van Meegerens been subtracted from the precedent-class for Vermeer, but also a precedent-class for Van Meegeren has been established. With these two precedent-classes before us, the characteristic differences become so conspicuous that telling other Van Meegerens from Vermeers offers little difficulty. Yesterday's expert might well have avoided his errors if he had had a few known Van Meegerens handy for comparison. And today's layman who so cleverly spots a Van Meegeren may well be caught taking some quite inferior school-piece for a Vermeer.

In answering the questions raised above, I have not attempted the formidable task of defining "aesthetic" in general,[7] but have simply argued that since the exercise, training, and development of our powers of discriminating among works of art are plainly aesthetic activities, the aesthetic properties of a picture include not only those found by looking at it but also those that determine how it is to be looked at. This rather obvious fact would hardly have needed underlining but for the prevalence of the time-honored Tingle-Immersion theory,[8] which tells us that the proper behavior on encountering a work of art is to strip ourselves of all the vestments of knowledge and experience (since they might blunt the immediacy of our enjoyment), then submerge ourselves completely and gauge the aesthetic potency of the work by the intensity and duration of the resulting tingle. The theory is absurd on the face of it and useless for dealing with any of the important problems of aesthetics; but it has become part of the fabric of our common nonsense.

Notes

1. And only for the sake of argument—only in order not to obscure the central issue. All talk of mere looking in what follows is to be understood as occurring within the scope of this temporary concession, not as indicating any acceptance of the notion on my part.

2. Germans learning English often cannot, without repeated effort and concentrated attention, hear any difference at all between the vowel sounds in "cup" and "cop". Like effort may sometimes be needed by the native speaker of a language to discern differences in color, etc., that are not marked by his elementary vocabulary. Whether language affects actual sensory discrimination has long been debated among psychologists, anthropologists, and linguists; see the survey of experimentation and controversy in Segall, Campbell, and Herskovits, *The Influence of Culture on Visual Perception* (Indianapolis and New York, The Bobbs-Merrill Co., Inc., 1966), pp. 34-48. The issue is unlikely to be resolved without greater clarity in the use of "sensory," "perceptual," and "cognitive," and more care in distinguishing between what a person can do at a given time and what he can learn to do.

3. In saying that a difference *between the pictures* that is thus relevant to my present experience in looking at them constitutes an aesthetic difference

between them, I am of course not saying that everything (e.g., drunkenness, snow blindness, twilight) that may cause my experiences of them to differ constitutes such an aesthetic difference. Not every difference in or arising from how the pictures happen to be looked at counts; only differences in or arising from how they are to be looked at. Concerning the aesthetic, more will be said later in this section and in VI, 3-6.

4. For a detailed and fully illustrated account, see P. B. Coremans, *Van Meegeren's Faked Vermeers and De Hooghs*, trans. A. Hardy and C. Hutt (Amsterdam. J. M. Meulenhoff, 1949). The story is outlined in Sepp Schüller, *Forgers, Dealers, Experts*, trans. J. Cleugh (New York, G. P. Putnam's Sons, 1960), pp. 95-105.

5. Not surprisingly, since a single quantum of light may excite a retinal receptor. See M. H. Pirenne and F. H. C. Marriott, "The Quantum Theory of Light and the Psycho-Physiology of Vision", in *Psychology*, ed. S. Koch (New York and London, McGraw-Hill Co., Inc., 1959), vol. I, p. 290; also Theodore C. Ruch, "Vision", in *Medical Psychology and Biophysics* (Philadelphia, W. B. Saunders Co., 1960), p. 426.

6. That the forgeries purported to have been painted during a period from which no Vermeers were known made detection more difficult but does not essentially alter the case. Some art historians, on the defensive for their profession, claim that the most perceptive critics suspected the forgeries very early; but actually some of the foremost recognized authorities were completely taken in and for some time even refused to believe Van Meegeren's confession. The reader has a more recent example now before him in the revelation that the famous bronze horse, long exhibited in the Metropolitan Museum and proclaimed as a masterpiece of classical Greek sculpture, is a modern forgery. An official of the museum noticed a seam that apparently neither he nor anyone else had ever seen before, and scientific testing followed. No expert has come forward to claim earlier doubts on aesthetic grounds.

7. I shall come to that question much later, in Chapter VI.

8. Attributed to Immanuel Tingle and Joseph Immersion (ca. 1800).

GEORGE DICKIE

The Myth of the Aesthetic Attitude

S OME RECENT ARTICLES[1] have suggested the unsatisfactoriness of the notion of the aesthetic attitude and it is now time for a fresh look at that encrusted article of faith. This conception has been valuable to aesthetics and criticism in helping wean them from a sole concern with beauty and related notions.[2] However, I shall argue that the aesthetic attitude is a myth and while, as G. Ryle has said, "Myths often do a lot of theoretical good while they are still new,"[3] this particular one is no longer useful and in fact misleads aesthetic theory.

There is a range of theories which differ according to how strongly the aesthetic attitude is characterized. This variation is reflected in the language the theories employ. The strongest variety is Edward Bullough's theory of psychical distance, recently defended by Sheila Dawson.[4] The central technical term of this theory is "distance" used as a verb to denote an action which either constitutes or is necessary for the aesthetic attitude. These theorists use such sentences as "He distanced (or failed to distance) the play." The second variety is widely held but has been defended most vigorously in recent years by Jerome Stolnitz and Eliseo Vivas. The *central* technical term of this variety is "disinterested"[5] used either as an adverb or as an adjective. This weaker theory speaks not of a special kind of action (distancing) but of an ordinary kind of action (attending) done in a certain way (disinterestedly). These first two versions are perhaps not as different as my classification suggests. However, the language of the two is different enough to justify separate discussions. My discussion of this second variety will for the most part make use of Jerome Stolnitz' book[6] which is a thorough, consistent, and large-scale version of the attitude theory. The weakest version of the attitude theory can be found in Vincent Tomas' statement "If looking at a picture and attending closely to how it looks is not really to be in the aesthetic attitude, then what on earth is?"[7] In the following I shall be concerned with

From *American Philosophical Quarterly*, I (1964), pp. 56-65. Reprinted by permission of American Philosophical Quarterly.

the notion of *aesthetic* attitude and this notion may have little or no connection with the ordinary notion of an *attitude*.

I

Psychical distance, according to Bullough, is a psychological process by virtue of which a person *puts* some object (be it a painting, a play, or a dangerous fog at sea) "out of gear" with the practical interests of the self. Miss Dawson maintains that it is "the beauty of the phenomenon, which captures our attention, puts us out of gear with practical life, and forces us, if we are receptive, to view it on the level of aesthetic consciousness."[8]

Later she maintains that some persons (critics, actors, members of an orchestra, and the like) "distance deliberately."[9] Miss Dawson, following Bullough, discusses cases in which people are unable to bring off an act of distancing or are incapable of being induced into a state of being distanced. She uses Bullough's example of the jealous ("under-distanced") hubsand at a performance of *Othello* who is unable to keep his attention on thc play because he keeps thinking of his own wife's suspicious behavior. On the other hand, if "we are mainly concerned with the technical details of its [the play's] presentation, then we are said to be over-distanced."[10] There is, then, a species of action—distancing—which may be deliberately done and which initiates a state of consciousness—being distanced.

The question is: Are there actions denoted by "to distance" or states of consciousness denoted by "being distanced"? When the curtain goes up, when we walk up to a painting, or when we look at a sunset are we ever induced into a state of being distanced either by being struck by thc beauty of the object or by pulling off an act of distancing? I do not recall committing any such special actions or of being induced into any special state, and I have no reason to suspect that I am atypical in this respect. The distance-theorist may perhaps ask, "But are you not usually oblivious to noises and sights other than those of the play or to the marks on the wall around the painting?" The answer is of course—"Yes." But if "to distance" and "being distanced" simply mean that one's attention is focused, what is the point of introducing new technical terms and speaking as if these terms refer to special kinds of acts and states of consciousness? The distance-theorist might argue further, "But surely you put the play (painting, sunset) 'out of gear' with your practical interests?" This question seems to me to be a very odd way of asking (by employing the technical metaphor "out of gear") if I attended to the play rather than thought about my wife or wondered how they managed to move the scenery about. Why not ask me straight out if I paid attention? Thus, when Miss Dawson says that the jealous husband under-

distanced *Othello* and that the person with a consuming interest in techniques of stagecraft over-distanced the play, these are just technical
and misleading ways of describing two different cases of inattention. In
both cases something is being attended to, but in neither case is it the
action of the play. To introduce the technical terms "distance," "under-
distance," and "over-distance" does nothing but send us chasing after
phantom acts and states of consciousness.

Miss Dawson's commitment to the theory of distance (as a kind of
mental insulation material necessary for a work of art if it is to be enjoyed aesthetically) leads her to draw a conclusion so curious as to throw
suspicion on the theory.

> One remembers the horrible loss of distance in *Peter Pan*—the moment
> when Peter says "Do you believe in fairies? . . . If you believe, clap your
> hands!" the moment when most children would like to slink out of the
> theatre and not a few cry—not because Tinkerbell may die, but because
> the magic is gone. What, after all, should we feel like if Lear were to leave
> Cordelia, come to the front of the stage and say, "All the grown-ups who
> think that she loves me, shout 'Yes'."[11]

It is hard to believe that the responses of any children could be as theory-
bound as those Miss Dawson describes. In fact, Peter Pan's request for
applause is a dramatic high point to which children respond enthusiastically. The playwright gives the children a momentary chance to become
actors in the play. The children do not at that moment lose or snap out
of a state of being distanced because they never had or were in any such
thing to begin with. The comparison of Peter Pan's appeal to the
hypothetical one by Lear is pointless. *Peter Pan* is a magical play in which
almost anything can happen, but *King Lear* is a play of a different kind.
There are, by the way, many plays in which an actor directly addresses
the audience (*Our Town, The Marriage Broker, A Taste of Honey,* for
example) without causing the play to be less valuable. Such plays are
unusual, but what is unusual is not necessarily bad; there is no point in
trying to lay down rules to which every play must conform independently
of the kind of play it is.

It is perhaps worth noting that Susanne Langer reports the reaction she
had as a child to this scene in *Peter Pan*.[12] As she remembers it, Peter
Pan's appeal shattered the illusion and caused her acute misery. However,
she reports that all the other children clapped and laughed and enjoyed
themselves.

II

The second way of conceiving of the aesthetic attitude—as the ordinary
action of attending done in a certain way (disinterestedly)—is illustrated
by the work of Jerome Stolnitz and Eliseo Vivas. Stolnitz defines "aesthetic

attitude" as "disinterested and sympathetic attention to and contemplation of any object of awareness whatever, for its own sake alone."[13]
Stolnitz defines the main terms of his defintion: "disinterested" means
"no concern for any ulterior purpose";[14] "sympathetic" means "accept
the object on its own terms to appreciate it";[15] and "contemplation"
means "perception directed toward the object in its own right and the
spectator is not concerned to analyze it or ask questions about it."[16]

The notion of disinterestedness, which Stolnitz has elsewhere shown[17]
to be seminal for modern aesthetic theory, is the key term here. Thus, it is
necessary to be clear about the nature of disinterested attention to the
various arts. It can make sense to speak, for example, of listening disinterestedly to music only if it makes sense to speak of listening interestedly to music. It would make no sense to speak of walking *fast* unless
walking could be done *slowly*. Using Stolnitz' definition of "disinterestedness," the two situations would have to be described as "listening with
no ulterior purpose" (distinterestedly) and "listening with an ulterior
purpose" (interestedly). Note that what initially appears to be a perceptual
distinction—listening in a certain way (interestedly or disinterestedly)—
turns out to be a motivational or an intentional distinction—listening for
or with a certain purpose. Suppose Jones listens to a piece of music for the
purpose of being able to analyze and describe it on an examination the
next day and Smith listens to the same music with no such ulterior purpose. There is certainly a difference between the motives and intentions
of the two men: Jones has an ulterior purpose and Smith does not, but this
does not mean Jones's *listening* differs from Smith's. It is possible that both
men enjoy the music or that both be bored. The attention of either or
both may flag and so on. It is important to note that a person's motive
or intention is different from his action (Jones's listening to the music,
for example). There is only one way to *listen* to (to attend to) music,
although the listening may be more or less attentive and there may be a
variety of motives, intentions, and reasons for doing so and a variety of
ways of being distracted from the music.

In order to avoid a common mistake of aestheticians—drawing a conclusion about one kind of art and assuming it holds for all the arts—
the question of disinterested attention must be considered for arts other
than music. How would one look at a painting disinterestedly or interestedly? An example of alleged interested viewing might be the case in
which a painting reminds Jones of his grandfather and Jones proceeds to
muse about or to regale a companion with tales of his grandfather's
pioneer exploits. Such incidents would be characterized by attitude-
theorists as examples of using a work of art as a vehicle for associations
and so on, i.e., cases of interested attention. But Jones is not looking
at (attending to) the painting at all, although he may be facing it with
his eyes open. Jones is now musing or attending to the story he is telling,
although he had to look at the painting at first to notice that it resembled
his grandfather. Jones is not now looking at the painting interestedly,

since he is not now looking at (attending to) the painting. Jones's thinking or telling a story about his grandfather is no more a part of the painting than his speculating about the artist's intentions is and, hence, his musing, telling, speculating, and so on cannot properly be described as attending to the painting interestedly. What attitude-aestheticians are calling attention to is the occurrence of irrelevant associations which distract the viewer from the painting or whatever. But distraction is not a special kind of attention, it is a kind of inattention.

Consider now distinterestedness and plays. I shall make use of some interesting examples offered by J. O. Urmson,[18] but I am not claiming that Urmson is an attitude-theorist. Urmson never speaks in his article of aesthetic attitude but rather of aesthetic satisfaction. In addition to aesthetic satisfaction, Urmson mentions economic, moral, personal, and intellectual satisfactions. I think the attitude-theorist would consider these last four kinds of satisfaction as "ulterior purposes" and, hence, cases of interested attention. Urmson considers the case of a man in the audience of a play who is delighted.[19] It is discovered that his delight is *solely* the result of the fact that there is a full house—the man is the impresario of the production. Urmson is right in calling *this* impresario's satisfaction economic rather than aesthetic, although there is a certain oddness about the example as it finds the impresario sitting *in the audience*. However, my concern is not with Urmson's examples as such but with the attitude theory. This impresario is certainly an interested party in the fullest sense of the word, but is his behavior an instance of interested attention as distinct from the supposed disinterested attention of the average citizen who sits beside him? In the situation as described by Urmson it would not make any sense to say that the impresario is attending to the play at all, since his *sole* concern at the moment is the till. If he can be said to be attending to anything (rather than just thinking about it) it is the size of the house. I do not mean to suggest that an impresario could not attend to his play if he found himself taking up a seat in a full house; I am challenging the sense of disinterested attention. As an example of personal satisfaction Urmson mentions the spectator whose daughter is in the play. Intellectual satisfaction involves the solution of technical problems of plays and moral satisfaction the consideration of the effects of the play on the viewer's conduct. All three of these candidates which the attitude-theorist would propose as cases of interested attention turn out to be just different ways of being distracted from the play and, hence, not cases of interested attention to the play. Of course, there is no reason to think that in any of these cases the distraction or inattention must be total, although it could be. In fact, such inattentions often occur but are so fleeting that nothing of the play, music, or whatever is missed or lost.

The example of a playwright watching a rehearsal or an out-of-town performance with a view to rewriting the script has been suggested to me as a case in which a spectator is certainly attending to the play (unlike our impresario) and attending in an interested manner. This case is unlike those just discussed but is similar to the earlier case of Jones (not Smith) listening to a particular piece of music. Our playwright— like Jones, who was to be examined on the music—has ulterior motives. Furthermore, the playwright, unlike an ordinary spectator, can change the script after the performance or during a rehearsal. But how is our playwright's *attention* (as distinguished from his motives and intentions) different from that of an ordinary viewer? The playwright might enjoy or be bored by the performance as any spectator might be. The playwright's attention might even flag. In short, the kinds of things which may happen to the playwright's attention are no different from those that may happen to an ordinary spectator, although the two may have quite different motives and intentions.

For the discussion of disinterested-interested reading of literature it is appropriate to turn to the arguments of Eliseo Vivas whose work is largely concerned with literature. Vivas remarks that "By approaching a poem in a nonaesthetic mode it may function as history, as social criticism, as diagnostic evidence of the author's neuroses, and in an indefinite number of other ways."[20] Vivas further notes that according to Plato "the Greeks used Homer as an authority on war and almost anything under the sun," and that a certain poem "can be read as erotic poetry or as an account of a mystical experience."[21] The difference between reading a poem *as* history or whatever (reading it nonaesthetically) and reading it aesthetically depends on how *we* approach or read it. A poem "does not come self-labelled,"[22] but presumably is a poem only when it is read in a certain way—when it is an object of aesthetic experience. For Vivas, being an aesthetic object means being the object of the aesthetic attitude. He defines the aesthetic experience as "an experience of rapt attention which involves the intransitive apprehension of an object's immanent meanings and values in their full presentational immediacy."[23] Vivas maintains that his definition "helps me understand better what I can and what I cannot do when I read *The Brothers [Karamazov]*" and his definition "forces us to acknowledge that *The Brothers Karamazov* can hardly be read as art. . . ."[24] This acknowledgment means that we probably cannot intransitively apprehend *The Brothers* because of its size and complexity.

"Intransitive" is the key term here and Vivas' meaning must be made clear. A number of passages reveal his meaning but perhaps the following is the best. "Having once seen a hockey game in slow motion, I am prepared to testify that it was an object of pure intransitive experience [attention]—for I was not *interested* in which team won the game and no external factors mingled with my interest in the beautiful rhythmic flow of the slow-moving men."[25] It appears that Vivas' "intransitive attention" has the same meaning as Stolnitz' "disinterested attention," namely, "attending with no ulterior purpose."[26] Thus, the question to ask is "How does one attend to (read) a poem or any literary work transitively?" One can certainly attend to (read) a poem for a variety of different purposes and because of a variety of different reasons, but can one attend to a poem transitively? I do not think so, but let us consider the examples Vivas offers. He mentions "a type of reader" who uses a poem or parts of a poem as a spring-board for "loose, uncontrolled, relaxed day-dreaming, wool-gathering rambles, free from the contextual control" of the poem.[27] But surely it would be wrong to say such musing is a case of transitively attending to a poem, since it is clearly a case of not attending to a poem. Another supposed way of attending to a poem transitively is by approaching it "as diagnostic evidence of the author's neuroses." Vivas is right if he means that there is no critical point in doing this since it does not throw light on the poem. But this is a case of *using* information gleaned from a poem to make inferences about its author rather than attending to a poem. If anything can be said to be attended to here it is the author's neuroses (at least they are being thought about). This kind of case is perhaps best thought of as a rather special way of getting distracted from a poem. Of course, such "biographical" distractions might be insignificant and momentary enough so as scarcely to distract attention from the poem (a flash of insight or understanding about the poet). On the other hand, such distractions may turn into dissertations and whole careers. Such an interest may lead a reader to concentrate his attention (when he does read a poem) on certain "informational" aspects of a poem and to ignore the remaining aspects. As deplorable as such a sustained practice may be, it is at best a case of attending to certain features of a poem and ignoring others.

Another way that poetry may allegedly be read transitively is by reading it as history. This case is different from the two preceding ones since poetry often *contains* history (makes historical statements or at least references) but does not (usually) contain statements about the author's neuroses and so on nor does it contain statements about what a reader's free associations are about (otherwise we would not call them "*free* associations"). Reading a poem as history suggests that we are attending to (thinking about) historical events by way of attending to a poem—the poem is a time-telescope. Consider the following two sets of lines:

> In fourteen hundred and ninety-two
> Columbus sailed the ocean blue.

> Or like stout Cortez when with eagle eyes
> He star'd at the Pacific—and all his men
> Look'd at each other with a wild surmise—
> Silent, upon a peak in Darien.

Someone might read both of these raptly and not know that they make historical references (inaccurately in one case)—might this be a case of intransitive attention? How would the above reading differ—so far as attention is concerned—from the case of a reader who recognized the historical content of the poetic lines? The two readings do not differ as far as attention is concerned. History is a part of these sets of poetic lines and the two readings differ in that the first fails to take account of an aspect of the poetic lines (its historical content) and the second does not fail to do so. Perhaps by "reading as history" Vivas means "reading *simply* as history." But even this meaning does not mark out a special kind of attention but rather means that only a single aspect of a poem is being noticed and that its rhyme, meter, and so on are ignored. Reading a poem as social criticism can be analyzed in a fashion similar to reading as history. Some poems simply are or contain social criticism, and a complete reading must not fail to notice this fact.

The above cases of alleged interested attending can be sorted out in the following way. Jones listening to the music and our playwright watching the rehearsal are both attending with ulterior motives to a work of art, but there is no reason to suppose that the attention of either is different in kind from that of an ordinary spectator. The reader who reads a poem as history is simply attending to an aspect of a poem. On the other hand, the remaining cases—Jones beside the painting telling of his grandfather, the gloating impresario, daydreaming while "reading" a poem, and so on—are simply cases of not attending to the work of art.

In general, I conclude that "disinterestedness" or "intransitiveness" cannot properly be used to refer to a special kind of attention. "Disinterestedness" is a term which is used to make clear that an action has certain kinds of motives. Hence, we speak of disinterested findings (of boards of inquiry), disinterested verdicts (of judges and juries), and so on. Attending to an object, of course, has its motives but the attending itself is not interested or disinterested according to whether its motives are of the kind which motivate interested or disinterested action (as findings and verdicts might), although the attending may be more or less close.

I have argued that the second way of conceiving the aesthetic attitude is also a myth, or at least that its main content—disinterested attention—is; but I must now try to establish that the view misleads aesthetic theory. I shall argue that the attitude-theorist is incorrect about (1) the way in which he wishes to set the limits of aesthetic relevance; (2) the relation of the critic to a work of art; and (3) the relation of morality to aesthetic value.

Since I shall make use of the treatment of aesthetic relevance in Jerome Stolnitz' book, let me make clear that I am not necessarily denying the relevance of the specific items he cites but disagreeing with his criterion of relevance. His criterion of relevance is derived from his definition of "aesthetic attitude" and is set forth at the very beginning of his book. This procedure leads Monroe Beardsley in his review of the book to remark that Stolnitz' discussion is premature.[28] Beardsley suggests "that relevance cannot be satisfactorily discussed until after a careful treatment of the several arts, their dimensions and capacities."[29]

First, what is meant by "aesthetic relevance"? Stolnitz defines the problem by asking the question: "Is it ever 'relevant' to the aesthetic experience to have thoughts or images or bits of knowledge which are not present within the object itself?"[30] Stolnitz begins by summarizing Bullough's experiment and discussion of single colors and associations.[31] Some associations absorb the spectator's attention and distract him from the color and some associations "fuse" with the color. Associations of the latter kind are aesthetic and the former are not. Stolnitz draws the following conclusion about associations:

> If the aesthetic experience is as we have described it, then whether an association is aesthetic depends on whether it is compatible with the attitude of "disinterested attention." If the association re-enforces the focusing of attention upon the object, by "fusing" with the object and thereby giving it added "life and significance," it is genuinely aesthetic. If, however, it arrogates attention to itself and away from the object, it undermines the aesthetic attitude.[32]

It is not clear how something could *fuse* with a single color, but "fusion" is one of those words in aesthetics which is rarely defined. Stolnitz then makes use of a more fruitful example, one from I. A. Richards' *Practical Criticism*.[33] He cites the responses of students to the poem which begins:

> Between the erect and solemn trees
> I will go down upon my knees;
> I shall not find this day
> So meet a place to pray.

The image of a rugby forward running arose in the mind of one student-reader on reading the third verse of this poem. A cathedral was suggested to a second reader of the poem. The cathedral image "is congruous with both the verbal meaning of the poem and the emotions and mood which it expresses. It does not divert attention away from the poem."[34] The rugby image is presumably incongruous and diverts attention from the poem.

It is a confusion to take compatibility with disinterested attention as a criterion of relevance. If, as I have tried to show, *disinterested attention* is a confused notion, then it will not do as a satisfactory criterion. Also, when Stolnitz comes to show why the cathedral image is, and the rugby image is not relevant, the criterion he actually uses is *congruousness with the meaning of the poem*, which is quite independent of the notion of disinterestedness. The problem is perhaps best described as the problem of relevance to a poem, or more generally, to a work of art, rather than aesthetic relevance.

A second way in which the attitude theory misleads aesthetics is its contention that a critic's relationship to a work of art is different in kind from the relationship of other persons to the work. H. S. Langfeld in an early statement of this view wrote that we may "slip from the attitude of aesthetic enjoyment to the attitude of the critic." He characterizes the critical attitude as "intellectually occupied in coldly estimating . . . merits" and the aesthetic attitude as responding "emotionally to" a work of art.[35] At the beginning of his book in the discussion of the aesthetic attitude, Stolnitz declares that if a percipient of a work of art "has the purpose of passing judgment upon it, his attitude is not aesthetic."[36] He develops this line at a later stage of his book, arguing that appreciation (perceiving with the aesthetic attitude) and criticism (seeking for reasons to support an evaluation of a work) are (1) distinct and (2) "psychologically opposed to each other."[37] The critical attitude is questioning, analytical, probing for strengths and weakness, and so on. The aesthetic attitude is just the opposite: "It commits our allegiance to the object freely and unquestioningly"; "the spectator 'surrenders' himself to the work of art."[38] "Just because the two attitudes are inimical, whenever criticism obtrudes, it reduces aesthetic interest."[39] Stolnitz does not, of course, argue that criticism is unimportant for appreciation. He maintains criticism plays an important and necessary role in preparing a person to appreciate the nuances, detail, form, and so on of works of art. We are quite right, he says, thus to read and listen perceptively and acutely, but he questions, "Does this mean that we must analyze, measure in terms of value-criteria, etc., *during* the supposedly aesthetic experience?"[40] His answer is "No" and he maintains that criticism must occur "*prior* to the aesthetic encounter,"[41] or it will interfere with appreciation.

How does Stolnitz know that criticism will always interfere with appreciation? His conclusion sounds like one based upon the observations of actual cases, but I do not think it is. I believe it is a logical consequence of his definition of aesthetic attitude in terms of disinterested attention (no ulterior purpose). According to his view, to appreciate an object aesthetically one has to perceive it with no ulterior purpose. But the critic has an ulterior purpose—to analyze and evaluate the object he perceives—hence, in so far as a person functions as a critic he cannot function as an appreciator. But here, as previously, Stolnitz confuses a perceptual distinction with a motivational one. If it were possible to *attend* disinterestedly or interestedly, then perhaps the critic (as percipient) would differ from other percipients. But if my earlier argument about attending is correct, the critic differs from other percipients only in his motives and intentions and not in the way in which he attends to a work of art.

Of course, it might just be a fact that the search for reasons is incompatible with the appreciation of art, but I do not think it is. Several years ago I participated in a series of panel discussions of films. During the showing of each film we were to discuss, I had to take note of various aspects of the film (actor's performance, dramatic development, organization of the screen-plane and screen-space at given moments, and so on) in order later to discuss the films. I believe that this practice not only helped educate me to appreciate subsequent films but that it enhanced the appreciation of the films I was analyzing. I noticed and was able to appreciate things about the films I was watching which ordinarily out of laziness I would not have noticed. I see no reason why the same should not be the case with the professional critic or any critical percipient. If many professional critics seem to appreciate so few works, it is not because they are critics, but perhaps because the percentage of good works of art is fairly small and they suffer from a kind of combat fatigue.

I am unable to see any significant difference between "perceptively and acutely" attending to a work of art (which Stolnitz holds enhances appreciation) and searching for reasons, so far as the experience of a work of art is concerned. If I attend perceptively and acutely, I will have certain standards and/or paradigms in mind (not necessarily consciously) and will be keenly aware of the elements and relations in the work and will evaluate them to some degree. Stolnitz writes as if criticism takes place and then is over and done with, but the search for and finding of reasons (noticing this fits in with that, and so on) is continuous in practiced appreciators. A practiced viewer does not even have to be looking for a reason, he may just notice a line or an area in a painting, for example, and the line or area becomes a reason why he thinks the painting better or worse. A person may be a critic (not necessarily a good one) without meaning to be or without even realizing it.

There is one final line worth pursuing. Stolnitz' remarks suggest that one reason he thinks criticism and appreciation incompatible is that they compete with one another for time (this would be especially bad in the cases of performed works). But seeking and finding reasons (criticism) does not compete for time with appreciation. First, to seek for a reason means to be ready and able to notice something and to be thus ready and able as one attends does not compete for time with the attending. In fact, I should suppose that seeking for reasons would tend to focus attention more securely on the work of art. Second, finding a reason is an achievement, like winning a race. (It takes time to run a race but not to win it.) Consider the finding of the following reasons. How much time does it take to "see" that a note is off key (or on key)? How long does it take to notice that an actor mispronounces a word (or does it right)? How much time does it take to realize that a character's action does not fit his already established personality? (One is struck by it.) How long does it take to apprehend that a happy ending is out of place? It does not take time to find any of these reasons or reasons in general. Finding a reason is like coming to understand—it is done in a flash. I do not mean to suggest that one cannot be mistaken in finding a reason. What may appear to be a fault or a merit (a found reason) in the middle of a performance (or during one look at a painting and so forth) may turn out to be just the opposite when seen from the perspective of the whole performance (or other looks at the painting).

A third way in which the attitude theory misleads aesthetic theory is its contention that aesthetic value is always independent of morality. This view is perhaps not peculiar to the attitude theory, but it is a logical consequence of the attitude approach. Two quotations from attitude-theorists will establish the drift of their view of morality and aesthetic value.

> We are either concerned with the beauty of the object or with some other value of the same. Just as soon, for example, as ethical considerations occur to our mind, our attitude shifts.[42]

> Any of us might reject a novel because it seems to conflict with our moral beliefs . . . . When we do so . . . We have *not* read the book aesthetically, for we have interposed moral . . . responses of our own which are alien to it. This disrupts the aesthetic attitude. We cannot then say that the novel is *aesthetically* bad, for we have not permitted ourselves to consider it aesthetically. To maintain the aesthetic attitude, we must follow the lead of the object and respond in concert with it.[43]

This conception of the aesthetic attitude functions to hold the moral aspects and the *aesthetic* aspects of the work of art firmly apart. Presumably, although it is difficult to see one's way clearly here, the moral aspects of a work of art cannot be an object of aesthetic attention because aesthetic attention is by definition disinterested and the moral aspects are somehow practical (interested). I suspect that there are a number of confusions involved in the assumption of the incompatibility of aesthetic attention and the moral aspects of art, but I shall not attempt to make these clear, since the root of the assumption—disinterested attention—is a confused notion. Some way other than in terms of the aesthetic attitude, then, is needed to discuss the relation of morality and aesthetic value.

David Pole in a recent article[44] has argued that the moral vision which a work of art may embody is *aesthetically* significant. It should perhaps be remarked at this point that not all works of art embody a moral vision and perhaps some kinds of art (music, for example) cannot embody a moral vision, but certainly some novels, some poems, and some films and plays do. I assume it is unnecessary to show how novels and so on have this moral aspect. Pole notes the curious fact that while so many critics approach works of art in "overtly moralistic terms," it is a "philosophical commonplace . . . that the ethical and the aesthetic modes . . . form different categories."[45] I suspect that many philosophers would simply say that these critics are confused about their roles. But Pole assumes that philosophical theory "should take notice of practice"[46] and surely he is right. In agreeing with Pole's assumption I should like to reserve the right to argue in specific cases that a critic may be misguided. This right is especially necessary in a field such as aesthetics because the language and practice of critics is so often burdened with ancient theory.

Perhaps *all* moralistic criticism is wrong but philosophers should not rule it out of order at the very beginning by use of a definition.

Pole thinks that the moral vision presented by a particular work of art will be either true or false (perhaps a mixture of true and false might occur). If a work has a false moral vision, then something "is lacking within the work itself. But to say that is to say that the [work] is internally incoherent; some particular aspect must jar with what—on the strength of the rest—we claim a right to demand. And here the moral fault that we have found will count as an aesthetic fault too."[47] Pole is trying to show that the assessment of the moral vision of a work of art is just a special case of coherence or incoherence, and since everyone would agree that coherence is an aesthetic category, the assessment of the moral vision is an aesthetic assessment.

I think Pole's conclusion is correct but take exception to some of his arguments. First, I am uncertain whether it is proper to speak of a moral vision being true or false, and would want to make a more modest claim —that a moral vision can be judged to be acceptable or unacceptable. (I am not claiming Pole is wrong and my claim is not inconsistent with his.) Second, I do not see that a false (or unacceptable) moral vision makes a work incoherent. I should suppose that to say a work is coherent or incoherent is to speak about how its parts fit together and this involves no reference to something outside the work as the work's truth or falsity does.

In any event, it seems to me that a faulty moral vision can be shown to be an aesthetic fault independently of Pole's consideration of truth and coherence. As Pole's argument implies, a work's moral vision is a *part* of the work. Thus, any statement—descriptive or evaluative—about the work's moral vision is a statement about the *work*; and any statement about a *work* is a critical statement and, hence, falls within the aesthetic domain. To judge a moral vision to be morally unacceptable is to judge it defective and this amounts to saying that the work of art has a defective part. (Of course, a judgment of the acceptability of a moral vision may be wrong, as a judgment of an action sometimes is, but this fallibility does not make any difference.) Thus, a work's moral vision may be an aesthetic merit or defect just as a work's degree of unity is a merit or defect. But what justifies saying that a moral vision is a part of a work of art? Perhaps "part" is not quite the right word but it serves to make the point clear enough. A novel's moral vision is an essential part of the novel and if it were removed (I am not sure how such surgery could be carried out) the novel would be greatly changed. Anyway, a novel's moral vision is not like its covers or binding. However, someone might still argue that even though a work's moral vision is defective and the moral vision is part of the work, that this defect is not an *aesthetic* defect. How is "aesthetic" being used here? It is being used to segregate certain aspects or parts of works of art such as formal and stylistic aspects from such aspects as a work's moral vision. But it seems to me that the separation is only nominal. "Aesthetic" has been selected as a name for a certain sub-set of characteristics of works of art. I certainly cannot object to such a stipulation, since an underlying aim of this essay is to suggest the vacuousness of the term "aesthetic." My concern at this point is simply to insist that a work's moral vision is a part of the work and that, therefore, a critic can legitimately describe and evaluate it. I would *call* any defect or merit which a critic can legitimately point out an aesthetic defect or merit, but what we call it does not matter.

It would, of course, be a mistake to judge a work solely on the basis of its moral vision (it is only one part). The fact that some critics have judged works of art in this way is perhaps as much responsible as the theory of aesthetic attitude for the attempts to separate morality from the aesthetic. In fact, such criticism is no doubt at least partly responsible for the rise of the notion of the aesthetic attitude.

If the foregoing arguments are correct, the second way of conceiving the aesthetic attitude misleads aesthetic theory in at least three ways.

III

In answer to a hypothetical question about what is seen in viewing a portrait with the aesthetic attitude, Tomas in part responds "If looking at a picture and attending closely to how it looks is not really to be in the aesthetic attitude, then what on earth is?"[48] I shall take this sentence as formulating the weakest version of the aesthetic attitude. (I am ignoring Tomas' distinction between appearance and reality. See footnote 7. My remarks, thus, are not a critique of Tomas' argument; I am simply using one of his sentences.) First, this sentence speaks only of "looking at a picture," but "listening to a piece of music," "watching and listening to a play," and so on could be added easily enough. After thus expanding the sentence, it can be contracted into the general form: "Being in the aesthetic attitude is attending closely to a work of art (or a natural object)."

But the aesthetic attitude ("the hallmark of modern aesthetics") in this formulation is a great letdown—it no longer seems to say anything significant. Nevertheless, this does seem to be all that is left after the aesthetic attitude has been purged of *distancing* and *disinterestedness*. The only thing which prevents the aesthetic attitude from collapsing into simple attention is the qualification *closely*. One may, I suppose, attend to a work of art more or less closely, but this fact does not seem to signify anything very important. When "being in the aesthetic attitude" is equated with "attending (closely)," the equation neither involves any mythical element nor could it possibly mislead aesthetic theory. But if the definition has no vices, it seems to have no virtues either. When the aesthetic attitude finally turns out to be simply attending (closely), the final version should perhaps not be called "the weakest" but rather "the vacuous version" of the aesthetic attitude.

Stolnitz is no doubt historically correct that the notion of the aesthetic attitude has played an important role in the freeing of aesthetic theory from an overweening concern with beauty. It is easy to see how the slogan, "Anything can become an object of the aesthetic attitude," could help accomplish this liberation. It is worth noting, however, that the same goal could have been (and perhaps to some extent was) realized by simply noting that works of art are often ugly or contain ugliness, or have features which are difficult to include within beauty. No doubt, in more recent times people have been encouraged *to take an aesthetic attitude toward a painting* as a way of lowering their prejudices, say, against abstract and non-objective art. So if the notion of aesthetic attitude has turned out to have no theoretical value for aesthetics, it has had practical value for the appreciation of art in a way similar to that of Clive Bell's suspect notion of significant form.

Notes

[George Dickie wishes] to thank both Monroe C. Beardsley and Jerome Stolnitz who read earlier drafts of this paper and made many helpful comments.

1. See Marshall Cohen, "Appearance and the Aesthetic Attitude," *Journal of Philosophy,* vol. 56 (1959), p. 926; and Joseph Margolis, "Aesthetic Perception," *Journal of Aesthetics and Art Criticism,* vol. 19 (1960), p. 211. Margolis gives an argument, but it is so compact as to be at best only suggestive.

2. Jerome Stolnitz, "Some Questions Concerning Aesthetic Perception," *Philosophy and Phenomenological Research,* vol. 22 (1961), p. 69.

3. *The Concept of Mind* (London, 1949), p. 23.

4. " 'Distancing' as an Aesthetic Principle," *Australasian Journal of Philosophy,* vol. 39 (1961), pp. 155-174.

5. "Disinterested" is Stolnitz' term. Vivas uses "intransitive."

6. *Aesthetics and Philosophy of Art Criticism* (Boston, 1960), p. 510.

7. "Aesthetic Vision," *The Philosophical Review,* vol. 68 (1959), p. 63. I shall ignore Tomas' attempt to distinguish between appearance and reality since it seems to confuse rather than clarify aesthetic theory. See F. Sibley, "Aesthetics and the Looks of Things," *Journal of Philosophy,* vol. 56 (1959), pp. 905-915; M. Cohen, op. cit., pp. 915-926; and J. Stolnitz, "Some Questions Concerning Aesthetic Perception," op. cit., pp. 69-87. Tomas discusses only visual art and the aesthetic attitude, but his remarks could be generalized into a comprehensive theory.

8. Dawson, op. cit., p. 158.

9. Ibid., pp. 159-160.

10. Ibid., p. 159.

11. Ibid., p. 168.

12. *Feeling and Form* (New York, 1953), p. 318.

13. *Aesthetics and the Philosophy of Art Criticism,* pp. 34-35.

14. Ibid., p. 35.
15. Ibid., p. 36.
16. Ibid., p. 38.
17. "On the Origins of 'Aesthetic Disinterestedness,' " *The Journal of Aesthetics and Art Criticism,* vol. 20 (1961), pp. 131-143.
18. "What Makes a Situation Aesthetic?" in *Philosophy Looks at the Arts,* Joseph Margolis (ed.), (New York, 1962). Reprinted from *Proceedings of the Aristotelian Society, Supplementary Volume* 31 (1957), pp. 75-92.
19. Ibid., p. 15.
20. "Contextualism Reconsidered," *The Journal of Aesthetics and Art Criticism,* vol. 18 (1959), pp. 224-225.
21. Ibid., p. 225.
22. Loc. cit.
23. Ibid., p. 227.
24. Ibid., p. 237.
25. Ibid., p. 228. (Italics mine.)
26. Vivas's remark about the improbability of being able to read *The Brothers Karamazov* as art suggests that "intransitive attention" may sometimes mean for him "that which can be attended to at one time" or "that which can be held before the mind at one time." However, this second possible meaning is not one which is relevant here.
27. Vivas, op. cit., p. 231.
28. *The Journal of Philosophy,* vol. 57 (1960), p. 624.
29. Loc. cit.
30. Op. cit., p. 53.
31. Ibid., p. 54.
32. Ibid., pp. 54-55.
33. Ibid., pp. 55-56.
34. Ibid., p. 56.
35. *The Aesthetic Attitude* (New York, 1920), p. 79.
36. Op. cit., p. 35.
37. Ibid., p. 377.
38. Ibid., pp. 377-378.
39. Ibid., p. 379.
40. Ibid., p. 380.
41. Loc. cit.
42. H. S. Langfeld, op. cit., p. 73.
43. J. Stolnitz, op. cit., p. 36.
44. "Morality and the Assessment of Literature," *Philosophy,* vol. 37 (1962), pp. 193-207.
45. Ibid., p. 193.
46. Loc. cit.
47. Ibid., p. 206.
48. Tomas, op. cit., p. 63.

MONROE C. BEARDSLEY

Aesthetic Experience Regained

THIS IS NOT the ideal historical moment for discoursing on aesthetic theory. That ought to be done with quietness and patience. But a quiet voice is all too easily drowned out by the cries of anguish and of anger we hear around us, and patience is a virtue that only those who live in a less terrified society can afford to cultivate. Even hardened aestheticians (an obvious oxymoron) may suffer from doubts that beauty or significant form is what the world needs most right now, when quite different goods—intelligence and charity, for instance—are more likely to restore our sense of community and stop us from creating a society whose answer to all problems—aesthetic and otherwise—will be violent repression. When so many of us in this troubled land do not seem to care very much even for one another—much less for the ravaged nature and crumbling cities our descendants will inherit—the aesthetic point of view becomes difficult to sustain. It may even seem absurd.

But though it would be more than human never to feel such doubts, it would be less than human to succumb to them. If all rational reflection on the domain of art must be indefinitely postponed, we have already lost our struggle, and reduced the chances that others can win theirs later. It is not as though we were shutting our eyes to reality by resolving to continue our aesthetic dialogue, but rather that we refuse to let certain important things be lost sight of.

It is in this spirit that I speak to you tonight. I draw some comfort—which it is yours to share—from the nature of my mission. I have cast myself in the role of do-gooder. Not quite as much of a do-gooder as my title suggests, of course: it's not salvation that I have to offer—but something more like hot soup. Call it a conceptual rescue operation—an attempt to rehabilitate or maybe even rejuvenate a concept that has played an important role in twentieth century aesthetics, but has lost its respectability in sophisticated circles, and is in peril of its very life.

From *Journal of Aesthetic and Art Criticism*, 28 (1969), pp. 3-11. Copyright 1969 by *Journal of Aesthetics and Art Criticism*. Reprinted by permission of the journal and the author.

I

It would be interesting to know who first used the term *aesthetic experience* with intent to mark out a kind of experience that is obtainable from some of the works of nature and some of the technological works of man, but is characteristically and preeminently afforded by works of art. Interest in the typical effects—both immediate and delayed—of music and tragic drama goes back, of course, a long way in the history of aesthetics. And the emergence of a quasiscientific psychology in the eighteenth century gave much impetus to this empirical inquiry. But these earlier students preferred narrower—some would say better—terms to describe the effects they were particularly interested in, whether, like Aristotle, they welcomed these effects or, like Plato, viewed them with alarm. They spoke of feeding and watering the passions (in Jowett's poetic version), of catharsis (to be sure), of instruction and delight, transport, pleasure, or peculiar operations of the transcendental faculties of understanding. But the concept of a kind of *experience* must be much more recent.

Whatever its origin, this concept undoubtedly achieved its fullest development and its richest application in the aesthetic theory of John Dewey. I think it is largely to his work that we owe the extensive adoption of the term by contemporary aestheticians, even though not all of us, of course, accept everything that Dewey said about aesthetic experience. Most of us, indeed, have—I think fortunately—refused to follow some of the more cryptic passages in *Art as Experience* where Dewey proposes to identify the work of art with an experience. It has become usual to talk about the experience, or an experience, *of* a work of art as something distinct from the work that is the object of, and in, the experience. In any case, it has been very widely accepted that there is such a thing as aesthetic experience, describable in its own terms and distinguishable, at least by the practiced introspecter, from other sorts of experience.

It may be that scholarly status-seeking, or academic social-climbing, has had some part in promoting the term *aesthetic experience*. The spread—and to my mind, the beneficent spread—of progressive education, with its early-Deweyan involvement with "interactions" and "transactions" and "doings and undergoings," had numerous consequences. On one education level it popularized expressions like "experiencing pictures" and "the musical experience." On a more elevated level, some aestheticians may have felt that if other university departments were to have their things, like "the religious experience" and "political man," then we ought to stake out a comparable segment of life as our own concern. Even if we found it no easy task to teach people how to tell when they were having an aesthetic experience, we were confident that to be in this glorious state is not the same as feeling tipsy or merely comfortable.

Our confidence, after all, was sustained by some phenomenological evidence. It seemed obvious that musical, literary, dramatic, plastic, and other such experiences, do have something rather special about them. And though they are not exact substitutes for each other, they seem to go together: the experience of listening to a song has more in common with the experience of looking at a piece of sculpture than it does, say, with that of walking in a picket line or that of driving down the Schuylkill Expressway. So perhaps it was a bit non sequiturish for W. E. Kennick to say, in his famous iconoclastic essay: "To put it dogmatically, there is no such thing as *the* Aesthetic Experience; different sorts of experiences are properly referred to as aesthetic."[1] I grant the differences: however, they leave open the question what there is about the different experiences that makes it "proper" to call them aesthetic.

Moreover, the concept of aesthetic experience provides a convenient and—to me—persuasive analysis of artistic goodness. Here lies, I think, its greatest philosophical significance. Those of us who are committed to a naturalistic metaphysical position, whatever our differences may be, will seek the ground of artistic goodness, as of all other forms of goodness, in the import of things for human welfare. Not that to be good is simply to have effects on human beings, but that to be good is to have the potentiality for such effects, assuming that the effects are desirable. And since works of art are typically destitute of any power to affect other objects, in the way a fork-lift truck or a stick of dynamite can, they must be classed among the consumer goods, rather than the production goods, of this world. Setting aside transcendent beauties or ineffable intuitions, the only ground that seems to be left for attributing goodness to works of art is the sort of experience they have it in them to provide. This is the use to be made of them. If artistic goodness is that sort of goodness that an object possesses in virtue of its capacity to provide aesthetic experience (which is here assumed to be desirable), then there can be no artistic goodness unless there can be aesthetic experiences.

I cannot, of course, deny that we could frame other naturalistic definitions of "artistic goodness" that dispense with the term *aesthetic experience* in favor, say, of *aesthetic satisfaction*. These alternatives, which are several, have been partly, though by no means fully, explored.[2] The difficulty common to those I know of—not perhaps an insuperable difficulty—is that of distinguishing between the relevant kind of satisfaction and other kinds. To know "What Makes a Situation Aesthetic," in J. O. Urmson's well-known words, we must first know what makes a *satisfaction* aesthetic, and that seems to depend entirely on the kind of properties that you take satisfaction in. But an experience is larger than a satisfaction, and more independently describable. Perhaps, then, we can distinguish an aesthetic experience from a non-aesthetic one in terms of its own internal properties, and thus decide whether or not an experience is aesthetic without having first to know whether or not the *object* of (and in) the experience has the properties that permit aesthetic experiences.

Despite the good uses it can undoubtedly be put to, if it will do the job, the notion of aesthetic experience is surely a queer one. There is first the difficulty in talking intelligibly about experiences as such. Dewey applies the most extravagant predicates to experiences, some of them metaphorically far-out (for example, "slack and discursive" and "having no holes, mechanical junctions, and dead centers").[3] Some of these may be taken metonymically as applied to the objects of the experience. Some cannot. An experience can have a certain duration; so much is clear. But what else can correctly be said about it? This is one puzzle. But even if we are allowed to apply some predicates to experiences, it may also be questioned whether they will be rich enough and exact enough to afford a reasonably clear distinction between aesthetic experiences and other kinds. That is the second puzzle.

And now another aesthetic iconoclast has come upon this scene to challenge the entire concept. In his provocative essay of a few years ago[4] —which still remains unanswered—George Dickie has directed his attack against "the causal conception of aesthetic experience" in general, and certain typical forms of it in particular. His critique is both sharp and forceful, and his arguments should move us all—either to give an adequate defense of aesthetic experience or to learn to do without it. It is this challenge that I take up now.

II

What does it mean to say that someone is having an aesthetic experience? Strangely enough, in all the literature on aesthetic experience, I cannot find a direct and concise answer to this question. In fact, when I make the attempt, I realize that it is by no means easy to give a satisfactory answer. What is worse, I have the uneasy feeling that my own answer has latent flaws, the ruthless examination of which might lead to just the consequence which this whole essay is aimed to ward off: namely, the abandonment of the concept of aesthetic experience. But we shall see.

I propose to say that a person is having an aesthetic experience during a particular stretch of time if and only if the greater part of his mental activity during that time is united and made pleasurable by being tied to the form and qualities of a sensuously presented or imaginatively intended object on which his primary attention is concentrated.

The structure of aesthetic experience, then, might be sketched in the following way. As someone listens to a piece of music, say, or watches a motion picture, he attends to various features of a phenomenally objective field: to sounds, pictures, etc. At the same time, he is aware of various phenomenally subjective events: his expectations are aroused and he feels satisfactions when they are fulfilled, or he has sympathy-like or anger-like emotions toward the events that occur in the film. We can describe the phenomenally objective qualities and forms: these are the properties of the work of art that appear in the experience. We can describe the phenomenally subjective feelings and emotions: they may be said to be "evoked by" or to be "responses to" the work of art, and in this special sense these *affects* can be said to be caused by the objective features. The experience, as such, consists of both objective and affective elements, and, indeed, of all the elements of awareness that occur in the perceiver during the time of exposure to the work of art, except those elements that are unconnected with that work of art (e.g., traffic noises or sudden thoughts of unpaid bills).

Now, it is agreed that some interesting things can be said about the work of art as experienced: that it may be more or less unified—i.e., that it may be more or less coherent, and more or less complete in itself. The difficulty is in my second assumption: that we can also apply these terms (and similar ones) to the experience as such. If that second application makes sense—if it is intelligible to speak of *experience* as having coherence and completeness, and not merely of *works of art* as having these properties—then it becomes possible to hold (as I have held) that the unity of an aesthetic experience is *due to,* is *determined by,* the unity of the work of art that it is the experience of. This would be a synthetic, empirical statement. But it is just this statement that Dickie rejects, because, according to him, the term *unified* cannot intelligibly be applied to experiences.

This philosophical mistake is described by Dickie as a simple, though serious, confusion. The word *experience* is a very convenient catch-all term which we use on many occasions when we do not require to describe what went on very definitely. But Dickie suggests that it must always be able to be cashed in:

> "It was a great experience" simply means "It (the game) was thrilling" or "It (the play) was exciting or moving," and so forth. "It was an experience that I shall never forget" simply means "I shall always remember the game (painting, play, or what ever)" and so on.

And so

> The harmless expression "the experience of unity," which is used as a general way of referring to the seeing of the unified design, the hearing of the sound pattern, and so on, is somehow inverted and becomes "the unity of experience."[5]

"Somehow" is not really the right word here; Dickie, in fact, attributes this error in Dewey to the lingering malign influence of German idealism, which made expressions like "the unity of experience" seem to mean something. As his examples show, Dickie thinks that statements about aesthetic experiences, to make sense, must be regarded as shorthand expressions either for (1) the work of art as perceived (the music was unified) or for (2) the affects evoked by the work (one was thrilled or moved). From this he concludes that *no* terms (including the crucial critical terms that interest us here) apply intelligibly and irreducibly to experiences as such. Let us, for convenience, call this Dickie's Experience Thesis, i.e., the thesis that the terms *unified, coherent,* and *complete* do not apply to aesthetic experiences as such. If it is correct, then we cannot, of course, use any of these concepts as criteria to distinguish aesthetic experiences from other sorts of experience.

Dickie also holds that we cannot intelligibly apply the terms *unified, coherent,* and *complete* to the phenomenally *subjective* features of the experience as such. Let us call this Dickie's Affect Thesis. Dickie, of course, does not deny that such affects occur in our encounters with works of art: we are, he says, thrilled and moved. But he does not think it makes sense to talk about the unity of sequences of such affects.

The relation between the two theses seems to me to be this: given a certain natural assumption, the Experience Thesis entails the Affect Thesis. Thus, suppose the Affect Thesis is false, and there are sequences of affects that are unified. Then it is possible for someone to perceive a unified piece of music and at the same time feel a unified sequence of affects. But if each of these sequences (of sounds and of affects) could be unified, they could also be so related as to be united with each other (this is my assumption), and in that case the experience as a whole would be unified. Hence the Experience Thesis would be false.

But though the falsity of the Affect Thesis implies the falsity of the Experience Thesis (if we make that one assumption), the *truth* of the Affect Thesis does not imply the *truth* of the Experience Thesis. For even if Dickie is right in thinking that it does not make sense to speak of sequences of affects as "unified," it may still make sense to speak of *experiences* (made up of both affects and phenomenally objective qualities) as "unified." And whether it does make sense is just what we wish to know.

III

Let us first consider Dickie's treatment of the concept of *coherence.* My position, briefly, is (1) that (for example) a musical composition, as heard, may be a highly coherent phenomenal object and (2) that the experience that involves close continued attention to the music may also be highly coherent, when the affective elements of the experience are under the control, so to speak, of the perceptual elements. A coherent experience is something more than an "experience of coherence"—though what makes an (aesthetic) experience coherent is that it is, in part, an experience of something coherent. In describing coherence of experience (relying, obviously, on John Dewey), I wrote that

> One thing leads to another; continuity of development, without gaps or dead spaces, a sense of overall providential pattern of guidance, an orderly cumulation of energy toward a climax, are present to an unusual degree.[6]

Dickie's comment is this:

> Note that everything referred to here is a perceptual characteristic (what Beardsley calls "the phenomenally objective presentation in experience") and not an effect of the perceived characteristics. Thus no ground is furnished for concluding that experiences can be unified in the sense of being coherent.[7]

On the contrary, it seems to me that some of these expressions apply not only to phenomenally objective fields. A feeling, for example, may vary in intensity over a certain stretch of time, and it may change by gentle degrees or abruptly; or it may be interrupted by quite opposed or irrelevant feelings; it may fluctuate in a random way, at the mercy of shifts in the phenomenally objective field, or it may begin as one feeling among many and slowly spread over the whole field of awareness. It seems to me that the terms *continuity* and *discontinuity* apply quite clearly to such sequences, and continuity makes for coherence, in affects as well as in objects.

In order to quiet the suspicion that this way of talking is due to philosophers' habitual high-handedness with plain language, let me appeal to the authority of a psychologist. In his studies of what he calls "peak-experiences"—among them experiences of works of art—Maslow has discriminated and generalized various characteristics of these experiences.[8] He says, for example:

> The person in the peak-experiences feels more integrated (unified, whole, all-of-a-piece) than at other times.
>
> He is now most free of blocks, inhibitions, cautions, fears, doubts, controls, reservations, self-criticisms, brakes. . . . This is both a subjective and an objective phenomenon, and could be described further in both ways.[9]

The phenomenology of this matter is no doubt very difficult to be clear about. But if it is true that the person in aesthetic experience feels a high degree of "integration" (which I construe as a kind of coherence), then it would seem that there is in fact an integration of his feelings; they feel closely related to each other, as though they belong with each other and to each other.

I turn now to Dickie's treatment of the concept of *completeness*. And, again, my position is (1) that a musical composition (for example) can be highly complete, in the sense of finishing what it starts and thus being sufficient unto iself, and (2) that a complete musical composition can help to provide an *experience* that is complete. But the experience of completeness (of the music) is only part of what constitutes the completeness of the experience (as a whole).

In my earlier treatment, I tried to describe two forms of completeness, or two patterns of experience that (it seemed to me) are highly complete. One of these was a "balance" or "equilibrium" of impulses or tendencies (say, the confrontation of opposed feelings about the same object). Dickie's critical analysis of this line of thought is devastating; he shows that I was thoroughly mistaken about it. The second pattern of experience, however, was the pattern of expectation-and-fulfillment. Again the phenomenology is elusive and subtle. It is agreed that a musical passage, for example, may arouse the expectation that certain other musical events are to follow (this is the kind of experience that is so fully studied by Leonard Meyer in his *Emotion and Meaning in Music*). It is also agreed that the promised events, when at last they occur, may fulfill the expectation and thus end the condition of suspense. This kind of thing is what I cited as a paradigm case of completeness. I said that music has (phenomenally objective) completeness, and the experience as a whole also has completeness. But Dickie objects:

> Now when an expectancy is satisfied a process is completed; i.e., over with; but is the process (the expectation and the satsifaction) complete in the sense of being unified?[10]

When the expected actually occurs, a gestalt has been completed: we have, says Dickie, the experience of a completion. This sense of finality may pervade both the objective and the affective parts of the whole field of awareness. But (he argues) the "experience of completion" is something that occurs at the end of the experience of the music (or of some well-defined part of it); so it cannot provide the further and quite distinct concept of the *completeness of the experience*.

But this is just the nature of an experience, considered as such: that its character is partly given by its end. When the gestalt completes itself, we now think of the whole experience as building to that end; the (musical) significance of much that we have heard is now at least revealed, and the recollection of our earlier expectations and the way the music played with them takes on a new intensity in the light of what is now happening, in the final moments. It is in something like this sense, I think, that the experience as such takes on the character of completeness. And I think this is what Maslow has in mind when he writes:

> All peak-experiences may be fruitfully understood as completions-of-the-act in David M. Levy's sense, or as the Gestalt psychologists' closure, or on the

paradigm of the Reichian type of complete orgasm, or as total discharge, catharsis, culmination, climax, consummation, emptying, or finishing.[11]

IV

This defense of aesthetic experience is far from being a whole brief; it mainly replies to certain key points in the indictment. The most fundamental point of all is Dickie's allegation that *unity* and its family of related terms do not even apply, strictly speaking. If that point can be rebutted, then we face the possibility that unity, while indeed a property of aesthetic experiences, is no more special to them than to any other experiences. This is the view, for example, of Marshall Cohen:

> Surely, the experience of riding a crowded subway, or of being badly beaten, has at least as great a degree of unity as (and is more surely pervaded by a single individualizing quality than) the experience of hearing many a sonata or symphonic suite, or of reading many a picaresque novel or chronicle play.[12]

This is the sort of example that contemporary critics of "aesthetic essences" are likely to toss out, like sausages to wolves chasing a Siberian sleigh, to keep the philosophic reader occupied while the argument rushes headlong on. The business about the "single individualizing quality" alludes, of course, to one of Dewey's more dubious statements about the unity of "*an* experience." But apart from that, does the experience of riding a crowded subway really have unity; or is it a mass of jarringly diverse and confused impressions, without dramatic structure or formal development? Even in a "chronicle play" the appearances and disappearances of important characters are far more interrelated than the arrival and departure of subway straphangers. (I must add that I checked this impression only last week while riding on the Broadway-7th Avenue subway.)

These brief remarks are only the beginning of an argument to show that, contrary to Marshall Cohen, our experiences of works of art, and especially our experiences of good works of art, are in fact generally of a high order of unity—of coherence and completeness—compared with most daily experiences. But even if I had time I would hesitate to present such an argument here: the point seems to me somewhat elementary, once we establish the propriety of discussing the question at all.

There is one further question that I think we should look into, however, because it grows so directly out of the line of thought we have been following. I said a while back that perhaps the main philosophic use to be made of the concept of aesthetic experience is in giving a satisfactory analysis of artistic goodness. But there remains the problem of artistic *betterness*. To attribute artistic goodness to an object is, I claim, to attribute to it the capacity to provide a certain desirable kind of experience. What, then, does it mean to say that one object is artistically better than another?

What we must look for, I suppose, is a dimension along which we can compare aesthetic experiences—call it the dimension of D-ness—so that we can say, justifiably, that it is X's capacity to provide aesthetic experiences with greater D-ness that gives it greater artistic goodness than Y has. Unless we can identify, and exhibit, such a dimension—whether simple or compound—we cannot claim to have provided a value theory adequate to the requirements of critical judgment.

So far as I can see, there is only one tenable answer: that D-ness is amount of pleasure. Other hedonistic terms may be preferable, at least in certain contexts where misunderstanding lurks: enjoyment, satisfaction, gratification, or delight. But the main thing to note is that the pleasure here involved is aesthetic pleasure, i.e., that kind of pleasure that is found in aesthetic experience. The view I propose, then, is that X is artistically better than Y if X is capable of providing a more pleasurable aesthetic experience than any that Y is capable of providing.

I realize that up to this point my discussion may have suggested a rather dry and solemn view of aesthetic experiences. I have not spoken, for example, of those delightful characteristics of Maslow's "peak-experiences": the sense of liberation, the joy of play, elation, fullness of power. Letting the term *pleasure* cover all such positive affective states, it seems to me plain that aesthetic experience is pleasurable, and indeed, essentially so. If the fabled businessman dragged to the opera by his wife does not enjoy himself, that is a reliable indication that he is not having an aesthetic experience—though, of course, the fact that his wife *does* enjoy herself does not show she *is* having one.

My proposed account of artistic betterness, then, presupposes that aesthetic experience is always pleasurable. But this has been denied, for example, by Marshall Cohen:

> But, as we may question whether beauty is, indeed, the essential property of art, we may question whether pleasure, which aestheticians have normally supposed to be characteristic of its apprehension is, truly, an essential feature of aesthetic experience.[13]

At this moment, beauty is not in question (fortunately), but pleasure is. Cohen's climactic example is that "The muzzles of the battleship *Potemkin,* pointed at the audience, are positively menacing." This is another one of those sacrificial sausages, though not meaty enough to detain us long. It is not the battleship *Potemkin* that confronts us when we go to a motion picture theater to see the Eisenstein film, but merely a picture of it. And this picture does not in any way menace us, but instead it offers us the *quality* of menace—a quality that we deeply enjoy in its dramatic context. If we recall Burke's or Kant's or Schopenhauer's account of the sublime, it becomes obvious enough that examples like this do not in any way show that aesthetic experience can be unpleasurable.

V

The more unsettling objection to the Hedonistic account of aesthetic experience comes from a very different source: the current avant-garde, including both practical and theoretical wings. The "new aesthetic" of contemporary art escapes (according to these thinkers) the bounds of mere Hedonism. The dimension of D-ness is not to be sought in pleasure, but in blowing the mind. It does not matter what sort of reaction a work of art evokes in us; the important thing is that it evoke *some* reaction, and as intense a reaction as possible. There is, for example, the psychedelic school of turning us on without drugs—one of the current impresarios of total environmental assaults (acid rock, strobe lights, incense, and multi-screen viewing) explains: "We try to vaporize the mind by bombing the senses." The more far-out sculptures and dramatic events are praised by avant-garde critics because they are so startling, terrifying, irritating, disgusting, shocking—or even stupefyingly boring. Never mind that boredom is no Maslow-type peak experience: at least it is a feeling. If Walter Kerr or Clive Barnes walks out of the play, or objects to its nonsensicalness, then the play is a success: it has provoked the very objection that was intended; it has wakened the conventional playgoer, if only for a moment, from his spiritual torpor. To turn away is to pay tribute to the "theater of cruelty" or the "living theater" that frees us from "bourgeois repressions"—like wearing clothes. When someone produces a film that makes everyone in the audience sick to his stomach, it may be hailed as supreme cinematic art.

This Reactionist position is, then, that intensity of feeling is the dimension of D-ness, the ground of artistic betterness. It follows that newness is a prime requisite for really good art, since shocks wear off in time; this is why, in fact, avant-garde writers seldom talk about the goodness of works of art but much about novelty and originality. The first box of dirt brought into the Metropolitan Museum as natural art is a surprise; the second is just more dirt; to save this little artistic movement from exhaustion you then have to fill the whole museum with dirt, or throw it at the visitors.

My object is not to dismiss these ideas with ridicule, for their existence presses upon us some basic aesthetic questions. Why not broaden our concept of aesthetic experience and its dimension of comparative value so that we can include all of these activities, so long as something is really happening? First let us distinguish. The fact is that being bored (or being beaten up or shot at by battleships) is a very different sort of experience from the experience of reading Wallace Stevens or watching the Pennsylvania Ballet Company perform. And whatever may be the hunger that is satisfied by ear-splitting noises, it is not the hunger that draws us to the compositions of Beethoven or Bartók. Many contemporary experiments are, of course, attempts to open up new qualities and forms, new sources of aesthetic experience. Others are really an abandonment of anything we can recognize as aesthetic objectives, in favor of something else. Perhaps there is a need for these forms of sensuous masochism, artifically induced insanity, desperate lunges toward interpersonal contact on the most primitive levels. Such questions must be left to the deep social prophets and the gurus—among whom I am not to be numbered. But it is up to us to study these contemporary developments—more openly, sympathetically, and thoroughly than we have done so far—and to point out similarities and differences. When the experience is largely painful, when it consists more in blowing the mind than in revitalizing it, when it involves no exercise of discrimination and control, we must frankly say that what it provides is not much of an *aesthetic* experience, however intense it may be. And so its goodness, if it has any, cannot strictly be artistic goodness.

You see that my attempt at a conceptual rescue operation turns out to be even more substantial—it is not only the term *aesthetic experience* whose future I am trying to assure, but even aesthetic experience itself. It seems on the face of it ridiculous to fear that a society, or a large part of it, could lose its understanding and desire for the kind of satisfaction that works of art afford. But there are times when a large part of the population, including its elected and unelected officials, seems to lose its grasp of what free scientific inquiry is all about or what is really at stake in enterprises like universities and churches. Similarly, under present social and economic conditions, we may forget that there is a kind of gratification that is something more than gags or shocks or kicks.

We can hardly be too often reminded (if I may paraphrase a splendid sentence from John Stuart Mill) that there have been serious creative artists between whom and the aesthetic authorities of their times there took place some memorable collisions. An eternal problem of philosophy —how to cope conceptually with change—is perhaps most acute in aesthetics, where the phenomena ultimately to be understood are in a constant, and necessary, flux. We must somehow achieve that most difficult intellectual stance which keeps us open to everything that may have worth or the seeds of worth, yet without relinquishing all distinctions that give order to our thought.

It may be that we are now living through a revolution comparable to the broadening of aesthetic appreciation from beauty to the sublime a few centuries ago. If so, then along with a willingness to extend our concept of art—keeping it an "open concept"—must go a willingness to extend our concept of aesthetic experience, assimilating whatever happens to us when we confront these novel works. Or perhaps we should let the concept of art expand freely—applying it to any sort of object that is made to be given our undivided attention—but at the same time keep our concept of aesthetic experience rather restricted: then we would accept the consquence that some contemporary artists are not concerned to provide aesthetic experience—either because they have a need to share their own boredom, or because they sincerely believe that beauty and significant form are no longer good for modern man. I am inclined, though without rigid conviction, to describe what is happening in this second way—though I do not accept its premises. No doubt other sorts of experience are important besides aesthetic experience. But if we concede the right of the artist to evoke them, we ought, by the same token, to insist that aesthetic experience is important, too—and we ought to do what can be done by such abstract labors as ours to insure that aesthetic experience does not disappear amidst the troubles that now try our civilization.

Notes

1. "Does Traditional Aesthetics Rest on a Mistake?" *Mind,* XVII (1958), 323. Cf. Marshall Cohen, "Aesthetic Essence," in Max Black, ed., *Philosophy in America,* Ithaca, 1965: "there is no reason to believe any property essential to aesthetic experience or certainly, to believe that such a property distinguishes aesthetic from, say, 'practical,' or intellectual experience" (116-17).

2. See, for example, J. O. Urmson, "What Makes a Situation Aesthetic?" *Proceedings of the Aristotelian Society,* Supplementary Volume 31 (1957), 75-92; M. C. Beardsley, "The Discrimination of Aesthetic Enjoyment," *British Journal of Aesthetics,* III (1963), 291-300.

3. For further examples see my essay on "Aesthetic Theory and Educational Theory," forthcoming in Ralph A. Smith, ed., *Aesthetic Concepts and Education.*

4. George Dickie, "Beardsley's Phantom Aesthetic Experience," *Journal of Philosophy,* LXII (1965), 129-36; cf. my *Aesthetics: Problems in the Philosophy of Criticism* (New York, 1958), pp. 527-30, 552-54. I wish to thank Dickie for his helpful critical comments on the present paper.

5. Dickie, p. 135.

6. *Aesthetics,* p. 528.

7. Dickie, p. 131; cf. p. 133.

8. Abraham H. Maslow, *Toward a Psychology of Being* (Princeton, N. J., 1962), p. 98.

9. Maslow, p. 101.

10. Dickie, p. 133.

11. Maslow, p. 104.

12. Cohen, p. 119.

13. Cohen, p. 118. There are some good remarks about the pleasure of aesthetic experinece in Pepita Haezrahi, *The Contemplative Activity* (New York, 1956), esp. p. 43.

On Aesthetic Experience

THE WORDS "AESTHETIC" AND "AESTHETICALLY" are qualifying expressions. We speak of something's being aesthetically graitfying *as opposed to* its being morally, religiously, personally, or politically gratifying, as well as of aesthetic pleasures or delights as opposed to those that are merely sensual or intellectual. We speak of someone's taking an aesthetic approach or adopting an aesthetic point of view toward something, and we intend to contrast this with some alternative approach or point of view. All these can be classified as (kinds of) experiences or can be described in the idiom of "experience." But what makes them *aesthetic* experiences, when they are? In other words, what warrants our qualifying them as "aesthetic"?

Philosophers have tried to define the aesthetic in roughly three ways: (1) by reference to a special class of objects; (2) by reference to a special class of properties; (3) by reference to certain (psychological) features of our reactions to or engagements with objects. As in the case of rival definitions of art, no definition of the aesthetic of any of these three types is widely, let alone universally, accepted, which leads us to wonder why this is the case and whether any such definition can be successful. What is the obstacle to finding one?

Are aesthetic experiences restricted to a specifiable class of objects? What objects? Works of art? Can flowers, seashells, and sunsets, then, not be objects of aesthetic delight? Or is it rather that no matter what class an object belongs to, it may be the object of an aesthetic experience? Is there any *kind* of object that *could* not provide one with an aesthetic experience?

And what about classes of properties, predicates, or predicate-concepts (regardless of the kind of object in question)? Are there any that are exclusively or distinctively aesthetic in that experience of one or more of them is *eo ipso* aesthetic experience? (This issue comes up in the next section in connection with Sibley's "Aesthetic Concepts," and full discussion of it should be postponed until then.) The favorite candidate for such a property has historically been beauty, but even Kant would not assert without considerable qualification that any experience of beauty is *eo ipso* aesthetic.[1]

Because aesthetic experiences are experiences and, hence, subjective or psychological phenomena, one might suppose that the way to find out what all aesthetic experiences have distinctively in common is introspection—a way suggested by Beardsley but questionably employed by him.[2] Unfortunately, those who have used this method have not come up with the same results. Even if they had, would this be of any philosophical interest? Would it tell us what makes an experience aesthetic, unless it is assumed that "aesthetic" is applied to experiences in virtue of their having some introspectable feature(s) in common? But is this assumption correct?

If it were, then must not anyone who knows how to apply the term "aesthetic" correctly to experiences know *before* he begins his investigation what the common psychological feature of such experiences is? (Consider trying to find out what fear is by introspecting. How would you know it was fear you were inwardly examining and not hate?) And if he already knows this, is it not pointless for him to search, by introspection or in any other way, for the common feature in question? In Saul Bellow's novel *Henderson the Rain King*, Henderson says of himself, "Certain emotions make my teeth itch. Aesthetic appreciation especially does it to me. Yes, when I admire beauty, I get these tooth pangs, and my gums are on edge."[3] It is possible that we should *all* have Henderson's "itch" and identify an aesthetic experience by its presence. But wouldn't this be identifying the presence of the experience by a symptom rather than by an essential or defining feature of it? And do we really tell whether we have had an aesthetic experience by introspecting?

Urmson's approach to defining (marking the boundaries or limits of) the aesthetic as opposed to the moral, and so on appears to be a variant of the second method cited above. "We find the criterion for distinguishing aesthetic from kindred reactions in the nature of the explanation of the reaction." But what about these distinguishing explanations: must they not refer to features or properties of the object being reacted to? Urmson suggests an affirmative answer when he says such things as, "We may recognize an aesthetic reaction by its being due to features of the thing contemplated . . . ". But if we look at his example of the man in the audience at a play, is this the picture of the relevant explanation that emerges? If the man is the impresario and he is beaming with satisfaction solely because "there is a full house, and the reaction of his audience indicates a long run," his satisfaction is economic. If, on the other hand, he was delighted solely because "his daughter was acquitting herself well in her first part as a leading lady," his delight was personal. And so on. But Dickie holds that Urmson's nonaesthetic cases are just cases of different ways of not attending to the play at all but to something else connected with it. And is there not some merit in this charge?

The kinds of reactions Urmson is interested in are what Tormey calls "intentional states," and as such they have "intentional objects." The impresario is satisfied *with* the full house and the prospect of a long run, not with the play. The proud father is delighted *with* his daughter's performance, not with the play. And the moralist is delighted *with* the good effect he thinks the play will have on the conduct of the audience, not with the play. Which suggests that the distinguishing feature of the aesthetic for Urmson lies not in a reaction's being due to features of the thing contemplated, if the "thing contemplated" is here supposed to be the *play*, but rather in the nature of the intentional object of the reaction. If this is so, then his view is actually a variant of the first kind cited; and the question then becomes, What must the intentional object of a reaction be if the reaction is to count as aesthetic? Must it be a work of art? Urmson certainly does not think so.

Urmson suggests that there is a principle, however vague, that determines the sort of explanation that is at least *sufficient* for a reaction to be counted as aesthetic, and this principle has to do with the *appearances* of things: what makes a reaction aesthetic "is that it is concerned with a thing's looking [sounding, tasting, feeling, smelling] somehow without concern for whether it really is like that." Works of literature, of course, will not fall under this rubric, as Kivy notes, but then the condition is offered as sufficient only. But what about music? According to Charles Rosen,

> Haydn needed *three* upbeats to write the finale with the most outrageous rhythmic effects, that of the Quartet in F flat major, op. 76 no. 6, which surpasses even the duplicity of the minuet of the *Oxford* Symphony in fooling the listener as to the place of the downbeat. The opening, indeed, sounds clearly not like three upbeats, but like *five*.[4]

Is what *makes* a listener's reaction aesthetic in this case the fact that it is concerned with the opening's sounding like five upbeats without concern for whether it really is like that? Does not appreciation of the duplicity in question require that one know that there are only three upbeats, albeit it sounds like five?

Even ignoring such cases where one can draw a distinction between appearance and reality in music, will Urmson's view do for music? Is it how a piece of music sounds—where how it sounds is analogous to how it smells in the case of a rose—that makes the appreciation of music aesthetic?

In his effort to cast doubt on the view that aesthetic perception is aspect-perception, as that view is spelled out by Tilghman, Kivy offers what he takes to be "two very obvious and fatal kinds of counterexample."

> First, let us imagine someone listening rather dreamily, and perhaps not
> too intently, to the lilting and seductive strains of Weber's *Invitation to
> the Dance.* He seems to be having a pleasant enough experience. But
> along comes a musician to disturb his revery and educate his percep-
> tion. . . . We would all agree that before the musician came along to
> instruct him, our listener was . . . having an *aesthetic* experience. . . .
> If that wasn't an aesthetic experience, what was it?

Well, would we all agree that our listener was having an aesthetic experience? Isn't his experience suspiciously like that of Dickie's imaginary
Jones who is reminded of his grandfather by a painting and "proceeds to
muse about . . . his grandfather's pioneer exploits"? Note that the
musician disturbs the listener's *revery.* Is it possible that Weber's *Invitation to the Dance* is part of a recorded collection labeled "Music to
Day-Dream By"? Is musing to music as obvious a case of aesthetic experience as Kivy thinks it is? Indeed, is it an aesthetic experience at all?
Wouldn't Tilghman be justified in rejecting this putative counterexample
out of hand, or at least asking for further details?

Kivy's second counterexample is one of a person who reads a novel
that he neither likes nor thinks good. This shows that "Tilghman's view
simply cannot accommodate unpleasant experiences of bad works of
art, at least it cannot accommodate them as 'aesthetic' experiences"—
which would appear to be "an absolutely fatal flaw." Whatever Tilghman
would say to this, we know what Beardsley would say, namely, that it is
no flaw at all, let alone a fatal one, and the counterexample is no counter-
example at all. For "aesthetic experience is pleasurable, and indeed,
essentially so." Here we have an interesting disagreement. Kivy holds that
it is possible to have an unpleasant aesthetic experience; Beardsley, that
it is not possible. Is there any way of resolving this antinomy?

At the end of his discussion Kivy remarks on "the continued failure
of philosophers to distinguish aesthetic perception from perception in
general." To say that they have failed is at least to suggest the possibility of success. But is there a difference between aesthetic perception
and perception in general that philosophers have failed adequately to
account for? Is looking at a painting, for example, different *in kind* from
looking at anything else? Or is it just that what is looked at is different?

Note that a different view of aesthetic perception (of pictures) has
been given by Kendall Walton: when you look at Breughel's *Haymaking*
you make-believedly see peasants working, and so on. Will Walton's
account do to distinguish aesthetic from ordinary perception, any better
than the appearance- or the aspect-view?

Although there may be many differences between an original painting
and a faithful or deceptive copy of it, if one can't *see* any difference, is
there any *aesthetic* difference between them? Goodman finds the question
as it stands too vague to admit an answer. Such questions as who's looking at them and under what conditions need to be answered first. He
finally narrows the question to this:

Is there any aesthetic difference between the two pictures for *x* at *t*, where *t* is a suitable period of time, if *x* cannot tell them apart at *t*? Or in other words, can anything that *x* does not discern by merely looking at the pictures at *t* constitute an aesthetic difference between them for *x* at *t*?

This is "the critical question."

To this Goodman replies that, although one may see no difference between the two now, he may learn to see a difference between them—which seems to be true enough. Hence, "the fact that I may later be able to make a perceptual distinction between the pictures that I cannot make now constitutes an aesthetic difference between them that is important to me now." But does it? *Ex hypothesi* they are *now* interchangeable as far as I am concerned. Suppose that I never see them again—which is often the case with pictures: we see them once only. How can the fact that I might have been taught to make a perceptual distinction between the pictures constitute an aesthetic difference between them that is important to me at the one and only time I see them?

Also, given Beardsley's view of aesthetic experience, what would his answer to Goodman's "critical question" have to be?

Suppose it could be proved that no one will *ever* be able to see any difference between the two pictures. Would there then be any aesthetic difference between them? Goodman is surely right in saying that search for such a proof would be futile—how would we recognize it if we found it? But the question is still of some theoretical interest. Goodman imagines someone's answering the question in the negative. His reply is that this will give the questioner no comfort. "For the net result would be that if no difference between the two pictures can be perceived, then the existence of an aesthetic difference between them will rest entirely upon what is or is not proved by means other than merely looking at them." But isn't this a non sequitur? The person who answers no presumably holds that aesthetic differences are perceptual differences only; hence, if *ex hypothesi*, no perceptual differences will *ever* be found, then no aesthetic differences will ever be found. Goodman assumes that "the aesthetic properties of a picture include not only those found by looking at it," and this seems to be his basic disagreement with the person who answers his question in the negative. But is he right about this?

One of the more interesting of Dickie's criticisms of the disinterested-attitude theory is his charge that it misrepresents the relation between aesthetic value and morality by holding that the two are independent. As Dickie sees it, "a work's moral vision [if it has one] is a *part* of the work"; hence, "any statement—descriptive or evaluative—about the work's moral vision is a statement about the work; and any statement about a *work* is a critical statement and, hence, falls within the aesthetic domain." But does the last statement—especially its second part—follow from the first two, unless "aesthetic" is made to mean "about or pertaining to a work of art"? In Book II of Plato's *Republic*, Homer and Hesiod are castigated for being tellers of wicked lies because

they give false representations of the gods, which have a deleterious effect
on the minds of young people.[5] This may be more theological than moral
criticism, but that should make no difference. The question here is
whether Plato's criticism is *aesthetic* criticism simply because it is about
the poems of Homer and Hesiod. Many people say it is not. Are they in
some way misusing the word "aesthetic"?

Monroe Beardsley defines the aesthetic experience as follows:

> . . . a person is having an aesthetic experience during a particular stretch
> of time if and only if the greater part of his mental activity during that
> time is united and made pleasurable by being tied to the form and
> qualities of a sensuously presented or imaginatively intended object
> on which his primary attention is concentrated.[6]

Although Beardsley bridles at examples of experiences other than those
of works of art as possibly fitting his definition of aesthetic experience,
are there not countless examples that, at least *prima facie*, satisfy Beardsley's definition? For example, consider a surgeon performing a successful
appendectomy, or an eager student listening to a brilliant lecture on
medieval cosmology, or a suitably excitable person watching the sleaziest
of pornographic movies. As Mark Sagoff says in another connection, "On
any non-question-begging ranking of pleasures, those least worth the
cost are afforded by art." So the experience of the pornography consumer "could certainly beat in intensity, duration, certainty, propinquity,
fecundity, purity, and extent the pleasure anyone gets from looking
at a painting" such as Picasso's *Guernica*.[7] The point is: can there be
aesthetic experiences, as defined, outside the realm of art, and generally
even more pleasant ones than inside that realm?

A difficulty one might have with Beardsley's notion of aesthetic experiences is that of individuating them. For example, suppose someone reads
one book of the *Iliad* each week at a single sitting until he has finished
the poem. Has he had twenty-four aesthetic experiences or just one? The
definition's reference to "a particular stretch of time" would seem to
suggest that the answer is twenty-four. But is this really tolerable? On
the other hand, if the answer is one, are we not going to have trouble
with the notion of the experience's being "unified"—as opposed to its
object's being unified?

Beardsley holds that such properties as unity, coherence, and completeness can belong to experiences in addition to their belonging to
objects of experience. A coherent experience, for example, is something
more than an experience of something's coherence, although what
"makes an . . . experience coherent is that it is, in part, an experience
of something coherent." But just what is the relation between the coherence of the object and that of the experience? Is it contingent or
necessary? Could one have a coherent experience that is "tied to" or
"under the control of" something incoherent, and could its very inco-

herence help "make" the experience coherent? A feeling, Beardsley assures us, can have continuity, "and continuity makes for coherence, in affects as well as in objects." Well, suppose someone has a continuous feeling of disgust with the incoherence of an object. Will that make the experience coherent?

Completeness of an experience for Beardsley is a function of expectation and fulfillment or satisfaction. But are experiences of music (and they are many) in which an expectation is not fulfilled thereby incomplete and, hence, defective as aesthetic experiences? Charles Rosen, again, writes that

> The clear, well-defined, eminently detachable shape of the finale-theme is the basis for one of Haydn's best-loved and most dramatic effects: the surprise return. A great deal of ingenuity is expended upon the return of the theme . . . : the trick is to keep suggesting the return but to delay it until the listener no longer knows when to expect it . . .[8]

If the return of a theme comes as a surprise, it can hardly be expected. Is listening to Haydn's *Surprise* Symphony therefore aesthetically inferior to listening to music that contains no surprises at all?

And what are we to say about experiences of works of art that are devoid of expectations, such as the experiences of at least some pictures? Are they incapable of being complete? Or, even more seriously, what are we to say of experiences of works of art that are devoid of "affect" altogether? No feelings or emotions, or at least none that are of any significance, none that are "under the control of" the work, are involved at all. Are these automatically ruled out as aesthetic, because aesthetic experience—in order to be unified, coherent, or complete at least—essentially involves affects or series of them? If so, can any theory of aesthetic experience that has this consequence be acceptable?

Notes

1. See the next section for Kant's distinction between "dependent" or "adherent" beauty and "free" beauty.

2. Beardsley says, "it has been widely accepted that there is such a thing as aesthetic experience, describable in its own terms and distinguishable, at least by the practiced introspecter, from other sorts of experience." But we hear no more about introspection from him, and Beardsley hardly presents his claims about aesthetic experience as those of a "practiced introspecter."

3. Saul Bellow, *Henderson the Rain King* (New York, 1959), p. 79.

4. Charles Rosen, *The Classical Style* (New York, 1972), p. 339.

5. For a modern example, see William Empson's *Milton's God* (London, 1961). Empson holds that "the Christian God the Father . . . is the wickedest thing yet invented by the black heart of man" (p. 251), hence "the reason why

the poem [Milton's *Paradise Lost*] is so good is that it makes God so bad" (p. 275). Is this aesthetic criticism of Milton?

6. George Dickie says that "Beardsley does not give a definition of 'aesthetic experience,' rather he gives directions for locating aesthetic experiences . . ." (*Art and the Aesthetic: An Institutional Analysis*, Ithaca, N.Y., 1974, p. 186). This may be true of Beardsley's book, *Aesthetics*, but it is hardly true of this essay, which Dickie also has under scrutiny. When a philosopher uses "if and only if" in the way that Beardsley does, he can be presumed to be defining, unless he makes clear what else he could be up to.

Some of the questions below are indebted to Dickie's criticism of Beardsley.

7. Mark Sagoff, "The Aesthetic Status of Forgeries," *J.A.A.C.*, 35 (1976), 179. The properties listed are the factors of Bentham's "Hedonic Calculus" involved in determining which of two pleasures is quantitatively the greater.

8. *Op. cit.*, p. 337.

Suggestions for Additional Reading

Virgil C. Aldrich, "Back to Aesthetic Experience," *J.A.A.C.*, 24 (1966), 365-371 and *Philosophy of Art* (Englewood Cliffs, N.J., 1963), Ch. 1; Monroe C. Beardsley, *Aesthetics* (New York, 1958), Ch. XI; Bernard Bosanquet, *Three Lectures on Aesthetic* (originally published in 1915), Ralph Ross, ed. (Indianapolis and New York, 1963); Laurence Buermeyer, *The Aesthetic Experience* (Merion, Pa., 1929); Edward Bullough, *Aesthetics: Lectures and Essays*, Elizabeth M. Wilkinson, ed. (London, 1957)—contains Bullough's famous essay, " 'Psychical Distance' as a Factor in Art and an Aesthetic Principle"; John Clammer, "On Defining the Aesthetic Experience," *B.J.A.*, 10 (1970), 147-151; Marshall Cohen, "Aesthetic Essence," *Philosophy in America*, Max Black, ed. (Ithaca, N.Y., 1965), 115-133 and "Appearance and the Aesthetic Attitude," *J. Phil.*, 56 (1959), 915-926; Sheila Dawson, " 'Distancing' as an Aesthetic Principle," *Aust. J. Phil.*, 39 (1961), 155-174; John Dewey, *Art as Experience* (New York, 1934); George Dickie, *Aesthetics: An Introduction* (Indianapolis and New York, 1971), Ch. 5, *Art and the Aesthetic* (Ithaca, N.Y., 1974), Chs. 4-8, "Attitude and Object: Aldrich on the Aesthetic," *J.A.A.C.*, 25 (1966), 89-91, "Beardsley's Phantom Aesthetic Experience," *J. Phil.*, 62 (1965), 129-136, "I. A. Richards's Phantom Double," *B.J.A.*, 8 (1968), 54-59, "Is Psychology Relevant to Aesthetics?," *Phil. Rev.*, 71 (1962), 285-302, "Psychical Distance: In a Fog at Sea," *B.J.A.*, 13 (1973), 17-29, and "Taste and Attitude: the Origin of the Aesthetic," *Theoria*, 39 (1973), 153-170; C. J. Ducasse, *The Philosophy of Art* (New York, 1929), Chs. IX-XII; J. N. Findlay, "The Perspicuous and the Poignant: Two Aesthetic Fundamentals," *B.J.A.*, 7 (1967), 3-19; Gerald N. Fisher, "Who Overlooks *The Fat Woman*?," *B.J.A.*, 8 (1968), 394-401; Nelson Goodman, *Languages of Art* (Indianapolis and New York, 1968), Ch. VI; Pepita Haezrahi, *The Contemplative Activity* (New York, 1956); Roman

Ingarden, "Aesthetic Experience and Aesthetic Object," *Phil. and Phen.*, 21 (1961), 289-313; Friedrich Kainz, *Aesthetics the Science*, H. M. Schueller, trans. (Detroit, 1962), 40-244; Peter Kivy, "Aesthetic Aspects and Aesthetic Qualities," *J. Phil.*, 65 (1968), 85-93; Joel J. Kupperman, "Art and Aesthetic Experience," *B.J.A.*, 15 (1974), 29-39; H. S. Langfeld, *The Aesthetic Attitude* (New York, 1920); Alfred Lessing, "What Is Wrong with a Forgery?," *J.A.A.C.*, 23 (1965), 461-471; David M. Levin, "More Aspects to the Concept of 'Aesthetic Aspects,' " *J. Phil.*, 65 (1968), 483-490; C. A. Mace, "The Aesthetic Attitude," *B.J.A.*, 12 (1972), 217-227; Joseph Margolis, "Aesthetic Perception," *J.A.A.C.*, 19 (1960), 209-213; and "Sibley on Aesthetic Perception," *J.A.A.C.*, 25 (1966), 155-158; Robert McGregor, "Art and the Aesthetic," *J.A.A.C.*, 32 (1974), 549-559; K. Mitchells, "Aesthetic Perception and Aesthetic Qualities," *P.A.S.*, 67 (1966-1967), 53-72; Milton C. Nahm, *Aesthetic Experience and Its Presuppositions* (New York, 1946); Harold Osborne, "The Elucidation of Aesthetic Experience," *J.A.A.C.*, 23 (1964), 145-151; D. L. Pole, "Varieties of Aesthetic Experience," *Philosophy*, 30 (1955), 238-248; Kingsley Price, "The Truth About Psychical Distance," *J.A.A.C.*, 35 (1977), 411-423; R. F. Racy, "The Aesthetic Experience," *B.J.A.*, 9 (1969), 345-352; Melvin Rader, "The Imaginative Mode of Awareness," *J.A.A.C.*, 33 (1974), 131-137; I. A. Richards, *Principles of Literary Criticism* (London, 1925), Chs. 2, 32; I. A. Richards, C. K. Ogden, and James Woods, *The Foundations of Aesthetics* (New York, 1925); Mark Sagoff, "The Aesthetic Status of Forgeries," *J.A.A.C.*, 35 (1976), 169-180; Frank Sibley, "Aesthetics and the Looks of Things," *J. Phil.*, 56 (1959), 905-915; Jerome Stolnitz, *Aesthetics and the Philosophy of Art Criticism* (Boston, 1960), Pt. I, "The Artistic Values in Aesthetic Experience," *J.A.A.C.*, 32 (1973), 5-15, "On the Origins of 'Aesthetic Disinterestedness,' " *J.A.A.C.*, 20 (1961), 131-143, and "Some Questions Concerning Aesthetic Perception," *Phil. and Phen.*, 22 (1961), 69-87; Benjamin R. Tilghman, "Aesthetic Perception and the Problem of the 'Aesthetic Object,' " *Mind*, 75 (1966), 351-367; Vincent Tomas, "Aesthetic Vision," *Phil. Rev.*, 68 (1959), 52-67; Eliseo Vivas, "A Definition of Aesthetic Experience," *J. Phil.*, 34 (1937), 628-634, reprinted in *Creation and Discovery* (New York, 1955); Dorothy Walsh, "Aesthetic Objects and Works of Art," *J.A.A.C.*, 23 (1974), 7-12.

V

Aesthetic Judgment

Introduction

IN THE COURSE OF WRITING about Pietro da Cortona's *The Rape of the Sabine Women* (c. 1629, Capitoline Museum, Rome), Rudolf Wittkower says, "A dynamic flow of movement and countermovement is integrated with a stable and organized distribution of groups and figures."[1] And in writing about Beethoven's *Kreutzer* Sonata, Charles Rosen says, "the *Kreutzer* Sonata has a first movement unequalled in formal clarity, grandeur, and dramatic force by anything that Beethoven had yet written; the beautiful slow movement, however, a set of variations in F major, belongs to a totally different style, elegant, brilliant, ornamental, and a little precious . . .".[2] These are typical of what some philosophers would call "aesthetic judgments," and they would single out such terms as "dynamic," "integrated," "stable," "organized," "formal clarity," "grandeur," "dramatic force," "beautiful," "elegant," "brilliant," "ornamental," and "precious" as marking them as aesthetic judgments.

Of the terms mentioned, "beautiful" is the one on which philosophers have concentrated most heavily since the time of Plato, and many philosophers, following Kant, have even identified "pure" aesthetic judgments with judgments of beauty. In recent years, however, more attention has been given to such terms as "elegant" and "integrated," and "beautiful" has tended to be ignored or to be thought of as simply one of a wide range of terms that can figure in aesthetic judgments. For at least the purposes of this book, the last view mentioned has been adopted. And, to put it as simply as possible, the problem is that of the nature of aesthetic judgment. What is it to judge something aesthetically?

Because judgments of beauty historically have been of such central importance, we begin with three theories of such judgments. The first is that of Hume as found in his principal work in aesthetics, the famous essay "Of the Standard of Taste" of 1757.

Judgments of beauty, according to Hume, are judgments of taste, and this makes them essentially subjective. Does it follow from this that there can be no such thing as a *standard* of taste, "a rule by which the various sentiments of men may be reconciled, [or] at least a decision afforded, confirming one sentiment and condemning another"? Hume thinks not. Just as not everyone is qualified "to decide concerning flavors" or "to give a verdict with regard to colors" (flavors and colors being for Hume also subjective), so not everyone is qualified to judge the beauty of something. It is "the joint verdict" of what we might call qualified critics that is "the true standard of taste and of beauty," and Hume spells out what he takes to be at least the necessary conditions of being a qualified critic. Although the verdicts of qualified critics will, Hume thinks, tend to coincide, he recognizes that they may on occasion not do so, which leaves us with a residuum of unresolvable disagreements. Still, the anarchic relativism that would appear to follow from the fact that judgments of beauty are judgments of taste is obviated by there being a standard of taste.

Judgments of beauty for Kant too are judgments of taste, for taste is "the faculty of judging the beautiful." They are a species of what Kant calls "aesthetic" as opposed to "logical" judgments, the latter being "objective" judgments, judgments that attribute determinable properties to objects, the former being "subjective" in that their "determining ground" is the pleasure or pain, satisfaction or dissatisfaction of the subject pronouncing them. Thus, "This wine is red" is a logical judgment; "This wine is pleasant (= pleases or is pleasing to me)," an aesthetic judgment. There are, however, two kinds of aesthetic judgments: "material," or "empirical," and "pure." The example just given is a material aesthetic judgment; judgments of beauty are pure ones.

To be a pure aesthetic judgment the pleasure on which the judgment is grounded must, Kant holds, be first of all disinterested. Being disinterested, the pleasure is one that any person can be expected to be capable of enjoying; hence, when I pronounce something to be beautiful I speak, Kant says, "with a universal voice." In this respect pure aesthetic judgments are impersonal and, hence, *like* logical judgments, even though they do not ascribe some determinable property to an object. Like logical judgments they purport to be "universally" and not merely "subjectively valid." Further, for the judgment of taste to claim universal validity, the pleasure on which it is grounded must be consequent upon an act of reflecting on the object, using the two cognitive capacities requisite for all experience of objects—imagination and understanding. Because this act of reflection is involved in an exercise of taste and not in any effort to determine what properties the object really has, the two faculties employed in it are said to be in "free play"; and if they discern a certain relevant pattern in the object as it is experienced, they are said to be in "harmony." It is really consciousness of this harmony that is the ground of the disinterested pleasure on which the judgment of taste is based.

But what is the relevant pattern that imagination and understanding in their free play are in search of? It is what Kant calls "purposiveness without purpose." If an object, for example, a typewriter, is fashioned according to some rule, plan, or determinate concept, it is said by Kant to have a purpose and also to be purposive. But an object may be purposive—"subjectively purposive"—without having a purpose if its structure or form as it appears to us is of the sort we generally think of as possible only as a result of the object's being fashioned according to some rule, that is, if its structure *looks as if* it were so fashioned. This means that, in reflecting on an object while exercising taste, we prescind from the question of whether the object actually has a purpose and attend solely to its "subjective" or apparent purposiveness. It is this feature that reflecting on the object seeks to discern through the free play of imagination and understanding, thereby effecting that harmony of these faculties that yields the disinterested pleasure on which the judgment of taste is grounded. The capacity to feel this disinterested pleasure is what Kant calls a "sense," and he argues that it must be supposed to be common to all persons—and hence be a "common sense"—if the judgment of taste is to have universal validity or what Kant also calls "exemplary necessity." In this way Kant tries to steer a course between the Scylla of pure subjectivism and the Charybdis of pure objectivism.

According to Kant there is no such thing as "a universal criterion of the beautiful." Guy Sircello disagrees. He holds that, if an object is judged to be beautiful (using "object" in a generous sense), we can always ask "What's beautiful about it?" or "In what respects is it beautiful?," and this question must in principle be answerable in terms of some property or properties of the object—which is diametrically opposed to Kant's view (for the purposiveness without purpose that is involved in judgments of taste is, Kant insists, subjective only). But not just any property will make an object beautiful in some respect. The only properties that will do this are what Sircello calls "properties of qualitative degree" (or "PQDs" for short), for example, the vividness, depth, or richness of something's color. Excluded from this class of beauty-making properties are properties of deficiency, lack, or defect (such as being unhealthy, mad, or silly), properties of "the 'appearance' of deficiency, lack, or defect" (such as being unhealthy-looking, being rotten-smelling, or being evil-looking), and, of course, "beauty and all of its synonyms." Given these restrictions, then any object that is not itself a PQD is beautiful only if it possesses at least one PQD to a very high degree.

Frank Sibley's "Aesthetic Concepts" has been one of the most influential essays in aesthetics written since World War II. Although he mentions beauty once, Sibley is concerned with a much wider range of judgments—or, as he prefers, concepts—than judgments of beauty. The concept of beauty as he sees it is merely one of an extensive realm of concepts that he calls aesthetic concepts, for example, "unified," "coherent," "balanced," "elegant," "dynamic," "graceful," "pretty." Sibley propounds two theses with respect to such concepts: (1) using them to judge objects "requires the exercise of taste, perceptiveness, or sensitivity, of aesthetic discrimination or appreciation"—or just taste for short and (2) the application of such concepts is not condition-governed, except negatively, in that there are no logically necessary and/or sufficient, or even defeasible, conditions for their application. Sibley also discusses some of the ways in which, in the absence of conditions or rules, we learn to apply such concepts and support judgments in which they figure.

Ted Cohen mounts a sustained attack on Sibley's view, specifically on Sibley's attempt to distinguish between aesthetic and nonaesthetic concepts according to whether taste is or is not required for their application. Cohen denies that there are any concepts—or, more precisely, terms —whose successful application invariably requires taste as Sibley construes it, because it is possible to find for any given term an application of it that could be managed without taste. The upshot is that the aesthetic/nonaesthetic distinction as Sibley conceives it comes to nothing.

If you were confronted with a work of art about the origins of which you knew absolutely nothing—a Tibetan painting, say, or a piece of ancient Chinese music—would you be in any position to judge it aesthetically, to tell, for example, whether it is coherent or incoherent, serene or agitated? Kendall Walton says no. Contrary to a widespread view that it is never even partly in virtue of the circumstances of a work's origin that it is coherent or serene, has the aesthetic features that it has, he argues that questions of aesthetic judgment of works of art cannot be separated from questions about their histories: "a work's aesthetic properties depend not only on its nonaesthetic ones [in some such way as that acknowledged by Sibley, say], but also on which of its nonaesthetic properties are 'standard,' which 'variable,' and which 'contrastandard' " in senses spelled out by Walton. His strategy is first to specify how features of a work of art are standard, variable, or contrastandard with respect to a *perceptually distinguishable* category of art, that is, a category in which it is perceived.[3] This allows him to argue that what aesthetic properties a work *seems* to have may depend on what category it is perceived in. But how then do we determine what aesthetic properties it *really* has? By determining what category it is *correct* to perceive it in. But how do we do this? In different ways in different situations, but Walton gives, and discusses, four criteria that count toward its being correct to perceive a work in a certain category. So "the aesthetic properties [a work] actually possesses are those that are to be found in it when it is perceived correctly."

If you know that I know that Borromini designed the church of S. Ivo della Sapienza in Rome, then you know that Borromini designed the church of S. Ivo. In this way knowledge is "transmissible." But if you know that I judge S. Ivo to be one of the most beautiful churches in Rome, does it follow that you judge S. Ivo to be one of the most beautiful churches in Rome? Alan Tormey says no: "critical judgments are non-transmissible." This means, among other things, that acquaintance with the object judged is requisite to aesthetic judgment—something Kant would appear to agree with. But although you cannot judge something aesthetically at secondhand, so to speak, you might as a result of knowing my judgment of S. Ivo believe that it is one of the most beautiful churches in Rome. Further, although aesthetic judgments are not amenable to *confirmation* in the way scientific hypotheses are amenable to confirmation, they are, according to Tormey, testable in that they are subject to *corroboration*. Thus you might corroborate my judgment of S. Ivo by going to Rome (or by examining plans and photographs of it) and judging it for yourself. In this way at least, aesthetic judgments can be said to be "cognitive."

Notes

1. Rudolf Wittkower, *Art and Architecture in Italy, 1600-1750*, third revised edition (Harmondsworth, England, 1973), p. 250.
2. Charles Rosen, *The Classical Style* (New York, 1971), p. 399.
3. It is widely held these days that nothing is, or can be, perceived except in some category, as Walton would put it. See Nelson Goodman, *Languages of Art* (Indianapolis and New York, 1968), p. 8: "Nothing is seen nakedly or naked. The myths of the innocent eye and of the absolute given are unholy accomplices. Both derive from and foster the idea of knowing as a processing of raw material received from the senses, and of this raw material as being discoverable either through purification rites or by methodological disinterpretation. But reception and interpretation are not separable operations; they are thoroughly interdependent. The Kantian dictum echoes here: the innocent eye is blind and the virgin mind empty. Moreover, what has been received and what has been done to it cannot be distinguished within the finished product. Content cannot be extracted by peeling off layers of comment."

DAVID HUME

Of the Standard of Taste

THE GREAT VARIETY of taste, as well as of opinion, which prevails in the world is too obvious not to have fallen under everyone's observation. Men of the most confined knowledge are able to remark a difference of taste in the narrow circle of their acquaintance, even where the persons have been educated under the same government, and have early imbibed the same prejudices. But those who can enlarge their view to contemplate distant nations and remote ages are still more surprised at the great inconsistency and contrariety. We are apt to call barbarous whatever departs widely from our own taste and apprehension, but soon find the epithet of reproach retorted on us. And the highest arrogance and self-conceit is at last startled on observing an equal assurance on all sides, and scruples, amidst such a contest of sentiment, to pronounce positively in its own favor.

As this variety of taste is obvious to the most careless inquirer, so will it be found, on examination, to be still greater in reality than in appearance. The sentiments of men often differ with regard to beauty and deformity of all kinds, even while their general discourse is the same. There are certain terms in every language which import blame, and others praise, and all men who use the same tongue must agree in their application of them. Every voice is united in applauding elegance, propriety, simplicity, spirit in writing, and in blaming fustian, affectation, coldness, and a false brilliancy. But when critics come to particulars this seeming unanimity vanishes, and it is found that they had affixed a very different meaning to their expressions. In all matters of opinion and science, the case is opposite. The difference among men is there oftener found to lie in generals than in particulars, and to be less in reality than in appearance. An explanation of the terms commonly ends the controversy, and the disputants are surprised to find that they had been quarrelling, while at bottom they agreed in their judgment.

From *Essays and Treatises on Several Subjects* (London, 1777). Punctuation, spelling, and capitalization have been modernized.

Those who found morality on sentiment, more than on reason, are inclined to comprehend ethics under the former observation, and to maintain that in all questions which regard conduct and manners, the difference among men is really greater than at first sight it appears. It is indeed obvious that writers of all nations and all ages concur in applauding justice, humanity, magnanimity, prudence, veracity, and in blaming the opposite qualities. Even poets and other authors whose compositions are chiefly calculated to please the imagination are yet found, from Homer down to Fenelon, to inculcate the same moral precepts, and to bestow their applause and blame on the same virtues and vices. This great unanimity is usually ascribed to the influence of plain reason which, in all these cases, maintains similar sentiments in all men, and prevents those controversies to which the abstract sciences are so much exposed. So far as the unanimity is real, this account may be admitted as satisfactory; but we must also allow that some part of the seeming harmony in morals may be accounted for from the very nature of language. The word *virtue*, with its equivalent in every tongue, implies praise, as that of *vice* does blame; and no one, without the most obvious and grossest impropriety, could affix reproach to a term which in general acceptation is understood in a good sense, or bestow applause where the idiom requires disapprobation. Homer's general precepts, where he delivers any such, will never be controverted, but it is obvious that when he draws particular pictures of manners, and represents heroism in Achilles and prudence in Ulysses, he intermixes a much greater degree of ferocity in the former and of cunning and fraud in the latter than Fenelon would admit of. The sage Ulysses in the Greek poet seems to delight in lies and fictions, and often employs them without any necessity or even advantage; but his more scrupulous son, in the French epic writer, exposes himself to the most imminent perils rather than depart from the most exact line of truth and veracity.

The admirers and followers of the *Alcoran* insist on the excellent moral precepts interspersed throughout that wild and absurd performance. But it is to be supposed that the Arabic words which correspond to the English *equity, justice, temperance, meekness, charity*, were such as, from the constant use of that tongue, must always be taken in a good sense; and it would have argued the greatest ignorance, not of morals, but of language, to have mentioned them with any epithets besides those of applause and approbation. But would we know whether the pretended prophet had really attained a just sentiment of morals? Let us attend to his narration and we shall soon find that he bestows praise on such instances of treachery, inhumanity, cruelty, revenge, bigotry, as are utterly incompatible with civilized society. No steady rule of right seems there to be attended to, and every action is blamed or praised so far only as it is beneficial or hurtful to the true believers.

The merit of delivering true general precepts in ethics is indeed very small. Whoever recommends any moral virtues really does no more than is implied in the terms themselves. That people who invented the word *charity* and used it in a good sense inculcated more clearly and much more efficaciously the precept, *be charitable*, than any pretended legislator or prophet who should insert such a *maxim* in his writings. Of all expressions, those which, together with their other meaning, imply a degree either of blame or approbation are the least liable to be perverted or mistaken.

It is natural for us to seek a *standard of taste*, a rule by which the various sentiments of men may be reconciled, [or] at least a decision afforded, confirming one sentiment and condemning another.

There is a species of philosophy which cuts off all hopes of success in such an attempt, and represents the impossibility of ever attaining any standard of taste. The difference, it is said, is very wide between judgment and sentiment. All sentiment is right, because sentiment has a reference to nothing beyond itself, and is always real, wherever a man is conscious of it. But all determinations of the understanding are not right, because they have a reference to something beyond themselves, to wit, real matter of fact, and are not always conformable to that standard. Among a thousand different opinions which different men may entertain of the same subject, there is one, and but one, that is just and true, and the only difficulty is to fix and ascertain it. On the contrary, a thousand different sentiments excited by the same object are all right, because no sentiment represents what is really in the object. It only marks a certain conformity of relation between the object and the organs or faculties of the mind, and if that conformity did not really exist, the sentiment could never possibly have being. Beauty is no quality in things themselves; it exists merely in the mind which contemplates them, and each mind perceives a different beauty. One person may even perceive deformity where another is sensible of beauty, and every individual ought to acquiesce in his own sentiment without pretending to regulate those of others. To seek the real beauty or real deformity is as fruitless an inquiry as to pretend to ascertain the real sweet or real bitter. According to the disposition of the organs, the same object may be both sweet and bitter, and the proverb has justly determined it to be fruitless to dispute concerning tastes. It is very natural, and even quite necessary, to extend this axiom to mental as well as bodily taste; and thus common sense, which is so often at variance with philosophy, especially with the skeptical kind, is found, in one instance at least, to agree in pronouncing the same decision.

But though this axiom, by passing into a proverb, seems to have attained the sanction of common sense, there is certainly a species of common sense which opposes it, [or] at least serves to modify and restrain it. Whoever would assert an equality of genius and elegance between Ogilby and Milton, or Bunyan and Addison, would be thought to defend no less an extravagance than if he had maintained a molehill to be as high as Teneriffe, or a pond as extensive as the ocean. Though there may be found persons who give the preference to the former authors, no one pays attention to such a taste, and we pronounce without scruple the sentiment of these pretended critics to be absurd and ridiculous. The principle of the natural equality of tastes is then totally forgotten, and while we admit it on some occasions, where the objects seem near an equality, it appears an extravagant paradox, or rather a palpable absurdity, where objects so disproportionate are compared together.

It is evident that none of the rules of composition are fixed by reasonings *a priori,* or can be esteemed abstract conclusions of the understanding from comparing those habitudes and relations of ideas which are eternal and immutable. Their foundation is the same with that of all the practical sciences, experience; nor are they anything but general observations concerning what has been universally found to please in all countries and in all ages. Many of the beauties of poetry and even of eloquence are founded on falsehood and fiction, on hyperboles, metaphors, and an abuse or perversion of terms from their natural meaning. To check the sallies of the imagination and to reduce every expression to geometrical truth and exactness would be the most contrary to the laws of criticism, because it would produce a work which, by universal experience, has been found the most insipid and disagreeable. But though poetry can never submit to exact truth, it must be confined by rules of art, discovered to the author either by genius or observation. If some negligent or irregular writers have pleased, they have not pleased by their transgressions of rule or order, but in spite of these transgressions; they have possessed other beauties, which were conformable to just criticism, and the force of these beauties has been able to overpower censure, and give the mind a satisfaction superior to the disgust arising from the blemishes. Ariosto pleases, but not by his monstrous and improbable fictions, by his bizarre mixture of the serious and comic styles, by the want of coherence in his stories, or by the continual interruptions of his narration. He charms by the force and clearness of his expression, by the readiness and variety of his inventions, and by his natural pictures of the passions, especially those of the gay and amorous kind; and however his faults may diminish our satisfaction, they are not able entirely to destroy it. Did our pleasure really arise from those parts of his poem which we denominate faults, this would be no objection to criticism in general; it would only be an objection to those particular rules of criticism which would establish such circumstances to be faults and would represent them as universally blamable. If they are found to please they cannot be faults, let the pleasure which they produce be ever so unexpected and unaccountable.

But though all the general rules of art are founded only on experience and on the observation of the common sentiments of human nature, we must not imagine that, on every occasion, the feelings of men will be comformable to these rules. Those finer emotions of the mind are of a very tender and delicate nature, and require the concurrence of many favorable circumstances to make them play with facility and exactness, according to their general and established principles. The least exterior hindrance to such small springs, or the least internal disorder, disturbs their motion, and confounds the operation of the whole machine. When we would make an experiment of this nature, and would try the force of any beauty or deformity, we must choose with care a proper time and place, and bring the fancy to a suitable situation and disposition. A perfect serenity of mind, a recollection of thought, a due attention to the object; if any of these circumstances be wanting, our experiment will be fallacious, and we shall be unable to judge of the catholic and universal beauty. The relation which nature has placed between the form and the sentiment will at least be more obscure, and it will require greater accuracy to trace and discern it. We shall be able to ascertain its influence, not so much from the operation of each particular beauty, as from the durable admiration which attends those works that have survived all the caprices of mode and fashion, all the mistakes of ignorance and envy.

The same Homer who pleased at Athens and Rome two thousand years ago is still admired at Paris and at London. All the changes of climate, government, religion, and language have not been able to obscure his glory. Authority or prejudice may give a temporary vogue to a bad poet or orator, but his reputation will never be durable or general. When his compositions are examined by posterity or by foreigners the enchantment is dissipated, and his faults appear in their true colors. On the contrary, a real genius, the longer his works endure and the more wide they are spread, the more sincere is the admiration which he meets with. Envy and jealousy have too much place in a narrow circle, and even familiar acquaintance with his person may diminish the applause due to his performances. But when these obstructions are removed the beauties which are naturally fitted to excite agreeable sentiments immediately display their energy, and while the world endures they maintain their authority over the minds of men.

It appears then that amidst all the variety and caprice of taste there are certain general principles of approbation or blame, whose influence a careful eye may trace in all operations of the mind. Some particular forms or qualities, from the original structure of the internal fabric, are calculated to please, and others to displease; and if they fail of their effect in any particular instance, it is from some apparent defect or imperfection in the organ. A man in a fever would not insist on his palate as able to decide concerning flavors; nor would one affected with the jaundice pretend to give a verdict with regard to colors. In each creature there is a sound and a defective state, and the former alone can be supposed to afford us a true standard of taste and sentiment. If in the sound state of the organ there be an entire or a considerable uniformity of sentiment among men, we may thence derive an idea of the perfect beauty; in like manner as the appearance of objects in daylight, to the eye of a man in health, is denominated their true and real color, even while color is allowed to be merely a phantasm of the senses.

Many and frequent are the defects in the internal organs which prevent or weaken the influence of those general principles on which depends our sentiment of beauty or deformity. Though some objects, by the structure of the mind, be naturally calculated to give pleasure, it is not to be expected that in every individual the pleasure will be equally felt. Particular incidents and situations occur which either throw a false light on the objects, or hinder the true from conveying to the imagination the proper sentiment and perception.

One obvious cause why many feel not the proper sentiment of beauty is the want of that *delicacy* of imagination which is requisite to convey a sensibility of those finer emotions. This delicacy everyone pretends to; everyone talks of it, and would reduce every kind of taste or sentiment to its standard. But as our intention in this essay is to mingle some light of the understanding with the feelings of sentiment, it will be proper to give a more accurate definition of delicacy than has hitherto been attempted. And not to draw our philosophy from too profound a source, we shall have recourse to a noted story in *Don Quixote*.

It is with good reason, says Sancho to the squire with the great nose, that I pretend to have a judgment in wine; this is a quality hereditary in our family. Two of my kinsmen were once called to give their opinion of a hogshead which was supposed to be excellent, being old and of a good vintage. One of them tastes it, considers it, and, after mature reflection, pronounces the wine to be good, were it not for a small taste of leather which he perceived in it. The other, after using the same precautions, gives also his verdict in favor of the wine, but with the reserve of a taste of iron, which he could easily distinguish. You cannot imagine how much they were both ridiculed for their judgment. But who laughed in the end? On emptying the hogshead, there was found at the bottom an old key with a leathern thong tied to it.

The great resemblance between mental and bodily taste will easily teach us to apply this story. Though it be certain that beauty and deformity, [no] more than sweet and bitter, are not qualities in objects, but belong entirely to the sentiment, internal or external, it must be allowed that there are certain qualities in objects which are fitted by nature to produce those particular feelings. Now as these qualities may be found in a small degree, or may be mixed and confounded with each other, it often happens that the taste is not affected with such minute qualities, or is not able to distinguish all the particular flavors, amidst the disorder in which they are presented. Where the organs are so fine as to allow nothing to escape them, and at the same time so exact as to perceive every ingredient in the composition, this we call delicacy of taste, whether we employ these terms in the literal or metaphorical sense. Here then the general rules of beauty are of use, being drawn from established models, and from the observation of what pleases or displeases when presented singly and in a high degree. And if the same qualities, in a continued composition and in a smaller degree, affect not the organs with a sensible delight or uneasiness, we exclude the person from all pretensions to this delicacy. To produce these general rules or avowed patterns of composition is like finding the key with the leathern thong which justified the verdict of Sancho's kinsmen and confounded those pretended judges who had condemned them. Though the hogshead had never been emptied, the taste of the one was still equally delicate, and that of the other equally dull and languid, but it would have been more difficult to have proved the superiority of the former to the conviction of every bystander. In like manner, though the beauties of writing had never been methodized or reduced to general principles, though no excellent models had ever been acknowledged, the different degrees of taste would still have subsisted, and the judgment of one man been preferable to that of another; but it would not have been so easy to silence the bad critic, who might always insist upon his particular sentiment, and refuse to submit to his antagonist. But when we show him an avowed principle of art, when we illustrate this principle by examples whose operation, from his own particular taste, he acknowledges to be conformable to the principle, when we prove that the same principle may be applied to the present case, where he did not perceive or feel its influence, he must conclude, upon the whole, that the fault lies in himself, and that he wants the delicacy which is requisite to make him sensible of every beauty and every blemish in any composition or discourse.

It is acknowledged to be the perfection of every sense or faculty to perceive with exactness its most minute objects, and allow nothing to escape its notice and observation. The smaller the objects are which become sensible to the eye, the finer is that organ, and the more elaborate its make and composition. A good palate is not tried by strong flavors but by a mixture of small ingredients, where we are still sensible of each part, notwithstanding its minuteness and its confusion with the rest. In like manner, a quick and acute perception of beauty and deformity must be the perfection of our mental taste; nor can a man be satisfied with himself while he suspects that any excellence or blemish in a discourse has passed him unobserved. In this case, the perfection of the man and the perfection of the sense or feeling are found to be united. A very delicate palate, on many occasions, may be a great inconvenience both to a man himself and to his friends, but a delicate taste of wit or beauty must always be a desirable quality, because it is the source of all the finest and most innocent enjoyments of which human nature is susceptible. In this decision the sentiments of all mankind are agreed. Wherever you can ascertain a delicacy of taste it is sure to meet with approbation, and the best way of ascertaining it is to appeal to those models and principles which have been established by the uniform consent and experience of nations and ages.

But though there be naturally a wide difference in point of delicacy between one person and another, nothing tends further to increase and improve this talent than *practice* in a particular art and the frequent survey or contemplation of a particular species of beauty. When objects of any kind are first presented to the eye or imagination the sentiment which attends them is obscure and confused, and the mind is, in a great measure, incapable of pronouncing concerning their merits or defects. The taste cannot perceive the several excellencies of the performance, much less distinguish the particular character of each excellency, and ascertain its quality and degree. If it pronounces the whole in general to be beautiful or deformed, it is the utmost that can be expected, and even this judgment a person so unpracticed will be apt to deliver with great hesitation and reserve. But allow him to acquire experience in those objects, his feeling becomes more exact and nice; he not only perceives the beauties and defects of each part, but marks the distinguishing species of each quality, and assigns it suitable praise or blame. A clear and distinct sentiment attends him through the whole survey of the objects, and he discerns that very degree and kind of approbation or displeasure which each part is naturally fitted to produce. The mist dissipates which seemed formerly to hang over the object; the organ acquires greater perfection in its operations and can pronounce, without danger of mistake, concerning the merits of every performance. In a word, the same address and dexterity which practice gives to the execution of any work is also acquired by the same means in the judging of it.

So advantageous is practice to the discernment of beauty that, before we can give judgment on any work of importance, it will even be requisite that that very individual performance be more than once perused by us and be surveyed in different lights with attention and deliberation. There is a flutter or hurry of thought which attends the first perusal of any piece, and which confounds the genuine sentiment of beauty. The relation of the parts is not discerned; the true characters of style are little distinguished; the several perfections and defects seem wrapped up in a species of confusion, and present themselves indistinctly to the imagination. Not to mention that there is a species of beauty which, as it is florid and superficial, pleases at first, but being found incompatible with a just expression either of reason or passion soon palls upon the taste, and is then rejected with disdain, [or] at least rated at a much lower value.

It is impossible to continue in the practice of contemplating any order of beauty without being frequently obliged to form *comparisons* between the several species and degrees of excellence, and estimating their proportion to each other. A man who has had no opportunity of comparing the different kinds of beauty is indeed totally unqualified to pronounce an opinion with regard to any object presented him. By comparison alone we fix the epithets of praise or blame and learn how to assign the due degree of each. The coarsest daubing contains a certain luster of colors and exactness of imitation, which are so far beauties and would affect the mind of a peasant or Indian with the highest admiration. The most vulgar ballads are not entirely destitute of harmony or nature, and none but a person familiarized to superior beauties would pronounce their numbers harsh or narration uninteresting. A great inferiority of beauty gives pain to a person conversant in the highest excellence of the kind and is for that reason pronounced a deformity, as the most finished object with which we are acquainted is naturally supposed to have reached the pinnacle of perfection and to be entitled to the highest applause. One accustomed to see and examine and weigh the several performances admired in different ages and nations can alone rate the merits of a work exhibited to his view and assign its proper rank among the productions of genius.

But to enable a critic the more fully to execute this undertaking, he must preserve his mind free from all *prejudice,* and allow nothing to enter into his consideration but the very object which is submitted to his examination. We may observe that every work of art, in order to produce its due effect on the mind, must be surveyed in a certain point of view, and cannot be fully relished by persons whose situation, real or imaginary, is not conformable to that which is required by the performance. An orator addresses himself to a particular audience, and must have a regard to their particular genius, interests, opinions, passions, and prejudices; otherwise he hopes in vain to govern their resolutions and inflame their affections. Should they even have entertained some prepossessions against him, however unreasonable, he must not overlook this disadvantage but, before he enters upon the subject, must endeavor to conciliate their affection, and acquire their good graces. A critic of a different age or nation who should peruse this discourse must have all these circumstances in his eye, and must place himself in the same situation as the audience in order to form a true judgment of the oration. In like manner, when any work is addressed to the public, though I should have a friendship or enmity with the author, I must depart from this situation, and considering myself as a man in general forget, if possible, my individual being and my peculiar circumstances. A person influenced by prejudice complies not with this condition, but obstinately maintains his natural position without placing himself in that point of view which the performance supposes. If the work be addressed to persons of a different age or nation, he makes no allowance for their peculiar views and prejudices, but, full of the manners of his own age and country, rashly condemns what seemed admirable in the eyes of those for whom alone the discourse was calculated. If the work be executed for the public, he never sufficiently enlarges his comprehension or forgets his interest as a friend or enemy, as a rival or commentator. By this means, his sentiments are perverted; nor have the same beauties and blemishes the same influence upon him as if he had imposed a proper violence on his imagination and had forgotten himself for a moment. So far his taste evidently departs from the true standard, and of consequence loses all credit and authority.

It is well known that in all questions submitted to the understanding, prejudice is destructive of sound judgment, and perverts all operations of the intellectual faculties. It is no less contrary to good taste, nor has it less influence to corrupt our sentiment of beauty. It belongs to *good sense* to check its influence in both cases, and in this respect, as well as in many others, reason, if not an essential part of taste, is at least requisite to the operations of this latter faculty. In all the nobler productions of genius, there is a mutual relation and correspondence of parts; nor can either the beauties or blemishes be perceived by him whose thought is not capacious enough to comprehend all those parts and compare them with each other in order to perceive the consistency and uniformity of the whole. Every work of art has also a certain end or purpose for which it is calculated, and is to be deemed more or less perfect as it is more or less fitted to attain this end. The object of eloquence is to persuade, of history to instruct, of poetry to please by means of the passions and the imagination. These ends we must carry constantly in our view when we peruse any performance, and we must be able to judge how far the means employed are adapted to their respective purposes. Besides, every kind of composition, even the most poetical, is nothing but a chain of propositions and reasonings; not always, indeed, the justest and most exact, but still plausible and specious, however disguised by the coloring of the imagination. The persons introduced in tragedy and epic poetry must be represented as reasoning and thinking and concluding and acting suitably to their character and circumstances, and without judgment, as well as taste and invention, a poet can never hope to succeed in so delicate an undertaking. Not to mention that the same excellence of faculties which contributes to the improvement of reason, the same clearness of conception, the same exactness of distinction, the same vivacity of apprehension, are essential to the operations of true taste, and are its infallible concomitants. It seldom or never happens that a man of sense who has experience in any art cannot judge of its beauty, and it is no less rare to meet with a man who has a just taste without a sound understanding.

Thus, though the principles of taste be universal and nearly, if not entirely, the same in all men, yet few are qualified to give judgment on any work of art or establish their own sentiment as the standard of beauty. The organs of internal sensation are seldom so perfect as to allow the general principles their full play and produce a feeling correspondent to those principles. They either labor under some defect or are vitiated by some disorder, and by that means excite a sentiment which may be pronounced erroneous. When the critic has no delicacy he judges without any distinction, and is only affected by the grosser and more palpable qualities of the object; the finer touches pass unnoticed and disregarded. Where he is not aided by practice his verdict is attended with confusion and hesitation. Where no comparison has been employed the most frivolous beauties, such as rather merit the name of defects, are the object of his admiration. Where he lies under the influence of prejudice all his natural sentiments are perverted. Where good sense is wanting he is not qualified to discern the beauties of design and reasoning, which are the highest and most excellent. Under some or other of these imperfections the generality of men labor, and hence a true judge in the finer arts is observed, even during the most polished ages, to be so rare a character. Strong sense, united to delicate sentiment, improved by practice, perfected by comparison, and cleared of all prejudice, can alone entitle critics to this valuable character, and the joint verdict of such, wherever they are to be found, is the true standard of taste and of beauty.

But where are such critics to be found? By what marks are they to be known? How distinguish them from pretenders? These questions are embarrssing, and seem to throw us back into the same uncertainty from which, during the course of this essay, we have endeavored to extricate ourselves.

But if we consider the matter aright, these are questions of fact, not of sentiment. Whether any particular person be endowed with good sense and a delicate imagination, free from prejudice, may often be the subject of dispute and be liable to great discussion and inquiry, but that such a character is valuable and estimable will be agreed in by all mankind. Where these doubts occur, men can do no more than in other disputable questions which are submitted to the understanding: they must produce the best arguments that their invention suggests to them; they must acknowledge a true and decisive standard to exist somewhere, to wit, real existence and matter of fact; and they must have indulgence to such as differ from them in their appeals to this standard. It is sufficient for our present purpose if we have proved that the taste of all individuals is not upon an equal footing, and that some men in general, however difficult to be particularly pitched upon, will be acknowledged by universal sentiment to have a preference above others.

But in reality, the difficulty of finding, even in particulars, the standard of taste is not so great as it is represented. Though in speculation we may readily avow a certain criterion in science and deny it in sentiment, the matter is found in practice to be much more hard to ascertain in the former case than in the latter. Theories of abstract philosophy, systems of profound theology, have prevailed during one age; in a successive period, these have been universally exploded, their absurdity has been detected, other theories and systems have supplied their place, which again gave place to their successors, and nothing has been experienced more liable to the revolutions of chance and fashion than these pretended decisions of science. The case is not be same with the beauties of eloquence and poetry. Just expressions of passion and nature are sure, after a little time, to gain public applause, which they maintain forever. Aristotle and Plato and Epicurus and Descartes may successively yield to each other, but Terence and Vergil maintain a universal, undisputed empire over the minds of men. The abstract philosophy of Cicero has lost its credit; the vehemence of his oratory is still the object of our admiration.

Though men of delicate taste be rare, they are easily to be distinguished in society by the soundness of their understanding and the superiority of their faculties above the rest of mankind. The ascendant which they acquire gives a prevalence to that lively approbation with which they receive any productions of genius and renders it generally predominant. Many men, when left to themselves, have but a faint and dubious perception of beauty, who yet are capable of relishing any fine stroke which is pointed out to them. Every convert to the admiration of the real poet or orator is the cause of some new conversion. And though prejudices may prevail for a time, they never unite in celebrating any rival to the true genius, but yield at last to the force of nature and just sentiment. Thus, though a civilized nation may easily be mistaken in the choice of their admired philosopher, they never have been found long to err in their affection for a favorite epic or tragic author.

But notwithstanding all our endeavors to fix a standard of taste and reconcile the discordant apprehensions of men, there still remain two sources of variation, which are not sufficient indeed to confound all the boundaries of beauty and deformity, but will often serve to produce a difference in the degrees of our approbation or blame. The one is the different humors of particular men; the other, the particular manners and opinions of our age and country. The general principles of taste are uniform in human nature; where men vary in their judgments, some defect or perversion in the faculties may commonly be remarked, proceeding either from prejudice, from want of practice, or from want of delicacy, and there is just reason for approving one taste and condemning another. But where there is such a diversity in the internal frame or external situation as is entirely blameless on both sides and leaves no room to give one the preference above the other, in that case a certain degree of diversity in judgment is unavoidable, and we seek in vain for a standard by which we can reconcile the contrary sentiments.

A young man whose passions are warm will be more sensibly touched with amorous and tender images than a man more advanced in years who takes pleasure in wise, philosophical reflections concerning the conduct of life and moderation of the passions. At twenty, Ovid may be the favorite author, Horace at forty, and perhaps Tacitus at fifty. Vainly would we, in such cases, endeavor to enter into the sentiments of others and divest ourselves of those propensities which are natural to us. We choose our favorite author as we do our friend, from a conformity of humor and disposition. Mirth or passion, sentiment or reflection; whichever of these most predominates in our temper, it gives us a peculiar sympathy with the writer who resembles us.

One person is more pleased with the sublime, another with the tender, a third with raillery. One has a strong sensibility to blemishes and is extremely studious of correctness; another has a more lively feeling of beauties and pardons twenty absurdities and defects for one elevated or pathetic stroke. The ear of this man is entirely turned toward conciseness and energy; that man is delighted with a copious, rich, and harmonious expression. Simplicity is affected by one, ornament by another. Comedy, tragedy, satire, odes, have each its partisans, who prefer that particular species of writing to all others. It is plainly an error in a critic to confine his approbation to one species or style of writing and condemn all the rest. But it is almost impossible not to feel a predilection for that which suits our particular turn and disposition. Such preferences are innocent and unavoidable, and can never reasonably be the object of dispute, because there is no standard by which they can be decided.

For a like reason, we are more pleased, in the course of our reading, with pictures and characters that resemble objects which are found in our own age or country than with those which describe a different set of customs. It is not without some effort that we reconcile ourselves to the simplicity of ancient manners, and behold princesses carrying water from the spring and kings and heroes dressing their own victuals. We may allow in general that the representation of such manners is no fault in the author nor deformity in the piece, but we are not so sensibly touched with them. For this reason, comedy is not easily transferred from one age or nation to another. A Frenchman or Englishman is not pleased with the *Andria* of Terence, or *Clitia* of Machiavelli, where the fine lady upon whom all the play turns never once appears to the spectators, but is always kept behind the scenes, suitably to the reserved humor of the ancient Greeks and modern Italians. A man of learning and reflection can make allowance for these peculiarities of manners, but a common audience can never divest themselves so far of their usual ideas and sentiments as to relish pictures which nowise resemble them.

But here there occurs a reflection which may, perhaps, be useful in examining the celebrated controversy concerning ancient and modern learning, where we often find the one side excusing any seeming absurdity in the ancients from the manners of the age, and the other refusing to admit this excuse, or at least admitting it only as an apology for the author, not for the performance. In my opinion, the proper boundaries in this subject have seldom been fixed between the contending parties.

Where any innocent peculiarities of manners are represented, such as those above-mentioned, they ought certainly to be admitted, and a man who is shocked with them gives an evident proof of false delicacy and refinement. The poet's *monument more durable than brass* must fall to the ground like common brick or clay were men to make no allowance for the continual revolutions of manners and customs, and would admit of nothing but what was suitable to the prevailing fashion. Must we throw aside the pictures of our ancestors because of their ruffs and fardingales? But where the ideas of morality and decency alter from one age to another and where vicious manners are described without being marked with the proper characters of blame and disapprobation, this must be allowed to disfigure the poem, and to be a real deformity. I cannot, nor is it proper I should, enter into such sentiments, and however I may excuse the poet on account of the manners of his age I never can relish the composition. The want of humanity and of decency so conspicuous in the characters drawn by several of the ancient poets, even sometimes by Homer and the Greek tragedians, diminishes considerably the merit of their noble performances, and gives modern authors an advantage over them. We are not interested in the fortunes and senti- ments of such rough heroes; we are displeased to find the limits of vice and virtue so much confounded; and whatever indulgence we may give to the writer on account of his prejudices, we cannot prevail on our- selves to enter into his sentiments, or bear an affection to characters which we plainly discover to be blamable.

The case is not the same with moral principles as with speculative opinions of any kind. These are in continual flux and revolution. The son embraces a different system from the father. Nay, there scarcely is any man who can boast of great constancy and uniformity in this particular. Whatever speculative errors may be found in the polite writings of any age or country, they detract but little from the value of those compositions. There needs but a certain turn of thought or imagination to make us enter into all the opinions which then prevailed and relish the sentiments or conclusions derived from them. But a very violent effort is requisite to change our judgment of manners, and excite sentiments of approbation or blame, love or hatred, different from those to which the mind from long custom has been familiarized. And where a man is confident of the rectitude of that moral standard by which he judges, he is justly jealous of it, and will not pervert the sentiments of his heart for a moment in complaisance to any writer whatsoever.

Of all speculative errors, those which regard religion are the most excusable in compositions of genius; nor is it ever permitted to judge of the civility or wisdom of any people, or even of single persons, by the grossness or refinement of their theological principles. The same good sense that directs men in the ordinary occurrences of life is not hearkened to in religious matters, which are supposed to be placed altogether above

the cognizance of human reason. On this account, all the absurdities of
the pagan system of theology must be overlooked by every critic who
would pretend to form a just notion of ancient poetry, and our posterity,
in their turn, must have the same indulgence to their forefathers. No
religious principles can ever be imputed as a fault to any poet while they
remain merely principles, and take not such strong possession of his heart,
as to lay him under the imputation of *bigotry* and *superstition*. Where
that happens, they confound the sentiments of morality and alter the
natural boundaries of vice and virtue. They are therefore eternal
blemishes, according to the principle above mentioned; nor are the
prejudices and false opinions of the age sufficient to justify them.

It is essential to the Roman Catholic religion to inspire a violent hatred
of every other worship, and to represent all pagans, mahometans, and
heretics as the objects of divine wrath and vengeance. Such sentiments,
though they are in reality very blamable, are considered as virtues by the
zealots of that communion, and are represented in their tragedies and
epic poems as a kind of divine heroism. This bigotry has disfigured two
very fine tragedies of the French theater, *Polieucte* and *Athalia*, where an
intemperate zeal for particular modes of worship is set off with all the
pomp imaginable, and forms the predominant character of the heroes.
"What is this?" says the sublime Joad to Josabet, finding her in discourse with Mathan the priest of Baal. "Does the daughter of David speak
to this traitor? Are you not afraid lest the earth should open and pour
forth flames to devour you both? Or lest these holy walls should fall and
crush you together? What is his purpose? Why comes that enemy of God
hither to poison the air which we breathe with his horrid presence?" Such
sentiments are received with great applause on the theater of Paris, but
at London the spectators would be full as much pleased to hear
Achilles tell Agamemnon that he was a dog in his forehead and a deer
in his heart, or Jupiter threaten Juno with a sound drubbing if she will
not be quiet.

Religious principles are also a blemish in any polite composition when
they rise up to superstition, and intrude themselves into every sentiment,
however remote from any connection with religion. It is no excuse for the
poet that the customs of his country had burdened life with so many
religious ceremonies and observances that no part of it was exempt from
that yoke. It must forever be ridiculous in Petrarch to compare his
mistress Laura to Jesus Christ. Nor is it less ridiculous in that agreeable
libertine, Boccace, very seriously to give thanks to God Almighty and the
ladies for their assistance in defending him against his enemies.

IMMANUEL KANT

Critique of the Aesthetical Judgment

FIRST DIVISION
Analytic of the Aesthetical Judgment[1]

FIRST BOOK
Analytic of the Beautiful

FIRST MOMENT
Of the Judgment of Taste,[2] According to Quality[3]

1. The Judgment of Taste is Aesthetical

In order to distinguish whether anything is beautiful or not, we refer the representation, not by the understanding to the object for cognition, but by the imagination (perhaps in conjunction with the understanding) to the subject and its feeling of pleasure or pain. The judgment of taste is therefore not a judgment of cognition, and is consequently not logical but aesthetical, by which we understand that whose determining ground can be *no other than subjective*.[4] Every reference of representations, even that of sensations, may be objective (and then it signifies the real element of an empirical representation), save only the reference to the feeling of pleasure and pain, by which nothing in the object is signified, but through which there is a feeling in the subject as it is affected by the representation.

2. The Satisfaction Which Determines the Judgment of Taste Is Disinterested

The satisfaction which we combine with the representation of the existence of an object is called "interest." Such satisfaction always has reference to the faculty of desire, either as its determining ground or as necessarily connected with its determining ground. Now when the question is if a thing is beautiful, we do not want to know whether anything depends or can depend on the existence of the thing, either for myself or for anyone else, but how we judge it by mere observation (intuition or reflection). If anyone asks me if I find that palace beautiful which I see before me, I may answer: I do not like things of that kind which are made merely to be stared at. . . . In fine, I could easily convince myself that if I found myself on an uninhabited island without the hope of ever again coming among men, and could conjure up just such a splendid building by my mere wish, I should not even give myself the trouble if I had a sufficiently comfortable hut. This may all be admitted and approved, but we are not now talking of this. We wish only to know if this mere representation of the object is accompanied in me with satisfaction, however indifferent I may be as regards the existence of the object of this representation. We easily see that, in saying it is *beautiful* and in showing that I have taste, I am concerned, not with that in which I depend on the existence of the object, but with that which I make out of this representation in myself. Everyone must admit that a judgment about beauty, in which the least interest mingles, is very partial and is not a pure judgment of taste. We must not be in the least prejudiced in favor of the existence of the things, but be quite indifferent in this respect, in order to play the judge in things of taste.[5]

We cannot, however, better elucidate this proposition, which is of capital importance, than by contrasting the pure disinterested satisfaction in judgments of taste with that which is bound up with an interest, especially if we can at the same time be certain that there are no other kinds of interest than those which are to be now specified.

3. The Satisfaction in the Pleasant Is Bound up with Interest

. . . If a determination of the feeling of pleasure or pain is called sensation, this expression signifies something quite different from what I mean when I call the representation of a thing (by sense, as a receptivity belonging to the cognitive faculty) sensation. For in the latter case the representation is referred to the object, in the former simply to the subject, and is available for no cognition whatever, not even for that by which the subject *cognizes* itself.

In the above elucidation we understand by the word "sensation" an objective representation of sense; and, in order to avoid misinterpretation, we shall call that which must always remain merely subjective and can constitute absolutely no representation of an object by the ordinary term "feeling." The green color of the meadows belongs to *objective* sensation, as a perception of an object of sense; the pleasantness of this belongs to *subjective* sensation by which no object is represented, i.e., to feeling, by which the object is considered as an object of satisfaction (which does not furnish a cognition of it).

Now that a judgment about an object by which I describe it as pleasant expresses an interest in it, is plain from the fact that by sensation it excites a desire for objects of that kind; consequently the satisfaction presupposes, not the mere judgment about it, but the relation of its existence to my state, so far as this is affected by such an object. Hence we do not merely say of the pleasant, *it pleases,* but, *it gratifies.* I give to it no mere assent, but inclination is aroused by it; and in the case of what is pleasant in the most lively fashion there is no judgment at all upon the character of the object, for those persons who always lay themselves out for enjoyment (for that is the word describing intense gratification) would fain dispense with all judgment.

4.   The Satisfaction in the Good Is Bound up with Interest

Whatever by means of reason pleases through the mere concept is *good.* That which pleases only as a means we call *good for something* (the useful), but that which pleases for itself is *good in itself.* In both there is always involved the concept of a purpose, and consequently the relation of reason to the (at least possible) volition, and thus a satisfaction in the *presence* of an object or an action, i.e., some kind of interest.

In order to find anything good, I must always know what sort of a thing the object ought to be, i.e., I must have a concept of it. But there is no need of this to find a thing beautiful. Flowers, free delineations, outlines intertwined with one another without design and called conventional foliage, have no meaning, depend on no definite concept, and yet they please. The satisfaction in the beautiful must depend on the reflection upon an object, leading to any concept (however indefinite), and it is thus distinguished from the pleasant, which rests entirely upon sensation.[6]

It is true, the pleasant seems in many cases to be the same as the good. Thus people are accustomed to say that all gratification (especially if it lasts) is good in itself, which is very much the same as to say that lasting pleasure and the good are the same. But we can soon see that this is merely a confusion of words, for the concepts which properly belong to these expresssions can in no way be interchanged. The pleasant, which, as such, represents the object simply in relation to sense, must first be brought by the concept of a purpose under principles of reason, in order to call it good, as an object of the will. But that there is involved a quite different relation to satisfaction in calling that which gratifies at the same time *good* may be seen from the fact that, in the case of the good, the question always is whether it is mediately or immediately good (useful or good in itself); but on the contrary in the case of the pleasant, there can be no question about this at all, for the word always signifies something which pleases immediately. (The same is applicable to what I call beautiful.). . .

However, notwithstanding all this difference between the pleasant and the good, they both agree in this that they are always bound up with an interest in their object; . . . For the good is the object of will (i.e., of a faculty of desire determined by reason). But to wish for something and to have a satisfaction in its existence, i.e., to take an interest in it, are identical.

5.   Comparison of the Three Specifically Different Kinds of Satisfaction

The pleasant and the good have both a reference to the faculty of desire, and they bring with them, the former a satisfaction pathologically conditioned (by impulses, *stimuli*), the latter a pure practical satisfaction which is determined not merely by the representation of the object but also by the represented connection of the subject with the existence of the object. It is not merely the object that pleases, but also its existence. On the other hand, the judgment of taste is merely *contemplative*; i.e., it is a judgment which, indifferent as regards the existence of an object, compares its character with the feeling of pleasure and pain. But this contemplation itself is not directed to concepts; for the judgment of taste is not a cognitive judgment (either theoretical or practical), and thus is not *based* on concepts, nor has it concepts as its *purpose*.

The pleasant, the beautiful, and the good designate then three different relations of representations to the feeling of pleasure and pain, in reference to which we distinguish from one another objects or methods of representing them. And the expressions corresponding to each, by which we mark our complacency in them, are not the same. That which *gratifies* a man is called *pleasant*; that which merely *pleases* him is *beautiful*; that which is *esteemed* or *approved* by him. i.e., that to which he accords an objective worth, is *good*. . . . We may say that, of all these three kinds of satisfaction, that of taste in the beautiful is alone a disinterested and *free* satisfaction; for no interest, either of sense or of reason, here forces our assent. Hence we may say of satisfaction that it is related in the three aforesaid cases to *inclination,* to *favor,* or to *respect.* Now *favor* is the only free satisfaction. An object of inclination and one that is proposed to our desire by a law of reason leave us no freedom in forming for ourselves anywhere an object of pleasure. All interest presupposes or generates a want, and, as the determining ground of assent, it leaves the judgment about the object no longer free. . . .

Explanation of the Beautiful Resulting from the First Moment

Taste is the faculty of judging of an object or a method of representing it by an *entirely disinterested* satisfaction or dissatisfaction. The object of such satisfaction is called *beautiful.*

SECOND MOMENT
Of the Judgment of Taste, According to Quantity

6. The Beautiful is That Which Apart from Concepts Is Represented as the Object of a Universal Satisfaction

This explanation of the beautiful can be derived from the preceding explanation of it as the object of an entirely disinterested satisfaction. For the fact of which everyone is conscious, that the satisfaction is for him quite disinterested, implies in his judgment a ground of satisfaction for all men. For since it does not rest on any inclination of the subject (nor upon any other premeditated interest), but since the person who judges feels himself quite *free* as regards the satisfaction which he attaches to the object, he cannot find the ground of this satisfaction in any private conditions connected with his own subject, and hence it must be regarded as grounded on what he can presuppose in every other person. Consequently he must believe that he has reason for attributing a similar satisfaction to everyone. He will therefore speak of the beautiful as if beauty were a characteristic of the object and the judgment logical (constituting a cognition of the object by means of concepts of it), although it is only aesthetical and involves merely a reference of the representation of the object to the subject. For it has this similarity to a logical judgment that we can presuppose its validity for all men. But this universality cannot arise from concepts; for from concepts there is no transition to the feeling of pleasure or pain (except in pure practical laws, which bring an interest with them such as is not bound up with the pure judgment of taste). Consequently the judgment of taste, accompanied with the consciousness of separation from all interest, must claim validity for every man, without this universality depending on objects. That is, there must be bound up with it a title to subjective universality.[7]

7. Comparison of the Beautiful with the Pleasant and the Good by Means of the Above Characterisitc

As regards the pleasant, everyone is content that his judgment, which he bases upon private feeling and by which he says of an object that it pleases him, should be limited merely to his own person. Thus he is quite contented that if he says, "Canary wine is pleasant," another man may correct his expression and remind him that he ought to say, "It is pleasant *to me*." And this is the case not only as regards the taste of the tongue, the palate, and the throat, but for whatever is pleasant to anyone's eyes and ears. To one, violet color is soft and lovely; to another, it is washed out and dead. One man likes the tone of wind instruments, another that of strings. To strive here with the design of reproving as incorrect another man's judgment which is different from our own, as if the judgments were logically opposed, would be folly. As regards the pleasant, therefore, the fundamental proposition is valid: *everyone has his own taste* (the taste of sense).

The case is quite different with the beautiful. It would (on the contrary) be laughable if a man who imagined anything to his own taste thought to justify himself by saying: "This object (the house we see, the coat that person wears, the concert we hear, the poem submitted to our judgment) is beautiful *for me*." For he must not call it *beautiful* if it merely pleases him. Many things may have for him charm and pleasantness—no one troubles himself at that—but if he gives out anything as beautiful, he supposes in others the same satisfaction; he judges not merely for himself, but for everyone, and speaks of beauty as if it were a property of things. Hence he says "the *thing* is beautiful"; and he does not count on the agreement of others with this his judgment of satisfaction, because he has found this agreement several times before, but he *demands* it of them. He blames them if they judge otherwise and he denies them taste, which he nevertheless requires from them. Here, then, we cannot say that each man has his own particular taste. For this would be as much as to say that there is no taste whatever, i.e., no aesthetical judgment which can make a rightful claim upon everyone's assent. . . .

8. The Universality of the Satisfaction Is Represented in a Judgment of Taste Only as Subjective

This particular determination of the universality of an aesthetical judgment, which is to be met with in a judgment of taste, is noteworthy, not indeed for the logician, but for the transcendental philosopher. It requires no small trouble to discover its origin, but we thus detect a property of our cognitive faculty which without this analysis would remain unknown.

First, we must be fully convinced of the fact that in a judgment of taste (about the beautiful) the satisfaction in the object is imputed to *everyone,* without being based on a concept (for then it would be the good). Further, this claim to universal validity so essentially belongs to a judgment by which we describe anything as *beautiful* that, if this were not thought in it, it would never come into our thoughts to use the expression at all, but everything which pleases without a concept would be counted as pleasant. In respect of the latter, everyone has his own opinion; and no one assumes in another agreement with his judgment of taste, which is always the case in a judgment of taste about beauty. I may call the first the taste of sense, the second the taste of reflection, so far as the first lays down mere private judgments and the second judgments supposed to be generally valid (public), but in both cases aesthetical (not practical) judgments about an object merely in respect of the relation of its representation to the feeling of pleasure and pain. Now here is something strange. As regards the taste of sense, not only does experience show that its judgment (of pleasure or pain connected with anything) is not valid universally, but everyone is content not to impute agreement with it to others (although actually there is often found a very extended concurrence in these judgments). On the other hand, the taste of reflection has its claim to the universal validity of its judgments (about the beautiful) rejected often enough, as experience teaches, although it may find it possible (as it actually does) to represent judgments which can demand this universal agreement. In fact it imputes this to everyone for each of its judgments of taste, without the persons that judge disputing as to the possibility of such a claim, although in particular cases they cannot agree as to the correct application of this faculty.

Here we must, in the first place, remark that a universality which does not rest on concepts of objects (not even on empirical ones) is not logical but aesthetical; i.e., it involves no objective quantity of the judgment, but only that which is subjective. For this I use the expression *general validity,* which signifies the validity of the reference of a representation, not to the cognitive faculty, but to the feeling of pleasure and pain for every subject. (We can avail ourselves also of the same expression for the logical quantity of the judgment, if only we prefix "objective" to "universal validity," to distinguish it from that which is merely subjective and aesthetical.)

A judgment with *objective universal validity* is also always valid subjectively; i.e., if the judgment holds for everything contained under a given concept, it holds also for everyone who represents an object by means of this concept. But from a *subjective universal validity,* i.e., aesthetical and resting on no concept, we cannot infer that which is logical because that kind of judgment does not extend to the object. But, therefore, the aesthetical universality which is ascribed to a judgment must be of a particular kind, because it does not unite the predicate of beauty with the concept of the object, considered in its whole logical sphere, and yet extends it to the whole sphere of judging persons.

In respect of logical quantity, all judgments of taste are *singular* judgments. For because I must refer the object immediately to my feeling of pleasure and pain, and that not by means of concepts, they cannot have the quantity of objective generally valid judgments. Nevertheless, if the singular representation of the object of the judgment of taste, in accordance with the conditions determining the latter, were transformed by comparison into a concept, a logically universal judgment could result therefrom. E.g., I describe by a judgment of taste the rose that I see as beautiful. But the judgment which results from the comparison of several singular judgments, "Roses in general are beautiful," is no longer described simply as aesthetical, but as a logical judgment based on an aesthetical one. Again the judgment, "The rose is pleasant" (to use) is, although aesthetical and singular, not a judgment of taste but of sense. It is distinguished from the former by the fact that the judgment of taste carries with it an *aesthetic quantity* of universality, i.e. of validity for everyone, which cannot be found in a judgment about the pleasant. It is only judgments about the good which, although they also determine satisfaction in an object, have logical and not merely aesthetical universality, for they are valid of the object as cognitive of it, and thus are valid for everyone.[8]

If we judge objects merely according to concepts, then all representation of beauty is lost. Thus there can be no rule according to which anyone is to be forced to recognize anything as beautiful. We cannot press upon others by the aid of any reasons or fundamental propositions our judgment that a coat, a house, or a flower is beautiful. People wish to submit the object to their own eyes, as if the satisfaction in it depended on sensation; and yet, if we then call the object beautiful, we believe that we speak with a universal voice, and we claim the assent of everyone, although on the contrary all private sensation can only decide for the observer himself and his satisfaction.

We may see now that in the judgment of taste nothing is postulated but such a *universal voice,* in respect of the satisfaction without the intervention of concepts, and thus the *possibility* of an aesthetical judgment that can, at the same time, be regarded as valid for everyone. The judgment of taste itself does not *postulate* the agreement of everyone (for that can only be done by a logically universal judgment because it can adduce reasons); it only *imputes* this agreement to everyone, as a case of the rule in respect of which it expects, not confirmation by concepts, but assent from others. The universal voice is, therefore, only an idea (we do not yet inquire upon what it rests). It may be uncertain whether or not the man who believes that he is laying down a judgment of taste is, as a matter of fact, judging in conformity with that idea; but that he refers his judgment thereto, and consequently that it is intended to be a judgment of taste, he announces by the expression "beauty." He can be quite certain of this for himself by the mere consciousness of the separating off everything belonging to the pleasant and the good from the satisfaction which is left; and this is all for which he promises himself the agreement of everyone—a claim which would be justifiable under these conditions, provided only he did not often make mistakes, and thus lay down an erroneous judgment of taste.

9. Investigation of the Question Whether in the Judgment of Taste the Feeling of Pleasure Precedes or Follows the Judging of the Object

The solution of this question is the key to the critique of taste, and so is worthy of all attention.

If the pleasure in the given object precedes, and it is only its universal communicability that is to be acknowledged in the judgment of taste about the representation of the object, there would be a contradiction. For such pleasure would be nothing different from the mere pleasantness in the sensation, and so in accordance with its nature could have only private validity, because it is immediately dependent on the representation through which the object *is given*.[9]

Hence it is the universal capability of communication of the mental state in the given representation which, as the subjective condition of the judgment of taste, must be fundamental and must have the pleasure in the object as its consequent. But nothing can be universally communicated except cognition and representation, so far as it belongs to cognition. For it is only thus that this latter can be objective, and only through this has it a universal point of reference, with which the representative power of everyone is compelled to harmonize. If the determining ground of our judgment as to this universal communicability of the representation is to be merely subjective, i.e., is conceived independently of any concept of the object, it can be nothing else than the state of mind, which is to be met with in the relation of our representative powers to each other, so far as they refer a given representation to *cognition in general*.

The cognitive powers, which are involved by this representation, are here in free play, because no definite concept limits them to a definite rule of cognition. Hence the state of mind in this representation must be a feeling of the free play of the representative powers in a given representation with reference to a cognition in general. Now a representation by which an object is given that is to become a cognition in general requires *imagination* for the gathering together the manifold of intuition, and *understanding* for the unity of the concept uniting the representations. This state of *free play* of the cognitive faculties in a representation by which an object is given must be universally communicable, because cognition, as the determination of the object with which given representations (in whatever subject) are to agree, is the only kind of representation which is valid for everyone.

The subjective universal communicability of the mode of representation in a judgment of taste, since it is to be possible without presupposing a definite concept, can refer to nothing else than the state of mind in the free play of the imagination and the understanding (so far as they agree with each other, as is requisite for *cognition in general*). We are conscious that this subjective relation, suitable for cognition in general, must be valid for everyone, and thus must be universally communicable, just as if it were a definite cognition, resting always on that relation as its subjective condition.

This merely subjective (aesthetical) judging of the object, or of the representation by which it is given, precedes the pleasure in the same and is the ground of this pleasure in the harmony of the cognitive faculties; but on that universality of the subjective conditions for judging of objects is alone based the universal subjective validity of the satisfaction bound up by us with the representation of the object that we call beautiful.

That the power of communicating one's state of mind, even though only in respect of the cognitive faculties, carries a pleasure with it, this we can easily show from the natural propension of man toward sociability (empirical and psychological). But this is not enough for our design. The pleasure that we feel is, in a judgment of taste, necessarily imputed by us to everyone else, as if, when we call a thing beautiful, it is to be regarded as a characteristic of the object which is determined in it according to concepts, though beauty, without a reference to the feeling of the subject, is nothing by itself. . . .

We now occupy ourselves with the easier question, in what way we are conscious of a mutual subjective harmony of the cognitive powers with one another in the judgment of taste—is it aesthetically by mere internal sense and sensation, or is it intellectually by the consciousness of our designed activity, by which we bring them into play?

If the given representation which occasions the judgment of taste were a concept uniting understanding and imagination in the judging of the object, into a cognition of the object, the consciousness of this relation would be intellectual . . . But then the judgment would not be laid down in reference to pleasure and pain, and consequently would not be a judgment of taste. But the judgment of taste, independently of concepts, determines the object in respect of satisfaction and of the predicate of beauty. Therefore that subjective unity of relation can only make itself known by means of sensation. The excitement of both faculties (imagination and understanding) to indeterminate but yet, through the stimulus of the given sensation, harmonious activity, viz., that which belongs to cognition in general, is the sensation whose universal communicability is postulated by the judgment of taste. An objective relation can only be thought, but yet, so far as it is subjective according to its conditions, can be felt in its effect on the mind; and, of a relation based on no concept (like the relation of the representative powers to a cognitive faculty in general), no other consciousness is possible than that through the sensation of the effect, which consists in the more lively play of both mental powers (the imagination and the understanding) when animated by mutual agreement. A representation which, as individual and apart from comparison with others, yet has an agreement with the conditions of universality which it is the business of the understanding to supply, brings the cognitive faculties into that proportionate accord which we require for all cognition, and so regard as holding for everyone who is determined to judge by means of understanding and sense in combination (i.e. for every man).

Explanation of the Beautiful Resulting from the Second Moment

The *beautiful* is that which pleases universally without requiring a concept.

THIRD MOMENT
Of Judgments of Taste, According to the Relation of the Purposes which are Brought into Consideration in Them

10. Of Purposiveness in General

If we wish to explain what a purpose is according to its transcendental determinations (without presupposing anything empirical like the feeling of pleasure), we say that the purpose is the object of a concept, in so far as the concept is regarded as the cause of the object (the real ground of its possibility); and the causality of a *concept* in respect of its *object* is its purposiveness (*forma finalis*). Where then not merely the cognition of an object but the object itself (its form and existence) is thought as an effect only possible by means of the concept of this latter, there we think a purpose. The representation of the effect is here the determining ground of its cause and precedes it. The consciousness of the causality of a representation, for *maintaining* the subject in the same state, may here generally denote what we call pleasure; while on the other hand pain is that representation which contains the ground of the determination of the state of representations into their opposite of restraining or removing them.[10]

The faculty of desire, so far as it is determinable to act only through concepts, i.e., in conformity with the representation of a purpose, would be the will. But an object, or a state of mind, or even an action is called purposive, although its possibility does not necessarily presuppose the representation of a purpose, merely because its possibility can be explained and conceived by us only so far as we assume for its ground a causality according to purposes, i.e., in accordance with a will which has regulated it according to the representation of a certain rule. There can be, then, purposiveness without purpose, so far as we do not place the causes of this form in a will, but yet can only make the explanation of its possibility intelligible to ourselves by deriving it from a will. Again, we are not always forced to regard what we observe (in respect of its possibility) from the point of view of reason. Thus we can at least observe a purposiveness according to form, without basing it on a purpose (as the material of the *nexus finalis*), and remark it in objects, although only by reflection.

11. The Judgment of Taste Has Nothing at its Basis but the Form of the Purposiveness of an Object (or of its Mode of Representation)

Every purpose, if it be regarded as a ground of satisfaction, always carries with it an interest—as the determining ground of the judgment —about the object of pleasure. Therefore no subjective purpose can lie at the basis of the judgment of taste. But also the judgment of taste can be determined by no representation of an objective purpose, i.e., of the possibility of the object itself in accordance with principles of purposive combination, and consequently by no concept of the good, because it is an aesthetical and not a cognitive judgment. It therefore has to do with no *concept* of the character and internal or external possibility of the object by means of this or that cause, but merely with the relation of the representative powers to one another, so far as they are determined by a representation.

Now this relation in the determination of an object as beautiful is bound up with the feeling of pleasure, which is declared by the judgment of taste to be valid for everyone; hence a pleasantness merely accompanying the representation can as little contain the determining ground of the judgment as the representation of the perfection of the object and the concept of the good can. Therefore it can be nothing else than the subjective purposiveness in the representation of an object without any purpose (either objective or subjective), and thus it is the mere form of purposiveness in the representation by which an object is *given* to us, so far as we are conscious of it, which constitutes the satisfaction that we without a concept judge to be universally communicable; and, consequently, this is the determining ground of the judgment of taste. . . .

13. The Pure Judgment of Taste is Independent of Charm and Emotion

Every interest spoils the judgment of taste and takes from its impartiality, especially if the purposiveness is not, as with the interest of reason, placed before the feeling of pleasure but grounded on it. This last always happens in an aesthetical judgment upon anything, so far as it gratifies or grieves us. Hence judgments so affected can lay no claim at all to a universally valid satisfaction, or at least so much the less claim, in proportion as there are sensations of this sort among the determining grounds of taste. That taste is always barbaric which needs a mixture of *charms* and *emotions* in order that there may be satisfaction, and still more so if it make these the measure of its assent.

Nevertheless charms are often not only taken account of in the case of beauty (which properly speaking ought merely to be concerned with form) as contributory to the aesthetical universal satisfaction, but they are passed off as in themselves beauties; and thus the matter of satisfaction is substituted for the form. This misconception, however, which like so many others, has something true at its basis, may be removed by a careful determination of these concepts.

A judgment of taste on which charm and emotion have no influence (although they may be bound up with the satisfaction in the beautiful)— which therefore has as its determining ground merely the purposiveness of the form—is a *pure judgment of taste*.

14. Elucidation by Means of Examples

Aesthetical judgments can be divided just like theoretical (logical) judgments into empirical and pure. The first assert pleasantness or unpleasantness; the second assert the beauty of an object or of the manner of representing it. The former are judgments of sense (material aesthetical judgments); the latter as formal are alone strictly judgments of taste.

A judgment of taste is therefore pure only so far as no merely empirical satisfaction is mingled with its determining ground. But this always happens if charm or emotion have any share in the judgment by which anything is to be described as beautiful.

Now here many objections present themselves which fallaciously put forward charm not merely as a necessary ingredient of beauty, but as alone sufficient to justify a thing's being called beautiful. A mere color, e.g., the green of a grass plot, a mere tone (as distinguished from sound and noise), like that of a violin, are by most people described as beautiful in themselves, although both seem to have at their basis merely the matter of representations, viz., simply sensation, and therefore only deserve to be called pleasant. But we must at the same time remark that the sensations of colors and of tone have a right to be regarded as beautiful only in so far as they are *pure*. This is a determination which concerns their form and is the only element of these representations which admits with certainty of universal communicability; for we cannot assume that the quality of sensations is the same in all subjects, and we can hardly say that the pleasantness of one color or the tone of one musical instrument is judged preferable to that of another in the same way by everyone. . . .

"Pure" in a simple mode of sensation means that its uniformity is troubled and interrupted by no foreign sensation, and it belongs merely to the form; because here we can abstract from the quality of that mode of sensation (abstract from the colors and tone, if any, which it represents). . . .

In painting, sculpture, and in all the formative arts—in architecture and horticulture, so far as they are beautiful arts—the *delineation* is the essential thing; and here it is not what gratifies in sensation but what pleases by means of its form that is fundamental for taste. The colors which light up the sketch belong to the charm; they may indeed enliven the object for sensation, but they cannot make it worthy of contemplation and beautiful. In most cases they are rather limited by the requirements of the beautiful form, and even where charm is permissible it is ennobled solely by this.

Every form of the objects of sense (both of external sense and also mediately of internal) is either *figure* [*Gestalt*] or *play* [*Spiel*]. In the latter case it is either play of figures (in space, viz., pantomime and dancing) or the mere play of sensations (in time). The *charm* of colors or of the pleasant tones of an instrument may be added, but the *delineation* in the first case and the composition in the second constitute the proper object of the pure judgment of taste. To say that the purity of colors and of tones, or their variety and contrast, seem to add to beauty does not mean that they supply a homogeneous addition to our satisfaction in the form because they are pleasant in themselves; but they do so because they make the form more exactly, definitely, and completely, intuitible, and besides, by their charm, excite the representation, while they awaken and fix our attention on the object itself.

Even what we call "ornaments," i.e., those things which do not belong to the complete representation of the object internally as elements, but only externally as complements, and which augment the satisfaction of taste, do so only by their form; as, for example, the frames of pictures or the draperies of statues or the colonnades of places. But if the ornament does not itself consist in beautiful form, and if it is used as a golden frame is used, merely to recommend the painting by its *charm*, it is then called *finery* and injures genuine beauty.

Emotion, that is a sensation in which pleasantness is produced by means of a momentary checking and a consequent more powerful outflow of the vital force, does not belong at all to beauty. And thus a pure judgment of taste has for its determining ground neither charm nor emotion—in a word, no sensation as the material of the aesthetical judgment.

15. The Judgment of Taste is Quite Inedpendent of the Concept of Perfection

Objective purposiveness can only be cognized by means of the reference of the manifold to a definite purpose, and therefore only through a concept. From this alone it is plain that the beautiful, the judging of which has at its basis a merely formal purposiveness, i.e., a purposiveness without purpose, is quite independent of the concept of the good, because the latter presupposes an objective purposiveness, i.e., the reference of the object to a definite purpose.[11]

Objective purposiveness is either external, i.e., the *utility*, or internal, i.e., the *perfection* of the object. That the satisfaction in an object, on account of which we call it beautiful, cannot rest on the representation of its utility is sufficiently obvious from the two preceding sections; because in that case it would not be an immediate satisfaction in the object, which is the essential condition of a judgment about beauty. But objective internal purposiveness, i.e., perfection, comes nearer to the predicate of beauty; and it has been regarded by celebrated philosophers as the same as beauty, with the proviso, *if it is thought in a confused way*. It is of the greatest importance in a critique of taste to decide whether beauty can thus actually be resolved into the concept of perfection.

To judge of objective purposiveness we always need, not only the concept of a purpose, but (if that purposiveness is not to be external utility but internal) the concept of an internal purpose which shall contain the ground of the internal possibility of the object. Now as a purpose in general is that whose *concept* can be regarded as the ground of the possibility of the object itself; so, in order to represent objective purposiveness in a thing, the concept of *what sort of thing it is to be* must come first. The agreement of the manifold in it with this concept (which furnishes the rule for combining the manifold) is the *qualitative perfection* of the thing. Quite different from this is *quantitative* perfection, the completeness of a thing after its kind, which is a mere concept of magnitude (of totality). In this *what the thing ought to be* is conceived as already determined, and it is only asked if it has *all* its requisites. The formal element in the representation of a thing, i.e., the agreement of the manifold with a unity (it being undetermined what this ought to be), gives to cognition no objective purposiveness whatever. For since abstraction is made of this unity as *purpose* (what the thing ought to be), nothing remains but the subjective purposiveness of the representations in the mind of the intuiting subject. And this, although it furnishes a certain purposiveness of the representative state of the subject, and so a facility of apprehending a given form by the imagination, yet furnishes no perfection of an object, since the object is not here conceived by means of the concept of a purpose. For example, if in a forest I come across a plot of sward around which trees stand in a circle and do not then represent to myself a purpose, viz., that it is intended to serve for country dances, not the least concept of perfection is furnished by the mere form. But to represent to oneself a formal *objective* purposiveness without purpose, i.e., the mere form of a *perfection* (without any matter and without the *concept* of that with which it is accordant, even if it were merely the idea of conformity to law in general), is a veritable contradiction.

Now the judgment of taste is an aesthetical judgment, i.e., such as rests on subjective grounds, the determining ground of which cannot be a concept, and consequently cannot be the concept of a definite purpose. Therefore by means of beauty, regarded as a formal subjective purposiveness, there is in no way thought a perfection of the object, as a purposiveness alleged to be formal but which is yet objective. And thus to distinguish between the concepts of the beautiful and the good as if they were only different in logical form, the first being a confused, the second a clear concept of perfection, but identical in content and origin, is quite fallacious. For then there would be no *specific* difference between them, but a judgment of taste would be as much a cognitive judgment as the judgment by which a thing is described as good; just as when the ordinary man says that fraud is unjust he bases his judgment on confused grounds, while the philosopher bases it on clear grounds, but both on identical principles of reason. I have already, however, said that an aesthetical judgment is unique of its kind and gives absolutely no cognition (not even a confused cognition) of the object; this is only supplied by a logical judgment. On the contrary, it simply refers the representation, by which an object is given, to the subject, and brings to our notice no characteristic of the object, but only the purposive form in the determination of the representative powers which are occupying themselves therewith. The judgment is called aesthetical just because its determining ground is not a concept, but the feeling (of internal sense) of that harmony in the play of the mental powers, so far as it can be felt in sensation. On the other hand, if we wish to call confused concepts and the objective judgment based on them aesthetical, we will have an understanding judging sensibly or a sense representing its objects by means of concepts both of which are contradictory. The faculty of concepts, be they confused or clear, is the understanding; and although understanding has to do with the judgment of taste as an aesthetical judgment (as it has with all judgments), yet it has to do with it, not as a faculty by which an object is cognized, but as the faculty which determines the judgment and its representation (without any concept) in accordance with its relation to the subject and the subject's internal feeling, in so far as this judgment may be possible in accordance with a universal rule.

16. The Judgment of Taste, by Which an Object Is Declared to Be Beautiful Under the Condition of a Definite Concept, Is Not Pure

There are two kinds of beauty: free beauty (*pulchritudo vaga*), or merely dependent beauty (*pulchritudo adhaerens*). The first presupposes no concept of what the object ought to be; the second does presuppose such a concept and the perfection of the object in accordance therewith. The first is called the (self-subsistent) beauty of this or that thing; the second, as dependent upon a concept (conditioned beauty), is ascribed to objects which come under the concept of a particular purpose.[12]

Flowers are free natural beauties. Hardly anyone but a botanist knows what sort of a thing a flower ought to be; and even he, though recognizing in the flower the reproductive organ of the plant, pays no regard to this natural purpose if he is passing judgment on the flower by taste. There is, then, at the basis of this judgment no perfection of any kind, no internal purposiveness, to which the collection of the manifold is referred. Many birds (such as the parrot, the humming bird, the bird of paradise) and many sea shells are beauties in themselves, which do not belong to any object determined in respect of its purpose by concepts, but please freely and in themselves. So also delineations *à la grecque*, foliage for borders or wall papers, mean nothing in themselves; they represent nothing—no object under a definite concept—and are free beauties. We can refer to the same class what are called in music phantasies (i.e., pieces without any theme), and in fact all music without words.

In the judging of a free beauty (according to the mere form), the judgment of taste is pure. There is presupposed no concept of any purpose which the manifold of the given object is to serve, and which therefore is to be represented in it. By such a concept the freedom of the imagination which disports itself in the contemplation of the figure would be only limited.

But human beauty (i.e., of a man, a woman, or a child), the beauty of a horse, or a building (be it church, palace, arsenal, or summer house), presupposes a concept of the purpose which determines what the thing is to be, and consequently a concept of its perfection; it is therefore adherent beauty. Now as the combination of the pleasant (in sensation) with beauty, which properly is only concerned with form, is a hindrance to the purity of the judgment of taste, so also is its purity injured by the combination with beauty of the good (viz., that manifold which is good for the thing itself in accordance with its purpose). . . .

Now the satisfaction in the manifold of a thing in reference to the internal purpose which determines its possibility is a satisfaction grounded on a concept; but the satisfaction in beauty is such as presupposes no concept, but is immediately bound up with the representation through which the object is given (not through which it is thought). If now the judgment of taste in respect of the beauty of a thing is made dependent on the purpose in its manifold, like a judgment of reason, and thus limited, it is no longer a free and pure judgment of taste.

It is true that taste gains by this combination of aesthetical with intellectual satisfaction, inasmuch as it becomes fixed; and though it is not universal, yet in respect to certain purposively determined objects it becomes possible to prescribe rules for it. These, however, are not rules of taste, but merely rules for the unification of taste with reason, i.e., of the beautiful with the good, by which the former becomes available as an instrument of design in respect of the latter. Thus the tone of mind which is self-maintaining and of subjective universal validity is subordinated to the way of thinking which can be maintained only by painful resolve, but is of objective universal validity. Properly speaking, however, perfection gains nothing by beauty, or beauty by perfection; but when we compare the representation by which an object is given to us with the object (as regards what it ought to be) by means of a concept, we cannot avoid considering along with it the sensation in the subject. And thus when both states of mind are in harmony our *whole faculty* of representative power gains.

A judgment of taste, then, in respect of an object with a definite internal purpose, can only be pure if either the person judging has no concept of this purpose or else abstracts from it in his judgment. Such a person, although forming an accurate judgment of taste in judging of the object as free beauty, would yet by another who considers the beauty in it only as a dependent attribute (who looks to the purpose of the object) be blamed and accused of false taste, although both are right in their own way—the one in reference to what he has before his eyes, the other in reference to what he has in his thought. By means of this distinction we can settle many disputes about beauty between judges of taste, by showing that the one is speaking of free, the other of dependent, beauty—that the first is making a pure, the second an applied, judgment of taste. . . .

Explanation of the Beautiful Derived from this Third Moment

Beauty is the form of the *purposiveness* of an object, so far as this is perceived in it *without any representation of a purpose.*[13]

FOURTH MOMENT
Of the Judgment of Taste, According to the Modality of the Satisfaction in the Object

18. What the Modality in a Judgment of Taste Is

I can say of every representation that it is at least *possible* that (as a cognition) it should be bound up with a pleasure. Of a representation that I call *pleasant* I say that it *actually* excites pleasure in me. But the *beautiful* we think as having a *necessary* reference to satisfaction. Now this necessity is of a peculiar kind. It is not a theoretical objective necessity, in which case it would be cognized *a priori* that everyone *will feel* this satisfaction in the object called beautiful by me. It is not a practical necessity, in which case, by concepts of a pure rational will serving as a rule for freely acting beings, the satisfaction is the necessary result of an objective law and only indicates that we absolutely (without any further design) ought to act in a certain way. But the necessity which is thought in an aesthetical judgment can only be called exemplary, i.e., a necessity of the assent of *all* to a judgment which is regarded as the example of a universal rule that we cannot state. Since an aesthetical judgment is not an objective cognitive judgment, this necessity cannot be derived from definite concepts and is therefore not apodictic. Still less can it be inferred from the universality of experience (of a complete agreement of judgments as to the beauty of a certain object). For not only would experience hardly furnish sufficiently numerous vouchers for this, but also, on empirical judgments, we can base no concept of the necessity of these judgments.[14]

19. The Subjective Necessity, Which We Ascribe to the Judgment of Taste, Is Conditioned

The judgment of taste requires the agreement of everyone, and he who describes anything as beautiful claims that everyone *ought* to give his approval to the object in question and also describe it as beautiful. The *ought* in the aesthetical judgment is therefore pronounced in accordance with all the data which are required for judging, and yet is only conditioned. We ask for the agreement of everyone else, because we have for it a ground that is common to all; and we could count on this agreement, provided we were always sure that the case was correctly subsumed under that ground as rule of assent.

20. The Condition of Necessity Which a Judgment of Taste Asserts Is the Idea of a Common Sense

If judgments of taste (like cognitive judgments) had a definite objective principle, then the person who lays them down in accordance with this latter would claim an unconditioned necessity for his judgment. If they were devoid of all principle, like those of the mere taste of sense, we would not allow them in thought any necessity whatever. Hence they must have a subjective principle which determines what pleases or displeases only by feeling and not by concepts, but yet with universal validity. But such a principle could only be regarded as a *common sense*, which is essentially different from common understanding which people sometimes call common sense (*sensus communis*); for the latter does not judge by feeling but always by concepts, although ordinarily only as by obscurely represented principles.

Hence it is only under the presupposition that there is a common sense (by which we do not understand an external sense, but the effect resulting from the free play of our cognitive powers)—it is only under this presupposition, I say, that the judgment of taste can be laid down.[15]

21. Have We Ground for Presupposing a Common Sense?

Cognitions and judgments must, along with the conviction that accompanies them, admit of universal communicability; for otherwise there would be no harmony between them and the object, and they would be collectively a mere subjective play of the representative powers, exactly as scepticism desires. But if cognitions are to admit of communicability, so must also the state of mind—i.e., the accordance of the cognitive powers with a cognition generally and that proportion of them which is suitable for a representation (by which an object is given to us) in order that a cognition may be made out of it—admit of universal communicability. For without this as the subjective condition of cognition, cognition as an effect could not arise. This actually always takes place when a given object by means of sense excites the imagination to collect the manifold, and the imagination in its turn excites the understanding to bring about a unity of this collective process in concepts. But this accordance of the cognitive powers has a different proportion according to the variety of the objects which are given. However, it must be such that this internal relation, by which one mental faculty is excited by another, shall be generally the most beneficial for both faculties in respect of cognition (of given objects); and this accordance can only be determined by feeling (not according to concepts). Since now this accordance itself must admit of universal communicability, and consequently also our feeling of it (in a given representation), and since the universal communicability of a feeling presupposes a common sense, we have grounds for assuming this latter. And this common sense is assumed without relying on psychological observations, but simply as the necessary condition of the universal communicability of our knowledge, which is presupposed in every logic and in every principle of knowledge that is not sceptical.

22. The Necessity of the Universal Agreement that Is Thought in a Judgment of Taste Is a Subjective Necessity, Which Is Represented as Objective Under The Presupposition of a Common Sense

In all judgments by which we describe anything as beautiful, we allow no one to be of another opinion, without, however, grounding our judgment on concepts, but only on our feeling, which we therefore place as its basis, not as a private, but as a common feeling. Now this common sense cannot be grounded on experience, for it aims at justifying judgments which contain an *ought*. It does not say that everyone *will* agree with my judgment, but that he *ought*. And so common sense, as an example of whose judgment I here put forward my judgment of taste and on account of which I attribute to the latter an *exemplary* validity, is a mere ideal norm, under the supposition of which I have a right to make into a rule for everyone a judgment that accords therewith, as well as the satisfaction in an object expressed in such judgment. For the principle which concerns the agreement of different judging persons, although only subjective, is yet assumed as subjectivly universal (an idea necessary for everyone), and thus can claim universal assent (as if it were objective) provided we are sure that we have correctly subsumed the particulars under it.

This indeterminate norm of a common sense is actually presupposed by us, as is shown by our claim to lay down judgments of taste. . . .

Explanation of the Beautiful Resulting from the Fourth Moment

The *beautiful* is that which without any concept is cognized as the object of a *necessary* satisfaction.

Notes

All notes in brackets have been supplied by the editor; the rest are Kant's.

1. [The translator uses the same English noun for two German nouns used by Kant: *Urteilskraft* and *Urteil*. Judgment = *Urteilskraft* is a mental, indeed a

cognitive, faculty: the ability or capacity to judge something, to make judgments. In the introduction (omitted here) Kant says, "Judgment (*Urteilskraft*) in general is the faculty of thinking the particular under the universal," for example, the ability to think that this (some item presented to us in sense experience, say) is a horse, or is brown. A judgment (*Urteil*) is either (1) an exercise of the faculty of judgment, that is, an act of judging or thinking a particular under a universal, or (2) the expression of such an act in the form of a statement or proposition.

Again in the introduction Kant distinguishes between two kinds of judgment (*Urteilskraft*): "If the universal . . . be given, the judgment which subsumes the particular under it . . . is *determinant*. But if only a particular be given for which a universal has to be found, the judgment is merely *reflective*." Thus if you possess the concept of a sonnet or of a symphony and you look for, and find, something answering to it, your judgment that this (Shakespeare's "When to the sessions of sweet silent thought . . . ," say) is a sonnet is determinant. But if you are presented with a poem or a piece of music and you try to find the concept that properly applies to it, your judgment that this (which happens to be Mozart's "Jupiter" Symphony, say) is a symphony is reflective.

The German title of Kant's book is *Der Kritik der Urteilskraft*.]

2. The definition of "taste" which is laid down here is that it is the faculty of judging of the beautiful. But the analysis of judgments of taste must show what is required in order to call an object beautiful. The moments to which this judgment has regard in its reflection I have sought in accordance with the guidance of the logical functions of judgment (for in a judgment of taste a reference to the understanding is always involved). I have considered the moment of quality first because the aesthetical judgment upon the beautiful first pays attention to it.

3. [According to the *Critique of Pure Reason*, the doctrine of which is presupposed by the *Critique of Judgment*, every judgment (proposition) can be classified as to its quality, that is, as to whether it is affirmative ("A is B"), negative ("A is not B"), or infinite ("A is non-B"); as to its quantity, that is, as to whether it is universal ("Every A is B"), particular ("Some A is B"), or singular ("This A is B"); as to its relation, that is, as to whether it is categorical ("A is B"), hypothetical ("If something is A, then it is B") or disjunctive ("Either something is A or it is B"); and as to its modality, that is, as to whether it is assertoric (asserts that something is, or is not, actually the case), problematic (asserts that something is possibly the case, or not the case), or apodictic (asserts that something is necessarily the case, or not the case). This classification provides the ostensible topics of the four "Moments" of the Analytic of the Beautiful, although Kant is not actually much interested in this classification of judgments of taste as to logical form. The discussion of the First Moment, for example, does not raise the question as to whether the judgment of taste is affirmative, negative, or infinite, but deals with other features of such a judgment.]

4. [When Kant applies the adjective "aesthetical" or "aesthetic" to *representations (Vorstellungen)*, by which, according to the *Critique of Pure Reason*, objects are given to us (in intuition) or are thought (through concepts), he means that they are "sensible." "Aesthetic" comes from the Greek AISTHETIKOS, which, in one of its senses, means perceptible by sense. There are two kinds of aesthetic or sensible representations: sensations (*Empfindungen*) and feelings (*Gefühle*). As applied to *judgments*, however, "aesthetic" means that they are "subjective" or, in a way, about the "subject" or person making the judgment. For example, "That is disgusting" is about the way in which the subject, or person pronouncing the judgment, is affected by the referent of "That," which is an "object." In other words, Kant seems to hold that an aesthetical judgment,

such as "This is pleasing (pleasant)," is an implicit avowal and says, in effect, "I am pleased by this." Judgments of taste are a species of aesthetic judgments, according to Kant, and the purpose of the Analytic of the Beautiful is to spell out how judgments of taste—or "pure" aesthetic judgments, as Kant calls them in #14—differ from other aesthetic judgments—which he calls "empirical" or "material"—as well as from what he calls "logical" or "objective" judgments, judgments that are wholly about objects, for example, "This is a liquid" or "That is a horse."]

5. [A judgment of taste, "This is beautiful," implicitly avows that the subject or person making it is pleased or satisfied by the object designated by "This." But for it to be a pure judgment of taste, the pleasure avowed must be disinterested or devoid of interest. Interested pleasures are pleasures we take in the existence of an object, or in the idea of its existence, and they are connected with desire, want, or need. For pleasures are distinguished from one another by that on which they are based. If they are based on interest, then they are interested pleasures; otherwise they are disinterested or "free." Interests, Kant seems to hold in the following two sections, are confined to that which is sensuously pleasant and to that which is good. The good is of two kinds: the good-for, or the useful, and the good-in-itself, which, Kant argues elsewhere, is restricted to the moral, or what he calls "a good will." For example, if something gives me sensuous pleasure—has a pleasing taste or smell, say—then I am delighted that it exists and desire it, or desire that it continue to exist. If I need a screwdriver to perform a certain task, I am delighted to find that one is at hand, exists; and, as a rational being, I inherently desire the existence of good wills (people who act morally) and am pleased to find them in existence, or even to think that they might exist. All of these pleasures or delights are interested.]

6. [This is an important paragraph and may be paraphrased as follows: To find something good, I must always know what sort of thing the object ought to be; which means that I must have a *definite* or *determinate (bestimmt)* concept of it. But to find something beautiful, I do not require a definite or determinate concept of it. Flowers and the like please us in such a way that we can rightly say they are beautiful, but our judgment does not depend on any definite concept of them (See #16). Still, the pleasure or satisfaction in the beautiful must depend on reflection upon an object (see #9), leading to *some* concept, albeit an *indefinite* one, and it is thus distinguished from the merely pleasant, which rests on sensation alone (as opposed to reflection on the object).

The indefinite or indeterminate concept to which reflection on the object leads and upon which the judgment of taste rests turns out to be (#10) that of "purposiveness without purpose." When Kant says, as he often does, that "the judgment of taste is not based upon concepts at all" he means that it is not based on *determinate* concepts at all, determinate concepts being the kind of concepts involved in *knowledge* of objects. For the distinction between definite and indefinite concepts, see #57.

(I am indebted for the substance of this note to a letter from Professor Donald W. Crawford, whose book, *Kant's Aesthetic Theory*, I have found to be the most helpful of commentaries on the first part of the *Critique of Judgment* and to which these notes are elsewhere indebted.)]

7. [Unlike "This is pleasant," which is an aesthetic judgment and is based on (avows) an interested pleasure and is, hence, personal (has what Kant calls "subjective, or private, validity only"), a judgment of taste, being based on (avowing) a distinterested pleasure, is impersonal. Being impersonal it is *like* a "logical" judgment, for example, "This is green" or "That is round," even though "_____ is beautiful," unlike "_____ is green" or

"_____ is round," does not express a concept, does not ascribe some publicly determinable property to an object. And, hence, just as my claim that something is green or is round (unlike my claim that it merely looks green or round to me), being impersonal, invites or calls for the agreement of everyone (even though it may do so unjustifiably in some cases, or may not actually receive general agreement), so my claim that something is beautiful (unlike the claim that it merely pleases me) invites or calls for the agreement of everyone, or, as Kant puts it, purports to be "universally valid." The difference is this: in the case of an objective judgment, the basis of the universal validity is some property ascribed to the object, the existence of which anyone can verify for himself; whereas in the case of a judgment of taste, the initial basis of the implicit claim to universal validity is a disinterested feeling of pleasure or satisfaction.]

8. [From a strictly logical point of view, as Kant notes at the beginning of this paragraph, every judgment of taste is, as regards its quantity, singular: its subject term is a demonstrative ("This," "That"), a proper name (*The School of Athens* by Raphael; *La Mer* by Debussy), or a definite description ("The last quartet composed by Mozart," "The Vermeer in the Frick Collection"). Neither "Some Bach fugues are beautiful" nor "All the paintings by Piero della Francesca are beautiful" is, strictly speaking, a judgment of taste; although each may be based collectively on a set of (singular) judgments of taste (See #33). Still, a judgment of taste "carries with it an *aesthetic quantity* of universality" in that it purports to be universally valid.]

9. [If a judgment of taste were merely an implicit avowal of pleasure excited by an object, then it would be nothing but an ordinary (material or empirical) aesthetic judgment; in which case it could have subjective or private validity only. What, in the heading of this section, Kant calls "the judging of the object" is, then, *not the same as* the judgment of taste. For the judgment of taste to claim universal validity, the pleasure involved in it must follow or be consequent upon the judging of the object. What is this judging of the object? It consists in reflecting on the object (is an act of *reflective* judgment), employing the two cognitive capacities requisite for all knowledge, or indeed for all experience, of objects, namely, imagination (by which a manifold of sensuous representations, of sensuous experiences of features of the object, are reproduced and brought together or "synthesized") and understanding (by which some significant pattern in the manifold is discerned—if possible). Because the activities of imagination and understanding are, in the reflection on an object that is involved in an exercise of taste, not guided by a concept (in which case the judgment would be determinant anyhow), or by a search for the kind of pattern or unity in the manifold that would justify the application of a (determinate) concept, as they would be in the case of cognition of the object (e.g., recognizing it as a church, or as a sonnet), the two faculties are said to be in "free play." Now if they are successful in discerning the relevant pattern (discussed in the next section) in the manifold of representations that constitutes experience of the object, they are said by Kant to be in "harmony," and it is consciousness of this harmony that is, or provokes, the pleasure implicitly avowed in the judgment of taste. Thus, as Kant argues in this section, (reflectively) judging of the object precedes the disinterested pleasure involved in the experience of the beautiful, the pleasure implicitly avowed in the judgment of taste. Because judging of the object is reflective (and not determinant), the judgment of taste that is consequent upon it is, by extension, reflective as well.

Further, since all human beings must be capable of exercising imagination and understanding and of experiencing their free play, this experience must be universally communicable, and its universal communicability makes possible the universal validity of the judgment of taste.]

10. [An object is said by Kant to have a purpose when it, and the organization of its parts or constituent elements (its *form*), is the result of an exercise of will according to some rule or plan, that is, a concept. Thus bridges, typewriters, churches, and other objects that have a specifiable use, have a purpose. A purpose, however, is not the same as a specifiable use; for objects that have no specifiable use, for example, symphonies, paintings, and the like, clearly have a purpose in Kant's sense. Objects that have a purpose are also said to be purposive. But purposiveness does not entail actual purpose: "X is purposive" does not imply "X has a purpose, that is, is the result of a will acting according to a rule or concept." For an object can be said to be purposive solely on the basis of its discerned structure or form, if that structure or form is of the sort that we generally think of as possible only as the result of a will acting according to a rule or concept. For an object to be apprehended as purposive we have merely to think of it, or its form, *as if* it were the result of a will acting according to a concept; we *need* not think of it as actually being such a result. Thus if a certain rock formation or a stand of trees were to look for all the world as if it had been fabricated or arranged by human hand, then, whether or not it was *actually* so fabricated or arranged, it would be purposive. This means that in reflectively judging an object we can ignore or prescind from the question of whether it has a purpose and attend solely to its possible purposiveness. It is this feature that the reflective judging of the object (discussed in #9) seeks to discern through the free play of imagination and understanding, thereby effecting that harmony of these faculties which yields the disinterested pleasure implicitly avowed in the judgment of taste.]

11. [In this section Kant distinguishes between objective and subjective purposiveness. Objective purposiveness does entail purpose; subjective purposiveness does not. Because objective purposiveness entails purpose, it also entails a concept, namely, the concept according to which a will fashioned the object in question. This concept is the concept of "what sort of thing it [the object] is to be," as Kant puts it. Thus a screwdriver and a sonnet both have objective purposiveness: each has a purpose, and the purpose in each case is specified by the concept of what sort of thing the object is to be. Both the maker of the screwdriver and the writer of the sonnet were guided in their activity by a concept. Since a judgment of taste, however, prescinds from any (determinate) concept of the object judged, it involves only its possible purposiveness apart from any purpose it may in fact have.]

12. [Kant recognizes that the adjective "beautiful" has at least two uses. "This (which may happen to be a sonnet) is beautiful" and "This is a beautiful sonnet," although they may on occasion be used synonymously, are not necessarily synonymous. Where they are not, the latter, as Kant sees it, presupposes the concept of a sonnet, of what a sonnet is to be, and hence of its perfection (from *perfectus* = finished or complete). It says in effect that the sonnet is a perfect, or nondefective, instance of its kind. Other examples: your dentist says, "That's a beautiful set of teeth you have there," or your tennis coach says, "That was a beautiful serve." This is what Kant calls "dependent" or "adherent" beauty. A judgment of taste, however, is "free," that is, determinate concept-free; it does not involve a concept of the object judged, except perhaps incidentally. To put it another way: if in a judgment of the form "This X is beautiful" or "This is a beautiful X," the concept of X is eliminable without affecting the sense or purport of the judgment, then the judgment is one of taste; otherwise it is a judgment of dependent beauty.]

13. It might be objected to this explanation that there are things in which we see a purposive form without cognizing any purpose in them, like the stone implements often gotten from old sepulchral tumuli with a hole in them, as if for a handle. These, although they plainly indicate by their shape a purposiveness of

which we do not know the purpose, are nevertheless not described as beautiful. But if we regard a thing as a work of art, that is enough to make us admit that its shape has reference to some design and definite purpose. And hence there is no immediate satisfaction in the contemplation of it. On the other hand a flower, e.g., a tulip, is regarded as beautiful, because in perceiving it we find a certain purposiveness which, in our judgment, is referred to no purpose at all.

[This is why the *free* beauty of a work of art is on all fours with the free beauty of natural objects. The fact that an object judged to be beautiful is a sonnet as opposed to a sonata is absolutely immaterial in the case of a judgment of taste.]

14. [The *logical* modality of the judgment of taste is actuality. But because the judgment purports to have universal validity that, unlike an ordinary logical judgment, is not grounded in determinate concepts, it has a necessity, as Kant puts it, "of a peculiar kind," an "exemplary" neecessity.]

15. [The exemplary necessity of a judgment of taste presupposes, or requires as a necessary condition of its possibility, a "common sense" present in all beings capable of cognition, this sense being the capacity to feel the disinterested pleasure that is, or has as its necessary ground, the harmony resulting from the free play of imagination and understanding in the reflective judgment of the object. The reason for this, as Kant argues in the next section, is that if the content or purport of a judgment is to admit of universal communicability, the state of mind on which it is based—be that state of mind cognitive or non-cognitive—must be universally communicable. It is this presupposition that allows us, when making judgments of taste to speak with what Kant has called (Section 8) "a universal voice." (And do we not assume that creatures incapable of having the kinds of experiences, or "states of mind," that we have are *ipso facto* incapable of understanding what we say? Wittgenstein remarks (*Philosophical Investigations*, G. E. M. Anscombe trans., p. 223e), "If a lion could talk, we could not understand him." That is, if a lion behaved in the way normal lions do, except that it occasionally uttered English sentences, would we be able to understand what, if anything, it had in mind? We might be able to understand the *sentences* it uttered; but would we be able to understand *it*?)]

GUY SIRCELLO

A New Theory of Beauty

Skepticism with Regard to Beauty

K ANT STARTED IT ALL by declaring that the judgment of beauty is not
determined by concepts.[1] He meant that no criteria of beauty can
be given in terms of features of the objects to which "beautiful" is applicable; and he thus opened the gates of subjectivism. This form of
skepticism with regard to beauty has dominated most of the up-to-date
thought of the last two centuries. At a certain level of superficiality, the
skepticism is reasonable. First, it's easy to see that no one has yet offered
a clear enough or a comprehensive enough theory of beauty. Second,
the task of finding a criterion of beauty seems, *prima facie*, beyond
human powers. For just consider the range of objects to which beauty
can be attributed: people, rocks, snakes, daisies, horses, trees, mountains,
rivers, paintings, symphonies, buildings, spoons, books, chairs, hats.
Confronted with this array, even the most intrepid theorist is likely to
despair of uncovering features that all beautiful objects share and that
constitute necessary and sufficient conditions for the correct attribution
of beauty. . . .

Beautiful "Objects"

The best way to refute skepticism is simply to provide a clear, comprehensive, and true theory that gives the criterion of beauty in things.
The way to do that, however, is not to search for features common to
all beautiful objects, for a moment's reflection will show that if we
restrict our attention only to beautiful objects, we shall miss much of
the world's beauty. Mountains, rivers, and symphonies may, in an
attenuated sense, be called objects. But the starry night, the ridgeline of
the Santa Ana Mountains against the morning sky, the way the Phila-

From Guy Sircello, *A New Theory of Beauty* (Copyright © 1975 by Princeton
University Press). Excerpts from pp. 4-81. Reprinted by permission of Princeton
University Press.

delphia Orchestra plays Strauss, the color of California hills in spring, a well-executed *arabesque penchée*, and the late afternoon sunlight reflecting off the waves are by no means objects. Of course, we *need* not construe "object" so pedantically. We could mean by "object" in these contexts merely anything denoted by the subject of a sentence in which "beautiful" is a predicate adjective. Let us, accordingly, enlarge the class of things we take to be objects. We will henceforth refer to members of this larger class as *"objects"*—with the scare quotes a part of the referring term. The class of beautiful "objects," then, includes much more than the class of beautiful objects.

With "object" so defined, however, skepticism looms even larger. The springtime hills are beautiful; their color is beautiful. Helen's skin is beautiful; the clearness of her skin is beautiful. But what do the hills and their color, or Helen's skin and its clarity, have in common that makes them both beautiful? . . .

"Beautiful Properties"

. . . In general, the beauty of an "object" X would seem to be nothing but the beauty of all its properties that are beautiful, or the beautiful properties of all those "objects," if any, with respect to which X is beautiful, or both. . .[2]

But, you ask, couldn't Helen's skin or the hills of home have beauty independent of the beauties of *any* of their respective properties? If so, it would also be possible for them to possess *no* beautiful properties and yet be beautiful. We would ask "What is there about the hills that is beautiful?" And a legitimate answer would be: "There is nothing about the hills that is beautiful; there is nothing with respect to which they are beautiful. They are, nevertheless, beautiful." I want to claim on the contrary that, at least for "objects" that are not themselves properties, such an answer is never warranted. That is, I am claiming that at least all beautiful "objects" that are not properties are beautiful with respect to some other beautiful "objects." I cannot, however, think of any convincing deductive argument that yields such a conclusion. My reasons for believing the claim are these: (1) For a great many beautiful "objects" we can indeed say what is beautiful about them by mentioning one or more of their beautiful parts, elements, or properties. Therefore, (2) it is not generally true that "beautiful" applies to all "objects" *in no respects.* Furthermore, (3) even of those beautiful "objects" about which we cannot specify the respect(s) in which they are beautiful, it is never impertinent to pose the questions "What about them is beautiful? In what respect(s) are they beautiful?" And this fact implies (4) that there might well be an answer to the questions, even if it does not *guarantee* that there is an answer. . . .

The Job of a Theory of Beauty

. . . If certain "objects" are beautiful only with respect to certain other beautiful "objects," a maximally comprehensive theory of beauty need not concern itself with the former "objects." Furthermore, if the whole class of beautiful "objects" were divisible, without remainder, into a class of beautiful "objects" that are beautiful with respect to other "objects" and a class of "objects" with respect to which ultimately all the "objects" of the first class are beautiful, then a maximally comprehensive theory of beauty need be a theory solely of the beauty of the latter class of "objects." And if, finally, we could specify in a general way the class of such "objects," we would thereby simplify and clarify the job of constructing a comprehensive theory of beauty. . . .

. . . Now it appears to be quite universally true that if, of any beautiful "object" X, *which is not clearly a property,* we ask "With respect to what is X beautiful?" or "What about X is beautiful?" then either (1) we can answer the question by naming one or more beautiful properties or (2) we can apply the question again to what we put forward as an answer. Furthermore, we can continue applying the question until the answer is given by naming a beautiful property (or properties). Thus what is beautiful about the hills, say, is their greenness and their soft look. What is beautiful about Helen is, say, only her skin, and what is beautiful about her skin, say, is only its clearness. What is beautiful about my eucalypt, say, is only the radial pattern I see when I look up its trunk. And what is beautiful about that pattern, say, is only its "explosive" look. We have here, then, many diverse beautiful "objects": the hills, their greenness, their soft look, Helen, her skin, its clearness, my tree, its pattern, the pattern's "explosive" look. But it would appear that a comprehensive theory of beauty could do its job perfectly well if it could account only for the beauty of the hills' greenness and their soft look, the clearness of Helen's skin, and the eucalypt's "explosive" look. It seems, thus, that beautiful "objects" can be ordered in such a way—namely, by asking a certain question about all non-properties—that beautiful properties acquire a privileged status in any theory of beauty.[3]

What we need at this point is a sufficiently precise determination of what counts as a property. The best tactic for now is simply to say that a property is whatever is signifiable by any adjectival word or phrase that can complete a sentence of the form X *is* _____. This stipulation lets into the range of properties more than we need or want, but it excludes much of the class of beautiful "objects." In any case, the class of properties we are interested in is further delimited by the requirement that they be *beautiful* properties. Thus, although "tiny," "late," "high," "pessimistic," and "dirty" all signify[4] properties, they are not, so far as I can see, properties that form part of the subject matter of a theory of beauty. This determination of "property" is more restrictive than most . . . This restricted notion of property may seem arbitrary, but reflection will prove that at least no beautiful properties are thereby excluded.

The phrase "beautiful properties" may bother some readers. Remember that the way we came to our present position was by first noticing that "beautiful" does apply to some properties—for example, a greenness and a clearness that make their objects beautiful. Now, of course, we have generalized the point. It may be that not *every* property brought to light by the question-asking procedure described above can, in some context or other, be said to be beautiful. But certainly most of them can; think of the beautiful trustfulness of her eyes, the beautiful mystery (mysteriousness) of the blue velvet she was wearing, the beautiful solid look ("solid-lookingness") of the bull against the sky, the beautiful stillness of *La Grande Jatte*. We need not insist on the general point, however. It is enough simply to say that a comprehensive theory of beauty need give an account only of those properties, whether in any context properly *called* "beautiful" or not, that can constitute what is beautiful about some beautiful "objects." When I say "beautiful properties," I shall mean such properties.

A much more fundamental point about the term "beautiful property" must be raised now. The term itself suggests that a beautiful property is to be considered beautiful "in general," that is, in any possible instance of it. Notice, however, that whenever we call a property "beautiful," we always apply the term to the property *as it is instantiated in a specified "object."* It is not greenness in general that is beautiful when the hills are beautiful. It is not clearness in general that is beautiful when Helen's skin is beautiful. It is not even clearness-of-skin in general that is said to be beautiful. It is the greenness *of those particular hills*, the clearness *of Helen's skin*, that is beautiful. And thus we say that there is *a* beautiful greenness in those hills and *a* beautiful clearness to Helen's skin. Therefore, calling greenness a beautiful property means only that it is *possible*[5] for it to be beautiful in some of its instantiations, not that it *is* beautiful in all of its instantiations.[6]

Now since a comprehensive theory of beauty needs to account only for beauty of properties, it requires no more than finding what is common to all beautiful properties in virtue . . . of which they are beautiful . . .

There is only one way . . .—as far as I can see—for a theory to grab hold of properties-as-they-are-instantiated and distinguish the beautiful ones from the non-beautiful ones. That way is to distinguish, for all F, *a way of being F* in virtue of which, for all X, X is beautifully F, from other ways of being F. This is, in other words, what a successful theory of beauty *must* do. What a successful theory of beauty *might* also do—and what might thereby also make its necessary task easier—is to determine the domain of F to be a certain subset of the set of all properties as defined earlier.

All that a perfectly comprehensive theory of beauty need do, therefore, is to determine what, for all X and all F such that X is beautiful with respect to F-ness and such that F-ness is beautiful as instantiated in X, makes X *beautifully F*. In a way, that is an astounding conclusion, for we have always known that if X is *beautiful* with respect to F, then X is *beautifully F*, and vice versa. But we have never paid any attention to this adjective-adverb interchangeability. We have taken the adjectival form *beautiful* to be irreducible, treating it like any other adjective (even though very few other adjectives admit the same kind of adverbial transformation), and have assumed beauty to be a property of things, like yellowness or rectangularity.[7] And it was, of course, by following where that assumption led that I came finally to see that we might understand all the beauty there is by not considering beauty a property at all but a way "objects" have of being F, for all F (whatever the domain of F may turn out to be). I have been able to conclude, in other words, that the adverbial form *beautifully* (as it applies to adjectives) is the basic linguistic form for the subject matter of a general theory of beauty. Note, however, that this conclusion still does not leave us with any guarantee that a comprehensive and true theory of beauty is possible. All that I have accomplished so far is to specify—in a way I think has never been done before—what the job of such a theory is. For all we know at this point, there is no way of being F that is a necessary and sufficient condition of any "object" beautiful with respect to F being *beautifully F*.

Another caveat should be entered here. Although a comprehensive theory of beauty can be given by a comprehensive theory of beautiful properties, it still might be necessary, in order to provide the latter, to reduce in turn the beauty of properties to the beauty of a special kind of property. In fact, it will be necessary to make such a reduction. Keep this in mind throughout the discussion of beauty of color. For there I shall be talking about properties-as-instantiated-in-a-specified-"object" that are themselves beautiful with respect to some further property or properties. Also remember that, although I have asserted that all "objects" that are *not* properties-as-instantiated are beautiful with respect to some other "objects" (including properties), it has been left open til now whether all beautiful properties are themselves beautiful with respect to other "objects." It will turn out, in fact, that some beautiful properties are indeed beautiful with respect to some other properties and that some are not.

Let us recall that all beautiful "objects" (including beautiful properties) that *are* beautiful with respect to some other "objects" are usually called (simply) beautiful. That is to say, the standard form of our judgments is X *is beautiful (simpliciter)*. I have argued that, at least with respect to those "objects" that can be beautiful with respect to some other "object," a statement of the form X *is beautiful (simpliciter)* implies one or more statements of the form X *is beautiful with respect to Y*. . . .

Vividness and the Beauty of Color

I will first work out a theory of beauty of color and later generalize the results to other properties. Eventually I will clarify the reasons for this strategy.

Imagine examples of the following kinds of things that you judge to be beautiful with respect to their color:

a) an orange cat,
b) a new red car,
c) green coastal hills of Southern California in February,
d) golden coastal hills of Southern California in June,
e) an orange sunset,
f) blue sky on a brilliant autumn day.

Now imagine conditions of the following descriptions. A rule for imagining correctly is that you must imagine the conditions as destroying, damaging, or diminishing (whether temporarily or permanently) the beauty of color imagined before.

a′) The cat comes in from a rainstorm spattered with mud and with grease from a car it has been hiding under.

b′) The car is two years old, has never been polished, and has been allowed to stand in the sun and rain.

c′) The rainy season is over, and the hot sun has begun to yellow the grass here and there.

d′) It is November; the rains have started, and the weeds of the fields have not only been bleached out by the summer sun but have begun to get those tiny, gray specks of decay.

e′) The sun is sinking, and the color is getting weaker.

f′) The weather has turned colder, a breeze has come up and blown a light veil of clouds over the sky. The sky remains blue but has a whitish cast to it.

So far we have imagined each of a series of things under two kinds of condition. Under one sort of condition the things are beautiful with respect to the colors, respectively, orange, red, green, golden, orange, and blue. Under the other sort of condition the things are no longer beautiful, or as beautiful, with respect to *those same colors*.[8] Notice, though, that it is, by hypothesis, still true of those things under the second sort of condition that they inded have the same color as under the first sort. This does not imply that they do *not* have *different* colors under the changed conditions. It merely implies that they are still, respectively, orange, red, green, golden, orange, and blue.

Nevertheless, under conditions (a′) through (f′) something does change in (a) through (f), and change specifically with respect to the colors that make (a) through (f) beautiful. The orange color of the cat becomes dingy and dull; the red of the car becomes faded; the green of the hills becomes pale and splotchy; the gold of the hills becomes bleached and dim; the orange of the sunset becomes faint and pale; the blue of the sky becomes insipid and washed out. There is a natural and straightforward way to generalize from these facts: the beautiful colors, in becoming less vivid, become less beautiful or even not beautiful. Vividness is thus an important respect in which color can be beautiful.

The first thing to notice about vividness is that it is a property of degree. One instance of color may be more or less vivid than another instance of color. Now since it is the case that the less vivid an instance of color is the less beautiful it is, then the more vivid an instance of color is, the more beautiful it is, at least with respect to the property of vividness. From this generalization it does not *follow* that a very high degree of vividness in the color of a thing is sufficient to make the color of that thing beautiful with respect to vividness. But the latter is, nevertheless, a reasonable hypothesis. . . .

Thus a thing may be beautiful with respect to its color, and the color of the thing may be beautiful with respect to its vividness. Furthermore, it appears that if the color of a thing has a very high degree of vividness, it is beautiful with respect to the property of vividness and, conversely, that if the color of a thing is beautiful with respect to its vividness, then it is vivid to a very high degree. At this stage of the argument the latter claim is only plausible. . . . I ultimately want to argue that, just as the beauty of "objects" that are not properties is nothing but the beauty of properties of those "objects," so the beauty of properties, of which beauty of color is an important subspecies, is reducible to the beauty of properties of degree like vividness.

Vividness and the Context of Color

Despite the plethora of colors, not every instance of color is vivid relative to some color for the good reason that vividness in an instance of color is not dependent only on color parameters like hue and saturation. The vividness of a thing's color also depends upon the environment of that thing. Since Plato's time people have known that what is beautiful is not always, and under all conditions, beautiful. This is strikingly so with respect to beauty of color. A flower that is gorgeous in the sunlight is nothing special on a gray day. Or a tie that is ugly and drab when worn against one shirt is eye-catching with another. The color in a painting that is uninteresting when seen from a distance of forty feet becomes luminously beautiful when viewed up close. These common-place facts are explainable in terms of the theory that one important feature of colors that makes them beautiful is their extreme vividness. For vividness, too, varies with respect to these sorts of context. . . .

Vividness and Appearance

In the preceding two sections I have argued that the vividness of a color of a thing depends upon contextual factors. I have not tried to give a comprehensive theory of the contextual conditions of vividness. I pointed out only some of the important kinds of context that condi-tion vividness: the quality and quantity of light on the color, the color surroundings of a color, and the position of an observer with respect to the color.

It may look at this point as if vividness of color, however closely re-lated to beauty of color, is only a matter of how color *appears* under certain conditions. Thus it is true to say that in sunlight any color ap-pears more vivid than under clouds, that a yellow spot will appear more vivid surrounded by a field of baby blue, and that the orange plastic appears more vivid when seen up close. So if one kind of beauty of color is extreme vividness of color, colors can *appear* more beautiful under some conditions than under others.

The latter consequence of my theory, of course, is one we should ex-pect. For nearly everything, including colors, does appear more beauti-ful under certain conditions and less so under others. This fact has also been known since at least as far back as Plato's time. . . .

Other Beauties of Color

So far I have argued that often, when the color of a thing is beautiful, it is beautiful because of its vividness, and that if the color is very vivid, it is likely, but not necessarily, beautiful (*simpliciter*). Not all color that is beautiful, however, is so because of its vividness. The cloud touched ever so lightly by the setting sun may be just barely rose-tinged. The cloud may still be beautiful, but beautiful not because of the vividness of the rose color. It might be the *delicacy* of the color in this context that provides the beauty. A dark blue fabric may be beautiful because of the *depth* of the color. An off-green color, grayish and yellowish at once, may be beautiful because of its *sultriness,* and an orange color may be beautiful precisely because of the *earthiness* that places it on the drab end of the vividness scale relative to the color orange.

Properties other than vividness are especially important in locating the beauties of those "colors" that contain little or no hue—the so-called neutrals: black, brown, gray, and white. "Vividness" does not properly apply to these colors. Instead, there are other properties, like the richness of a brown, the depth or intensity of a black, the purity or brilliance of a white, that make them beautiful. . . .

The properties other than vividness that can make colors beautiful may be unlimited; there may be no way to list them all. But there would be no point in listing them all in any case. For they all share with vividness a crucial feature; they are all properties of degree. Just as the color in a thing can be more or less vivid, color can be more or less deep, delicate, mysterious, bold, earthy, sultry, smoldering, fresh, naive, subtle, brilliant, or rich. And with respect to every one of these properties, if the color in a thing has the property to a very high degree, there is beauty in the color with respect to that property. . . .

Properties of Qualitative Degree

Thus far we have one element of a theory of beautiful color, namely, that if the color of a thing is beautiful, it possesses at least one property in a very high degree. I am ready now to formulate a general theory of beauty. In order to do so, however, I must clarify a key concept in that theory, the notion of a "property of qualitative degree" (henceforth PQD). All the properties with respect to which the color of a thing may be beautiful are PQDs. A generic feature of any PQD F is that it be possible for one "object" to be more or less F than another "object." A specific feature of any PQD F is that the degree to which one "object" is more or less F than another is not numerically determinable according to a single scale that can measure the degree to which any given "object" is more or less F than any other "object." The generic feature excludes from the class of PQDs such nondegree properties as *being square, being full,* and *being pregnant.* The specific feature excludes such properties of quantitative degree as *being heavy, being hot, being tall,* and *being large.* The specific feature of PQDs, moreover, means that there is no *uniform* and *general* scale of measurement for the degrees of a PQD. Without this feature the distinction between PQDs and properties of quantitative degree cannot be made. The reason is that, given a sufficiently narrowing set of conditions, a numerical degree scale could easily be constructed to measure the difference of degree in which any two "objects" that meet those conditions possess any PQD. . . .

We have then isolated a class of properties, the PQDs. Let me further divide the class of PQDs by distinguishing all those that are deficiencies, lacks, or defects from those that are not. Properties may be deficiencies, lacks, or defects in either of two ways: either universally, or relative to sorts of "objects" to which they apply. *Being blemished, being deformed, being uncouth, being dilapidated, being unhealthy, being silly, being imprecise, being sallow* are examples of the former. Examples of the latter are *being rough* (applied to a skin, or a road, but not to eucalyptus bark), *being shiny* (applied to a gabardine fabric, but not to an automobile finish), *being fat* (applied to adults, but not to babies), *being smooth* (applied to tire treads, but not to roads), *being sad* (applied to days, but not to music and not necessarily to people).

One more division is necessary. We shall also want to distinguish those properties that signify the *appearance* of lack, deficiency, or defect from those properties that signify neither lacks, deficiencies, nor defects nor their appearance. I have in mind here such properties as *being unhealthy-looking, being sallow-looking, being rotten-smelling, being putrid-tasting, being evil-looking.* The latter sort of properties, like properties of lack, deficiency, or defect, may also be either "universal" or "relative."

The New Theory of Beauty Stated

In Section 5 I concluded that a perfectly comprehensive theory of beauty could be a theory of the beauty of properties because there is no beauty in "objects" that is not beauty with respect to one or more properties of the "objects." The analysis of beauty in color allows us to think that even the beauty of some "beautiful properties," like color properties, can be further reduced. For we can say that there is no beauty of color that is not beauty with respect to one or more PQDs. Generalizing from beauty of color, then, we can say that a perfectly comprehensive theory of beauty can be a theory of beautiful PQDs.

Before stating the theory, however, I must make one important delimitation of the notion of a PQD. As thus far delimited, the class of PQDs includes whatever is signified by "beautiful." But since we have determined that the subject matter of a theory of beauty is located by the class of beautiful PQDs, we do not want beauty to be both the analysans and the analysand. We must, therefore, exclude beauty and all of its synonyms, whatever they may turn out to be in particular, from the class of PQDs. What this restriction will amount to is that any adjective or adjectival phrase that can be modified by "more" or "less," where these terms are taken in the qualitative sense explained earlier, will *not* count as signifying a PQD if what is so signified can, like beauty, be construed as a way *of being F.* And we will take the following as the formal *mark* of the possibility of such a construction: the adjective (or adjectival phrase) cannot be placed, without creating a redundancy, in the blank of sentences of the form "X *is beautifully* _____." This test will exclude from the class of PQDs *beauty, gorgeousness, exquisiteness,* as well as (some of the time) *brilliance, radiance,* and others.

Most succinctly expressed, then, the New Theory of Beauty I am putting forth is: *A PQD of an "object" is beautiful if and only if (1) it is not a property of deficiency, lack, or defect, (2) it is not a property of the "appearance" of deficiency, lack, or defect, and (3) it is present in that "object" in a very high degree; and any "object" that is not a PQD is beautiful only if it possesses, proximately or ultimately,*[9] *at least one PQD present in that "object" to a very high degree.*

Note that the New Theory specifies only a necessary, not a sufficient, condition for an "object" that is not a PQD to be beautiful. Thus I am explicitly distinguishing between a comprehensive theory of beauty and a theory that lays down necessary *and sufficient* conditions for the proper application of the predicate "beautiful" and all of its cognates and synonyms. This is to say again that the theory takes as its subject matter only beauty, not all of the utterances in which "beauty" and its synonyms and cognates are used.

The Argument Strategy

The strategy of my argument in support of the New Theory has already been launched and shall be continued in the following sections. I want here . . . to specify exactly what it would take to disconfirm the New Theory (henceforth NTB). . . .

It can be disconfirmed by discovering (a) one or more beautiful "objects" that are not PQDs and that are beautiful but not with respect to one or more PQDs, or (b) one or more "objects" that possess an extremely high degree of one or more PQDs (which are not properties of lack, defect, or deficiency) but that are not beautiful with respect to those PQDs. . . .

Qualifications for Judging Beauty

. . . It is not difficult to imagine a person whose eyes literally hurt when he looks at bright colors and who therefore must always take care to surround himself with pastels. Such a person would presumably be able to judge beauty with respect to any color in the less (absolutely) vivid range, but not with respect to the (relative) vividness of even the spectral colors. In this case the pain of seeing vivid spectral colors functions as an obstacle in perceiving their beauty. And a similar situation obtains, but much more frequently, with respect to properties of taste, touch, and smell.

A natural objection to this line of argument is that since what is beautiful is always enjoyable (likeable, pleasant, agreeable), these various dislikes are actually counterexamples to NTB. And, of course, if this objection has any force, then the whole structure of NTB is completely shattered. For the dislike of properties of taste, touch, and smell is by no means the only kind of dislike available. Some persons dislike green, or blue, or red; dislike pale colors, dark colors, bright colors; dislike mountains, plains, hills, lakes, seashores—the list is endless. But if the fact that some person finds a whole category of "object" or some property or other disagreeable is allowed to tell against that sort of "object" or those properties being beautiful, then there will surely remain no PQD of a thing at all that, even if present in an extreme degree, is beautiful.

What is at issue here is the precise nature of the relation between the beauty of anything and the enjoyment (delight, pleasure, agreeableness, etc.) customarily associated with beauty. Now I think everyone must admit that it is not only no contradiction, but that it might often be the case, that a thing is beautiful with respect to some PQD and that some person finds that thing, precisely in that respect, disagreeable or in some way unpleasant. Furthermore, that person may find the thing disagreeable in that respect because he finds every instance of that PQD, or every instance with a relatively high degree of that PQD, at least as relativized to a sort of "object," similarly unpleasant. For if there were no such possibilities, there would be no point in saying that so-and-so is insensitive to the beauties of, say, Berloiz, of Renaissance chamber music, of succulents, of desert landscapes, of collie dogs, or of Abstract Expressionist painting. . . .

It is therefore possible that X be beautiful with respect to F and that some person find X disagreeable precisely with respect to F. But then it is possible that X be beautiful with respect to F and that I find X disagreeable precisely with respect to F. And yet there is *something wrong* in *my* saying that blue color on the chair is beautiful but I dislike it. What exactly is wrong, however, cannot be that I am contradicting myself or implying a contradiction; "X is beautiful" does not entail "X is agreeable to me." In the same way "It is raining" does not entail "I believe it is raining"; but there is *something wrong* with saying that it is raining but I don't believe it. What is wrong in the latter case is that my saying and meaning that it is raining implies (no matter what "implies" here *really* means) that I believe it is raining. And likewise my saying and meaning (that is, "judging") that X is beautiful implies that I find X agreeable at least in the respect that X is beautiful. It is, in other words, a necessary condition of a person's *judging* something as beautiful with respect to F that he find it agreeable with respect to F. . . .

Beauty and Goodness

In the discussion thus far I have suggested several times that beauty and goodness are closely related. Traditionally theorists of beauty have noted a close relationship between the two ideas. Some philosophers have even identified the two notions. Others have claimed that they are coextensive, that whatever is beautiful is good and the converse.[10] Neither of these theses is correct; the truth is more complex and various than either of these theses make it out to be. For some classes of beautiful "objects" (and of good "objects") there is no connection between beauty and goodness. For the others, though the connection is close, it is different for different kinds of beautiful "objects."

If I say the hills are beautiful because of their vivid green or vivid golden color, if I say the bull against the sky or the bare hills in the afternoon sun on a clear day are very solid-looking, I imply nothing about whether the hills are good hills or the bulls good bulls. The only connection between these sorts of beauties and goodness is that what is beautiful is presumably good to look at.

But a bull may be beautiful because it is so very strong-looking and healthy-looking. And then it follows that the bull is also *good-looking,* and good-looking with respect to some properties that make it beautiful. Note, though, that if a bull is good-looking with respect to PQDs F and G, it may or may not be the case that it is beautiful with respect to F or G. "Good-looking" and "beautiful," even when applied by virtue of the same properties, mark different segments of the degree scales of those properties. . . .

It is instructive to note how my conclusions about the relation between beauty and goodness compare with those of the most influential modern philosopher of beauty, Immanuel Kant. Unlike most ancient and medieval philosophers, Kant made a radical distinction between a judgment of beauty and a judgment of goodness. The distinction ultimately boils down to the doctrine that the latter judgments are "objective" and "cognitive," and therefore express *knowledge about objects,* whereas the former are "subjective" and merely "aesthetical," and therefore express *feelings of subjects.* What is interesting, though, is that Kant recognized the fact that beauty is attributed to things both in virtue of their *utility* (what they are *good for*) and in virtue of their possessing qualities according to which they are *good specimens* of their respective kinds. Moreover, Kant admitted that the judgments of these varieties of goodness—that is, being good for something and being a good specimen of a kind—are indeed objective because they are determined by concepts, namely, the concept of the "external" *purpose* that a thing is good for and the concept of the *kind* of thing to which it belongs. To square these facts with his subjective theory of beauty Kant distinguishes between two "kinds" of beauty: "free" or "self-subsistent" beauty, on the one hand, and "dependent," "conditioned," or "adherent" beauty, on the other. It seems clear to me that under "free beauty" Kant would include just those beauties that I said above are unrelated to goodness except in being good to look at or listen to (a sort of goodness that Kant, too, I'm sure, would concede to them).[11]

It is obvious from the Kantian text that in the part of the *Critique of Judgment* dealing with beauty Kant is interested chiefly in free beauty. And it is his doctrines about free beauty that have been most influential in modern aesthetics. In fact, beauty in modern times has come to be commonly identified with "free" beauty, and philosophers have dropped all interest in "adherent beauty." What NTB does against Kantian doctrines is to show that there is no distinction, as Kant has drawn it, between "free" and "adherent" beauty, because *all* varieties of beauty are "determined by concepts"—indeed, by the same concept. By showing the unity among what Kant had sharply separated, moreover, NTB yanks the rug out from under the chief support for the nearly universal modern faith in the splendid isolation and precious purity of everything "genuinely" aesthetic.

Notes

1. I pick on Kant only because his particular views have been so influential. But, as Jerome Stolnitz has shown in an interesting article, " 'Beauty': Some Stages in the History of an Idea," *Journal of the History of Ideas,* xxii (1961), subjectivism with respect to beauty had become a widely shared opinion among philosophers by the end of the eighteenth century.

2. This general statement, of course, can hold only for beautiful "objects" that are in fact beautiful with respect to properties. At this point in the discussion, it is certainly an open question whether all beautiful "objects" are beautiful in such a respect.

3. I admit to having no *argument* for this absolutely crucial step. I rest the claim on an "inspection" of the field of beautiful "objects" and on my own failure to find counterexamples to the proposition.

4. "Signify," by the way, does not mean "name"; "dirty" *signifies* the property that "dirtiness" *names.*

5. Only possible, not actually the case. For if tomorrow all the "objects" beautiful with respect to their greenness were annihilated, greenness would still be a beautiful property.

6. It could happen that at any given time all "objects" possessing a property might be beautiful with respect to that property. But it could not happen that every possible instance of a property might be beautiful with respect to it. Why this is so will become clear later.

7. Even philosophers like Plato and Plotinus, who are finally led to believe that the nominal form *beauty* is basic, and hence that beauty is essentially a substance and only accidentally a property, were led to this view by taking the adjectival form *beautiful* as, in some sense, an unquestionable given.

8. I stress this phrase because they might, under the second condition, yet be beautiful with respect to color, but with respect to some other color, for example, sea green in (c′), or oatmeal in case (d′), or bronze in (e′). I shall have more to say about this point later. They might, of course, also still (under the second kind of condition) be beautiful with respect to some properties other than color properties. But that is irrelevant to the present point.

9. An "object" possesses a PQD *proximately* if, when the question-procedure

described earlier is applied, the first result is that PQD. An "object" possesses a PQD *ultimately* if the question-procedure must be applied more than once to yield that PQD.

10. The scholastic philosophers William of Auvergne and William of Auxerre, according to Tatarkiewicz [*History of Aesthetics*, The Hague, 1970], identified "good" and "beautiful" (II, 219), while Aquinas, among others, thought the concepts were merely coextensive (II, 246). Again, Tatarkiewicz's two volumes (*passim*) are very informative on this whole topic.

11. Immanuel Kant, *Critique of Judgment,* tr. J. H. Bernard (New York: Hafner, 1951) pp. 62-68.

FRANK SIBLEY

Aesthetic Concepts

THE REMARKS WE MAKE about works of art are of many kinds. For the purpose of this paper I wish to indicate two broad groups. I shall do this by examples. We say that a novel has a great number of characters and deals with life in a manufacturing town; that a painting uses pale colors, predominantly blues and greens, and has kneeling figures in the foreground; that the theme in a fugue is inverted at such a point and that there is a stretto at the close; that the action of a play takes place in the span of one day and that there is a reconciliation scene in the fifth act. Such remarks may be made by, and such features pointed out to, anyone with normal eyes, ears, and intelligence. On the other hand, we also say that a poem is tightly-knit or deeply moving; that a picture lacks balance, or has a certain serenity and repose, or that the grouping of the figures sets up an exciting tension; that the characters in a novel never really come to life, or that a certain episode strikes a false note. It would be natural enough to say that the making of such judgments as these requires the exercise of taste, perceptiveness, or sensitivity, of aesthetic discrimination or appreciation; one would not say this of my first group. Accordingly, when a word or expression is such that taste or perceptiveness is required in order to apply it, I shall call it an *aesthetic* term or expression, and I shall, correspondingly, speak of *aesthetic* concepts or *taste* concepts.[1]

Aesthetic terms span a great range of types and could be grouped into various kinds and sub-species. But it is not my present purpose to attempt any such grouping; I am interested in what they all have in common. Their almost endless variety is adequately displayed in the following list: *unified, balanced, integrated, lifeless, serene, somber, dynamic, powerful, vivid, delicate, moving, trite, sentimental, tragic.* The list of course is not limited to adjectives; expressions in artistic contexts like *telling contrast,*

Reprinted from *The Philosophical Review*, Vol. LXVIII (1949) and revised by the author.

sets up a tension, conveys a sense of, or *holds it together* are equally good illustrations. It includes terms used by both laymen and critic alike, as well as some which are mainly the property of professional critics and specialists.

I have gone for my examples of aesthetic expressions in the first place to critical and evaluative discourse about works of art because it is there particularly that they abound. But now I wish to widen the topic; we employ terms the use of which requires an exercise of taste not only when discussing the arts but quite liberally throughout discourse in everyday life. The examples given above are expressions which, appearing in critical contexts, most usually, if not invariably, have an aesthetic use; outside critical discourse the majority of them more frequently have some other use unconnected with taste. But many expressions do double duty even in everyday discourse, sometimes being used as aesthetic expressions and sometimes not. Other words again, whether in artistic or daily discourse, function only or predominantly as aesthetic terms; of this kind are *graceful, delicate, dainty, handsome, comely, elegant, garish.* Finally, to make the contrast with all the preceding examples, there are many words which are seldom used as aesthetic terms at all: *red, noisy, brackish, clammy, square, docile, curved, evanescent, intelligent, faithful, derelict, tardy, freakish.*

Clearly, when we employ words as aesthetic terms we are often making and using metaphors, pressing into service words which do not primarily function in this manner. Certainly, also, many words *have come* to be aesthetic terms by some kind of metaphorical transference. This is so with those like "dynamic," "melancholy," "balanced," "tightly-knit" which, except in artistic and critical writings, are not normally aesthetic terms. But the aesthetic vocabulary must not be thought wholly metaphorical. Many words, including the most common (*lovely, pretty, beautiful, dainty, graceful, elegant*), are certainly not being used metaphorically when employed as aesthetic terms, the very good reason being that this is their primary or only use, some of them having no current non-aesthetic uses. And though expressions like "dynamic," "balanced," and so forth *have come* by a metaphorical shift to be aesthetic terms, their employment in criticism can scarcely be said to be more than quasi-metaphorical. Having entered the language of art description and criticism as metaphors they are now standard vocabulary in that language.[2]

The expressions I am calling aesthetic terms form no small segment of our discourse. Often, it is true, people with normal intelligence and good eyesight and hearing lack, at least in some measure, the sensitivity required to apply them; a man need not be stupid or have poor eyesight to fail to see that something is graceful. Thus taste or sensitivity is somewhat more rare than certain other human capacities; people who exhibit a sensitivity both wide-ranging and refined are a minority. It is over the application of aesthetic terms, too, that, notoriously, disputes and differences sometimes go helplessly unsettled. But almost everybody is able to exercise taste to some degree and in some matters. It is surprising therefore that aesthetic terms have been so largely neglected. They have received glancing treatment in the course of other aesthetic discussions; but as a broad category they have not received the direct attention they merit.

The foregoing has marked out the area I wish to discuss. One warning should perhaps be given. When I speak of taste in this paper, I shall not be dealing with questions which center upon expressions like "a matter of taste" (meaning, roughly, a matter of personal preference or liking). It is with an ability to *notice* or *see* or *tell that* things have certain qualities that I am concerned.

I

In order to support our application of an aesthetic term, we often refer to features the mention of which involves other aesthetic terms: "it has an extraordinary vitality because of its free and vigorous style of drawing," "graceful in the smooth flow of its lines," "dainty because of the delicacy and harmony of its coloring." It is as normal to do this as it is to justify one mental epithet by other epithets of the same general type, *intelligent* by *ingenious, inventive, acute,* and so on. But often when we apply aesthetic terms, we explain why by referring to features which do *not* depend for their recognition upon an exercise of taste: "delicate because of its pastel shades and curving lines," or "it lacks balance because one group of figures is so far off to the left and is so brightly illuminated." When no explanation of this latter kind is offered, it is legitimate to ask or search for one. Finding a satisfactory answer may sometimes be difficult, but one cannot ordinarily reject the question. When we cannot ourselves quite say what non-aesthetic features make something delicate or unbalanced or powerful or moving, the good critic often puts his finger on something which strikes us as the right explanation. In short, aesthetic terms always ultimately apply because of, and aesthetic qualities always ultimately depend upon, the presence of features which, like curving or angular lines, color contrasts, placing of masses, or speed of movement, are visible, audible, or otherwise discernible without any exercise of taste or sensibility. Whatever kind of dependence this is, and there are various relationships between aesthetic qualities and non-aesthetic features, what I want to make clear in this paper is that there are no non-aesthetic features which serve in *any* circumstances as logically *sufficient conditions* for applying aesthetic terms. Aesthetic or taste concepts are not in *this* respect condition-governed at all.

There is little temptation to suppose that aesthetic terms resemble words, which, like "square," are applied in accordance with a set of necessary and sufficient conditions. For whereas each square is square in virtue of the *same* set of conditions, four equal sides and four right angles, aesthetic terms apply to widely varied objects; one thing is graceful because of these features, another because of those, and so on almost endlessly. In recent times philosophers have broken the spell of the strict necessary-and-sufficient model by showing that many everyday concepts are not of that type. Instead, they have described various other types of concepts which are governed only in a much looser way by conditions. However, since these newer models provide satisfactory accounts of many familiar concepts, it might plausibly be thought that aesthetic concepts are of some such kind and that they similarly are governed in some looser way by conditions. I want to argue that aesthetic concepts differ radically from any of these other concepts.

Amongst these concepts to which attention has recently been paid are those for which no *necessary-and-sufficient* conditions can be provided, but for which there are a number of relevant features, A, B, C, D, E, such that the presence of some groups or combinations of these features is *sufficient* for the application of the concept. The list of relevant features may be an open one; that is, given A, B, C, D, E, we may not wish to close off the possible relevance of other unlisted features beyond E. Examples of such concepts might be "dilatory," "discourteous," "possessive," "capricious," "prosperous," "intelligent" (but see below p. 549). If we begin a list of features relevant to "intelligent" with, for example, ability to grasp and follow various kinds of instructions, ability to master facts and marshall evidence, ability to solve mathematical or chess problems, we might go on adding to this list almost indefinitely.

However, with concepts of this sort, although decisions may have to be made and judgment exercised, it is always possible to extract and state, from cases which have already clearly been decided, the sets of features or conditions which were regarded as sufficient in those cases. These relevant features which I am calling conditions are, it should be noted, features which, though not sufficient *alone* and needing to be combined with other similar features, nevertheless carry some weight and can count only in one direction. Being a good chess player can count only *towards* and not *against* intelligence. Whereas mention of it may enter sensibly along with other remarks in expressions like "I say he is intelligent because . . ." or "the reason I call him intelligent is that . . . ," it cannot be used to complete such negative expressions as "I say he is *un*intelligent because. . . ." But what I want particularly to emphasize about features which function as conditions for a term is that *some* group or set of them *is* sufficient fully to ensure or warrant the application of that term. An individual characterized by some of these features may not yet qualify to be called lazy or intelligent, and so on, beyond all question, but all that is needed is to add some further (indefinite) number of such characterizations and a point is reached where we have enough. There are individuals possessing a number of such features of whom one cannot deny, cannot but admit, that they are intelligent. We have left necessary-and-sufficient conditions behind, but we are still in the realm of sufficient conditions.

But aesthetic concepts are not condition-governed even in this way. There are no sufficient conditions, no non-aesthetic features such that the presence of some set or number of them will beyond question logically justify or warrant the application of an aesthetic term. It is impossible (barring certain limited exceptions, see below p. 551) to make any statements corresponding to those we can make for condition-governed words. We are able to say "If it is true he can do this, and that, and the other, then one just cannot deny that he is intelligent," or "if he does A, B, and C, I don't see how it can be denied that he is lazy," but we cannot make *any* general statement of the form "If the vase is pale pink, somewhat curving, lightly mottled, and so forth, it will be delicate, cannot but be delicate." Nor again can one say *any* such things here as "Being tall and thin is not enough *alone* to ensure that a vase is delicate, but if it is, for example, slightly curving and pale colored (and so forth) as well, it cannot be denied that it is." Things may be described to us in non-aesthetic terms as fully as we please but we are not thereby put in the position of having to admit (or being unable to deny) that they are delicate or graceful or garish or exquisitely balanced.[3]

No doubt there are some respects in which aesthetic terms *are* governed by conditions or rules. For instance, it may be impossible that a thing should be garish if all its colors are pale pastels, or flamboyant if all its lines are straight. There may be, that is, descriptions using only non-aesthetic terms which are incompatible with descriptions employing certain aesthetic terms. If I am told that a painting in the next room consists solely of one or two bars of very pale blue and very pale grey set at right angles on a pale fawn ground, I can be sure that it cannot be fiery or garish or gaudy or flamboyant. A description of this sort may make certain aesthetic terms *in*applicable or *in*appropriate; and if from this description I inferred that the picture was, or even might be, fiery or gaudy or flamboyant, this might be taken as showing a failure to understand these words. I do not wish to deny therefore that taste concepts may be governed *negatively* by conditions.[4] What I am emphasizing is that they quite lack governing conditions of a sort many other concepts possess. Though on *seeing* the picture we might say, and rightly, that it is delicate or serene or restful or sickly or insipid, no *description* in non-aesthetic terms permits us to claim that these or any other aesthetic terms must undeniably apply to it.

I have said that if an object is characterized *solely* by certain sorts of features this may count decisively against the possibility of applying to it certain aesthetic terms. But of course the presence of *some* such features need not count decisively; other features may be enough to outweigh those which, on their own, would render the aesthetic term inapplicable. A painting might be garish even though much of its color is pale. These facts call attention to a further feature of taste concepts. One *can* find general features or descriptions which in some sense count in one direction only, only *for* or only *against* the application of certain aesthetic terms. Angularity, fatness, brightness, or intensity of color are typically *not* associated with delicacy or grace. Slimness, lightness, gentle curves, lack of intensity of color are associated with delicacy, but not with flamboyance, majesty, grandeur, splendor or garishness. This is shown by the naturalness of saying, for example, that someone is graceful *because* she's so light, but, *in spite of* being quite angular or heavily built; and by the corresponding oddity of saying that something is graceful *because* it is so heavy or angular, or delicate *because* of its bright and intense coloring. This may therefore sound quite similar to what I have said already about conditions in discussing terms like "intelligent." There are nevertheless very significant differences. Although there is this sense in which slimness, lightness, lack of intensity of color, and so on, count only towards, not against, delicacy, these features, I shall say, at best count only *typically* or *characteristically* towards delicacy. They do not count towards in the same sense as condition-features count towards laziness or intelligence; that is, no group of them is ever logically sufficient.

One way of reinforcing this is to notice how features which are characteristically associated with one aesthetic term may also be similarly associated with other and rather different aesthetic terms. "Graceful" and "delicate" may be on the one hand sharply contrasted with terms like "violent," "grand," "fiery," "garish," or "massive" which have characteristic non-aesthetic features quite unlike those for "delicate" and "graceful." But on the other hand "graceful" and "delicate" may also be contrasted with aesthetic terms which stand much closer to them, like "flaccid," "weakly," "washed out," "lanky," "anaemic," "wan," "insipid"; and the range of features characteristic of *these* qualities, pale color, slimness, lightness, lack of angularity and sharp contrast, is virtually identical with the range for "delicate" and "graceful." Similarly many of the features typically associated with "joyous," "fiery," "robust," or "dynamic" are identical with those associated with "garish," "strident," "turbulent," "gaudy," or "chaotic." Thus an object which is described very fully, but exclusively in terms of qualities characteristic of delicacy, may turn out on inspection to be not delicate at all, but anaemic or insipid. The failures of novices and the artistically inept prove that quite close similarity in point of line, color, or technique gives no assurance of gracefulness or delicacy. A failure and a success in the manner of Degas may be generally more alike, so far as their non-aesthetic features go, than either is like a successful Fragonard. But it is not necessary to go even this far to make my main point. A painting which has only the kind of features one would associate with vigor and energy but which even so fails to be vigorous and energetic *need* not have some other character, need not be instead, say, strident or chaotic. It may fail to have any particular character whatever.

It may employ bright colors, and the like, without being particularly lively and vigorous at all; but one may feel unable to describe it as chaotic or strident or garish either. It is, rather, simply lacking in character (though of course this too is an aesthetic judgment; taste is exercised also in seeing that the painting has no character) .

There are of course many features which do not in these ways characteristically count for (or against) particular aesthetic qualities. One poem has strength and power because of the regularity of its meter and rhyme; another is monotonous and lacks drive and strength because of its regular meter and rhyme. We do not feel the need to switch from "because of" to "in spite of." However, I have concentrated upon features which are characteristically associated with aesthetic qualities because, if a case could be made for the view that taste concepts are in any way governed by sufficient conditions these would seem to be the most promising candidates for governing conditions. But to say that features are associated only *characteristically* with an aesthetic term *is* to say that they can never amount to sufficient conditions; no description however full, even in terms characteristic of gracefulness, puts it beyond question that something is graceful in the way a description may put it beyond question that someone is lazy or intelligent.

It is important to observe, however, that in this paper I am not merely claiming that no sufficient conditions can be stated for taste concepts. For if this were all, taste concepts might not be after all really different from one kind of concept recently discussed. They could be accommodated perhaps with those concepts which Professor H. L. A. Hart has called "defeasible"; it is a characteristic of defeasible concepts that we cannot state sufficient conditions for them because, for any sets we offer, there is always an (open) list of defeating conditions any of which might rule out the application of the concept. The most we can say schematically for a defeasible concept is that, for example, A, B, and C together are sufficient for the concept to apply *unless* some feature is present which overrides or voids them. But, I want to emphasize, the very fact that we *can* say this sort of thing shows that we are still to that extent in the realm of conditions.[5] The features governing defeasible concepts can ordinarily count only one way, *either* for *or* against. To take Hart's example, "offer" and "acceptance" can count only towards the existence of a valid contract, and fraudulent misrepresentations, duress, and lunacy can count only against. And even with defeasible concepts, if we are told that there are no voiding features present, we can know that some set of conditions or features, A, B, C, . . . is enough, in this absence of voiding features, to ensure, for example, that there is a contract. The very notion of a defeasible concept seems to require that some group of features *would* be sufficient *in certain circumstances*, that is, in the absence of overriding or voiding features. In a certain way defeasible concepts lack sufficient conditions then, but they are still, in the sense described, condition-governed. My claim about taste concepts is stronger; that they are not, except negatively, governed by conditions at all. We could not conclude even *in certain circumstances*, e.g., if we were told of the absence of all "voiding" or uncharacteristic features (no angularities, and the like), that an object *must* certainly be graceful, no matter how fully it was described to us as possessing features characteristic of gracefulness.

My arguments and illustrations so far have been rather simply schematic. Many concepts, including most of the examples I have used *(intelligent,* and so on, p. 545), are much more thoroughly open and complex than my illustrations suggest. Not only may there be an open list of relevant conditions; it may be impossible to give precise rules telling how many features from the list are needed for a sufficient set or in which combinations; impossible similarly to give precise rules covering the extent or degree to which such features need to be present in those combinations. Indeed, we may have to abandon as futile any attempt to describe or formulate anything like a complete set of precise conditions or rules, and content ourselves with giving only some general account of the concept, making reference to samples or cases or precedents. We cannot fully master or employ these concepts therefore *simply* by being equipped with lists of conditions, readily applicable procedures or sets of rules, however complex. For to exhibit a mastery of one of these concepts we must be able to go ahead and apply the word correctly to new individual cases, at least to central ones; and each new case may be a uniquely different object, just as each intelligent child or student may differ from others in relevant features and exhibit a unique combination of kinds and degrees of achievement and ability. In dealing with these new cases mechanical rules and procedures would be useless; we have to exercise our judgment, guided by a complex set of examples and precedents. Here then there is a marked *superficial* similarity to aesthetic concepts. For in using aesthetic terms too we learn from samples and examples, not rules, and we have to apply them, likewise, without guidance by rules or readily applicable procedures, to new and unique instances. Neither kind of concept admits of a simply "mechanical" employment.

But this is *only* a superficial similarity. It is at least noteworthy that in applying words like "lazy" or "intelligent" to new and unique instances we say that we are required to exercise *judgment*; it would be indeed odd to say that we are exercising *taste.* In exercising judgment we are called upon to weigh the pros and cons against each other, and perhaps sometimes to decide whether a quite new feature is to be counted as weighing on one side or on the other. But this goes to show that, though we may learn from and rely upon samples and precedents rather than a set of stated conditions, we are not out of the realm of general conditions and guiding principles. These precedents necessarily embody, and are used by us to illustrate, a complex web of governing and relevant conditions which it is impossible to formulate completely. To profit by precedents we have to understand them; and we must argue consistently from case to case. This is the very function of precedents. Thus it is possible, even with these very loosely condition-governed concepts, to take clear or paradigm cases of X and to say "this is X because . . . ," and follow it up with an account of features which logically clinch the matter.

Nothing like this is possible with aesthetic terms. Examples undoubtedly play a crucial role in giving us a grasp of these concepts; but we do not and cannot derive from these examples conditions and principles, however complex, which will enable us if we are consistent, to apply the terms even to some new cases. And when, with a clear case of something which *is* in fact graceful or balanced or tightly-knit, someone tells me why it is, what features make it so, it is always possible for me to wonder whether, in spite of these features, it really is graceful, balanced, and so on. No such features logically clinch the matter.

The point I have argued may be reinforced in the following way. A man who failed to realize the nature of aesthetic concepts, or someone who, knowing that he lacked sensitivity in aesthetic matters, did not want to reveal this lack might by assiduous application and shrewd observation provide himself with some rules and generalizations; and by inductive procedures and intelligent guessing, he might frequently say the right things. But he could have no great confidence or certainty; a slight change in an object might at any time unpredictably ruin his calculations, and he might as easily have been wrong as right. No matter how careful he has been about working out a set of consistent principles and conditions, he is only in a position to think that the object is very possibly delicate. With concepts like *lazy, intelligent,* or *contract,* someone who intelligently formulated rules that led him aright appreciably often *would* thereby show the beginning of a grasp of those concepts; but the person we are considering is not even beginning to show an awareness of what delicacy is. Though he sometimes says the right thing, he has not seen, but guessed, that the object is delicate. However intelligent he might be, we could easily tell him wrongly that something was delicate and "explain" why without his being able to detect the deception. (I am ignoring complications now about negative conditions.) But if we did the same with, say, "intelligent" he could at least often uncover some incompatibility or other which would need explaining. In a world of beings like himself he would have no use for concepts like delicacy. As it is, these concepts would play a quite different role in his life. He would, for himself, have no more reason to choose tasteful objects, pictures, and so on, than a deaf man would to avoid noisy places. He could not be praised for exercising taste; at best his ingenuity and intelligence might come in for mention. In "appraising" pictures, statuettes, poems, he would be doing something quite different from what other people do when they exercise taste.

At this point I want to notice in passing that there are times when it may look as if an aesthetic word could be applied according to a rule.

These cases vary in type; I shall mention only one. One might say, in using "delicate" of glassware perhaps, that the thinner the glass, other things being equal, the more delicate it is. Similarly, with fabrics, furniture, and so on, there are perhaps times when the thinner or more smoothly finished or more highly polished something is, the more certainly some aesthetic term or other applies. On such occasions someone might formulate a rule and follow it in applying the word to a given range of articles. Now it may be that sometimes when this is so, the word being used is not really an aesthetic term at all; "delicate" applied to glass in this way may at times really mean no more than "thin" or "fragile." But this is certainly not always the case; people often *are* exercising taste even when they say that glass is very delicate because it is so thin, and know that it would be less so if thicker and more so if thinner. These instances where there appear to be rules are peripheral cases of the use of aesthetic terms. If someone did merely follow a rule we should not say he was exercising taste, and we should hesitate to admit that he had any real notion of delicacy until he satisfied us that he could discern it in other instances where no rule was available. In any event, these occasions when aesthetic words can be applied by rule are exceptional, not central or typical, and there is still no reason to think we are dealing with a logical entailment.[6]

It must not be thought that the impossibility of stating any conditions (other than negative) for the application of aesthetic terms results from an accidental poverty or lack of precision in language, or that it is simply a question of extreme complexity. It is true that words like "pink," "bluish," "curving," "mottled," do not permit of anything like a specific naming of each and every varied shade, curve, mottling, and blending. But if we were to give special names much more liberally than either we or even the specialists do (and no doubt there are limits beyond which we could not go), or even if, instead of names, we were to use vast numbers of specimens and samples of particular shades, shapes, mottlings, lines, and configurations, it would still be impossible, and for the same reasons, to supply any conditions.

We do, indeed, in talking about a work of art, concern ourselves with its individual and specific features. We say that it is delicate not simply because it is in pale colors but because of *those* pale colors, that it is graceful not because its outline curves slightly but because of *that* particular curve. We use expressions like "because of *its* pale coloring," "because of *the* flecks of bright blue," "because of *the* way the lines converge" where it is clear we are referring not to the presence of general features but to very specific and particular ones. But it is obvious that even with the help of precise names, or even samples and illustrations, of particular shades of color, contours and lines, any attempt to state conditions would be futile. After all, the very same feature, say a color or shape or line of a particular sort, which helps make one work may quite spoil another. "It would be quite delicate if it were not for that pale color there" may be said about the very color which is singled out in another picture as being largely responsible for its delicate quality. No doubt one way of putting this is to say that the features which make something delicate or graceful, and so on, are combined in a peculiar and unique way; that the aesthetic quality depends upon exactly this individual or unique combination of just these specific colors and shapes so that even a slight change might make all the difference. Nothing is to be achieved by trying to single out or separate features and generalizing about them.

I have now argued that in certain ways aesthetic concepts are not and cannot be condition- or rule-governed.[7] Not to be so governed is one of their essential characteristics. In arguing this I first claimed in a general way that no non-aesthetic features are possible candidates for conditions, and then considered more particularly both the "characteristic" *general* features associated with aesthetic terms and the individual or *specific* features found in particular objects. I have not attempted to examine what relationship these specific features of a work do bear to its aesthetic qualities. An examination of the locutions we use when we refer to them in the course of explaining or supporting our application of an aesthetic term reinforces with linguistic evidence the fact that we are certainly not offering them as explanatory or justifying *conditions*. When we are asked why we say a certain person is lazy or intelligent or courageous, we are being asked in virtue of what we *call* him this; we reply with "because of the way he regularly leaves his work unfinished," or "because of the ease with which he handles such and such problems," and so on. But when we are asked to say why, in our opinion, a picture lacks balance or is somber in tone, or why a poem is moving or tightly organized, we are doing a different kind of thing. We may use similar locutions: "his verse has strength and variety *because of the way* he handles the meter and employs the caesura," or "it is nobly austere *because of* the lack of detail and the restricted palette." But we can also express what we want to by using quite other expressions: "it is the handling of meter and caesura which is *responsible for* its strength and variety," "its nobly austere quality is *due to* the lack of detail and the use of a restricted palette," "its lack of balance *results from* the highlighting of the figures on the left," "those minor chords *make it* extremely moving," "those converging lines *give it* an extraordinary unity." These are locutions we cannot switch to with "lazy" or "intelligent"; to say *what makes* him lazy, what is *responsible for* his laziness, what it is *due to*, is to broach another question entirely.

One after another, in recent discussions, writers have insisted that aesthetic judgments are not "mechanical": "Critics do not formulate general standards and apply these mechanically to all, or to classes of, works of art." "Technical points can be settled rapidly, by the application of rules," but aesthetic questions "cannot be settled by any mechanical method." Instead, these writers on aesthetics have emphasized that there

is no "substitute for individual judgment" with its "spontaneity and speculation" and that "The final standard . . . [is] the judgment of personal
taste."[8] What is surprising is that, though such things have been repeated
again and again, no one seems to have said what is meant by "taste" or
by the word "mechanical." There are many judgments besides those requiring taste which demand "spontaneity" and "individual judgment"
and are not "mechanical." Without a detailed comparison we cannot see
in what particular way aesthetic judgments are not "mechanical," or how
they differ from those other judgments, nor can we begin to specify what
taste is. This I have attempted. It is a characteristic and essential feature
of judgments which employ an aesthetic term that they cannot be made
by appealing, in the sense explained, to non-aesthetic conditions.[9] This, I
believe, is a logical feature of aesthetic or taste judgments in general,
though I have argued it here only as regards the more restricted range of
judgments which employ aesthetic terms. It is part of what "taste" means.

II

A great deal of work remains to be done on aesthetic concepts. In the
remainder of this paper I shall offer some further suggestions which may
help towards an understanding of them.

The realization that aesthetic concepts are governed only negatively by
conditions is likely to give rise to puzzlement over how we manage to
apply the words in our aesthetic vocabulary. If we are not following rules
and there are no conditions to appeal to, how are we to know when they
are applicable? One very natural way to counter this question is to point
out that some other sorts of concepts also are not condition-governed. We
do not apply simple color words by following rules or in accordance with
principles. We see that the book is red by looking, just as we tell that the
tea is sweet by tasting it. So too, it might be said, we just see (or fail to
see) that things are delicate, balanced, and the like. This kind of comparison between the exercise of taste and the use of the five senses is indeed familiar; our use of the word "taste" itself shows that the comparison is age-old and very natural. Yet whatever the similarities, there are
great dissimilarities too. A careful comparison cannot be attempted here
though it would be valuable; but certain differences stand out, and writers who have emphasized that aesthetic judgments are not "mechanical"
have sometimes dwelt on and been puzzled by them.

In the first place, while our ability to discern aesthetic features is dependent upon our possession of good eyesight, hearing, and so on, people
normally endowed with senses and understanding may nevertheless fail
to discern them. "Those who listen to a concert, walk round a gallery,
read a poem may have roughly similar sense perceptions, but some get a
great deal more than others," Miss Macdonald says; but she adds that she

is "puzzled by this feature 'in the object' which can be seen only by a specially qualified observer" and asks, "What is this 'something more'?"[10]

It is this difference between aesthetic and perceptual qualities which in part leads to the view that "works of art are esoteric objects . . . not simple objects of sense perception."[11] But there is no good reason for calling an object esoteric simply because we discern aesthetic qualities in it. The *objects* to which we apply aesthetic words are of the most diverse kinds and by no means esoteric: people and buildings, flowers and gardens, vases and furniture, as well as poems and music. Nor does there seem any good reason for calling the *qualities* themselves esoteric. It is true that someone with perfect eyes or ears might miss them, but we do after all say we *observe or notice* them ("Did you notice how very graceful she was?" "Did you observe the exquisite balance in all his pictures?"). In fact, they are very familiar indeed. We learn while quite young to use many aesthetic words, though they are, as one might expect from their dependence upon our ability to see, hear, distinguish colors, and the like, not the earliest words we learn; and our mastery and sophistication in using them develop along with the rest of our vocabulary. They are not rarities; some ranges of them are in regular use in everyday discourse.

The second notable difference between the exercise of taste and the use of the five senses lies in the way we support those judgments in which aesthetic concepts are employed. Although we use these concepts without rules or conditions, we do defend or support our judgments, and convince others of their rightness, by talking; "disputation about art is not futile," as Miss Macdonald says, for critics do "attempt a certain kind of explanation of works of art with the object of establishing correct judgments."[12] Thus even though this disputation does not consist in "deductive or inductive inference" or "reasoning," its occurrence is enough to show how very different these judgments are from those of a simple perceptual sort.

Now the critic's talk, it is clear, frequently consists in mentioning or pointing out the features, including easily discernible non-aesthetic ones, upon which the aesthetic qualities depend. But the puzzling question remains how, by mentioning these features, the critic is thereby justifying or supporting his judgments. To this question a number of recent writers have given an answer. Stuart Hampshire, for example, says that "One engages in aesthetic discussion for the sake of what one might see on the way. . . . [I]f one has been brought to see what there is to be seen in the object, the purpose of discussion is achieved. . . . The point is to bring people to see these features."[13] The critic's talk, that is, often serves to support his judgments in a special way; it helps us to *see* what he has seen, namely, the aesthetic qualities of the object. But even when it is agreed that this is one of the main things that critics do, puzzlement tends to break out again over *how* they do it. How is it that by talking about features of the work (largely non-aesthetic ones) we can manage to bring others to see what they had not seen? "What sort of endowment is this which *talking* can modify? . . . Discussion does not improve eyesight and hearing" (my italics) .[14]

Yet of course we do succeed in applying aesthetic terms, and we frequently do succeed by talking (and pointing and gesturing in certain ways) in bringing others to see what we can see. One begins to suspect that puzzlement over the "esoteric" character of aesthetic qualities too, arises from bearing in mind inappropriate philosophical models. When someone is unable to see that the book on the table is brown, we cannot get him to see it is by talking; consequently it seems puzzling that we might get someone to see that the vase is graceful by talking. If we are to dispel this puzzlement and recognize aesthetic concepts and qualities for what they are, we must abandon unsuitable models and investigate how we actually employ these concepts. With so much interest in and agreement about *what* the critic does, one might expect decriptions of *how* he does it to have been given. But little has been said about this, and what has been said is unsatisfactory.

Miss Macdonald,[15] for example, subscribes to this view of the critic's task as presenting "what is not obvious to casual or uninstructed inspection," and she does ask the question "What sort of considerations are involved, *and how,* to justify a critical verdict?" (my italics) . But she docs not in fact go on to answer it. She addresses herself instead to the different, though related, question of the interpretation of art works. In complex works different critics claim, often justifiably, to discern different features; hence Miss Macdonald suggests that in critical discourse the critic is bringing us to see what he sees by offering new interpretations. But if the question is "what (the critic) does and how he does it," he cannot be represented either wholly or even mainly as providing new interpretations. His task quite as often is simply to help us appreciate qualities which other critics have regularly found in the works he discusses. To put the stress upon *new* interpretations is to leave untouched the question how, by talking, he can help us to see *either* the newly appreciated aesthetic qualities *or* the old. In any case, besides complex poems or plays which may bear many interpretations, there are also relatively simple ones. There are also vases, buildings, and furniture, not to mention faces, sunsets, and scenery, about which no questions of "interpretation" arise but about which we talk in similar ways and make similar judgments. So the "puzzling" questions remain: how do we support these judgments and how do we bring others to see what we see?

Hampshire,[16] who likewise believes that the critic brings us "to see what there is to be seen in the object," does give some account of how the critic does this. "The greatest service of the critic" is to point out, isolate, and place in a frame of attention the "particular features of the particular object which *make* it ugly or beautiful"; for it is "difficult to see and hear all that there is to see and hear," and simply a prejudice to suppose that while "things really do have colours and shapes . . . there do not exist literally and objectively, concordances of colours and perceived rhythms and balances of shapes." However, these "extraordinary qualities" which the critic "may have seen (in the wider sense of 'see') " are "qualities which are of no direct practical interest." Consequently, to bring us to see them the critic employs "an unnatural use of words in description"; "the common vocabulary, being created for practical purposes, obstructs any disinterested perception of things"; and so these qualities "are normally described metaphorically by some transference of terms from the common vocabulary."

Much of what Hampshire says is right. But there is also something quite wrong in the view that the "common" vocabulary "obstructs" our aesthetic purposes, that it is "unnatural" to take it over and use it metaphorically, and that the critic "is under the necessity of building . . . a vocabulary *in opposition to the main tendency of his language*" (my italics). First, while we do often coin new metaphors in order to describe aesthetic qualities, we are by no means always under the necessity of wresting the "common vocabulary" from its "natural" uses to serve our purposes. There does exist, as I observed earlier, a large and accepted vocabulary of aesthetic terms some of which, whatever their metaphorical origins, are now not metaphors at all, others of which are at most quasi-metaphorical. Second, this view that our use of metaphor and quasi-metaphor for aesthetic purposes is unnatural or a makeshift into which we are forced by a language designed for other purposes misrepresents fundamentally the character of aesthetic qualities and aesthetic language. There is nothing unnatural about using words like "forceful," "dynamic," or "tightly-knit" in criticism; they do their work perfectly and are exactly the words needed for the purposes they serve. We do not want or need to replace them by words which lack the metaphorical element. In using them to describe works of art, the very point is that we are noticing aesthetic qualities related to their literal or common meanings. If we possessed a quite different word from "dynamic," one we could use to point out an aesthetic quality unrelated to the common meaning of "dynamic," it could not be used to describe that quality which "dynamic" does serve to point out. Hampshire pictures "a colony of aesthetes, disengaged from practical needs and manipulations" and says that "descriptions of aesthetic qualities, which for us are metaphorical, might seem to them to have an altogether literal and familiar sense"; they might use "a more directly descriptive vocabulary." But if they had a new and "directly descriptive" vocabulary lacking the links with non-aesthetic properties and interests which our vocabulary possesses, they would have to remain silent about many of the aesthetic qualities we can describe; further, if they were more completely "disengaged from practical needs" and other non-aesthetic awarenesses and interests, they would perforce be blind to many aesthetic qualities we can appreciate. The links between aesthetic qualities and non-aesthetic ones are both obvious and vital. Aesthetic concepts, all of them, carry with them attachments and in one way or another are tethered to or parasitic upon non-aesthetic features. The fact that many aesthetic terms are metaphorical or quasi-metaphorical in no way means that common language is an ill-adapted tool with which we have to struggle. When someone writes as Hampshire does, one suspects again that critical language is being judged against other models. To use language which is frequently metaphorical might be strange for some *other* purpose or from the standpoint of doing something else, but for the purpose and from the standpoint of making aesthetic observations it is not. To say it is an unnatural use of language for doing *this* is to imply there is or could be for this purpose some other and "natural" use. But these *are* natural ways of talking about aesthetic matters.

To help understand what the critic does, then, how he supports his judgments and gets his audience to see what he sees, I shall attempt a brief description of the methods we use as critics.[17]

(1) We may simply mention or point out non-aesthetic features: "Notice these flecks of color, that dark mass there, those lines." By merely drawing attention to those easily discernible features which make the painting luminous or warm or dynamic, we often succeed in bringing someone to see these aesthetic qualities. We get him to see B by mentioning something different, A. Sometimes in doing this we are drawing attention to features which may have gone unnoticed by an untrained or insufficiently attentive eye or ear: "Just listen for the repeated figure in the left hand," "Did you notice the figure of Icarus in the Breughel? It is very small." Sometimes they are features which have been seen or heard but of which the significance or purpose has been missed in any of a variety of ways: "Notice how much darker he has made the central figure, how much brighter these colors are than the adjacent ones," "Of course, you've observed the ploughman in the foreground; but had you considered how he, like everyone else in the picture, is going about his business without noticing the fall of Icarus?" In mentioning features which may be discerned by anyone with normal eyes, ears, and intelligence, we are singling out what may serve as a kind of key to grasping or seeing something else (and the key may not be the same for each person).

(2) On the other hand we often simply mention the very qualities we want people to see. We point to a painting and say, "Notice how nervous and delicate the drawing is," or "See what energy and vitality it has." The use of the aesthetic term itself may do the trick; we say what the quality or character is, and people who had not seen it before see it.

(3) Most often, there is a linking of remarks about aesthetic and non-aesthetic features: "Have you noticed this line and that, and the points of bright color here and there . . . don't they give it vitality, energy?"

(4) We do, in addition, often make extensive and helpful use of similes and genuine metaphors: "It's as if there are small points of light burning," "as though he had thrown on the paint violently and in anger," "the

lights shimmer, the lines dance, everything is air, lightness and gaiety," "his canvases are fires, they crackle, burn, and blaze, even at their most subdued always restlessly flickering, but often bursting into flame, great pyro-technic displays," and so on.

(5) We make use of contrasts, comparisons, and reminiscences: "Suppose he had made that a lighter yellow, moved it to the right, how flat it would have been," "Don't you think it has something of the quality of a Rembrandt?", "Hasn't it the same serenity, peace, and quality of light of those summer evenings in Norfolk?" We use what keys we have to the known sensitivity, susceptibilities, and experience of our audience.

Critics and commentators may range, in their methods, from one extreme to the other, from painstaking concentration on points of detail, line and color, vowels and rhymes, to more or less flowery and luxuriant metaphor. Even the enthusiastic biographical sketch decorated with suitable epithet and metaphor may serve. What is best depends on both the audience and the work under discussion. But this would not be a complete sketch unless certain other notes were added.

(6) Repetition and reiteration often play an important role. When we are in front of a canvas we may come back time and again to the same points, drawing attention to the same lines and shapes, repeating the same words, "swirling," "balance," "luminosity," or the same similes and metaphors, as if time and familiarity, looking harder, listening more carefully, paying closer attention may help. So again with variation; it often helps to talk round what we have said, to build up, supplement with more talk *of the same kind.* When someone misses the swirling quality, when one epithet or one metaphor does not work, we throw in related ones; we speak of its wild movement, how it twists and turns, writhes and whirls, as though, failing to score a direct hit, we may succeed with a barrage of near-synonyms.

(7) Finally, besides our verbal performances, the rest of our behavior is important. We accompany our talk with appropriate tones of voice, expression, nods, looks, gestures. A critic may sometimes do more with a sweep of the arm than by talking. An appropriate gesture may make us see the violence in a painting or the character of a melodic line.

These ways of acting and talking are not significantly different whether we are dealing with a particular work, paragraph, or line, or speaking of an artist's work as a whole, or even drawing attention to a sunset or scenery. But even with the speaker doing all this, we may fail to see what he sees. There may be a point, though there need be no limit except that imposed by time and patience, at which he gives up and sets us (or himself) down as lacking in some way, defective in sensitivity. He may tell us to look or read again, or to read or look at other things and then come back again to this; he may suspect there are experiences in life we have missed. But these are the things he does. This is what succeeds if anything does; indeed it is all that can be done.

By realizing clearly that, whether we are dealing with art or scenery or people or natural objects, this is how we operate with aesthetic concepts, we may recognize this sphere of human activity for what it is. We operate with different kinds of concepts in different ways. If we want someone to agree that a color is red we may take it into a good light and ask him to look; if it is viridian we may fetch a color chart and make him compare; if we want him to agree that a figure is fourteen-sided we get him to count; and to bring him to agree that something is dilapidated or that someone is intelligent or lazy we may do other things, citing features, reasoning and arguing about them, weighing and balancing. These are the methods appropriate to these various concepts. But the ways we get someone to see aesthetic qualities are different; they are of the kind I have described. With each kind of concept we can describe what we do and how we do it. But the methods suited to these other concepts will not do for aesthetic ones, or vice versa. We cannot prove by argument or by assembling a sufficiency of conditions that something is graceful; but this is no more puzzling than our inability to prove, by using the methods, metaphors, and gestures of the art critic, that it will be made in ten moves. The questions raised admit of no answer beyond the sort of decription I have given. To go on to ask, with puzzlement, how it is that *when* we do these things people come to see, is like asking how is it that, when we take the book into a good light, our companion agrees with us that it is red. There is no place for this kind of question or puzzlement. Aesthetic concepts are as natural, as little esoteric, as any others. It is against the background of different and philosophically more familiar models that they seem queer or puzzling.

I have described how people justify aesthetic judgments and bring others to see aesthetic qualities in things. I shall end by showing that the methods I have outlined are the ones natural for and characteristic of taste concepts from the start. When someone tries to make me see that a painting is delicate or balanced, I have some understanding of these terms already and know in a sense what I am looking for. But if there is puzzlement over how, by talking, he can bring me to see these qualities in this picture, there should be a corresponding puzzlement over how I learned to use aesthetic terms and discern aesthetic qualities in the first place. We may ask, therefore, how we learn to do these things; and this is to inquire (1) what natural potentialities and tendencies people have and (2) how we develop and take advantage of these capacities in training and teaching. Now for the second of these, there is no doubt that our ability to notice and respond to aesthetic qualities is cultivated and developed by our contacts with parents and teachers from quite an early age. What is interesting for my present purpose is that, while we are being taught in the presence of examples what grace, delicacy, and so on are, the methods used, the language and behavior, are of a piece with those of the critic as I have already described them.

To pursue these two questions, consider first those words like "dynamic," "melancholy," "balanced," "taut," or "gay" the aesthetic use of which is quasi-metaphorical. It has already been emphasized that we could not use them thus without some experience of situations where they are used literally. The present inquiry is how we shift from literal to aesthetic uses of them. For this it is required that there be certain abilities and tendencies to link experiences, to regard certain things as similar, and to see, explore, and be interested in these similarities. It is a feature of human intelligence and sensitivity that we do spontaneously do these things and that the tendency can be encouraged and developed. It is no more baffling that we should employ aesthetic terms of this sort than that we should make metaphors at all. Easy and smooth transitions by which we shift to the use of these aesthetic terms are not hard to find. We suggest to children that simple pieces of music are hurrying or running or skipping or dawdling, from there we move to lively, gay, jolly, happy, smiling, or sad, and, as their experiences and vocabulary broaden, to solemn, dynamic, or melancholy. But the child also discovers for himself many of these parallels and takes interest or delight in them. He is likely on his own to skip, march, clap, or laugh with the music, and without this natural tendency our training would get nowhere. Insofar, however, as we do take advantage of this tendency and help him by training, *we do just what the critic does.* We may merely need to persuade the child to pay attention, to look or listen; or we may simply *call* the music jolly. But we are also likely to use, as the critic does, reiteration, synonyms, parallels, contrasts, similes, metaphors, gestures, and other expressive behavior.

Of course the recognition of similarities and simple metaphorical extensions are not the only transitions to the aesthetic use of language. Others are made in different ways; for instance, by the kind of peripheral cases I mentioned earlier. When our admiration is for something as simple as the thinness of a glass or the smoothness of a fabric, it is not difficult to call attention to such things, evoke a similar delight, and introduce suitable aesthetic terms. These transitions are only the beginnings; it may often be questionable whether a term is yet being used aesthetically or not. Many of the terms I have mentioned may be used in ways which are not straightforwardly literal but of which we should hesitate to say that they demanded much yet by way of aesthetic sensitivity. We speak of warm and cool colors, and we may say of a brightly colored picture that at least it is gay and lively. When we have brought someone to make this sort of metaphorical extension of terms, he has made one of the transitional steps from which he may move on to uses which more obviously deserve to be called aesthetic and demand a more obviously aesthetic appreciation. When I said at the outset that aesthetic sensitivity was rarer than some other natural endowments, I was not denying that it varies in degree from the rudimentary to the refined. Most people learn easily to make the kinds of remarks I am now considering. But when someone can call bright canvases gay and lively without being able to spot the one which is really vibrant, or can recognise the obvious outward vigor and energy of a student composition played *con fuoco* while failing to see that it lacks inner fire and drive, we do not regard his aesthetic sensitivity in these areas as particularly developed. However, once these transitions from common to aesthetic uses are begun in the more obvious cases, the domain of aesthetic concepts may broaden out, and they may become more subtle and even partly autonomous. The initial steps, however varied the metaphorical shifts and however varied the experiences upon which they are parasitic, are natural and easy.

Much the same is true when we turn to those words which have no standard non-aesthetic use, "lovely," "pretty," "dainty," "graceful," "elegant." We cannot say that these are learned by a metaphorical shift. But they still are linked to non-aesthetic features in many ways and the learning of them also is made possible by certain kinds of natural response, reaction, and ability. We learn them not so much by noticing similarities, but by our attention being caught and focussed in other ways. Certain phenomena which are outstanding or remarkable or unusual catch the eye or ear, seize our attention and interest, and move us to surprise, admiration, delight, fear or distaste. Children begin by reacting in these ways to spectacular sunsets, woods in autumn, roses, dandelions, and other striking and colorful objects, and it is in these circumstances that we find ourselves introducing general aesthetic words to them, like "lovely," "pretty," and "ugly." It is not an accident that the first lessons in aesthetic appreciation consist in drawing the child's attention to roses rather than to grass; nor is it surprising that we remark to him on the autumn colors rather than on the subdued tints of winter. We all of us, not only children, pay aesthetic attention more readily and easily to such outstanding and easily noticeable things. We notice with pleasure early spring grass or the first snow, hills of notably marked and varied contours, scenery flecked with a great variety of color or dappled variously with sun and shadow. We are struck and impressed by great size or mass, as with mountains or cathedrals. We are similarly responsive to unusual precision or minuteness or remarkable feats of skill, as with complex and elaborate filigree, or intricate wood carving and fan-vaulting. It is at these times, taking advantage of these natural interests and admirations, that we first teach the simpler aesthetic words. People of moderate aesthetic sensitivity and sophistication continue to exhibit aesthetic interest mainly on such occasions and to use only the more general words ("pretty," "lovely," and the like). But these situations may serve as a beginning from which we extend our aesthetic interests to wider and less obvious fields, mastering as we go the more subtle and specific vocabulary of taste. The principles do not change; the basis for learning more specific terms like "graceful," "delicate," and "elegant" is also our interest in and admiration for various non-aesthetic natural properties ("She seems to move *effortlessly*, as if floating," "So very *thin* and *fragile*, as if a breeze might destroy it," "So *small* and yet so *intricate*," "So *economical* and perfectly *adapted*").[18] And even with these aesthetic terms which are not metaphorical themselves ("graceful," "delicate," "elegant"), we rely in the same way upon the critic's methods, including comparison, illustration, and metaphor, to teach or make clear what they mean.

I have wished to emphasize in the latter part of this paper the natural basis of responses of various kinds without which aesthetic terms could not be learned. I have also outlined what some of the features are to which we naturally respond: similarities of various sorts, notable colors, shapes, scents, size, intricacy, and much else besides. Even the non-metaphorical aesthetic terms have significant links with all kinds of natural features by which our interest, wonder, admiration, delight, or distaste is aroused. But in particular I have wanted to urge that it should not strike us as puzzling that the critic supports his judgments and brings us to see aesthetic qualities by pointing out key features and talking about them in the way he does. It is by the very same methods that people helped us develop our aesthetic sense and master its vocabulary from the beginning. If we responded to those methods then, it is not surprising that we respond to the critic's discourse now. It would be surprising if, by using this language and behavior, people could *not* sometimes bring us to see the aesthetic qualities of things; for this would prove us lacking in one characteristically human kind of awareness and activity.

Notes

1. I shall speak loosely of an "aesthetic term," even when, because the word sometimes has other uses, it would be more correct to speak of its *use* as an aesthetic term. I shall also speak of "non-aesthetic" words, concepts, features, and so on. None of the terms other writers use, "natural," "observable," "perceptual," "physical," "objective" (qualities), "neutral," "descriptive" (language), when they approach the distinction I am making, is really apt for my purpose.

2. A contrast will reinforce this. If a critic were to describe a passage of music as chattering, carbonated, or gritty, a painter's coloring as vitreous, farinaceous, or effervescent, or a writer's style as glutinous, or abrasive, he *would* be using live metaphors rather than drawing on the more normal language of criticism. Words like "athletic," "vertiginous," "silken" may fall somewhere between.

3. In a paper reprinted in *Aesthetics and Language,* ed. by W. Elton (Oxford, 1954), pp. 131-146, Arnold Isenberg discusses certain problems about aesthetic concepts and qualities. Like others who approach these problems, he does not isolate them, as I do, from questions about verdicts on the *merits* of works of art, or from questions about *likings* and *preferences.* He says something parallel to my remarks above: "There is not in all the world's criticism a single purely descriptive statement concerning which one is prepared to say beforehand, 'if it is true, I shall *like* that work so much the better'" (p. 139, my italics). I should think *this* is highly questionable.

4. Isenberg (*op. cit.*, p. 132) makes a somewhat similar but mistaken point: "If we had been told that the colours of a certain painting are garish, it would be *astonishing* to find that they are *all* very pale and unsaturated" (my italics). But if we say "all" rather than "predominantly," then "astonishing" is the wrong word. The word that goes with "all" is "impossible"; "astonishing" might go with "predominantly."

5. H. L. A. Hart, "The Ascription of Responsibility and Rights" in *Logic and Language*, First Series, ed. by A. G. N. Flew (Oxford, 1951). Hart indeed speaks of "conditions" throughout, see p. 148.

6. I cannot in the compass of this paper discuss the other types of apparent exceptions to my thesis. Cases where a man *lacking* in sensitivity might learn and follow a rule, as above, ought to be distinguished from cases where someone who *possesses* sensitivity might know, from a non-aesthetic description, that an aesthetic term applies. I have stated my thesis as though this latter kind of case never occurs because I have had my eye on the logical features of *typical* aesthetic judgments and have preferred to over- rather than understate my view. But with certain aesthetic terms, especially negative ones, there may be perhaps some rare genuine exceptions when a description enables us to visualize very fully, and when what is described belongs to certain restricted classes of things, say human faces or animal forms. Perhaps a description like "One eye red and rheumy, the other missing, a wart-covered nose, a twisted mouth, a greenish pallor" may justify in a strong sense ("must be," "cannot but be") the judgments "ugly" or "hideous." If so, such cases are marginal, form a very small minority, and are uncharacteristic or atypical of aesthetic judgments in general. Usually when, on hearing a description, we say "it *must* be very beautiful (graceful, or the like)," we mean no more than "it surely must be, it's only remotely possible that it isn't." Different again are situations, and these are very numerous, where we can move quite simply from "bright colors" to "gay," or from "reds and yellows" to "warm," but where we are as yet only on the borderline of anything that could be called an expression of taste or aesthetic sensibility. I have stressed the importance of this transitional and border area between non-aesthetic and obviously aesthetic judgments below (p. 369).

7. Helen Knight says (Elton, *op. cit.*, p. 152) that "piquant" (one of my "aethetic" terms) "depends on" various features (a *retroussé* nose, a pointed chin, and the like) and that these features are *criteria* for it; this is what I am denying. She also maintains that "good," when applied to works of art, depends on *criteria* like balance, solidity, depth, profundity (my aesthetic terms again; I should place piquancy in this list). I would deny this too, though I regard it as a different question and do not consider it in this paper. The two questions need separating: the relation of non-aesthetic features (*retroussé*, pointed) to aesthetic qualities, and the relation of aesthetic qualities to "aesthetically good" (verdicts). Most writings which touch on the nature of aesthetic concepts have this other (verdict) question mainly in mind. Mrs. Knight blurs this difference when she says, for example. " 'piquant' is the same kind of word as 'good.' "

8. See articles by Margaret Macdonald and J. A. Passmore in Elton, *op. cit.*, pp. 118, 119, 40, 41.

9. As I indicated, I have dealt only with the relation of *nonaesthetic* to aesthetic features. Perhaps a description in *aesthetic* terms may occasionally suffice for applying another aesthetic term. Johnson's Dictionary gives "handsome" as "beautiful with dignity"; Shorter O. E. D. gives "pretty" as "beautiful in a slight, dainty, or diminutive way."

10. Macdonald in Elton, *op. cit.*, pp. 114, 119. See also pp. 120, 122.

11. Macdonald, *ibid.*, pp. 114, 120-123. She speaks of non-aesthetic properties

here as "physical" or "observable" qualities, and distinguishes between "physical object" and "work of art."

12. *Ibid.*, pp. 115-116; cf. also John Holloway, *Proceedings of the Aristotelian Society*, Supplementary Vol. XXIII (1949), pp. 175-176.

13. Stuart Hampshire in Elton, *op. cit.*, p. 165. Cf. also remarks in Elton by Isenberg (pp. 142, 145), Passmore (p. 38), in *Philosophy and Psycho-analysis* by John Wisdom (Oxford, 1953), pp. 223-224, and in Holloway, *op. cit.* p. 175. [Hampshire's paper appears in Section VI of this book. Ed.]

14. Macdonald, *op. cit.*, pp. 119-120.

15. *Ibid.* See pp. 127, 122, 125, 115. Other writers also place the stress on interpretations, cf. Holloway, *op. cit.*, p. 173 ff.

16. *Op. cit.*, pp. 165-168.

17. Holloway, *op. cit.*, pp. 173-174, lists some of these briefly.

18. It is worth noticing that most of the words which in current usage are primarily or exclusively aesthetic terms had earlier non-aesthetic uses and gained their present use by some kind of metaphorical shift. Without reposing too great weight on these etymological facts, it can be seen that their history reflects connections with the responses, interests, and natural features I have mentioned as underlying the learning and use of aesthetic terms. These transitions suggest both the dependence of aesthetic upon other interests, and what some of these interests are. Connected with liking, delight, affection, regard, estimation or choice—*beautiful, graceful, delicate, lovely, exquisite, elegant, dainty*; with fear or repulsion—*ugly*; with what notably catches the eye or attention—*garish, splendid, gaudy*; with what attracts by notable rarity, precision, skill, ingenuity, elaboration—*dainty, nice, pretty, exquisite*; with adaptation to function, suitability to ease of handling—*handsome*.

TED COHEN

Aesthetic / Non-aesthetic and the Concept of Taste: A Critique of Sibley's Position

Introduction to Sibley

SIBLEY'S THEORY is a *kind* of theory characteristic of a strain of mid-twentieth century aesthetics (and ethics), and it is as such philosophizing that I would like to discredit it. I am less interested in the conclusions reached from views like Sibley's than in those views' conception of the framework within which to raise questions which lead to conclusions. This conception does *lead*, I think, in a way which renders any conclusion pernicious. Roughly this approach is dictated: Given that there are aesthetic judgments, (i) one must decide whether they are "objective" or "cognitive" or whatever, or, broadly speaking, whether they are things that have truth-values; and if they do have truth-values, (ii) one must determine whether an aesthetic judgment ever can be inferred from any conjunction of non-aesthetic judgments. This is likely to require that (iii) one determine how the terms found in aesthetic judgments are related to other terms.

This sketch is familiar to anyone acquainted with recent analytic aesthetics, and it outlines the thoughts (and despair) of those who have "done" aesthetics as students. Sibley is one among dozens whose work fits this pattern. I choose his position to discuss for five reasons.

(1) It is, I think, the best, most careful work in this vein.

(2) It has been very influential: the principal essay, "Aesthetic Concepts," is included in most standard anthologies published since its appearance, and much of the "mainstream" literature in aesthetics of the 1960's is addressed to Sibley in one way or another.

(3) It exemplifies what one might call "conceptual" aesthetics, paral-

From *Theoria*, 39 (1973), pp. 113-152. Reprinted by permission of *Theoria*.

lelling—or following after—what we have been taught to think of as meta-ethics. I should like my work to suggest that there is some point in wondering whether there is any point in aesthetics going through the same moves ethics has gone through (as well as wondering what ethics has done to itself).

(4) Although by now Sibley's view has begun to look like one among a variety of possible (standard) meta-aesthetic theories, it remains special in its studied characterization of aesthetic judgments without reference to their status as verdicts or evaluations.

(5) Sibley's approach recalls eighteenth century British philosophy of art—up to a point. This part of the Tradition, largely ignored in recent philosophy of art before Sibley, animates Sibley's work, giving it the depth, plausibility, and appeal so conspicuously and characteristically missing from recent aesthetics. I hope to show that the ultimate collapse of Sibley's view coincides with his departure from the pivotal notion in Hume's analysis, the conception of taste.

With regard to (4) and (5) I believe Sibley's view to be unique. This will be discussed in some detail once the view itself has been outlined.

The paper which has been for me the *locus classicus* of the aesthetic/non-aesthetic distinction in its respectably analytic version is "Aesthetic Concepts." In fact Sibley's view has been presented and extended in three papers, two major ones and a short response, all of which first appeared in the *Philosophical Review*: "Aesthetic Concepts," "Aesthetic Concepts: A Rejoinder," and "Aesthetic and Nonaesthetic."[1] These are the only papers I shall be drawing on. Since the latest of them, "Aesthetic and Nonaesthetic," Sibley has produced a number of papers, some of which derive from these three, but none of which change the original view.

Outline of Sibley's Theory

Abstracting and condensing, to isolate the themes I will be examining, I take Sibley to be making three moves (though, as shall be seen, Sibley does not think of the first as a *move*): (1) invoking an aesthetic/non-aesthetic distinction, (2) asking whether the items thus distinguished are related in certain specific ways, (3) answering that they are not so related. In more detail—

(1) The distinction works on many levels, applying at least to qualities, descriptions, judgments, terms, and concepts. Which level Sibley takes as basic or independent is unclear, in spite of the ostensible concern with concepts. (The paper is called "Aesthetic Concepts.") The most natural account I can give of the distinction, consistent with Sibley's intentions but coherent, is this.

An aesthetic quality (or feature) is one which is noted in an aesthetic judgment (or description or remark). An aesthetic judgment is a judgment in which an aesthetic concept is used. An aesthetic concept is a concept whose related term—the term used when one applies the concept—is an aesthetic term. An aesthetic term is one whose use (perhaps correct use) requires the possession of taste. Taste is perceptiveness, sensitivity, aesthetic discrimination, aesthetic appreciation. Sibley says that it is "an ability to *notice* or *see* or *tell* that things have certain qualities" (AC, p. 65). Finally, a quality, judgment, concept, or term is non-aesthetic if and only if it is not an aesthetic one.

That Sibley intends something like this quasi-formal apparatus is clear from the opening passages of "Aesthetic Concepts."

> The remarks we make about works of art are of many kinds. . . . We say that a novel has a great number of characters and deals with life in a manufacturing town; that a painting uses pale colors, predominantly blues and greens, and has kneeling figures in the foreground; that the theme in a fugue is inverted at such a point and that there is a stretto at the close; that the action of a play takes place in the span of one day and that there is a reconciliation scene in the fifth act. Such remarks may be made by, and such features pointed out to, anyone with normal eyes, ears, and intelligence. On the other hand, we also say that a poem is tightly-knit or deeply moving; that a picture lacks balance, or has a certain serenity and repose, or that the grouping of the figures sets up an exciting tension; that the characters in a novel never really come to life, or that a certain episode strikes a false note. It would be neutral enough to say that the making of such judgments as these requires the exercise of taste, perceptiveness, or sensitivity, of aesthetic discrimination or appreciation; one would not say this of my first group. Accordingly, when a word or expression is such that taste or perceptiveness is required in order to apply it, I shall call it an *aesthetic* term or expression, and I shall, correspondingly, speak of *aesthetic* concepts or *taste* concepts. (AC, pp. 63-64)

Still, my technical-looking rectified version of Sibley's aesthetic/non-aesthetic distinction requires considerable justification, for there is no way to take it straightforwardly from his text. Most controversial points are non-exegetical, I think, since around them turn various possible defences of Sibley against my criticisms. So, I shall not deal with them until they arise in the course of the argument. There are, however, two points to be mentioned immediately.

(i) The quotation seems to show clearly that the fundamental distinction is between concepts, or at least that concepts are as basic as terms for Sibley, while in my version concepts are ultimately supplanted by terms. I reserve discussion of this until later, when I hope to show that it is a critical matter. Here I simply point out that Sibley is unclear about the relation of terms to concepts as well as about what either a term or a concept is. In a later paper, Sibley alludes to the passages from which the above quotation came, saying, "the distinction I set out to make

in the introductory section was between *terms* or *expressions* of two kinds"
(ACR, p. 80).

(ii) Whatever the relation of terms to concepts, it seems a mistake to
say for Sibley that every aesthetic judgment contains an aesthetic term—
as I do. In ACR, which is addressed to H. R. G. Schwyzer,[2] Sibley complains of just this misinterpretation.

> Nothing I said, that is, implied the doctrine Schwyzer attributes to me, that
> 'an aesthetic remark always involves the use of an aesthetic term.' Indeed,
> not only did I suppose it obvious that, as he says, 'the class of remarks *the
> making of which* requires perceptiveness is different from, indeed far larger
> than, the class of remarks that contain *words and expressions whose ap-
> plication* requires perceptiveness'; I said so myself at the end of Part I
> where I pointed out that I had not been discussing 'aesthetic or taste judg-
> ments in general' but only 'the more restricted range of judgments which
> employ aesthetic terms.' (ACR, p. 40)

In the context of this essay my recasting of the distinction is immune
to this complaint. It is with regard only to aesthetic judgments which
do contain aesthetic terms that Sibley takes a stand, and it is only as such
that I will claim that his argument is defective. However, more generally,
Sibley and Schwyzer seem to me much too quick to recognize aesthetic
judgments which contain no aesthetic terms. They have in mind remarks
like "how very gradually the stem curves" and "it is a big picture." It is
simple to imagine circumstances in which sensitivity and pedagogical
insight are behind these remarks, and yet none of the constituent words
seem to require for their successful use what Sibley calls taste. But this
is not so clear. I shall be arguing that Sibley has no convincing reason
for refusing to call these words aesthetic terms. Until that argument appears, perhaps this will suffice to preserve my rendering of Sibley's distinction: although Sibley (and Schwyzer) seem to use "term" as roughly
interchangeable with "word" (or "words"), I am using it in the sense of
"open sentence."[3] Thus in any remark of the form "x is F," "is F" is a
term. This being so, it seems clear that a remark is aesthetic only if its
term is aesthetic. When this construction becomes contentious I will
return to it. So long as attention is confined to those judgments which,
according to Sibley, are aesthetic *and* contain aesthetic terms, his terms
and my terms (roughly) coincide.

(2) About aesthetic terms Sibley says "I am interested in what they all
have in common" (AC, p. 64).

(3) Eleven pages later he announces that he has found it: "I have now
argued that in certain ways aesthetic concepts are not and cannot be
condition- or rule-governed" (AC, p. 75). (This means that the applicability of an aesthetic concept cannot be inferred, in any of a variety of
standard ways, from the applicability of any number of non-aesthetic
concepts.)

It should be clear that Sibley's work fits the conception and approach sketched earlier. In his view aesthetic judgments do have truth-values. They are in the ordinary sense, descriptions; their characteristic terms—aesthetic terms—apply to certain properties—aesthetic properties. Since the presence of a particular aesthetic property is never guaranteed by the presence of any given non-aesthetic properties, it follows that neither the applicability of an aesthetic term nor the truth of an aesthetic judgment (which on my view of "term" comes to the same thing) can be inferred from the applicability of non-aesthetic terms. Only taste will suffice in making aesthetic judgments.

Seen in terms of the sketch Sibley looks like an intuitionist or non-naturalist, if one imports the all too handy categories of meta-meta-ethics, as has been noted by various readers.[4] However his characterization of aesthetic judgments and, correlatively, his conception of "taste" make Sibley's view untypical. He treats aesthetic judgments explicitly without regard to their connection with value or praise. He says,

> About a third and much-discussed class of judgments, however, I have nothing to say in this paper. These are the purely evaluative judgments: whether things are aesthetically good or bad, excellent or mediocre, superior to others or inferior, and so on. Such judgments I shall call *verdicts.* Nor shall I raise any other questions about evaluation: about how verdicts are made or supported, or whether the judgments I am dealing with carry evaluative implications. (AN, p. 136)

Then this is not so much like ethical intuitionists' discussions of "good" and "right," nor is it obviously commensurate with Hume's naturalistic account of beauty so that it might be taken as a straightforward alternative. I will return to this at the end of the essay.

Criticism of Sibley's Argument

Sibley's conclusion is that there are and can be no necessary, sufficient or defeasible non-aesthetic conditions for the use of an aesthetic term. He offers a number of observations in support of this, but until just before the conclusion is announced he presents no *argument*. In fact he says, "My arguments and illustrations so far have been rather simply schematic" (AC, p. 71). And so they have, in general coming to statements like these—

> There is little temptation to suppose that aesthetic terms resemble words which, like 'square,' are applied in accordance with a set of necessary and sufficient conditions. For whereas each square is square in virtue of the *same* set of conditions, four equal sides and four right angles, aesthetic terms apply to widely varied objects; one thing is graceful because of these features, another because of those, and so on almost endlessly. (AC, p. 66)

There are no sufficient conditions, no non-aesthetic features such that the presence of some set or numbers of them will beyond question logically justify or warrant the application of an aesthetic term. It is impossible (barring certain limited exceptions, . . .) to make any statements corresponding to those we can make for condition-governed words. We are able to say 'If it is true he can do this, and that, and the other, then one just cannot deny that he is intelligent,' or 'if he does A, B, and C, I don't see how it can be denied that he is lazy,' but we cannot make *any* general statement of the form 'If the vase is pale pink, somewhat curving, lightly mottled, and so forth, it will be delicate, cannot but be delicate' (AC, pp. 67-68)

Although there is this sense in which slimness, lightness, lack of intensity of color, and so on, count only towards, not against, delicacy, these features, I shall say, at best count only *typically* or *characteristically* towards delicacy; they do not count towards in the same sense as condition-features count towards laziness or intelligence; that is, no group of them is even logically sufficient. (AC, p. 69)

The very notion of a defeasible concept seems to require that some group of features *would* be sufficient *in certain circumstances,* that is, in the absence of overriding or voiding features. In a certain way defeasible concepts lack sufficient conditions then, but they are still, in the sense described, condition-governed. My claim about taste concepts is stronger; that they are not, except negatively, governed by conditions at all. We could not conclude even in certain circumstances, e.g., if we were told of the absence of all 'voiding' or uncharacteristic features (no angularities and the like), that an object *must* certainly be graceful, no matter how fully it was described to us as possessing features characteristic of gracefulness. (AC, p. 71)

The obvious way to quarrel with these remarks is to produce a counter-example. I have none. Indeed I do not say that they are wrong (though I expect to show that they are vacuous). I note only that they are, as Sibley says, simply schematic, and pass on to what seems to me Sibley's only real argument. Perhaps Sibley does not regard this as an argument at all; he calls it a reinforcement of his argument. However, I believe it schematizes all the argument Sibley has, and it will do to show that there is no arguing, only a kind of running in place.

The point I have argued may be reinforced in the following way. A man who failed to realize the nature of aesthetic concepts, or someone who, knowing he lacked sensitivity in aesthetic matters, did not want to reveal this lack might by assiduous application and shrewd observation provide himself with some rules and generalizations; and by inductive procedures and intelligent guessing, he might frequently say the right things. But he could have no great confidence or certainty; a slight change in an object might at any time unpredictably ruin his calculations, and he might as easily have been wrong as right. No matter how careful he has been about working out a set of consistent principles and conditions, he is only in a position to think that the object is very possibly delicate. . . . Though he sometimes says the right thing, he has not seen, but guessed, that the object is delicate. (AC, pp. 72-73)

Again, I do not say that Sibley is wrong, but that he has said nothing (new). To show this concisely it will help to use some symbols.

Let E be an aesthetic term naming the aesthetic quality E-ness.

Let N_1, N_2, . . . , and N_n be non-aesthetic terms naming the non-aesthetic qualities N_1-ness, N_2-ness, . . . , and N_n-ness.

There are four distinct relations to consider.

(1) E means (or means the same as) N_1 and N_2 and . . . N_n.

(2) The meaning of 'E' is carried in (or is contained in) the meaning of N_1 and N_2 and . . . and N_n.

I do not claim to have an account of "meaning," "containment of meaning," etc., nor that there is an account. It will be clear that this is not an important matter.

(3) $(x)(Ex \equiv . N_1 \& N_2 \& \ldots \& N_n)$. (Things are E if and only if they are N_1 and N_2 and . . . and N_n.)

(4) $(x)(N_1 \& N_2 \& \ldots \& N_n . \supset E)$. (Anything which is $N_1 \& N_2 \& \ldots \& N_n$ is also E.)

With this in hand, let us argue.

Since taste is required to detect E-ness but not to detect any of N_1-ness, . . . , N_n-ness (for that is exactly the difference between aesthetic and non-aesthetic terms)—it follows immediately that,

From the fact that someone can apply all of N_1, . . ., N_n we cannot infer that he can detect E-ness.

That seems to be Sibley's point. But he must intend more, because it remains possible that,

From the fact that N_1, . . ., N_n apply we can infer that E applies.

Why? Because it may happen that E-ness always accompanies the joint presence of N_1-ness and . . . and N_n-ness. That is, it may be that (4) or even (3) is true and is known to be true. It is senseless to suppose that (1) or (2) be true but not be known to be true, and perhaps both (1) and (2) must be false, as Sibley would have it. But the truth of (4), or even of (3), requires the truth of neither (1) or (2). Then Sibley's argument is inadequate.

The point is simple, but perhaps too simple to be appreciated easily, for it is startling to find it undercutting Sibley's argument. An illustration of the point in a parallel example is helpful.

Suppose that all cylindrical objects are red, that Smith knows this, and that Smith is blind. Now Smith can tell that something is red even though Smith can't detect redness and even though "red" and "cylindrical" are unconnected in meaning. Sibley's position is that of citing the existence of Smith as a proof, or a reinforcement of a proof, that not all cylinders are red. That is, Smith "has not seen" that the object is red. But what point could this reinforce?—beyond the claim that Smith is blind?[5]

One might feel like saying that after all Smith only guesses or predicts that a given cylinder is red because in fact it might not be red. Then suppose that cylinders have to be red, that it is a law of nature that cylinders are red. This puts it in order, I suppose, to aver that if such were the case, "cylindrical" and "red" might not be altogether unconnected in meaning. No matter: the point remains that the existence, or imaginability, of a blind man is not—as things stand—proof that some cylinders are not red.

Another possible rejoinder is that Smith can't fit the description, can't tell that something is red, because being blind Smith can't know the meaning of "red." Whether or not there is any reason to believe that "acquaintance" with something is a necessary condition of knowing the meaning of a term which applies to that thing, the point can be made irrelevant. Amend the example so that Smith occasionally has seen, and seen red things, but in this case doesn't see that the object is red. (This could be because Smith has only recently gone blind, or perhaps he is not blind but the object is poorly lit or too far away.) Then why deny that Smith can tell that "red" applies though he does not detect (see) any redness?

Sibley can be rescued—and I should like him to be rescued—in this way. Let apply E and detect E-ness be interchangeable. This will make it true that,

From the fact that $N_1, \ldots, N_n$ apply, it does not follow that E applies.

This is Sibley's conclusion: E is not condition-governed. But the maneuver which gets there, construing being able to apply 'E' as being able to detect E-ness, is of no help to Sibley, for it leaves us with this:

To apply an aesthetic term is to detect an aesthetic quality; it takes taste to do this.

To apply a non-aesthetic term does not require taste, only normality (whether or not one must detect N_1-ness in order to apply N_1).

Now we can say that being able to apply non-aesthetic terms never guarantees that one can apply aesthetic terms; but we can say this because—and only because,

From the fact that one is normal it does not follow that one has taste.

Or, to be more exact,

> From the fact that one is exercising one's normal capacities it does not
> follow that one is exercising taste.

This is an unhappy but telling form for Sibley's conclusion, for it is nothing but the aesthetic/non-aesthetic distinction itself. If there were no difference between exercising one's taste and exercising one's (merely) normal capacities, there would have been no difference between aesthetic and non-aesthetic terms.

This argument against Sibley is oblique and it may be misleading. I must not be taken to be advancing "naturalism" as against Sibley's "intuitionism." I have not shown that Sibley is wrong in denying that aesthetic judgments can be inferred from non-aesthetic ones, if this would be to show that they can be inferred. One may conceive all these petrified views—naturalism, property-intuitionism, rule-intuitionism, etc.—as answers to one question: How, if at all, are aesthetic and non-aesthetic judgments, concepts, or terms related to one another? What I wish to do, if not to bury this question, is at least to divest it of its innocence. To this end I have now made clear that whatever Sibley has *shown* was shown in the drawing of the aesthetic/non-aesthetic distinction and only reflected in the putative argument following the appearance of the distinction.

Criticism of Sibley's Distinction

To rehearse: Suppose in discussing a painting someone refers to one of its lines, saying "That line is curved," and later adds "That line is graceful." The latter is an aesthetic judgment, the former is not. Why? Because only the latter (or its making) is the application of an aesthetic concept, the use of an aesthetic term. How does one tell? By noting that "graceful" is an aesthetic term while "curved" is not. Which is to say that taste is required to apply "graceful" but no more than normal eyes and intelligence is required to apply "curved."

That is the aesthetic/non-aesthetic distinction at work, identifying judgments like "That is graceful" and thereby sorting out what Sibley calls the "subject matter" of aesthetics (AN, p. 135). It is not itself part of aesthetics, on Sibley's view; rather, drawing it is a precondition of beginning aesthetics. If the preceding section of this essay succeeded, then what Sibley does after invoking the distinction is ignorable: the distinction itself is all the philosophy Sibley has and it is the ultimate cause of whatever uneasiness one feels with Sibley's position. How does one "attack" this distinction (or any other)? Only, I think, by showing that it does nothing—in particular, that it does not do what is demanded of it in its context.

One thing the distinction should do (according to my rectified version of it)[6] is to identify a given judgment as aesthetic or non-aesthetic by discerning the presence or absence of aesthetic terms. I think the distinction fails to do this, or even to begin to do this, for there seems to me no sensible and important way of dividing terms according to whether taste or only normality is needed to apply them. (One may think that "sense" and "importance" are not definite enough notions to underwrite a critique. I had thought of supplanting them with the technical notion of an effective procedure, and then criticizing Sibley for supplying nothing remotely like even a quasi-mechanical routine. But this would be a mistake. Sibley is altogether unspecific about the nature of the distinction and its application. My leaving the terms of appraisal vague seems fairer and more generous to Sibley, and it allows me to encompass some efforts to rescue the distinction. And finally, it is the burden of this essay to persuade you that Sibley's distinction has become far too prominent and that its sense (and sensibility) have been too readily acknowledged.)

With regard to the application of the distinction Sibley acknowledges "the expected debatable, ambiguous, or borderline cases" (AN, p. 135). But I cannot see that he has any clearcut cases. Take "graceful," to start, which is one of the words which, according to Sibley, "whether in artistic or daily discourse, function only or predominantly as aesthetic terms" (AC, p. 64). Suppose I show this figure and ask which is the graceful line, or whether any is a graceful line. No doubt you have taste, but do you need it? Virtual insensitivity will do, I think, to manage "(c) is the graceful one" or "(c) is graceful" or "(c) is more graceful than (a) or (b)."

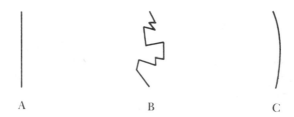

A   B   C

If you are unsatisfied with my figure you must make your own. Keep in mind that the aim is not to make (c) better than the others, nor is it to make (c) more likeable. Good and bad, and likes and dislikes have nothing to do with the conception of taste as used in drawing the distinction. Taste is more than normal ability to notice or detect things. Taste is required to notice gracefulness (and so to use the aesthetic term "graceful"). I ask you to produce an example in which "(c) is graceful" is accessible upon a merely normal view. This may seem to beg the question against Sibley but I think it does not. It is to take the question seriously, disingenously, pre-theoretically: is it always the case with "graceful" that taste is needed to apply it? I say no.

Sibley would say, perhaps, that in such an example "(c) is graceful" is not an aesthetic judgment. Then what about "graceful"? There are answers at Sibley's disposal. One, which seems to me painfully clumsy, is that "graceful" is a term associated with (at least) two concepts, the aesthetic concept $graceful_a$ and the non-aesthetic concept $graceful_n$. Sibley says that, given the definition of "aesthetic term" he "shall, correspondingly, speak of *aesthetic* concepts" (AC, p. 64). About the correspondence between terms and concepts Sibley says nothing; perhaps he would say that "graceful" can correspond to either of (at least) two concepts. Then he could hold that "(c) is graceful" is a non-aesthetic judgment with "graceful" a non-aesthetic term being used to apply the non-aesthetic concept $graceful_n$.

To this one may object that it renders the distinction inoperative. It is no longer possible to identify aesthetic judgments by noting the presence of aesthetic terms, for there is no way of noting aesthetic terms by inspection. I prefer to object that no legitimate reason has been given for claiming that "graceful" has two concepts or senses. What motivation is there for multiplying the senses of "graceful" beyond a desire to preserve the aesthetic/non-aesthetic distinction? I am not raising those involuted questions about meaning which require technical accounts of polysemy backed by a "theory of meaning." What is wanted (and, I think, is lacking) is an informal rationale for identifying extra concepts for "graceful." What *reason* is there for distinguishing $graceful_a$ and $graceful_n$? They are distinguished so far, in this hypothetical response on Sibley's behalf, by the fact that only one of them requires taste for its application. Is that sufficient? Shall we say that whenever an otherwise ordinary term is used in a context in which more than normal competence is needed to handle the term, the term has changed its meaning or been affixed to a different concept? Although I think the general answer to this question is clear, it is a vexed question even when taken informally. Since it will recur in this essay, it may be helpful to take time now to consider a battery of illustrations.

First, consider some terms which can be managed readily on the strength of normal intelligence, eyes, etc., but whose use on occasion signals more than mere normality. (I shall be claiming that this description fits virtually all of Sibley's aesthetic terms.)

The terms applying to a variety of racial, geographical, and sexual groups of people are common, and are learned and used by everyone. Some observers, however, are much more accurate than others at recognizing members of these groups. They can tell on sight, by attending to people's size, shape, posture, gestures, gait, etc., Jews, Northern Europeans, homosexuals, New Yorkers, etc. Phonetic descriptions are a special case. Some professional linguists and many amateurs with good ears can identify East Texans, Canadians, native Bavarians, etc., by hearing them speak English.

Another auditory case is pitch, in music. Regardless of what minimal ability one supposes could be cultivated in any normal person, beyond that there are differences in abilities to "hear" absolute and relative pitch, to identify pitches in chord constructions, etc.

Handwriting identification is, visually, a partial analogue. A handwriting expert can identify signatures and match writing samples with far more facility than those with no more than normal intelligence and eyes.

It is helpful to consider some terms all of whose uses are relatively esoteric. Some examples are medical terms applied to patients after examination, i.e., the names of diseases, syndromes, "conditions," etc. A few doctors, the best internists, are much better than their colleagues at detecting, say, diabetes and hypoglycemia. From external examinations they obtain results nearly as accurate as those obtained by lesser diagnosticians aided by laboratory analysis.

The fact that these examples may involve terms which apply to properties which are not purely perceptual is irrelevant. Sibley's examples of aesthetic terms include ones which refer to qualities not literally seen or heard (e.g., "tightly-knit," said of a poem; "has characters who never really come to life," said of a novel). (A relevant passage from Sibley is quoted above, p. 567 f.)

Also irrelevant, but probably harder to ignore, is the fact that the examples involve terms which, allegedly unlike "graceful," seem clearly to be condition-governed. But being unconditioned is not what makes "graceful" an aesthetic term. Sibley first sorts out aesthetic terms and then argues that these terms are unconditioned. We have seen that the argument goes nowhere beyond the distinction, and we are now back at the beginning, looking into Sibley's way of sorting out aesthetic terms. Taking Sibley literally, "graceful" is an aesthetic term—whether or not it is condition-governed—because taste is needed to apply it. In response to the suggested counter-example ["(c) is graceful"] one might look for two concepts to go with 'graceful.' The budget of cases just gone through is meant to illustrate an implausibility in that response.

The cases mainly concern terms—"Jew," "East Texan," "G-sharp," "written by Lincoln"—whose use frequently requires no special capacity, but whose use in the examples is effected by means of special capacities and talents (something beyond mere normality). The (rhetorical) question is, shall we say that in these examples the terms are being used to apply different concepts?

It may be suggested that the fact that these terms have conditions, perhaps even necessary and sufficient ones, renders the examples defective. The argument would be that each of the terms does have two senses, the proof being that in their ordinary use one applies them with reference to their defining conditions, while this does not happen when they are used by a specialist in difficult cases. This suggestion is mistaken, but it has an interesting twist.

The mistake is, simply, to conflate unreasonably the meaning of a term and the way in which—in some actual case—someone decides whether to apply it. "Square" does not change its meaning when I apply it to a figure without measuring the sides. Surely the brilliant diagnostician and the routine laboratory worker are not using "diabetes" to apply different concepts. Knowing the meaning of a term is not a guarantee of being able to decide whether it correctly applies; nor is inability to tell whether a term applies a proof of ignorance of the term's meaning.

However, if the suggestion were acceptable it would have an unwanted effect on Sibley's argument. All aesthetic terms, including "graceful," are non-condition-governed, Sibley argues. Then if alteration in the conditions governing application of a term—in general, or in particular cases—were the sign of a multiplicity of concepts associated with the term, this would be of no help in urging that "graceful" is associated with more than one concept.

I conclude that Sibley has no reason to discount "(c) is graceful" (as a counter-example to "graceful's" being an aesthetic term) by claiming that it is the application of *graceful*$_n$, for I see no reason to suppose that there is a *graceful*$_n$ (or a *graceful*$_a$).

A simpler, more direct response, in Sibley's interest, is that "graceful" is indeed an aesthetic term but that aesthetic terms can appear in non-aesthetic judgments, as, for example, "graceful" appears in "(c) is graceful."

This response obviously ruins the program for identifying aesthetic and non-aesthetic judgments by the presence or absence of aesthetic terms. That is a minor objection. The decisive objection is not that the distinction ceases to function, but that it functions inconsistently. Sibley says that both judgments and terms are to be defined as aesthetic by means of the "Is-taste-required?" test. Since a non-aesthetic judgment can be made without exercising taste, but an aesthetic term cannot be applied without exercising taste, it follows that if "graceful" is an aesthetic term then making the judgment that (c) is graceful both does and does not require taste.

No doubt Sibley would deal with "(c) is graceful" in neither of the ways just discussed, but it is hard to see what response, right or wrong, he would find congenial. His most relevant remark occurs in a footnote. He says,

> I shall speak loosely of an 'aesthetic term,' even when, because the word sometimes has other uses, it would be more correct to speak of its *use* as an aesthetic term. (AC, p. 64, n. 1)

This suggests that there are times when one might speak of an aesthetic term and not be speaking loosely. This would occur, presumably, when one were speaking of a term whose use invariably requires taste. I doubt that there are any such terms, whatever taste is; and I am fairly certain that there are no such terms when the notion of taste is the one Sibley uses.

Two aspects of the notion of taste are expressly removed from consideration by Sibley (though he does not deny that they would come up in a more complete analysis of taste). The first is taste as it has to do with likes and dislikes, the second is taste as it has to do with good and bad.[7] Taste, as that which is exercised in the use of an aesthetic term, is "an ability to *notice* or *see* or *tell* that things have certain qualities" (AC, p. 65). Whether this constricts or distorts the notion of taste, and how that affects one's notion of the relative complexity of the apprehension of art works, is an implicit theme throughout this essay, and it will become explicit shortly. Here I want only to get clear about what one of Sibley's aesthetic terms would be like if there were one. If there are any, they are terms whose (successful) application invariably requires an "ability to notice" which is something more than the abilities that go with normal intelligence and sense organs. I said that I think there are no such terms. My reason is simply that I seem to be able to find, for any given term (or at least any of the terms Sibley considers), an application of it which could be managed by any normal man. I doubt that this reason will convince you straightway (though I have no idea what other reason could be given). You have to think it over until you agree that something like what I did with "graceful"—or what you did to satisfy yourself about "graceful"—can be done with any term. But what Sibley means by "taste" must be kept in mind or it may not be clear when a "non-aesthetic" use has been found. I believe Sibley himself may have overlooked this.

Sibley says that "lovely," "pretty," "beautiful," "dainty," "graceful," and "elegant" "are certainly not being used metaphorically when employed as aesthetic terms, the very good reason being that this is their primary or only use, some of them having no current non-aesthetic use" (AC, p. 65). That is, at least some of these terms are—*strictly speaking*—aesthetic terms.

We have dealt with "graceful." The others seem no more difficult. Can't you imagine situations in which it would be natural, easy, and obvious to say—"It's a lovely day today"; "This glove is too big; you have a rather dainty hand"; "He's an elegant old gentleman"; "The sun has finally broken through and now the sky is pretty"; "I couldn't see the vessels clearly on the last one, but this earthworm is a beautiful specimen."

Do you insist that taste is required to make these judgments? (In fact, do you feel like calling them aesthetic judgments at all?) Why? Remember that whether the speaker is expressing personal satisfaction or gratification and whether he is evaluating or ranking things are irrelevant. Perhaps in the situation you imagine the speaker of "It's a lovely day" is clearly happy about it and in addition is lauding the climate and ranking this day above others. Those features of the utterance seem to me the only ones which make it even faintly plausible to call it an aesthetic judgment. But those features are irrelevant (as is the fact—if you think it is one—that "lovely" is not condition-governed, that the speaker couldn't *prove* that the day is lovely). From none of these features does it follow that what Sibley calls an aesthetic judgment has been made. The only question is whether *taste* has been exercised, and it needn't have been if normal intelligence and senses are enough. I don't see why they should not be enough.

What difference does this make in the intelligibility of the aesthetic/non-aesthetic distinction? This: if no term invariably requires taste for its application, then what, after all, is an *aesthetic term?* Is it a term which usually requires taste for its application? Then what of Sibley's formula for speaking correctly (not loosely) of such a term. We are, he says, to speak of a term's *use* as an aesthetic term. That, now, will be to speak of a term's being used as a term which is usually used as an aesthetic term. A minor objection to this version of the distinction is, again, that it will not support the program for identifying aesthetic judgments by picking out aesthetic terms. The major objection this time is not that the distinction functions inconsistently, but that it functions not at all: it will pick out nothing as an aesthetic term.

Before giving up on Sibley's version of the aesthetic/non-aesthetic distinction we must consider two final, meager, efforts to rescue it.

In the footnote quoted from above, Sibley says something which suggests that, speaking more correctly, the aesthetic/non-aesthetic distinction is to be made out with regard, not to terms, but to the "uses" of terms (AC, p. 64, n. 1; quoted above, p. 577). Could we say that on certain occasions the use of (some) terms manifests an exercise of taste, and thereby effect a distinction between aesthetic and non-aesthetic uses? Perhaps—though to what point I don't know, but in any case this subverts Sibley's program. All the talk of terms, judgments, descriptions, remarks, and concepts becomes idle at best. There are no terms which are always used in that way, and, I think, there are none that are never used in that way. Part of the spirit of Schwyzer's objection is right, after all (though he has left himself open to Sibley's rebuttal). He says,

> Sibley's preoccupation with words (both aesthetic and non-aesthetic) and their uses, and the features to which they allegedly 'apply,' has led him to lose sight of the nature of actual critical utterances.[8]

If we turn from terms to terms-as-they-are-used-in-specific circumstances, or some such, then can we identify a class of performances, actual utterances, which are exhibitions of taste? If so, then it will be not that "graceful" is an aesthetic term, but that the use of "graceful" upon some occasion is an aesthetic use. There will also be non-aesthetic uses. There is no reason to call these *other* uses in any but a numerical sense. Still, is there now a serviceable aesthetic/non-aesthetic distinction? It

will not serve Sibley's purposes, for he wants to isolate and then discuss
more abstract things than particular actual uses of terms. And indeed
it is only about terms considered generally that his question about
conditions is sensible. We can ask, Why does Churchill call Mussolini a
utensil? but we can't ask, What are the necessary and sufficient conditions for applying "utensil" to Mussolini as opposed to applying "utensil"
in general?

Schwyzer's criticism fails to get deep enough, I think, because in spite
of his aversion to classifying words, he is willing to classify, and to accept
Sibley's formula for going about it. He agrees, that is, that

> the distinction between aesthetic and non-aesthetic discourse is clearly
> to be located in the area of what we can and cannot say given normal
> eyesight, normal hearing, normal intelligence . . .⁹

Classifying discourse is as problematic as classifying terms. In either
case the conception of taste does the work. Whatever defects have been
uncovered in Sibley's distinction, it will be good to take up this conception
in examining one last possible defense of the distinction.

The "(c) is graceful" judgment and all the others might be met head
on: one might insist that "graceful" and the others are aesthetic terms as
defined by Sibley, that these judgments are aesthetic judgments and that
they can be made by any normal speaker because any normal speaker will
have taste enough to do so. Sibley does say that "almost everybody is able
to exercise taste to some degree and in some matters" (AC, p. 65).

This reply fails, I think, because it places on Sibley's conception of
taste more weight than it can bear. A distinction is now forced between
being a merely normal man and exercising one's merely normal capacities.
The fact that the most pedestrian observer can manage "(c) is graceful"
shows nothing; the question remains, does he in judging that (c) is graceful
make use of more than "normal eyes and intelligence"? I do not know
what to make of this question. I am prepared to claim (or to repeat) that
Sibley has given no reason to suppose that an extra perceptivity is required
—or used—in making the judgment. Why suppose that?

Again I point out that the presence or absence of conditions governing
this, or any, use of "graceful" is irrelevant. It is especially likely that one
will begin to think of the possibility of stating conditions when the issue
concerns the relative ease with which terms can be mastered. That is, it is
tempting to suppose that some terms are learned and used readily because
there are clear (perhaps necessary and sufficient) conditions to be learned;
and conversely, that when conditions can be given, the terms are readily
mastered. This is probably, in general, an error. Sibley says, "We do not
apply simple color words by following rules or in accordance with principles" (AC, p. 77). Surely he is right. Even if such words do have necessary and sufficient conditions, this is not what accounts for the ease with

which they are mastered. On the other hand, various esoteric terms like "primitive recursive function," "quadrature of a parabola," and "abelian group" obviously do have necessary and sufficient conditions, having been introduced in terms of such conditions, and yet their fully competent use exceeds the competence of many people. A bothersome point here is that examples of mathematical terms are examples of terms whose necessary and sufficient conditions are themselves stated in mathematical terms, so that inability to master, say, "primitive recursive function" is likely to be accompanied by an inability to master "value of a function," etc.; while the conditions ostensibly sought for aesthetic terms are non-aesthetic conditions. This point must simply be ignored, for it is the intelligibility of the aesthetic/non-aesthetic distinction itself which is at issue; and I mean only to remind you of the irrelevance of the question of conditions (of any kind) in appraising that distinction. The distinction must be sensible antecedently. If the question of conditions is to be part of the initial characterization of aesthetic terms, then, as has been seen in the preceding section, the subsequent argument is aimless. But still, the distinction remains unclear. We shall now need a way of picking aesthetic terms out of the class of non-condition-governed terms, and this will lead us back to taste. Aesthetic terms will be those unconditioned terms whose use requires taste.

And so, what about taste? How are we to decide whether some judgment requires only normal eyes, ears, etc., or more, when any normal observer can make the judgment? I sympathize with anyone trying to give a convincing answer. It would be understandable if Sibley were to fall back on our sense that there is a difference, whether or not we can mark it. However, I do not share this sense, and I have little sympathy for anyone trying to construct a "theory" atop the distinction if it's drawn in this way.

On the strength of this and the preceding section, I conclude (1) that his aesthetic/non-aesthetic distinction is the soul of Sibley's view, and (2) that that distinction comes to nothing. If this conclusion seems hasty, perhaps the next section will help, where the question of what to require of a "distinction" is met more directly.

Discussion of the Distinction in General

Before attempting some cautious generalizations about the aesthetic/non-aesthetic distinction I would like to fend off a misunderstanding to which my view seems susceptible. I do not claim (nor do I think) that the word "aesthetic" is meaningless or ambiguous or vague. I am not asking to extrude the word from ordinary talk, or even from philosophical talk. Here are some sample remarks which, whether or not they are true, are understandable; and I have no reason or wish to ask that they not be made. (i) "Some proofs, though not defective on strictly formal grounds, are objectionable on aesthetic grounds: they are inelegant." (ii) "One must resist treating the Mass as an occasion for an aesthetic experience, for this will likely preclude a religious response." (iii) "In the first part of *Either/ Or* Kierkegaard is exhibiting what it is to be a man for whom all the world's objects—including people—are aesthetic objects." (iv) "Our traditional way of approaching paintings is exactly what comes between us and much of contemporary art. This, now classical, aestheticizing compromises one's response, and destroys one's chances with a work which will submit to nothing but a perfectly human approach."

These remarks are intelligible; one can understand them, argue over them, etc.; and it isn't clear how some of them could be supplanted by substitutes devoid of "aesthetic." What follows from that? Nothing much, I think, and certainly not that people who say such things are committed to anything like the existence of a definition of "aesthetic" which would underwrite an aesthetic/non-aesthetic distinction. (An irony: if there were such things as Sibley's aesthetic terms, "aesthetic" might well be one.)

Then what of the distinction? I am not *against* it as, so to speak, a matter of principle, because I cannot see what point—or sense—there could be in saying I reject it (or I accept it)—period. There is a time to say something, and that is when the distinction is being used and it matters how far we are willing to be led. I have shown that when Sibley uses the distinction we have gone the whole route if we fail to balk at the outset. This is not because of some simple blunder of Sibley's. If he has begged an important question, it is not the ostensible question, Is the applicability of non-aesthetic terms ever sufficient to justify applying an aesthetic term?—though that question was dealt with in the asking. What has been begged is the question of raising that question, and that involves a complex of questions about what the world is like, what art is like, and what it's like to come to terms with either. It is not Sibley's conclusion but his approach which is deep, and this is especially dangerous because that approach not only looks innocuous but is explicitly presented by Sibley as pre-philosophical trivia. Thus he seems to me disingenuous when he says,

> I make this broad distinction by means of *examples* of judgments, qualities, and expressions. There is, it seems to me, no need to defend the distinction. . . . Those who in their theoretical moments deny any such distinction usually show in their practice that they can make it quite adequately. (AN, p. 135)

This will not do, for these are theoretical moments. Summing up the first section of "Aesthetic Concepts," Sibley says,

> Without a detailed comparison we cannot see in what particular way *aesthetic* judgments are not 'mechanical,' or how they differ from those other judgments, nor can we begin to specify what taste is. This I have

attempted. It is a characteristic and essential feature of judgments which employ an aesthetic term that they cannot be made by appealing, in the sense explained, to non-aesthetic conditions. This, I believe, is a logical feature of aesthetic or taste judgments in general, though I have argued it here only as regards the more restricted range of judgments which employ aesthetic terms. It is part of what 'taste' means. (AC, p. 76)

These seem to be theoretical remarks concerning the nature of "aesthetic language," and I have been trying to show that the arguments supporting these remarks require that the underlying aesthetic/non-aesthetic distinction be at least relatively unproblematic. Even granting that one makes, or can make, the distinction in practice—which I do not grant—Sibley's claim that no further defense is needed warrants the (irresistible) reply, That may be well and good in practice but it seems not to work in theory. Before looking at distinctions, theoretical ones and also those obviously exemplified in one's practice, I want to try to take seriously Sibley's claim about one's practice. What does this mean, that one shows in one's practice that one can make the aesthetic/non-aestheic distinction? That one uses "aesthetic" is not enough, nor would it help if one also used "non-aesthetic" (which no one does).

What Sibley means, I think, is that most people (or perhaps most people who have much taste) could, upon being given a series of terms, descriptions, or judgments, sort them into two groups, the aesthetic ones and the non-aesthetic ones, and that with some exceptions the groupings would be the same. Is this so? We can imagine two ways of getting started.

(1) The person is given two sheets of paper, both blank except for *aesthetic* and *non-aesthetic* written in as headings. We give him instructions: "You are to enter on the first list any term whose use requires taste. Taste is an ability to. . . . All other terms go on the second list."

I cannot accept this procedure, obviously, for I have been arguing for several pages that the given instructions are not going to produce the desired results, if indeed they produce anything at all. Perhaps it is better, and clearer, here, to object to the procedure on the grounds that the assumption that it might be implemented begs the question—regardless of what results would ensue. I say that I cannot get a grip on the notion that some terms require taste and others do not. That means that I cannot receive and use the given instructions. If this brings us to a point at which it is simply Sibley's sense that the instructions are clear and usable against my inability to find this sense, then we are at an impasse. After sketching a second way of getting started, I will try to swing the issue my way by imagining more concretely the use of the distinction in practice.

There is a feeling that the first way of getting started somehow takes too much for granted, because instead of straightforwardly resting the burden of the distinction on common practice it first indoctrinates that practic with the distinction itself. This feeling might be relieved by imagining a procedure reminiscent of one suggested by Katz in his effort to reconstitute the analytic/synthetic distinction.[10]

(2) The person is given two sheets of paper, headed *aesthetic* and *non-aesthetic,* each containing the first few entries in a list. Each begins with the terms that Sibley has already sorted for us. Under *aesthetic* are "lovely," "pretty," "beautiful," "dainty," etc.; under *non-aesthetic* are "red," "noisy," "brackish," etc.[11] We give the person instructions: "Go on making these two lists." We might add that what we mean is that he is to continue the lists in conformity with the rule obviously employed, or exhibited, in their beginnings.

What will happen? I submit that the subject will have no idea how to proceed. What if "noisy" were not on either initial list and when he came to "noisy" he happened to think not of pneumatic drills but of a section of some Mahler symphony? Or what if he came to "flat" and thought of a Mondrian?[12]

Perhaps you feel like saying: why not stop this pussyfooting, this pseudo-philosophical by-play, with the distinction without examples or examples without the distinction; Sibley is not doing technical philosophy of language, he is presenting a simple, obvious fact in the informal tone appropriate to such a right-minded announcement. This is not a novel objection. In coming to my view of the distinction (that there is none worth drawing), I have often felt that I was being perverse, raising niggling points of unimportant detail. But no longer. I can find no other way to show that there is no sensible and important way of dividing terms in line with Sibley's aesthetic/non-aesthetic distinction. Sibley says,

> Once examples have been given to illustrate it [the distinction], I believe almost anyone could continue to place further examples—barring of course the expected debatable, ambiguous, or borderline cases—in one category or the other. (AN, p. 135)

Let us try, try it with ourselves. We combine ways (1) and (2): we tell ourselves what Sibley says taste is, we illustrate for ourselves the necessity, or lack of it, of using taste with reference to any of Sibley's examples we find convincing, and then we try to go on. Try going on with these terms.

allegorical	introspective	religious
baroque	Kafkaësque	restful
by Beethoven	linear	rhythmic
(in the style of	lyrical	riddle canon
Beethoven)	mechanical	Romanesque
Christian	metaphysical	romantic
classical	modernist	sad
climactic	moralistic	sentimental
colorful	murky	serious
daring	muted	sincere
derivative	nationalistic	soothing

didactic	obscene	suggestive
dissonant	painterly	surrealist
funny	philosophical	(surrealistic)
geometrical	poetic	suspenseful
Gothic	pompous	symbolist
(Île-de-France	popular	(symbolistic,
Gothic)	powerful	symbolical)
ideological	pretentious	youthful
impressionist	realist	
(impressionistic)	(realistic)	

These terms were collected, not at random, but not with malice or con-trivance either. They are terms used in talking about art works (and other things). How do you class them—aesthetic or non-aesthetic? It is important to imagine as fully as possible contexts for their use. (In cases where a term is accompanied by related terms in parentheses, try imagin-ing cases where all the terms will do, and then where one will do but not the other.) An inexperienced listener mismanages "by Beethoven," withholding it from Beethoven's *First Symphony* and applying "by Haydn" instead. Is that a failure or taste? The fact that "by Beethoven" does not apply to a "property-of-the-work," if that fact can be made out, is irrelevant, I think. The issue concerns only the correct use of terms. We can avoid the problem by looking at "in the style of Beethoven." Not everything by Beethoven is Beethovian, nor is everything in the style of Beethoven by Beethoven. What is required to apply "in the style of Beethoven" to various works of Lizst and Brahms? Obviously some train-ing or informed experience is needed. But what is that: the development of taste or the directed training of one's normal faculties? What kind of question is this? I want to say not that it is a hard question, but that it is a phony. To suppose that it must "in principle" have an answer is to ask to be smitten with a theory.

There is little point in my going on about these terms. At best I can help in imagining cases in which the aesthetic/non-aesthetic distinction becomes tortured. ("Stevens is metaphysical" seems harder than "Donne is metaphysical" which is harder than "Donne is Metaphysical." Is this a diminution in a term's "taste component"?) So I assert, but can only nudge you to accept, that we do not show in our practice that we make or can make Sibley's distinction. . . .

Schematic Summary of the Argument

The argument I've given against Sibley has been rambling and some-times indirect, as I think it must be if it is to be persuasive (that is, liberating). Appraising the argument may be helped by having a more

concise and consecutive statement, not a substitute for the argument but
a kind of guide to it.

(1) Sibley divides terms into aesthetic and non-aesthetic ones (A-terms
and N-terms; "At" for "t is an A-term"). I take seriously the idea that
there is some way of doing this: that is, there is something—call it P—
which every A-term is (or has). (This is the property of requiring taste
for its successful application.) So,

$$(t)(At \equiv Pt).$$

(2) Subsequently Sibley argues that A-terms have a common property—
call it P'. (This is the property of being non-condition-governed.) This
is not a unique feature; some N-terms possess it. So, we have not
$(t)(At \equiv P't)$, but

$$(t)(At \supset P't).$$

(3) More to the point,

$$(t)(Pt \supset P't).$$

The obvious refutation would consist in showing that

$$(\exists t)(Pt \ \& \sim P't).$$

I have not done that. An obvious kind of counterargument, less specifically a refutation, would consist in first dispensing with Sibley's explicit
characterization of A-terms, taking that as a reference to a generally
understood characterization of A-terms, and then showing, with regard
to any likely characterization, that

$$(\exists t)(At \ \& \sim P't).$$

I have not done that.

What I have shown about $(t)(Pt \supset P't)$ is that Sibley's only argument
in its favor begs the question. I have wanted to suggest that so does any
likely argument for $(t)(At \supset P't)$, however aesthetic terms are characterized.

The more difficult and more important point I've tried to make is that

if $(t)(At \equiv Pt)$,
then $\sim (\exists t)At.$

And, again, I have wanted to suggest, though less confidently, that even
if Sibley's explicit characterization of A-terms is replaced by some

assumedly common characterization, it will turn out that there are no such terms.

It is my argument that there are no aesthetic terms when $(t)(At \equiv Pt)$ that figures most obscurely. It was first made clear to me by G. E. L. Owen that this is not an independent argument for me, but is one step in a kind of pragmatic *reductio*. When I claim that one of Sibley's aesthetic terms (e.g., *"graceful"*) can be applied without taste, I am not claiming that the term is non-aesthetic. It is not the classifying, but the distinction I want to assault. The form of the argument is roughly this:

(i)   There is an aesthetic/non-aesthetic distinction.
(ii) There are aesthetic terms.
(iii) t is an aesthetic term.
(iv) t is a non-aesthetic term.

Therefore,

(v) There is not an aesthetic/non-aesthetic distinction.

This is not a strict *reductio*; it is not a strict text argument at all. (ii) seems an unexceptionable step, and I have argued for (iv). But then all that follows is that either (i) or (iii) is false: perhaps (i) is true but t has been chosen ineptly. I call the argument "pragmatic" because I claim that no matter what is chosen as t to satisfy (iii), (iv) will still be true. I have no "proof" of this. I have tried to show that Sibley is mistaken about every example he gives of t (where t is to be an A-term and $(x)(At \equiv Pt)$), and that he would be mistaken about any other example I can think of.

The other murky matter is my claim to find a defect in Sibley's argument that $(t)(Pt \supset P't)$ while I also disavow showing or believing that $(\exists t)(Pt \ \& \sim P't)$. The part about Sibley's begging the question, about his having begun, in effect, with $(t)(At \supset P't)$, is as clear as I can make it. The difficulty is in seeing why anyone, outside an examination or a dissertation, should care to show a defect in the argument unless he wanted to maintain that some aesthetic terms are condition-governed. I have cared to do it in order to locate the interest, and discomfort, in Sibley's view in the aesthetic/non-aesthetic distinction, and not in what follows. And then I have tried to undermine the distinction. There seems to be a connection between undermining the distinction and showing that $(\exists t)(Pt \ \& \sim P't)$, and this frequently clouds my argument, even for me. I think I can account for this.

The practice of asking about the logical connections between two classes of terms and/or judgments is entrenched in recent philosophy, a paradigm being the work of classical "logicism" in the philosophy of mathematics. The effort to "reduce" mathematics to logic is variously judged to have been a failure or a partial success. Had it been a complete success, the axioms (and so the theorems) of elementary number theory could be read off as theorems of logic, with no appreciable change in logic.[13] Mathematical statements—those containing the special terms of mathematics which do not appear in logic—could be understood as abbreviations of purely logical statements. Adapting Sibley's terminology, one could say that mathematical judgments would have been shown to be condition-governed: from the truth of every member of a set of non-mathematical (i.e., logical) judgments it would follow that some mathematical statement was true; and there would be such a set of necessary and sufficient non-mathematical conditions for each mathematical judgment. But then it could be said that the effect of this success would be to show that there are no mathematical judgments, or at least that the distinction between mathematics and the part of non-mathematics called logic must be given up. Accordingly, one associates the legitimacy of the mathematics/logic distinction with the fact that mathematical terms and judgments are not, in this sense, condition-governed. So, too, with the aesthetic/non-aesthetic distinction: one may suppose the best—or only—way of showing the distinction illegitimate to be showing that aesthetic terms are condition-governed. This is a misapprehension.

I am not claiming that an enterprise like Sibley's cannot begin, at least not quite. One might say that if A's and N's can be distinguished clearly enough to allow inquiry into the logical connection between A's and N's, then it must turn out that A's and N's are not closely connected —or else there could have been no initial distinction. But I do not say quite that. In the case of logicism the initial distinction is given: the N's are, roughly, the statements in Frege's logical theory, and the A's are the statements in what is called classical mathematics. In the beginning (though not ultimately, according to Quine—see footnote 13), there is nothing in the way A's and N's are distinguished that prejudices the question whether A's and N's are related in certain ways. Not so with Sibley. I have argued that the initial distinction between A's and N's is not well founded, but this is not to deny that there are A-terms in the sense that logicism might deny that there is any mathematics; it is to deny that the notions of A-terms and N-terms have any even initial application. And so of course I do not show, or believe, that (∃ t)(Pt & ~ P't).

Brief Comparison of Sibley on Taste with with Hume and Kant

Sibley's essays, in reinvoking the notion of taste, as well as in the somewhat pre-Victorian character of their examples and illustrations, serve, I hope, to reinvigorate a great period in the Tradition, the last half of the eighteenth century. They also, however, ignore some salient insights of that period, and perhaps this can be seen as the source of the flaws in Sibley's view.

Hume's philosophy of art is a theory of taste. Like Sibley, Hume is interested in whether, and how, judgments of taste can be supported, and his description of a "true judge" and the claim that "the joint verdict of such, wherever they are to be found, is the true standard of taste and beauty"[14] is like Sibley's eventual effort to locate a criterion for the presence of aesthetic qualities in the judgments of a group of elite critics.[15] And in construing taste to be an ability to notice, Sibley preserves a central feature of Hume's conception of taste. But there is more to Hume's conception: it is richer, if more elusive. Taste as a special capacity to notice is a theme throughout "Of the Standard of Taste," appearing in passages like this.

> Where the organs are so fine as to allow nothing to escape them, and at the same time so exact as to perceive every ingredient in the composition, this we call delicacy of taste . . . (p. 240)

However, equally prominent is the conception of taste as a special capacity to feel.

> Though it be certain that beauty and deformity, more than sweet and bitter, are not qualities in objects, but belong entirely to the sentiment, internal or external, it must be allowed, that there are certain qualities in objects which are fitted by nature to produce those particular feelings. (p. 240)

> . . . and if the same qualities, in a continued composition, and in a smaller degree, affect not the organs with a sensible delight or uneasiness, we exclude the person from all pretensions to this delicacy. (p. 240)

This conception of taste as sensibility is most explicit in "Of the Delicacy of Taste and Passion" and it is the only conception formulated there.

> In short, delicacy of taste has the same effect as delicacy of passion. It enlarges the sphere both of our happiness and misery, and makes us sensible to pains as well as pleasures which escape the rest of mankind. (p. 4)

What, then, is Hume's view? If you, having more delicate taste, respond to a work to which I am indifferent, must it be that you notice something which escapes me, or could it be that everything to be noticed is seen by us both while only you also feel pleasure? To take this question seriously as it arises in Hume requires taking Hume seriously, and that enlarges the question beyond the purview of this essay. Hume's theory of mind and mental activity does not yield a ready distinction between feeling and seeing. If we are restricted to the general categories of *ideas* and *impressions,* and their subdivisions, then, as always with Hume, the simplicity gained masks fantastic subtleties. If you respond and I don't, then mustn't you be acquiring an impression I don't get? Perhaps we each have some visual impression but yours is accompanied by—causes, in Hume's sense—another, a pleasure impression. Or is the number of impressions the same though yours is received in a different "mode"? But this is irrelevant to the difference between Hume and Sibley I wish to point out, and so is their apparent disagreement over where to locate the qualities referred to by "beauty," "deformity," etc. (How much disagreement there is depends partly on how we understand Sibley's notion of "emergent" qualities, and mostly on how, given the *Treatise,* we suppose Hume to effect a significant epistemological distinction between qualities in and not in objects.)

The point of interest is that, however he analyzes the act, Hume regards feeling as an ineliminable part of any taste judgment. Sibley excludes this and the matter of praise as well, which Hume also retains.

> It appears, then, that amidst all the variety and caprice of taste, there are certain general principles of approbation or blame, whose influence a careful eye may trace in all operations of the mind. (p. 238)

Hume finds three components, or aspects, in the exercise of taste: noticing, feeling, evaluating. An exercise of taste is an act of appreciation, in the fullest sense. How far Hume thinks it reasonable to isolate the three parts is hard to say. He may regard them as three ways of looking at the same thing, as at times in the moral philosophy he identifies a feeling of pleasure with a judgment that someone is virtuous. Sibley, however, in his characterization of taste judgments, eliminates the last two features, leaving taste as a capacity to notice. I have already said that he seems to have reneged on this, if he finds it obvious that judgments like "It's a lovely day" are aesthetic, since whatever special character such judgments may have is due to their relation to feeling and evaluation. A deeper point emerges if we try to understand why Sibley seems to reject out of hand the possible existence of what Hume calls a standard of taste.

According to Hume we can find "a rule by which the various sentiments of men may be reconciled" (p. 234) if we can identify the legitimate authors of such a rule, the "true judges." And we can do this. When men are in dispute over whether someone is a proper critic (an exemplar of a standard of taste), says Hume,

> . . . they must acknowledge a true and decisive standard to exist somewhere, to wit, real existence and matter of fact . . . (p. 248)

In the section criticizing Sibley's argument (pp. 569 ff.) I argued that Sibley has no argument against there being such a rule or its being discovered, and that given such a rule a man without taste (in Sibley's sense) can apply (what Sibley calls) taste terms. Why does Sibley simply overlook or disregard this "empirical possibility"? Why does he consider the possibility conceptually irrelevant? It must be, I think, because he thinks that a judgment made in this way, depending on a rule (judging "x is E" without seeing E-ness but because one sees that x is N_1 & N_2 & . . . & N_n and also knows that any such x is also E), is not an aesthetic judgment. Why? Because it seems clear that such a derivative judgment could not take the place of a taste judgment, could not do or express or "mean" the same thing: Knowing that x is E in this roundabout way is not the same as seeing that x is E. But this is not enough. Knowing that x is square or red or lazy or immense is not the same as seeing that x is any of these, at least not always. One's conviction that no inferred judgment could be, or be a surrogate for, a judgment of taste must be more deeply rooted.

The one who is clearest about this, both as it bears on the characterization of the exercise of taste and as it determines the outlines of subsequent arguments about the possibility of justifying or vindicating one's exercise of taste, is Kant. The two aspects of taste eliminated from Sibley's discussion are the most prominent in Kant's account. About evaulation:

> The definition of taste here relied upon is that it is the faculty of estimating the beautiful [*das Vermögen der Beurteilung des Schönen sei*]. (p. 41)[16]

About feeling:

> If we wish to discern whether anything is beautiful or not, we do not refer the representation of it to the Object by means of understanding with a view to cognition, but by means of the imagination (acting perhaps in conjunction with understanding) we refer the representation to the Subject and its feeling of pleasure or displeasure. (p. 41)

Given this, Kant immediately adds,

> The judgement of taste, therefore, is not a cognitive judgement, and so not logical, but is aesthetic—which means that it is one whose determining ground *cannot be other than subjective*. (pp. 41-42)

And so, from the beginning, there is no question—not even a philosopher's academic question—of reasons in support of a taste judgment. This is in fact a partially defining feature of taste judgments for Kant. I believe Sibley agrees, in spite of his mistaking the point and so presenting an argument which doesn't succeed and is superfluous anyway. The striking difference is that the aspects of the conception of taste which for Kant make this a characterizing feature are exactly the ones explicitly eliminated from Sibley's discussion. And so for Kant the difference between taste judgments and other judgments cannot be a difference between using one kind of concept and using a more ordinary kind. The exercise of taste is the application of no concept at all. Taste involves noticing. It is not merely a manipulation of oneself. But it is a kind of noticing evinced in a feeling. One might say that Kant thinks it is a special feeling but for the fact that he claims that its signal attribute is that it is so un-special that one can demand to find it in all other people.

This is no defense or exegesis of Hume or Kant. It is a suggestion that what is most appealing in Sibley's view echoes them, while unheard from them are the points needed to support the appeal.

Notes

1. "Aesthetic Concepts," *Philosophical Review,* Vol. 68, No. 4 (October, 1959); "Aesthetic Concepts: A Rejoinder," ibid., Vol. 72, No. 1 (January, 1963); "Aesthetic and Nonaesthetic," ibid., Vol. 74, No. 2 (April, 1965). Hereafter, to facilitate brief references in the body of the text, these will be referred to by AC, ACR, and AN, respectively.

Shortly after its initial appearance AC was reprinted with the author's "extensive minor revisions" in *Philosophy Looks at the Arts,* edited by Joseph Margolis (New York: Scribner's, 1962). References to AC will cite pages in the Margolis volume, references to ACR and AN will be to the *Philosophical Review.*

2. H. R. G. Schwyzer, "Sibley's 'Aesthetic Concepts,'" *Philosophical Review,* Vol. 72, No. 1 (January, 1963).

3. For an account of this use see Willard Van Orman Quine, *Methods of Logic* (New York: Holt, Rinehart and Winston, 1950—revised edition, 1956), sections 12 and 17, especially pp. 64 and 89 ff.

4. For instance, R. David Broiles in "Frank Sibley's 'Aesthetic Concepts,'" *Journal of Aesthetics and Art Criticism,* Vol. 23, No. 2 (Winter, 1964), and Peter Kivy in "Aesthetic Aspects and Aesthetic Qualities," *Journal of Philosophy,* Vol. 65, No. 4 (February 22, 1968).

5. This parallel illustration is hard to keep a grip on. Perhaps it is of help to have the analogy laid out. Being blind: Being without taste; "Red": An aesthetic term; "Cylindrical": A non-aesthetic term.

6. See pp. 566 ff. above.

7. "When I speak of taste in this paper, I shall not be dealing with questions which center upon expressions like 'a matter of taste' (meaning, roughly, a matter of personal preference or liking)" (AC, p. 65). For his extrusion of questions of evaluation, see his remark quoted above on p. 569.

8. Schwyzer, op. cit., p. 75.

9. Ibid., p. 75.

10. See Jerrold J. Katz, "Some Remarks on Quine on Analyticity," *The Journal of Philosophy,* vol. 64 (1967), pp. 36-52.

11. See AC, pp. 64-65 for Sibley's examples.

12. Paul Ziff has intriguing remarks on the significance of flatness in Mondrian

in his "Reasons in Art Criticism," first published in *Philosophy and Education,* edited by Israel Scheffler (Boston: Allyn and Bacon, Inc., 1958), and reprinted in Ziff's self-anthology *Philosophic Turnings* (Ithaca: Cornell University Press, 1966).

13. In this account I follow Quine's account, for the most part. According to him the reduction of mathematics to logic depends upon whether set theory is counted as part of logic. In his *Philosophy of Logic* (Englewood Cliffs, N. J.: Prentice-Hall, Inc., 1970), he says that "Frege, Whitehead, and Russell made a point of reducing mathematics to logic. . . . But the logic capable of encompassing this reduction was logic inclusive of set theory" (pp. 65-66), and then goes on to argue that set theory does not belong to logic. The technical details of the logicist program and Quine's assessment of it do not bear on the general comparison of logicism with some meta-aesthetic theories, though this situation —the "reduction" of N's to A's by way of intermediates themselves not obviously N's or A's—is of interest, or would be if one recognized any initial distinction between N's and A's.

14. These quotations are from "Of the Standard of Taste," p. 247. This essay appeared in *Four Dissertations,* published in 1757. I give references to this essay and to "Of the Delicacy of Taste and Passion" as they occur in David Hume, *Essays Moral, Political and Literary* (Oxford: Oxford University Press, 1963).

15. This part of Sibley's view is not developed in any of the papers considered so far. It appears in Sibley's contribution to "Objectivity and Aesthetics" (*Proceedings of the Aristotelian Society,* supplementary volume 62, 1968).

16. All references to Kant are to the first two pages of the First Book of the *Critique of Judgment* (first published in 1790); pp. 41-42 in James Creed Meredith's translation (Oxford: Oxford University Press, 1952), pp. 37-38 in J. H. Bernard's translation (New York: Hafner Publishing Co., 1951). I quote and cite pages from the Meredith translation. I prefer the Bernard translation, but Meredith's use of "estimating" for *"Beurteil(ung)"* is more judicious—given the context—than Bernard's "judging."

KENDALL L. WALTON

Categories of Art

I. Introduction

> False judgments enter art history if we judge from
> the impression which pictures of different epochs,
> placed side by side, make on us. . . . They speak a
> different language.[1]

PAINTINGS AND SCULPTURES are to be looked at; sonatas and songs are to be
heard. What is important about such works of art is what can be seen
or heard in them.[2] This apparent truism has inspired attempts by
aesthetic theorists to purge from criticism of works of art supposedly
extraneous excursions into matters not available to inspection of the
works and to focus attention narrowly on the works themselves. Circumstances connected with a work's origin, in particular, are frequently held
to have no essential bearing on an assessment of its aesthetic nature. Thus
critics are advised to ignore how and when a work was created, the
artist's intentions in creating it, his philosophical views, psychological
state and personal life, the artistic traditions and intellectual atmosphere
of his society, and so forth. Once produced, it is argued, a work must
stand or fall on its own; it must be judged for what it is, regardless of
how it came to be as it is.

Arguments for this position need not involve the claim that how and
in what circumstances a work comes about is not of "aesthetic" interest
or importance. One might consider an artist's action of producing a work
to be aesthetically interesting, an "aesthetic object" in its own right, while
vehemently denying its relevance to an aesthetic investigation of the work.
Robert Rauschenberg once carefully obliterated a drawing by de Kooning, titled the bare canvas *Erased De Kooning Drawing*, framed it, and
exhibited it.[3] His doing this might be taken as symbolic or expressive
(of an attitude toward art, or toward life in general, or whatever) in an

A revised version of the paper that appeared in *The Philosophical Review*,
79 (1970), pp. 334-367. Reprinted by permission of *The Philosophical Review*
and the author.

"aesthetically" significant manner, and yet thought to have no bearing whatever on the aesthetic nature of the finished product. The issue I am here concerned with is how far critical questions about works of art can be *separated* from questions about their histories.[4]

One who wants to make a sharp separation here may regard the basic facts of art along the following lines. Works of art are simply objects with various properties, of which we are primarily interested in perceptual ones—visual properties of paintings, audible properties of music, and so forth.[5] A work's perceptual properties include "aesthetic" as well as "non-aesthetic" ones—the sense of mystery and tension of a painting as well as its dark coloring and diagonal composition; the energy, exuberance, and coherence of a sonata, as well as its meters, rhythms, pitches, timbres; the balance and serenity of a Gothic cathedral as well as its dimensions, lines, and symmetries.[6] Aesthetic properties are features or characteristics of works of art just as much as non-aesthetic ones are.[7] They are *in* the works, to be seen, heard, or otherwise perceived there. Seeing a painting's sense of mystery or hearing a sonata's coherence might require looking or listening longer or harder than does perceiving colors and shapes, rhythms and pitches; it may even require special training or a special kind of sensitivity. But these qualities must be discoverable simply be examining the works themselves if they are discoverable at all. It is never even partly *in virtue of* the circumstances of a work's origin that it has a sense of mystery or is coherent or serene. Such circumstances sometimes provide hints concerning what to look for in a work, what we might reasonably expect to find by examining it. But these hints are always theoretically dispensable; a work's aesthetic properties must "in principle" be ascertainable without their help. Surely (it seems) a Rembrandt portrait does not have (or lack) a sense of mystery in virtue of the fact that Rembrandt intended it to have (or to lack) that quality, any more than a contractor's intention to make a roof leakproof makes it so; nor is the portrait mysterious in virtue of any other facts about what Rembrandt thought or how he went about painting the portrait or what his society happened to be like. Such circumstances are important to the result only in so far as they had an effect on the pattern of paint splotches that became attached to the canvas, and the canvas can be examined without in any way considering how the splotches got there. It would not matter in the least to the aesthetic properties of the portrait if the paint had been applied to the canvas not by Rembrandt at all, but by a chimpanzee or a cyclone in a paint shop.

The view sketched above can easily seem very persuasive. But the tendency of critics to discuss the histories of works of art in the course of justifying aesthetic judgments about them has been remarkably persistent. This is partly because hints derived from facts about a work's history, however dispensable they may be "in principle," are often crucially important in practice. (One might not think to listen for a recurring series of intervals in a piece of music, until he learns that the composer meant the work to be structured around it.) No doubt it is partly due also to genuine confusions on the part of critics. But I will argue that certain facts about the origins of works of art have an *essential* role in criticism, that aesthetic judgments rest on them in an absolutely fundamental way. For this reason, and for another as well, the view that works of art should be judged simply by what can be perceived in them is seriously misleading. Nevertheless there is something right in the idea that what matters aesthetically about a painting or a sonata is just how it looks or sounds.

II. Standard, Variable, and Contra-Standard Properties

I will continue to call tension, mystery, energy, coherence, balance, serenity, sentimentality, pallidness, disunity, grotesqueness, and so forth, as well as colors and shapes, pitches and timbres *properties* of works of art, though "property" is to be construed broadly enough not to beg any important questions. I will also, following Sibley, call properties of the former sort "aesthetic" properties, but purely for reasons of convenience I will include in this category "representational" and "resemblance" properties, which Sibley excludes—for example, the property of representing Napoleon, that of depicting an old man stooping over a fire, that of resembling, or merely suggesting, a human face, claws (the petals of Van Gogh's sunflowers), or (in music) footsteps or conversation. It is not essential for my purposes to delimit with any exactness the class of aesthetic properties (if indeed any such delimitation is possible), for I am more interested in discussing particular examples of such properties than in making generalizations about the class as a whole. It will be obvious, however, that what I say about the examples I deal with is also applicable to a great many other properties we would want to call aesthetic.

Sibley points out that a work's aesthetic properties depend on its nonaesthetic properties; the former are "emergent" or "*Gestalt*" properties based on the latter.[8] I take this to be true of all the examples of aesthetic properties we will be dealing with, including representational and resemblance ones. It is because of the configuration of colors and shapes on a painting, perhaps in particular its dark colors and diagonal composition, that it has a sense of mystery and tension, if it does. The colors and shapes of a portrait are responsible for its resembling an old man and its depicting an old man. The coherence or unity of a piece of music (for example, Beethoven's *Fifth Symphony*) may be largely due to the frequent recurrence of a rhythmic motive, and the regular meter of a song plus the absence of harmonic modulation and of large intervals in the voice part may make it serene or peaceful.

Moreover, a work *seems* or *appears* to us to have certain aesthetic properties because we observe in it, or it appears to us to have, certain nonaesthetic features (though it may not be necessary to notice consciously all the relevant nonaesthetic features). A painting depicting an old man may not look like an old man to someone who is color-blind, or when it is seen from an extreme angle or in bad lighting conditions which distort or obscure its colors or shapes. Beethoven's *Fifth Symphony* performed in such a sloppy manner that many occurrences of the four-note rhythmic motive do not sound similar may seem incoherent or disunified.

I will argue, however, that a work's aesthetic properties depend not only on its nonaesthetic ones, but also on which of its nonaesthetic properties are "standard," which "variable," and which "contra-standard," in senses to be explained. I will approach this thesis by way of the psychological point that what aesthetic properties a work seems to us to have depends not only on what nonaesthetic features we perceive in it, but also on which of them are standard, which variable, and which contra-standard *for us* (in a sense also to be explained).

It is necessary to introduce first a distinction between standard, variable, and contra-standard properties relative to perceptually distinguishable categories of works of art. A category is perceptually distinguishable if membership in it is determined solely by features of works that can be perceived in them when they are experienced in the normal manner. The categories of painting, cubist painting, Gothic architecture, classical sonatas, painting in the style of Cézanne, music in the style of late Beethoven, and most other media, genre, styles, and forms can be construed as perceptually distinguishable. If we do construe them this way we must, for example, regard whether a piece of music was written in the eighteenth century as irrelevant to whether it belongs to the category of classical sonatas, and we must take whether or not a work was produced by Cézanne or Beethoven to have nothing essential to do with whether or not it is in the style of Cézanne or late Beethoven. The category of etchings as normally understood is not perceptually distinguishable in the requisite sense, for to be an etching is, I take it, to have been produced in a particular manner. But the category of *apparent* etchings, works that *look* like etchings from the quality of their lines, whether or not they are etchings, is perceptually distinguishable.[9]

A feature of a work of art is *standard* with respect to a (perceptually distinguishable) category just in case it is among those in virtue of which works in that category belong to that category—that is, just in case the absence of that feature would disqualify, or tend to disqualify, a work from that category. A feature is *variable* with respect to a category just in case it has nothing to do with works' belonging to that category; the possession or lack of the feature is irrelevant to whether a work qualifies for the category. Finally, a *contra-standard* feature with respect to a category is the absence of a standard feature with respect to that category—that is, a feature whose presence tends to *disqualify* works as members of the category. Needless to say, it will not be clear in *all* cases whether a feature of a work is standard, variable, or contra-standard relative to a given category, since the criteria for classifying works of art are far from precise. But clear examples are abundant. The flatness of a painting and the motionlessness of its markings are standard, and its particular shapes and colors are variable, relative to the category of painting. A protruding three-dimensional object or an electrically driven twitching of the canvas would be contra-standard relative to this category. The straight lines in stick-figure drawings and squarish shapes in cubist paintings are standard with respect to those categories respectively, though they are variable with respect to the categories of drawing and painting. The exposition-development-recapitulation form of a classical sonata is standard, and its thematic material is variable, relative to the category of sonatas.

In order to explain what I mean by features being standard, variable, or contra-standard *for a person on a particular occasion,* I must introduce the notion of perceiving a work in, or as belonging to, a certain (perceptually distinguishable) category. To perceive a work in a certain category is to perceive the *"Gestalt"* of that category in the work. This needs some explanation. People familiar with Brahmsian music—music in the style of Brahms (notably, works of Johannes Brahms)—or impressionist paintings can frequently recognize members of these categories by recognizing the Brahmsian or impressionist *Gestalt* qualities. Such recognition is dependent on perception of particular features that are standard relative to these categories, but it is not a matter of *inferring* from the presence of such features that a work is Brahmsian or impressionist. One may not notice many of the relevant features, and he may be very vague about which ones are relevant. If I recognize a work as Brahmsian by first noting its lush textures, its basically traditional harmonic and formal structure, its superimposition and alternation of duple and triple meters, and so forth, and recalling that these characteristics are typical of Brahmsian works, I have not recognized it by hearing the Brahmsian *Gestalt.* To do that is simply to recognize it by its Brahmsian *sound,* without necessarily paying attention to the features ("cues") responsible for it. Similarly, recognizing an impressionist painting by its impressionist *Gestalt,* is recognizing the impressionist *look* about it, which we are familiar with from other impressionist paintings; not applying a rule we have learned for recognizing it from its features.

To *perceive* a *Gestalt* quality in a work—that is, to perceive it in a certain category—is not, or not merely, to *recognize* that *Gestalt* quality. Recognition is a momentary occurrence, whereas perceiving a quality is a continuous state which may last for a short or long time. (For the same reason, seeing the ambiguous duck-rabbit figúre as a duck is not, or not merely, recognizing a property of it.) We perceive the Brahmsian or impressionist *Gestalt* in a work when, and as long as, it *sounds* Brahmsian or looks impressionist to us. This involves perceiving (not necessarily being aware of) features standard relative to that category. But it is not *just* this, nor this plus the intellectual realization that these features make the work Brahmsian, or impressionist. These features are perceived combined into a single *Gestalt* quality.

We can of course perceive a work in several or many different categories at once. A Brahms sonata might be heard simultaneously as a piece of music, a sonata, a romantic work, and a Brahmsian work. Some pairs of categories, however, seem to be such that one cannot perceive a work as belonging to both at once, much as one cannot see the duck-rabbit both as a duck and as a rabbit simultaneously. One cannot see a photographic image simultaneously as a still photograph and as (part of) a film, nor can one see something both in the category of paintings and at the same time in the category (to be explained shortly) of *guernicas*.

It will be useful to point out some of the *causes* of our perceiving works in certain categories. (a) In which categories we perceive a work depends in part, of course, on what other works we are familiar with. The more works of a certain sort we have experienced, the more likely it is that we will perceive a particular work in that category. (*b*) What we have heard critics and others say about works we have experienced, how they have categorized them, and what resemblances they have pointed out to us is also important. If no one has ever explained to me what is distinctive about Schubert's style (as opposed to the styles of, say, Schumann, Mendelssohn, Beethoven, Brahms, Hugo Wolf), or even pointed out that there is such a distinctive style, I may never have learned to hear the Schubertian *Gestalt* quality, even if I have heard many of Schubert's works, and so I may not hear his works as Schubertian. (*c*) How we are introduced to the particular work in question may be involved. If a Cézanne painting is exhibited in a collection of French Impressionist works, or if before seeing it we are told that it is French Impressionist, we are more likely to see it as French Impressionist than we would be if it is exhibited in a random collection and we are not told anything about it beforehand.

I will say that a feature of a work is standard for a particular person on a particular occasion when, and only when, it is standard relative to some category in which he perceives it, and is not contra-standard relative to any category in which he perceives it. A feature is variable for a person just when it is variable relative to *all* of the categories in which he perceives it. And a feature is contra-standard for a person just when it is contra-standard relative to *any* of the categories in which he perceives it.[10]

III. A Point about Perception

I turn now to my psychological thesis that what aesthetic properties a work seems to have, what aesthetic effect it has on us, how it strikes us aesthetically often depends (in part) on which of its features are standard, which variable, and which contra-standard for us. I offer a series of examples in support of this thesis.

(1) Representational and resemblance properties provide perhaps the most obvious illustration of this thesis. Many works of art look like or resemble other objects—people, buildings, mountains, bowls of fruit, and so forth. Rembrandt's "Titus Reading" looks like a boy, and in particular like Rembrandt's son; Picasso's "Les Demoiselles d'Avignon" looks like five women, four standing and one sitting (though not *especially* like any particular women). A portrait may even be said to be a *perfect* likeness of the sitter, or to capture his image *exactly*.

An important consideration in determining whether a work *depicts* or *represents* a particular object, or an object of a certain sort (for example, Rembrandt's son, or simply *a* boy), in the sense of being a picture, sculpture, or whatever of it[11] is whether the work resembles that object, or objects of that kind. A significant degree of resemblance is, I suggest, a necessary condition in most contexts for such representation or depiction,[12] though the resemblance need not be obvious at first glance. If we are unable to see a similarity between a painting purportedly of a woman and women, I think we would have to suppose either that there is such a similarity which we have not yet discovered (as one might fail to see a face in a maze of lines), or that it simply is not a picture of a woman. Resemblance is of course not a *sufficient* condition for representation, since a portrait (containing only one figure) might resemble both the sitter and his twin brother equally but is not a portrait of both of them. (The title might determine which of them it depicts.)[13]

It takes only a touch of perversity, however, to find much of our talk about resemblances between works of art and other things preposterous. Paintings and people are *very* different sorts of things. Paintings are pieces of canvas supporting splotches of paint, while people are live, three-dimensional, flesh-and-blood animals. Moreover, except rarely and under special conditions of observation paintings and people *look* very different. Paintings look like pieces of canvas (or anyway flat surfaces) covered with paint and people look like flesh-and-blood animals. There is practically no danger of confusing them. How, then, can anyone seriously hold that a portrait resembles the sitter to any significant extent, let alone that it is a perfect likeness of him? Yet it remains true that many paintings strike us as resembling people, sometimes very much or even exactly—despite the fact that they look so very different!

To resolve this paradox we must recognize that the resemblances we perceive between, for example, portraits and people, those that are relevant in determining what works of art depict or represent, are resemblances of a somewhat special sort, tied up with the categories in which we perceive such works. The properties of a work which are standard for us are ordinarily irrelevant to what we take it to look like or resemble in the relevant sense, and hence to what we take it to depict or represent. The properties of a portrait which make it *so* different from, so easily distinguishable from, a person—such as its flatness and its *painted* look—are standard for us. Hence these properties just do not count with regard to what (or whom) it looks like. It is only the properties which are variable for us, the colors and shapes on the work's surface, that make it look to us like what it does. And these are the ones which are relevant in determining what (if anything) the work represents.[14]

Other examples will reinforce this point. A marble bust of a Roman emperor seems to us to resemble a man with, say, an aquiline nose, a wrinkled brow, and an expression of grim determination, and we take it to represent a man with, or as having, those characteristics. But why don't we say that it resembles and represents a perpetually motionless man, of uniform (marble) color, who is severed at the chest? It is similar to such a man, it seems, and much more so than to a normally colored, mobile, and whole man. But we are not struck by the former similarity when we see the bust, obvious though it is on reflection. The bust's uniform color, motionlessness, and abrupt ending at the chest are standard properties relative to the category of busts, and since we see it as a bust they are standard for us. Similarly, black-and-white drawings do not look to us like colorless scenes and we do not take them to depict things as being colorless, nor do we regard stick-figure drawings as resembling and depicting only very thin people. A cubist work might look like a person with a cubical head to someone not familiar with the cubist style. But the standardness of such cubical shapes for people who see it as a cubist work prevents them from making that comparison.

The shapes of a painting or a still photograph of a high jumper in action are motionless, but these pictures do not look to us like a high jumper frozen in midair. Indeed, depending on features of the pictures which are variable for us (the exact positions of the figures, swirling brush strokes in the painting, slight blurrings of the photographic image) the athlete may seem in a frenzy of activity; the pictures may convey a vivid sense of movement. But if static images exactly like those of the two pictures occur in a motion picture, and we see it as a motion picture, they probably would strike us as resembling a static athlete. This is because the immobility of the images is standard relative to the category of still pictures and variable relative to that of motion pictures. (Since we are so familiar with still pictures it might be difficult to see the static images as motion pictures for very long, rather than as [filmed] still pictures. But we could not help seeing them that way if we had no acquaintance at all with the medium of still pictures.) My point here is brought out by the tremendous aesthetic difference we are likely to experience between a film of a dancer moving *very* slowly and a still picture of him, even if "objectively" the two images are very nearly identical. We might well find the former studied, calm, deliberate, laborious, and the latter dynamic, energetic, flowing, or frenzied.

In general, then, what we regard a work as resembling, and as representing, depends on the properties of the work which are variable, and not on those which are standard for us.[15] The latter properties serve to determine what *kind* of a representation the work is, rather than what it represents or resembles. We take them for granted, as it were, in representations of that kind. This principle helps to explain also how clouds can look like elephants, how diatonic orchestral music can suggest a conversation or a person crying or laughing, and how a twelve-year-old boy can look like his middle-aged father.

We can now see how a portrait can be an *exact* likeness of the sitter, despite the huge differences between the two. The differences, in so far as they involve properties standard for us, simply do not count against likeness, and hence not against exact likeness. Similarly, a boy not only can resemble his father but can be his "spitting image," despite the boy's relative youthfulness. It is clear that the notions of resemblance and exact resemblance that we are concerned with are not even cousins of the notion of perceptual indistinguishability.[16]

(2) The importance of the distinction between standard and variable properties is by no means limited to cases involving representation or resemblance. Imagine a society that does not have an established medium of painting but does produce a kind of work of art called "guernicas." Guernicas are like versions of Picasso's *Guernica* done in various bas-relief dimensions. All of them are surfaces with the colors and shapes of Picasso's *Guernica*, but the surfaces are molded to protrude from the wall like relief maps of different kinds of terrain. Some guernicas have rolling surfaces, others are sharp and jagged, still others contain several relatively flat planes at various angles to each other, and so forth. If members of this society should come across Picasso's *Guernica*, they would count it as a guernica—a perfectly flat one—rather than as a painting. Its flatness is variable and the figures on its surface are standard relative to the category of guernicas. Thus the flatness, which is standard for us, would be variable for members of the other society, and the figures on the surface, which are variable for us, would be standard for them. This would make for a profound difference between our aesthetic reaction to *Guernica* and theirs. It seems violent, dynamic, vital, disturbing to us. But I imagine it would strike them as cold, stark, lifeless, or serene and restful, or perhaps bland, dull, boring—but in any case *not* violent, dynamic, and vital. We do not pay attention to or take note of *Guernica*'s flatness; this is a feature we take for granted in paintings. But for the other society, this is *Guernica*'s most striking and noteworthy characteristic—what is *expressive* about it. Conversely, *Guernica*'s color catches, which we find noteworthy and expressive, are insignificant to them.

It is important to notice that this difference in aesthetic response is not due *solely* to the fact that we are much more familiar with flat works of art than they are and that they are more familiar with *Guernica*'s colors and shapes. Someone equally familiar with paintings and guernicas might, I think, see Picasso's *Guernica* as a painting on some occasions and as a guernica on others. On the former occasions it will probably look dynamic, violent, and so forth to him, and on the latter cold, serene, bland, or lifeless. Whether he sees the work in a museum of paintings or a museum of guernicas, or whether he has been told that it is a painting or a guernica, may influence how he sees it. But I think he might be able to shift at will from one way of seeing it to the other, somewhat as one shifts between seeing the duck-rabbit as a duck and seeing it as a rabbit.

This example and the previous ones might give the impression that in general only features of a work that are variable for us are aesthetically important—that these are the expressive, aesthetically active properties, as far as we are concerned, whereas features standard for us are aesthetically inert. But this notion is quite mistaken, as the following examples will demonstrate. Properties standard for us are not aesthetically lifeless, though the life that they have, the aesthetic effect they have on us, is typically very different from what it would be if they were variable for us.

(3) Because of the very fact that features standard for us do not seem striking or noteworthy, that they are somehow expected or taken for granted, they can contribute to a work a sense of order, inevitability, stability, correctness. This is perhaps most notably true of large-scale structural properties in the time arts. The exposition-development-recapitulation form (including the typical key and thematic relationships) of the first movements of classical sonatas, symphonies, and string quartets is standard with respect to the category of works in sonata-allegro form, and standard for listeners, including most of us, who hear them as belonging to that category. So proceeding along the lines of sonata-allegro form seems *right* to us; to our ears that is how sonatas are *supposed* to behave. We feel that we know where we are and where we are going throughout the work—more so, I suggest, than we would if we were not familiar with sonata-allegro form, if following the strictures of that form were variable rather than standard for us.[17] Properties standard for us do not always have this sort of unifying effect, however. The fact that a piano sonata contains only piano sounds, or uses the Western system of harmony throughout, does not make it seem unified to us. The reason, I think, is that these properties are *too* standard for us in a sense that needs explicating (cf. note 10). Nevertheless, sonata form is unifying partly because it is standard rather than variable for us.

(4) That a work (or part of it) has a certain determinate characteristic (of size, for example, or speed, or length, or volume) is often variable relative to a particular category, when it is nevertheless standard for that category that the variable characteristic falls within a certain range. In such cases the aesthetic effect of the determinate variable property may be colored by the standard limits of the range. Hence these limits function as an aesthetic catalyst, even if not as an active ingredient.

Piano music is frequently marked *sostenuto, cantabile, legato,* or *lyrical.*

But how can the pianist possibly carry out such instructions? Piano tones diminish in volume drastically immediately after the key is struck, becoming inaudible relatively promptly, and there is no way the player can prevent this. If a singer or violinist should produce sounds even approaching a piano's in suddenness of demise, they would be nerve-wrackingly sharp and percussive—anything but *cantabile* or lyrical! Yet piano music *can* be *cantabile, legato,* or lyrical nevertheless; sometimes it is extraordinarily so (for example, a good performance of the *Adagio Cantabile* movement of Beethoven's *Pathétique* sonata). What makes this possible is the very fact that the drastic diminution of piano tones cannot be prevented, and hence never is. It is a standard feature for piano music. A pianist can, however, by a variety of devices, control a tone's rate of diminution and length within the limits dictated by the nature of the instrument.[18] Piano tones may thus be *more or less* sustained within these limits, and *how* sustained they are, how quickly or slowly they diminish and how long they last, within the range of possibilities, is variable for piano music. A piano passage that sounds lyrical or *cantabile* to us is one in which the individual tones are *relatively* sustained, given the capabilities of the instrument. Such a passage sounds lyrical only because piano music is limited as it is, and we hear it as piano music; that is, the limitations are standard properties for us. The character of the passage is determined not merely by the "absolute" nature of the sounds, but by that in relation to the standard property of what piano tones can be like.[19]

This principle helps to explain the lack of energy and brilliance that we sometimes find even in very fast passages of electronic music. The energy and brilliance of a fast violin or piano passage derives not merely from the absolute speed of the music (together with accents, rhythmic characteristics, and so forth), but from the fact that it is fast *for that particular medium.* In electronic music different pitches can succeed one another at any frequency up to and including that at which they are no longer separately distinguishable. Because of this it is difficult to make electronic music *sound* fast (energetic, violent). For when we have heard enough electronic music to be aware of the possibilities we do not feel that the speed of a passage approaches a limit, no matter how fast it is.[20]

There are also visual correlates of these musical examples. A small elephant, one which is smaller than most elephants with which we are familiar, might impress us as charming, cute, delicate, or puny. This is not simply because of its (absolute) size, but because it is small *for an elephant.* To people who are familiar not with our elephants but with a race of mini-elephants, the same animal may look massive, strong, dominant, threatening, lumbering, if it is large for a mini-elephant. The size of elephants is variable relative to the class of elephants, but it varies only within a certain (not precisely specifiable) range. It is a standard property of elephants that they do fall within this range. How an elephant's size affects us aesthetically depends, since we see it as an elephant, on whether it falls in the upper, middle, or lower part of the range.

(5) Properties standard for a certain category which do not derive from physical limitations of the medium can be regarded as results of more or less conventional "rules" for producing works in the given category (for example, the "rules" of sixteenth-century counterpoint, or those for twelve-tone music). These rules may combine to create a dilemma for the artist which, if he is talented, he may resolve ingeniously and gracefully. The result may be a work with an aesthetic character very different from what it would have had if it had not been for those rules. Suppose that the first movement of a sonata in G major modulates to C-sharp major by the end of the development section. A rule of sonata form decrees that it must return to G for the recapitulation. But the keys of G and C-sharp are as unrelated as any two keys can be; it is difficult to modulate smoothly and quickly from one to the other. Suppose also that while the sonata is in C-sharp there are signs that, given other rules of sonata form, indicate that the recapitulation is imminent (motivic hints of the return, an emotional climax, a cadenza). Listeners who hear it as a work in sonata form are likely to have a distinct feeling of unease, tension, uncertainty, as the time for the recapitulation approaches. If the composer with a stroke of ingenuity accomplishes the necessary modulation quickly, efficiently, and naturally, this will give them a feeling of relief—one might say of deliverance. The movement to C-sharp, which may have seemed alien and brashly adventurous at the time, will have proven to be quite appropriate, and the entire sequence will in retrospect have a sense of correctness and perfection about it. Our impression of it is likely, I think, to be very much like our impression of a "beautiful" or "elegant" proof in mathematics. (Indeed the composer's task in this example is not unlike that of producing such a proof.)

But suppose that the rule for sonatas were that the recapitulation must be *either* in the original key *or* in the key one half-step below it. Thus in the example above the recapitulation could have been in F-sharp major rather than G major. This possibility removes the sense of tension from the occurrence of C-sharp major in the development section, for a modulation from C-sharp to F-sharp is as easy as any modulation is (since C-sharp is the dominant of F-sharp). Of course, there would also be no special *release* of tension when the modulation to G is effected, there being no tension to be released. In fact, that modulation probably would be rather surprising, since the permissible modulation to F-sharp would be much more natural.

Thus the effect that the sonata has on us depends on which of its properties are dictated by "rules," which ones are standard relative to the category of sonatas and hence standard for us.

(6) I turn now to features which are contra-standard for us—ones which

have a tendency to disqualify a work from a category in which we nevertheless perceive it. We are likely to find such features shocking, or
disconcerting, or startling, or upsetting, just because they are contra-
standard for us. Their presence may be so obtrusive that they obscure
the work's variable properties. Three-dimensional objects protruding
from a canvas and movement in a sculpture are contra-standard relative
to the categories of painting and (traditional) sculpture respectively.
These features are contra-standard for us, and probably shocking, if
despite them we perceive the works possessing them in the mentioned
categories. The monochromatic paintings of Yves Klein are disturbing
to us (at least at first) for this reason: we see them as paintings, though
they contain the feature contra-standard for paintings of being one solid
color.[21] Notice that we find other similarly monochromatic surfaces—
walls of living rooms, for example—not in the least disturbing, and indeed
quite unnoteworthy.

If we are exposed frequently to works containing a certain kind of
feature which is contra-standard for us, we ordinarily adjust our categories
to accommodate it, making it contra-standard for us no longer. The first
painting with a three-dimensional object glued to it was no doubt
shocking. But now that the technique has become commonplace we
are not shocked. This is because we no longer see these works as *paintings,*
but rather as members of either *(a)* a new category—*collages*—in which
case the offending feature has become standard rather than contra-
standard for us, or *(b)* an expanded category which includes paintings
both with and without attached objects, in which case that feature is
variable for us.

But it is not just the rarity, unusualness, or unexpectedness of a feature
that makes it shocking. If a work differs *too* significantly from the norms
of a certain category we do not perceive it in that category and hence
the difference is not contra-standard for us, even if we have not previously
experienced works differing from that category in that way. A sculpture
which is constantly and vigorously in motion would be so obviously
and radically different from traditional sculptures that we probably would
not perceive it as one even if it is the first moving sculpture we have
come across. We would either perceive it as a *kinetic* sculpture, or simply
remain confused. In contrast, a sculpted bust which is traditional in every
respect except that one ear twitches slightly every thirty seconds would
be perceived as an ordinary sculpture. So the twitching ear would be
contra-standard for us, and it would be considerably more unsettling
than the much greater movement of the other kinetic sculpture. Similarly,
a very small colored area of an otherwise entirely black-and-white drawing would be very disconcerting. But if enough additional color is added
to it we will see it as a colored rather than a black-and-white drawing,
and the shock will vanish.

This point helps to explain a difference between the harmonic aber-
rations of Wagner's *Tristan and Isolde,* and those of Debussy's *Pelléas et*

Mélisande and Schoenberg's *Pierrot Lunaire* as well as Schoenberg's later twelve-tone works. The latter are not merely *more* aberrant, *less* tonal, than *Tristan*. They differ from traditional tonal music in such respects and to such an extent that they are not heard as tonal at all. *Tristan*, however, retains enough of the apparatus of tonality, despite its deviations, to be heard as a tonal work. For this reason its lesser deviations are often the more shocking.[22] *Tristan* plays on harmonic traditions by selectively following and flaunting them, while *Pierrot Lunaire* and the others simply ignore them.

Shock then arises from features that are not just rare or unique, but ones that are contra-standard relative to categories in which objects possessing them are perceived. But it must be emphasized that to be contra-standard relative to a certain category is not merely to be rare or unique *among things of that category*. The melodic line of Schubert's song, *Im Walde*, is probably unique; it probably does not occur in any other songs, or other works of any sort. But it is not contra-standard relative to the category of songs, because it does not tend to disqualify the work from that category. Nor is it contra-standard relative to any other category to which we hear the work as belonging. And clearly we do not find this melodic line at all upsetting. What is important is not the rarity of a feature, but its connection with the classification of the work. Features contra-standard for us are perceived as misfits in a category which the work strikes us as belonging to, as doing *violence* to such a category. Being rare in a category is not the same thing as being a misfit in it.

It should be clear from the above examples that how a work affects us aesthetically—what aesthetic properties it seems to us to have and what ones we are inclined to attribute to it—depends in a variety of important ways on which of its features are standard, which variable, and which contra-standard for us. Moreover, this is obviously not an isolated or exceptional phenomenon, but a pervasive characteristic of aesthetic perception. I should emphasize that my purpose has not been to establish general principles about how each of the three sorts of properties affects us. How any particular feature affects us depends also on many variables I have not discussed. The important point is that in many cases whether a feature is standard, variable, or contra-standard for us has a great deal to do with what effect it has on us. We must now begin to assess the theoretical consequences of this.

IV. Truth and Falsity

The fact that what aesthetic properties a thing seems to have may depend on what categories it is perceived in raises a question about how to determine what aesthetic properties it really does have. If *Guernica* appears dynamic when seen as a painting, and not dynamic when seen as a guernica, is it dynamic or not? Can one way of seeing it be ruled correct, and the other incorrect? One way of approaching this problem is to deny that the apparently conflicting aesthetic judgments of people who perceive a work in different categories actually do conflict.[23]

Judgments that works of art have certain aesthetic properties, it might be suggested, implicitly involve reference to some particular set of categories. Thus our claim that *Guernica* is dynamic really amounts to the claim that it is dynamic *as a painting,* or for people who see it as a painting. The judgment that it is not dynamic made by people who see it as a guernica amounts simply to the judgment that it is not dynamic *as a guernica.* Interpreted in these ways, the two judgments are of course quite compatible. Terms like "large" and "small" provide a convenient model for this interpretation. An elephant might be both small as an elephant and large as a mini-elephant, and hence it might be called truly either "large" or "small," depending on which category is implicitly referred to.

I think that aesthetic judgments are in *some* contexts amenable to such category-relative interpretations, especially aesthetic judgments about natural objects (clouds, mountains, sunsets) rather than works of art. (It will be evident that the alternative account suggested below is not readily applicable to most judgments about natural objects.) But most of our aesthetic judgments can be forced into this mold only at the cost of distorting them beyond recognition.

My main objection is that category-relative interpretations do not allow aesthetic judgments to be mistaken often enough. It would certainly be natural to consider a person who calls *Guernica* stark, cold, or dull, because he sees it as a guernica, to be *mistaken;* he misunderstands the work because he is looking at it in the wrong way. Similarly, one who asserts that a good performance of the *Adagio Cantabile* of Beethoven's *Pathetique* is percussive, or that a Roman bust looks like a unicolored, immobile man severed at the chest and depicts one as such, is simply wrong, even if his judgment is a result of his perceiving the work in different categories from those in which we perceive it. Moreover, we do not accord a status any more privileged to our own aesthetic judgments. We are likely to regard cubist paintings, or Japanese *gagaku* music, as formless, incoherent, or disturbing on our first contact with these forms largely because, I suggest, we would not be perceiving the works as cubist paintings, or as *gagaku* music. But after becoming familiar with these kinds of art, we would probably *retract* our previous judgments, admit that they were mistaken. It would be quite inappropriate to protest that what we meant previously was merely that the works were formless or disturbing for the categories in which we then perceived them, while admitting that they are not for the categories of cubist paintings, or *gagaku* music. The conflict between apparently incompatible aesthetic judgments made while perceiving a work in different categories does not simply evaporate when the difference of categories is pointed out, as does the conflict between the claims that an animal is large and that it is small, when it is made clear that the person making the first claim regarded it as a mini-elephant and the one making the second regarded it as an elephant. The latter judgments do not (necessarily) reflect a real disagreement about the size of the animal, but the former do reflect a real disagreement about the aesthetic nature of the work.

Thus it seems that, at least in some cases, it is *correct* to perceive a work in certain categories and *incorrect* to perceive it in certain others; that is, our judgments of it when we perceive it in the former are likely to be true, and those we make when perceiving it in the latter false. This provides us with absolute senses of *standard, variable,* and *contra-standard:* features of a work are standard, variable, or contra-standard absolutely just in case they are standard, variable, or contra-standard, respectively, for people who perceive the work correctly. (Thus an absolutely standard feature is standard relative to some category in which the work is correctly perceived and contra-standard relative to none, an absolutely variable feature is variable relative to all such categories, and an absolutely contra-standard feature is contra-standard relative to at least one such category.)

How is it to be determined in which categories a work is correctly perceived? There is certainly no very precise or well-defined procedure to be followed. Different criteria are emphasized by different people and in different situations. But there are several fairly definite considerations which typically figure in critical discussions and which fit our intuitions reasonably well. I suggest that the following circumstances count toward its being correct to perceive a work, W, in a given category, C:

(*i*) The presence in W of a relatively large number of features standard with respect to C. The correct way of perceiving a work is likely to be that in which it has a minimum of contra-standard features for us. I take the relevance of this consideration to be obvious. It cannot be correct to perceive Rembrandt's *Titus Reading* as a kinetic sculpture, if this is possible, just because that work has too few of the features which make kinetic sculptures kinetic sculptures. But of course this does not get us very far. *Guernica,* for example, qualifies equally well on this count for being perceived as a painting and as a guernica.

(*ii*) The fact that W is better, or more interesting or pleasing aesthetically, or more worth experiencing when perceived in C than it is when perceived in alternative ways. The correct way of perceiving a work is likely to be the way in which it comes off best.

(*iii*) The fact that the artist who produced W intended or expected it to be perceived in C, or thought of it as a C.

(*iv*) The fact that C is well established in and recognized by the society in which W was produced. A category is well established in and recognized by a society if the members of the society are familiar with works in that category, consider a work's membership in it a fact worth mentioning, exhibit works of that category together, and so forth—that is, roughly if that category figures importantly in their way of classifying works of art. The categories of impressionist painting and Brahmsian music are well established and recognized in our society; those of guernicas, paintings with diagonal composition containing green crosses, and pieces of music containing between four and eight F-sharps and at least seventeen quarter notes every eight bars are not. The categories in which a work is correctly perceived, according to this condition, are generally the ones in which the artist's contemporaries did perceive or would have perceived it.

In certain cases I think the mechanical process by which a work was produced, or (for example, in architecture) the nonperceptible physical characteristics or internal structure of a work, is relevant. A work is probably correctly perceived as an apparent etching[24] rather than, say, an apparent woodcut or line drawing, if it was produced by the etching process. The strengths of materials in a building, or the presence of steel girders inside wooden or plaster columns counts (not necessarily conclusively) toward the correctness of perceiving it in the category of buildings with visual characteristics typical of buildings constructed in that manner. I will not discuss these considerations further here.

What can be said in support of the relevance of conditions (*ii*), (*iii*), and (*iv*)? In the examples mentioned above, the categories in which we consider a work correctly perceived probably meet all of these conditions. I would suppose that *Guernica* is better seen as a painting than it would be seen as a guernica (though this would be hard to prove). In any case, Picasso certainly intended it to be seen as a painting rather than a guernica, and the category of paintings is well established in his (that is, our) society, whereas that of guernicas is not. But this of course does not show that (*ii*), (*iii*), and (*iv*) *each* is relevant. It tends to indicate only that one or other of them, or some combination, is relevant.

The difficulty of assessing each of the three conditions individually is complicated by the fact that by and large they can be expected to coincide, to yield identical conclusions. Since an artist usually intends his works for his contemporaries he is likely to intend them to be perceived in categories established in and recognized by his society. Moreover, it is reasonable to expect works to come off better when perceived in the intended categories than when perceived in others. An artist tries to produce works which are well worth experiencing when perceived in the intended way and, unless we have reason to think he is totally incompetent, there is some presumption that he succeeded at least to some extent. But it is more or less a matter of chance whether the work comes off well when perceived in some unintended way. The convergence of the three conditions, however, at the same time diminishes the *practical* importance of justifying them individually, since in most cases we can decide how to judge particular works of art without doing so. But the theoretical question remains.

I will begin with (*ii*). If we are faced with a choice between two ways of perceiving a work, and the work is very much better perceived in one way than it is perceived in the other, I think that, at least in the absence of contrary considerations, we would be strongly inclined to settle on the former way of perceiving it as the *correct* way. The process of trying to determine what is in a work consists partly in casting around among otherwise plausible ways of perceiving it for one in which the work is good. We feel we are coming to a correct understanding of a work when we begin to like or enjoy it; we are finding what is really there when it seems worth experiencing.

But if (*ii*) is relevant, it is quite clearly not the *only* relevant consideration. Take any work of art we can agree is of fourth- or fifth- or tenth-rate quality. It is very possible that if this work were perceived in some far-fetched set of categories that someone might dream up, it would appear to be first-rate, a masterpiece. Finding such *ad hoc* categories obviously would require talent and ingenuity on the order of that necessary to produce a masterpiece in the first place. But we can sketch how one might begin searching for them. (*a*) If the mediocre work suffers from some disturbingly prominent feature that distracts from whatever merits the work has, this feature might be toned down by choosing categories with respect to which it is standard, rather than variable or contra-standard. When the work is perceived in the new way the offending feature may be no more distracting than the flatness of a painting is to us. (*b*) If the work suffers from an overabundance of clichés it might be livened up by choosing categories with respect to which the clichés are variable or contra-standard rather than standard. (*c*) If it needs ingenuity we might devise a set of rules in terms of which the work finds itself in a dilemma from which it ingeniously escapes, and we might build these rules into a set of categories. Surely, however, if there are categories waiting to be discovered which would transform a mediocre work into a masterpiece, it does not follow that the work really is a hitherto unrecognized masterpiece. The fact that when perceived in such categories it would appear exciting, ingenious, and so forth, rather than grating, cliché-ridden, pedestrian, does not make it so. It *cannot* be correct, I suggest, to perceive a work in categories which are totally foreign to the artist and his society, even if it comes across as a masterpiece in them.[25]

This brings us to the historical conditions (*iii*) and (*iv*). I see no way of avoiding the conclusion that one or the other of them at least is relevant in determining in what categories a work is correctly perceived. I consider both relevant, but I will not argue here for the independent relevance of (*iv*). (*iii*) merits special attention in light of the prevalence of disputes about the importance of artists' intentions. To test the relevance of (*iii*) we must consider a case in which (*iii*) and (*iv*) diverge. One such instance occurred during the early days of the twelve-tone movement in music. Schoenberg no doubt intended even his earliest twelve-tone works to be heard as such. But this category was certainly not then well established or recognized in his society: virtually none of his contemporaries (except close associates such as Berg and Webern), even musically sophisticated ones, would have (or could have) heard these works in that category. But it seems to me that even the very first twelve-tone compositions are correctly heard as such, that the judgments one who hears them otherwise would make of them (for example, that they are chaotic, formless) are mistaken. I think this would be so even if Schoenberg had been working entirely alone, if *none* of his contemporaries had any inkling of the twelve-tone system. No doubt the first twelve-tone compositions are much better when heard in the category of twelve-tone works than when they are heard in any other way people might be likely to hear them. But as we have seen this cannot *by itself* account for the correctness of hearing them in the former way. The only other feature of the situation which could be relevant, so fas as I can see, is Schoenberg's intention.

The above example is unusual in that Schoenberg was extraordinarily self-conscious about what he was doing, having explicitly formulated rules—that is, specified standard properties—for twelve-tone composition. Artists are not often so self-conscious, even when producing revolutionary works of art. Their intentions as to which categories their works are to be perceived in are not nearly as clear as Schoenberg's were, and often they change their minds during the process of creation. In such cases (as well as ones in which the artists' intentions are unknown) the question of what categories a work is corectly perceived in is left by default to condition (*iv*), together with (*i*) and (*ii*). But it seems to me that in almost all cases at least one of the historical conditions, (*iii*) and (*iv*), is of crucial importance.

My account of the rules governing decisions about what categories works are correctly perceived in leaves a lot undone. There are bound to be a large number of undecidable cases on my criteria. Artists' intentions are frequently unclear, variable, or undiscoverable. Many works belong to categories which are borderline cases of being well established in the artists' societies (perhaps, for example, the categories of rococo music—for instance, C.P.E. Bach—of music in the style of early Mozart, and of very thin metal sculpted figures of the kind that Giacometti made). Many works fall between well-established categories (for example, between impressionist and cubist paintings), possessing *some* of the standard features relative to each, and so neither clearly qualify nor clearly fail to qualify on the basis of condition (*i*) to be perceived in either. There is, in addition, the question of what relative weights to accord the various conditions when they conflict.

It would be a mistake, however, to try to tighten up much further the rules for deciding how works are correctly perceived. To do so would be simply to legislate gratuitously, since the intuitions and precedents we have to go on are highly variable and often confused. But it is important to notice just where these intuitions and precedents are inconclusive, for doing so will expose the sources of many critical disputes. One such dispute might well arise concerning Giacometti's thin metal sculptures. To a critic who sees them simply as sculptures, or sculptures of people, they look frail, emaciated, wispy, or wiry. But that is not how they would strike a critic who sees them in the category of thin metal sculptures of that sort (just as stick figures do not strike us as wispy or emaciated). He would be impressed not by the thinness of the sculptures, but by the expressive nature of the positions of their limbs, and so forth, so he would no doubt attribute very different aesthetic properties to them. Which of the two ways of seeing these works is correct is, I suspect, undecidable. It is not clear whether enough such works have been made and have been regarded sufficiently often as constituting a category for that category to be deemed well established in Giacometti's society. And I doubt whether any of the other conditions settle the issue conclusively. So perhaps the dispute between the two critics is essentially unresolvable. The most that we can do is to point out just what sort of a difference of perception underlies the dispute, and why it is unresolvable.

The occurrence of impasses like this is by no means something to be regretted. Works may be fascinating precisely because of shifts between equally permissible ways of perceiving them. And the enormous richness of some works is due in part to the variety of permissible, and worthwhile, ways of perceiving them. But it should be emphasized that even when my criteria do not clearly specify a *single* set of categories in which a work is correctly perceived, there are bound to be possible ways of perceiving it (which we may or may not have thought of) that they definitely rule out.

The question posed at the outset of this section was how to determine what aesthetic properties a work has, given that which ones it seems to have depends on what categories it is perceived in, on which of its properties are standard, which variable, and which contra-standard for us. I have sketched in rough outline rules for deciding in what categories a work is *correctly* perceived (and hence which of its features are absolutely standard, variable, and contra-standard). The aesthetic properties it actually possesses are those that are to be found in it when it is perceived correctly.[26]

V. Conclusion

I return now to the issues raised in Section I. (I will adopt for the remainder of this paper the simplifying assumption that there is only one correct way of perceiving any work. Nothing important depends on this.) If a work's aesthetic properties are those that are to be found in it when it is perceived correctly, and the correct way to perceive it is determined partly by historical facts about the artist's intention and/or his society, no examination of the work itself, however thorough, will by itself reveal those properties.[27] If we are confronted by a work about whose origins we know absolutely nothing (for example, one lifted from the dust at an as yet unexcavated archaeological site on Mars), we would simply not be in a position to judge it aesthetically. We could not possibly tell by staring at it, no matter how intently and intelligently, whether it is coherent, or serene, or dynamic, for by staring we cannot tell whether it is to be seen as a sculpture, a guernica, or some other exotic or mundane kind of work of art. (We could attribute aesthetic properties to it in the way we do to natural objects, which of course does not involve consideration of historical facts about artists or their societies. [Cf. p. 608.] But to do this would not be to treat the object as a *work* of art.)

It should be emphasized that the relevant historical facts are not merely useful aids to aesthetic judgment; they do not simply provide hints concerning what might be found in the work. Rather they help to *determine* what aesthetic properties a work has; they, together with the work's nonaesthetic features, *make* it coherent, serene, or whatever. If the origin of a work which is coherent and serene had been different in crucial respects, the work would not have had these qualities; we would not merely have lacked a means for *discovering* them. And of two works which differ *only* in respect of their origins—ones which are perceptually indistinguishable—one might be coherent or serene, and the other not. Thus, since artists' intentions are among the relevant historical considerations, the "intentional fallacy" is not a fallacy at all. I have of course made no claims about the relevance of artist's intentions as to the aesthetic properties that their works should have. I am willing to agree that whether an artist intended his work to be coherent or serene has nothing essential to do with whether it is coherent or serene. But this must not be allowed to seduce us into thinking that *no* intentions are relevant.

Aesthetic properties, then, are not to be found in works themselves in the straightforward way that colors and shapes or pitches and rhythms are. But I do not mean to deny that we perceive aesthetic properties in works of art. I *see* the serenity of a painting and *hear* the coherence of a sonata, despite the fact that the presence of these qualities in the works depends partly on circumstances of their origin which I cannot (now) perceive. Jones's marital status is part of what makes him a bachelor, if he is one, and we cannot tell his marital status just by looking at him, though we can thus ascertain his sex. Hence, I suppose, his bachelorhood is not a property we can be said to perceive in him. But the aesthetic properties of a work do not depend on historical facts about it in anything like the way Jones's bachelorhood depends on his marital status. The point is not that the historical facts function as *grounds* in any ordinary sense for aesthetic judgments. By themselves they do not, in general, count either for or against the presence of any particular aesthetic property. And they are not part of a larger body of information (also including data about the work derived from an examination of it) from which conclusions about the works' aesthetic properties are to be deduced or inferred. We must learn to *perceive* the work in the correct categories, as determined in part by the historical facts, and judge it by what we then perceive in it. The historical facts help to determine whether a painting is coherent or serene *only* (as far as my arguments go) by affecting what way of perceiving the painting must reveal these qualities if they are truly attributable to the work.

We must not, however, expect to judge a work simply by setting ourselves to perceive it correctly, once it is determined what the correct way of perceiving it is. For one cannot, in general, perceive a work in a given set of categories simply by setting himself to do it. I could not possibly, merely by an act of will, see *Guernica* as a guernica rather than as a painting, nor could I hear a succession of street sounds in any arbitrary category one might dream up, even if the category has been explained to me in detail. Indeed, I cannot even imagine except in a rather vague way what it would be like, for example, to see *Guernica* as a guernica. One cannot merely decide to respond appropriately to a work—to be shocked or unnerved or surprised by its (absolutely) contra-standard features, to find its standard features familiar or mundane, and to react to its variable features in other ways—once one knows the correct categories. Perceiving a work in a certain category or set of categories is a skill that must be acquired by training, and exposure to a great many other works of the category or categories in question is ordinarily, I believe, an essential part of this training. (But an effort of will may facilitate the training, and once the skill is acquired one may be able to decide at will whether or not to perceive it in that or those categories.) This has important consequences concerning how best to approach works of art of kinds that are new to us—contemporary works in new idioms, works from foreign cultures, or newly resurrected works from the ancient past. It is no use just immersing ourselves in a particular work, even with the knowledge of what categories it is correctly perceived in, for that alone will not enable us to perceive it in those categories. We must become familiar with a considerable variety of works of similar sorts.

When dealing with works of more familiar kinds it is not generally necessary to undertake deliberately the task of training ourselves to perceive them in the correct categories (except perhaps when those categories include relatively subtle ones). But this is, I think, only because we have been trained unwittingly. Even the ability to see paintings as paintings had to be acquired, it seems to me, by repeated exposure to a great many paintings. The critic must thus go beyond the work before him in order to judge it aesthetically, not only to discover what the correct categories are, but also to be able to perceive it in them. The latter does not require consideration of historical facts, or consideration of facts at all, but it requires directing one's attention nonetheless to things other than the work in question.

Probably no one would deny that *some* sort of perceptual training is necessary, in many if not all instances, for apprehending a work's serenity or coherence, or other aesthetic properties. And of course it is not only *aesthetic* properties whose apprehension by the senses requires training. But the kind of training required in the aesthetic cases (and perhaps some others as well) has not been properly appreciated. In order to learn how to recognize gulls of various kinds, or the sex of chicks, or a certain person's handwriting, one must have gulls of those kinds, or chicks of the two sexes, or examples of that person's handwriting pointed out to him, practice recognizing them himself, and be corrected when he makes mistakes. But the training important for discovering the serenity or coherence of a work of art that I have been discussing is not of this sort. Acquiring the ability to perceive a serene or coherent work in the correct categories is not a matter of having had serene or coherent things pointed out to one, or having practiced recognizing them. What is important is not (or not merely) experience with other serene and coherent things, but experience with other things of the appropriate categories.

Much of the argument in this paper has been directed against the seemingly common-sense notion that aesthetic judgments about works of art are to be based solely on what can be perceived in them, how they look or sound. That notion is seriously misleading, I claim, on two different counts. I do not deny that paintings and sonatas are to be judged solely by what can be seen or heard in them—when they are perceived correctly. But examining a work with the senses can by itself reveal neither how it is correct to perceive it, nor how to perceive it that way.

Notes

1. Heinrich Wölfflin, *Principles of Art History*, trans. by M. D. Hottinger (7th ed.; New York, 1929), p. 228.
2. "[W]e should all agree, I think, . . . that any quality that cannot even in principle be heard in it [a musical composition] does not belong to it as music." Monroe Beardsley, *Aesthetics: Problems in the Philosophy of Criticism* (New York, 1958), pp. 31-32.
3. See Calvin Tompkins, *The Bride and the Bachelors* (New York, 1965), pp. 210-211.
4. Monroe Beardsley argues for a relatively strict separation (*op. cit.*, pp. 17-34). Some of the strongest recent attempts to enforce this separation are to be found in discussions of the so-called "intentional fallacy," beginning with William Wimsatt and Beardsley, "The Intentional Fallacy," *Sewanee Review*, LIV (1946), which has been widely cited and reprinted. Despite the name of

the "fallacy" these discussions are not limited to consideration of the relevance of artists' *intentions*.

5. The aesthetic properties of works of literature are not happily called "perceptual." For reasons connected with this it is sometimes awkward to treat literature together with the visual arts and music. (The notion of perceiving a work in a category, to be introduced shortly, is not straightforwardly applicable to literary works.) Hence in this paper I will concentrate on visual and musical works, though I believe that the central points I make concerning them hold, with suitable modifications, for novels, plays, and poems as well.

6. Frank Sibley distinguishes between "aesthetic" and "nonaesthetic" terms and concepts in "Aesthetic Concepts," *Philosophical Review,* LXVIII (1959).

7. Cf. Paul Ziff, "Art and the 'Object of Art,' " in Ziff, *Philosophic Turnings* (Ithaca, N.Y., 1966), pp. 12-16 (originally published in *Mind,* N. S. LX [1951]).

8. "Aesthetic and Nonaesthetic," *Philosophical Review,* LXXII (1965).

9. A category will not count as perceptually distinguishable in my sense if, in order to determine perceptually whether something belongs to it, it is necessary (in some or all cases) to determine, on the basis of nonperceptual considerations, which categories it is correctly perceived in. This prevents the category of serene things, for example, from being perceptually distinguishable.

10. I am ignoring some considerations that might be important at a later stage of investigation. In particular, I think it would be important at some point to distinguish between different *degrees* or *levels* of standardness, variableness, and contra-standardness for a person; to speak, e.g., of features being *more* or *less* standard for him. At least two distinct sorts of grounds for such differences of degree should be recognized. (1) Distinctions between perceiving a work in a certain category to a greater and lesser extent should be allowed for, with corresponding differences of degree in the standardness for the perceiver of properties relative to that category. (2) A feature which is standard relative to more, and/or more specific, categories in which a person perceives the work should thereby count as more standard for him. Thus, if we see something as a painting and also as a French Impressionist painting, features standard relative to both categories are more standard for us than features standard relative only to the latter.

11. This excludes, e.g., the sense of "represent" in which a picture might represent justice or courage, and probably other senses as well.

12. This does not hold for the special case of photography. A photograph is a photograph of a woman no matter what it looks like, I take it, if a woman was in front of the lens when it was produced.

13. Nelson Goodman denies that resemblance is necessary for representation—and obviously not merely because of isolated or marginal examples of nonresembling representations (p. 5). I cannot treat his arguments here, but rather than reject *en masse* the common-sense beliefs that pictures do resemble significantly what they depict and that they depict what they do partly because of such resemblances, if Goodman advocates rejecting them, I prefer to recognize a sense of "resemblance" in which these beliefs are true. My disagreement with him is perhaps less sharp than it appears since, as will be evident, I am quite willing to grant that the relevant resemblances are "conventional." See Goodman, *Languages of Art* (Indianapolis, 1968), p. 39, n. 31.

14. The connection between features variable for us and what the work looks like is by no means a straightforward or simple one, however. It may involve "rules" which are more or less "conventional" (e.g., the "laws" of perspective). See E. H. Gombrich, *Art and Illusion* (New York, 1960) and Nelson Goodman, *op. cit.*

15. There is at least one group of exceptions to this. Obviously features of a

work which are standard for us because they are standard relative to some *representational* category which we see it in—e.g., the category of nudes, still lifes, or landscapes—do help determine what the work looks like to us and what we take it to depict.

16. Since the original publication of this paper I have changed my views concerning resemblance in representational art. See my "Pictures and Make-Believe," *Philosophical Review,* LXXXII, (1973).

17. The presence of clichés in a work sometimes allows it to contain drastically disorderly elements without becoming chaotic or incoherent. See Anton Ehrenzweig, *The Hidden Order of Art* (London, 1967), pp. 114-116.

18. The timing of the release of the key affects the tone's length. Use of the sustaining pedal can lessen slightly a tone's diminuendo by reinforcing its overtones with sympathetic vibrations from other strings. The rate of diminuendo is affected somewhat more drastically by the force with which the key is struck. The more forcefully it is struck the greater is the tone's relative diminuendo. (Obviously the rate of diminuendo cannot be controlled in this way independently of the tone's initial volume.) The successive tones of a melody can be made to overlap so that each tone's sharp attack is partially obscured by the lingering end of the preceding tone. A melodic tone may also be reinforced after it begins by sympathetic vibrations from harmonically related accompanying figures, contributed by the composer.

19. "[T]he musical media we know thus far derive their whole character and their usefulness as musical media precisely from their limitations." Roger Sessions, "Problems and Issues Facing the Composer Today," in Paul Henry Lang, *Problems of Modern Music* (New York, 1960), p. 31.

20. One way to make electronic music sound fast would be to make it sound like some traditional instrument, thereby trading on the limitations of that instrument.

21. This example was suggested by Göran Hermerén.

22. Cf. William W. Austin, *Music in the 20th Century* (New York, 1966), pp. 205-206; and Eric Salzman, *Twentieth-Century Music: An Introduction* (Englewood Cliffs, N.J., 1967), pp. 5, 8, 19.

23. I am ruling out the view that the notions of truth and falsity are not applicable to aesthetic judgments, on the ground that it would force us to reject so much of our normal discourse and common-sense intuitions about art that theoretical aesthetics, conceived as attempting to understand the institution of art, would hardly have left a recognizable subject matter to investigate. (See the quotation from Wölfflin, above.)

24. See p. 597.

25. To say that it is incorrect (in my sense) to perceive a work in certain categories is not necessarily to claim that one *ought not* to perceive it that way. I heartily recommend perceiving mediocre works in categories that make perceiving them worthwhile whenever possible. The point is that one is not likely to *judge* the work correctly when he perceives it incorrectly.

26. This is a considerable oversimplification. If there are two equally correct ways of perceiving a work, and it appears to have a certain aesthetic property perceived in one but not the other of them, does it actually possess this property or not? There is no easy general answer. Probably in some such cases the question is undecidable. But I think we would sometimes be willing to say that a work is, e.g., touching or serene if it seems so when perceived in one acceptable way (or, more hesitantly, that there is "something very touching, or serene, about it"), while allowing that it does not seem touching or serene when perceived in another way which we do not want to rule incorrect. In some cases works have aesthetic properties (e.g., intriguing, subtle, alive, interesting, deep)

which are not apparent on perceiving it in any *single* acceptable way, but which depend on the multiplicity of acceptable ways of perceiving it and relations between them. None of these complications relieves the critic of the responsibility for determining in what way or ways it is correct to perceive a work.

27. But this, plus a general knowledge of what sorts of works were produced when and by whom, might.

ALAN TORMEY

Critical Judgments

THIS PAPER IS ADDRESSED primarily to two related questions concerning the logic of aesthetic or critical judgments. The expressions "aesthetic judgment" and "critical judgment" I shall regard as synonymous in this discussion and to spare redundancies I shall use only the latter. The questions that I shall raise concern the transmissibility of critical judgments from one person to another and the mooted "cognitive" status of critical judgments. What I shall say about the second of these issues will be discursive and inconclusive. What I have to say about the first will, hopefully, be more focused and more decisive. The ensuing discussion also carries some significant implications for the question of the role or function of the critic, and suggests a challenge to a widely held view of the importance of critical activity. To avoid premature foreclosure of potentially relevant questions I have made no attempt to define or to delimit the extension of "critical judgment," trusting that the following set of examples will be sufficient to illustrate what I understand by that expression:

A. The bright robe of the central foreground figure in Pietro Lorenzetti's *Deposizione dalla Croce* clashes with the sombre mood of the subject.

B. Brahms' F Minor Piano Quintet is a more poised and tightly knit work than Schumann's Opus 44.

C. The choir of Santa Maria in Organo is the most refined example of Veronese marquetry.

D. The studied and polemical murals of Rivera are monumental exaggerations of the banal.

E. The developmental sections of Bruckner's *Fourth Symphony* are stretched further than the thematic material can bear.

F. The *Gnossiennes* of Erik Satie are among the most subtle and transparent of his piano works.

From *Theoria*, 39 (1973), pp. 35-49. Reprinted by permission of *Theoria*.

First, then, to set the stage: In his study of epistemic logic, *Knowledge and Belief*,[1] Hintikka contends that the expression (1)*"KaKbp⊃Kap"* (if *a* knows that *b* knows that *p*, then *a* knows that *p*) is "self-sustaining," viz., that it is an epistemic analog of a logically valid sentence form, whereas the expression (2) *"BaBbp⊃Bap"* (if *a* believes that *b* believes that *p* then *a* believes that *p*) is "indefensible," i.e., not self-sustaining. Hintikka argues convincingly for his reading of these two expressions. Indeed, the inadmissibility of (2) seems transparently evident given the standard sense of "believes that *p*," and (1) is logically defensible once the entailment between knowledge and truth is granted. I shall not be further concerned with the details of Hintikka's argument here, except to caution that it is the strictly formal acceptability of (1) that has been established, and that it must not be taken to be a schematic expression of temporal or epistemological priority. (1) can tell us nothing about the temporal order or the epistemic conditions under which someone may come into the possession of a bit of knowledge, only that the conditions expressed in the antecedent cannot obtain unless the conditions expressed in the consequent obtain as well. Thus, when Hintikka describes his demonstration of (1) as an argument for the transmissibility of knowledge we must resist his implication that a kind of epistemic transfusion is being described, whereby *a* comes to know that *p* by first coming to know that *b* knows that *p*. (1), then, we may agree, is logically "self-sustaining" where (2) is not.[2]

The first question about critical judgments may now be posed in the following form: using "*J*" for "judges that" and "*q*" as a variable ranging over critical judgments, and substituting in (1) we obtain the expression (3) *"KaJbq⊃Jaq"* (if *a* knows that *b* judges that *q* then *a* judges that *q*). Now I think it is apparent that (3) is *not* self-sustaining. We do not, for whatever reasons, regard "*Jaq*" as logically similar to "*Kap*" (Nor, as it will emerge, can we regard it as reducible to "*Baq*"). Suppose, for example, that I know that a certain reputable critic judges that the choir of Santa Maria in Organo is a masterpiece of Veronese marquetry. What follows from that regarding my own critical judgments? Surely, *nothing* follows logically. No knowledge of mine, however extensive, of the critical judgments of others *entails* any particular critical judgment on my part. I may concur with some, or many, or all of the critical judgments of someone else, but it cannot be *inferred* that I do from what I know of his judgments. "I know that Berenson judges *φ* to be an insignificant display of decorative design, *and I judge it to be so as well*." is intelligible and informative, since it adds "*Jaq*" to "*KaJbq*" forming the acceptable expression "*KaJbq • Jaq*." But there is no way to *derive* this conjunction from "*KaJbq*" and an acceptable implication linking the conjuncts. Now, consider the same maneuver applied to an instance of "*KaKbp*": "I know that Jones knows that his wife is unfaithful, *and I know that she is as well*." Here, since "*Kap*" is *entailed* by *"KaKbp"* the italicized clause is redundant and merely rhetorical. *"KaKbp • Kap"* is formally derivable from *"KaKbp,"* given the acceptability of (1), while *"KaJbq • Jaq"* cannot be derived from *"KaJbq"* since (3) is unacceptable.

So much then for the logical underpinnings of the first question. It remains now to explain why critical judgments should display the logical behavior that they do, and to see whether there might still be a reason to entertain a defense of the transmissibility of critical judgments that relies on a relation weaker than that of entailment.

Let us suppose that I have just recently come to know that an art historian and critic for whom I have great respect (call him W) reports that a newly uncovered fresco at Mantova by an anonymous 15th century master outstrips in subtlety, scope, conception, and expressive depth anything that was accomplished in that idiom by Perugino or Pinturicchio. Now, I have every reason to believe that W knows what he's talking about. His sensitivity and historical knowledge are unrivaled, and moreover I have found in the past that my own judgments concur with his much of the time. So, even though we have seen that my knowledge that W judges that *q* fails to ensure, logically, that I too judge that *q*, surely it might seem that knowledge may constitute an *entitlement* for me to *adopt* the judgment that *q*. That is, it might seem on purely inductive grounds that I have excellent reasons to espouse *q* and make it my own. That, after all, is the rational procedure in so many other matters. But now, suppose that I tell someone else, M, that the Mantovan fresco is superior in scope, subtlety, composition and expressiveness to the frescos of Perugino and Pinturicchio, and that I present this *as* a critical judgment of my own. M reacts with surprise: "I didn't know you'd been to Italy recently." "I haven't," I admit, "but, you see, I have it from W, and W as you know . . ."

It is, I think, quite evident that I am flying here under false colors, and that I have been caught out. But just what is the *source* of our reluctance to allow for even this weaker form of transmissibility of critical judgments? The source, I believe, lies among the conditions that are presupposed in the making and considering of critical judgments. There are, certainly, conditions in the *absence* of which a critical judgment may not be taken seriously, or weighed and acknowledged by others— conditions of knowledge, sensitivity, training, and so on; but these are not the conditions that are at issue here. There is another, more primitive condition that is presupposed whenever we offer or accept an utterance *as* a genuine critical judgment, whatever the actual merits of that judgment may be: acquaintance with the object. Permissible substitution instances of *"Jaq"* require that *a* have, or have had direct perceptual access to the object (or objects) about which *q* is a judgment.[3] In art, unlike the law, we do not admit judgments in the absence of direct or immediate experience of the object of the judgment. We require critical judgments to be rooted in "eye-witness" encounters, and the epistemically indirect avenues of evidence, inference and authority that are permissible elsewhere are anathema here. This demands an immediate qualification, however. In some instances reproductions or representations of the object may, for *critical* purposes, be adequate surrogates for the object of the critical judgment. But the term "surrogate" must be taken seriously. Acceptable surrogates must possess properties that are at least perceptual analogs of the original work (in those arts where there *is* an object to be referred to as the original). This is admittedly a very loose criterion, but its importance lies largely in its negative force. It serves, for example, to bar *descriptions*, however accurate, from standing as surrogates for the objects of critical judgment (and thus, incidentally, contributes to the distinction between *critical* judgments and *moral* judgments, since a reasonably full and accurate description of an action *may* be sufficient grounds for a moral judgment). There is little more to be said generally about the parameters of adequacy for surrogate objects since these will obviously display manifold variations from case to case, except to note that a surrogate object must bear sufficient similarities to the work to which it stands as a surrogate so that a critical judgment formed on acquaintance with the surrogate will, or *would*, stand unaltered if the surrogate were replaced by the original.

To return to our example, I may come to suspect, or believe, that the newly discovered Mantovan fresco must indeed be superior in just those respects that q asserts that it is on the ground that W's critical discrimination has proven so reliable in the past; but this belief is rooted in my faith in W's competence as an art critic. It is not an independent *judgment* that q. (It is conceivable that someone might come to *believe* that q by coming to know that someone else has *judged* that q, but it does not follow that he thereby also judges that q. Judging that q implies believing that q, but the converse does not hold. And thus "Jaq" is not equivalent to, or reducible to "Baq," since the latter may be true while the former is false.) However strong such beliefs or suspicions may be, they can never be sufficient to entitle one to *judge* that q in the absence of direct perceptual experience of the object or an acceptable surrogate. Critical judgments then are essentially first-person affairs, and consequently, non-transmissible.

Now, I think this says something about the "cognitive" status of critical judgments, though something oblique and inconclusive. If critical judgments *are* non-transmissible, i.e., if "$KaJbq \supset Jaq$" is indefensible *and* if "$KaJbq$" is, by itself, insufficient to entitle a to judge that q, that would imply that critical judgments of the form "Jaq" have no share in a characteristic aspect of the logical behavior of the standard epistemic expression "Kap." Does this then show conclusively that critical judgments are not, or cannot be "cognitive"? It was perhaps an analogous problem that prompted Kant, in the third *Critique,* to adopt an uneasy compromise and to suggest that critical judgments are, in a way, cognitive and yet are not, in a way, cognitive at all. But one can share Kant's perplexity and respect his sensitivity to the problem without borrowing his rather cumbersome apparatus for exploring it. I want here to attempt something far less ambitious than Kant, though something, I should like to think, in the spirit of Kantian perplexity.

It might seem tempting to argue that, since critical judgments are non-transmissible and lack the status of knowledge claims, they should be classed with reports or expressions of private states—of feelings, hunches, headaches, musings, and the like. For there *are* similarities. I can no more borrow your authority for issuing my critical judgments than I can borrow your authority for reporting or expressing my pains or my whims, and thus it might appear that privacy and privileged access are as characteristic of the one as of the other. But the appearance is illusory, and the real similarities do nothing to fix the cognitive status of critical judgments. Unless one is committed to a primitive emotivism, it will be evident that critical judgments are not, *simpliciter,* reports or expressions of private states though they may be evidence for the existence of such states. One does not introspect, notice, observe, feel or detect that he judges that *q.* Critical judgments are *formed,* not found, and though the process of forming a critical judgment may be private, the target of the judgment—the art work, the object judged—is not.

But if critical judgments are neither reports (or expressions) of private states, nor epistemically transmissible from one person to another, where does that leave them on the map of cognitive/non-cognitive distinctions?

It seems reasonably clear that critical judgments, when asserted, are *claims* of a certain kind about particular objects or classes of object. Further, they are claims that are open to test. Indeed, we test them regularly. Their peculiarity is that the relevant tests are uniformly what I should call phenomenally direct tests, or "eye-witness" tests. And this is a characteristic of critical judgments that marks them off from apparently similar claims which concern the way something *appears* under stipulated conditions.

Consider the following two claims:

C_1. Woodwind instruments sound muffled in Philharmonic Hall.

C_2. The unison B at the close of Act III, Scene II, of *Wozzeck* sounds dissonant.

Minimally, both C_1 and C_2 are statements about how something sounds or appears. Other differences aside for the moment, let us consider how these claims might be tested, or rather, how *I* might test them. I could of course test C_1 by going to Philharmonic Hall and attending to the woodwinds during an orchestral performance. But I could equally well send someone else, or a number of others to make the relevant observations and report them back to me. I do not *need* to hear for myself to have adequate grounds for accepting and asserting C_1, for C_1 is a claim about how something appears or would appear to normal and qualified observers under stipulated observational conditions, and that knowledge is both indirectly obtainable and logically transmissible. C_2, however, is a critical judgment, and here it is impossible for me to ground *my* assertion of C_2 entirely on the reports of others. Overwhelming agreement among sensitive and trustworthy listeners can provide me with nothing stronger than a presumption of the likelihood *were* I to attend a performance of *Wozzeck*, I too would judge that C_2. But nothing can *entitle* me to make that judgment in the absence of a phenomenally direct test. Critical judgments and claims about how things appear under given conditions then are logically distinct claims, since the latter are indirectly testable and logically transmissible while the former are neither. This conclusion, if correct, is significant for aesthetic inquiry, and brings us around again to the cognitivity issue.

The strain that philosophers since Kant have felt here arises from the recognition that critical judgments *are* claims of a sort—claims about public and observable objects. And the immediate and predictable implication is that such judgments must then be classifiable as true/false, right/wrong, or correct/incorrect. And this of course flies in the teeth of the notorious difficulties of establishing sufficient or even necessary conditions for the truth, rightness or correctness of such judgments.

This is not, I am convinced, a pseudo-problem, and it will not evaporate with a wave of the linguistic wand. But our distress can be somewhat alleviated by a better view of the ground on which the difficulty rests. Critical judgments are not "subjective" if that is meant to denote such things as first-person sensation reports, expressions of occurrent feelings, affirmations of preference, and exclamatory effusions of appreciation. Critical judgments are claims about, and purport to be claims about, public objects. Hence they must be testable in principle if they are to be sustained. I have contended that they *are* in fact testable claims, but that their logical distinctiveness lies in their being testable, for each of us, only by direct inspection of the object (or an acceptable surrogate) and in the non-transmissibility of the ensuing judgments. Conversely, critical judgments are not "objective" either if that is taken to refer to indirectly testable and logically transmissible knowledge claims of the sort that may be substitution instances of (1). Thus, the relevant tests of critical judgments are *corroborative* tests rather than *confirmative* tests, and the *case* for a critical judgment rests on the extent of its acceptance among independent judgers and not on something like "degree of confirmation."

This last point is crucial and merits some exposition. I have argued that critical judgments require phenomenally direct access to the object of the judgment and that they are independent and nontransmissible. *Testing* the judgment that q then consists in adopting q as an hypothesis with respect to the object, O, scrutinizing O (or an O surrogate) and affirming or denying q. The reasons for describing this procedure as corroborative rather than confirmative are these: Since critical judgments are non-transmissible they fail to enter into implication relations that are common to sentences that may be substituted for p in "*Kap*." Consequently, two characteristics of confirmable sentences are missing in the case of critical judgments: disconfirmability and predictive power. (I am assuming here that what is confirmable is knowable and vice versa.)

A sentence subject to confirmative tests, such as "Metals of atomic weight greater than 27 expand when heated" is of course open to reasonably decisive disconfirmation by a negative instance. Also, a high degree of confirmation of the sentence invests it with predictive power enabling us to make projections concerning future instances.[4] All this is well-known and need not be elaborated. The point I wish to make here is that neither significant predictive power nor disconfirmability are attributable to critical judgments. That critical judgments are not, strictly, disconfirmable I think is generally conceded. No individual judgment that not-q is sufficient to *refute* or *disconfirm* a prior judgment or set of judgments that q. (At least no one to my knowledge has ever argued it to be sufficient.) It merely *fails* to contribute to the collective support for q, or as I should prefer to say, it fails to *corroborate* q.[5]

The second point, that even highly corroborated critical judgments fail to provide adequate bases for prediction, is less obvious and perhaps disputable. It might seem that such highly corroborated judgments as "Impressionism was the high point in the development of a distinctively French musical language" would entitle us to predict with a good deal of confidence that future judgments will affirm this as well. But one need only recall some of the more notorious vagaries of criticism to have second thoughts about the projectability of judgments that are *currently* highly corroborated. (Consider, for example, the fate of Fragonard or Wagner.) Certainly, we could limit our projections to the immediate future and to those persons whose training and tastes are comfortably close to our own, but that, too, weakens the case for the projectability of critical judgments. No sentence in science—or elsewhere—that has the status of an effective predictive base can accept such radical spatial and temporal limitations on its scope and continue to remain useful.

Critical judgments then are immune from anything as threatening as disconfirmation, but they retain this immunity at the price of remaining relatively useless as predictive bases from which to project critical judgments of the future.

From the fact that critical judgments are closed to *confirmative* tests however we should not conclude that they are open to no tests at all. Indeed, if we are to regard them as claims about public objects and not mere effusions of private states they *must* be open to tests of some sort. I have argued that the relevant tests of a critical judgment, *q*, are rooted in independent, phenomenally direct encounters with the object or surrogate object issuing in non-transmissible affirmations or denials of *q*; and it is the strength of the set of independent judgments that *q* that determines the degree of corroboration for *q*.

(*Theoretically* it should be possible to construct a calculus for determining the strength or degree of corroboration for a critical judgment along the following lines: Assigning a relative "weight" to each judgment based on the expertise of the judge—for example, with respect to judgments of Venetian painting Carli and Berenson are assigned greater weights than Tormey—we can postulate that

$$\text{degree of corroboration for } q = \frac{\text{(number of affirmative judgments that } q) \times \text{(mean weight of affirmative judgments)}}{\text{(total number of judgments affirming or denying that } q) \times \text{(mean weight of all such judgments)}}$$

Of course, the actual degree of corroboration at any given time is a function of the number of judgments formulated by that time, and tells us little or nothing about the worth of the object or about the potential fate of *q*. Also, and equally obviously, the practical difficulties of assigning weights to the individual judgments renders the calculus inoperable. But even though a precise measurement of *degree* of corroboration is not to be expected, we may justifiably continue to describe the procedure outlined above as constituting *corroborative tests* of critical judgments, so long as the distinction between corroboration and confirmation is kept in mind.)

If we are to distinguish, as I have proposed, between corroboration and confirmation, the danger remains that corroboration may be construed as mere convergence of critical judgments, and it might be argued that such convergent judgments are nothing more than contingent agreements among those who have formulated independent judgments about particular works of art, and thus nothing more, logically, than, say, the contingent agreement among those who share a penchant for pineapples or Porsches. But if this objection is admitted, there is nothing to prevent it from being extended to confirmative tests as well, and it is hardly reasonable to maintain, e.g., that the testing of postulated stellar parallax carried out during the recent international geo-physical year resulted in nothing more than mere agreement with priorly formulated statements. Analogously, positive instances of corroborative tests of critical judgments are not reducible to *mere* agreement either. What distinguishes a positive test—corroborative or confirmative—from contingent agreement is the occurrence and propriety of certain operations. Some prescribed procedures are required in both instances before a resultant judgment may be acknowledged as confirmative or corroborative. And in both cases, supportive reasons may be legitimately adduced or demanded before the judgment is admitted. Neither of these conditions is a requisite for merely contingent agreement. Corroboration, then, though logically weaker than confirmation is stronger than contingent agreement, and for that reason recommends itself as an appropriate characterization of the manner in which critical judgments, even though autonomous and nontransmissible, may be mutually supportive.

I have argued that although critical judgments can be subsumed as instances of neither knowledge nor belief, they can, and should, be regarded as testable claims about phenomenally public objects. The latter contention rescues critical judgments from radical subjectivism; the former prevents their forcible conscription by an uncompromising cognitivism. Neither of these alternatives does justice to the logical status of critical judgments. Indeed, much of the agonizing over the "cognitive" status of critical judgments is traceable to a misleading polarization of tensions between the common (and accommodating) senses of "subjective" and "objective." Neither label, if the preceding arguments have any force, adequately or unambiguously attaches to critical judgments; and until there is willingness to forgo the imposition of both this crude dichotomy and the related pair, cognitive/noncognitive, we shall continue to hear complaints of the elusive nature of critical judgments as we continue to witness the attempt to force the fit of one or the other of a pair of old and misshapen categories.

The role (or function, or purpose) of criticism has been widely discussed in recent years, and sustained arguments have arisen over whether the critic is, or ought to be, an arbiter of taste, an awarder of prizes, an aesthetic taxonomist, or a public educator. Without entering these lists at full tilt the foregoing discussion does, I believe, generate a challenge that deserves consideration.

If critical judgments are autonomous, non-transmissible claims about public objects and subject to corroborative tests on acquaintance with the object (or appropriate surrogate) then there is good reason to place the greatest value on those judgments that are both semantically rich and novel, disconcerting, provocative, revelatory or suggestive—in short, on the more test-worthy judgments. And the *good* critic is therefore someone who is able to *formulate* such judgments for our scrutiny. An analogy here between the formulation of a critical judgment and the formulation of a scientific hypothesis would not be unduly stretched. Testability of a scientific hypothesis is a function, in part, of its semantic content. Where there is little or no semantic content there can be no question of confirmation or (more importantly, according to Popper) of disconfirmation. And although critical judgments are open to neither confirmation nor disconfirmation, semantic content is as requisite to corroborative testability as it is to confirmative testability, and the good critic, like the good scientist, is often distinguished by his ability to formulate semantically rich and test-worthy statements.

Now, if this assessment of the relative value of critical judgment is correct, it threatens to displace the heavily entrenched view that the most significant critical judgments are those that instantiate such open-sentence exemplars as "X is good." But consider again the judgments expressed in examples A—F. Each of these examples is richer in semantic content than "X is good" and all of them whether supportable or not, if the preceding arguments are fair, are more valuable as critical judgments than a substitution instance of "X is good." As Goodman has noted in another context:[6]

> To say that a work of art is good or even to say how good it is does not after all provide much information, does not tell us whether the work is evocative, robust, vibrant, or exquisitely designed, and still less what are its salient specific qualities of color, shape, or sound. Moreover, works of art are not race-horses, and picking a winner is not the primary goal.

In art, as in science, statements that do not provide much information are not, after all, very testable, and, consequently, not very valuable. "X is good" (however "good" is to be analysed) would best be regarded as standing at the lower end of the scale of significant critical pronouncements and not at its apex. And I think it is reasonably clear that the practice of better art critics sustains this assessment. Systematic scrutiny of the writings of leading critics of the major art forms reveals a high incidence of semantically rich judgments and a paucity of expressions of the form "X is good." To cite one, not atypical, example:[7]

> It is remarkable that in de Kooning tenacity is matched by a mastery of the rapidly executed, almost instantaneous, gesture; in many of the landscape-figure-abstractions of the last few years he has achieved through speed a lightning clarity and briskness unattainable in his more pressured compositions. One of de Kooning's outstanding qualities (compared, for instance, to Pollock or Kline) is the variety of tempo he has been able to introduce into his action without destroying its continuity. . . . His compositions devour everyday sights, odd thoughts, moods, theories old and new, paintings and sculptures of the past. He has the hungry multifariousness of the Renaissance humanists, the "vulgarity" of Rabelais and Cervantes. His abstractions and female figures are no less accumulations than if they had been put together out of newsprint, rags and rubbish (some de Koonings do incorporate strips of tabloids, cutouts of magazine advertisements, sections of discarded canvases). Ready-made materials are, however, too clumsy a medium to carry the "slipping glimpses" of de

Kooning's insight. The constant interchange of image and symbol, direct impression and analytical generalization, can be seized only through the action of the brush.

Pure evaluations are of necessity semantically poor, and if, as critical practice seems to show, we prefer our criticism to exhibit semantic richness it should be clear why "X is good" and similar expressions must rank as low-grade critical judgments.

The implications of the preceding arguments then constitute direct challenge to the view that criticism is essentially or even centrally occupied with the rating or grading of art works or with the bestowal of aesthetic merit badges. Moreover, if critical judgments are epistemically non-transmissible, then the critic who hopes to canonize his pronouncements is destined to failure, for there can be neither logically compelling reasons for accepting them nor indirect means of transmitting them. And even universal corroboration of a critical judgment is not so much the *acknowledgement* of its propriety as the *establishment* of it.

But if, finally, the analysis of critical judgments forces us to abandon the view that the passing of evaluative verdicts is the principal or final object of criticism, it also restores to it a crucial function that is eclipsed by that inverted thesis: the formulation of semantically rich and testworthy statements; and the ability to achieve that is as difficult and rare in music or drama as it is in microbiology or fluid dynamics.

Notes

1. Jaakko Hintikka, *Knowledge and Belief* (Ithaca, New York: Cornell University Press, 1962).

2. Also, it could easily be shown, though Hintikka does not trouble to do so, that none of the following set of mixed cases is self-sustaining: "*BaKbp ⊃ Kap*," "*KaBbp ⊃ Kap*," "*KaBbp ⊃ Bap*." (The remaining mixed case "*BaKbp ⊃ Bap*" is interestingly problematic, and it is not pre-analytically evident whether it should be regarded as self-sustaining or not.)

3. The addition of the plural is necessary to accommodate comparative critical judgments where acquaintance must extend to all of the relevant members of the comparison class.

4. It is unimportant here whether "degree of confirmation" is understood in the logical or the statistical sense. (See Carl Hempel, "Studies in the Logic of Confirmation," in *Aspects of Scientific Explanation And Other Essays in the Philosophy of Science* (New York: The Free Press, 1965), pp. 3-46.

5. It is, I think, significant that there is no common antonym for "corroboration" analogous to "disconfirmation" or "falsification."

6. Nelson Goodman, *Languages of Art* (Indianapolis and New York: The Bobbs-Merrill Company, Inc., 1968), pp. 261 f.

7. Harold Rosenberg, *The Anxious Object,* A Mentor Book (New York and Toronto: The New American Library, 1966), pp. 104 f.

On Aesthetic Judgment

GETTING CLEAR about just what Hume's view of beauty is is not an easy matter. In his master work in philosophy, *A Treatise of Human Nature*, he says:

> beauty is such an order and construction of parts [of something], as either by the *primary constitution* of our nature, by *custom,* or by *caprice* is fitted to give a pleasure and satisfaction to the soul. This is the distinguishing character of beauty, and forms all the difference betwixt it and deformity, whose natural tendency is to produce uneasiness. Pleasure and pain, therefore, are not only necessary attendants of beauty and deformity, but constitute their very essence.[1]

Here beauty is an order and construction of parts fitted to give pleasure and satisfaction. This appears to allow for the possibility that something might be *fitted* to give pleasure and satisfaction and yet fail to do so; that is, that something might be beautiful and yet not give pleasure and satisfaction. Or is to say something is *fitted* to give pleasure to say that it actually gives pleasure, in that it could not be fitted to do so if it did not do so? And does that then mean that beauty is really an order and construction of parts that actually does give pleasure and satisfaction? To whom? To everyone? To anyone? We cannot answer these questions on the basis of what Hume says here.

When we turn to "Of the Standard of Taste" we find a similar, but still significantly different, statement about beauty:

> Though it be certain that beauty and deformity . . . are not qualities in objects, but belong entirely to the sentiment, internal or external, it must be allowed that there are certain qualities in objects which are fitted by nature to produce these particular feelings.[2]

Because "these particular feelings" are obviously pleasure and pain, satisfaction and dissatisfaction, it would appear that pleasure here con-

stitutes the very essence of beauty in that something is beautiful only if
it gives pleasure. This is, of course, not the end of the matter, but before
proceeding we might ask whether this is so. Is it not possible for something to be beautiful and to give pleasure to no one? Does a proposition
of the form "X is beautiful but X pleases no one" imply a contradiction?
Further, what would happen to the statement "People are pleased with
certain things because they are beautiful"? Would it not reduce to
"People are pleased with certain things because they are pleased with
them"? But is that what the original statement means?[3]

Now Hume does not want to say that "X is beautiful" means simply
that whoever says that X is beautiful is pleased with X, for this would
leave him with the unhappy conclusion that "each mind perceives a
different beauty" and that it would be "fruitless to dispute concerning
tastes," which Hume rejects. For "few are qualified to give judgment
on any work of art or establish their own sentiment as the standard of
beauty," and "the taste of all individuals is not upon an equal footing."
So it is possible for something to please me and not be beautiful and for
something to be beautiful and not please me, because I may lack the
proper qualifications to judge its beauty or be defective in some way.
"In each creature there is a sound and a defective state, and the former
alone can be supposed to afford us a true standard of taste and sentiment." Hume likens beauty to flavor and color. Something can look red
to me and not be red or be red and not look red to me, if either I suffer
from some defect of vision or the conditions under which I see it are
abnormal. The "true and real color" of an object is the color it appears
to have "in daylight, to the eye of a man in health." (Is this correct, by
the way?) Similarly, something can look beautiful to me (please me) and
not really be beautiful or really be beautiful and not look beautiful to
me (please me).

What is it, then, for something to be *really* beautiful? To be really
beautiful something must look beautiful (please) all those possessed of
"strong [or good] sense, united to delicate sentiment, improved by practice, perfected by comparison, and cleared of all prejudice." But will
this do? Is this what we mean by saying that something is really beautiful? If so, how are we common, garden variety folk to recognize those
few who are qualified to establish their own sentiment as the standard
of beauty?

Because he holds the same view of all other terms used to judge, appraise, or evaluate, for example, "virtuous,"[4] as he does of "beautiful,"
Hume has a further difficulty on his hands. As Hume himself puts it,

> Now it may . . . be objected to the present system, that if virtue and vice
> be determin'd by pleasure and pain, these qualities must, in every case,
> arise from the sensations; and consequently any object, whether animate
> or inanimate, rational or irrational, might become morally good or evil,
> provided it can excite a satisfaction or uneasiness.[5]

That is, if to say that something is virtuous is merely to avow pleasure or satisfaction, then if a stone pleases one it should be proper to judge it as virtuous, which is absurd. Hume's reply is,

> 'tis evident, that under the term *pleasure,* we comprehend sensations, which are very different from each other, and which have only such a distant resemblance, as is requisite to make them be express'd by the same abstract term. A good compositoin of music and a bottle of good wine equally produce pleasure; and what is more, their goodness is determin'd merely by the pleasure. But shall we say upon that account, that the wine is harmonious, or the music of a good flavour?[6]

A pleasure must be of a "peculiar" or "particular" kind to justify the use of "virtuous" as opposed to "beautiful," say. But on what basis are pleasures to be sorted into *kinds*? Is there some peculiar feature of a pleasure, apart from the object that provokes it and/or the way in which that object is regarded, that marks it as of a certain kind? This seems most unlikely. Or is it the nature of the object and/or the way in which it is regarded that marks it as of a certain kind? Hume seems to opt for the latter alternative:

> 'Tis only when a *character* [or an action by a human being] is *considered in general, without reference to our particular interest,* that it causes such a feeling or sentiment, as denominates it morally good or evil.[7]

That is, only the characters or actions of human beings considered disinterestedly are proper subjects of the terms "virtuous" and "vicious." But, as "Of the Standard of Taste" makes clear, it is only when things are considered disinterestedly or "free from all prejudice" that they are the proper subjects of "beautiful" and "deformed" or "ugly." So the difference between something's being beautiful as opposed to virtuous must have to do with the nature or properties of the thing (which is precisely what Sircello says it does have to do with). But does Hume tell us what kinds of things can be the proper subjects of "beautiful" and "deformed" alone?

Although it would be anachronistic to do so, there just might be some point in thinking of Kant's discussion of judgments of taste as an essay in speech-act analysis; that is, as an attempt not say what the *locution* "This is beautiful" means (and it's not clear that that's what he is doing in any case) but to spell out some of the features of "This is beautiful" when it is used to perform the *illocutionary* act of *judging* something to be beautiful.[8] From this point of view Kant's initial distinction between "logical" and "aesthetic" judgments becomes a distinction between what we may generically call "assertions"[9] and speech acts in which the feelings of the agent are intrinsically involved, are what Kant calls their "determining ground." Thus, "Some people smoke cigarettes" would typically be used to assert that some people smoke cigarettes, whereas

"I disapprove of smoking" would typically be used to avow one's disapproval of smoking. The distinction between "material" and "pure" aesthetic judgments would then become one, in part at least, between different ways in which the feelings of the speaker are involved: in "material" judgments they would be involved directly, as it were, these judgments being straightforward avowals of feelings ("This is delightful," "That is disgusting"), whereas in "pure" judgments they would be involved only by implication.[10]

What then is the force of Kant's saying that the pleasure on which a pure judgment of taste is "grounded" must be disinterested? Although he tries to spell out the distinction between interested and disinterested pleasures in terms of interest in or indifference to the existence of the object judged (which seems rather far-fetched), it seems to turn out that disinterested pleasures—or better, disinterested judgments of beauty—are either simply ones that are not "grounded" on the simply sensuously pleasant and are not judgments of goodness (utility or moral goodness), or that they are disinterested in Hume's sense, namely, "free from prejudice." In the former case, they would not qualify as aesthetic judgments, properly speaking, at all, but rather as straightforward avowals ("This wine has a very pleasant taste") or as moral judgments ("Spinoza was a good man, but Nero most certainly was not") or as judgments of nonmoral goodness ("Aspirin is good for a headache"). In the latter case, judgments of beauty would be subject to the general requirement that *acceptable* judgments of any kind be disinterested; and note that it is the general acceptability of the pure judgment of taste that Kant is trying to guarantee by insisting that the pleasure on which it is grounded be disinterested.

This approach may account for still further features of judgments of beauty that Kant insists on; for example, that they require locutions, or, to use the more common word, propositions that are categorical and singular for their performance, and that they "immediately accompany intuition." For hypothetical and disjunctive propositions do not lend themselves (readily) to the performance of acts of judgment. "If the picture is beautiful, I'll buy it" and "Either the picture is beautiful or I won't buy it" can hardly be used to judge the picture.[11] As for the singularity requirement, it is closely tied to the requirement that judgments of beauty be about objects of "intuition," objects one is experiencing or has experienced. As Tormey puts it,

> Permissible substitution instances of "*Jaq*" require that *a* have, or have had direct perceptual access to the object (or objects) about which *q* is a judgment. In art, unlike the law, we do not admit judgments in the absence of direct or immediate experience of the object of the judgment. We require critical judgments to be rooted in "eye-witness" encounters, and the epistemically indirect avenues of evidence, inference and authority that are permissable elsewhere are anathema here.

Isn't this precisely Kant's point? If it is, then it is easy to see why he says that judgments of beauty must be singular (or reducible to a concunction of singular judgments, for example, "All of these pictures are beautiful," which is equivalent to "This one is beautiful, and so is that one, and that one too").

Still further similarities between Kant and Tormey emerge. Kant's claim "that a thing has pleased others could never serve as the basis of an aesthetical judgment" is surely similar to Tormey's claim that "critical judgments are non-transmissible." And Kant's view that "the judgment of taste does not postulate the agreement of everyone . . . ; it only imputes this agreement to everyone, as a case of the rule in respect of which it expects, not confirmation by concepts, but assent from others" is close to Tormey's idea that critical judgments are amenable to corroboration but not to confirmation.

I have suggested one way of approaching Kant's treatment of judgments of beauty, a way that he, admittedly, would not recognize, but I have not tried here to work it out in detail. I offer it, however, as a suggestion to be tested for possible fruitfulness by further comparison between what Kant says and what we might want independently to hold about the nature of (the illocutionary act of) aesthetic judging.

The most controversial part of what Kant has to say about aesthetic judgment, as I see it, has to do with his restriction of aesthetic appreciation (pleasure) to only one feature of an object as it is experienced, namely, its form, specifically its apprehended "purposiveness without purpose" or "purposiveness according to form," which Kant construes narrowly to be either *Gestalt*, the structure of a spatial object, or *Spiel*, the structure of a temporal object. Is there really anything in the nature of judging the beauty of something that necessitates this restriction, or is it simply an oddity of Kant's? And a related question is, Is there really any difference between Kant's "free" and "dependent" beauty? (Note that according to Sircello, "there is no distinction, as Kant has drawn it, between 'free' and 'adherent' beauty. . . .")

Further, suppose that you casually invert a bag of black marbles on the floor and that they (improbably) fall in the following pattern:

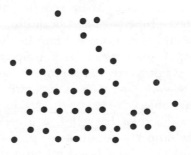

You put your imagination and understanding freely to work on this pattern, and you make the following sense out of it:

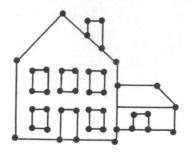

You are delighted! Here we have the apprehension of "subjective purposiveness without purpose" (if this isn't a case of it, what could be?), accompanied by pleasure. Does this mean that you must find this pattern *beautiful?*

An important assumption on which Sircello's theory of beauty rests is that with respect to anything—at least anything that is not a property—that is said to be beautiful we can always ask, "What's beautiful about it?" or "In what respect(s) is it beautiful?," and this question must in principle be answerable.[12] It must be answerable, however, immediately or ultimately, "by naming a beautiful property (or properties)." But is this true? If what is beautiful about a leaf is its color, does it follow that its color is beautiful? It may well be that what is beautiful about a leaf is its color, and that its color is beautiful, and that what makes the leaf beautiful is its beautiful color. But what now is beautiful about its color? Sircello wants to hold that "just as the beauty of 'objects' that are not properties is nothing but the beauty of properties of those 'objects,' so the beauty of properties, of which beauty of color is an important subspecies, is reducible to the beauty of properties of degree like vividness." So the color of the leaf is beautiful with respect to its vividness, say. Does this mean that the *vividness* is now beautiful? Does "The vividness of the leaf's color is beautiful" make any sense at all?[13]

Sircello has a rider that may get him off this hook. "A comprehensive theory of beauty," he says, "need give an account only of those properties, whether in any context properly *called* 'beautiful' or not, that can constitute what is beautiful about some beautiful 'objects.' When I say 'beautiful properties,' I shall mean such properties." So a beautiful property may be either a property that is properly called 'beautiful' or one that is not properly so called, so long as it constitutes what is beautiful about some beautiful "objects." Hence, the vividness of the leaf's color, which is what makes the color beautiful, is a beautiful property, even though it may not be properly so called.

But is this confusing talk about beautiful properties really essential to Sircello's thesis at all? Can't it be completely dispensed with in favor of what he later calls "beauty-making properties," some of which may, of course, be properly called "beautiful"?

Sircello wishes to exclude from the class of PQDs all properties of "deficiency, lack, or neglect"—the notorious "privations" of ancient philosophy. But does he make clear at all what such properties are? Are wickedness, cruelty, stinginess, rudeness, effeminacy (in a man) or masculinity (in a woman), poverty, shortness (relative to the general population), inability to play basketball, or ignorance of higher mathematics such properties? How can we tell? Of course, if one is stingy then he lacks generosity; but if he's generous, then he lacks stinginess. And if he's poor, he's not rich; and if rich, not poor. So that won't do. Because the exclusion of properties of deficiency, lack, or defect, as well as properties of their "appearance," is important to the New Theory of Beauty, is that theory adequate or persuasive until some criterion has been provided for the recognition of such properties?

The New Theory of Beauty can be disconfirmed, according to Sircello,

by discovering (a) one or more beautiful "objects" that are not PQDs and that are beautiful but not with respect to one or more PQDs, or (b) one or more "objects" that possess an extremely high degree of one or more PQDs (which are not properties of lack, defect, or deficiency) but that are not beautiful with respect to those PQDs.

First, consider the following pattern of dots:

o o o o o o o o o o o o o o o o

o o o o o o o o o o o o o o o o

It is a regular and symmetrical pattern, indeed has a very high degree of regularity and symmetry. Regularity and symmetry are PQDs (there are degrees of them, and there is no "*uniform* and *general* scale" for measuring them), and (I assume) they are not properties of deficiency, lack, or defect. But is the pattern beautiful with respect to its regularity and symmetry? Isn't it really just dull? And don't its regularity and symmetry make it dull? Or imagine a deep hole, perhaps a coal mine, which is very dark. Darkness is a PQD. Does it follow that the hole is beautiful with respect to its darkness? Perhaps darkness is a property of lack or deficiency—Aristotle thought it was ("darkness is merely the privation of light"). So imagine the hole being very, very deep. Depth we know is a PQD. Does it follow that the hole is beautiful with respect to its depth? Finally, imagine a man with a bulgy midriff. Bulginess is a PQD. Does it follow that his midriff is beautiful with respect to its bulginess? ("You've got a beautiful midriff there, Jack" is surely ironic.)

Of course I have not really *discovered* anything that runs counter to the NTB; all my cases are imaginary. But isn't that enough? Ignoring properties of deficiency, lack, and defect (and their "appearances"), the

NTB tells us that a PQD of an "object" is beautiful, which means that a PQD constitutes what is beautiful about an "object," if and only if it is present in that object in a high degree; and any "object" that isn't a PQD is beautiful only if it possesses at least one PQD to a very high degree. This gives us, according to Sircello, a necessary condition for an "object" that is not a PQD to be beautiful. And the necessity in question must be logical necessity, the kind of necessity that exists between being a father and being a parent, or being a square and having four sides. In that case, to "disconfirm" the NTB, is it not enough to ask ourselves whether a proposition of either of the following forms implies a contradiction? (1) "X is a beautiful 'object' and X is not a PQD, but X is not beautiful with respect to one or more PQDs;" (2) "X is an 'object' and X possesses an extremely high degree of at least one PQD, but X is not beautiful with respect to that PQD." Of course, *if* the NTB is correct, then a proposition of either of these forms will imply a contradiction. But isn't that precisely what is at issue?

Ted Cohen's criticism of Sibley apparently takes the claim that aesthetic concepts are taste concepts as a putative definition. But is he justified in doing this? Sibley begins his essay by saying:

> The remarks we make about works of art are of many kinds. For the purpose of this paper I wish to indicate two broad groups. *I shall do this by examples.* (Italics mine.)

He then gives some examples and generalizes over them: some of the remarks can be made by "anyone with normal eyes, ears, and intelligence," whereas making the others "requires the exercise of taste, perceptiveness, or sensitivity, of aesthetic discrimination or appreciation." Suppose we take this as a, perhaps too hasty, generalization based on the examples given (as well as those given in the course of the paper), and also take the claim that aesthetic concepts are not condition-governed as a similar generalization. Will Cohen's strategy work, or work as effectively as he thinks it does?

Of course, even if "Aesthetic concepts are taste concepts" is a generalization of the sort described, Cohen's example of the three lines will show that it is false—that at best only some aesthetic concepts are taste concepts—if the example is allowed (just as Sircello's theory of beauty will show that "Aesthetic concepts are not condition-governed" is false if *it* is allowed). But does Cohen's example of the three lines show what he takes it to show? Is (c) graceful? Is it the graceful one of the three? Is it more graceful than the other two? Suppose, if only for the sake of argument, that the answer to one or more of the three questions is yes. Now imagine a child "with normal eyes, ears, and intelligence" who can recognize (a) as straight, (b) as wiggly, and (c) as curved, but who just looks blank when asked which of the three is graceful. What's the obstacle? Is it that he hasn't yet learned to apply "graceful" to anything? If so, could we teach him to do so by using *this* case? Is it quite as certain as Cohen seems to think it is that acquisition of at least a modicum of "taste, perceptiveness, or sensitivity, of aesthetic discrimination or appreciation" is *not* required to manage "graceful" correctly?

Leaving aside the question of whether aesthetic terms (always) require taste for their proper application, consider Cohen's view that the aesthetic/nonaesthetic distinction comes to nothing. Take his second procedure for trying to give the distinction some substance:

> The person is given two sheets of paper, headed *aesthetic* and *non-aesthetic,* each containing the first few entries in a list. Each begins with the terms that Sibley has already sorted for us. . . . We give the person instructions: "Go on making these two lists."

"What will happen?," asks Cohen. "I submit that the subject will have no idea how to proceed." Perhaps. But that might be due to the fact that the subject is a child or an illiterate adult. There may be all sorts of reasons for a subject's inability to proceed. But if we take only persons who are educated in the arts and are articulate, is it quite so certain that they will have *no* idea how to proceed? Maybe. But let's make the test more interesting: each time the subject adds a term to either list we ask him to give an example of its use in some context. This will allow the same term, for example, "noisy" or "flat," to appear in both lists. But is it now clear that "taste" will not be required for the uses specified under the heading *aesthetic*?[14]

Sibley's approach to aesthetic concepts or terms or judgments is a wholesale one. Is the gravamen of Cohen's criticism, perhaps, that only a piecemeal approach is likely to yield any significant results?

Kendall Walton argues that a work of art's "aesthetic properties depend not only on its non-acsthetic ones, but also on which of its non-aesthetic properties are 'standard,' which 'variable,' and which 'contra-standard'." Does Cohen's attack on the aesthetic/nonaesthetic distinction spoil Walton's program in any way?

Walton gives four considerations that, he holds, always (?) count towards its being correct to perceive a work, W, in a given category, C. The third is "the fact that the artist who produced W intended or expected it to be perceived in C, or thought of it as a C." But is it not the case that most historical categories, that is, categories of art history, come after the fact, and thereby come too late for artists to have been able to intend or expect their work to be perceived in those categories, or to think of them as belonging to those categories. Could Bernini, for example, have intended or expected his major work to be perceived in the category of High Baroque, or could he have thought of it as High Baroque work? Or could Bach have thought of his music in the same way? Could Mozart and Haydn have thought of their music as Classical, or Donne his poetry

as Metaphysical? If not, won't this difficulty affect the fourth consideration as well? For, after all, none of these categories was established in and
recognized by the societies in which the works in question were produced.
But if (iii) and (iv) are seriously compromised in this way, what happens
to Walton's claim that "it *cannot* be correct . . . to perceive a work in
categories which are totally foreign to the artist and his society . . ."?

Alan Tormey claims that aesthetic or critical judgments are non-
transmissible: if I know that Wittkower has judged the flow of movement
and counter-movement in Cortona's *The Rape of the Sabine Women* to be
dynamic, this does not imply that I judge that flow of movement to be
dynamic. But could it not follow, given suitable assumptions about the
person making the judgment, that I *know* on Wittkower's authority that
the flow of movement in Cortona's picture is dynamic? Tormey allows
that on the basis of someone else's judgment that q I can come to believe
that q. But if I can come to believe it, is there any obstacle in principle to
my coming to know it? In other words, given suitable assumptions about
the person(s) making a critical judgment, is not the following formula
acceptable: $KaJbq \supset Kaq$? How else do we know the qualities of David
Garrick's or Mrs. Siddons' acting, for example, except from the judgments
of contemporaries who witnessed their acting?

Notes

1. David Hume, *A Treatise of Human Nature*, L. A. Selby-Bigge, ed. (Oxford,
1888), p. 299. This edition has been frequently reprinted.
2. See "Euclid has fully explained all the qualities of the circle, but he has
not, in any proposition, said a word of its beauty. The reason is evident. The
beauty is not a quality of the circle. It lies not in any part of the line whose
points are equally distant from a common center. It is only the effect which
the figure produces upon the mind, whose peculiar fabric and structure renders
it susceptible to such sentiments. In vain would you look for it in the article,
or seek it, either by your senses or by mathematical reasonings, in all the
properties of that figure." This passage appears, word for word, twice in
Hume's works: once in his essay "The Sceptic" *(Essays Moral, Political, and
Literary*, T. H. Green and T. H. Grose, eds., London, 1882, Vol. I, p. 219) and
again in his *An Enquiry Concerning the Principles of Morals (Hume's Enquiries Concerning Human Understanding and Concerning the Principles of
Morals*, L. A. Selby-Bigge, ed., Oxford, 1902, pp. 291-292).
3. I am here making the widespread assumption that what Hume is doing
is trying to say what "_____ is beautiful" *means*. It is just possible, however, that that is not what he is doing; that what he is doing is trying to
say what it is to *judge* or *call* something "beautiful." (Many hints are given in
his essay that this is what he is really up to.) If this is so, then it's not that
pleasure and pain constitute the very essence of beauty and deformity, but rather
that they constitute the very essence of *calling* something "beautiful" or "deformed" ("ugly")—which is a far more plausible view. As John Searle points out
in the course of discussing the use of "good": "Calling something 'good' is char-

acteristically praising, or commending, or recommending, or expressing approval of the thing so called. Furthermore, this seems not to be just a contingent fact, as is shown by the fact that the word 'good' itself is sometimes described as a term of praise" (*Speech Acts: An Essay in the Philosophy of Language,* Cambridge, 1969, p. 150). This is also true of "beautiful."

Searle goes on to point out (p. 151) that there are "two classes of illocutionary verbs" that are relevant to this context. In the first are "such verbs as 'grade,' 'evaluate,' 'assess,' 'judge,' 'rate,' 'rank,' and 'appraise';" in the second "such verbs as 'commend,' 'praise,' 'laud,' 'extol,' 'express approval,' 'express satisfaction,' and 'recommend'." To perform one of the acts named in the second group is (usually) to perform one of the acts named in the first group; but not conversely, because "I may evaluate something favourably or unfavourably, but I cannot extol it unfavourably. I may grade it as excellent or bad, but I cannot praise it as bad." Now "beautiful," like "good," is typically used to perform one of the acts named in the second group (and hence also one of the acts named in the first group), which is why, as Sircello puts it, "a *necessary* condition of one's legitimately judging something as beautiful is that he take pleasure (or some comparable positive feeling) in apprehending it."

But it does not follow from the fact that to *call* something "beautiful" or to *judge* it as beautiful is to imply that one is pleased or satisfied with it that "*X* is beautiful" *means* "I am pleased with *X*." To suppose otherwise is to commit what Searle calls "the speech-act fallacy," for a full discussion of which see Searle, *op. cit.,* Ch. 6.

4. See, for example, *A Treatise of Human Nature,* p. 471.

5. *Ibid.*

6. *Op. cit.,* p. 472.

7. *Ibid.* Italics mine.

8. Kant does use the German equivalents of "judgment" and "to judge," but it is questionable how much this proves. For he uses "judgment," for example, in the way many philosophers use "proposition." Still, this linguistic point is not, I think, to be disregarded entirely, especially in view of the fact that in the *Critique of Judgment* Kant regards judgment (*Urteilskraft*) as a faculty having a special employment.

9. "Assertions" covers statements, descriptions, reports, and the like—illocutionary acts in which, roughly, factual information is at issue.

10. For the kind of implication at issue, see note 3. The proposition "This is beautiful" does not imply the proposition "This pleases me," but the proposition "I judge this to be beautiful" typically does.

11. There is, however, a kind of hypothetical that can be so used, for example, "If that's beautiful, then I'm a monkey's uncle." But this is in effect to judge something as not beautiful.

12. See Renford Bambrough, *Reason, Truth and God* (London, 1969), p. 52: "I cannot say that there is no difference between two pictures except that one of them is beautiful and the other is not, or that one of them is ugly and the other is not. A claim that a picture has or lacks a certain aesthetic quality has to be supported by pointing out that it has or lacks certain other . . . qualities."

13. The color might be said to be beautifully vivid, perhaps, but according to the principle of "adjective-adverb interchangeability," "The color is beautifully vivid" = "The vividness of the color is beautiful."

It is not clear why Sircello excludes properties from the domain of the question "What's beautiful about it?" Of course, if he held both (1) that *X* is beautiful only if it's beautiful with respect to some *F*, and (2) that "*X* is beautiful with respect to *F*" implies that *F* is beautiful, then (1) and (2) would lead to a vicious infinite regress; for we could then ask "With respect to what is *F* beautiful?," and so on. But since, as it turns out, he does not really hold (2), there's no reason for the exclusion of properties.

14. Other possible procedures: (1) have a pile of cards with a term inscribed on each and give the cards to the subject one by one, asking him to file them as *aesthetic* or *nonaesthetic;* (2) give the subject sheets of paper headed *aesthetic, moral, religious, economic, mathematical,* and so on and ask him to list terms accordingly; (3) or give him sheets of paper headed *visual and aesthetic/visual but nonaesthetic, aural and aesthetic/aural but nonaesthetic,* and so on. It's anyone's guess what would happen, but, whatever the results, what would (could) they show? That there is no such thing as a special class of aesthetic terms or uses of terms?

Suggestions for Additional Reading

On Hume and Kant:

Peter Jones, "Hume's Aesthetics Reassessed," *Phil. Quart.,* 26 (1976), 48-62; Peter Kivy, "Hume's Standard of Taste: Breaking the Circle," *B.J.A.,* 7 (1967), 57-66; Carolyn W. Korsmeyer, "Hume and the Foundations of Taste," *J.A.A.C.,* 35 (1976), 201-215; H. Osborne, "Hume's Standard and the Diversity of Aesthetic Taste," *B.J.A.,* 7 (1967), 50-56; Mary Carmen Rose, "The Importance of Hume in the History of Western Aesthetics," *B.J.A.,* 16 (1976), 218-229; Harry Blocker, "Kant's Theory of the Relation of Imagination and Understanding in Aesthetic Judgments of Taste," *B.J.A.,* 5 (1965), 37-45; H. W. Cassirer, *A Commentary on Kant's Critique of Judgment* (London, 1938); Francis X. J. Coleman, *The Harmony of Reason: A Study in Kant's Aesthetics* (Pittsburgh, Pa., 1974); Donald W. Crawford, *Kant's Aesthetic Theory* (Madison, Wisc., 1974), and "Reason-Giving in Kant's Aesthetics," *J.A.A.C.,* 28 (1970), 505-510; R. K. Elliott, "The Unity of Kant's 'Critique of Aesthetic Judgment,'" *B.J.A.,* 8 (1968), 244-259; John Fisher and Jeffrey Maitland, "The Subjectivist Turn in Aesthetics: a Critical Analysis of Kant's Theory of Appreciation," *Rev. Met.,* 27 (1974), 726-751; D. W. Gotshalk, "Form and Expression in Kant's Aesthetics," *B.J.A.,* 7 (1967), 250-260; I. Knox, *The Aesthetic Theories of Kant, Hegel, and Schopenhauer* (New York, 1936); Berel Lang, "Kant and the Subjective Objects of Taste," *J.A.A.C.,* 25 (1967), 247-253; Jeffrey Maitland, "Two Senses of Necessity in Kant's Aesthetics," *B.J.A.,* 16 (1976), 347-353; Michael R. Neville, "Kant's Characterization of Aesthetic Experience," *J.A.A.C.,* 33 (1974), 193-202; H. Osborne, "On Mr. Elliott's Kant," *B.J.A.,* 8 (1968), 260-268; Stuart J. Petock, "Kant, Beauty, and the Object of Taste," *J.A.A.C.,* 32 (1973), 183-186; Ingrid Stadler, "Perception and Perfection in Kant's Aesthetics," *Kant: A Collection of Critical Essays,* Robert Paul Wolff, ed. (New York, 1967), 339-384; Robert L. Zimmerman, "Kant: the Aesthetic Judgment," *J.A.A.C.,* 21 (1963), 333-344, reprinted in Wolff, ed., *op. cit.,* 365-406.

On beauty:

Virigil C. Aldrich, "Beauty as Feeling," *Kenyon Review*, 1 (1939), 300-307; S. Alexander, *Beauty and Other Forms of Value* (London, 1933), Pt. I; Monroe C. Beardsley, *Aesthetics* (New York, 1958), 502-512; E. F. Carritt, *The Theory of Beauty* (London, 1928); G. P. Henderson, "The Concept of Ugliness," *B.J.A.*, 6 (1966), 219-229, and "An 'Orthodox' Use of the Term 'Beautiful'," *Philosophy*, 35 (1960), 114-121; T. E. Jessop, "The Definition of Beauty," *P.A.S.*, 33 (1932-1933), 159-172; Vernon Lee, *The Beautiful* (Cambridge, 1931); G. E. Moore, *Principia Ethica* (Cambridge, 1903), 183-202; H. Osborne, *Theory of Beauty* (London, 1952); George Santayana, *The Sense of Beauty* (New York, 1896), often reprinted; F. E. Sparshott, *The Structure of Aesthetics* (Toronto and London, 1963), Ch. III; Jerome Stolnitz, "Beauty: History of an Idea," *Journal of the History of Ideas*, 23 (1961), 185-204; Wladyslaw Tatarkiecwicz, "The Great Theory of Beauty and Its Decline," *J.A.A.C.*, 31 (1972), 165-180—on the "classical" theory of beauty; Ludwig Wittgenstein, *Lectures and Conversations on Aesthetics, Psychology and Religious Belief*, Cyril Barrett, ed. (Oxford, 1966), 1-36; E. M. Zemach, "The Pragmatic Paradox in Aesthetics," *B.J.A.*, 7 (1967), 215-224—on "It's beautiful, but I don't like it."

On aesthetic judgments:

Monroe C. Beardsley, *Aesthetics* (New York, 1958), Ch. II, and "What is an Aesthetic Quality?," *Theoria*, 39 (1973), 50-70; E. J. Bond, "Some Words Used in Appraising Works of Art," *B.J.A.*, 16 (1976), 108-116; R. David Broiles, "Frank Sibley's 'Aesthetic Concepts'," *J.A.A.C.*, 23 (1964), 219-225; Allan Casebier, "The Alleged Specific Logic for Aesthetic Terms," *J.A.A.C.*, 31 (1973), 357-364—critical of Sibley; Marcia Cavell, "Critical Dialogue," *J. Phil.*, 67 (1970), 339-351—develops a position similar to that of Tormey's "Critical Judgments;" George Dickie, "Taste and Attitude: the Origin of the Aesthetic," *Theoria*, 39 (1973), 153-170; Marcia P. Freedman, "The Myth of the Aesthetic Predicate," *J.A.A.C.*, 27 (1968), 49-55; Isabel Creed Hungerland, "Once Again, Aesthetic and Non-Aesthetic," *J.A.A.C.*, 26 (1968), 285-295; Göran Hermerén, "Aesthetic Qualities, Value and Emotive Meaning," *Theoria*, 39 (1973), 71-100; Gary Iseminger, "Aesthetic Judgments and Non-Aesthetic Conditions," *Analysis*, 33 (1972-1973), 129-132—critical of Sibley; Peter Kivy, "Aesthetic Aspects and Aesthetic Qualities," *J. Phil.*, 65 (1968), 85-93—on Sibley, and "Aesthetics and Rationality," *J.A.A.C.*, 34 (1975), 51-57, and *Speaking of Art* (The Hague, 1973), esp. Chs. 1-3—an extended attack on the claim that aesthetic concepts are not condition-governed, and "What Makes Aesthetic Terms 'Aesthetic'?," *Phil. and Phen.*, 36 (1975), 197-211; J. F. Logan, "More on Aesthetic Concepts," *J.A.A.C.*, 25 (1967), 401-406; Colin Lyas, "Personal Qualities and the Intentional Fallacy," *Philosophy and the Arts*, Royal Institute of Philosophy Lectures, 6, 1971/72 (New York, 1973), 194-210—

deals with such terms as 'responsible.' 'intelligent,' 'witty,' 'shallow,' 'immature,' 'smug'; Joseph Margolis, *The Language of Art and Art Criticism* (Detroit, 1965), Pt. IV; R. Meager, "Aesthetic Concepts," *B.J.A.*, 10 (1970), 303-322; A. G. Pleydel-Pearce, "Objectivity and Value in the Judgments of Aesthetics," *B.J.A.*, 10 (1970), 25-38; Francis B. Randall, "The Goofy in Art," *B.J.A.*, 11 (1971), 327-340; Eva Schaper and Frank Sibley, "Symposium: About Taste," *B.J.A.*, 6 (1966), 55-69; H. R. G. Schwyzer, "Sibley's 'Aesthetic Concepts'," *Phil. Rev.*, 72 (1963), 72-78; Frank Sibley, "Aesthetic Concepts: a Rejoinder," *Phil. Rev.*, 72 (1963), 79-83, and "Aesthetic and Non-Aesthetic," *Phil Rev.*, 74 (1965), 135-159; Frank Sibley and Michael Tanner, "Objectivity and Aesthetics," *P.A.S.*, Suppl. Vol. 62 (1968), 31-72; Eva Simpson, "Aesthetic Appraisal," *Philosophy*, 50 (1975), 189-204; Guy Sircello, "Subjectivity and Justification in Aesthetic Judgments," *J.A.A.C.*, 27 (1968), 3-12; Kenneth M. Stamp, Jr., "Unity as a Virtue," *J.A.A.C.*, 34 (1975), 191-197, and "Unity as a Necessary Condition," *J.A.A.C.*, 27 (1968), 141-143; Sasha Talmor, "The Aesthetic Judgment and Its Criteria of Value," *Mind*, 78 (1969), 102-115; Morris Weitz, "Interpretation and the Visual Arts," *Theoria*, 39 (1973), 101-112.

VI

Critical Judgment

Introduction

T HE MATERIAL OF THIS SECTION is continuous with that of the last, as the reader will quickly see. For editorial purposes, an arbitrary distinction has been drawn between aesthetic judgments and critical judgments, restricting the latter to such judgments as "Paris Bordone's *Venus and Cupid* is a good painting," "Giorgione's *Sleeping Venus* is a better picture than Bordone's *Venus and Cupid*," or "*Don Giovanni* is the best of Mozart's operas." If we accept the concluding paragraphs of Tormey's "Critical Judgments," however, the distinction is not entirely arbitrary but, rather, is one of the relative "semantic richness" of what we have called "aesthetic judgments" as against the relative semantic poverty of what we here call "critical judgments," a fact that is accounted for by Lycan and Machamer in their essay.

The words "good" and "bad" (together with their comparative and superlative forms) have no inherent connection with art criticism, which could be—and usually is, as Tormey points out—carried on without them. They are, however, for whatever reason, terms on which much of the philosophy of art criticism has concentrated; and the following selections, representative of recent work in this area, are principally about the meaning and justification of such propositions as "That is a good painting," when in using it one is judging, evaluating, appraising, or pronouncing a verdict on the painting in question. What is it to call a work of art good? With what kinds of reasons alone can one back up, substantiate, or justify a critical or verdictive judgment of a work of art? And what is the relation between reason and verdict? Closely connected with these issues is the question of the very purpose or function of art criticism or verdictive judgment. Is it, like moral appraisal, directed at affecting choice and behavior, the behavior of artists and the choices of spectators? Or is it rather directed at enlightening the spectator's looking, listening, and reading?

Stuart Hampshire deals mainly with the function of art criticism. Critical appraisal, as he sees it, is not analogous to moral judgment, although it has often been thought to be: "aesthetic [i.e., critical] judgments are not comparable in purpose with moral judgments." There are no principles or standards of art criticism comparable with the principles or standards of right conduct; hence there are no reasons why a work of art is good comparable with the reasons why an action is right. This is because "a work of art is gratuitous. It is not *essentially* [i.e., *qua* work of art] the answer to a question or the solution of a presented problem." So the aim of criticism is to display or call attention to, to get the spectator to see, the unique features of the work being criticized—a view with which the other authors in this section tend to agree.

Isenberg is concerned with "the content of the critic's argument": "What claim does he transmit to us? How does he expect us to deal with this claim?" He opposes a "widely held" view of criticism according to which the critical process has three parts: "There is the value judgment or *verdict* (V): 'This picture or poem is good _____'; there is a particular statement or *reason*: (R), '_____ because it has such-and-such a quality _____' [of the sort discussed in the previous section of this book]; and there is a general statement or *norm* (N): '_____ and any work which has that quality is *pro tanto* good.'"

According to this view, what makes R critically useful and relevant is that it is backed up by N. Isenberg rejects this: N is expendable. He comes to this conclusion by drawing a distinction between *explaining* and *justifying* a critical response or judgment. Whereas N (which Isenberg construes as based upon an inductive generalization) may be necessary for *explaining* a critical judgment, it has no parallel role in *justification*. As for R, its truth, according to Isenberg, "never adds the slightest [logical] weight to V," in the way that the premises of a deductive or inductive argument lend weight to the conclusion; because R never designates any quality "the perception of which might induce us to assent to V." R has a different role to play—to induce in the audience that experience of the work that led the critic to make the judgment he did, and thereby to bring about, in so far as it can be brought about, agreement with respect to V.

Where Isenberg holds that we can't be sure that there is any *kind* of statement about art that cannot acts as R, that is, "which cannot influence aesthetic appreciation," Ziff, in a way, disagrees. Isenberg, as he sees it, confuses *appreciation* with *evaluation*. Any fact about a work of art may be relevant to appreciation, and it will be so relevant if knowledge of it tends to facilitate or enhance appreciation; but it does not follow from this that it will be directly relevant to evaluation, only that it may be indirectly relevant—although every fact directly relevant to evaluation will be similarly relevant to appreciation. To be directly relevant to evaluation, R must point to some aspect of a painting, say, that can be contemplated in it; a reason that does not guide one in the contemplation of the painting is worthless. This is because a good painting is simply one that is worth contemplating (for its own sake). Ziff also distinguishes between reason for *supposing* that a painting is good (worth contemplating), and reasons *why it is good,* and tries to define or circumscribe the latter.

Lycan and Machamer offer what they call "a preliminary account of the logic and function of reasons in art criticism." They first state and criticize the positions of Isenberg and Ziff. They then compare the logic of critical reasons with that of "criteria" (in a special sense of the term introduced by Wittgenstein) and find six respects in which they are similar or "parallel," the upshot of which is that the reasons why a work of art, say, a painting, is good partly determine the sense of "   is a good painting." They draw a distinction between "detachable" and "nondetachable" reasons for which a painting is good, a detachable reason being a more or less straightforward statement of fact—for example, "Pietro da Cortona studied the works of the Venetian masters"—which "could be replaced . . . without loss of critical efficacy" by another statement more obviously about some contemplable feature of a painting—for example, "The scene [of Cortona's *The Rape of the Sabine Women*] is . . . permeated by a sense of Venetian romanticism."[1] They then hold, with some qualifications, that " a fact can serve as a critical reason *why some painting, P, is good* if and only if it is *about P* and *nondetachable.*"

They also introduce the notion of a "continuum of reasons" ranging from "_____ is a good painting" at the top (which, of course, is not actually a reason why the painting is good) to thoroughly detachable reasons at the bottom, for example, "_____ was painted in 1629." In the light of the two notions of detachability and continuum of reasons, they then draw certain conclusions about the purported difference between descriptions and evaluations, about the universalizability of critical reasons, and about the putative distinction between the "aesthetic" and the "nonaesthetic." They also show how the viable insights of Isenberg and Ziff can be accommodated to their theory.

Is Beethoven's *Hammerklavier* sonata as good a work of art as, or better than, Piero della Francesca's *Montefeltro Altarpiece*? Is Shakespeare's *Coriolanus* as good as, or better than, either of these? Such questions seem rather far-fetched. We're not sure what the point of the comparison is meant to be. And yet it is sometimes supposed that there is not merely goodness as a piano sonata, goodness as a painting, or goodness as a play, but goodness as a work of art *qua* art, or, for short, "aesthetic goodness." If so, then it would seem that the works cited, or even more divergent ones, should be comparable with respect to their aesthetic or artistic goodness. This fascinating problem is explored by Bruce Vermazen.

Operating on the assumption that there is such a property as "aesthetic goodness" in general, Vermazen first raises the question whether it has a precise, or only a vague, metric and concludes that it has only a vague metric. He proposes to "offer an explanation of this fact."

He offers what he takes to be three independently plausible theses about what we are doing when we call something a good work of art and purports to show how they entail the difficulty of comparing the aesthetic merits of different works, that is, how they reinforce the claim that "roughly speaking, the more dissimilar in such ways as medium, period, genre, and so on, the more respects there are in which they [works of art] are incomparable, and the more hesitant we are to compare them on the whole." Central to his theses is the distinction between "independently" and "dependently" valued aspects or properties of a work of art, that is, aspects or properties with respect to which a work of art is good. Roughly, the dependently valued aspects are those that, as it were, borrow their value from the independently valued ones. So it's the independently valued ones that really count. The three theses are (1) some aspects of works of art are valued independently; (2) works of art almost always have at least two aspects that are valued independently; and (3) while it's generally possible to rank works with respect to the degree of a single independently valued aspect, it's not generally possible to rank them with respect to the degree of two or more different independently valued aspects.

Given these theses, Vermazen shows, borrowing the model of "commodity bundles" from economics, how the value assigned to the independently valued aspects of a work can be represented. Given this model and the three theses, together with the further claim (which Vermazen defends) that "a judgment that a work of art is aesthetically good does not in any important way go beyond those judgments that rank a work with respect to the degree in which it possesses independently valued properties," he purports to explain why the examples we began with are indeed far-fetched.

Note

1. The second statement comes from Rudolf Wittkower, *Art and Architecture in Italy, 1600-1750* (Harmondsworth, England, 1973), p. 250. It is itself only relatively detachable, however.

STUART HAMPSHIRE

Logic and Appreciation

IT SEEMS THAT there *ought* to be a subject called "Aesthetics." There is an alexandrianism which assumes that there are so many classified subjects waiting to be discussed and that each one ought to have its place in the library and in the syllabus. There is moral philosophy—the study of the nature of the problems of conduct—in every library and in every syllabus; there ought surely to be a philosophical study of the problems of Art and Beauty—if there are such problems; and this is the question which comes first. That there are problems of conduct cannot be doubted; people sometimes wonder what they ought to do and they find reasons for solving a moral problem to their own satisfaction; one can discuss the nature of these problems, and the form of the arguments used in the solution of them; and this is moral philosophy. But what is the subject-matter of aesthetics? Whose problems and whose methods of solution? Perhaps there is no subject-matter; this would fully explain the poverty and weakness of the books. Many respectable books can be, and have been, written on subjects which have no subject-matter; they may be written for the sake of system and completeness, to round off a philosophy, or simply because it is felt that there ought to be such a subject.

There is a simple and familiar way of finding the subject-matter of aesthetics, by begging the question. One may invent a kind of judgment called a value judgment, and let it be either a judgment about conduct or a judgment about Art and Beauty: a single genus with two species. From this beginning, one may go on to distinguish value judgments from other kinds of judgment. But the existence of the genus has been assumed, the assimilation of moral to aesthetic judgment taken for granted. One has certainly not isolated the subject-matter of aesthetics by this method; the original material has simply been dropped from view. What questions under what conditions are actually answered by aesthetic judgments? This must be the starting-point. I shall argue that aesthetic judg-

Reprinted from *The World Review*, October 1952.

ments are not comparable in purpose with moral judgments, and that there are no problems of aesthetics comparable with the problems of ethics.

There are artists who create and invent, and there are critics and a wider audience who appraise and enjoy their work. An artist has the technical problems of the medium in which he works; he may discuss these technical problems with other artists working in the same medium and with those who intimately understand the difficulties of his material. As an artist, he has his own conception of what his own work is to be; clearly or confusedly, he has set his own end before himself; even if his work must satisfy some external demand, he has his own peculiar conception of it, if he is to be regarded as more than a craftsman in some applied art. He has therefore created his own technical problems; they have not been presented to him; they arise out of his own conception of what he is to do. He did not set himself to create Beauty, but some particular thing. The canons of success and failure, of perfection and imperfection, are in this sense internal to the work itself, if it is regarded as an original work of art. In so far as the perfection of the work is assessed by some external criterion, it is not being assessed as a work or art, but rather as a technical achievement in the solution of some presented problem. A work of art is gratuitous. It is not *essentially* the answer to a question or the solution of a presented problem. Anyone may dance for any reason and to achieve any variety of purposes; but a spectator may attend to the movements of the dance for the sake of their own intrinsic qualities, and disregard the purposes which lie outside; and, so regarded, the dance becomes gratuitous; it ceases to be an action, and becomes a set of movements; the subject of the spectator's attention has changed.

Compare the subject-matter and situation of moral judgment. Throughout any day of one's life, and from the moment of waking, one is confronted with situations which demand action. Even to omit to do anything positive, and to remain passive, is to adopt a policy; Oblomov had his own solution to the practical problems confronting him; his was one possible solution among others. One can suspend judgment on theoretical questions and refuse either to affirm or deny any particular solution; but no one can refuse to take one path or another in any situation which confronts him; there must always be an answer to the question "What did you do in that situation?" even if the answer is: "I ignored it and did nothing; I went to bed and to sleep." If that is the answer, that was the solution adopted. One can always describe, first, the situation and the possibilities open, and, secondly, the solution of the problem which the agent adopted. Action in response to any moral problem is not gratuitous; it is imposed; that there should be some response is absolutely necessary. One cannot pass by a situation; one must pass *through* it in one way or another.

When there are unavoidable problems, a rational man looks for some general method of solving them; a rational man may be defined as a man who adheres to general methods, allotting to each type of problem its own method of solution. Unless general methods of solution are recognized, there can be no grounds for distinguishing a valid from an invalid step in any argument in support of any solution. To be irrational is either to have no reasons at all for preferring one solution to another, or to give utterly different reasons in different cases of the same type; to refuse any general method of solving problems of a particular type is to accept either caprice or inconsistency in that domain. "Must there be some general method of solving problems of conduct?" Or "Must to act rightly be to act rationally and consistently?"—these have always been the principal questions in moral philosophy. Aristotle, the most accurate of moral philosophers, gave a carefully ambiguous answer, Kant an unambiguous "Yes," Hume a qualified "No"; for Hume held that morality was ultimately a matter of the heart and not of the head, of sympathy and not of consistency. But none of these philosophers denied that it always makes sense to ask for the reasons behind any practical decision; for constant ends may be served by a variety of different means. Actions (unlike works of art) do not bear their justification on the face of them; one must first inquire into reasons and purposes. Even if it is not necessary, at least it is always possible, to adopt some general ends of action, or (it is ultimately the same) to acknowledge some universal principles. Since any action susceptible of moral judgment can be viewed as the solution of a problem presented, one can always criticize and compare different methods of solution. Consistent policies are needed in order to meet common human predicaments; men may discuss the reasons which have inclined them to solve the same problem in different ways. Their arguments (since arguments must be consistent) will lead them to general principles; anyone, therefore, who moralizes necessarily generalizes; he "draws a moral"; in giving his grounds of choice, he subsumes particular cases under a general rule. Only an aesthete in action would comfortably refuse to give any grounds of decision; he might refer the questioner to the particular qualities of the particular performance; precisely this refusal to generalize would be the mark of his aestheticism. Virtue and good conduct are essentially repeatable and imitable, in a sense in which a work of art is not. To copy a right action is to act rightly; but a copy of a work of art is not necessarily or generally a work of art.

In a moralizing climate there will always be a demand, based on analogy, for principles of criticism, parallel with principles of conduct. But this analogy must be false. Where it makes sense to speak of a problem, it makes sense to speak of a solution of it; and where solutions are offered, it makes sense to ask for reasons for preferring one solution to another; it is possible to demand consistency of choice and general principles of preference. But if something is made or done gratuitously, and not in response to a problem posed, there can be no question of preferring one solution to another; judgment of the work done does not involve a choice, and there is no need to find grounds of preference. One may, as a spectator, prefer one work to another, but there is no *necessity* to decide between them; if the works themselves are regarded as free creations, to be enjoyed or neglected for what they are, then any grading is inessential to the judgment of them; if they are not answers to a common problem, they do not compete and neither need be rejected, except on its own merits. A critical judgment is in this sense noncommital and makes no recommendation; the critic may reject the work done without being required to show what the artist ought to have done in place of the work rejected. But the moralist who condemns an action must indicate what ought to have been done in its place; for something had to be done, some choice between relative evils made. All practical decision is choice between relative evils or relative goods; if what was done was wrong, the agent must have failed to do what he ought to have done. Any moral comment has therefore some force of recommendation and is itself a practical judgment. A moral censor must put himself in the place of the agent and imaginatively confront the situation which the agent confronted; the censor and the agent censored have so far the same problem. But a critic is not another artist, as the moral censor is another agent; he is a mere spectator and he has the spectator's total irresponsibility; it is only required that he should see the object exactly as it is. Nothing which he says in judgment and description necessarily carries any exclusions with it, or necessarily reflects upon the merit of other work; the possible varieties of beautiful and excellent things are inexhaustible. He may therefore discuss any work on its merits alone, in the most strict sense of this phrase; he need not look elsewhere and to possible alternatives in making his judgment. On the contrary, his purpose is to lead people *not* to look elsewhere, but to look here, at precisely this unique object; not to see the object as one of a kind, but to see it as individual and unrepeatable.

One engages in moral argument in order to arrive at a conclusion— what is to be done or ought to have been done; one had the practical problem to begin with, and the conclusion ("this is better than that") is always more important than the route by which one arrives at it; for one *must* decide one way or the other. But a picture or poem is not created as a challenge or puzzle, requiring the spectator to decide for or against. One engages in aesthetic discussion for the sake of what one might see on the way, and not for the sake of arriving at a conclusion, a final verdict for or against; if one has been brought to see what there is to be seen in the object, the purpose of discussion is achieved. Where the logicians' framework of problem and conclusion does not apply, the notion of "reason" loses some of its meaning also; it is unnatural to ask *"why* is that picture or sonata good?" in parallel with "why was that the right thing to do?" There are no reasons why some object is ugly in the sense that there are reasons why some action is wrong. Perhaps it may be said that there are particular features of the particular object which *make* it ugly or beautiful, and these can be pointed out, isolated, and placed in a frame of attention; and it is the greatest service of the critic to direct attention in this analytical way. But when attention is directed to the particular features of the particular object, the point is to bring people to see these features, and not simply to lead them to say: "That's good." There is no point in arguing that the object is good *because* it possesses these qualities, if this involves the generalization that all objects similar in this respect are good; for if one generalizes in this manner, one looks away from the particular qualities of the particular thing, and is left with some general formula or recipe, useless alike to artist and spectator. One does not need a formula or recipe unless one needs repetitions; and one needs repetitions and rules in conduct, but not in art; the artist does not need a formula of reproduction and the spectator does not need a formula of evaluation.

The spectator-critic in any of the arts needs gifts precisely the opposite of the moralist's; he needs to suspend his natural sense of purpose and significance. To hold attention still upon any particular thing is unnatural; normally, we take objects—whether perceived by sight, touch, hearing, or by any combination of the senses—as signs of possible actions and as instances of some usable kind; we look through them to their possible uses, and classify them by their uses rather than by sensuous similarities. The common vocabulary, being created for practical purposes, obstructs any disinterested perception of things; things are (in a sense) recognized before they are really seen or heard. There is no practical reason why attention should be arrested upon a single object, framed and set apart; attention might always be practical attention, and therefore always passing from one thing to the next; in the sense in which thunder "means" rain, almost everything means something else; "what does it mean?" is the primitive reaction which prevents perception. One may always look through a picture as if it were a map, and look through a landscape towards a destination; for everything presented through the senses arouses expectations and is taken as a signal of some likely reaction. Nothing but holding an object still in attention, by itself and for its own sake, would count as having an aesthetic interest in it. A great part of a critic's work, in any of the arts, is to place a frame upon the object and upon its parts and features, and to do this by an unnatural use of words in description. Perception, of any kind and on any level, has degrees; some perceive more than others, and it is difficult to see and hear all that there is to see and hear. There is a metaphysical prejudice that the world consists of so many definite objects possessing so many definite qualities, and that, if we perceive and attend to the objects, we necessarily notice their qualities; as if the things and their qualities were somehow already isolated and labelled for us, ready for the camera-brain to record. So it seems that in principle a vast inventory might be made of all the things in the world with their qualities, passively received and recorded; when one had gone

through the inventory of literal description, any further statements about
the furniture of the world would be subjective impression and metaphor.
There is the prejudice that things really do have colours and shapes, but
that there do not exist, literally and objectively, concordances of colours
and perceived rhythms and balances of shapes; these are supposed to be
added by the mind. It seems that the more recondite qualities of form,
expression, style, atmosphere, cannot properly be entered in the inventory
of the world, alongside the weights and measures of things; the relations
of stress and balance between masses in sculpture or building cannot
really be seen in any literal sense; the expression of a voice is not as much
a perceptible reality as its loudness. The qualities which are of no direct
practical interest are normally described metaphorically, by some transference of terms from the common vocabulary; and the common vocabulary is a vocabulary of action, classifying by use and function. The
assumption is that only these literal descriptions are descriptions of realities; so descriptions of aesthetic qualities become subjective impressions.
But a colony of aesthetes, disengaged from practical needs and manipulations, would single out different units of attention (things), and they
would see different resemblances and make different comparisons (qualities). Descriptions of aesthetic qualities, which for us are metaphorical,
might seem to them to have an altogether literal and familiar sense. They
might find complete agreement among themselves in the use of a more
directly descriptive vocabulary, singling out different units of attention. A
critic in any one of the arts is under the necessity of building such a vocabulary in opposition to the main tendency of his language; he needs
somehow to convince himself that certain isolated objects of his attention
really do have the extraordinary qualities which they seem to have; to this
end he will need to discuss his perceptions with others, and to try to bring
others to notice these qualities. He may have seen (in the wider sense of
"see") more than there is to be seen; and the only test of whether the
qualities are really there must be some agreement among careful and disinterested observers. This is the point at which an aesthetic judgment is
made—what are the relationships of elements here? What pattern or arrangement of elements is there to be seen, when one attends to the thing
carefully and disinterestedly? Anything may be seen or heard or read in
many different ways, and as an arrangement of any number of elements
of different kinds. The picking out of the elements and of their pattern,
in defiance of habit and practical interest, is a work of practice and skill;
and the use of words in description is an aid to this perception. Anything
whatever may be picked out as an object of aesthetic interest—anything
which, when attended to carefully and apart altogether from its uses, provides, by the arrangement of its elements and their suggestion to the imagination, some peculiar satisfaction of its own. An aesthetic judgment
has to point to the arrangement of elements, and to show what constitutes
the originality of the arrangement in this particular case; what one calls

originality in one case may bear little analogy to originality found elsewhere; for there was no common problem to be solved and the achievements were essentially different.

But a moralist in criticism (and there exist such critics) will always be
making unnecessary choices and laying down principles of exclusion, as a
moralist must. He will make "value judgments," and a value judgment is
essentially a grading of one thing as better than another. If the judgment
is an assessment of the particular excellences of works which are very
similar, it may be enlightening and useful; but there can be larger comparisons of scale and greatness between things which are in themselves
very different. Judgments of this second kind may be taken as practical
advice that certain things ought to be read, seen, and heard, and the advice must involve some reference to the whole economy of human needs
and purposes; but at this point the critic has actually become a moralist, and the arguments supporting his recommendations are the subject-
matter of ethics. "Is this thing more worth attention than other objects of
its kind?" is one question, and "What is the peculiar arrangement of elements here and what are the effects of this arrangement?" is another.
Most aesthetic theories have involved a confusion of answers to these two
very different questions; no positive answer to the second by itself entails
any answer to the first. One would need to add some further premises
about changing human needs and interests; and there is no reason to assume that all works of art satisfy the same needs and interests at all times
and for all people. The objects themselves, and the artists who made
them, make no unavoidable claim on the spectator's interest, and anyone
may neglect the work done when it is of no interest to him. But the peculiar features of particular objects, with their own originality of arrangement, remain constant and unaffected by the spectator's choices and
priorities; and there can be no place for exclusive theories and general
principles in identifying their originality; they must be seen as they are,
individually, and not judged as contestants in a single race called Art or
The Novel or Painting.

I conclude that everyone needs a morality to make exclusions in conduct; but neither an artist nor a critical spectator unavoidably needs an
aesthetic; and when in Aesthetics one moves from the particular to the
general, one is travelling in the wrong direction.

ARNOLD ISENBERG

Critical Communication

T HAT QUESTIONS ABOUT MEANING are provisionally separable, even if
finally inseparable, from questions about validity and truth, is shown
by the fact that meanings can be exchanged without the corresponding
convictions or decisions. What is imparted by one person to another in an
act of communication is (typically) a certain idea, thought, content, meaning, or claim—not a belief, expectation, surmise, or doubt; for the last
are dependent on factors, such as the checking process, which go beyond
the mere understanding of the message conveyed. And there is a host of
questions which have to do with this message: its simplicity or complexity,
its clarity or obscurity, its tense, its mood, its modality, and so on. Now,
the theory of art criticism has, I think, been seriously hampered by its
headlong assault on the question of validity. We have many doctrines
about the objectivity of the critical judgment but few concerning its import, or claim to objectivity, though the settlement of the first question
probably depends on the clarification of the second. The following remarks are for the most part restricted to meeting such questions as: What
is the content of the critic's argument? What claim does he transmit to us?
How does he expect us to deal with this claim?

A good starting point is a theory of criticism, widely held in spite of its
deficiencies, which divides the critical process into three parts. There is
the value judgment or *verdict* (*V*): "This picture or poem is good—";
There is a particular statement or *reason* (*R*): "—because it has such-and-
such a quality—"; and there is a general statement or *norm* (*N*): "—and
any work which has that quality is *pro tanto* good."[1]

V has been construed, and will be construed here, as an expression of
feeling—an utterance manifesting praise or blame. But among utterances
of that class it is distinguished by being in some sense conditional upon *R*.
This is only another phrasing of the commonly noted peculiarity of

From *The Philosophical Review*, 58 (1949), pp. 330-344. Reprinted by permission of *The Philosophical Review*.

aesthetic feeling: that it is "embodied" in or "attached" to an aesthetic content.

R is a statement describing the content of an art work; but not every such descriptive statement is a case of *R*. The statement, "There are just twelve flowers in that picture" (and with it nine out of ten descriptions in Crowe and Cavalcaselle), is without critical relevance, that is, without any bearing upon *V*. The description of a work of art is seldom attempted for its own sake. It is controlled by some purpose, some interest; and there are many interests by which it might be controlled other than that of reaching or defending a critical judgment. The qualities which are significant in relation to one purpose—dating, attribution, archaeological reconstruction, clinical diagnosis, proving or illustrating some thesis in sociology—might be quite immaterial in relation to another. At the same time, we cannot be sure that there is any *kind* of statement about art, dictated by no matter what interest, which cannot also act as *R*; or, in other words, that there is any *kind* of knowledge about art which cannot influence aesthetic appreciation.

V and *R*, it should be said, are often combined in sentences which are at once normative and descriptive. If we have been told that the colors of a certain painting are garish, it would be astonishing to find that they were all very pale and unsaturated; and to this extent the critical comment conveys information. On the other hand, we might find the colors bright and intense, as expected, without being thereby forced to admit that they are garish; and this reveals the component of valuation (that is, distaste) in the critical remark. This feature of critical usage has attracted much notice and some study; but we do not discuss it here at all. We shall be concerned exclusively with the descriptive function of *R*.

Now if we ask what makes a description critically useful and relevant, the first suggestion which occurs is that it is *backed up by N*. *N* is based upon an inductive generalization which describes a relationship between some aesthetic quality and someone's or everyone's system of aesthetic response. Notice: I do not say that *N* is an inductive generalization; for in critical evaluation *N* is being used not to predict or to explain anybody's reaction to a work of art but to vindicate that reaction, perhaps to someone who does not yet share it; and in this capacity *N* is a precept, a rule, a *generalized value statement*. But the *choice* of one norm, rather than another, when that choice is challenged, will usually be given some sort of inductive justification. We return to this question in a moment. I think we shall find that a careful analysis of *N* is unnecessary, because there are considerations which permit us to dismiss it altogether.

At this point it is well to remind ourselves that there is a difference between *explaining* and *justifying* a critical response. A psychologist who should be asked "why *X* likes the object *Y*" would take *X*'s enjoyment as a datum, a fact to be explained. And if he offers as explanation the presence in *Y* of the quality *Q*, there is, explicit or latent in this causal argument, an appeal to some generalization which he has reason to think is true, such as "*X* likes any work which has that quality." But when we ask *X* as a critic "why he likes the object *Y*," we want him to give us some reason to like it too and are not concerned with the causes of what we may so far regard as his bad taste. This distinction between the genetic and the normative dimension of inquiry, though it is familiar to all and acceptable to most of us, is commonly ignored in the practice of aesthetic speculation; and the chief reason for this—other than the ambiguity of the question, Why do you like this work?—is the fact that some statements about the object will necessarily figure both in the explanation and the critical defense of any reaction to it. Thus, if I tried to explain my feeling for the line

> But musical as is Apollo's lute

I should certainly mention "the pattern of u's and l's which reinforces the meaning with its own musical quality," because this quality of my sensations is doubtless among the conditions of my feeling response. And the same point would be made in any effort to convince another person of the beauty of the line. The remark which gives a reason also, in this case, states a cause. But notice that, though as criticism this comment might be very effective, it is practically worthless as explanation, because we have no phonetic or psychological laws (nor any plausible "common-sense" generalizations) from which we might derive the prediction that such a pattern of u's and l's should be pleasing to me. In fact, the formulation ("pattern of u's and l's," and so forth) is so vague that one could not tell just what general hypothesis it is that is being invoked or assumed; yet it is quite sharp enough for critical purposes. On the other hand, suppose that someone should fail to be "convinced" by my argument in favor of Milton's line. He might still readily admit that the quality which I mentioned might have something to do with *my* pleasurable reaction, given my peculiar psychology. Thus the statement which is serving both to explain and to justify is not equally effective in the two capacities; and this brings out the difference between the two paths of discussion. Coincident at the start, they diverge in the later stages. A *complete* explanation of any of my responses would have to include certain propositions about my nervous system, which would be irrelevant in any critical argument. And a critically relevant observation about some configuration in the art object might be useless for explaining a given experience, if only because the experience did not yet contain that configuration.[2]

Now it would not be strange if, among the dangers of ambiguity to which the description of art, like the rest of human speech, is exposed, there should be some which derive from the double purpose—critical and psychological—to which such description is often being put. And this is, as we shall see, the case.

The necessity for sound inductive generalizations in any attempt at aesthetic explanation is granted. We may now consider, very briefly, the parallel role in normative criticism which has been assigned to N. Let us limit our attention to those metacritical theories which *deny* a function in criticism to N. I divide these into two kinds, those which attack existing standards and those which attack the very notion of a critical standard.

1. It is said that we know of no law which governs human tastes and preferences, no quality shared by any two works of art that makes those works attractive or repellent. The point might be debated; but it is more important to notice what it assumes. It assumes that if N *were* based on a sound induction, it would be (together with R) a real ground for the acceptance of V. In other words, it would be reasonable to accept V on the strength of the quality Q if it could be shown that works which possess Q tend to be pleasing. It follows that criticism is being held back by the miserable state of aesthetic science. This raises an issue too large to be canvassed here. Most of us believe that the idea of progress applies to science, does not apply to art, applies, in some unusual and not very clear sense, to philosophy. What about criticism? Are there "discoveries" and "contributions" in this field? It is reasonable to expect better evaluations of art after a thousand years of investigation than before? The question is not a simple one: it admits of different answers on different interpretations. But I do think that some critical judgments have been and are every day being "proved" as well as in the nature of the case they ever can be proved. I think we have already numerous passages which are not to be corrected or improved upon. And if this opinion is right, then it could not be the case that the validation of critical judgments waits upon the discovery of aesthetic laws. Let us suppose even that we *had* some law which stated that a certain color combination, a certain melodic sequence, a certain type of dramatic hero has everywhere and always a positive emotional effect. To the extent to which this law holds, there is of course that much less disagreement in criticism; but there is no better method for resolving disagreement. We are not more fully convinced in our own judgment because we know its explanation; and we cannot hope to convince an imaginary opponent by appealing to this explanation, which by hypothesis does not hold for him.

2. The more radical arguments against critical standards are spread out in the pages of Croce, Dewey, Richards, Prall, and the great romantic critics before them. They need not be repeated here. In one way or another they all attempt to expose the absurdity of presuming to judge a work of art, the very excuse for whose existence lies in its *difference* from everything that has gone before, by its degree of *resemblance* to something that has gone before; and on close inspection they create at least a very strong doubt as to whether a standard of success or failure in art is either necessary or possible. But it seems to me that they fail to provide a positive interpretation of criticism. Consider the following remarks by

William James on the criticism of Herbert Spencer: "In all his dealings
with the art products of mankind he manifests the same curious dryness
and mechanical literality of judgment. . . . Turner's painting he finds
untrue in that the earth-region is habitually as bright in tone as the air-
region. Moreover, Turner scatters his detail too evenly. In Greek statues
the hair is falsely treated. Renaissance painting is spoiled by unreal
illumination. Venetian Gothic sins by meaningless ornamentation." And
so on. We should most of us agree with James that this is bad criticism.
But *all* criticism is similar to this in that it cites, as reasons for praising
or condemning a work, one or more of its qualities. If Spencer's reasons
are descriptively true, how can we frame our objection to them except in
some such terms that "unreal illumination does not make a picture bad,"
that is, by attacking his standards? What constitutes the relevance of a
reason but its correlation with a norm? It is astonishing to notice how
many writers, formally committed to an opposition to legal procedure
in criticism, *seem* to relapse into a reliance upon standards whenever
they give reasons for their critical judgments. The appearance is inevitable; for as long as we have no alternative interpretation of the
import and function of R, we must assume *either* that R is perfectly
arbitrary *or* that it presupposes and depends on some general claim.

With these preliminaries, we can examine a passage of criticism. This
is Ludwig Goldscheider on *The Burial of Count Orgaz:*

> Like the contour of a violently rising and falling wave is the outline of the
> four illuminated figures in the foreground: steeply upwards and downwards
> about the grey monk on the left, in mutually inclined curves about the
> yellow of the two saints, and again steeply upwards and downwards about
> . . . the priest on the right. The depth of the wave indicates the optical
> center; the double curve of the saints' yellow garments is carried by the
> greyish white of the shroud down still farther; in this lowest depth rests
> the bluish-grey armor of the knights.[3]

This passage—which, we may suppose, was written to justify a favorable judgment on the painting—conveys to us the idea of a certain
quality which, if we believe the critic, we should expect to find in a
certain painting by El Greco. And we do find it: we can verify its presence by perception. In other words, there is a quality in the picture which
agrees with the quality which we "have in mind"—which we have been
led to think of by the critic's language. But the same quality ("a steeply
rising and falling curve," and so on) would be found in any of a hundred
lines one could draw on the board in three minutes. It could not be the
critic's purpose to inform us of the presence of a quality as banal and
obvious as this. It seems reasonable to suppose that the critic is thinking
of another quality, no idea of which is transmitted to us by his language,
which he *sees* and which by his use of language he *gets us to see*. This
quality is, of course, a wavelike contour; but it is not the quality desig-

nated by the expression "wavelike contour." Any object which has this quality will have a wavelike contour; but it is not true that any object which has a wavelike contour will have this quality. At the same time, the expression "wavelike contour" *excludes* a great many things: if anything is a wavelike contour, it is not a color, it is not a mass, it is not a straight line. Now the critic, besides imparting to us the idea of a wavelike contour, gives us directions for perceiving and does this *by means* of the idea he imparts to us, which narrows down the field of possible visual orientations and guides us in the discrimination of details, the organization of parts, the grouping of discrete objects into patterns. It is as if we found both an oyster and a pearl when we had been looking for a seashell because we had been told it was valuable. It *is* valuable, but not because it is a seashell.

I may be stretching usage by the senses I am about to assign to certain words, but it seems that the critic's *meaning* is "filled in," "rounded out," or "completed" by the act of perception, which is performed not to judge the truth of his description but, in a certain sense, to *understand* it. And if *communication* is a process by which a mental content is transmitted by symbols from one person to another, then we can say that it is a function of criticism to bring about communication at the level of the senses, that is, to induce a sameness of vision, of experienced content. If this is accomplished, it may or may not be followed by agreement, or what is called "communion"—a community of feeling which expresses itself in identical value judgments.

There is a contrast, therefore, between critical communication and what I may call normal or ordinary communication. In ordinary communication, symbols tend to acquire a footing relatively independent of sense-perception. It is, of course, doubtful whether the interpretation of symbols is at any time completely unaffected by the environmental context. But there is a difference of degree between, say, an exchange of glances which, though it means "Shall we go home?" at one time and place, would mean something very different at another—between this and formal science, whose vocabulary and syntax have relatively fixed connotations. With a passage of scientific prose before us, we may be dependent on experience for the definition of certain simple terms, as also for the confirmation of assertions; but we are not dependent on experience for the interpretation of compound expressions. If we are, this exposes semantic defects in the passage—obscurity, vagueness, ambiguity, or incompleteness. (Thus: "Paranoia is marked by a profound egocentricity and deep-seated feeling of insecurity"—the kind of statement which makes every student think he has the disease—is suitable for easy comparison of notes among clinicians and all who know how to recognize the difference between paranoia and other conditions; but it does not explicitly set forth the criteria which they employ.) Statements about immediate experience, made in ordinary communication, are no exception. If a theory requires that a certain flame should be blue, then we have to report whether it is or is not blue—regardless of shades or variations which may be of enormous importance aesthetically. We are bound to the letters of our words. Compare with this something like the following:

> "The expression on her face was delightful."
> "What was delightful about it?"
> "Didn't you see that smile?"

The speaker does not mean that there is something delightful about smiles as such; but he cannot be accused of not stating his meaning cleary, because the clarity of his language must be judged in relation to his purpose, which in this case is the *evaluation* of the immediate experience; and for that purpose the reference to the smile will be sufficient if it gets people to feel that they are "talking about the same thing." There is understanding and misunderstanding on this level; there are marks by which the existence of one or the other can be known; and these are means by which misunderstanding can be eliminated. But these phenomena are not identical with those that take the same names in the study of ordinary communication.

Reading criticism, otherwise than in the presence, or with direct recollection, of the objects discussed, is a blank and senseless employment—a fact which is concealed from us by the cooperation, in our reading, of many noncritical purposes for which the information offered by the critic is material and useful. There is not in all the world's criticism a single purely descriptive statement concerning which one is prepared to say beforehand, "If it is true, I shall like that work so much the better"—and *this* fact is concealed by the play of memory, which gives the critic's language a quite different, more specific, meaning than it has an ordinary communication. The point is not at all similar to that made by writers who maintain that value judgments have no objective basis because the reasons given to support them are not logically derivable from the value judgments themselves. I do not ask that R be related *logically* to V. In ethical argument you have someone say, "Yes, I would condemn that policy if it really did cause a wave of suicides, as you maintain." Suppose that the two clauses are here only psychologically related —still, this is what you never have in criticism. *The truth of R never adds the slightest weight to V*, because R does not designate any quality the perception of which might induce us to assent to V. But if it is not R, or what it designates, that makes V acceptable, then R cannot possibly require the support of N. The critic is not committed to the general claim that the quality named Q is valuable, because he never makes the particular claim that a work is good in virtue of the presence of Q.

But he, or his readers, can easily be misled into *thinking* that he has made such a claim. You have, perhaps, a conflict of opinion about the merits of a poem; and one writer defends his judgment by mentioning vowel sounds, metrical variations, consistent or inconsistent imagery. Another critic, taking this language at its face value in ordinary communication, points out that "by those standards" one would have to condemn famous passages in *Hamlet* or *Lear* and raise some admittedly bad poems to a high place. He may even attempt what he calls an "experiment" and, to show that his opponents' grounds are irrelevant, construct a travesty of the original poem in which its plot or its meter or its vowels and consonants, or whatever other qualities have been cited with approval, are held constant while the rest of the work is changed. This procedure, which takes up hundreds of the pages of our best modern critics, is a waste of time and space; for it is the critic abandoning his own function to pose as a scientist—to assume, in other words, that criticism explains experiences instead of clarifying and altering them. If he saw that the *meaning* of a word like "assonance"—the quality which it leads our perception to discriminate in one poem or another—is in critical usage never twice the same, he would see no point in "testing" any generalization about the relationship between assonance and poetic value.

Some of the foregoing remarks will have reminded you of certain doctrines with which they were not intended to agree. The fact that criticism does not actually designate the qualities to which it somehow directs our attention has been a ground of complaint by some writers, who tell us that our present critical vocabulary is woefully inadequate.[4] This proposition clearly looks to an eventual improvement in the language of criticism. The same point, in a stronger form and with a different moral, is familiar to readers of Bergson and Croce, who say that it is impossible by means of concepts to "grasp the essence" of the artistic fact; and this position has seemed to many people to display the ultimate futility of critical analysis. I think that by returning to the passage I quoted from Goldscheider about the painting by El Greco we can differentiate the present point of view from both of these. Imagine, then, that the painting should be projected onto a graph with intersecting coordinates. It would then be possible to write complicated mathematical expressions which would enable another person who knew the system to construct for himself as close an approximation to the exact outlines of the El Greco as we might desire. Would this be an advance toward precision in criticism? Could we say that we had devised a more specific terminology for drawing and painting? I think not, for the most refined concept remains a concept; there is no vanishing point at which it becomes a percept. It is the idea *of* a quality, it is not the quality itself. To render a critical verdict we should still have to perceive the quality; but Goldscheider's passage already shows it to us as clearly as language can. The idea of a new and better means of communication presupposes the absence of the sensory contents we are talking about; but criticism always assumes the presence of these contents to both parties; and it is upon this assumption that the vagueness or precision of a critical statement must be judged. Any further illustration of this point will have to be rough and hasty. For the last twenty or thirty years the "correct" thing to say about the metaphysical poets has been this: They think with their senses and feel with their brains. One hardly knows how to verify such a dictum: as a psychological observation it is exceedingly obscure. But it does not follow that it is not acute criticism; for it increases our awareness of the difference between the experience of Tennyson and the experience of Donne. Many words—like "subtlety," "variety," "complexity," "intensity"—which in ordinary communication are among the vaguest in the language have been used to convey sharp critical perceptions. And many expressions which have a clear independent meaning are vague and fuzzy when taken in relation to the content of a work of art. An examination of the ways in which the language of concepts mediates between perception and perception is clearly called for, though it is far too difficult to be attempted here.

We have also just seen reason to doubt that any aesthetic quality is ultimately ineffable. "What can be said" and "what cannot be said" are phrases which take their meaning from the purpose for which we are speaking. The aesthetics of obscurantism, in its insistence upon the incommunicability of the art object, has never made it clear what purpose or demand is to be served by communication. If we devised a system of concepts by which a work of art could be virtually reproduced at a distance by the use of language alone, what human intention would be furthered? We saw that *criticism* would not be improved: in the way in which criticism strives to "grasp" the work of art, we could grasp it no better then than now. The scientific *explanation* of aesthetic experiences would not be accomplished by a mere change of descriptive terminology. There remains only the *aesthetic* motive in talking about art. Now if we set it up as a condition of communicability that our language should *afford* the experience which it purports to describe, we shall of course reach the conclusion that art is incommunicable. But by that criterion all reality is unintelligible and ineffable, just as Bergson maintains. Such a demand upon thought and language is not only preposterous in that its fulfillment is logically impossible; it is also baneful, because it obscures the actual and very large influence of concepts upon the process of perception (by which, I must repeat, I mean something more than the ordinary *reference* of language to qualities of experience). Every part of the psychology of perception and attention provides us with examples of how unverbalized apperceptive reactions are engrained in the content and structure of the perceptual field. We can also learn from psychology how perception is affected by verbal cues and instructions. What remains unstudied is the play of critical comment in society at large; but we have, each of us in his own experience, instances of differential emphasis and selective grouping which have been brought about through the concepts imparted to us by the writings of critics.

I have perhaps overstressed the role of the critic as teacher, that is, as one who affords *new* perceptions and with them new values. There is such a thing as discovering a community of perception and feeling which already exists; and this can be a very pleasant experience. But it often happens that there are qualties in a work of art which are, so to speak, neither perceived nor ignored but felt or endured in a manner of which Leibniz has given the classical description. Suppose it is only a feeling of monotony, a slight oppressivenes, which comes to us from the style of some writer. A critic then refers to his "piled-up clauses, endless sentences, repetitious diction." This remark shifts the focus of our attention and brings certain qualities which had been blurred and marginal into distinct consciousness. When, with a sense of illumination we say "Yes, that's it exactly," we are really giving expression to the *change* which has taken place in our aesthetic apprehension. The postcritical experience is the true commentary on the precritical one. The same thing happens when, after listening to Debussy, we study the chords that can be formed on the basis of the whole-tone scale and then return to Debussy. New feelings are given which bear some resemblance to the old. There is no objection in these cases to our saying that we have been made to "understand" why we liked (or disliked) the work. But such understanding, which is the legitimate fruit of criticism, is nothing but a second moment of aesthetic experience, a retrial of experienced values. It should not be confused with the psychological study which seeks to know the causes of our feelings.

Notes

1. Compare, for instance, C. J. Ducasse, *Art, the Critics, and You* (New York: Liberal Arts Press, 1944), p. 116: "The statement that a given work possesses a certain objective characteristic expresses at the same time a judgment of value if the characteristic is one that the judging person approves, or as the case may be, disapproves; and is thus one that he regards as conferring, respectively, positive or negative value on any object of the given kind that happens to possess it." See, further, pp. 117-120.

2. I should like to add that when we speak of "justifying" or "giving reasons" for our critical judgments, we refer to something which patently does go on in the world and which is patently different from the causal explanation of tastes and preferences. We are not begging any question as to whether the critical judgment can "really" be justified, that is, established on an objective basis. Even if there were no truth or falsity in criticism, there would still be agreement and disagreement; and there would be argument which arises out of

disagreement and attempts to resolve it. Hence, at least there exists the purely "phenomenological" task of elucidating the import and intention of words like "insight," "acumen," "obtuseness," "bad taste," all of which have a real currency in criticism.

3. Ludwig Goldscheider, *El Greco* (London: Phaidon Press, 1949), p. 13.
4. See D. W. Prall, *Aesthetic Analysis* (New York: Crowell, 1936). p. 201.

PAUL ZIFF

Reasons in Art Criticism

HSIEH HO SAID one of the principles of painting is that "through organization, place and position should be determined." Le Brun
praised Poussin's paintings to the French Academy, saying the figures
were faithful copies of Roman and Greek statues.

If someone now says "P.'s painting is a faithful copy of a Roman
statue," he is not apt to be offering a reason why the work is either good
or bad. "The painting has a touch of blue," ". . . is a seascape," ". . . a
picture of peasants," ". . . conforms to the artist's intentions," ". . . will
improve men's morals": these too are not apt to be offered, and if offered
cannot be accepted as reasons why the painting is good or bad.

But if someone says "P.'s painting is disorganized," he is apt to be offering a reason why the work is bad (he need not be; this might be part of
an answer to "Which one is P.'s?"). Even if it is right to say "P.'s painting
is disorganized," it may be wrong to conclude "P.'s painting is bad," or
even "P.'s painting is not good." Some good paintings are somewhat disorganized; they are good in spite of the fact that they are somewhat disorganized. But no painting is good because it is disorganized and many
are bad primarily because they are disorganized.

To say "P.'s painting is disorganized" may be to offer a good reason
why P.'s painting is bad. It is a consideration. It need not be conclusive.
But it is a reason nonetheless. Much the same may be said of reference to
the balance, composition, proportions, etc., of a painting; but much the
same may not be said of certain references to the subject matter, of any
reference to the size, shape, effect on morals, etc., of a painting. Why is
this so? Is this so?

From *Philosophy and Education*, Israel Scheffler, ed., pp. 219-36. Copyright,
1958, by Allyn and Bacon, Inc., Boston. Reprinted by permission of the publisher.

I

Someone might say this: "If a painting were disorganized and had no redeeming features, one would not call it 'a good painting.' To understand the relevant uses of the phrase 'a good painting' is to understand, among other things, that to say 'P.'s painting is disorganized' may be to offer a reason in support of an unfavorable opinion of P.'s painting."

This won't do at all even though it is plainly true that someone would not—I would not—call a painting "a good painting" if it were disorganized and had no redeeming features.

Maybe certain persons use the phrase "a good painting" in such a way that they would call a painting "a good painting" even if it were disorganized and had no redeeming features. Maybe some or even many or most in fact use the phrase "a good painting" in a way that no painting is good if it is not a seascape. Many people probably use the phrase "a good painting" in many different ways.

It is true that I and my friends would not call a painting "a good painting" if it were merely disorganized, unredeemed. That is no reason why anyone should accept the fact that a painting is disorganized as a reason in support of an unfavorable opinion of it. To say one would not call it "a good painting" if it were disorganized and had no redeeming features is primarily a way of indicating how strongly one is committed to the acceptance of such a fact as a reason, it is a way of making clear precisely what attitude one has here: it does not show the attitude is reasonable.

Why use the phrase in one way rather than another? Why bother with organization? Why not concentrate on seascapes? on pictures of peasants? Is it merely a linguistic accident that one is concerned with organization? This is not a matter of words. (And this is not to say that the words do not matter: "That is a good painting" can be queried with "According to what standards?"; "That is a magnificent painting" cannot be so queried and neither can "That is an exquisite painting," ". . . a splendid painting," etc.)

Only some of the remarks sometimes made while discussing a work of art are reasons in support of a critical evaluation of the work: to evaluate a work one must understand it, appreciate it; much of what is said about a work is directly relevant only to an appreciation of it.

Any fact is relevant to an appreciation of a work if a knowledge of it is likely to facilitate, to enhance, the appreciation of the work. A critic may direct attention to many different facts: the role of the supporting continuo is the central point in Tovey's discussion of Haydn's chamber music. Tovey points out that the supporting continuo was used to fill a crucial gap in the musical structure:

The pioneers of instrumental music in the years 1600-20 showed an accurate instinct by promptly treating all groups of instruments as consisting of a firm bass and a florid treble, held together by an unobtrusive mass of harmony in the middle. Up to the death of Handel and beyond, throughout Haydn's boyhood, this harmonic welding was entrusted to the continuo player, and nobody ever supposed that the polyphony of the "real" orchestral parts could, except accidentally or by way of relief, sound well without this supplement.[1]

When Tovey then says: in the later chamber music Haydn abandoned the use of a supporting continuo, he is saying something of relevance to an appreciation of any one of Haydn's chamber works: who can then listen to an early Haydn quartet and not hear it in a new way? The supporting continuo acquires a new prominence in the structure of the whole work. But the end product of this process of re-examining the interrelations of the various parts, to which one has been impelled by the critic's information, is a keener feeling for the texture of the whole.

This is one instance of how historical information can be of value in directing and enlightening the appreciation of a work; there are others: the music of Bach has been compared with that of Schütz, Donne's poetry with that of Cavalcanti, Matisse's work with Egyptian wall paintings. Comparative studies are useful; they provide fresh means of directing and arousing interest in certain aspects of the works under consideration. When a critic shows that work *A* is intimately related or similar in some important respects to work *B*, this is of interest not only in that one is then aware of this particular relation between *A* and *B*, but more significantly, one may then see both *A* and *B* in a different way: *A* seen in the light of its relation to *B* can acquire a new lucidity.

Any fact may be relevant to an appreciation of a work, may thereby be indirectly relevant in evaluating it. Presumably every fact directly relevant in evaluating the work is also relevant to an appreciation of it. But the converse is not true, e.g. that the work was executed while the artist was in Rome may be relevant to an appreciation of it but is likely to be relevant in no other way to an evaluation of it. What further requirements must a fact relevant to an appreciation of a work satisfy if it is also to be relevant in evaluating the work?

To say a painting is a good painting is here simply to say it is worth contemplating. (Strictly speaking, this is false but for the time being I am not concerned to speak strictly, but only for the time being. See II below.) Nothing can be a reason why the painting is good unless it is a reason why the painting is worth contemplating. (One can add: for its own sake, but that is redundant.)

Suppose we are in a gallery with a friend looking at P.'s painting; he somewhat admires the work, is inclined to claim that it is good; we wish to deny this, to claim it is a bad painting. We might attempt to support our counter claim by saying "The painting is clearly disorganized," offering this as a reason in support of our opinion of the work.

Saying this to him would be a way of drawing his attention to the organization of the painting, to the lack of it, a way of pointing to this aspect of the painting, saying "Notice this, see the disorder," not merely this, of course, but at least this.

> ("Here you see a single great curving diagonal holds together in its sweep nearly everything in the picture. And this diagonal is not built up by forms that are at the same distance from the eye. The forms are arranged so as to lead the eye gradually backwards until we pass out of the stable into the open air beyond. Here . . ."[2]

said Roger Fry, discussing a painting by Rubens, focusing the listening eye on the single great curving diagonal, drawing it back and forth across the picture plane, levelling the attention, directing it freely throughout the painting.)

This pointing is a fundamental reason why "The painting is clearly disorganized" is a reason, and the fact that it is indicates why "The work was executed while the artist was in Rome," ". . . conforms to the artist's intentions," ". . . is liked by Bernard," even though possibly relevant to an appreciation of the work, are not reasons why the painting is good or bad; for all this is not directly relevant. One cannot contemplate the fact that the work was done while the artist was in Rome in the painting; this is not an aspect of the painting, not a characteristic of it which one can either look at or look for. Suppose one were told: "Notice that the work was done while the artist was in Rome," one could only reply: "But what am I supposed to look at?"

Of course one could do this: I say to you "Think of Rome; then look for things in the picture that will fit in with what you've just been thinking"; you might find a great deal in some pictures, little in others. If I want you to make out a lion in the picture which you seem not to have seen I could say this: "Remember the work was done in Africa," "The artist was much interested in animals," etc. So it won't do, in one sense, to say that remarks like "Notice that the work was done while the artist was in Rome" are not reasons because they do not direct or guide one in the contemplation of the work. But in another sense it is obvious that such remarks do not guide or direct one in the contemplation of a work; to suppose that they do is to suppose certain familiar locutions to be signifying in somewhat extraordinary ways.

What is important here is this: one looks at paintings; nothing can be a reason why a painting is good or bad unless it is concerned with what can be looked at in the painting, unless it is concerned with what can, in some sense, be seen.

If it be asked: "Why insist on this? How does this show that 'The work was done while the artist was in Rome' is not a reason why the painting is good?," a sufficient answer is: only in this way can the reason direct or guide one in the contemplation of the work; a "reason" that failed to do this would not be worth asking for, not worth giving; there would be no reason to be concerned with such a "reason."

But this is not to say that "The work was done while the artist was in Rome," ". . . is liked by Bernard," etc., are necessarily, apart from questions of appreciation, altogether irrelevant; these matters may in many ways be indirectly relevant to an evaluation of a work.

That the work was done while the artist was in Rome, is liked by Bernard, was done in the artist's old age, is detested by people of reputed good taste . . . may be indications, signs, that it is a poor work; these may be very good and important reasons to suppose the work is defective. It is for such reasons as these that one decides not to see a certain exhibition, not to read a certain book, not to hear a certain concert. But such facts as these do not in themselves constitute reasons why the painting is a poor work: indications or signs are never reasons why the painting is good or bad, but at best only reasons to suppose it is good or bad. The fact that *C* cannot remember *D*'s name is often an indication or a sign of the fact that *C* dislikes *D*; it is a reason to suppose *C* dislikes *D*; in odd cases it may also be a reason why *C* dislikes *D* in that it is a contributing cause of the dislike: an indication or a sign is a reason why only when it is a cause. But one is not here concerned with causes: "What causes this to be a good painting?" has no literal meaning; "What makes this a good painting?" asks for the reason why it is a good painting, and this kind of question cannot be answered by citing indications or signs.

This pointing is not the only reason why certain facts are, and others are not, reasons why a painting is good or bad: "The painting is a seascape" points to a characteristic of the painting, directs one's attention to certain features of the work; for saying this to him could be a way of saying "Notice this, see that it is a seascape," yet this is not a reason why the painting is either good or bad.

To say to him "The painting is a seascape" could be a way of directing his attention to the subject matter of the painting, indicating that the painting was of a certain kind. While contemplating a painting one may consider what kind of work it is, who painted it, what kind of organization it has, what kind of subject matter (if any), what kind of pigmentation, etc. To learn that a painting is by a certain artist, has a certain kind of organization, subject matter, pigmentation, etc., may be relevant to an appreciation of the work; it may enable one to recognize, discern, make out, identify, label, name, classify things in the painting, aspects of the painting; such recognition, identification, classification, may be important in the appreciation of a painting; one who failed to recognize or discern or make out the man in Braque's *Man with a Guitar*, the printed letters in a cubist painting, a horse in *Guernica*, would be apt to misjudge the balance and organization of these works, would fail to appreciate or understand these works, would be in no position to evaluate them.

That a painting is of a certain kind may be an excellent reason to suppose it is good or bad. But is it ever a reason why the painting is good or bad? Is the fact that the painting is of a certain kind directly relevant to the contemplation of the painting? Does "The painting is a seascape" direct or guide one in the contemplation of the painting?

Being of a certain kind matters here primarily in connection with the recognition, identification, classification, etc., of various elements of the work. Shall we then say: "Contemplating the subject matter of a painting (or its organization, or its pigmentation, etc.) is not merely a matter of recognizing, identifying, the subject matter, not merely a matter of labelling, naming, classifying"?

That is not enough; it is not that contemplating a painting is not merely a matter of this or that, it is not a matter of recognizing or identifying or classifying or labelling at all.

Contemplating a painting is something one does, something one may be engaged in; one can and does say things like "I am contemplating this painting," "I have been contemplating this painting for some time." But in this sense, recognizing is not something one does; even though it may be true that while contemplating a painting (which has subject matter) I may recognize, or fail to recognize, or simply not recognize, the subject matter of the painting, it is never true that I am recognizing the subject matter; and this is a way of saying one cannot say "I am recognizing the subject matter of this painting," or "I am recognizing this painting," or "I have been recognizing it for some time," etc.

Recognition is like an event, whereas contemplation is like an activity (much the same may be said of identification, classification, etc., in certain relevant senses, though not in all senses, of these terms) ; certain events may occur during the course of an activity, recognition may or may not take place during the course of contemplation. While contemplating Braque's *Man with a Guitar* one may suddenly (or slowly and at great length) recognize, discern, make out, a figure in the painting; analytical cubistic works often offer such difficulties. If on Monday one recognizes a figure in the Braque painting, on Tuesday there is ordinarily no question of recognition; it has occurred, is over and done with, for the time being; "I recognize it every time I see it" would be sensible if each time it appeared in a fresh disguise, if I suffered from recurrent amnesia, if it appeared darkly out of a haze. (In the sense in which one can speak of "recognizing" the subject matter of an abstract or semi-abstract work, one often cannot speak of "recognizing" the subject matter of a characteristic Chardin still-life: one can see, look at, study, examine the apple in the Chardin painting, but there is not likely to be any "recognition.")

This is not to deny that if a work has recognizable elements, recognition may occur during the course of contemplation, nor that if it does occur then the contemplation of the work is, for some people at least, likely to be somewhat enhanced. If recognition is ever a source of delight, that is certainly true; this, too, would be true: the second time one contemplates the work the contemplation of it may be less worthwhile. But whether this is true or not does not really matter here. It appears to be of interest owing only to an ambiguity of "contemplating."

"Contemplating" may be employed to refer simply to contemplating, or to someone's contemplation of a work at a certain time and place and under certain conditions. "In contemplating the work one attends to the organization" is about contemplating, about what one is doing in contemplating the work; to speak of "contemplating a work," or of "the contemplation of a work," is a way of referring only to certain aspects of one's contemplation of a work at a certain time and place and under certain conditions; it is a way of abstracting from considerations of person, place and time. "In contemplating the work one recognizes a figure in the foreground" is not about contemplating the work; it is not about what one is doing in contemplating the work; it is about something like an event that may occur while someone is contemplating the work for the first or second time under certain conditions. (Contrast "In walking one's leg muscles are continually being tensed and relaxed" with "In walking one finds an emerald.")

To say "Since the work has recognizable elements, recognition is likely to occur while contemplating the work and thus the contemplation of the work will be enhanced" would not be to refer to the contemplation of the work, it would not be to abstract from considerations of time; for it is not the contemplation of the work that would be enhanced, but only and merely the contemplation of the work on that particular occasion when recognition occurred. It is for this reason the fact that the work has recognizable elements—and thus admits of the possibility of recognition occurring during the course of contemplation, so enhancing the contemplation—is not a reason why the work is worth contemplating. To say "The work is worth contemplating," or "Contemplating the work is worthwhile," is here and ordinarily to speak of contemplating the work, it is here and ordinarily to abstract from considerations of person, place and time.

Were *Guernica* hung in Hell, contemplating it would hardly be worthwhile, would there be altogether tedious; yet it is not the work that would be at fault, rather the contemplation of the work in the galleries of Hell. But whether this would be the case has no bearing on whether *Guernica* is worth contemplating. It would ordinarily be at best foolish to reply to "*Guernica* is well worth contemplating" by asking "When?" or "Where?" or even "For whom?" That a certain person, at a certain time and place, finds *Guernica* not worth contemplating may be a slight reason to suppose *Guernica* is not worth contemplating, but it is not a reason why the work is not worth contemplating. If one knows that no one ever has found, or ever will find, *Guernica* worth contemplating, one has excellent reason to suppose *Guernica* is not worth contemplating; one can be absolutely sure it is not worth contemplating; yet this is not even the most trifling reason why *Guernica* is not worth contemplating. This does not ever entitle anyone to say "I know *Guernica* is not worth contemplating." All this is but an elaborate way of saying that in saying "The work is worth contemplating" one is abstracting from considerations of person, place and time.

What has been said of "recognition" could be said, in one way or another, of "identification," "classification," "labelling," "naming," etc.; thus identification, as well as recognition, may occur during the course of contemplation, may enhance the contemplation, is over and done with after a time. But this is never a reason why the painting is good or bad. If recognition, identification, classification, etc. all fail, as they do in fact all fail, to be such a reason, and if nothing can be such a reason unless it is a fact about the work that directs or guides one in the contemplation of the work—thus comparisons, associations, etc., are out of order—it follows that the fact that a work is of a certain kind is also incapable of being a reason why the work is worth contemplating. "There can be no objective rule of taste by which what is beautiful may be defined by means of concepts," said Kant,[3] and he was right (but for the wrong reasons).

Let it be clear that nothing has been said to deny that one can be concerned only with recognition, or identification, or classification, or comparisons, etc., when contemplating paintings; one can treat a painting in the way an entomologist treats a specimen spider, or be concerned only with puzzle pictures, with conundrums. Nor has it been maintained that to say "The work is worth contemplating" is necessarily to abstract from considerations of person, place, and time; that this is what is here and ordinarily intended in speaking of "contemplating a painting" is primarily (though not exclusively) a verbal point and does not signify. There are other ways of speaking: a person may choose to say "The work is worth contemplating" and abstract only from considerations of person, or of place, or of time, or not at all. But if so, he cannot then say what one now wants to say and does say about paintings; for if a person fails or refuses to abstract from such considerations at all, it will be impossible either to agree or disagree with him about the worth of paintings; refusing to abstract from considerations of person, place, and time is tantamount to refusing ever to say, as one now says, "The work is worth contemplating," but insisting always on saying things like "The work is worth contemplating for me, here and now," or ". . . for him, yesterday, at two o'clock," etc. One can speak in this way if one chooses; one can do what one wills with paintings. But none of this has anything to do with art.

To state that a painting is a seascape, if it is simply to state that the work is of a certain kind, is not to state a reason why it is good or bad; for that the painting is of a certain kind cannot be such a reason. What can?

Contrast "The painting is a seascape" with "The painting is disorganized." To say the former to someone could be a way of directing his attention to the subject matter of the painting, indicating that it had a certain kind of subject matter; to say the latter not only could but would be a way of directing his attention to the organization of the painting, but it would not be indicating that it had a certain kind of organization.

The sense of "organization" with which one is here primarily concerned is that in which one can say of any painting "Notice the organization" without thereby being committed to the view that the painting is in fact organized; one can and does say things like "The main fault to be found with Pollock's paintings is in the organization: his work is completely disorganized." (Just so one can on occasion say "Notice the balance" of a certain painting, and yet not be committed to saying the painting is balanced.) Every work has an organization in the sense that no matter what arrangement there may be of shapes, shades, etc., there is necessarily a particular configuration to be found in the painting. In this sense, the organization is an aspect, a feature, of every painting; something that may be contemplated, studied, and observed, in every painting.

There are various kinds of organization, for the organization of a work is something which may be described, classified, analyzed:

> The chief difference between the classical design of Raphael and the Baroque lay in the fact that whilst the artists of the high Renaissance accepted the picture plane and tended to dispose their figures in planes parallel to that—Raphael's cartoons, for instance, almost invariably show this method—the Baroque designers disposed their figures along lines receding from the eye into the depths of the picture space.[4]

"Horizontally, crossing the picture plane," or "Primarily rectangular," or "Along a single curving diagonal," could be answers to the question "What kind of organization does it have?" in a way that "Organized" or "Disorganized" could not. "Organized" and "Disorganized" are more like states than like kinds of organization ("organized" is more like "happy" than like "healthy," and more like "healthy" than like "human").

Yet this is not to deny what cannot be denied, that a sensible answer to "What kind of painting is it?" might be "A fairly well organized seascape, somewhat reminiscent of the Maine coast." "What kind of painting is it?" is often a request not only to describe the painting, to identify it, name it, classify it, point out its similarities and dissimilarities to other paintings, but also to evaluate the painting, to say whether it is worth bothering with, etc.

But seascapes are a kind of painting in a way disorganized or organized paintings are not; crocodiles are a kind of animal in a way healthy animals are not: unlike "seascape" and "crocodile," "organized" and "healthy" admit of questions of degree; one can say "He is quite healthy," "It is somewhat disorganized," "It would be less well organized if that were done," etc.; there are and can be no corresponding locutions employing the terms "seascape" and "crocodile." (One could introduce the terms "seascapish" and "crocodilish," but this is to say: one could invent a use for them.) One cannot discriminate between seascapes on the basis of their being seascapes, whereas one can and does discriminate between disorganized paintings on the basis of their being disorganized, for some are more and some are less.

That "organized," and "disorganized," unlike "seascape," admit of questions of degree is important (thus Tolstoi, who knew what art was, and knowing crucified it, spoke of ". . . those infinitely minute degrees of which a work of art consists");[5] here it indicates that determining whether a painting is disorganized, unlike determining whether it is a seascape, is not a matter of recognition or identification, though it may, on occasion, presuppose such recognition or identification. In order to determine whether a painting is disorganized, it is necessary to contemplate the organization of the painting. To determine whether a painting is a seascape, it is sufficient to recognize or identify the subject matter of the work; it is not necessary to contemplate the subject matter. To say to someone "The painting is a seascape" could be a way of drawing his attention to the subject matter of the painting, but it would be a way of inviting recognition or identification of certain things in the painting, not a way of inviting contemplation of an aspect of the painting.

"Disorganized," unlike "seascape," reports on an aspect of the painting; one might also say: it refers to a point in a dimension, the particular dimension being that of organization; another point in this dimension is referred to by "clearly organized," another by "an incoherent organization," etc.; to say "The organization of the painting is defective," or "The painting has a defective organization," or "The painting is defectively organized," are ways—different ways—of attributing approximately the same location to the painting in the dimension of organization. To say "The painting is a seascape" is not to direct attention to a certain dimension, that of subject matter; it may direct attention to the subject matter, but not to the dimension of subject matter: such a dimension is found when one considers not the kind but the treatment or handling of subject matter (contrast "The painting is a seascape" with "The figures are too stiff, too impassive") ; for it does not refer to a point in that dimension; it does not locate the painting in that dimension. (Just so to say "The painting has a diagonal organization" is not to direct attention to a certain dimension.)

But not any report on any aspect of the painting can be a reason why the painting is good or bad; "The painting is quite green, predominantly green" reports on an aspect of the painting, yet it is not a reason why the work is good or bad.

To say "The painting is quite green" could be somewhat like saying "Notice the organization of the painting" for it could serve to direct attention to an aspect of the painting; but it is not apt to be the relevant kind of report on this aspect. It is not such a report if it does not lead one either to or away from the work: if it were a reason, would it be a reason why the painting is a good painting or a reason why the painting is a bad painting?

But it would not be correct to say it is never a report, in a relevant sense; it is not apt to be, but it might; if someone were to claim that a painting were good and if, when asked why, replied, "Notice the organization!" it could be clear he was claiming that the painting was organized, perhaps superbly organized, that the organization of the work was delightful, etc.; just so if he were to claim "The painting is quite green, predominantly green," it could be quite clear he was claiming that the greenness of the painting was delightful, that the work was "sufficiently green," etc. "The painting is quite green" would here be a report on an aspect of the painting, a report leading in one direction. Even so, it is not a reason why the painting is good or bad.

This is not to deny that someone might offer such a statement as the statement of a reason why the painting is good. Nor is it to deny that "The painting is quite green" has all the marks of such a reason: it points to the painting: it directs one's attention to an aspect of the painting, an aspect that can be contemplated; it reports on this aspect of the painting and thus directs one to the contemplation of the painting. It could be a reason why the painting is good. But it is not. Is it because one simply does not care whether the painting is quite green? because it makes no difference?

One would not ordinarily say to someone "The painting is clearly disorganized" unless one supposed he had somehow not sufficiently attended to the organization of the work. But more than this: ordinarily one would not attempt to draw his attention to the organization of the painting, to the lack of it, unless one took for granted that if he did sufficiently attend to the organization and did in fact find the work to be disorganized, he would then realize that the painting was indeed defective.

One sometimes takes for granted that the absence of organization in a painting, once it is attended to, will in fact make much difference to a person; that he will be less inclined and perhaps even cease to find the work worth contemplating. And this is in fact sometimes the case; what one sometimes takes for granted is sometimes so.

This is one reason that a reference to the organization of the work may be a reason, and why a reference to the greenness of the painting is not; one ordinarily neither finds nor takes for granted one will find the fact that the painting is or is not quite green will make any such difference.

Being green or not green is not likely to make any difference to anyone in his contemplation of the painting; but the same is not true of being huge, or of having a sordid subject. Suppose a work were three miles high, two miles long: one simply could not contemplate it; suppose the subject matter of a work were revolting; certainly many could not contemplate it; or again, what if one knew that contemplating a work would have an insidious and evil influence: could one, nonetheless, contemplate it calmly?

There are many factors that may prevent and hinder one from contemplating a work; there are also certain factors that may facilitate the contemplation of a work; e.g., figure paintings, the Italian treatment of the figure, Raphael's, Signorelli's, Piero's handling, smoothes the path of contemplation.

> Therefore the nude, and best of all the nude erect and frontal, has through all the ages in our world—the world descended from Egypt and Hellas—been the chief concern of the art of visual representation.[6]

One is inclined to contemplate the nude (though not the naked—there is a difference).

That a painting has revolting subject matter, may seduce the beholder, is too large, too small, etc., does make much difference, but a difference of a different kind. That a painting is too large is in fact a reason why the painting is not good; yet it is a reason of a different kind, for it is also a reason why the painting is not bad: that the painting is too large is not a reason why the contemplation of the work is not worthwhile; rather it is a reason why one cannot contemplate the painting, a reason why one simply cannot evaluate the work.

That a painting is not too large, not too small, is not apt to seduce and is even apt to improve one, has splendid subject matter, etc., are not, in themselves, or in isolation, reasons why a work is a good work, why the work is worth contemplating. Yet such factors as these, by rendering the work accessible to contemplation, can tend to enhance its value. (Memling's *Lady with a Pink* would be less lovely were it larger; *Guernica* would be less majestic were it smaller.) Such factors as these cannot stand alone; alone they are not reasons why the painting is a good painting. That the neighbouring woods are nearby does not prove them lovely, but if lovely, then by being nearby they are that much lovelier, and if ugly, that much uglier.

It is here, perhaps, that the locus of greatness, of sublimity, is to be found in art; a painting with a trivial subject, a shoe, a cabbage, may be a superb work, but its range is limited: even if it succeeds, it is not great, not sublime; and if it fails, its failure is of no consequence; it may be trivial, it may be delightful—nothing more. But a figure painting, Signorelli's Pan, was a great, a sublime painting; had it failed, its failure would have been more tragic than trivial.

Such factors as these often do make a difference, but unlike the fact that the work is well or poorly organized, they do not indicate that the work is or is not worth contemplating: they indicate only that if the work is worth contemplating, it will be well worth contemplating; and if it is not worth contemplating, then possibly it will be not merely not worth contemplating, but distressing.

One sometimes takes for granted that the presence or absence of organization will make a difference to the person. But what if it does not?

It is quite possible that it will not. It is possible that to some people it makes no difference at all whether a painting is disorganized. It may even be that some people prefer what are in fact disorganized paintings (though they might not call them "disorganized"). Perhaps some people greatly admire quite green paintings; the fact that a painting is or is not quite green will make much difference to them.

Someone might now want to say this: "even though you may happen to like a disorganized painting at a time, you won't like it after a time; disorganized paintings do not wear well." Or this: "Even though you may happen to like a disorganized painting, your liking of it will interfere with and narrow the range of your appreciation of many other paintings." Or even this: ". . . your liking of it is unlike that of someone who likes an organized painting; for such a person will not only like it longer, but will like it in a different and better way: 'not merely a difference in quantity, but a difference in quality.' Thus the satisfaction, the value, he finds in contemplating an organized painting is unlike and better than that you find in contemplating a disorganized painting."

It is sometimes true that disorganized paintings do not wear well, but it sometimes is not true; some people persist in liking unlikable paintings. Will perseverance do to transmute vice to virtue? It is sometimes true that a taste for disorganized paintings is apt to interfere with and narrow the range of one's appreciation of other paintings; but is it not likely that one who likes both organized and disorganized paintings will have the more catholic taste? Is it wise to be a connoisseur of wine and cut one's self off from the pleasures of the poor? There is a sense in which it is certainly true that the satisfaction one finds in contemplating an organized painting is unlike and superior to that one finds in contemplating a disorganized painting, but in the sense in which it is, it is here irrelevant: for of course it is certainly true that the satisfaction and value found in connection with a good painting is superior to that found in connection with a bad painting—this of course being a necessary statement. But apart from the fact that the satisfaction found in connection with a good painting is of course superior to that found in connection with a bad painting, what reason is there to suppose in fact—and not merely of course—this is the case? I find no satisfaction in connection with a bad painting, so how shall I compare to see which is superior?

One sometimes says: "Last year I found satisfaction in connection with what I now see to be a bad painting. Now I can see that my satisfaction then was inferior to my satisfaction now found in connection with a good painting." So you might predict to someone: "Just wait! Cultivate your taste and you will see that the satisfaction found in connection with good-*A* will be superior to the satisfaction, value, you now find in connection with bad-*B*."

And what if he does not? (Is it not clear that here aesthetics has nothing to do with consequences?) A man might say: "I find the very same kind of satisfaction in this 'disorganized' painting that you find in that 'organized' one: I too am greatly moved, greatly stirred. You may say of course your satisfaction, the value you find, is superior to mine; in fact it is not." He might be lying, but could he be mistaken?

There is then an inclination to say this: "If being organized or being disorganized does make much difference to a person then for him it is a reason, whereas if it does not make any such difference, it is not." This would be to say that instead of speaking of "the reasons why the painting is good," one would have to speak of "his reasons why" and "my reasons why" and "your reasons why" if one wished to speak precisely. This will not do at all.

I or you or he can have a reason to suppose (think, believe, etc.) the work is worth contemplating; but neither I nor you nor he can have a reason why the work is worth contemplating; anyone may know such a reason, discover, search for, find, wonder about such a reason, but no one can ever have such a reason; even when one has found such a reason, one can only point to it, present it, never appropriate it for one's own; "What are your reasons?" makes sense in reply to "I believe it is worth contemplating," but it has no literal sense if asked of "I know it is worth contemplating." "My reasons why the work is worth contemplating . . . ," "The reason for me the work is worth contemplating . . . ," are also here without relevant literal meaning.

(It would be absurd to describe this fact by saying that what is a reason for me must be a reason for everyone else—as though what no one ever could own must therefore be owned by all alike. What one could say here is that a reason must be as abstract as the judgment it supports.)

If being organized or being disorganized does make much difference to a person then, not "for him" nor "in that case," nor "then and there," it is apt to be a reason, for in that case, then and there, one can forget about him then and there; whereas if it does not make any such difference then, for him, in that case, then and there, it is not apt to be a reason, for in that case, then and there, one cannot forget about him then and there.

To say "The work is worth contemplating" is here and ordinarily to abstract from considerations of person; but such abstraction is, as it were, a minor achievement, an accomplishment possible only when there either is or can be a community of interest. I can ignore the ground I walk on so long as it does not quake. This fact cannot be ignored: contemplating a painting is something that people do, different people.

Paradise gardens are not ever simply a place (one could not be there not knowing it, and it is in part because I know I am not there that I am not there) ; not being simply a place, paradise gardens are proportioned to everyman's need, even though these requirements may at times be incompatible. But these lesser perfections that paintings are are less adaptable, answer only to some men's need.

Reasoning about works of art is primarily a social affair, an attempt to build and map our common Eden; it can be carried on fruitfully only so long as there is either a common care or the possibility of one. But Kant was wrong in saying aesthetic judgments presuppose a common sense: one cannot sensibly presuppose what is often not the case. A community of interest and taste is not something given, but something that can be striven for.

II

And now I can be more precise, and that is to say, more general, for we speak of "good poems," "good quartets," "good operas," etc., as well as "good painting." But the problem is always the same. A good anything is something that answers to interests associated with it. In art, this is always a matter of performing certain actions, looking, listening, reading, etc., in connection with certain spatio-temporal or temporal entities, with paintings, poems, musical compositions, etc.

Formulaically, there is only this: a person p_i, performs an action, a_i, in connection with an entity, c_i, under conditions, c_i; e.g. George contemplates Fouquet's *Madonna* in the gallery at Antwerp. e_i is good if and only if the performance of the relevant a_i by p_i under c_i is worthwhile for its own sake. To state a reason why e_i is good is simply to state a fact about e_i in virtue of which the performance of the relevant a_i by p_i under c_i is worthwhile for its own sake.

Someone says, pointing to a painting, "That is a good painting." There is (at least) a triple abstraction here, for neither the relevant persons, nor actions, nor conditions, have been specified. Is it any wonder we so often disagree about what is or is not a good painting.

Persons: George and Josef disagree about a Breughel. Say Josef is color-blind. Then here I discount Josef's opinion: I am not color-blind. But if they were concerned with a Chinese ink drawing, color-blindness would be irrelevant. George is not a peasant, neither does he look kindly on peasants, not even a Breughel painting of peasants. Well, neither do I, so I would not, for that reason, discount his opinion. Josef is a prude, that is, a moralist, and he looks uncomfortably at the belly of a Titian nude. I would discount his opinion, for I am not. (This is why it is horrible nonsense to talk about "a competent observer" in matters of art appreciation: no one is competent or not competent to look at the belly of a Titian nude.) But George has no stomach for George Grosz's pictures of butchers chopping up pigs, and neither do I, so I would not discount his opinion there. George has a horror of churches: his opinion of stained glass may be worthless. Not having an Oedipus complex, George's attitude towards Whistler's Mother is also eccentric. And so on.

If e_i is good then the performance of a_i by p_i under c_i is worthwhile for its own sake. But this obviously depends on the physical, psychological, and intellectual, characteristics of p_i. If p_i and p_j are considering a certain work then the relevant characteristics of p_i depend on the particular p_j, e_i, a_i and c_i involved. It is worse than useless to stipulate that p_i be "normal": what is that to me if I am not normal? and who is? To be normal is not necessary in connection with some limited works, and it is not enough to read *Finnegan's Wake*. Different works make different demands on the person. The popularity of "popular art" is simply due to the fact that it demands virtually nothing: one can be as ignorant and brutish as a savage and still deal with it.

But there is no point in worrying about persons for practically nothing can be done about them. Actions are what matter. Art education is a matter of altering the person's actions, and so, conceivably the person.

Actions: here we have a want of words. Aestheticians are fond of "contemplate," but one cannot contemplate an opera, a ballet, a cinema, a poem. Neither is it sensible to contemplate just any painting, for not every painting lends itself to contemplation. There is only one significant problem in aesthetics, and it is not one that an aesthetician can answer: given a work e_i under conditions c_i what are the relevant a_i? An aesthetician cannot answer the question because it depends on the particular e_i and c_i: no general answer exists.

Roughly speaking, I survey a Tintoretto, while I scan an H. Bosch. Thus I step back to look at the Tintoretto, up to look at the Bosch. Different actions are involved. Do you drink brandy in the way you drink beer? Do you drive a Jaguar XKSS in the way you drive a hearse?

A generic term will be useful here: "aspection," to aspect a painting is to look at it in some way. Thus to contemplate a painting is to perform one act of aspection; to scan it is to perform another; to study, observe, survey, inspect, examine, scrutinize, etc., are still other acts of aspection. There are about three hundred words available here in English, but that is not enough.

Generally speaking, a different act of aspection is performed in connection with works belonging to different schools of art, which is why the classification of style is of the essence. Venetian paintings lend themselves to an act of aspection involving attention to balanced masses; contours are of no importance, for they are scarcely to be found. The Florentine school demands attention to contours, the linear style predominates. Look for light in a Claude, for color in a Bonnard, for contoured volumes in a Signorelli.

George and Josef are looking at Van der Weyden's *Descent from the Cross*. Josef complains, "The figures seem stiff, the Christ unnatural." George replies, "Perhaps. But notice the volumes of the heads, the articulation of the planes, the profound movement of the contours." They are not looking at the painting in the same way, they are performing different acts of aspection.

They are looking at the *Unicorn Tapestry*. Josef complains "But the organization is so loose!" So Spenser's great *Faerie Queene* is ignored because fools try to read it as though it were a sonnet of Donne, for the *Queene* is a medieval tapestry, and one wanders about in it. An epic is not an epigram.

George says "A good apple is sour" and Josef says "A good apple is sweet," but George means a cooking apple, Josef means a dessert apple. So one might speak of "a scanning-painting," "a surveying-painting," etc., and just so one speaks of "a Venetian painting," "a sonata," "a lyric poem," "an improvisation," etc.

If e_i is good then the performance of a_i by p_i under c_i is worthwhile for its own sake. If p_i performs a_i under c_i in connection with e_i, whereas p_j performs a_j under c_i in connection with e_i, p_i and p_j might just as well be looking at two different paintings (or poems, etc.). It is possible that the performance of a_i under c_i in connection with e_i is worthwhile for its own sake, while the performance of a_j under c_i in connection with e_i is not worthwhile for its own sake.

There is no easy formula for the relevant actions. Many are possible: only some will prove worthwhile. We find them by trial and error. The relevant actions are those that prove worthwhile in connection with the particular work, but we must discover what these are.

Imagine that *Guernica* had been painted in the time of Poussin. Or a Mondrian. What could the people of the time have done with these works? The question the public is never tired of asking is: "What am I to look at? look for?" and that is to say: what act of aspection is to be performed in connection with e_i?

Before 1900, El Greco was accredited a second-rate hack whose paintings were distorted because he was blind in one eye. Who bothered with Catalonian frescoes? The Pompeian murals were buried.

Modern art recreates the art of the past, for it teaches the critics (who have the ear of museum and gallery directors who pick the paintings the public consents to see) what to look for and at in modern works. Having been taught to look at things in a new way, when they look to the past, they usually find much worth looking at, in this new way, that had been ignored. So one could almost say that Lehmbruck did the portal of Chartres, Daumier gave birth to Hogarth, and someone (unfortunately) did Raphael in.

Artists teach us to look at the world in new ways. Look at a Mondrian, then look at the world as though it were a Mondrian and you will see what I mean. To do this, you must know how to look at a Mondrian.

And now I can explain why a reason why a work is good or bad is worth listening to. One reason why a (good) Mondrian is good is that it is completely flat. If that sounds queer to you, it is because you do not know how to look at a Mondrian. And that is why the reason is worth considering.

A reason why e_1 is good is a fact about e_1 in virtue of which the performance of a_1 by p_1 under c_1 is worthwhile for its own sake. So I am saying that the fact that the Mondrian is completely flat indicates that the performance of a_1 by p_1 under c_1 is worthwhile in connection with the Mondrian painting. In telling you this, I am telling you something about the act of aspection to be performed in connection with the work, for now you know at least this: you are to look at the work spatially, three-dimensionally. (Without the painting to point to, I can only give hints: look at it upside down! Right side up, each backward movement into space is counterbalanced by an advancing movement. The result is a tense, dynamic, and dramatic picture plane held intact by the interplay of forces. Turn the painting upside down and the spatial balance is destroyed: the thing is hideous.)

Reasons in criticism are worthwhile because they tell us what to do with the work, and that is worth knowing. Yao Tsui said:

> It may seem easy for a man to follow the footsteps of his predecessors, but he does not know how difficult it is to follow the movements of curved lines. Although one may chance to measure the speed of the wind which blows through the Hsiang Valley, he may have difficulty in fathoming the water-courses of the Lü-liang mountain. Although one may make a good beginning by the skilful use of instruments, yet the ultimate meaning of an object may remain obscure to him until the end. Without knowing the song completely, it is useless to crave for the response of the falling dust.

Notes

1. *Essays and Lectures on Music,* pp. 3-4.
2. *French, Flemish and British Art,* p. 125.
3. *Critique of Aesthetic Judgment,* Bk. I, sec. 17.
4. R. Fry, *op. cit.,* p. 22.
5. *What is Art?,* Oxford Univ. Press, p. 201.
6. B. Berenson, *Aesthetics and History,* pp. 81-82.

WILLIAM G. LYCAN
and PETER K. MACHAMER

A Theory of Critical Reasons

I N THIS ESSAY we shall put forward a preliminary account of the logic and function of reasons in art criticism.[1] We intend to apply it, in passing, to several traditional questions of aesthetics, for example, those of the publicity of reasons, the role of universalizability in the logic of art, and the usefulness of the "aesthetic"/"nonaesthetic" distinction.

In section one we explicate and criticize two views that have elicited a good deal of comment: Paul Ziff's[2] and Arnold Isenberg's.[3] Ziff engages in a *logical* treatment of the way in which reason statements are related to critical value judgments; Isenberg, by contrast, views that same relation *psychologically.* Each of their essays contains many isolated claims that are both true and important, but we find that neither author is able to explain the importance of his statements in any unified way. In our discussion we shall point out how both Isenberg and Ziff falter at crucial junctures in their own attempts to account for what goes on in art criticism; we hope to show later, though, exactly what is good about each article, and give the reasons why.

In section two we begin to expound our own view of critical reasons by drawing a parallel between their logic and that of "criteria" in everyday life. This parallel sets the stage for section three, in which we spell out our account schematically. We introduce the notion of a "continuum" of reasons,[4] and bring out the way in which we can put the positive points made by Ziff and Isenberg into a coherent pattern. In terms of the "continuum" idea and the related concept of "detachability," we offer our embryonic solutions to the more general problems set earlier. In section four we put more flesh on our theory by making some remarks on the relation between *teaching* and *justifying* in art.

From *Language and Aesthetics: Contributions to the Philosophy of Art*, Edited by Benjamin R. Tilghman, pp. 87-112. Reprinted by permission of the Regents Press of Kansas.

We wish to note that while we restrict our discussion to the criticism of paintings, we are not necessarily left open to the "one-sided diet of cases" charge. Our examples of painting and of criticism have been chosen at random from a large selection; the reader may substitute his own examples if he likes.

I

Ziff distinguishes between *appreciating* and *evaluating* a painting (his point here is echoed by Isenberg, who talks about the "difference between *explaining* and *justifying* a critical response"), and goes on to try to mark off that class of facts that are relevant to evaluation. Any fact about a painting can be relevant to our appreciation of it; but, he feels, only some kinds of facts are (logically speaking) admissible as bona-fide reasons why a painting is good. His argument may be paraphrased as follows:

A_1 To call a painting "good" is, roughly, just to say that the painting is "worth contemplating" (for its own sake).

A_2 An acceptable reason must direct the audience's attention, "directly guide one in the contemplation of the work." (This is a logical point: "a 'reason' that failed to do this would not be worth asking for, not worth giving; there would be no reason to be concerned with such a 'reason.'")

A_3 "Reason"-facts must be contemplable *"in the painting"*; they must be "concerned with what can, in some sense, be seen" (pp. 222-23).

This condition precludes our offering "———was done while the artist was in Rome" or "———conforms to the artist's intentions" or "——— is liked by Bernard" as a reason why the painting is worth contemplating. More generally, it rules out most, if not all, facts about size, subject matter, photographic accuracy, effect on morals, and so forth, as irrelevant to evaluation (although in some cases such considerations may be reasons why one cannot contemplate the work in question *at all*). And Ziff claims that contemplating never *essentially* involves recognizing, identifying, or classifying; so he adds, as another corollary to A^3, that recognitions, identifications, and classifications can never stand alone as reasons in themselves.

Ziff later puts his claim "formulaically":

A_4 "A person, p_i, performs an action, a_i, in connection with entity, e_i, under conditions, c_i. . . . To state a reason why e_i is good is simply to state a fact about e_i in virtue of which the performance of the relevant a_i by p_i under c_i is worthwhile for its own sake" (p. 233).

This seems right, but it gets us into boggier terrain. Ziff does not want to say that *any* fact that meets condition A_3 is a good "goodmaking" reason. A good reason must, in addition, "make a difference" to the critic's audience (p. 229). Have we any guarantee that the same fact "makes a difference" to one and all? Or that it ever will "make a difference" to everyone alike, even if we have all been educated in exactly the same way? The answer seems to be no, and this leaves Ziff with a residual logical gap between good reason and responsible evaluation. In trying to bridge it he hazards three more claims:

A_5 Reasons are not owned by or appropriate to isolated persons. The expression "reason *for me*" has not literal sense. "A reason must be as abstract [vis-à-vis persons] as the judgment it supports" (p. 232).

But

A_6 Since "reasoning about works of art is primarily a social affair," we can perform this abstraction successfully only if the possibility of a "community of interest and taste" fills in the background. ("It is worse than useless to stipulate that p_i be 'normal': what is that to me if I am not normal? and who is?" [p. 233].) Formula A_4 is a function of the personal characteristics of p_i. So in some sense a good reason must be "a reason for me and my friends."

A_7 Formula A_4 must also be relativized to the type of contemplation or "aspection" performed. A *good* reason indicates the most worthwhile aspective act (surveying, scanning, inspecting, scrutinizing, examining, and so forth, and so forth); and it will be understood qua reason if and only if the audience "knows how to look at" the work in question.

This A_7 is a very pregnant point, and we shall discuss it in some detail below. But first we shall outline what we find to be the principal deficiencies in Ziff's account, and then go on to see whether Isenberg fares any better.

We see no reason, first of all, why a fact must be something visible in the painting in order to be able to guide contemplation in an evaluative way. That a particular painting was done while the artist was in Rome may not per se be a reason why the painting is good, but a critic might well call attention to the fact in order to get his audience to see how well the artist has assimilated some aspect of style. Similarly, to say that artist *A* liked *B*'s work might easily be a way (in fact, the best way) of getting one's audience, if they are familiar with *A*, to see something evaluatively good about *B*. To say that Picasso found a forceful way of depicting the horror of the Spanish Civil War is certainly to guide contemplation of *Guernica*.

Now Ziff explicitly recognizes such facts as these, but he wants to say that each of the three "critical" statements we cite is (though relevant to appreciation) only "indirectly" relevant to evaluation (pp. 222-23). What he means by "indirectly" is not quite clear.[5] He seems to hold that such statements are, on closer scrutiny, logically superfluous to the critic's enterprise. The critic could just say, "Notice the influence of Michelangelo in *the solidity of his bodies,*" or, "See how similar Rubens's painting is to Titian's work in *the way they build up flesh out of color,*" or, "Look— the horror of the War! *the screaming, contorted horse,* etc.," dismissing the reference to the artist's geographical location or to his intentions or to his admirers as being purely pedagogical frosting. But it is not obvious to us that such a useful distinction can be made, at least in art criticism, between the method of teaching and the "descriptive" cash value of what is being taught. We shall argue in section three that although a distinction similar to Ziff's can perhaps be made out, it is neither critically nor philosophically crucial.

In any case, this move just will not work in the more central cases that Ziff himself picks out. A good icon is good, in a sense, just *because* it is small. Or *try* to imagine a 3" x 5" *Guernica*; Ziff is just wrong in saying that such a work would not be deficient insofar as it was too small. It is surely not true, moreover, that the possible effect of a painting upon someone's morals is necessarily, or even always, irrelevant to its worth (look at Clive Bell's use of the predicate "good taste" in his *An Account of French Painting*).[6] There is no quality that we can think of, in fact, that could not *conceivably* guide our contemplation of some painting or other. So we hold that Ziff's move from A_2 to A_3 is illicit and that A_3 is entirely too restrictive.

The second and most important difficulty is one that Ziff seems to recognize, but that he is not apparently inclined to do anything about. The logical lacuna mentioned above raises a dilemma for him: A_5 and A_6 are prima facie incompatible, and it is hard to see how he purports to escape self-contradiction. Are reasons public or are they not?

There is a strong temptation to say that by virtue of the logic of the word "because," or some such, good critical reasons must be universalizable over persons, period. ("Psychological" reasons need not be, of course, since the differences between persons are expressly part of their subject matter.) If we subscribe to this view, we must conclude that Ziff's distaste for peasants can explain, but cannot critically justify, his dislike of a Breughel painting, since he presumably would not accept the universalization "Any painting that depicts peasants has two strikes against it (from an objective critical point of view)." So, his "reason" is not a critical reason.

On the other hand, it is not so easy to be sure that he would reject the universalization. He does accept (albeit wrongly) a similar one concerning the depiction of shoes (p. 230). So it may be hard, in general, to use the Universalizability Principle *in vacuo* as a criterion of reasonhood.

Moreover, if the Principle is true, it is trivially so. This has led many philosophers to deny its usefulness in any context; Ziff would have to give a *further* reason why he would or would not accept some universalization, and it is this further reason that would be aesthetically crucial. Traditionally, it has also been maintained that universalizability has (pragmatically speaking) no substantial application to works of art, because their value lies largely in their "uniqueness," in their *difference* from other works. (Are there no conceivable cases in which a painting might be either good or bad, in part, *because* it portrayed peasants rather than, say, squires? The relevance of "————portrays peasants" is *entirely* dependent upon the particular painting under study.) So the Universalizability Principle demands more examination. We shall take it up again in section three.

Isenberg distinguishes, as we have said, between explaining and justifying one's liking of a painting. Explanation, he says, is psychological, while justification is normative and critical; an explanation involves a causal argument, while a justification is meant to be in a sense more universal ("We want him [the critic] to give us some reason to like it [the painting] too and are not concerned with the causes of what we may so far regard as his bad taste" [p. 332]). At the same time, however, Isenberg rejects the commonly held "Verdict-Reason-Norm" view. (This theory asserts in essence that a critical value claim or verdict is supported by a reason, which in turn must be supported by some generalized normative statement. This "norm" is said to be based on an inductive generalization which relates aesthetic qualities to people's aesthetic responses.) First he shows that even those philosophers who have tried to reject the notion of critical "norms" or standards have tended covertly to fall back on it at crucial points. So long as we have the idea that the invocation of a reason, R, is necessary for the validation of the verdict, V, he says that "we must assume *either* that R is perfectly arbitrary *or* that it presupposes and depends on some general claim" (p. 335). He therefore sets out to prove, more radically, that *"the truth of R never adds the slightest weight to V"* (p. 338).

He begins by quoting a passage from Goldscheider about *The Burial of Count Orgaz,* and then argues more or less as follows:

B_1 Goldscheider wants to convey to us "the idea of a certain quality" in the painting.

B_2 His passage claims importance for the presence of certain wavelike line groupings (wlg's).

B_3 We can verify the presence of these wlg's by ordinary perception.

But

B_4 We could draw isomorphic wlg's on a blackboard; we do not need Goldscheider to show us that "containing lines like these" is a quality of painting.

B_5 Goldscheider must be trying to point out *another* quality, different from the one suggested by his language. That is, he must be using his language to try to get us to see what he sees (and this cannot be merely the wlg's, which could be seen anywhere by anyone).

Isenberg expresses B_5 again by saying that the critic is giving us "directions for perceiving" by means of the idea he imparts, which idea cannot be put directly or literally (p. 336). The critic's meaning is thus "filled out" or "completed" by perception; perception is necessary for understanding what he says. It is this idea that leads Isenberg into the fundamentally true but overstated claim that "reading criticism, otherwise than in the presence, or with direct recollection, of the objects discussed is a blank and senseless employment" (p. 337).

This general idea of the critic's function as inducing a sameness of vision between himself and his audience is needed in order to account at all for Isenberg's strong statement that the truth of a reason never adds the slightest weight to a verdict; he can now hold that a reason does not indicate any conventionally describable quality the perception of which might induce us to assent to the verdict (p. 338). The critic, as it were, is not trying to point out qualities that we can then go and see, but is rather trying to draw our attention to something much more general (cf. pp. 341-43): what he is striving for is the inducement of a *way of perceiving* in his audience, a way that will vary from context to context. Thus Isenberg says that the meaning of a critical word is "never twice the same" (p. 339).

Isenberg admits (p. 341) that perhaps he overemphasizes the idea of the critic as teacher, as the psychologically illuminating conjurer whose words induce people to express the changes in their aesthetic attitudes by saying things like, "Yes, that's it; now I see it as it is meant to be." Nevertheless, he gives us no hint as to how this idea should be qualified. In fact, given the situation as Isenberg has set it up, leaving us with the problem of understanding how the concepts used in critical language are related to the percepts induced in a person apprehending a work of art, it would be hard to see how such qualification is possible. Isenberg, though he carefully distinguishes between the psychological and the logical or philosophic questions of criticism, might be characterized as holding a purely psychological view of the critic's function.

Isenberg's emphasis on the relation of concepts (in the critic's language) to "aesthetic" percepts (in the minds of the audience) brings out the main difference between himself and Ziff, who ultimately wants to say that this relation is a logical one. Following up our psychological interpretation of Isenberg, we might recast his point in the vernacular of the psychology of "set."[7] The critic, so construed, is concerned not with pointing out qualities in the work directly but with getting his audience to have the *proper* set for perceiving the work. His method involves using language "indirectly" (almost metaphorically), using words that only *seem* to be about qualities present in the work itself. So Isenberg's view here is quite the opposite of Ziff's.

And this point brings out clearly the dilemma that he has caught himself in. Is the conceptual language of the critic "indirect" because it fails to describe a visible quality in the work itself or because it fails to describe literally the quality of the desired perceptual response? Isenberg seems to have both in mind at various times. But if he means merely the former, then it is hard to see where perceptual response or "mental set" fits into the scheme; if he means the latter, as it seems more reasonable to suppose, then he finds himself in difficulty about the following two problems of privacy.

If it is not the critic's reason that supports his verdict, it must be something else, something that the critic "has in mind." If this something cannot directly and literally be communicated to his audience, how are we ever really to know that he has been successful in any given case, that the mysterious quality apprehended by the audience is exactly the same quality that he has in mind? If his perception of the quality is private in the way Isenberg seems to think, then we are deprived of any identity criteria for aesthetic qualities; therefore (on grounds similar to those appealed to by Wittgenstein in his attack on "private language"), it does not even make sense to suppose that a critic can ever be successful, *if* he is operating on the Isenberg model.

There is yet a further difficulty in that if our previous contention is correct, the Isenbergian critic's own claims about some aesthetic quality are logically immune to public corroboration; they cannot be corrected by, for example, another critic. And if this is so, then (again on Wittgensteinian grounds) the original critic *himself* cannot properly be said to know what quality it is that he has in mind. There is no possible check. On Isenberg's view, the possibility of communication itself, critical though it may be breaks down *tout court*.

Isenberg takes great pains to make the point that perception of the *painting* is needed in order for an audience to understand the critic's assertions. One does not perceive in order to judge the truth or falsity of what the critic has said (p. 336). But in discussing the Goldscheider example, Isenberg says that our perception "verifies" the presence of the critic's *aesthetic quality* as well as that of the easily describable configuration of lines. Now, verification that is unconcerned with judging the truth value of what is being verified is a most puzzling notion.

Perhaps Isenberg will want to evade our "privacy" criticisms by saying that we have complex but workable behavioral criteria for telling when an audience has got the right way of seeing, the right percept, just as we have criteria for talking about more everyday aspect-seeing. It is still quite clear when we reconstruct Isenberg's position along the lines of "set," that it is much too broad and allows for many possibilities that both he and we should like to rule out. Suppose that an audience is looking at Tintoretto's *Crucifixation* and wishes to know why it is said to be well balanced; suppose that someone happens by and (pointing to the painting) says, "Look! Christ looks like a hippie!" and that this utterance, for some bizarre neurophysiological reason, "sets" the audience for the appropriate aesthetic response to *Crucifixion*. By no imaginative stretch would one want to conclude here that the speaker was a critic, or that his language was critically communicative; yet on Isenberg's view one must conclude just that.

One final perplexing note: Isenberg remarks that even if the critic has induced in us the same vision as is in himself, this "may or may not be followed by agreement, . . . [by] a community of feeling which expresses itself in identical value judgments" (p. 336). But if such a possibility of conflicting evaluations is open even *after* there is agreement about the way in which a work is to be seen, what is there, on Isenberg's view, that needs to be added in order to produce evaluative agreement? He gives us no hint of an answer.

It is worth remarking that Isenberg's disdain for logical connections, his claim that reasons do not "support" or "add weight to" verdicts, may just as well be paraphrased as, "We don't ever really give *reasons* for our critical judgments." But it seems quite plain that we usually do; therefore, something must be wrong with Isenberg's presentation. We feel that almost all of the faults we have listed are manifestations of the same problem: There is in Isenberg a tendency to mix up the *grammar* of the critic's function with the psychology of the critical responses he induces (though Isenberg does make some good points in this latter regard). The nature of this actual conflation is hard to make clear, but it is exactly this murky area between the logical and the psychological that needs exploration.

It is just in this borderland that both Ziff's and Isenberg's insights fail them, and here, too, that many, if not most, of the crucial problems of aesthetics arise. All the difficulties of relating "facts" to "values," and those involved in spelling out Ziff's "appreciation"/"evaluation" distinction, are examples of this; the universalizability issue raised above is another.

A more specific example of such a problem: If we are to maintain a tentative distinction between de facto and de jure value judgments (or, as Ziff would have it, between appreciation and evaluation), we are more or less committed to saying that a "good" painting is one that *ought* to be liked. And this seems reasonable. Logically speaking, "good" and "worth contemplating (for its own sake)" and "ought to be liked when contemplated" are roughly equivalent predicates. But how can we give this "ought" any substance? Where does it get its force?

The easy answer is this: "A ought to like P" means, "If A doesn't like P, and if either P is a good painting or A admits that P is a good painting, then there must be some 'nonaesthetic' or 'psychological' fact about A which accounts for his dislike of P." For example, A's reason for not liking P_i might be that though P_i is an excellent painting on the whole, P_i is slightly garish, and slightly garish paintings are particularly repugnant to A. In such a case we want to say that A ought to like P_i nonetheless, that A is exaggerating the importance of garishness, that A has got things all out of proportion. The situation demands that there be some fact about A himself which, when conjoined with certain facts about the painting, explains A's *aesthetically* unaccountable violation of "A

ought to like P_i." Now, what does the "easy" analysis tell us about the meaning of this curious "ought"? Not much. It gives us neither an indication of what real force the "ought" is supposed to have (what the consequences of violating it are) nor an account of how "*A* ought to like *P*" fits into the broader outline of aesthetic theory. Moreover, the analysis seems to presuppose some acquaintance on our part with the extremely suspect "aesthetic"/"nonaesthetic" distinction. So the problem is to explain why the "easy" analysis appears to be so unsatisfactory. We shall offer our solution in section three.

II

In this section we shall compare the logic of critical reasons to that of criteria, in the hope of clearing the way for our more general claims to follow. (We allude here to the notion of a "criterion" invoked in Wittgenstein's remarks on "other minds" and later elucidated by Shoemaker, Coburn, Kenny, Pollock, and others.) We shall not argue in behalf of the criteriological view, but merely outline a few properties that Wittgensteinian criteria are supposed to have, and point out that critical reasons share them in a relaxed sort of way.

Suppose that X is a criterion of Y (where X and Y are states of affairs). Then, according to the criteria theorists,

C_1 X is a kind of *grounds* for the claim that Y obtains, and X's logical status is said to be "between" that of a constitutive or defining characteristic and that of an inductive correlate or "symptom."

C_2 It is necessarily true that whenever X obtains and circumstances are "normal," Y obtains as well. That is, if someone claims X-but-not-Y in some situation, then the onus is on *him* to show something extraordinary about the situation in order to make good his claim.

C_3 Criteria earn this privileged logical status, as asserted in C_1 and C_2, by playing an essential role in the way certain concepts are formed, or in the way certain words are learned. (If the criterial relation between pain behavior and pain did not usually hold, no one could have taught me to use the word "pain" as it is in fact used.)

C_4 A "symptom" is what we have (experimentally) *found to be* evidence for Y; a criterion, by contrast, is what we have (in ostensive definition) *learned to call* evidence for Y. The falling barometer and the water leaking through the ceiling have been found (inductively) to be signs of concurrent rain; but we have been taught to say, "It's raining" when it "looks [and feels] like *that* outside."

Wittgenstein was careful to point out that

C_5 Y is not deductively *entailed* by any disjunctive set of criteria X_i v X_j v . . . This would vitiate the special status that criteria are supposed to have.

One of the important consequences of C_4 is that

> C_6 criteria can give us certain knowledge that entitles us even to override a judgment about Y made by someone who (preanalytically) has "privileged access" to the truth of the matter. If a person claims to be in excruciating pain, but manifests no pain behavior *and yet* refuses to admit to radically successful stoicism or to the possibility that there is some disorder in his motor nerves, then I am warranted in contradicting him, in telling him that he is *not* in pain, even though he is supposed (by the skeptic anyway) to be the authority on this. To contradict him thus presumably involves my holding that for some reason he does not know how to use the word "pain" properly (more boldly, that he does not know what pain is), provided we have established his sincerity.

The corresponding facts about critical reasons seem to be these:

> C_1* A reason, R, is in some sense grounds for the value judgment V in question (*pace,* Isenberg); and R neither deductively entails V nor can be construed as being merely inductive evidence for V.
>
> C_2* If some critic admits (R) that a certain painting is well organized, and yet denies (V) that it is a good painting, then the onus is on him to show some independent reason why the painting is unworthy despite its good organization.
>
> C_3* If the relation between R and V did not usually hold, then our concept of V (say, of goodness) would not be the way it is at present— our "goodness"-grammar would have to be at least slightly readjusted.
>
> C_4* In our art education we have learned to call certain kinds of paintings good and to see what makes them good. This partially ostensive learning process is quite different from that through which we come to know that paintings that hang in the Louvre are usually good.
>
> C_5* No V is deductively entailed by any disjunctive set of reasons R_i v R_j v . . .
>
> C_6* In arguing with a less enlightened pupil, the critic can reach a point at which he is forced to conclude that the pupil just does not know what a good painting is. He must simply tell the truth, "Look *again,*" or better, "Go and take another course in art history."

With this logical parallel in mind, we may now proceed to the body of our theory of the critic's function.

III

A bit of terminology is suggested by our earlier remarks on Ziff's condition A_3. We supposed that he might hold that "————was painted while the artist was in Rome" could be replaced by "————was influenced by Michelangelo in *this* way" (or better, "————looks *this* way") without loss of critical efficacy. Let us express this claim by saying that the artist's presence in Rome is a "detachable" fact.[8] When a critic effects such a replacement (see also the ones we have attributed to Ziff on pp. 689–690), let us say that he has *detached* the fact in question. We do not want to be more precise about detachability until we have presented more of our own theory; we hope that the reader will get the idea from the examples for now. Later on we shall employ a grammatical way of marking off the concept.

Now we can offer a new, more liberal version of A_3: A fact can serve as a critical reason *why some painting, P, is good* if and only if it is *about P* and *nondetachable*. This is *not* to deny that detachable facts in a sense "encapsulate" good reasons, or that to call attention to a detachable fact may, in particular cases, be the *best* way to get one's audience to see something (we grant Isenberg this).

But even when these two qualifications have been added, our new condition must remain a very loose one. Why is this so? Isenberg would say that the critic can indicate the percept, the aesthetic quality that he wants his audience to see, in many different indirect ways depending on the context of discussion, and that the meaning of a word "is in critical usage never twice the same." A more realistic hint is given by F. A. Siegler in his critique of Isenberg's article:[9] he points out that the meanings of such "purely descriptive" terms as "short," "thin," and "dark" are entirely relative to the painting under consideration. (A line that is unequivocally thin in the context of one of Rubens's larger works would look quite gross if superimposed upon one of his watercolor studies.) And this point suggests that in order to know why a certain line is called "thin," we must understand at least a little of the background information about the painting in question (its size, its medium, perhaps something about its style). Much more generally, it seems to us that critical reasons vary in the degree to which their significance depends upon a context *larger* than that provided by the painting itself. Reasons in general cannot easily be categorized on this basis, but, we feel, the particular reasons in any individual piece of criticism can be arranged in a continuum of sorts. Let us look at a few examples of how reasons may be assigned places on such a continuum.

(1) In order to understand what it means to say that some painting, *P,* is *well organized* (in giving a reason why *P* is good), we need to know what kind of "organization" is appropriate to *P's* period and style; we need to have been educated, to have had many well-organized paintings of similar type pointed out to us. We need to know, in fact, what sorts of *reasons* properly support the judgment that such a painting is well organized. (2) Suppose a critic calls some feature of *P* "exquisite." What he means will be determined largely by whether it is a line or a color or a texture or whatever that the term is being applied to; but his audience will, in general, need less artistic training in order to understand him, since the word "exquisite" is more closely tied to more descriptive words (for example, "delicate" or "graceful") than is the term "well organized." Nonetheless, the audience may well ask *why* such and such

a line is exquisite, and the critic must cite more subreasons to explain this. So, in order to appreciate the statement that the line is exquisite, the audience still needs to understand (to have been taught) something about the artistic background of the term "exquisite." And they are taught this by being shown examples of delicate lines, graceful lines, and so forth. (3) Now let us take a detachable reason. By its very nature a detachable reason demands no artistic sophistication of one who would understand its meaning. One does not need to ask for a *critical* reason why the artist had such and such intentions, or why he went to Rome in the first place.

With these examples in mind, let us catalogue the general features which give a continuum its character. D_1: As the examples suggest, the higher a reason is on the continuum (let us hereafter say, "the more loaded it is"), the more context-dependent it is; the more artistic education is presupposed; the more one needs to know about the period, style, and medium of the painting in question; the more subreasons may be needed to support the original reason. A reason is located on the continuum, in short, according to how much critical and historical background one must have in order to *understand* it. At the very top of the continuum is, of course, "————is good" (or one of its superlatives), which is almost entirely context-dependent. "————is good" is not itself a reason why *P* is good; it requires the longest string of reasons in its support if the audience is to understand what it means *when applied to P*. Detachable reasons appear at the bottom of the continuum, since they are fully intelligible independent of one's artistic background. D_2: The more loaded a reason is, the more indefeasible it is as a reason why *P* is good. It is more difficult for a well-organized painting not to be good than it is for one merely containing exquisite lines, while it is not notoriously hard for a painting done in Rome to be utterly bad.

D_3: It will now be seen that our continuum based on "loadedness" or context dependence coincides quite neatly with the evaluate-descriptive continuum. (It is plain that the hope for a firm distinction between descriptive and evaluative *words*—or, as Austin called it, the "fact/value fetish"—is totally unfounded.) This coincidence can be seen both a priori and by looking at the more specific examples of particular continua below. The more loaded a reason is, the more closely it is tied to "————is good" and the more straightforwardly and obviously it counts as a reason for *P*'s being called good; the less loaded it is, the more purely factual content it has.

Now for a few examples. An interchange between audience and critic about an El Greco might go something like this:

A. "What makes this good?"
c. "Well, among other things, it's well balanced."
A. "What makes it well balanced?"
c. "Its well-defined composition."

A. "What makes the composition well defined?"
C. "Mostly the forceful lines."
A. "What makes the lines forceful?"
C. "Look at the triangular form here."
A. "Why is there this triangular form?"
C. "Probably because of the Trinitarian influence."
A. "Where does the Trinitarian influence come from?"
C. "That's not surprising; it comes out of a medieval Christian doctrine prevalent at the time of El Greco's training."

Here we see how the critic, in justifying each of his reasons, moves lower and lower down the continuum. He starts with very loaded facts and ends up with detachable ones. Notice the change in the form of the audience's fifth and sixth questions: it indicates that the critic is no longer being called upon to give nondetachable reasons, but rather to fill in some of the historical background in order to set the stage for further discussion of this painting and similar ones. (He *cannot* give any more nondetachable reasons, in fact, since his fourth one was almost purely factual. It would not make sense to ask "What makes this form triangular?")

Each reason is justified in a quasi-criterial way by the one immediately subsequent to it.[10] It is especially important to see that in the string of claims that connects "———is basically triangular in form" with "——— is good," there is no one place at which a positivist could drive in the fact/value wedge, saying, "Ha! There! Now you've made the illicit leap from *description* to *evaluation*," and going on to add that "brute" facts never lend conceptual support to commendatory verdicts. No one "leap" up or down the continuum is more significant than any other in that respect. Consider another continuum: "———is beautiful," "———is exquisite," "———is delicate and graceful," "———has these sweeping, yet fragile lines," "———employs such and such brush techniques," and so forth. This example shows even more clearly that it is pointless and mistaken to hold that the vocabulary of criticism can be exhaustively and exclusively divided into "fact" words and "value" words; and it is this division that lets the traditional "problem" of justifying critical verdicts get a foothold in the first place.

Of course, our El Greco critic above has picked only one of the many possible continua leading away from the audience's first question, "What makes this good?" Another one is actually offered about an El Greco by Roger Fry:[11] he moves down the continuum from the *purity* of the painting through the *stubbornly unsoftened violent form* to El Greco's *indifference to public opinion*. No doubt we could find many other continua of this kind, all of which fill in the meaning of "This is a good painting."

Now how does this notion of a "continuum" of reasons tie in with our earlier remarks about the parallel between reasons and Wittgensteinian criteria? It seems that we can construct similar cases.

Q. "How do you know he's in pain?"
A. "He's exhibiting pain behavior."
Q. "How do you know that's pain behavior?"
A. "Well, he's grimacing."
Q. "Why do you call that a grimace?"
A. "He's frowning, and his lips are twitching."
Q. "What do you mean by 'frowning'?"
A. "The corners of his mouth are turning down." And so forth.

It will be seen that the reasons given are successively less and less loaded, that is, they presuppose less and less familiarity with our common "pain"-grammar in order to be intelligible. And the more loaded one of these answers is, the more unexceptionable it is as a reason for believing that the person in question is in pain. So the logic of reasons exhibits one more similarity to that of criteria.

But why is it that we never have to go through an interchange like this last one when we talk about someone's being in pain, while we usually do have to appeal to a hierarchy of reasons when we talk about a painting? The answer seems to be just that "pain"-talk (like sensation talk in general) is more basic to our "form of life" than is art. Painting is an ancillary or gratuitous activity, and art criticism is the product only of a sophisticated, leisured, perhaps jaded society. So an important difference is that the linguistic education pertaining to sensations is almost mandatorily undergone by everyone at a very early (tropistic) age, while art education is forced on no one and undergone by few. A second relevant difference is that the phenomenon of pain is a very simple one, compared to the incredibly complex mass of perceptual, psychological, and ratiocinative considerations that enter into one's critical appreciation of a painting.

It now appears that we must qualify C_2^* in the light of what we have said so far about continua: C_2^* holds only at the heavily loaded end of the continuum. If we substitute "——is basically triangular in form" for "——is well organized" as an example, C_2^* is falsified. This should not worry us, of course, if we understand how the "continuum" model applies to actual instances of art criticism. Nor is our parallel between reasons and criteria weakened: C_2 and C_3 are similarly vitiated if we try to talk about a criterial connection between pain and *frowning*, instead of the more straightforward one between pain and (to use the maximally loaded expression) pain behavior.

Now it is time to make good on our earlier promises and use our model to illuminate some more general aesthetic issues. We shall begin with that of (1) universalizability, which seems to yield fairly readily to our treatment. D_2 clearly indicates that the more loaded a reason is, the fewer exceptions its universalization will admit of; the less loaded a reason is, the sillier its universalization will be. Compare "Any painting that is well organized is to that extent a good one," "Any painting containing exquisite lines is to that extent a good one," and "Any painting done in Rome is to that extent a good one." The fact that the usefulness of universalizability varies directly in this way with loadedness may serve to explain the difficulty that philosophers have found in making general claims about the function of the Universalizability Principle in the logic of what might be called "the" aesthetic reason *simpliciter*. It also accounts for why the Principle is unhelpful even when our "continuum" model is brought to the fore: The universalization of a reason near the bottom of the continuum must be qualified practically out of existence (this is another way of putting the traditional "uniqueness" charge); but in the case of a more loaded R, we already know (*ex hypothesi*) what R contributes to the worth of the painting if we understand R, and $R's$ universalization can add nothing to our critical appreciation.

(2) We can easily connect our doctrine to Ziff's idea that we can distinguish between facts that are relevant only to appreciation and those that are relevant to justification as well. Let us say that the former class comprises just those facts that might be used to *give* us the context in which the justificatory facts acquire their meaning. For example, if van Gogh's painting did not portray a pair of shoes, we could not point to the way in which his lines and colors convey a sense of the soil, of hard work, and so forth. In general, although Ziff may be right in holding that detachable reasons are not per se reasons why a painting is good, they are usually the reasons why the reasons that Ziff *would* accept are true.

(3) Now we are also in a position to fit Ziff's claim A_7 into our scheme. This is quite simple: What he says is that a good reason will be understood qua reason if and only if the audience "knows how to look at" the work in question. We may paraphrase this last condition as "if and only if the audience has the artistic background to know what the reason means in this context." And if we understand A_7 in this way, it becomes axiomatic for us; it is just what the "continuum" view asserts.

(4) Let us return to the "aesthetic"/"nonaesthetic" distinction. We have already denied that we can pick out a class of "facts about a painting" that cannot have any relevance at all to the evaluation of the painting. Therefore we do not buy the traditional version of the distinction. However, we might readjust it by stipulating that the "nonaesthetic" coincide with the detachable. So a rough "aesthetic"/"nonaesthetic" distinction can be made out on this basis. Can this revised distinction be called upon to bear any philosophical weight? We do not see how it could be used in a rule book for critics or to define "work of art" or to display to us the essence of the beautiful; and once we have learned to apply the "continuum" model, there is no further job that "aesthetic"/ "nonaesthetic" could do for us. Though this revised distinction is more precise, it is no more useful than the traditional version.

(5) What can we now say about the meaning of "A ought to like P"?

The "easy" analysis discussed in section one seems to be accurate so far as it goes, but it does not clarify the nature of the "obligation" in question; it only asserts the necessity of there being an explanatory psychological fact about A, in the event that A violates the "ought" by disliking P. At this point an anomaly arises, somewhat reminiscent of one to be found in Kant: One cannot give an aesthetic reason or make an aesthetic judgment, as Ziff suggests in A_5, without demanding that one's reason or judgment be universally accepted, without "legislating" for all mankind. But the judgments of even the most undisputedly good critics are frequently not accepted by all of their contemporaries. More strongly, someone might say that the "ought" *has* no more force than the easy analysis awards it; in aesthetics one is not obliged to make *any* judgments whatever (a fact often emphasized by those who stress the differences between aesthetics and ethics).

A tentative resolution of the anomaly is this: Reasons are public and universal in that they can be conceptually connected to verdicts by continua of quasi-criterial linkages, as we have argued above. These continua can be appealed to by any number of people who seek to agree in their evaluative judgments; the truth of the component statements of a continuum is not relative to individual persons. However, if someone refuses to assent to a critic's move upwards or downwards on a continuum at some point, we and the critic can only say that the dissenter lacks or abjures the aesthetic concepts in question (or, more charitably, that he and the critic do not share the same conceptual structure vis-à-vis this aspect of art). In such a case, the two can come to be able to communicate and to agree, if they engage in the more or less ordinary teaching process that we shall describe in section four (see especially our elaboration on the claim $C_6{}^*$). In any event, the frequent occurrence of knowledgeable disagreements should not surprise or puzzle us; against the background of the "continuum" model, the tension of the Kantian anomaly is somewhat lessened, in that such disputes can always, in principle, be resolved—in fact, we believe, they usually *are* eventually resolved in this way.

(6) The apparent incompatibility between Ziff's A_5 and A_6 can be undercut similarly. A_5 is straightforwardly true, on the "continuum" view. A_6 is accounted for by the fact that continua have their bases in fundamental aesthetic "forms of life," just as Wittgensteinian criteria have their bases in more everyday "forms of life." The appraisal of some critic's judgment or reason is logically bound up in our understanding of it, just as the meaning of a term is inextricably bound to its application criteria (though these criteria do not *exhaust* the term's meaning). Radical aesthetic disagreements, then, must be disputes about meanings, about aesthetic concepts in part; concepts and their meanings can always, in principle, be transmitted. It is in this sense that critical reasons *need* not be reasons "for me and my friends" alone, though a "community of taste" *is* presupposed, as A_6 asserts.

Our claims in paragraphs (5) and (6) may seem facile, until we have built our account of the artistic teaching process into the "continuum" view. We shall do so shortly.

IV

We have not yet dwelt upon the way in which Isenberg is correct. In his insistence that the critic's function is to prime the audience into the proper "mental set," he seems to focus his attention on the less loaded end of the continuum. The reasons he is thinking of are less directly connected with the final verdict; it is both a fault and a virtue of Isenberg's that he emphasizes this kind of reason to the exclusion of the more loaded type. There is a clear sense in which detachable and only lightly loaded reasons do not directly add weight to the verdict—they function rather as reasons underlying those reasons which do add weight to the verdict. And the reason for giving detachable reasons at all is, as Isenberg points out, to give the audience a standpoint from which they are able to understand and evaluate the painting.

So it is that these detachable reasons have initial pride of place in teaching someone. The art-appreciation courses given at any university start out with a survey of such "nonaesthetic" truths as facts about the artist's life, about other painting that was going on at the time, and, in general, those social and historical facts which are going to be used to explain more detailed points about the artist's particular style, choice of subject matter and materials, and so forth. In the abstract (though this will never be so neat in actual practice) a teacher starts out with the facts that are most distant from the painting, and then turns to those observable within the painting itself. For example: "And here, class, we see the result of El Greco's Christian training; the continual use of triangles, which symbolize the Trinity, always pointing toward heaven. The forceful lines. . . ." The teacher usually presents the detachable facts, and then goes on to detach them. He wants to spell out in terms of less loaded facts what a term like "well balanced" will mean in certain particular paintings; in filling in and explaining these less loaded facts he may start not with the painting but with history. In this way he can bring out how *this* painting is well balanced, and avoid giving anyone the impression that there is one right way for a painting to be well balanced. Examples of this technique can be found in any textlike book on art, especially in surveys.[12]

Justifying a judgment about a painting might be characterized as "teaching in reverse"; one goes through the same steps, but in the opposite order. The teacher starts at the less loaded end of the continuum and works upwards. The critic, whose primary purpose is not education but evaluation (note how many critics are also assessors and guarantors of a painting's worth), starts with the painting itself and pronounces such judgments as "It's good," "It's a classic," "It's well balanced." Then he travels *down* the continuum in supporting his judgment.[13] This inverse parallelism between teaching and justifying is not surprising, given that the continuum along which both move is founded on graded degrees of background knowledge, which must be learned before it can be appealed to.

Of course, we have presented the difference between teaching and justifying in a very idealized way. Critics quite often function as educators as well, and educators are concerned not only with teaching their students about painting in general, but about good painting in particular. This duality of roles would lead one to suspect that it is frequently hard to see the difference between the two enterprises, and this is indeed so. But in general, the more a book or article is meant to function as a text or teaching aid, rather than as a piece of critical appraisal, the more detachable facts it will contain.[14]

Now we must reiterate and expand a little on the point we made in advancing C_6^* as a parallel to C_6. In cases of evaluation there is always the *possibility* of disagreement. A's claim that the Goya is well balanced might be met with B's saying, "You really think so? I don't." In support of his judgment, A may move down the continuum, citing the relevant facts which fill in his more loaded claims. This may suffice to convince B of the truth of A's verdict; but what can we say about a case in which B disagrees with all of A's further claims? He may even hold that they are not relevant in support of the judgment. What is called for in such a situation is not a further attempt at justification (no new facts need to be brought to light), but A must begin to teach B exactly what kind of statement he has made. He must try to give B the concept, what it is for a painting to be well balanced.[15]

A few words more about the idea of "mental set" that we have ascribed to Isenberg: The class of detachable reasons, we have said, is coextensive with the class of facts that would be cited in giving someone the proper background for perceiving the painting in question. Such reasons, then, function as "inducers" for a certain mental set. The necessity of the audience's having the proper set for viewing a particular work is nicely brought out in an article by Edward Lucie-Smith, in which he points out that in order to be in a position to judge icons, one must be educated in (or set for) the nature of icons in general.[16] The fact, for example, that they are not attempts to create new designs or variations on subject matter, but that rather they are produced from older icons almost by copying, is relevant here. Were this fact not brought out and appreciated, one would never be able to judge icons properly, because there would always be a tendency to judge them as "little paintings." To induce the proper set needed for viewing them is to rule out such a tendency. More generally, E. H. Gombrich points out in great detail how the psychological background and the set of particular artists and audiences affects what is *actually seen*.[17] Gombrich's concern is with the artist, and he tries to show how one might be able to pick out the emphases which characterize the various sets that may in turn be used to give an account of *style*.

A last similarity between reasons and criteria becomes manifest in the light of all this. Many philosophers who hold a basically criteriological view (including, we believe, Wittgenstein and Austin) think that it is mistaken to call a criterial connection an "evidential" one at all, that a logically adequate answer to "How do you know he's in pain?" is simply, "I'm *looking* at him." We have been trained (as we learned English) to see certain kinds of gross physical behavior "as" pain behavior, and that is all there is to the matter. In other words, we have acquired a certain mental set vis-à-vis pain facts. And this notion parallels what we have said above about reasons: a reason is understood for what it is because we have been taught the appropriate mental set, the appropriate aspect-seeing ability.

Notes

1. A brief extract from this paper was read at the 1969 meeting of the American Society for Aesthetics; Walter H. Clark, Jr., was the commentator. We have profited greatly from many discussions with Ted Cohen. We are also grateful to Jack Nelson, to Richard Suiter, and to Richard Garner, who commented helpfully on earlier drafts. Of course, these men are in no way responsible for whatever inaccuracies or inelegance may remain.

2. Paul Ziff, "Reasons in Art Criticism," pp. 219-36 in *Philosophy of Education*, ed. Israel Scheffler (Boston: Allyn & Bacon, 1958).

3. Arnold Isenberg, "Critical Communication," *Philosophical Review* 58 (1949): 330-44.

4. The notion of a "continuum" owes much to the work of John Wisdom. Relevant points are to be found in two of his unpublished works: "Proof and Explanation" (lectures at the University of Virginia, 1957, mimeograph prepared by S. F. Barker) and a set of notes on ethics. Naturally, we do not want to saddle Professor Wisdom with any uses of the concept of a continuum which he might not sanction. John Casey (in *The Language of Criticism* [London: Methuen, 1966]) has also made some use of the notion; but our view diverges from his.

5. Earlier Ziff says: "That the work was executed while the artist was in Rome may be relevant to an appreciation of it but is likely to be relevant *in no other way* to an evaluation of it" (p. 221; italics ours).

6. Clive Bell, *An Account of French Painting* (London: Chatto & Windus, 1931).

7. The psychology of "set" is explicated in the writings of the Gestalt psychologists (especially in those of Koffka and Köhler). The idea has been recently taken up and elaborated by cognitive psychologists, who stress the influence of a percipient's values, needs, and dispositions upon what he sees.

8. Our use of this term is not to be confused with that of H. P. Grice in "The Causal Theory of Perception" (*Aristotelian Society Supplementary Volume* 25 [1961]), although the two notions are very distantly related.

9. F. A. Siegler, "On Isenberg's 'Critical Communication,'" *British Journal of Aesthetics* 8 (1968): 173.

10. Stanley Cavell ("Aethetic Problems of Modern Philosophy," in *Philosophy in America,* ed. Max Black [Ithaca, N.Y.: Cornell University Press, 1965]) hints that he holds a similar view, though he does not pursue our line: "You call it psychology just because it so obviously is not logic, and it must be one or the other. Contrariwise, I should admit that I call it 'logic' mostly because it so obviously is not 'psychology' in the way I think you mean it. I do not really think it is either of those activities, in the senses we attach to them now; but I cannot describe to anyone's satisfaction *what* it is. Wittgenstein called it 'grammar'; others might call it 'phenomenology'" (p. 94).

11. Roger Fry, "El Greco," in *Vision and Design* (New York: Meridian Books, 1956), pp. 209-10.

12. E.g., Michael Levey, *A Concise History of Painting from Giotto to Cézanne* (New York: Praeger, 1962); see his discussion of Rubens, pp. 178-84.

13. A good example is Kenneth Clark's treatment of Botticelli's *The Birth of Venus (The Nude* [Garden City, N.Y.: Doubleday Anchor Books, 1956], p. 173).

14. This can easily be seen by comparing a text, such as that referred to in note 12, to a monograph that stresses detail (e.g., H. Knackfus, *Holbein,* trans. Campbell Dodgson [London: H. Grevel & Co., 1899]), or to a critical exhibition catalogue (e.g., *Catalogue* of the Arts Council of Great Britain's show of Joan Miró, 1964).

15. It is worth pointing out explicitly where the Wittgensteinian remarks about "seeing as" fit into this whole picture. To see a painting *as* well balanced, or *as* containing a triangle, obviously involves a certain amount of training. One must have grasped the requisite concept in order to see a thing as an instance of that concept. The more loaded a reason is, the "less phenomenal" it is (to borrow Hanson's phrase) and the more specialized training is required. Toward the less loaded end of a continuum less specialized training is needed, and agreement on what is seen (heard, and so forth) is more readily forthcoming. It is for this reason that fundamental disagreements, those at the less loaded end of a continuum, often betoken revolutionary action. One who disgrees with such minimal, less loaded claims (unless he has completely failed to grasp the concept, which is improbable since these are quite basic) is usually attempting to change the established concept. He is attempting to show us by his refusal to agree that we are seeing the work in the wrong way.

16. *Times* (London), Dec. 7, 1965.

17. E. H. Gombrich, *Art and Illusion* (2nd ed.; London: Phaidon Press, 1962).

BRUCE VERMAZEN

Comparing Evaluations
of Works of Art

IT IS SOMETIMES SUPPOSED that there is one value-property that belongs to works of art *qua* works of art, and that any other value-property that belongs to a work of art is somehow unimportant when one is assessing it as a work of art.[1] "Beauty" is one expression used in the attempt to refer to this property (though it has other uses). Other expressions are "aesthetic goodness," "aesthetic excellence," "being a (true or good) work of art (on the whole)," and (an expression students use) "being aesthetic." I will call this supposed property "aesthetic goodness." I should not be understood as claiming that all these expressions mean the same, since they seem to me all to be used to mean different things at different times. My claim is just that on many occasions they are used to pick out a property with the characteristics I have mentioned. If there were such a property, we could expect one of two situations to obtain: either it would be a degreeless property, so that if two objects had it, it wouldn't be possible for one to have more of it than the other, like the property of being an oak tree; or it would be a property that admits of degrees, like warmth or softness. Aesthetic goodness may be degreeless. But much critical practice treats it as if it had degrees, as if there were an associated metric. We judge one poem better on the whole than another, one picture more beautiful than another, Rossetti's sonnets truer works of art than his paintings. I want to take this critical practice as a datum.

If there is such a property, and if it has a metric, the metric could be either precise or vague. I would call the metric precise if and only if it is possible, epistemic difficulties aside, to say of any two bearers of the property that one of them had more or less of the property than the other, or that they had the same amount. A vague metric is one that is

From *Journal of Aesthetics and Art Criticism,* 34 (1975), pp. 7-14. Copyright 1975 by Journal of Aesthetics and Art Criticism. Reprinted by permission of the journal and the author.

not precise in this sense. It is sometimes supposed that aesthetic goodness has a precise metric, e.g., by Birkhoff in *Aesthetic Measure*[2] (where
he hesitantly calls the property "beauty") and by Leonard Meyer in
"Some Remarks on Value and Greatness in Music"[3] (where he calls it
"greatness"). But there are many apparent counterexamples. We hesitate
to compare even two rather similar works, like a sonnet by Donne and
one by Shakespeare, and the hesitation grows stronger as the dissimilarity
increases. Is *Coriolanus* aesthetically better or worse, on the whole, than
Twelfth Night? Or are they equally good? What about Donatello's *David*
and a Caravaggio *St. John*? Bernini's fountains in the Piazza Navona and
Mozart's 40th Symphony? Given that much dissimilarity, the question
seems almost senseless. On the face of it, then, aesthetic goodness has
only a vague metric. What I want to do in this paper is to offer an
explanation of this fact. It won't do just to say that after all the concept
of aesthetic goodness is itself rather vague, for there are vague concepts
with precise metrics, e.g., those of warmth and coldness. Nor will it do to
attribute the vagueness to some sort of *practical* difficulty in assessing the
degree of aesthetic goodness that an object has, as we might hesitate to
compare the redness of two color samples in a dim light. For we don't
reject the invitation to compare two works of art by saying that it's
difficult to tell just how good the play (for example) is, but by pointing
out that the works in question are just different sorts of things: maybe
the verse in *Coriolanus* is better than in *Twelfth Night,* and maybe the
characterization is deeper, but after all, the relation of each play to its
audience is different, and though each one succeeds in affecting its audience in its own way, there are really two different sorts of success involved,
and they aren't really comparable. The general strategy of rejection in
this case, and, I think, in the others, is to show that despite the possibility
of comparing the works in several respects and coming up with a judgment of comparative value in those respects, there is no hope for a comparison on the whole because of their incomparability in yet other
respects. Roughly speaking, the more dissimilar the works in such ways
as medium, period, genre, and so on, the more respects there are in
which they are incomparable, and the more hesitant we are to compare
them on the whole.

I want to maintain several independently plausible theses about what
we *are* doing when we call something a good work of art and to show
how these theses entail the difficulty of comparing the aesthetic value of
works of art. I don't want to maintain that this is the only source of the
difficulty, but I do think it is the principal one.

Thesis 1: Some aspects of works of art are valued independently of their
relations to other aspects of the work. I want to argue for this thesis by
giving some examples and contrasting independently valued aspects
with aspects whose value depends on their relations to other aspects.
Let me supply a work of art. Yeats's poem "When You are Old."[4]

When you are old and grey and full of sleep,
And nodding by the fire, take down this book,
And slowly read, and dream of the soft look
Your eyes had once, and of their shadows deep;

How many loved your moments of glad grace,
And loved your beauty with love false or true,
But one man loved the pilgrim soul in you,
And loved the sorrows of your changing face;

And bending down beside the glowing bars,
Murmur, a little sadly, how Love fled
And paced upon the mountains overhead
And hid his face amid a crowd of stars.

I hope you agree that this is a good poem and a good work of art, but if you don't, I think the points I make about it can be made about some work that you consider good.

If I were to defend my judgment that this is a good work of art, I would cite such things as Yeats's handling of the verse, the unity or integration of the whole, the evocative and mysterious quality of the ending (especially as contrasted with the literal, every-day quality of the first nine lines), and the way in which the poem manages to express the former (perhaps spurned) lover's regret (and perhaps his desire for revenge). We might even interpret the poem in such a way that it is a suitable instrument of revenge, and cite that as a reason for calling it good. All these reasons can be rephrased so that they cite properties of the poem, viz., having well-handled verse, being integrated, having an evocative ending, expressing a certain state of mind, being an instrument of revenge. It will be convenient to interpret the rather vague word "aspects" in Thesis 1 as meaning properties of this sort, although it sounds odd to say that we value these properties. It is more comfortable to talk about valuing the work, and to bring in the properties by saying that we value the work because of the properties, or value it as a thing with such properties. But it is not so uncomfortable to speak of valuing the unity of a work, or its verse, or its expressiveness, and it is this sort of thing I want to capture by talking about valuing the work's properties.

Now let me contrast an independently valued property with a dependently valued one. Instead of saying that the verse was well-handled, I could have pointed out that the verse starts out a little slow with all those monosyllables, gets a little slower when the rhythm is interrupted by the relatively strong stress required on "take" in line 2, "soft" in line 3, "glad" in line 5, and so on, and that in the second stanza the words "love" and "loved" create a superimposed rhythm, and so on. That is, I have described the characteristics of the verse that led me to say it was well handled. But these characteristics are not what I want to call independently valued properties, in that they are only valued given that the poem has certain other properties, viz., such properties as some-how require or make it desirable that the verse start out slow and that there be a rhythm to the occurrences of "love"; in this case, the property of expressing a certain state of mind and the speaker's employment of a certain subject-matter. That is, the poem is addressed to someone sleepy and is about love; that is why just this sort of verse is good. So the property of having slow (etc.) verse is only dependently valued, since the relation of the verse to subject-matter, tone of voice, emotional content, and whatever else it may be related to must already be assessed before it can safely be said that the verse is well-handled. Of the other four properties I gave as reasons for valuing the poem, I would maintain (with-out going into it) that two of them—being integrated and expressing a certain state of mind—are independently valued, whereas the other two —having an evocative ending and being an instrument of revenge— depend for their value (their being valued) on the poem having other properties.

The property of being independently valued must not be confused with that of being intrinsically valued. An object or property is intrinsi-cally valued when it is valued apart from its relation to anything else whatever. A property is independently valued when it is valued apart from its relation to any other property of the work in question, although the property's being valued may depend on its relation to something outside the work. The power a work has to move us, for example, may be independently valued without being intrinsically valued, if its power to move is held to be valuable only because being moved is valued. Being moved may in turn be valued either intrinsically or for some further reason; the point is that being moved is not itself a property of the work.

Thesis 2: Works of art nearly always have at least two aspects that are independently valued. This is a claim only about what is typically the case, so the appropriate defense would be a sweeping survey of critical commentary on a vast number of works of art. Failing this, I ask you to remember what I said about the Yeats poem, and reflect whether it wasn't a reasonable sort of thing to say, and whether there are not analogous kinds of commentary on nearly every work you can call to mind. The beginning of a counter-argument could be made by finding some work of art which is valued for a single reason, perhaps a supreme one—its sheer beauty, or, its unity-in-variety (a song without words or one of Clive Bell's Sung pots). But even if such an example could be presented convincingly, it is doubtful that it could serve as a model for the evaluation of every work of art. We just do seem to offer multiple inde-pendently valued properties as reasons for valuing most works.

In a discussion of an earlier version of this paper, Professor Albert Hofstadter pointed out that for many painters, the ultimate judgment of value on a piece is the claim "It works." Working, in this sense, is a degreeless property and the single independently valued property of an art object, since any object that doesn't work is a failure, and hence not valued at all.

This objection clearly contradicts Thesis 2. I could respond by narrowing my enterprise to an explanation of the practice of those critics who don't take such a severe view of artistic success. But I think that my theses can be modified to explain one important facet of the practice of Hofstadter's painter-critics: their ranking of works that don't work by degree of failure.

Thesis 1 must be rewritten thus: Some aspects of a failed work of art count as reasons for ranking that work vis-à-vis other failed works independently of that aspect's relations to other aspects of the work. Thesis 2 becomes this: There are nearly always at least two aspects of a failed work of art that can count as reasons of the sort mentioned in Thesis 1. In the remainder of this paper, I shall not make any special mention of the position cited by Hofstadter. I am confident that everything I claim can be converted to fit the practice of the adherents of working; the formal properties of comparisons between nonworking works are the same as those of comparisons between better and worse works in a system of judgments with no supreme or absolute rank.

Thesis 3: While it is generally possible to rank works with respect to the degree of a single independently valued property they possess, it is not generally possible to rank them with respect to the degree of two different independently valued properties. That is, in general it is possible to single out an independently valued property and say which of two works possesses a greater degree of it, or which of two works is better in that respect (which of two poems has better managed verse, which of two songs has a more suitable accompaniment); but we reject requests to rank one poem's verse vis-à-vis another poem's expression, or the modelling in a Masaccio vis-à-vis the portrayal of light in a Turner. Such comparisons don't seem to make sense, except in extreme cases, where one of the properties is present in a very high degree and the other only in a very low degree. It isn't that finer discriminations are difficult to make, but that there aren't discriminations to be made. This incomparability of degrees of different properties may seem to be an echo of the incomparability of degrees of aesthetic goodness, but I will maintain that the latter is the echo of the former.

There are also cases (pointed out by Professor James Bogen in his commentary on an earlier version of this paper) where we say that (e.g.) two poems are roughly as good as each other even though one is unmusical and full of vivid and effective images while the other is wonderfully musical but relatively barren of images, and they rank about the same in all other respects. Here we seem to be comparing two different properties and deciding that they balance each other, without being able to make finer discriminations, e.g., to decide at what point musicality would no longer balance wealth of imagery; for we can say only that the two poems are roughly as good as each other. It seems to me that in such cases we are assuming commensurability of two properties. The roughness of the measuring is present even in cases where it is the same property being measured: one might find it difficult to say how much more beautiful than Puccini's melodies Rossini's would have to be before we would call his operas better in that respect. My claim is not that no two independently valued properties are commensurable, but only that they are not commensurable in all cases.

If the judging situation is as I have described it, we can represent the value assigned to the independently valued properties of a single work of art as an ordered n-tuple of numbers, where n = the number of independently valued properties the work has, each slot in the n-tuple represents a different independently valued property, and the number in each slot represents the rank of this object with respect to this property vis-à-vis all the other objects that have the same independently valued property.[5] For example, we might compare the poem I read with another which has better handled verse, is just as well integrated (but no better), and is not as good at expressing a state of mind. Supposing (somewhat artificially) that these are the only independently valued properties of either poem, we could represent these judgments by the ordered triples (2, 1, 3) and (3, 1, 2). The absolute size of numbers is not significant here, but only the order: larger numbers represent greater degrees of the property. This is a standard way of representing judgments of value in economics: the n-tuples are usually called "commodity bundles". If we know which slot corresponds to which property, these n-tuples give a good representation of judgments where several internally rank-ordered but pair-wise incommensurable factors are involved. And, I have argued, that is just the situation with many judgments as to what is good *about* works of art.

The interesting thing I want you to notice about a set of such n-tuples is that there is a simple condition for imposing a partial ordering on the set: if every member of some n-tuple N is equal to or greater than the corresponding member of some n-tuple M, and if some member of N is strictly greater than the corresponding member of M, then N is strictly greater than M. This seems to represent well many situations in which we would say that one work was clearly better, all things considered, than another: it is at least as good with respect to every independently valued property, and clearly better with respect to at least one. This seems to be a natural condition on ordering, and indeed seems to be the only natural condition. For orderings that are not based on the numbers in the n-tuples would seem arbitrary, since they would lack any relation to the information about value that the numbers encode. And orderings that were based on the numbers would involve crucial reference to some relationship between the numbers that went beyond their role as mere representations of rank, e.g., to a relationship that was equivalent to the assumption of commensurability.[6]

Hence, the natural condition on ordering is the only condition that introduces an ordering without introducing new assumptions about the numbers in the n-tuples. So we can expect at *best* only a partial ordering of works of art based solely on the judgments we make about their independently valued properties.

It will be convenient to talk about the bundles of degrees of properties represented by these n-tuples as value-bundles. Obviously value-bundles for different works of art will differ not only with respect to the rank assigned to a given embodiment of a property, but also with respect to which properties are represented at all. The value-bundle for an opera, for example, will likely include a ranking of its beauty of melody, but the value-bundle for a painting will not. So the bare interpretation of the slots in the n-tuple will present comparison difficulties aside from those already rehearsed about the incommensurability of the numbers in recognizably different slots.

It should be obvious by this point how the three theses I have presented are supposed to explain the incomparability of overall value of works of art, if one further claim can be made plausible, namely that a judgment that a work is aesthetically good does not in any important way go beyond those judgments that rank a work with respect to the degree in which it possesses independently valued properties. Let me refer to these latter as the subordinate judgments.

The most important way in which such a judgment could go beyond the subordinate judgments is that it could be the attribution to the work of a further property. If it is such an attribution, however, it must be noted that the property is of a special sort: it isn't independent of the properties attributed in the subordinate judgments in that we can't conceive of aesthetic goodness being present in a thing where other independently valued properties were not also present. The counter-instances that tempt us, like Bell's Sung pots or an unaccompanied piece for cello, seem to me to be cases where perhaps there is only a single independently valued property, and where therefore one identifies the judgment that the object has this property with the judgment that it is aesthetically good. That the judgments really are distinct seems to me to be suggested by this: that the pot has the relevant property is perceived by sight, and that the song has it by hearing, and this is generally good evidence that the properties are distinct. To say that beauty, truth, and goodness are counterinstances is to issue a denial, not an argument.

If that point is accepted, then we can see the dependence of the aesthetic goodness of a work on at least some other properties of the work. We can remind ourselves, also, that it is a fairly tight dependence, in that an object whose value-bundle differed in just one rank-designation from another object would also differ from it in its aesthetic goodness ranking, and the second difference would be in the same direction as the first. A familiar way to account for this dependence, or at least to label it, is to talk about the supervenience of aesthetic goodness on the properties attributed by the subordinate judgments (or more usually on the non-valued properties that give the work its independently valued properties). I think that such a claim in this case is empty. There are clearly cases in which the claim is not empty, however. Redness, for example, is said to supervene on certain surface properties of an object whose surface reflects light of a certain wavelength. The property of being a mental event is said (by materialists) to supervene on certain sets of physical properties of events in the brain. The supervenient property is not the same as the cluster of properties on which it supervenes, yet they are as tightly stuck together as if they were the same. The justification for positing the supervenient property seems to be that we have some sort of epistemic access to it independent of what we may know or perceive in the way of the properties on which is supervenes. I can tell that something is red or is a mental event without any inkling as to the other properties of the surface or physical person that is the subject of my judgment. So if properties are to be used as entities to explain such perceiving and judging, we will want to avail ourselves of supervenient properties as well as properties supervened upon.

There are other cases, however, where the situation is similar, but the epistemic justification is missing. Take the supposed property of being colorful or that of being complicated. The judgment that an object is colorful or complicated depends on the judgment that it has a certain variety and number (vaguely specified) of color areas or of a certain class of relationships among its parts. But being colorful or complicated is not the same as having *just those* colors or relationship-properties, so one wants perhaps to say that colorfulness and complexity supervene on the lower-level properties. The proposal lacks the urgency it has in the cases of redness and mentality, however, just because one has no access to colorfulness without access to the subordinate color-properties, and no access to complexity without access to the relations among the parts of the complex object. If we are using properties as part of a theory to explain how the world is constituted and how knowledge about the world is possible, we don't really need supervenient properties like colorfulness and complexity. We can explain remarks about these supposed properties as mere summaries of the remarks we could make about the properties on which they supposedly supervene—which we can't do for mentality and redness. Knowing that something is colorful is just knowing that it has a sufficient variety of colors of a certain sort.

It seems to me that aesthetic goodness is in the same boat as colorfulness and complexity. Although it has the right sort of dependence on lower-level properties to qualify as supervenient, it lacks the epistemic justification: there is no access to the aesthetic goodness of a work aside from access to its independently valued properties. I may not be able to say in a given case just what is good about a work I judge good, or what it is that makes it good, but I must at least allow that there is something good about it, and even that I have noticed some good things about it. It seems reasonable, then, to treat "aesthetically good" just as I proposed treating "colorful" and "complicated": not as an expression that picks out a property, but as a convenient way of referring to certain *bona fide* attributions of properties which for some reason or other one is refraining from expressing. Perhaps "summary expression" is a good term to use to pick out this class of words.

Working is not in the same boat. It seems to me that, in the case of a work that "works," the judgments citing reasons of the kind one would cite for ranking one failed work above another are not subordinate to the judgment "It works," but coordinate (though less important). For the supposed subordinate judgments are not offered as reasons to back up the judgment that the painting works, even though working has the same tight dependence as aesthetic goodness on the properties cited in the "subordinate" judgments. In regard to epistemic access, working is intermediate between colorfulness and redness. Presumably one can't tell that a painting works without noting any of its other properties, for that would keep one from seeing the painting at all. But if Clive Bell is talking about working under the rubrics "rightness and necessity" and "good" in the following passage, it must be possible to decide that a painting works without the kind of detailed attention that goes into the judgment that it is aeshetically good (in the sense I am exploring), so there is some justification for counting working as a true supervenient property:

> Before we feel an aesthetic emotion for a combination of forms, do we not perceive intellectually the rightness and necessity of the combination? If we do, it would explain the fact that passing rapidly through a room we recognize a picture to be good, although we cannot say that it has provoked much emotion. We seem to have recognized intellectually the rightness of its forms without staying to fix our attention . . . (Clive Bell, *Art*, London, 1914, p. 26.)

There is, of course, one obvious way in which the assertion that a thing is aesthetically good goes beyond the assertion that there is some value-bundle or other associated with it, and that is that such an assertion ranks the object vis-à-vis other objects whose value-bundles only warrant the appelation "aesthetically bad" or "aesthetically mediocre." And similar remarks can be made about calling something "colorful" versus calling it "drab" or "complicated" vs. "simple." So these expressions function as slightly more than summaries, but we still don't need to posit corresponding properties. We can understand remarks about aesthetic goodness as classifying objects together because they have a certain (vaguely specified) range of value-bundles, not because they share the property of aesthetic goodness.

How, then, does my explanation explain? I claim that value-bundles by themselves can furnish only a vague metric (a partial ordering), and that to judge that a thing is aesthetically good is just to group it with other things (actual and possible) having associated value-bundles that fall within a certain range. Since the criterion for so grouping these objects is just that their value-bundles do fall within this range, there is nothing at hand to furnish a metric independent of the one furnished by the value-bundles. So our reluctance to compare arbitrary pairs of works of art as to their aesthetic goodness is plausibly traced back to the impossibility of inducing more than a partial ordering on the set of value-bundles without implicitly treating them as more than value-bundles.

I do not claim that viable comparisons can be made only between objects with value-bundles of the same sort, for there is the possibility that while one of the properties (call it P) in the bundle associated with one object is *different* from some property (call it Q) in the bundle associated with another, yet P and Q are commensurable (or at least commensurable in the range within which the given degrees of P and Q lie). If the value-bundle-sorts are otherwise the same, it may be possible, given this commensurability, to rank the two with respect to each other solely on the basis of the numbers expressing the measurement.

Bogen, in the commentary mentioned earlier, felt that the account I have given of ranking doesn't allow for the following situation. It seems to be possible to take a group of works whose value-bundles are incommensurable[7] on my account and sort them into sub-groups of good, middling, and poor works, with the result that one is willing to say of any work in the "good" group that it is better than any work in the "middling" group or the "poor" group, of any work in the "middling" group that it is worse than any in the "good" group, etc.; and this is possible without any assumptions being made about the commensurability of different properties.

This loose ordering of the set of value-bundles does not contradict my thesis, since it does not entail that arbitrary pairs of art objects can be ranked with respect to one another. But on the other hand, the roots of the loose ordering are not to be found merely in the characteristics I have assigned to value-bundles themselves. Something must also be said about the sorts of value-bundles represented in the whole set.

What is needed here is an account of how one determines what value-bundles will make the associated works fall in the "good," "middling," and "poor" ranges. It seems to me there are two sorts of questions involved: one is the relatively factual one how high the work ranks among conceivable[8] works with a certain sort of value-bundle (two bundles being of the same sort if each slot in each bundle can be paired with a slot in the other in such a way that the numbers paired measure the same or commensurable properties); the other is the clearly normative one how good anything with that sort of value-bundle can be. Suppose that a certain performance of a puppet show ranks very high among works with puppet-show-like bundles; it may be that nothing with such a bundle (something with only those properties to value) can rank any higher than "middling." But in a case where two value-bundle-sorts can both be associated with good works, and where two works, however disparate in kind, rank relatively high among conceivable works with that sort of bundle, we can call them both "good." Thus the import of the judgment that two works are both good is just that each one ranks high for its value-bundle-sort, and that each one's value-bundle-sort has a relatively high ranking among all value-bundle-sorts. This is enough, I think, to support claims that any good work is better than any middling work and so on. Thus my account allows for situations like the one Bogen suggests, but before it can really accommodate them, it must be supplemented by an account of the ranking of value-bundle-sorts.

The proposed account is somewhat reminiscent of claims that it is only appropriate to judge works of art within their own kind, and that attributions of aesthetic goodness are at bottom attributions of goodness-of-a-kind. But the resemblance is only structural. Genre criticism established the *kind* of a work not by what its independently valued properties were, but by such criteria as whether it was in the narrative or dramatic mode, whether the diction was noble or colloquial, whether the subject matter was pastoral or heroic, what meter was employed, and so on. Then the work was judged against other works of the same kind, at least partly on the basis of how well it exemplified the kind. I am calling attention to an impasse in judgment that affects any critic whose practice is described by Theses 1-3, and such a critic need not be a genre critic.[9]

Notes

1. I have in mind particularly Clive Bell and George Birkhoff. But the view is widespread, and I want to discuss it here without attention to the special twists given to it in the writings of these men.

2. (Cambridge, 1933).

3. *Journal of Aesthetics and Art Criticism* 17 (1959): 486-500.

4. *Poems* (London, 1912): 136.

5. It is possible for a work to have a certain property and for it to be independently valued while another work has the same property and it is only dependently valued. In this case the second work would not be included in the ranking with respect to the property.

6. That is, the condition would look like this: $N > M \longleftrightarrow [(x, y, z \ldots \varepsilon N)$ & $(w \varepsilon N \to w = xV \ w = y \ V \ w = zV \ldots)$ & $(t, u, v \ldots \varepsilon M)$ & $(s \varepsilon M \to s = tV \ s = uV \ s = vV \ldots)$ & $R (x, y, z \ldots)$ & $R' (t, u, v \ldots)]$. Insofar as R and R' are relations constructible in terms of the role assigned to the numbers, they can't be used to construct a weak ordering of the domain of n-tuples; insofar as they are relations of another sort, they are going beyond the roles assigned to the numbers.

7. Two value-bundles (B and B') are commensurable if and only if the slots in B can be exhaustively paired off with the slots in B' in such a way that the

property represented by the slot drawn from B is commensurable with the property represented by the slot drawn from B'. Otherwise the value-bundles are incommensurable.

8. We need to talk about conceivable works, since it may be that at a point early in the history of a category of work with a novel value-bundle, even the best work available is not very good, e.g., early computer-generated music or domestic architecture.

9. A version of this paper was read at the Pacific Division meeting of the American Society for Aesthetics on April 11, 1974. I wish to thank those present at the reading for their comments and criticism.

On Critical Judgment

HOW DO WE TELL good from bad in art? The quick and easy answer is: by looking in the case of painting, by listening in the case of music, by reading (or listening) in the case of poetry, and so on; in short, as Ziff points out, by performing some activity appropriate to the work in question. For it is surely a truism that a painting is something to be looked at (or "aspected," as Ziff would have it), a symphony something to be listened to, a poem something to be read (or heard), and so on. But an interesting philosophical question arises immediately: What is the relation between, on the one hand, what we see when we look, what we hear when we listen, what we apprehend when we read, and, on the other hand, a work of art's being good, bad, or indifferent?

First, telling whether a work of art is good or bad is not the same as supposing, believing, or even knowing that it is good or bad. (I can see no reason for saying, as some philosophers have said, that one cannot *know* whether a work of art is good or bad. Can you?) For one can know at secondhand, as it were, whether Bishop King's "Exequy" is a good poem, for example, by being told by a reliable critic that it is, just as one can know at secondhand what the results of an election were by reading an account of the results in a reliable newspaper. But one cannot *tell* at secondhand whether a work of art is good, except, as Tormey points out in the previous section, in the uninteresting sense that one can sometimes tell whether it is from photographs, copies, models, translations, and the like—although not, except perhaps in very special circumstances, from a description, even one couched in terms that would place it at the upper end of a Lycan-Machamer continuum. From an appropriate description one can infer or conclude whether a work is good, but that is not the same as telling whether it is. To tell whether it is is, at least typically, to judge whether it is, and to judge a work of art calls for firsthand acquaintance with it, or some suitable surrogate for firsthand acquaintance, as Tormey has pointed out.

Second, to judge a work of art one must be in a position to do so.

This too I take to be a truism. Trouble awaits us, however, when we try to specify what it is to be in a position to judge a work of art. But surely at least this can be said: to be in a position to judge a work of art one must be able to appreciate or understand what he is looking at or listening to; a capacity that calls for more than normal eyesight or hearing.[1] What you see is not independent of what you know or believe. What is seen or heard (at least at the human level) is seen or heard under a possible description, in that one must in principle be able to describe, classify, or categorize what he sees or hears *as* he sees or hears it; and this is a function of knowledge or belief. There is a difference between merely seeing, say, a building (let alone merely seeing an object, whatever it would be to do that), and seeing a church, seeing a High Baroque church, seeing a church in the manner of Borromini (perhaps a church *by* Barromini), and seeing a church in the manner of Borromini in which Gothic-like structural principles are exemplified (as they are in Borromini's Church of the Propaganda Fide in Rome).

Although there are many ways in which a given object or event may be perceived, some of them—the most interesting and important ones as far as criticism is concerned—are determined at least partly by historical knowledge, as Kendall Walton has pointed out in the preceding section. Imagine a native Nepalese with no knowledge of American culture trying to understand the cartoons, say, those of Hamilton or Saxon, in a typical isue of *The New Yorker* (even assuming that the captions are translated into Nepalese), and you will have some measure of the magnitude of the point at issue. So, although "I don't know anything about art, but I know what I like" may be unexceptionable, "I don't know anything about art, but I can tell a good painting when I see one" is not unexceptionable.

Now back to the question of the relation between discerning that a work of art has certain properties and telling whether it is good. This is the notorious issue often characterized as that between facts and values, or between descriptive and normative or evaluative statements. The issue is that of the logical relation between a sentence of roughly the form "This work of art (lyric poem, Impressionist painting, Baroque church, or what have you) has the set of properties, P" (where goodness is not a member of the set P) and a sentence of roughly the form "This is a good work of art (lyric poem, Impressionist painting, Baroque church, or what have you)," where the former sentence is used to *describe* the work, whereas the latter is used to *judge*, or express a judgment of, it; that is, where the two sentences are used in different "semantic moods," as they are sometimes called, or used to perform different illocutionary acts.

Before proceeding let us pause to consider what Lycan and Machamer have to say about the evaluative-descriptive distinction. The "hope for a firm distinction between descriptive and evaluative *words*," they say, "is totally unfounded." And this would appear to be true. But what about their own approach to the distinction? According to their "D₃" the "continuum based on 'loadedness' or context dependence coincides quite neatly with the evaluative-descriptive continuum"; although they also hold that "there is no one place at which a positivist could drive in the fact/value wedge . . .". This suggests that the higher a statement is in the continuum of reasons, the more evaluative it is—and the lower, the more descriptive. Perhaps, *relative to a continuum of reasons* (all of which would tend to be declaratives), but would it not be a mistake to suppose that propositions that would typically take their place at the upper end of a Lycan-Machamer continuum are in all contexts value judgments, whereas those that would typically take their place at the lower end are similarly descriptions? For, first, is it really true that a proposition of the form "*A* is a good *X*" is never descriptive? Why couldn't "She's a good dancer" figure as, or in, a description of a woman? Is there any implication of the meaning of "description" that disallows this? Second, the propositions in question can figure as antecedent or consequent of a hypothetical and as disjuncts of a disjunction; for example, "If the painting is well organized, then it is a good one—at least to that extent." Lycan and Machamer would consider this "a matter of grammar," as Wittgenstein might say; but leaving that aside, is it not apparent that "the painting is well organized" and "it is a good one" (both of which would be placed at the top of a Lycan-Machamer continuum) do not *here* figure as "value judgments" at all?

Perhaps Lycan and Machamer mean to say that a proposition that would characteristically take its place at the upper end of their continuum lends itself to being used in making a "value judgment," whereas a proposition that would characteristically take its place at the lower end would not lend itself to being used in making a "value judgment," but would lend itself to being used to describe something, although any proposition that could figure in a continuum might be used to describe something. Can there be any objection to this?[2]

The first thing to note about propositions of the form "That is a good *X*," that is, about so-called value judgments, is that, irrespective of the semantic mood in which they may be uttered, they do not behave analogously to at least some grammatically similar sentences (so-called descriptive statements), for example, "This is a red Volvo." For where it makes sense to say "This Volvo is exactly like that one except that this one is red whereas that one is green," it makes no sense to say of two impressions of the same etching, say, "This impression is exactly like that one except that this one is a good one whereas that one is not (or this one is better than that one)." Where something is called good, it always makes sense to ask "What's good about it?," "What's it good for?," "In what respects is it good?," or something of the sort.[3] If one thing is good where another is not, or one is better than the other, must there not be some difference between them in virtue of which the one is good where the other is not, or in virtue of which the one is better than the other? This point is sometimes made by referring to goodness as a "supervenient" property.

Vermazen is not entirely happy with this notion. He has two models of supervenience: that according to which "redness . . . is said to supervene on certain surface properties of an object whose surface reflects light of a certain wavelength" and that according to which colorfulness supervenes on an object's having "a certain variety and number (vaguely specified) of color areas." And he notes that speaking of supervenience in the latter case "lacks the urgency it has" in the former. And in a way this seem to be right. "This is red" (according to the common meaning is "_____ is red") does not entail, and is not entailed by, "The surface of this reflects light of a certain wavelength." The connection between the two propositions is contingent, which allows the second to explain the fact expressed in the first, whereas "This is colorful" just *means* "This has a sufficient variety of colors of a certain sort." But what, now, about goodness? Vermazen thinks it is

> in the same boat as colorfulness: Although it has the right sort of dependence on lower-level properties to qualify as supervenient, it lacks the epistemic justification: there is no access to the aesthetic goodness of a work aside from access to its independently valued properties [roughly, those properties that directly make something aesthetically good].

But is this quite right? One might know, on unimpeachable authority, say, that something is aesthetically good (and thereby have epistemic access to its goodness) without knowing what makes it good, what is good about it, or in what respects it is good, which is not to say that he might know it is good where there is nothing that makes it good, where there is nothing good about it, where it is good in no respect. In knowing that it is good, he knows that there is *some* respect in which it is good, but he does not know in *what* respect. For him, "_____ is aesthetically good" is not just a "summary expression" for "_____ is *P*, *Q*, and *R*" (where "*P*," "*Q*," and "*R*" stand for the properties that make it good), although it might become such were he to ask "What is good about it?" and be told "It is good because it is *P*, *Q*, and *R*." So, whereas "_____ is good" may entail "_____ has some properties that make it good," it does not, or need not, entail "_____ is *P*, *Q*, and *R*," even where *P*, *Q*, and *R* are what make it good. (Indeed, if Lycan and Machamer are right, the one never entails the other, or the other the one.) So, will the supervenience of goodness really fit either of Vermazen's models?

A good place to start looking at the relation, or relations, between the reasons why something is good and its goodness lies in considering the goodness of a functional object, especially a single-purpose or single-function object, for example, a thermometer. A thermometer is by definition an instrument for measuring temperatures. Although it may have any number of properties, only some of these will be good-making. As a measuring instrument it will necessarily be either accurate or inaccurate, but it will not necessarily cost less than three dollars. If it is an accurate thermometer, it will (to that extent) be a good one; otherwise it will be a poor one or a bad one, depending on the degree of inaccuracy. Price has nothing to do with whether it is a good one. Further, if the instrument were illegible, we would be unable to use it to measure temperatures; so, to be a good one it must also be legible. If the instrument is to be used over a period of time, it must, in order to be a good one, be consistent rather than erratic in performance, and durable rather than short lasting. And if it is to be used under varying conditions of wear and tear, it must be sturdy rather than fragile. Given these conditions (there may be still others, of course), if a thermometer is accurate, legible, consistent in performance, durable, and sturdy, it is a good one, and conversely. These features *make* it a good thermometer; and we call these features the *standards* of judgment for thermometers, which means that any thermometer that satisfies these standards is a good one.

In this kind of case it is easy to see how, in Vermazen's words, "_____ is a good thermometer" is a "summary expression" of "_____ is a thermometer that is accurate, legible, consistent, durable, and sturdy." For could anyone be said to know what a good thermometer is if he did not know that it is one that is accurate, and so on? Does "good" add semantically anything that is not captured by "accurate, legible, consistent, durable, and sturdy"?[4]

What we have said about thermometers applies to other single-function objects, as well as to multifunction objects such as food processors, the proper changes being made.[5]

But where does this get us with respect to telling good art from bad? Not very far, unless art *qua* art has some single purpose or function. According to Tolstoy it does, namely, to transmit emotions. And according to the other theorists represented in the body of Part One of this book, with the exception of Dickie, it does. And according to Beardsley also, it would seem, it does; for he holds that the function of a work of art is to provide (pleasurable) aesthetic experience. But does it? Hampshire says it does not: that is the force of his claim "that a work of art is gratuitous." If art is gratuitous, then, except in special circumstances, there is no way of judging a work of art comparable to the way we have of judging thermometers, or to the way we have of morally judging human conduct, that is assessed according to rules and principles (that work in a way similar to the way standards work, and are even sometimes called "standards").

From the thesis that art is gratuitous and that therefore there are in general no standards, rules, or principles to appeal to in judging art (which appears to be the consensus of the authors represented in this section), Hampshire sometimes moves toward the stronger thesis that anyone who says that a painting is good or that one poem is better than another is being "a moralist in criticism"; value judgments are in effect practical advice about what to read, look at, or listen to. Because such advice "must involve reference to the whole economy of human needs and purposes," the critic is actually a moralist. But is this so?

That works of art are gratuitous in Hampshire's sense does not mean, of course, that no work of art provides an answer to a problem. Artists set problems for themselves and have problems set for them by others, for example, patrons. In the light of these problems their work may be judged as successful or unsuccessful. But these are what Hampshire calls *technical* problems, and criticism based on them is technical criticism, which is to suggest that there is a difference between technical criticism of something and criticism of it as a work of art. What is this difference?

One type of technical criticism has to do with the way(s) an artist does something—how he achieves, or why he fails to achieve, certain results or effects. But might not the techniques employed in fashioning a work of art—those of painting, etching, building, casting, and the like—be faultless and yet the work of art be a poor one for all that? Technique may be a *condition* of artistic merit in that, unless an artist meets certain technical standards (and here there often are standards), it is unlikely that he will achieve satisfactory artistic results. But is there not a difference between *conditions of* and *reasons for* artistic goodness or failure? "Because the glazes were improperly applied" may explain why a painting is a failure, but is it a reason why it is not a good painting?

A second type of technical criticism has to do with technical accomplishment. One might try to draw a study in linear perspective, write a sestina, or compose a fugue, and there would be a question as to how well he succeeded. Might not something be a good or accomplished sestina, fugue, or linear perspective drawing, however, and not be a good work of art?[6]

The same applies to technical problems of an even wider sort. Tolstoy urged artists to create works that would "unite men with God and with one another"; other artists—Virgil, Dante, Goya, and Daumier among them—have created works to stir men's consciences, to make them aware of social injustices, or to mobilize their energies toward political or religious ends. Apart from the fact that art may be incapable of doing what some have wanted it to do, is it not one thing to judge a work of art from some such perspective as the ones indicated and another to judge it as a work of art?

Now what is it to criticize art *as art*? Hampshire's suggested answer is: to criticize it apart from any problems—the artist's or the spectator's—that the work of art is purported to solve. Does this imply that critical judgments, unless they are simply indicative of, or call our attention to, or induce us to grasp, particular features of unique works of art, are out of place in criticism? Or that they are really moral judgments?

All natural objects are gratuitous in Hampshire's sense. Apples, lakes, fishes, trees, and rubies are not *essentially* the solution to a problem. Many of them, of course, we use to solve problems, and we often judge them in that light; but many we do not. May not one ruby be superior to another apart from any task to be accomplished by the use of rubies? Does this not suggest that Hampshire implicitly misrepresents the function of critical judgments by construing them as relevant only to problem solving? Even if a critical judgment is essentially the grading of one thing as better than another, is it always in effect a piece of practical advice, or a moral judgment? If to judge a painting as good is to be a moralist in criticism, is not to judge typewriters, hunting dogs, and mathematicians also to be a moralist? In that case, does not the notion of a critical moralist become vacuous?

Hampshire's main target is not critical judgments as such, however, but something like what Isenberg calls "norms," generalizations about artistic goodness: there are no universal *principles* of art criticism.[7] If this is so, is it because art is gratuitous; or is it rather because not all works of art "satisfy the same needs and interests at all times and for all people"?

To satisfy or answer to an interest is not the same as to solve a problem. An interest in cats may be met by cats, pictures of cats, books about cats, and so on; the problem of ridding a barn of mice may be solved by a good mouser. Now are not different interests taken in different works of art? And do not different works of art answer to different interests? Do a sonnet of Shakespeare, a symphony of Mozart, and a painting by Rubens meet the same interests? Can we reasonably expect them to?[8]

Some might want to say that all works of art should (or must) answer to aesthetic interests, or even the aesthetic interest. But is not "aesthetic" here a generic term covering a wide diversity of distinct interests? Are the reasons why one work of art is good, bad, or superior to another always the same as the reasons why another work of art is good, bad, or superior to still another, even in those contexts, for example, a competition for prizes, where works are judged comparatively?

Vermazen seems to go along with the idea "that there is one value-property that belongs to works of art *qua* works of art, and that any other value-property that belongs to a work is somehow unimportant when one is assessing it as a work of art." But does anything he says really rest on this assumption? Isn't it really dispensable for him? Is not the upshot of his argument, in fact, an undermining of this very idea; for works of art are comparable (usually) only with respect to a single independently valued property that they share?

Finally, does not critical moralism presuppose the existence of a non-moralistic art criticism? To advise people to devote their time and energies to certain works of art as opposed to others may be moralism, but does it not assume that we can distinguish in art the good from the bad, the better from the worse, irrespective of how we ought to spend our time?

Lycan's and Machamer's criticisms raise most of the important questions posed by the essays of Isenberg and Ziff, and it would be otiose to repeat them here. Suffice it to point to a couple of matters not broached by Lycan and Machamer.

Isenberg construes a "verdict" as "an expression of feeling—an utterance manifesting praise or blame," and presumably the "feeling" in question is liking or enjoyment; for "when we ask X as a critic 'why he likes the object Y,' we want him to give us some reason to like it too. . . ." First, in what way is a verdict "an utterance manifesting praise or blame"? (This harks back to Hume on beauty, as does the matter of liking.) Second, is expressing a liking for something the same as praising it, as Isenberg suggests? Third, is expressing a liking for something the same as judging it to be good? Is there not a world of difference between "I like that painting" and "That is a good painting"? For example, will reasons why I like it always coincide with the reasons why it's good, and conversely? If not, what is the relation between liking something and judging it to be good?

Ziff says, "If e_i is good then the performance of a_i by p_i under c_i is worthwhile for its own sake." This is equivalent to: If the performance of a_i by p_i under c_i is not worthwhile for its own sake, then e_i is not good. First, is this really acceptable? Second, if the performance of a_i by p_i under c_i is worthwhile for its own sake, does it follow that e_i is good? Ziff suggests that it does when he says such things as "To say a painting is good is here simply to say it is worth contemplating" and "A good anything is something that answers to interests associated with it." But now if the performance of a_i by p_i under c_i is worthwhile for its own sake but the performance of a_i by p_j under c_i is not worthwhile for its own sake, is p_i both good and not good? How can this be?

As for Lycan and Machamer, consider their C_4* and C_6*. Are these really parallel to C_4 and C_6 as they claim? C_4* tells us that "in our art education we have learned to call certain kinds of paintings good and to see what makes them good." But, as we all know, art education varies widely and is far less "free from prejudice," as Hume would put it, than is teaching people what "   is in pain" means. So in art education may it not be—is it not usually the case—that I learn to call certain kinds of paintings good and to see what makes my teacher call them "good," whereas you learn to call certain other paintings good and to see what makes your teacher call them "good"? If so, then isn't C_6* in trouble? "In arguing with the less enlightened pupil, the critic can reach a point at which he is forced to conclude that the pupil just does not know what a good painting is." Yes; but this presumes that the teacher/critic does know what a good painting is, and what guarantee does the pupil, or anyone else, have of that? It is easy for me, the less enlightened pupil, to learn what he *means by* "a good painting"; but that's not necessarily what "a good painting" means.

Notes

1. To dramatize the point, put it this way. A person's cat or his two-year-old child may have normal eyesight and hearing, but neither his cat nor his child is in a position to judge the pictures on his walls or the music he plays on his phonograph. And some adults are in much the same position as a cat or a two-year-old with respect to all art, and most of us are in much the same position with respect to some art. With respect to Japanese music or Tibetan painting, for example, I am in much the same position, as far as being in a position to judge goes, as a small child. I may find some of it mildly pleasant to listen to or to look at, but like a child I simply do not understand what I am listening to or looking at; and that makes all the difference. As Ziff puts it, "to evaluate a work one must understand it." Can there be any arguing with this?

2. It is important to note that a proposition, sentence, utterance, or locution need not (and usually does not) change its *meaning* depending on which semantic mood it is used in, on which illocutionary act it is used to perform. For example, if a man accused of murder says to the police or before a judge in suitable circumstances, "I killed my uncle for his money," he is legally *confessing* to a felony, whereas if he says the very same words in confidence to his attorney, he is not, although he may be *admitting* that he committed one. *What* he says in either case, however, is the *same*.

3. In this way "_____ is good" resembles "_____ is beautiful."

According to Ziff, " 'That is a good painting' can be queried with 'According to what standards?'; 'That is a magnificent painting' cannot be so queried and neither can 'That is an exquisite painting,' '. . . a splendid painting,' etc." Perhaps. But isn't the word "standards" doing all the work here? Can't "That is a magnificent (exquisite, splendid) painting" always be queried with "What's magnificent (exquisite, splendid) about it?" or "Wherein is it magnificent (exquisite, splendid)?" And is "According to what standards?" always really appropriate? Do we always have *standards* for the judgment of paintings? Isn't it quite possible for a painting to be good but according to no standards at all? Not all reasons why a painting is good are *standards*, surely.

4. It does not follow from this, as Aristotle seems to have thought, that "good" here means "accurate, legible, consistent, durable, and sturdy," and that it would mean something else in "_____ is a good vacuum cleaner," and so on. That "good thermometer" means one thing and "good vacuum cleaner" another, does not imply that "good" means something different in the two cases. On this point see P. T. Geach, "Good and Evil," *Analysis*, 17 (1956), 33-42. And for an illuminating discussion of Aristotle on this point, see J. L. Ackrill, "Aristotle on 'Good' and the Categories," *Islamic Philosophy and the Classical Tradition*, S. M. Stern, Albert Hourani, and Vivian Brown, eds. (Columbia, S.C., 1973), pp. 17-25; reprinted in *Articles on Aristotle 2: Ethics and Politics*, Jonathan Barnes, Malcolm Schofield, and Richard Sorabji, eds. (London, 1977), pp. 17-24.

5. It, or something like it, will also apply to some nonfunctional objects and activities, such as diving (e.g., in diving competitions), where uniform, and sometimes even arbitrary, demands are made on the object or activity. There may even, at certain times and in certain places and among a certain group of people, be standards, rules, or principles for the judgment of works of art, for example, works of architecture. But, as history has shown, these standards and rules usually turn out to be more honored in the breach than in the observance.

6. The kind of goodness at issue here might, following Kant, be called "adherent" or "dependent" goodness, the kind of goodness that, when achieved, is called "perfection" (which is perfection as a *kind*). A perfect sonnet, for example, is simply one that satisfies the definition or defining rules of a sonnet.

7. By a principle, or canon, of criticism is usually meant a statement of one of the following forms: "Something is a good work of art if and only if it possesses the property *p*"; "If something does not possess the property *p*, then it is not a good work of art"; "If something is a work of art and possesses the property *p*, then it is a good work of art"; where "*p*" represents either a single property or a conjunction of properties and is not definitive, wholly or in part, of "good work of art."

8. According to Ziff, "A good anything is something that answers to interests associated with it. In art, this is always a matter of performing certain actions, looking, listening, reading, etc., in connection with certain spatio-temporal or temporal entities, with paintings, poems, musical compositions, etc." Can there be any objection to this?

Suggestions for Additional Reading

Henry D. Aiken, "A Pluralistic Analysis of Aesthetic Value," *Phil. Rev.*, 59 (1950), 493-513; Virgil C. Aldrich, *Philosophy of Art* (Englewood Cliffs, N.J., 1963), Ch. 4; Cyril Barrett, "Are Bad Works of Art 'Works of Art'?," *Philosophy and the Arts*, Royal Institute of Philosophy Lectures, Vol. 6, 1971-72 (New York, 1973), 182-193—the answer is, in a way, no; Monroe C. Beardsley, *Aesthetics* (New York, 1958), Chs. X, XI, and *The Possibility of Criticism* (Detroit, 1970), 62-111; George Boas, *A Primer for Critics* (Baltimore, 1937); Marcia Cavell, "Taste and the Moral Sense," *J.A.A.C.*, 34 (1975), 29-33—on Hampshire; Francis X. J. Coleman, "A Phenomenology of Aesthetic Reasoning," *J.A.A.C.*, 25 (1966), 197-203; George Dickie, *Aesthetics: An Introduction* (Indianapolis and New York, 1971), Pt. V; T. J. Diffey, "Evaluations and Aesthetic Appraisals," *B.J.A.*, 7 (1967), 358-373; C. J. Ducasse, *Art, the Critics, and You* (New York, 1944) and *The Philosophy of Art* (New York, 1929), Ch. XV; Hans Eichner, "The Meaning of 'Good' in Aesthetic Judgments," *B.J.A.*, 3 (1963), 301-316; Nelson Goodman, *Languages of Art* (Indianapolis and New York, 1968), Ch. VI; A. H. Hannay, John Holloway, and Margaret Macdonald, "What Are the Distinctive Features of Arguments Used in Art Criticism?," a symposium, *P.A.S.*, Suppl. Vol. 23 (1949), 165-194; Bernard Harrison, "Some Uses of 'Good' in Criticism," *Mind*, 69 (1960),

206-222; Donald F. Henze, "The Art Work as a Rule," *Ratio*, 11 (1969), 69-74 Bernard C. Heyl, "The Critic's Reasons," *J.A.A.C.*, 16 (1957), 169-179; I. C. Jarvie, "The Objectivity of Criticism of the Arts," *Ratio*, 9 (1967), 67-83; Peter Jones, "Comments on Meynell," *B.J.A.*, 8 (1968), 347-352—reply to Meynell paper listed below; Helen Knight, "The Use of 'Good' in Aesthetic Judgments," *P.A.S.*, 36 (1935-36), 207-222; Joel J. Kupperman, "Reasons in Support of Evaluations of Works of Art," *The Monist*, 50 (1966), 222 ff.; Joseph Margolis, "Proposals on the Logic of Aesthetic Judgment," *Phil. Quart.*, 9 (1959), 208-216, and *The Language of Art and Art Criticism* (Detroit, 1965), Ch. 10; R. Meager, "The Uniqueness of a Work of Art," *P.A.S.*, 59 (1959), 49-70; Hugo Meynell, "Remarks on the Foundations of Aesthetics," *B.J.A.*, 8 (1968), 16-34—"the goodness of a work of art may be *defined* as its tendency, given opportunity, to satisfy the public in the long run"; H. Morris-Jones, "The Logic of Criticism," *The Monist*, 50 (1966), 213-221; H. Osborne, *Aesthetics and Art Criticism* (London, 1954) and "Reasons and Description in Criticism," *The Monist*, 50 (1966), 204-212; Albert Tsugawa, "The Objectivity of Aesthetic Judgments," *Phil. Rev.*, 70 (1961), 3-22; Michael Scriven, "The Objectivity of Aesthetic Evaluation," *The Monist*, 50 (1966), 159-187; F. A. Siegler, "On Isenberg's 'Critical Communication'," *B.J.A.*, 8 (1968), 161-174; Anita Silvers, "Aesthetic *Akrasia*: On Disliking Good Art," *J.A.A.C.*, 31 (1972), 227-234; Michael A. Slote, "The Rationality of Aesthetic Value Judgments," *J. Phil.*, 68 (1971), 821-839; Jerome Stolnitz, *Aesthetics and the Philosophy of Art Criticism* (Boston, 1960), Pt. VI; P. F. Strawson, "Aesthetic Appraisal and Works of Art," *Freedom and Resentment and Other Essays* (London, 1974), 178-188; Dorothy Walsh, "Critical Reasons," *Phil. Rev.*, 69 (1960), 386-393—on Isenberg; Morris Weitz, "Reasons in Criticism," *J.A.A.C.*, 20 (1961), 429-437; Paul Ziff, *Semantic Analysis* (Ithaca, N.Y., 1960), Ch. VI.

On criteria:

Gordon Baker, "Criteria: a New Foundation for Semantics," *Ratio*, 16 (1974), 159-189; Anthony Kenny, "Criterion," *The Encyclopedia of Philosophy*, Paul Edwards, ed. (New York, 1967), Vol. 2, 258-261; W. Gregory Lycan, "Noninductive Evidence: Recent Work on Wittgenstein's 'Criteria,'" *Am. Phil. Quart.*, 8 (1971), 109-125—contains a full bibliography.